British Cultural Studies

British Cultural Studies

British
Cultural Studies

Geography, Nationality,
and Identity

Edited by David Morley and Kevin Robins

OXFORD
UNIVERSITY PRESS

OXFORD
UNIVERSITY PRESS

Great Clarendon Street, Oxford OX2 6DP

Oxford University Press is a department of the University of Oxford.
It furthers the University's objective of excellence in research, scholarship,
and education by publishing worldwide in

Oxford New York

Athens Auckland Bangkok Bogotá Buenos Aires Cape Town
Chennai Dar es Salaam Delhi Florence Hong Kong Istanbul Karachi
Kolkata Kuala Lumpur Madrid Melbourne Mexico City Mumbai Nairobi
Paris São Paulo Shanghai Singapore Taipei Tokyo Toronto Warsaw
with associated companies in Berlin Ibadan

Oxford is a registered trade mark of Oxford University Press
in the UK and in certain other countries

Published in the United States
by Oxford University Press Inc., New York

© David Morley and Kevin Robins 2001

The moral rights of the authors have been asserted
Database right Oxford University Press (maker)

First published 2001

A catalogue record for this book is available from the British Library

Library of Congress Cataloging in Publication Data
Data available
ISBN 0-19-874206-1

10 9 8 7 6 5 4 3 2 1

Typeset in Dante and Officina
by RefineCatch Limited, Bungay, Suffolk
Printed in Great Britain
on acid-free paper by
TJ International Ltd., Padstow, Cornwall

Acknowledgements

We would like to thank Andrew Lockett and Angela Griffin for their parts in this enterprise, and also thank all our contributors for their forbearance during this manuscript's gestation.

Most particularly, though, we would like to thank our Research Assistant at Goldsmiths College, Richard Smith—without whose good-humoured and resourceful approach we could never have produced this book. We can only hope that it will prove to have been worth the wait.

D.M.
K.R.

Contents

Notes on Contributors   xi

Introduction: The National Culture in its New
Global Context   1
DAVID MORLEY   KEVIN ROBINS

Section I: How British is it? Geographies of Identity   17

Introduction   19

1. British Cultural Identities and the Legacy of
   the Empire   27
   CATHERINE HALL

2. 'Englishness' and English National Identity   41
   KRISHAN KUMAR

3. Rituals and Representations of Black 'Britishness'   57
   JIM PINES

4. British Asian Identities: Something Old, Something
   Borrowed, Something New   67
   TARIQ MODOOD

5. No Longer 'Ourselves Alone' in Northern Ireland   79
   KEVIN DAVEY

6. Scotland and the Union: Changing Identities in the
   British State   97
   DAVID McCRONE

7. Welsh Politics in the New Millennium 109
   JOHN OSMOND

8. Which Britain? Which England? Which North? 127
   PETER J. TAYLOR

9. Rurality and English Identity 145
   ALUN HOWKINS

10. Britain, America, and Europe 157
    BILL SCHWARZ

**Section II: When Will We Be Modern? Culture,
Tradition, and Heritage** 171

   Introduction 173

11. 'Proper English' and the Politics of Standard Speech 181
    LYNDA MUGGLESTONE

12. Religious Culture in Contemporary Britain 195
    STEVE BRUCE

13. The Mediated Monarchy 207
    DAVID CHANEY

14. Everyday Royal Celebrity 221
    NICK COULDRY

15. Cartels and Lotteries: Heritage and Cultural Policy
    in Britain 235
    KEN WORPOLE

16. Heritage Cinema and Television 249
    ANDREW HIGSON

17. Television and Culture: Duties and Pleasures 261
    JOHN CORNER

18. British Popular Music and National Identity 273
    DAVID HESMONDHALGH

19. 'Young British Art' in the 1990s 287
    ROSEMARY BETTERTON

20. Writing Britains 305
BERNARD SHARRATT

**Section III: In the Place of Britishness? Lifestyles,
Subcultures, and Cultural Politics** 317

Introduction 319

21. Geographies of Consumption 327
PHILIP CRANG AND PETER JACKSON

22. Changing Cultures of Work: Employment, Gender,
and Lifestyle 343
LINDA McDOWELL

23. Good Girls, Bad Girls? Female Success and the
New Meritocracy 361
ANGELA McROBBIE

24. Resignifying Masculinity: From 'New Man' to
'New Lad' 373
SEAN NIXON

25. Gay Cultures/Straight Borders 387
KEN PLUMMER

26. Sport, Leisure, and Style 399
ALAN TOMLINSON

27. The Control of Space: Travellers, Youth, and
Drug Cultures 417
DAVID SIBLEY

28. Green Politics: Animal Rights, Vegetarianism,
and Naturism 431
LINDA MERRICKS

29. Against Enclosure: Rethinking the Cultural Commons 443
GRAHAM MURDOCK

30. Blair and 'Britishness' 461
STEVEN DRIVER AND LUKE MARTELL

Contents ix

Endnote: To London: The City beyond the Nation   473
KEVIN ROBINS

Afterword   495
SUSAN BASSNETT

Chronology   503
Index   511

Notes on Contributors

Susan Bassnett is Pro-Vice-Chancellor at the University of Warwick and Professor in the Centre for British and Comparative Cultural Studies, which she founded in the 1980s, She is the author of over twenty books and her *Translation Studies*, which first appeared in 1980, has become the most important textbook around the world in this expanding field. Her recent books include *Studying British Cultures: An Introduction* (1997), *Constructing Cultures* (1998, written with André Lefevere), and *Postcolonial Translation* (with Harish Trivedi, 1999). She also writes for several national newspapers, and contributes an education column to the *Independent*.

Rosemary Betterton is Reader in Women's Studies at Lancaster University. She has published widely on gender and visual culture including her book *An Intimate Distance: Women, Artists and the Body* (1996) and, most recently, 'A Matter of Paint: The Carnal Subject of Aesthetics', in P. Florence and N. Foster (eds.), *Differential Aesthetics: Art Practice, Philosophies and Feminist Understandings* (2000).

Steve Bruce is Professor of Sociology, University of Aberdeen. His books include *God Save Ulster! The Religion and Politics of Paisleyism* (1986), *The Rise and Fall of the New Christian Right: Protestant Politics in America, 1978–88* (1988), *The Red Hand: Loyalist Paramilitaries in Northern Ireland* (1992), *The Edge of the Union: The Ulster Loyalist Political Vision* (1994), and *Conservative Protestant Politics* (1998).

David Chaney is Professor of Sociology, University of Durham. He has published widely on the nature of cultural change and its implications for forms of collective identity in the modern era; his most recent work is *Cultural Change and Everyday Life* (forthcoming).

John Corner is Professor of Communications, University of Liverpool. He has published widely in international journals and is an editor of *Media, Culture and Society*. His books include *Television Form and Public Address* (1995), *The Art of Record* (1996), *Studying Media: Problems of Theory and Method* (1998), and *Critical Ideas in Television Studies* (1999).

Nick Couldry is a Lecturer in Media and Communications, London School of Economics. His publications include *The Place of Media Power: Pilgrims and Witnesses of the Media Age* (2000) and *Inside Culture: Reimagining the Method of Cultural Studies* (2000).

Philip Crang is Reader in Cultural Geography at Royal Holloway, University of London. He edits the journal *Ecumene: a journal of cultural geographies*. He is currently researching questions of transnationality in commodity culture.

Kevin Davey is a journalist, author and new media strategist. His *English Imaginaries: Six Studies in Anglo British Modernity* was published by Lawrence & Wishart in 1999. He is currently working on *Euroanxieties*, a book on Britain's response to Europeanization.

Stephen Driver is a Senior Lecturer in the School of Sociology and Social Policy at the University of Surrey Roehampton. He is the author, with Luke Martell, of *New Labour: Politics after Thatcherism* (1998). Currently, he is writing a book on the philosophy of social science.

Catherine Hall is Professor of Modern British Social and Cultural History, University College London. She has recently published *Defining the Victorian Nation: Class, Race, Gender and the Reform Act of 1867* with Keith McClelland and Jane Rendall (2000) and has edited *Cultures of Empire: A Reader* (2000). Her new book, *Civilizing Subjects: Colony and Metropole in the English Imagination 1830–1867*, will be published by Polity in 2001.

David Hesmondhalgh is Lecturer in Sociology at the Open University. He is co-editor (with Georgina Born) of *Western Music and its Others: Difference, Representation and Appropriation in Music* (2000) and author of *The Cultural Industries* (forthcoming).

Andrew Higson is Professor of Film Studies at University of East Anglia. He is author of *Waving the Flag: Constructing a National Cinema in Britain* (1995), editor of *Dissolving Views: Key Writings on British Cinema*, and co-editor (with Richard Maltby) of *'Film Europe' and 'Film America': Cinema, Commerce and Cultural Exchange, 1920–1939* (1999) and (with Justine Ashby) *British Cinema, Past and Present* (2000). He is currently completing *English Heritage, English Cinema* for Oxford University Press.

Alun Howkins is Professor of Social History, University of Sussex. He is on the editorial board of *History Workshop Journal* and his books include *Poor Labouring Men: Rural Radicalism in Norfolk, 1872–1923* (1985) and *Reshaping Rural England: A Social History, 1850–1925* (1992). He is currently working on a study of the socio-cultural history of rural England since 1918.

Peter Jackson is Professor of Human Geography at the University of Sheffield, where he teaches social and cultural geography. Recent research projects have included ESRC-funded studies of shopping, magazine reading, and transnational commodity culture. His latest publications are: *Commercial Cultures* (2000) and *Making Sense of Men's Magazines* (2001).

Krishan Kumar is Professor of Sociology at the University of Virginia. He was previously Professor of Social and Political Thought at the University of Kent at Canterbury. Among his more recent publications are *From Post-industrial to Post-modern Society* (1995) and (edited with Jeff Weintraub) *Private and Public in Thought and Practice* (1997). There is a volume of essays, *1989: Revolutionary Ideas and Ideals*, forthcoming with the University of Minnesota Press in autumn 2001. He is currently completing a book, *The Question of English National Identity*, to be published by Cambridge University Press.

David McCrone is Professor of Sociology, University of Edinburgh. His recent works include *The Sociology of Nationalism* (1998), *The Scottish Electorate: The 1997 General Election and Beyond* (1999), *Politics and Society in Scotland* (2nd edition, 1998), and *Scotland—the Brand: The Making of Scottish Heritage* (1995).

Linda McDowell is Professor of Economic Geography, University College, University of London. She has just completed a study for the Joseph Rowntree Foundation about the labour market entry behaviour of working-class youths and is currently looking at women's work in the 1950s. Her recent books include *Capital Culture* (1997), *Gender Identity and Place* (1999), and *A Feminist Glossary of Human Geography* (edited with Jo Sharp, 1999).

Angela McRobbie is Professor of Communications, Goldsmiths College, London, and author of *British Fashion: Design Rag Trade or Image Industry?* (1998), *In the Culture Society* (1999), and co-editor of *Without Guarantees: In Honour of Stuart Hall* (2000).

Luke Martell is Senior Lecturer in Sociology at the University of Sussex. He is author of *Ecology and Society* (1994) and co-author, with Stephen Driver, of *New Labour: Politics after Thatcherism* (1998).

Linda Merricks is Director of Undergraduate Programmes in the School of Educational Studies, University of Surrey. Her current research interests include lifelong and experimental learning. She has been a frequent contributor to *Rural History* and her books include *The World Made New: Frederick Soddy, Science, Politics, and Environment* (1996).

Tariq Modood is Director of the Research Centre for the Study of Ethnicity and Citizenship, University of Bristol. His books include *Not Easy Being British* (1992), *Changing Ethnic Identities* (with S. Beishon and S. Virdee, 1994), *Ethnic Minorities in Higher Education* (with M. Shiner, 1994, and *Asian Self-Employment* (with H. Metcalf and S. Virdee). He has edited *Church, State and Religious Minorities* (1997), *Debating Cultural Hybridity* and *The Politics of Multiculturalism in the New Europe* (both with P. Webner, 1997), and *Race and Higher Education* (with T. Acland, 1998).

David Morley is Professor of Communications at Goldsmiths College, University of London. He is the author of *Home Territories: Media, Mobility and Identity* (2000) co-author (with Kevin Robins) of *Spaces of Identity* (1995) and the co-editor (with Kuan-Hsing Chen) of *Stuart Hall: Critical Dialogues in Cultural Studies* (1996).

Lynda Mugglestone is Fellow in English Language and Literature at Pembroke College, Oxford, and News International Lecturer in Language and Communication. She has written widely on nineteenth-century language and is the author of *'Talking Proper': The Rise of Accent as Social Symbol* (1997) and editor of *Lexicography and the OED: Pioneers in the Untrodden Forest*, (2000). She is currently preparing a new edition of *'Talking Proper'*. and writing a new book on the history of the *Oxford English Dictionary*.

Graham Murdock is Reader in the Sociology of Culture, Loughborough University. He has written extensively on the organization of the mass media industries and on the press and television coverage of terrorism, riots, and other political events. His current work is on advertising and on the social impact of new communications technologies. His recent books include *The Economy of the Media* (2 volumes, edited with Peter Golding, 1997) and *Television across Europe: A Comparative Introduction* (edited with Jan Wieten and Peter Dahlgren, 2000).

Sean Nixon is Senior Lecturer in the Department of Sociology, University of Essex, and author of *Hard Looks: Masculinities, Spectatorship and Contemporary Consumption* (1996) and *Creative Cultures: Gender and Creativity at Work in Advertising* (forthcoming).

John Osmond is Director of the Institute of Welsh Affairs (Sefydliad Materion Cymreig), an independent think tank and research institute with whom he has written and edited numerous books and research papers including *Coalition Politics Come to Wales: Monitoring the National Assembly Sept to Dec 2000, Devolution Looks Ahead: Monitoring the National Assembly May to August 2000*, and *The National Assembly Agenda: A Handbook for the First Four Years* (1998).

Jim Pines is Senior Lecturer in the Department of Media Arts, University of Luton. He has written numerous articles on the presence and representation of black people in film and television. His books include *Black and White in Colour: Black People in British Television since 1936* (1992) and *The Essential Framework: Classic Film and TV Essays* (edited with Paul Willemen, 1998).

Ken Plummer is Professor of Sociology at the University of Essex. He is author and editor of some ten books including *Sexual Stigma* (1975), *The Making of the Modern Homosexual* (1981), *Modern Homosexualities* (1992), and *Telling Sexual Stories* (1995). Most recently he has published *Documents of Life—2: An Invitation to a Critical Humanism* (2001) and he is the founder-editor of a new journal *Sexualities*.

Kevin Robins is Professor of Communications, Goldsmiths College, University of London, and is the author of *Into the Image: Culture and Politics in the Field of Vision* (1996) and (with Frank Webster) *Times of the Technoculture* (1999).

Bill Schwarz is Reader in Communications, Goldsmiths College, University of London. He is an editor of *History Workshop Journal*, *New Formations* and *Cultural Studies*. His latest book is *Memories of Empire in Twentieth-Century England* (forthcoming).

Bernard Sharratt was Reader in English and Cultural Studies, University of Kent at Canterbury until taking early retirement in 1999. He currently works as a freelance multimedia producer. His best-known books are *Reading Relations: Structures of Literary Production* (1982) and *The Literary Labyrinth: Contemporary Critical Discourses* (1984).

David Sibley is Professor of Human Geography at the University of Hull. His principal research interests are the marginal spaces of nomadism and childhood and regimes of spatial control. His publications include *Geographies of Exclusion* (1995) and he is currently editing a volume *Critical Concepts in Cultural Geography* (forthcoming).

Peter Taylor is Professor of Geography at Loughborough University. His recent books included *Modernities: A Geohistorical Interpretation* (1999) and *The American Century: Coercion and Consensus in the Projection of American Power* (edited with David Slater, 1999). He is an editor of *Political Geography* (formerly *Political Geography Quarterly*).

Alan Tomlinson is Professor of Sport and Leisure Studies and Head of the Chelsea School Research Centre, University of Brighton. He has authored and edited many books on sport, leisure, and consumption, including *FIFA and the Contest for World Football: Who Rules the Peoples' Game?* (with John Sugden, 1998), *The Game's up: Essays in the Cultural Analysis of Sport, Leisure and Popular Culture* (1999), and *Sport and Leisure Cultures: Global, National and Local Dimensions* (forthcoming).

Ken Worpole is a researcher and consultant with Comedia, an independent research and consultancy organization specializing in urban strategy and cultural policy. His recent publications include *In our Backyard: The Social Promise of Environmentalism* (2000), *The Cemetery in the City* (1997), and *Towns for People: Transforming Urban Life* (1992).

The National Culture in its New Global Context

DAVID MORLEY AND KEVIN ROBINS

Introduction

THE objective of this book is to provide an overview of significant developments in British culture in recent decades, and to raise key issues for the future. What are the pressing issues to be confronted by the national culture, and how are they to be articulated with the already complex and contradictory heritage of Britishness? We have chosen to organize our material thematically, rather than as a narrative history, as we have not wanted to duplicate the many historical accounts of British society and culture. However, this is not a self-reflexive book about 'British Cultural Studies' as an intellectual formation. While many of our contributors are associated with that tradition, the emphasis here is on the application of cultural studies perspectives to a range of phenomena in contemporary British culture and society. There are now a number of texts to which the interested reader can turn for an introduction to the specifically British tradition of cultural studies (see Further Reading 1).

The contributors to this volume consider the contemporary development of British culture in the context of the rapidly changing world order. How, they ask, is Britain (and Britishness) being reshaped in the new global context? What tensions and contradictions are emerging as a consequence of Britain's involvement in the European Union? In what ways are British culture and identity being recast as a consequence of the nation's colonial heritage? What is the significance of the new forms of devolution, regionalism, and nationalism that are now emerging? This book aims to map the state of British culture now, seeking to identify its new configurations and to trace its new fault lines (see Further Reading 2).

Although we make no claim to offer a systematic history of British culture, the contemporary developments with which we are concerned could hardly be addressed without reference to the past. Thus, one set of issues addressed in the book concerns the significance of the British past and heritage. The key question here is to do with whose heritage we should now be counting as British. Here we also encounter issues concerning landscape, nature, and rurality (classic markers of the national culture). Important debates have emerged around these issues, involving both traditional conservationists and a new generation of militant campaigners for 'Nature'. A further set of key issues addressed concerns changes in the political culture of Britain: it seems that we are now seeing the break-up of the national public sphere, through which the nation historically saw and imagined itself as a national culture.

Over the last two decades, British political culture has also been massively transformed by the forces of privatization and consumerism. At the same time, and because of the moral vacuum this has created, there has been an increasing concern with the question of 'values'. Thus, the last two decades have witnessed yet another 'moral panic' around the idea of the decline of family and community values, associated with the nostalgic desire to recover 'lost' traditions. Amongst other things, these anxieties arise in relation to new and emerging forms of sexual and lifestyle identity that have been widely perceived as threatening to the 'British way of life'. In the last decade, we have seen the cultural consequences of the free-market Thatcherite agenda come home to roost. For many, identities have become increasingly centred on consumption and consumer culture, leading to the partial dissolution of other ('traditional') forms of social connection. On the one hand, then, we have the forces of 'privatization' and individualism moving through all spheres of life, and, on the other, the invocation of community and of communitarian values.

The 'structure of feeling' of the era in which Thatcherism transformed the political and cultural agenda of British life was well captured in John Corner and Sylvia Harvey's (1991) collection of essays on British culture in the 1980s, with its core themes of a struggle between the principles of 'enterprise' and 'heritage' in the national culture. While some glimpses of the shape of a new political and cultural agenda are now available, its overall form is, as yet, unclear. As Marx noted, in periods between unravelling of one hegemony and the installing of another, strange (and as yet unclassifiable) phenomena stalk the land—both harbingers of what might come and throwbacks to earlier patterns (from lottery fever to road rage and fuel protests). The question is how we are to read these strange portents.

David Morley and Kevin Robins

In political terms, the arrival of the New Labour government in 1997 seemed to mark the end of the decade-and-a-half-long hegemony of Thatcherism (despite desperate calls by the faithful to wake the ghost and even occasional sightings of the ghost herself, in what have sometimes seemed close to self-parodic modes). And yet New Labour has still found it necessary to operate, in many ways, within the terms of the cultural hegemony of that previous period. Moreover, each of the main British political parties continues to be riven by conflicts between their 'modernizers' and those who wish to drive them back towards some previous fundamentalism—the Tory Right espousing ever more shrill and narrow forms of anti-European nationalism, the Labour Left still trying to stem the 'modernizing' tide of the Third Way.

Dreams of the future are on offer, to be sure, some of them cutting across the party divide. At the level of global politics, we have seen an increasing (and, many would say, overdue) recognition that modernity may no longer necessarily have its 'natural home' in the West. Here we might note, in passing, the common conviction in the mid-1990s, among followers of both the Left and the Right, that the model for Britain's future economic regeneration was to be found in the societies of South East Asia. Increasingly, there is an awareness that post-imperial nations, such as Britain, are no longer assured any privileged place in the global geography of the future. The grandiose dreams of a 'New World Order', in which it was presumed that all the world would follow America and the West into the 'End of History', characterized by the untroubled hegemony of liberalism and market capitalism (cf. Fukuyama 1993), are now well and truly exposed for the ethnocentric fantasies they always were (see Ryan 1992). As western culture comes to be recognized as but one particular form of modernity, rather than as some universal template for humankind, and as Britain attempts to adapt to its sense of displacement from the centre of the world stage—and, at the same time, tries to come to terms with its own ethnic and cultural complexity—a whole new scenario begins to emerge.

At a local level, in its initial period in office, the New Labour government in Britain responded to these dilemmas by engaging in an exercise of what was described as 'rebranding Britain'—focusing on Britain's distinctive strengths in the creative and cultural industries, to create a new image for Britain as (in the now toe-curlingly embarrassing phrase) 'Cool Britannia' (Leonard 1997). As the shine wore off New Labour's initially cosy relationship with the showbiz worlds of fashion and music, this whole exercise came to be seen as something of an embarrassment. However, one could argue that, initially, it was at least founded on the recognition that, rather than Britain having any naturally dominant position in the world economy, 'Britishness' is but one of a large number of 'brands' on sale in the global marketplace and thus stands as much in need of marketing as the average soap powder.

At the core of many of the contradictions in play about what exactly 'Britishness' might be made to mean in the contemporary world is a central dilemma about how to combine the past and the future—the Internet and the remnants of family life, tele-democracy and the rising tide of fundamentalisms (among which we would also include the New Labour creed of communitarian-ism). This book brings together the work of leading scholars in the field of cultural studies in an attempt to map out the geography of these new cultural dynamics and dilemmas, now increasingly occupying the centre stage of Britain's cultural landscape.

Given the nature of the power relations between the English state and the constituent parts of the UK, 'Englishness' has long been the hegemonic component in the supposedly broader term of 'Britishness'. In a rich survey of empirical definitions of the content of English culture offered by commentators at different stages of the twentieth century, on which we draw heavily below, Blake Morrison traces the continuities between a series of emblematic lists of the constituents of Englishness. He begins with Conserva-tive Prime Minister Stanley Baldwin, who, in the 1920s, referred to 'the tinkle of the hammer on the anvil in the country smithy, the corncrake on a dewy morning, the sound of the scythe against the whetstone and the sight of the plough team coming over the hill' (Baldwin quoted in Morrison 2000). Ten or so years later, Baldwin's rustic imagery was transposed into an urban populism, in J. B. Priestley's defining image of 'bungalows with tiny garages, cocktail bars, Woolworths, motorcoaches, the wireless, hiking, factory girls looking like actresses, greyhound racing and dirt tracks' (see Priestley 1977: 375). But the image of Englishness as rooted in the countryside, in a kind of 'Constable country' of the mind (cf. Okely 1997), dies very hard. Still in 1943, John Betjeman identified Englishness with 'oil-lit churches, Women's Institutes, modest village inns, arguments about cow parsley on the altar, the noise of mowing machines on Saturday afternoons'. This is clearly very close to George Orwell's image of 'old maids biking to Holy Communion through the mists of the autumn morning' as one of the 'characteristic fragments of the English scene' (see Orwell 1969: 57). By 1948, T. S. Eliot, in his well-known evocation, felt able to characterize English culture more demotically, as comprising 'Derby Day, Henley Regatta, Cowes, the twelfth of August, a cup final, the dog races, the pin table, the dart board, Wensleydale cheese, boiled cabbage cut into sections, beetroot in vinegar, nineteenth-century Gothic churches and the music of Elgar' (Eliot 1948: 31).

Much of this imagery survives. Even in 1999, Jeremy Paxman was still characterizing Englishness in terms of 'village cricket, do-it-yourself, punk, irony, brass bands, Cumberland sausages, double-decker buses, dry-stone walls, fell running [and] crumpets' (Morrison 2000, summarizing Paxman 1998). Already in the mid-1980s, however, Geoff Mulgan and Ken Worpole were posing the question as to whether British culture might not better be characterized by reference to commercial institutions such as 'Next shops, Virgin, W. H. Smiths, News International, Benetton, Channel 4, Saatchi and Saatchi, the Notting Hill Carnival and Virago Books', rather than as comprised by the 'official' culture of 'the Wigmore Hall, the Arts Council, National Theatre . . . and the Royal Opera House' (Mulgan and Worpole 1986). Writing in the autumn of 2000, Morrison himself offers the following as his own characterization of the essence of contemporary Englishness:

mobile phones, speed cameras, cropped hair, wheel clamping, Harry Potter, estuary English, car-boot sales, squeegee merchants, up-and-over garage doors, walnut oil, grated Parmesan, Wonderbras, men in shorts, women with tattoos, Princess Di commemorative mugs, double-glazed conservatories, exercise bikes, chat shows, satellite dishes, rural post offices open three days a week, floral tributes by roadsides, pig-farms, out-of-town shopping malls, fields yellow with rape or blue with linseed, central locking, Sunday opening, privatised trains, farm shops, barbecues, chicken tikka masala, on-line shopping and Bridget Jones. (Morrison 2000)

What are we to make of this cornucopia of the rural and the (sub)urban, the traditional and the modern, the public and the private?

Questions of Identity

The question of what 'Britishness' or 'Englishness' is now to be taken to mean—and of how the relation between those two terms is to be understood—has been addressed extensively in recent years (one might say obsessively). If the 'knowledge industries' are the key to Britain's new cultural economy, in which we have to learn to 'live on thin air' (Leadbeater 2000), the output of books, television programmes, and journalism addressing these questions of identity has recently undergone a boom in production of phenomenal scale. The old hegemonies which secured taken-for-granted meanings for the terms 'British' or 'English', which hardly ever needed to be spelt out explicitly, are clearly now fractured. The authors collected together here are concerned to explore (and, where appropriate, celebrate) the positive potentials for 'new ethnicities' (Hall 1989) created by the rupturing of these old categories of race, ethnicity, and nationality.

At the same time, we see politicians of all sorts attempting to repair and reconstruct those old identities—repolishing old shibboleths for new times. Thus, it was not only John Major, when Prime Minister in 1992, who famously drew on George Orwell's imagery (quoted above) as bespeaking some supposedly eternal verity of English life. When the Runnymede Trust's report on *The Future of Multi-ethnic Britain* was published in the autumn of 2000, amidst a furore of protest at its analytic deconstruction of the taken-for-granted meaning of Britishness as a racial category, the Labour Home Secretary Jack Straw similarly reached for his Orwell—this time to excoriate 'the Left' for their supposed lack of patriotism or national pride.

However, at least these older definitions of nationalism or ethnicity can now no longer be left unspoken, and, to that extent, their power as the unquestioned assumptions constituting the very horizon of 'common sense' is much diminished. The more hysterically Norman Tebbit et al. insist on the older, exclusionary definitions of British nationality or English ethnicity, the more they seem like simply one partisan voice among many in an ongoing argument. The very words themselves which are used to describe 'our' identity are now plainly exposed as 'multi-accentual' in Volosinov's (1973) terminology, as different social and cultural forces struggle to pull the meaning of 'Britishness' in contradictory directions. Plainly, the key issue concerns the question of cultural power: who has command over the cultural, educational, and political resources that will determine how the meaning of these terms is to be understood. Here we see a similar struggle to that fought out during Mrs Thatcher's term of office, over how British history (and especially its imperial history) was to be taught in schools. The particular story that we tell our children and ourselves about our national history makes an enormous difference to our contemporary sense of who 'we' are. Evidently Mrs Thatcher's call for the story of empire to be taught in British schools without apology, as a story of the nation's 'civilizing' mission in the world at large, would sit very uneasily

David Morley and Kevin Robins

with any concept of contemporary Britain as a genuinely multi-cultural society. The difficult and contradictory dynamics of current debates about our national identity simply cannot be understood, we would argue, if one starts from such a wilfully perverse and traduced understanding of our imperial past. The relations of power which have been responsible for the patterns of immigration and settlement that have laid the basis for Britain's contemporary demographic profile cannot be so easily wished away. Nor can the imperial history of the English state, within the local confines of the 'United Kingdom' itself.

It is in this context that this book addresses the (increasingly) vexed question of what 'Britishness' is. The focus here is on how, historically, the particular forms of British culture and identity with which we are now familiar have been continuously reinvented. A central concern here is with the internal tensions, divisions, and contradictions that have been held in check, but which increasingly seek to reassert themselves as the United Kingdom begins to break up (for an early statement of this thesis, see Nairn 1977). In this connection, the essays collected here address questions of national-ity, regionality, statehood, empire, race, ethnicity, and religion, as they have all developed within Britain. In the opening section of the book, particular chapters deal with the relations between the nations of 'the Isles'—crucially with the relationship of Irish, Welsh, and Scottish culture to the dominant English culture, and with the significance of the forces of devolution and regionalism—while others offer a consideration of the problematical nature of English identity and ethnicity. These essays explore both the com-plexities of cultural encounter and confrontation within the British context and the potential for cultural transformation made possible by this cultural complexity. It is, of course, also necessary to con-sider British identity in terms of its key external reference points—from the imperial and colonial periods and their legacies, through to its problematical relations to American culture, and to con-temporary issues concerning Britain's ambivalent and awkward relation to current scenarios for the future of Europe.

We have addressed elsewhere (Morley and Robins 1995) the con-tradictions inherent in the European Union's attempts to reconstruct itself as an integrated space of 'Euroculture', and the implicitly racist and ethnocentric dangers which necessarily attend any attempt to create a white, Christian, 'Fortress Europe'. For all those dangers, it remains the case that the strength of the fearful 'Little Englandism' which, within both the main political parties, continues to hold back any prospect of Britain's closer and positive involvement with Europe is one of the most depressing features of the British political landscape. The media-generated moral panic, at the turn of the millennium, about 'illegal immigrants' and asylum-seekers 'invading' the symbolic white cliffs of Dover has been one of the most shameful episodes in recent British history. It would seem that there are still many who wish that the Channel Tunnel linking Dover to the French port of Calais ran only in one direction—so that British holidaymakers could have access to 'the Continent' when they wished, without permitting any but the most utilitarian, commercial traffic in the other direction. As Neil Ascherson has put it, 'the river of Eurosceptic xenophobia is beginning to converge with the river of intolerant English nationalism' (Ascherson 1996: 29).

Culture, Heritage, and the Arts

In the wake of the Thatcherite call for a return to 'Victorian Values' in the mid-1980s, Patrick Wright's path-breaking work announced the beginning of an overdue consideration of what it means to be living in an 'Old Country', where 'heritage culture' has come to be central to our understanding of who we are (Wright 1985). In subsequent years, the work of writers such as Robert Hewison (1987) and Raphael Samuel (1994), among others, has offered a significant development of this theme, and a number of the contributors to this volume pursue this issue. The key point is why the question of 'heritage culture' has become so very significant in recent years. The essays here also explore those forces of 'modernization' that are working against British heritage—the role of the media in dissolving the traditional 'symbolic distance' of the monarchy, for example; and the 'dissolving force' of commercialism in its new forms (such as the National Lottery). It is in the context of these new tensions between the forces of 'tradition' and of 'modernization', that we need to understand how 'traditions' are continuously reinvented (Hobsbawm and Ranger 1983). This is particularly so in the case of the monarchy, on which two of our essays focus, given the centrality of this institution in British culture. The story of Charles and Diana—from global, celebratory televising of their 'royal wedding' through the sad denouement of Diana's televised *Panorama* interview, after their separation, to the thoroughly mediated drama of the mourning of her death—perhaps condenses this tension most dramatically. Heritage has become a key word in our national vocabulary; it is what Britain sells—to the tourists who come to visit its stately homes and, in the audio-visual industries, in the form of costume drama (the films of Merchant–Ivory et al.). These images affect not only how others see us, but also how we see ourselves and our future, and our authors are concerned to trace the shifts in how we have attempted to symbolize our identity in (changing) 'modern' forms, from the post-war period (the Festival of Britain, for example), through the (mainly commercialized) cultural forms of the National Lottery, to the millennium celebrations. These issues are perhaps most notably symbolized by the tawdry shell of the Millennium Dome itself in Greenwich, which was made to carry so many impossible expectations as the symbol of Labour's 'New Britain' (Sinclair 1999).

However, our focus is not only on the public forms of politics and their institutional symbols but also on key developments in various art forms—music, literature, and the visual arts—that reflect the state of British culture now. There are profound ambivalences here, surrounding the repeated calls for some 'return' to established or traditional cultural identities. It is also important to place these current artistic developments in the context of wider developments beyond Britain (cultural globalization, Europeanization), involving the repositioning of British identity. Thus, in the field of music, while many celebrated the rise of 'Britpop' in the 1990s (see David Hesmondhalgh's discussion, Ch. 18), it is significant that this was an almost exclusively white musical form, while Britain's multicultural identity has found its articulation in quite different areas of musical expression (from bhangra to jungle and the 'New Asian Underground'). Similarly, in literature, if Martin Amis has been central to one thread of recent British literature, then writers such as Salman Rushdie, Hanif Kureishi, Meera Syal, and Zadie Smith have been crucial in giving voice to other non-white British cultures. In the realm of the visual arts, the work of 'young British artists' has been widely held to have been undergoing something of a renaissance in recent years (or at least, under the influence of the Saatchis and the annual televisual ritual of the Turner Prize, the visual arts have been much more publicly visible and commercially successful). The essays collected here focus on some key aspects of the musical, literary, and visual cultures of contemporary Britain. While they make no claim to offer a comprehensive account of their respective fields, they work by picking out emblematic examples and case-studies of key trends and issues in the contemporary arts.

Consumer Culture, Identity, and Lifestyle

The rise of shopping culture, and the physical 'rise', in the place of old industries, of new temples of consumerism—the shopping malls—has been one of the key stories of recent years. Consumerism and the retail industry are now central to how we see ourselves. The ways in which we are catered to as consumers and the range of available identities that we can now buy 'off the peg' has extended dramatically. On the one hand, we see here the rise of forms of standardization and globalization—the reach of global companies and brands, such as Nike and Benetton—into high streets all over the land. On the other hand, we also see around us greater forms of flexibility, new forms of 'personalized' identity, available to us in commercial forms, in a seemingly endless expansion of the realm of consumer choice, into new arenas of consumption.

To take but one example of a field which has been transformed by these forces, we might note that among the changes of recent years, there has been an increasing focus on the body itself as an object to be trained, moulded, and perfected. Sport and athleticism have been revalued within the culture: we are surrounded by a whole new pattern of activity in which 'working out' at the gym, body-building, and various forms of physical self-improvement are now taken for granted, as part of ordinary life, for a growing number of people. Sportswear itself—trainers, tracksuits, and all—has now become an item of fashion: the signs and symbols of athleticism have been aestheticized as part of a consumer culture in which we are now invited to continually remake and rebuild our physical selves. The 'entrepreneurial self' (cf. Rose 1999) is no mere ideological phantasm—here we also see the shaping of the entrepreneurial body as one of the key forms of cultural capital in which we are nowadays encouraged to invest our identities.

If global consumer capitalism has in some ways encouraged, in commodified forms, a certain loosening of personal identities from their traditional anchorages, nevertheless, many of the recent transformations in the fields of social, bodily, and sexual identities still continue to be matters of profound cultural anxiety and contention. Thus, alongside a certain liberalization with respect to the toleration of a wider range of sexual identities and lifestyles in the marketplace, we have also seen, in recent years, strident calls for a return to 'family values'. Accompanying the (sometimes grudging) recognition that, with an increasing number of women in the labour force, our understanding of gendered roles has to be fundamentally transformed, we have also seen a series of attempts, by politicians and commentators of all types, to reinstate the traditional nuclear family as the normative template for all households. Clearly these calls for a 'return' to tradition fly in the face of the actual realities we see around us (an increasing number of single-person households, a shrinking proportion of nuclear families of the 'traditional' kind, the decreasing availability of full-time work for many men). In recent years, to take but one example, the domestic home, long established as the ideological site of security and respite from the tribulations of the outside world, has itself been considerably transformed. As Donna Haraway puts it, nowadays, when we say the word 'home' we have to think of

Women-headed households, serial monogamy, the flight of men, old *+ men coming* women alone, technology of domestic work, paid homework, [the] re-emergence of home sweat-shops, home-based businesses and telecommuting, electronic cottage[s], urban homelessness, migration, module architecture, reinforced (simulated) nuclear family, intense domestic violence. (Haraway 1985: 194)

In the face of these transformations of our 'home life', calls for a return to 'family values' clearly articulate a profound sense of anxiety—they express a persistent cultural fantasy in which, if only we could go 'home', all would be well. In this picture, sexual abuse is what 'strangers' do, not one of the family's own dark secrets. Evidently, in this context, it is necessary also to invoke rather different perspectives on these issues. As Ken Worpole and Liz Greenhalgh note, in the wake of the Jamie Bulger child murder, and the subsequent 'Just Say "No" to Strangers' campaign, British parents are now so paranoid about their children's safety in public spaces that those children are allowed out of the house a shorter distance than children in any other European country (Worpole and Greenhalgh 1996). Nonetheless, the home is still, statistically, by far the most dangerous place, not only for children, but for all its inhabitants (Williams 1994; Chapman and Hockey 1999).

A generation has now passed since the feminism of the 1960s and 1970s. Our culture has seen various new gender identities come and go in that period—the post-feminist, the babe, and the ladette, as well as the 'new man' and the subsequent celebration of 'lad' culture, through magazines like *Loaded* and television programmes like *Men Behaving Badly*. The essays here address the contemporary transformation of our understandings of these issues of gender, sexual identity, sexual and gender relations. In these transformations, it is, as so often, no question of simple progress. As Angela

McRobbie points out (see Ch. 23), the new possibilities for young women in the workplace still remain, on the whole, closed to those from disadvantaged backgrounds—whose own 'failure' is then all the more readily disregarded, as a matter of their personal inadequacies, in an individualized and supposedly meritocratic culture.

Cultural Politics for a 'New Age'?

Over the last two decades the politics of the environment has moved increasingly to the centre of the British political stage, whether in the form of new environmentalist protests against road-building schemes or marches by the traditionalist countryside lobby in defence of fox-hunting. The politics of the pastoral also brings together, on occasion, strange alliances of rural conservatives and youth cultures (such as the participants in some 'animal rights' protests)—alliances that do not fit at all neatly onto any established political map. As this map is shaken up, there are, of course, also 'governmental' and legal attempts to redraw its contours and boundaries—from the Criminal Justice Act (1994) onwards, we have seen a series of legislative interventions designed to police the limits of acceptable forms of expression of new youth cultures— 'outlawing' participants in 'rave' and 'traveller' cultures—and a whole series of attempts to reassert control over these new, mobile, and fluid lifestyles. At the same time, members of these new groups often assert a set of values with close connections to old traditions of mysticism, pacifism, and astrology—condensed in the form of 'new age' religions. The contributions in this volume that are concerned with these issues aim to unravel some of the key threads that weave in and out of this mobile cultural tapestry, which mixes together the old (references to the very English tradition of the Diggers) and the new (road protesters' use of sophisticated communications technologies to co-ordinate their activities) in strange and hybrid cultural forms.

The construction of a distinctive political culture and public sphere has been central to the imagination of Britishness. For long, our public culture served as a binding and unifying force, working against the centrifugal cultural forces that have threatened, or seemed to threaten, disintegration. In the context of broader economic and social transformations (globalization, consumerism, privatization), this overarching political bond is now much weakened. This is particularly apparent in media culture, with the BBC, long the symbolic figurehead of all things British on the world stage, being undermined by the forces of commercialism and techno-logical change. Public culture in all its forms has been weakened by the growth of 'privatized' consumerism and its inherent individual-ism. Many forms of public provision (e.g. education, public trans-port, the railway system after its privatization), have become increasingly discredited. This is true of both the symbolic and material forms of public culture. As Ken Worpole and his col-leagues have demonstrated in their studies of town centres and other public spaces, these are increasingly felt to be 'no-man's [sic] land', at the mercy of colonization by aggressive forms of mascu-line culture quite at odds with traditional conceptions of the 'pub-lic' as a space of sociability and trust. In this context, the very idea of community has become a focus of attention, again signalling a crisis in our sense of collective belonging. This problematization of the traditional forms of political culture has still not been adequately confronted, and we see around us desperate attempts to shore up and reinvigorate the political frameworks of the past. The essays here address these issues directly, focusing on key examples such as the contrast between the shared symbolic space of public service media and the privatized commercial space of the user/consumer of the Internet. In political life, when national politics is dwarfed by the forces of the global market, rather than looking to the state to represent the 'public good', we are now inclined to accept a reduced model of the state's role, where the individual must buy many more things (health, education, pension rights) in the private marketplace. Developing a fuller understanding of the cultural consequences of the privatization of much that was for-merly public is, we would argue, one of the key intellectual tasks of our time.

Further Reading

1. British Cultural Studies

Baker, Houston, Diawara, Manthia, and Lindeberg, Ruth (eds.) (1996), *Black British Cultural Studies*, Chicago: University of Chicago Press.

Barker, Martin, and Beezer, Anne (eds.) (1995), *Reading into Cultural Studies*, London: Arnold.

Ferguson, Marjorie, and Golding, Peter (eds.) (1997), *Cultural Studies in Question*, London: Sage.

Grossberg, Lawrence, et al. (eds.) (1992), *Cultural Studies*, London: Routledge.

Inglis, Fred (1993), *Cultural Studies*, Oxford: Blackwell.

Kraniauskas, John (1998), 'Globalisation is Ordinary: the Transnationalisation of Cultural Studies', *Radical Philosophy*, 90.

Morley, David, and Chen, Kuan-Hsing (eds.) (1996), *Stuart Hall: Critical Dialogues in Cultural Studies*, London: Routledge.

Mulhearn, Francis (2000), *Metaculture*, London: Routledge.

Turner, Graham (1990), *British Cultural Studies*, London: Arnold.

Storey, John (ed.) (1996), *What is Cultural Studies?*, London: Arnold.

2. British Culture and Society

Alibhai-Brown, Yasmin (2000), *Who Do We Think We Are? Imagining the New Britain*, London: Allen Lane.

Bassnett, Susan (1997), *Studying British Culture*, London: Routledge.

Bracewell, Michael (1996), *England is Mine*, London: Harper Collins.

British Council (1997), *Reinventing Britain*, London: British Council.

—— (2000), *Looking into England*, London: British Council.

Buruma, Ian (1999), *Voltaire's Coconuts: Anglomania in Europe*, London: Weidenfeld & Nicolson.

Christopher, David (1997), *British Culture*, London: Routledge.

Cohn, Nick (2000), *Yes, We Have No: Adventures in Other England*, London: Secker.

Colley, Linda (1994), *Britons: Forging the Nation, 1707–1837*, London: Pimlico.

Davey, Kevin (1999), *English Imaginaries*, London: Lawrence & Wishart.

Davies, Alistair, and Sinfield, Alan (eds.) (2000), *British Culture in the Postwar Period*, London: Routledge.

Davies, Norman (1999), *The Isles: A History*, London: Macmillan.

Dodd, Philip (1995), *The Battle over Britain*, London: Demos.

Granta (1996), *What Happened to Us? Britain's Valedictory Realism*, London: Granta Books.

Lee, A. Robert (ed.) (1995), *Other Britain, Other British*, London: Pluto.

Leonard, Mark (1997), *Britain™: Reviewing our Identity*, London: Demos.

Longford, Paul (2000), *Englishness Identified 1650–1850*, Oxford: Oxford University Press.

Marr, Andrew (1999), *The Day Britain Died*, London: Profile Books.

Oakland, John (1998), *British Civilisation*, London: Routledge,

Owusu, Kwesi (ed.) (2000), *Black British Culture and Society*, London: Routledge.

Parr, Martin (2000), *Think of England*, London: Phaidon.

Paxman, Jeremy (1999), *The English: Portrait of a People*, London: Michael Joseph.

Philips, Caryl (1997), *A Literature of Belonging*, London: Faber.

Richards, Jeffrey (1997), *Films and British National Identity*, Manchester: Manchester University Press.

Runnymede Trust (2000), *The Future of Multi-ethnic Britain*, London: Profile Books.

Samuel, Raphael (1998), *Island Stories: Unravelling Britain*, London: Verso.

Scruton, Roger (2000), *England: An Elegy*, London: Chatto & Windus.

Storry, Michael, and Childs, Peter (eds.) (1997), *Studying British Identities*, London: Routledge.

Younge, Gary (2000), *No Place Like Home*, London: Picador.

References

Ascherson, Neil (1996), 'When was Britain?', *Prospect*, May.

Chapman, Tony, and Hockey, Jenny (eds.) (1999), *Ideal Homes? Social Change and Domestic Life*, London: Routledge.

Corner, John, and Harvey, Sylvia (1991), *Enterprise and Heritage: Crosscurrents of National Culture*, London: Routledge.

Eliot, T. S. (1948), *Notes towards the Definition of Culture*, London: Faber.

Fukuyama, Francis (1993), *The End of History and the Last Man*, Harmondsworth: Penguin

Hall, Stuart (1989), 'New Ethnicities', in Kobena Mercer (ed.), *Black Film, British Cinema*, London: Institute of Contemporary Arts.

Haraway, Donna (1985), 'Homes for Cyborgs', in Elizabeth Weed (ed.), *Coming to Terms: Feminism, Theory, Politics*, New York: Routledge.

Hewison, Robert (1987), *The Heritage Industry*, London: Methuen.

Hobsbawm, Eric, and Ranger, Terence (eds.) (1983), *The Invention of Tradition*, Cambridge: Cambridge University Press.

Leadbeater, C. (2000), *Living on Thin Air: The New Economy*, Harmondsworth: Penguin.

Leonard, Mark (1997), *Britain^{TM}: Renewing our Identity*, London: Demos.

Morley, David, and Robins, Kevin (1995), *Spaces of Identity*, London: Routledge.

Morrison, Blake (2000), 'England at Sea', *Independent on Sunday*, 27 Aug.

Mulgan, Geoff, and Worpole, Ken (1986), *Saturday Night or Sunday Morning?*, London: Comedia.

Nairn, Tom (1977), *The Break-up of Britain*, London: Verso.

Okely, Judith (1997), 'Constable Country', in Karen Fog Olwig and Kirsten Hastrup (eds.), *Siting Culture: The Shifting Anthropological Object*, London: Routledge.

Orwell, George (1969), 'The Lion and the Unicorn', in *The Collected Essays, Journalism and Letters of George Orwell*, ed. Sonia Orwell and Ian Angus, vol. ii, London: Secker & Warburg (1st pub. 1941).

Paxman, Jeremy (1998), *The English*, London: Michael Joseph.

Priestley, J. B. (1977), *An English Journey*, Harmondsworth: Penguin (1st pub. 1934).

Rose, Nikolas (1999), *Governing the Soul*, London: Free Association Books.

Runnymede Trust (2000), *The Future of Multi-ethnic Britain*, London: Profile Books.

Ryan, Alan (ed.) (1992), *After the End of History*, London: Collins & Brown.

Samuel, Raphael (1994), *Theatres of Memory*, i: *Past and Present in Contemporary Culture*, London: Verso.

Sinclair, Iain (1999), *Sorry Meniscus: Excursions to the Millennium Dome*, London: Profile Books.

Volosinov, V. N. (1973), *Marxism and the Philosophy of Language*, New York: Seminar Press.

Williams, Val (ed.) (1994), *Who's Looking at the Family?*, London: Barbican Art Gallery.

Worpole, Ken, and Greenhalgh, Liz (1996), *The Freedom of the City*, London: Demos.

Wright, Patrick (1985), *On Living in an Old Country*, London: Verso.

Section I

How British is it? Geographies of Identity

Introduction

THE first section begins with Catherine Hall's analysis of the legacy of empire and the various ways in which Britain and its population is still inevitably shaped by its imperial history, and to an extent that is often not acknowledged—as if what happened in India or elsewhere was somehow a mere adjunct to a domestic history essentially shaped by 'internal dynamics'. The signs of this imperial past, which belie our 'island story', are, as Hall notes, everywhere about us—in street names, monuments, buildings, and cemeteries. Hall demonstrates the deep roots of empire in everyday life. Taking the city of Birmingham as her example, she shows the extent to which the town's prosperity depended on its export trade to the colonies and the ways in which, historically, the popular press, public lectures by returned adventurers, exhibitions of imperial plunder, and letters from emigrated friends and family all functioned as media for the representation of empire at home. Taking the case of one particular family, Hall offers a compelling example of how the fine web of personal connections was established and maintained across the far-flung empire, through correspondence and travel, however arduous—providing vectors through which stories of colonial life could circulate on the 'home territory'. In all of this what is clear is the importance of race and ethnicity in the ways that white Anglo-Saxons defined their identities in opposition to those of the peoples they had conquered. The issue for Hall is how that imperial legacy is now to be reinterpreted in our postcolonial times, and she thus argues for the profound importance of this kind of 'memory work' on empire in the reconstitution of contemporary cultural identities.

Following Hall's address to British cultural identity, Krishan Kumar focuses specifically on the question of 'Englishness', its historical origins and particularities. He poses questions about how and why this form of identity arose, about its relationship to 'Britishness' and other ethnicities in the UK, and how it has defined itself in relation to European or 'continental' identities. Like Hall, Kumar argues that we need to abandon conventional methods of delineating national culture 'from the inside' and rather work 'from the outside in'—seeing English identity as a residue created by the whole imperial venture (or, in another terminology, 'mission'). It is from this perspective, he argues, that we can also best address the question of England's hegemony over the rest of the British Isles, and the history of its annexation of the territories and subjugation of the populations of Wales, Scotland, and Ireland. Kumar traces some of the complexities of the rise of a specifically English nationalism, arguing that it was never a populist form as it was in post-revolutionary France and elsewhere. As he notes it was only for a time a specifically Protestant identity, defined against the Catholic nationalisms of Europe, and that religious dimension of its identity has now been in decline for many years (see the later contributions by Modood and Bruce). Kumar argues that it was in the late nineteenth century, at the height of Britain's imperial power, when England's own hegemony over the rest of the UK was most securely enshrined, that we see the rise of English nationalism, both as a popular form of patriotism and through institutionalized forms enshrined in dictionaries, school curricula, and books of 'national verse'. Drawing on Collini, Kumar calls this process of institutionalization of 'Englishness' the 'Whig interpretation of English literature'—a self-congratulatory myth of Englishness as a 'blessed inheritance' which still provides the cultural vocabulary from which the current revival of embattled 'Little Englandism' draws (from Powell, through Thatcher and Major to Hague). The issue for the future is how such ideas of 'Englishness' will fare now that, in the wake of the (cultural, if not yet political) 'break up of Britain', as Kumar puts it, 'England stands exposed, no longer protected by a surrounding carapace of Britishness'.

The issue of the implications of the break-up of Britain for the politics of black Britishness is addressed by Jim Pines. His initial focus is on the symbolization and representation of 'race' and ethnicity in the context of international sporting competitions and how they can be read as 'barometers' of the rearticulation of national identities. In this context he traces the modalities through which, at some key moments in recent years, the flag of St George—the symbol of a specifically English, rather than British, identity—has replaced the Union Jack in public visibility. While the St George's Cross has principally been associated with negative images of English football hooliganism, Pines also shows how, at other moments, this symbol has allowed new and mobile forms of multi-ethnic inclusiveness which transcend the Union Jack's uniquely problematic exclusion of blackness. Shifting from the realm of sport to that of popular culture, he then traces some of the key changes in the cinematic representation of black Britishness over the last twenty-five years, from Horace Ove's *Pressure* (1975) onwards, showing how the question at issue has shifted from the representation of what it is to be 'black in Britain' to the quite different question of what it is to be 'black' and 'British'. In considering the work of black British film-makers of recent years he examines the new politics of representation and memory exhibited in these films' attempt to address issues of diaspora and diversity. As he notes, in the wake of the public discussions engendered by the Macpherson Report on the murder of Stephen Lawrence and the Runnymede Trust's report on *The Future of Multi-ethnic Britain*, the questions of black Britishness and black Englishness are central to the contemporary political agenda.

Tariq Modood's article is based on detailed large-scale survey work which offers rich and valuable insights into the views of a wide range of ethnic minorities in the UK. As he notes, ethnic identities have in many ways been politicized in the broader context of the rise of identity politics, and we see here new forms of political and religious assertiveness seeking not just toleration but recognition and respect as legitimate elements of contemporary British culture. Many members of the ethnic minorities surveyed here feel a keen sense of their 'racialization' by white Britain and feel that, despite all the claims about the emergence of a multicultural 'New Britain', they still in fact suffer from a variety of forms of cultural (if not colour-based) racism. The relationship between ethnic and religious identities here is complex. Some of the British-Asians surveyed here reject an ethnic in favour of a Muslim identity. Compared with white Britons for whom, as Steve Bruce observes in his chapter in Section II, religion is a rapidly declining factor in their lives, and even more than for Afro-Caribbean respondents, religion emerges as central to the self-description of the vast majority of south Asians in the UK. Moreover, this is also true for young south Asians, to an extent that contrasts particularly strongly with the almost total secularization of white British youth. However, Modood argues that these ethnic identities do not necessarily compete with a sense of 'Britishness'—many respondents happily espouse a hyphenated British-Asian identity, despite their anxieties about the extent to which their claims on Britishness are in fact accepted by white Britons.

The complexities of political and cultural identities in Northern

Ireland are examined by Kevin Davey, who traces the contours and schisms which continue to rend the landscape of that outpost of the United Kingdom. In his attempt to assess the fragile potential of the 'peace process', in its various phases in recent years, Davey draws on the work of Julia Kristeva. Thus, using her theoretical framework, he poses the question of whether the antagonistic elements that go so reluctantly together to make up the fractious 'communities' of Northern Ireland, with their 'fragile and threatened imaginaries' and embattled siege mentalities, can ever become, as Kristeva puts it, 'strangers to themselves' sufficiently to recognize and live with the Others against whom they have historically defined their identities. Beyond providing an outline of the recent history of Northern Ireland's 'Troubles', Davey also outlines the long-term forces—creeping deindustrialization and demographic change—which are already transforming the society. Moreover, as he notes, exogenous changes are also transforming the broader context of Irish politics. Transnational forces such as the growing importance of the Irish diaspora in North American politics, economic pressures towards future European integration, along with the reality of Eire's already strong EU involvement, all work towards the gradual transformation of the region. As Davey notes, the hybridizing, centrifugal forces of world markets mean that, ingrained hostilities notwithstanding, it seems likely that Northern Ireland's future may well be driven by forces originating far outside its own borders.

Recent developments in Scotland are considered by David McCrone. He starts out from the exceptional nature of the British state, and from the characteristically fuzzy quality of identities within that state. What the chapter argues is that the British state in fact suffers from an arrested political development—he points to the antiquated nature of state mechanisms. It is a state in which the people remain (pre-modern) 'subjects of the crown', rather than citizens of a modern democracy. McCrone also argues that Britain should be seen as a state-nation, rather than a nation-state, with a state identity having been imposed over an array of internal differences. One of the central reasons for the deformed nature of the British polity, in McCrone's view, is the imperial history of the country. The British state has been an empire state, defined and created in the context of warfare and imperial expansion. After empire, the strains within the British state formation have begun to show more and more. As McCrone puts it, 'layers of the British imperium [have been] peeling off, first the white Dominions, then the challenge from the Celtic countries'. This brings the argument to a consideration of the position of Scotland now. McCrone recognizes that Scotland received a relatively comfortable accommodation in the context of the British state formation, being able to run its own internal affairs (the legal, educational, and religious systems, as well as local government). But, now, in the context of Europeanization and globalization, Scotland is seeking to renegotiate its place in the Union. With the setting up of the Scottish Parliament, we have seen a significant shift in the politics of identity in these islands. What McCrone argues is that Scotland is now leading the way in resolving the contradictions of the British state formation.

John Osmond is concerned with similar developments in Wales, which have brought a National Asssembly into being. Osmond charts the developments in Welsh culture and identity in the period between 1979, when the vote was overwhelmingly against devolution, and 1997, when the Welsh, like the Scots, voted for the Assembly. In what is a very upbeat survey, Osmond identifies a number of key developments—up to the point of the first elections for the National Assembly in 1999—that have reshaped the national mood. First, there was a shift in identity politics, particularly in the context of Europeanization (and the idea of a Europe of the regions). The very meaning of 'British' and 'Welsh' became transformed, Osmond argues, and a new sense of European-oriented Welshness came into existence. There were also significant economic transformations, with the emergence of new sectors and new forms of industrial organization, and again these developments propelled the Welsh in a European direction. A further factor of change was the shift in generational consciousness that came about by 1997, with the old generation, shaped by the Second World War and the consciousness and then loss of Empire, fading from the scene. Osmond sees all of these developments as part of a 'modernization' of Welsh society. Many of the developments are, of course, akin to those that were happening in Scotland. What Osmond emphasizes, however, is that the Welsh were in a more disadvantaged position with respect to the new possibilities that were offering themselves. Welsh society was institutionally weaker, and, compared to Scotland, it had an underdeveloped press. Being Welsh has been 'much more diffuse and fractured' than is the case with being Scottish. Nonetheless, Osmond argues, things have changed significantly. The development of the Welsh television channel S4C, as well as of Welsh-language rock groups, has even meant that the Welsh language has become associated with the new processes of 'modernization'. In Osmond's view, the developments that culminated in the establishment of the National Assembly have opened up a new civic space for a truly Welsh politics—as indicated by the surge of support for Plaid Cymru in the May 1999 elections to the Assembly. They have, at the same time, profoundly affected the future of Britishness.

The 'English problem' in British society, culture, and identity is analysed by Peter Taylor. Englishness, he argues, is presenting all the inhabitants of these islands with profound dilemmas—dilemmas that are badly in need of clarification and resolution. Taylor wonders whether the period between 1980 and 2020 might be a watershed for Britishness, a period of politico-cultural choice for citizens of the UK. He sets about the task of clarifying the dynamics of English/British culture through a discussion of what he regards as three fundamental presumptions at its core. First, there is the English presumption, by which Englishness commonly and easily comes to substitute for Britishness (among the English). This discursive shift has resulted in a cultural politics that is patronizing to the non-English—one that in fact turns them into invisible peoples. Taylor's second presumption is what he calls the rural presumption, whereby Englishness has come to be associated with the countryside and its village culture (on this see Howkins's chapter, below). The rural presumption has underpinned the polarized North–South divide in English society, setting the Home Counties—the Crown Heartland—against the Other of the industrial and urban 'North'. The third presumption is the monolithic presumption, which regards this northern elsewhere as a single and unitary entity, disavowing its internal complexity and diversity. Having diagnosed the sickness at the heart of the national culture, Taylor then moves on to make some suggestions as to how these cultural-political dilemmas might be overcome. For Taylor, what is significant is the logic of economic and cultural globalization, which has given a new importance to city regions. He puts his hopes, not in regional or national futures, but in a new urbanism, with cosmopolitan and multicultural possibilities. For Taylor, the symbols of cultural modernization are devolution, 'Cool Britannia', and shopping malls—all of which contradict the old logic of national identity. There is a city solution to the problem of English/British national identity.

An account of the significance of rural culture in the construction of the national culture during the twentieth century is provided by Alun Howkins. In this context, Englishness, or even more specifically southern Englishness, often comes to stand in for Britishness. Here, of course, Howkins is developing a similar argument to that made in the previous chapter by Peter Taylor. The chapter traces the ways in which the southern ruralist imagination has insinuated itself into the national imagination—such that the wartime refrain 'Bluebirds over the White Cliffs of Dover' could symbolize the national spirit. Howkins notes how the ruralist spirit even informed the early socialist movement, inspiring the healthy, recreational culture of rambling and cycling clubs in the inter-war years. A central concern of the chapter is with how, in the early years of the century, the years before the Great War, the ideal of rurality assumed its great resonance in relation to what was regarded as the unnatural, and often degenerate, space of the city—in relation to the city regarded as a space of problems. Howkins argues that, throughout the century, the culture of ruralism has competed effectively against the culture and values of urbanism as an organizing principle in the national identity. The countryside has constantly asserted itself against the city—from the Surrey Anti-Litter League, fulminating against the unrural dispositions of trippers from London, to the massive rally of the Countryside Alliance in Hyde Park in 1997. The chapter invites us to reflect on the significance of rural culture and values today. There are those who now seek to mobilize the ideal of 'Deep England', invoking 'a core of ideas around which appeals to the "natural" heart of England can be based'. But Howkins notes that this pastoral ideal is also very much at odds with the multicultural nature of contemporary Britain—of contemporary urban Britain, that is to say. The issue of ruralism remains a central one in English/British culture: for some, it remains crucial to the maintenance of an 'enduring' national home: and for others, it represents a fundamental obstacle to the creation of more accommodating and cosmopolitan cultural order in Britain.

Finally in this Section, Bill Schwarz considers the position of Britain in its new global context, in a discussion that is concerned with changing centres and peripheries in a changing world order. The high point of British global hegemony was in what Schwarz dubs the Atlantic epoch, the period when it had maritime power and prestige. It was this maritime aspect of British society that at the same time made the country regard itself (narcissistically) as a marginal European culture. Britain has always had a difficult and ambivalent relation to the Europe that it is so close to—the United States and the empire have always been far more resonant points of reference. Yet now things are changing, and Britain is having to suffer a decline of authority and a decentring of its position in the new global order. And it is proving extremely difficult for the country to adapt to the new cultural conditions. Schwarz argues that the relative historical stability of the culture—which is what makes it an 'old country'—stands in the way of change now. Britain is struggling in its attempt to Europeanize itself, as the sense of its own providential history weighs it down in an almost metaphysical relation to its own cultural sovereignty. At the same time, however, there have had to be pragmatic accommodations, with respect to the European Union and the 'special relationship' to the United States. This has brought about a situation, Schwarz argues, in which there has been a certain divergence between the (more pragmatic) projects of the state and the (more archaic) imperatives of the nation. Interestingly, Schwarz argues that the development of cultural studies in Britain was a consequence of the progressive decentring of the national culture. There have been those who have seen possibilities inherent in the dislocations of British culture—possibilities of more realistic, and at the same time cosmopolitan, cultural arrangements. The question is whether Britain can now come to terms with the discomforts that have accompanied its cultural decentring.

British Cultural Identities and the Legacy of the Empire

CATHERINE
HALL

THE legacy of the British Empire is highly visible in the 1990s. The British population itself is shaped by imperial history: the African-Caribbean and South Asian presence, the result of the post-war migrations when Britain's labour shortages were met by Jamaican and Trinidadian bus drivers, building labourers, hospital workers, and nurses, Indian and Pakistani factory workers and cleaners; the Irish presence, the sign of the migrations of the mid-nineteenth century and the post-war period, and of the constant movement across the Irish channel over centuries. The cemeteries which provide multiple reminders of the diasporic lives of nineteenth-century English, Scottish, and Irish men particularly, soldiers who served in India or Africa, sailors who spent their lives crossing oceans, missionaries who returned and died back home. The buildings which offer material reminders of imperial connections, the Bank of England and the Royal Exchange symbolizing the financial centre of the globe, the reliefs of Africans' heads with elephants on the façade of the Liverpool Exchange marking the significance of the slave trade to that city's wealth, the great museums of London, packed with imperial treasures, the Hyderabad Barracks in Colchester, reminding us of the links between Britain and India, the West India Dock Company's elegant building just by Canary Wharf, once the meeting place of slave traders and sugar merchants, now the site of refurbished flats for city folks. The streets in every town which mark historic battles and moments, from Trafalgar to Mafeking, signalling the ways in which national identity in Britain has been so profoundly shaped by imperial expansion and danger. The novels which form the national literature, from Jane Austen's *Mansfield Park*, an English country home financed from the sugar plantations of Antigua, to Charles Dickens's unfinished novel *The Mystery of Edwin Drood*, touched with the racial fear engendered by the 'Indian Mutiny' of 1857 when 'natives' serving in the British army rebelled against their colonial masters. The quintessential national beverage, tea, imported from Ceylon and India, the demand for it changing the shape of whole regions as tea gardens were laid out, the sugar served with it which transformed the British Caribbean islands into a gigantic sugarmill, and changed the economy and society of Africa and the Caribbean for ever.

But what does that legacy mean and how can it be interpreted now in the postcolonial moment? Postcolonial for Britain in the sense that Britain is no longer a major colonial power, only the remnants of the empire remain, and even Ireland, the oldest colony with its very particular position both inside and outside the United Kingdom, begins to look different. In the time after the empire how does that imperial history now look and how might it be rethought? What difference does the understanding of nations as constituted through inclusions and exclusions, their fictional homegeneities constructed through discursive work, make? What difference does the history of being colonizers make to the constitution of British cultural identities? How significant were ideas about race to the making of English or British identities? If the history is everywhere it has also been strangely absent from our 'island stories', those stories as to who 'we' are, in which the empire seems tangential. Whenever colonial questions were discussed, historians assure us, the Houses of Parliament emptied. Domestic history was shaped by internal questions, by class conflict, by party political struggles, by the antagonism between the country and the city. What happened in India, or Ireland, or Egypt, or Jamaica, or Australia or New Zealand, was for the most part irrelevant to the national story. Of course *their* histories were shaped by the metropolis but that was different. But was it? Or were English, Scottish, and Welsh identities shaped by that empire as well as by the class and gender antagonisms, the European rivalries, which were part of everyday life?

In 1815, after the defeat of Napoleon, Britain had made a remarkable recovery from the loss of the North American colonies in the War of Independence. It had significantly added to its territories during the wars with France. British dominions included an estimated 26 per cent of the world's population in 1820 and stretched from India and Australia to Jamaica and Canada. The empire comprised both what came to be defined as colonies, those terrains where British settlers had formed new societies which they were making into a home from home, the white settler societies such as Australia and Canada, frequently constructed as the children of the 'mother country', and dependencies, those terrains where 'natives' formed the majority population and which were seen as in need of rule, India and the British Caribbean islands. The empire continued to grow throughout the nineteenth century so that, for example, New Zealand, South Africa, Ceylon, and Egypt were all incorporated.

But what effects did this ever growing empire have at home? In what sense might it be argued that British identities were in part constituted through this empire, that ordinary men and women recognized their own national identities through their difference from colonial others, that race and ethnicity were crucial markers of difference, that white Anglo-Saxons defined themselves in opposition to those they believed they ruled? My focus here is on British/English identities, for English, I suggest, constituted the dominant identity in the nineteenth century, claiming for itself the characteristics of Britishness. Take Birmingham in the nineteenth century, hardly an imperial city in any conventional sense. It did not depend on slavery as Liverpool and Bristol had done, or on raw materials from the colonies like Glasgow. It had no black population of any significance, no dockers or sailors, unlike London or Cardiff. Indeed it was a matter to be noted in the local press when a black person, a missionary or an entertainer, was sighted in the town. Yet Birmingham was *of* the empire, situated within the empire, defining itself through its relation to nation and empire, its townspeople imbricated with empire, long before Joseph Chamberlain articulated its political identity as imperial in the late nineteenth century. By the mid-nineteenth century its export market was closely linked to the colonies, its citizens formed a diaspora across those colonies, many of them closely maintaining their connections with home town, families, and friends, its political and cultural life deeply inflected with issues of race, nation, and empire.

Birmingham's fame, in so far as it had any, depended on its metals and its trades, its reputation that of an industrial and commercial centre, its visitors' first ports of call its manufactories and its workshops. The town's prosperity was closely tied to its ability to export and quantities of its goods went to the colonies. By the mid-1860s townsmen were proud to be able to claim that, within a radius of about 30 miles, 'nearly the whole of the hardware wants of the world are practically supplied': indeed, 'almost every metallic article, whether used in the shop or in the house, whether at home or abroad, is more or less directly connected with some of the Birmingham trades'. The casters, hinges, and latches, the railings, rods, and fireguards, the jewellery, steel pens, and brass bedsteads, the guns, lamps, and gas fittings, the buttons and buckles, the plated dinner services and cutlery, the needles, springs, small tools, and umbrella frames, the screws and nails, the kettles, pots, and pans which graced the homes of rich and poor, all had their origins in the workshops of Birmingham. Such items were required the world over and colonies provided a particularly significant market for Birmingham entrepreneurs. By the 1860s Australia and New Zealand led the demand for doorknobs while India led the sales of iron padlocks. Australia and India provided excellent markets for chains, cables, and anchors and Australia was second only to Britain for the jewellery and gilt toy trades while iron and brass-bed manufacturers depended for their sales on both the colonies and dependencies of the British Empire.

But the empire was part of the everyday world of Birmingham men and women in the nineteenth century and commerce was only one of the multiple ways in which that empire figured in the minds and imagined landscapes of Birmingham people. Local newspapers reported regularly on events in the empire, often with excerpts from national newspapers and editorial comment; they reviewed the new books of explorers and travellers, commented in myriad ways on the differences between 'them' and 'us'. The *Birmingham Journal*, a weekly liberal newspaper, saw it as part of its task to educate its readers on matters colonial and provided special features, sometimes with maps included, for those who were not sure where such places as the principality of Oude or the region of the Punjab were. The editors confidently characterized peoples, placing them in relation to their own assumptions about nation and 'civilization'. The liberal press was on the whole sympathetic to the notion of the universal family of man, a notion which was most powerfully articulated through the antislavery movement in the nineteenth century, committed as it was to the belief that black people could be educated and 'civilized' to become 'like us'. Other sections of the press provided a conduit for the new racial science which was emerging, a science which maintained that the races were biologically distinct and that black, brown, or yellow people would always be different from and inferior to white. *The Times*, for example, could always be relied on for a harsh vision of racial difference, whether in relation to the Africans of the Caribbean or the Irish in London or Dublin. The meanings of race and empire were always debated and contested, both locally and nationally. At certain moments particular representations came to carry the status of truth, as in 1857 when the Indian sepoy became a byword for treachery. Birmingham newspaper readers could enter the imagined community of nation and empire as well as that of the town as they read their morning papers, both local and national, read of strange doings elsewhere, and reflected on their own different and not so different daily lives. Englishmen and Brummagems did not have the same 'peculiarities of character' as 'the Hindoo', were not locked in prejudice like 'the Sepoy', were not barbaric in the ways the Irish were.

If newspapers were one of the major sites of representation of empire there were many others, from the novels of the circulating libraries to the penny dreadfuls of popular fiction, from the periodicals of the middle-class reading public to the sermons of the missionary societies which circulated so widely. Exhibitions, theatrical productions, the myriad shows, panoramas, and dioramas beloved by the Victorians, lectures and readings such as those of Dickens from his work, all of these provided spaces for imperial representations, and for the exploration of racial difference. Public meetings were held in the town to discuss imperial issues, from emigration to the 'Indian Mutiny', the American Civil War, and the conduct of Governor Eyre in the aftermath of the rebellion at Morant Bay in Jamaica, all of these were opportunities for debate over the conduct of empire and moments to reflect collectively on the differences between 'them' and 'us'.

But perhaps family and friends were the most intimate connection for Birmingham people with the empire and a remarkable number either knew or had relatives or friends who knew that empire personally. From the families of those in the army or navy to the emigrants of the 1830s and 1840s who despaired of life in Birmingham and opted for a new life elsewhere in Australia or New Zealand, or the congregations attached to missionaries in Jamaica or India, or those radicals who were transported to Australia, each emigrant took something of Birmingham with them and negotiated a new life with that cultural capital. Some maintained close connections with families and friends left at home, others made breaks but then reconnected to their roots, others again probably had no further contact with their home town. But the personal connections which were established across the empire, and the letters and gifts which passed between the different sites of empire, provided a tangible web of knowledges about peoples and places.

The linkages between metropolis and colonies were myriad and played a part in the constitution of British identities. The colonizers were made by the colonial encounter quite as much as those they colonized.

Take the Parkes family, living in Edgbaston, the new and leafy suburb of Birmingham, from the mid-1820s. John Parkes, son of a Warwickshire yeoman family and devoted Unitarian, was running a large lace and worsted factory in Warwick in the early nineteenth century. Together with his partners he employed 500 hundred hands. In 1825 the business went down in the national economic crisis and he retired with his wife to Harborne Road, Edgbaston, where there were strong Unitarian connections, for congregations formed one of the major places of belonging in the burgeoning industrial towns. There it was possible to live genteelly on limited means. The fourth son of the Parkeses was Joseph, born in 1796, who had studied at Glasgow University and then been articled to a solicitor in London. When his father's business collapsed he gave up his hopes of the Chancery Bar and became a county attorney working from Birmingham. In 1824 he married Elizabeth Rayner Priestley, the granddaughter of the celebrated radical Unitarian scientist Joseph Priestley, and they lived in the town until 1833. Joseph Parkes was very actively involved in Utilitarian and reforming initiatives and played a major part in securing municipal reform both locally and nationally. In 1833 he moved to London with his wife and two young children when he was appointed secretary to the Municipal Corporations Commission.

One of Joseph's sisters, Mary, married William Swainson, who was in the army and then became a naturalist. In 1835 Mary died leaving three boys and a girl and William lost most of his money in speculations in Mexico. In the late 1830s he decided to make a new life, to emigrate and marry his children's governess, Miss Grasby. This was a time when there was great interest in New Zealand and it was there that Swainson decided to go. The new world of Australia and New Zealand had very recently become a site for middle-class emigrants, hopeful of a better future in another place. The efforts of Edward Gibbon Wakefield, an energetic enthusiast for what became known as 'systematic colonization', a plan for the export of capital and labour to the colonies, had borne fruit in the New Zealand Association of 1837 which became the New Zealand Company in 1838. Wakefield was very enthusiastic about middle-class emigrants, and, indeed, about families as well as the young single English women who could provide suitable wives for settlers and bear children who would fill the so-called empty lands of the

New World. Young single men should be strongly encouraged to marry so that women's virtue would be protected, men's better habits encouraged. Every 'pair of immigrants' would then have 'the strongest motives for industry, steadiness and thrift'. In his vision:

the mother country and the colony would become partners in a new trade—the creation of happy human beings; one country furnishing the raw material—that is, the land, the dust of which man is made; the other furnishing the machinery—that is, men and women, to convert the unpeopled soil into images of God. (Wakefield 1833: ii. 216)

The 'unpeopled soil' of New Zealand turned out to be peopled with Maori but the scheme for the 'creation of happy human beings' chimed well with Unitarian and Utilitarian preoccupations as to the making of a better and more rational world. Birmingham had a number of great enthusiasts for the cause including the Hills, protagonists of educational reform, of political reform, of prison and of postal reform. The Hills and the Parkeses belonged to the same Unitarian congregation and a Hill daughter was one of the first group to settle in South Australia, a colony which was designed for reforming dissenters. William Swainson's decision to emigrate to New Zealand, therefore, was entirely in line with family and friends.

The New Zealand Company was pressuring strongly for British intervention in the period leading up to the Treaty of Waitangi of 1840, the historic pact between the Crown and Maori which opened the way for British domination of the islands. They dispatched their first immigrant ship in 1839. Their primary interest was to secure cheap land and protection for the settlers. Between 1840 and 1842 they were responsible, along with their affiliates, for founding Wellington, named after the Duke who had been very sympathetic to the settlement of South Australia, and two other new towns. Each had a population of between 1,000 and 4,000 within two years of settlement. These then became bases for secondary colonization, initially using the sea as there were no roads. In the 1840s settlers moved out from Wellington to Wanganui, Wairarapa, and Marlborough, areas in which Maori were enthusiastically selling land in the 1840s. The first settlers in Wellington took up sheep farming and found that trade with Maori was vital for them. Pakeha (white settlers) were as yet a tiny proportion of the population: by 1844 there were 12,000 concentrated in a number of settlements; the rest of the islands were ruled by Maori. As James Belich argues, there were in effect three New Zealands in this period: Aotearoa, independently run by Maori, 'Old New Zealand', the area of interface between Maori and Pakeha, and the new New Zealand of mass European settlement. It was not until the 1860s that Maori substantially lost power and the new New Zealand emerged triumphant.

Control over Wellington was disputed in the 1840s between Sir George Grey, the energetic Governor who arrived in 1845, and Te Rauparaha. In the 1820s Te Rauparaha had moved south in search of land, guns, and greenstone and established himself with a strategic base on Kapiti Island, key to the Cook Strait region between the North and South Islands. By the early 1840s he was overlord of extensive territories both sides of the Cook Strait, a bigger empire than Britain had in New Zealand at this time. Settlers around Wellington were encroaching on land which they believed they had bought. Te Rauparaha and his lieutenant Te Rangihaeata stopped one such encroachment at Wairau in 1843. Twenty-two settlers were killed including Captain Arthur Wakefield and the 'Wairau massacre' became enshrined in settler memory. At this point the Governor, Fitzroy, to the great annoyance of the settlers upheld Maori rights. When Grey arrived he was determined to shift the balance of power, bringing in more troops and enforcing British dominion in the areas of settlement. In 1846 he seized Te Rauparaha, who was imprisoned for two years and never fully recovered his power, dying in 1849.

The Swainsons arrived in New Zealand in 1841 and started farming in the Wellington area. Mary Swainson, born in Warwick in 1826 and 14 when she set out for her new life, kept closely in touch with her maternal grandparents in Edgbaston, writing by nearly every ship. In addition she wrote to friends and to her childhood friend and cousin Bessie Rayner Parkes, the daughter of Joseph Parkes. Writing letters 'home' was part of the construction of the settler identity, telling dear ones about the rigours of life in the colony, mapping that place as one of white settlement, and making a claim to be there. It was also a way of asserting connections with the 'mother country', reminding the letter writer of how different life was in the metropolis and yet how intimate the associations were, linking the identity of colonizer to that of the family and friends, distancing colonizers from the colonized. At the same time such letters were an important source of knowledge about empire, not only to their immediate recipients but also to a circle of family and friends, and church or chapel communities, who would pass the stories of colonial life around their own overlapping networks. Furthermore, such letters, particularly if they came from known families in the town, were sometimes excerpted in the local press.

Thus the *Birmingham Journal* published extracts from the letters of the Clark family, related by marriage to the Hills and known to many in Birmingham, and Brummagems learned one aspect of what it was to be a colonizer.

Mary started recording her impressions from the time of preparation for the voyage. On board she kept a diary and once established in New Zealand she wrote accounts of the new life providing a picture of the world of the settlers for those at home, reassuring would-be emigrants that it was possible, provided there was a willingness for hard work, to 'make a competence', though no one should imagine that they could make a fortune. Maori figured significantly in her descriptions and Mary provided a picture for her Midland relatives and friends who had never themselves seen indigenous people. Her descriptions could be put alongside the fiction and travel writings, the missionary reports and news items which shaped the imperial imagination. Writing to her friend Isabel Percy who had enquired what kind of people the natives were, Mary instructed her that 'for savages they are universally allowed to be the most intelligent', apart from the Tahitians. 'They are much better looking than any of the Australian or African tribes,' she continued confidently (though of course she was relying on hearsay):

they are in colour rather darker than the Creoles, with black hair and eyes, and generally good teeth, their stature varies very much, but I should think averaged that of the English, they are mostly tatooed, some of them all over their faces, others only partly. Their expression is certainly intelligent and sometimes cunning. It is astonishing to see how quickly they learn to read and write . . . they are a very dirty people and I am afraid this generation never will become anything like clean.[1]

While the early 1840s were relatively peaceful, by 1845 there was more open military conflict and scare stories amongst the settlers. 'Most horrible it is to be obliged to say', wrote 19-year-old Mary to her grandparents, 'that the Natives have returned to all their old habits of cannibalism, that they mutilated the body of Capt. Grant, and scalped Mr. Philpotts besides other atrocities, it is a most dreadful thing'. 'There is a faint hope', she added, that the story about the mutilation might not be true, 'but it is very much to be feared that it is only too true'. 'The Governor', she reported, who was at this time Fitzroy, 'makes every endeavour to hide every thing that is bad on the native side.' Here was a classic settler complaint: that the appointees of the Colonial Office were always more ready to 'excuse the natives' than were the settlers who really understood their ways.

1 M. F. Swainson, 'Letters to her grandparents in England 1840° 1850', M. F. Marshall, 'Letters to Mary de Lys and Isabel Percy, Warwick, from Hutt Valley and Kaewharawhara 1843–1854', Auckland Institute and Museum Library, MS 198. I am grateful to Raewyn Dalziel for pointing me in the direction of these letters.

The Legacy of the Empire

By 1846 local troubles with 'the natives' meant that the Swain-sons were very pleased to have a military camp established close to their house and were requesting armed men in the house for pro-tection. Two of Mary's brothers were meanwhile serving in the militia. Mary told her grandparents, perhaps partly to calm her own fears, that they 'must not stop sending for fear of the Natives' as the troubles would last for a long time. Besides which, 'there really is no fear' for the new Governor, George Grey, was constructing military roads so that areas would not be cut off, establishing an armed police force, and training 'natives' within that. This was part of Grey's policy of amalgamation, a policy which involved the attempted deculturation of Maori in the expectation that they would eventually become 'like us'.

By the early 1850s when Pakeha–Maori relations were less tense in the Wellington area Mary was prepared to be generous about the experiment of a reforming bishop in training 'native' boys. 'Being such savages it is of the first importance', she wrote, 'to establish faith and trust in us amongst them—especially poor things as their experience has been amongst the worst of our race—whalers and traders of no principle.' But she added that she was still entirely convinced that they were cannibals and indeed she had heard it from an eyewitness. She had come to believe, she told her friends in England, in the extinction of races. As the Maori population declined, despite reduced internal conflicts and a decline in canni-balism, it seemed to her, however painful, that 'it was in the order of God's providence it should be so'. In 1854 she described an encounter with an old whaler who had been married to a 'native' woman. She had died leaving him to grieve and to care for their six children. Mary was moved by his feelings for one who was not his colour and reflected that feelings seemed to be the same whatever the colour of the skin. He was caring tenderly for his mixed-race children, washing and dressing them every morning, teaching them every evening, and telling them terrifying stories of savage life in the recent past including cannibalism. His most dramatic tale was of Te Rangihaeata, the wicked protagonist of the Wairau massacre, who shot a slave girl, kicked her down the hill, and made a feast of her that very evening. As this story was passed round in Birming-ham how could the 'natives' of that town not be thankful that such practices were being banished by the civilities of settler life? Mary Swainson was in part working out for herself what she thought of Maori in her letters home, drawing not only on new settler wisdom but also on the racial discourses of the 'mother country'. Her voice was not consistent, her certainties as a very young woman no doubt disturbed by Pakeha dependence on and fear of 'the natives'. Grey's policy of amalgamation seems to have gained her support and by the 1850s she shared the commonsense assumption of many colonizers, both in the metropolis and the 'peripheries', that savage races would conveniently disappear in the wake of the march of progress.

Mary's letters must have been one of the many sources of knowledge about emigrants and colonists, about New Zealand and Maori, for her cousin Bessie Rayner Parkes. Brought up in the radical reforming tradition of her father, who was however quite clear as to the proper activities of young ladies, she was one of the 'Langham Place' feminists who publicly took up the 'Woman Question' in the 1850s. English feminists of this generation were shaped by the traditions of women's activism in philanthropy and antislavery, by the experience of working with their fathers and brothers on issues of reform from support for European nationalisms to running fund-raising activities for the Anti-Corn Law League. They were also shaped by their position at the heart of the empire and by the notions of civilization which had been framed by the Scottish Enlightenment and the colonial encounter. Feminists began to claim the right to work, the right to vote, the right to own their own property and to be full members of the nation, and nation was integrally linked to empire. The British nation was defined by its imperial task: it was this which raised the British above other nations. The empire was itself a sign of the conquering and colonizing genius of the Anglo-Saxon race. Its existence gave white Anglo-Saxons a particular responsibility, to civilize others, and their pursuit of this task imbued them with moral authority. The race was indeed a missionary race. In claiming their place in the national firmament English feminists had to contend with notions of their inferiority as a sex: their superiority as a race was a powerful counter to this. Victorian women's 'otherness', as Antoinette Burton argues, could be undermined by their identification with the self of nation and empire. Mary Swainson's determination to mark the boundaries between 'them' and 'us', 'savage' and 'civilized', reminds us of the efforts of those Victorian women missionaries and reformers who devoted themselves to improving the lot, as they saw it, of the 'native' women, whether in the Caribbean, India, Australia, the Cape, or New Zealand, who were seen as symbols of the barbarism of indigenous cultures.

Bessie Rayner Parkes and her dear friend Barbara Leigh Smith were central to the first women's periodical devoted to women's issues, the *English Woman's Journal*. They wanted work for women above all. They wanted women to have economic independence and to be saved from a life of 'redundancy', unsupported by husband or father, the fate which appeared to threaten many women after the revelations of the 1851 Census as to the numbers of spinsters. They wanted the kind of education and training that men had, and they wanted men's occupations to be open to women. Together with others they organized the first petition to Parliament for women's suffrage, they published pamphlets, and they used the rooms they rented in Langham Place to organize a multitude of activities. One of their activities concerned emigration, for the white settler colonies seemed to offer a possible avenue of employment for middle-class women. Bessie Parkes joined Maria Rye in organizing both the Society for Promoting the Employment of Women and the Female Middle Class Emigration Society. Arrangements were made for women to emigrate to Natal, British Columbia, India, Australia, and the Cape. In 1862 Maria Rye sailed for New Zealand to investigate the potential for female emigrants: her discoveries as to the inadequacies of the provision on arrival were publicized in *The Times* and she was disappointed to realize that the major demand was for working-class women who would be servants.

Mary Swainson had no doubts as to her right to be in New Zealand: it was the right of 'the civilized' to improve 'the savage'. Similarly generations of imperial feminists claimed these rights for themselves. Imperial identities were made both in the metropolis and the colonies. Those Birmingham men and women who feasted on scary stories of Maori cannibalism, who sold their products to the colonies, who consumed colonial goods, who enjoyed theatrical productions which centred on imperial questions, who debated the place of slavery in the American Civil War, were creating boundaries between 'them' and 'us' and proving to themselves in diverse ways the British right to rule over others.

Colonial rule was the rule of the colonizers over the colonized: it depended on the army and the navy, on economic power and on political might, on habits of mind and feeling which distanced the rulers from the ruled and legitimized patterns of domination and subordination. Colonial rule was not chosen by the colonized, it was imposed through conquest and the exercise of diverse forms of power. It was fought over and resisted, in the multiple 'small wars', as colonial wars were named in the metropolis in the nineteenth century, in the full-scale conflicts over decolonization of the twentieth century. In this process of colonial exploration and settlement, as Frantz Fanon has helped us to understand, the identities of both colonizer and colonized were made and remade. 'Europe', he argued, 'was literally the creation of the Third World.' This process of mutual constitution, the white woman settler who 'knows' and names the Maori warrior, yet cannot hold him in that place, the English feminist who bemoans the fate of other women less advanced than herself, some of whom actively refused that depiction, has shaped national and imperial identities. Such narratives were a part of the interlinked histories of metropolis and colony. Myths of the 'docility' of the Indian man or woman, or the sexual prowess of the African-Caribbean man have long histories, yet live on in the present.

Imperial identities, made over centuries, are not easy to unravel. They live on in reworked forms in the postcolonial moment. The long history of representations of Irish, African-Caribbean, and South Asian peoples, of Maori and of white settlers, inflect the ways in which race is lived in twenty-first-century Britain. This history demands our attention. If cultural identities are to be reconstructed and we are to learn to live with difference some memory work on empire is essential.

Further Reading

Belich, J. (1996), *Making Peoples: A History of the New Zealanders. From Polynesian Settlement to the End of the Nineteenth Century*, Auckland: Allen Lane. This book provides an excellent introduction to the history of New Zealand.

Burton, A. (1994), *Burdens of History: British Feminists, Indian Women, and Imperial Culture, 1865–1915*, Chapel Hill: University of North Carolina Press. Burton demonstrates the intimate connections between feminism and imperialism in the late nineteenth and early twentieth centuries.

Fanon, F. (1986), *Black Skin, White Masks*, London: Pluto (1st pub. 1952).

—— (1967), *The Wretched of the Earth*, Harmondsworth: Penguin. These two books together provide a powerful account and theorization of the relation between colonizer and colonized.

Hall, Catherine (ed.) (2000), *Cultures of Empire: Colonisers in Britain and the Empire in the Nineteenth and Twentieth Centuries. A Reader*, Manchester: Manchester University Press..This reader gives a way in to some of the best recent writing on the cultures the colonizers made.

Mendus, S., and Rendall, J. (eds.) (1989), *Sexuality and Subordination*, London: Routledge. Jane Rendall's article on Leigh Smith and Parkes in this volume provides an illuminating portrait of these two young women and their development as feminists.

References

Wakefield, E. G. (1833), *England and America*, 2 vols., London.

'Englishness' and English National Identity

KRISHAN KUMAR

Englishness and Britishness

'ENGLISH, I mean British'—this familiar locution alerts us immediately to one of the enduring perplexities of English national identity. How to separate 'English' from 'British'? Note that the reverse problem is nowhere near as acute. Non-English members of the United Kingdom rarely say 'British' when they mean 'English', or 'English' when they mean 'British'. On the contrary, they are usually only too gratingly aware of what is peculiarly English, and are ultra-sensitive to the lordly English habit of subsuming British under English. For them it is a constant reminder of what they perceive to be—rightly, of course—England's hegemony over the rest of the British Isles.

So the confusion is a peculiarly English one, and is rich in historical and cultural resonances. It tells of the difficulty that most English people have in distinguishing themselves, in a collective sense, from the other inhabitants of the British Isles. They are of course perfectly well aware that there are Welsh, Scots, Irish, and even Manxmen and Jersey Islanders. They make jokes about them, imitate their accents, and call upon them for special effects, as when they lend colour to poverty by portraying it in a Glasgow slum, or intone passages from Dylan Thomas's *Under Milk Wood* in a mock-Welsh voice. But these are particular exceptions to the general rule, which is to see all the major events and achievements of national life as English. Other ethnic groups are brought on in minor or supporting roles.

Though when it is brought to their attention the English are properly uneasy and even apologetic about this practice, they can also on occasion offer a robust defence. Fowler's celebrated view, in his *Modern English Usage*, is likely to strike a chord in the heart of every native Englishman (if not all Englishwomen). It is natural, says Fowler, to speak of the *British* Commonwealth or the *British* navy or *British* trade, and to boast that *Britons* never never shall be slaves.

But it must be remembered that no Englishman . . . calls himself a Briton without a sneaking sense of the ludicrous, or hears himself referred to as a Britisher without squirming. How should an Englishman utter the words *Great Britain* with the glow of emotion that goes for him with *England*? His sovereign may be Her *Britannic* Majesty to outsiders, but to him is Queen of *England*; he talks the *English* language; he has been taught *English* history as one continuous tale from Alfred to his own day; he has heard of the word of an *Englishman* and aspires to be an *English* gentleman; and he knows that *England* expects every man to do his duty . . . In the word *England*, not in *Britain*, all these things are implicit. It is unreasonable to ask forty millions of people to refrain from the use of the only names that are in tune with patriotic emotion, or to make them stop and think whether they mean their country in a narrower or wider sense each time they name it.

This defence, from the heart as it were, certainly tells us something important about Englishness, and its relation to Britishness. But it describes, rather than explains. Why, given the objective situation of a multinational state, did 'Britain' and 'Britishness' not gain the ascendancy? Why does 'patriotic emotion' attach itself so fervently to 'England' and not to 'Britain'? If 'Britain' sounds—as it does—colourless and boring, why is that so and why on the contrary is 'England' so glowingly sonorous (and not, let it be said, just to the English)? And if neither 'Britain' nor 'England' will do, what else? The mystery is deepened, not diminished, by the accurate observation that *none* of the available names for the United Kingdom is really suitable, for various reasons and from the differing points of view of the various inhabitants of the country. We live, says Tom Nairn, in a state

with a variety of titles having different functions and nuances—the U.K. (or 'Yookay', as Raymond Williams relabelled it), Great Britain (imperial robes), Britain (boring lounge-suit), England (poetic but troublesome), the British Isles (too geographical), 'This Country' (all-purpose within the Family), or 'This Small Country of Ours' (defensive-Shakespearian): (Nairn 1994: 93)

As a remedy Nairn proposes, with calculated malice, 'Ukania', a deliberate echo of the 'Kakania' of Robert Musil's famous end-of-empire novel *The Man without Qualities* (1930). This was Musil's notoriously satirical (and scatological) coinage for the Habsburg Empire, a baggy, unwieldy domain that also suffered from a plethora of names (Austria, Austria-Hungary, 'the Empire', etc.).

The allusion to Austria is helpful not just in the matter of names. It recalls also the significance of empire, and the role it plays in the development of national identities. Britain, like Austria, was and to some extent still is an empire, at its height in the early twentieth century the largest the world had ever known. It ruled over a vast array of peoples of every conceivable ethnicity. Its identity had to be related to its imperial character. It could not afford to be too closely identified with any one ethnic group, however influential and powerful (cf. Crick 1991: 92). The British state is the classic example of the 'state-nation', the state identified not by ethnicity but by state institutions such as Parliament and the monarchy.

But the British state was imperial in a double sense. There was the British Empire, in the well-known sense of a state with far-flung colonies. There was also Great Britain or the United Kingdom, a political entity that from several points of view could also be regarded as an empire—an 'internal empire', the result of 'internal colonialism' (Hechter 1975). England in this view was the imperial nation that had annexed the territories and subjugated the populations of Wales, Scotland, and Ireland.

The question of English national identity is bound up with this double identification. England and Englishness have to be seen within the framework of this imperial history, in all its complexity. This means that we should abandon, at least initially, conventional methods of delineating national characteristics or the national culture 'from the inside', as it were. Works such as J. B. Priestley's *English Journey* (1934), George Orwell's *The Lion and the Unicorn* (1941), and, most gloriously, W. C. Sellar and R. J. Yeatman's *1066 and All That* (1930) are instructive, entertaining, and, in the end, indispensable. But they cannot be the starting point. They attempt to trace the contours of Englishness through a discerning and imaginative exploration of some of the principal features of the national culture—its manners and morals, its landscape and townscape, the key episodes of its history. Of such stuff are works on 'national character' generally made.

But there is a prior task—or, to put it differently, one has to begin from a different direction. One has to work from the outside in.

One has to see English national identity as a kind of residue; the response to and the result of England's engagement with its imperial venture, and of its perception of its mission in the world. Probably this approach is necessary in the examination of any case of national identity. Nations are formed by a combination of attractions and repulsions, by a fusion of what they wish to be with what the like aspirations of other nations allow them to be. Certainly in the case of England it is impossible to understand its self-perception and its sense of identity without taking into account this wider picture.

The Protestant Nation

The very idea of English nationalism is problematic. For many people there is no such thing (see e.g. Newman 1987: pp. xvii–xviii). England, they say, has had patriotism, royalism, even imperialism, but not nationalism as that came to be known from its nineteenth-century development on the Continent.

Certainly announcements of a flourishing English nationalism before the nineteenth century are suspect. Attempts have been made to show that the English were nationalistic, indeed that they invented nationalism, in Elizabethan times (Greenfeld 1992: 29–87), in the seventeenth century, especially during the Civil War (Kohn 1940), and in the latter half of the eighteenth century, as a result of the growing rivalry with France (Newman 1987). Clearly these cannot all be right, which suggests that they are looking at different things. In one important sense they must all be wrong, at least if they want to make their accounts consistent with what is generally known and agreed about nationalism.

In all its varieties, one thing is clear about nationalism: it is a populist doctrine, in the sense that it asserts a natural bond between *all* the members of a nation (however defined). If blood, or language, or religion, or history, defines the quality of belonging, then all who share in it must be admitted as members of the nation, and must on that account be participant members of any state—'nation-state'—formed by the nation. It is for this reason that most theorists date the rise of nationalism to the aftermath of the French Revolution, with its fundamental doctrine of the equality of all citizens (see e.g. Alter 1994: 39–41; Brubaker 1992: 35–49).

England before the late nineteenth century—if not later—was not populist in this sense. It could not therefore know nationalism. The English nation, the political nation, was a class—or more accurately perhaps an estate—concept, and remained so for at least a century after the French Revolution. There were moments of patriotic fervour at the time of the Spanish Armada, and on several other occasions during Elizabeth's reign. There were claims for equality during the English Civil War, though quickly stifled and in any case couched mostly in religious terms. There was a popular mobilization against the French during the Revolutionary and Napoleonic wars. But none of these amounts to an instance of nationalism proper, and certainly generated nothing like a persisting national consciousness. Monarchs and statesmen might invoke 'the nation' when occasion called, but English society throughout this time was highly resistant to the notion that 'the people' constituted an equal body of citizens with equal rights (and duties) of participation in civic life. A good part—perhaps as much as two-thirds or three-quarters—of the English people did not 'belong' in this sense to the English nation, which remained largely the preserve of the upper and middle classes (the latter notoriously for much of the time in the cultural embrace of the former).

English national consciousness did, I shall argue, develop at some point towards the end of the nineteenth century. But what kinds of identity were available to the English before that time? Thanks especially to the work of Linda Colley (1992) we can offer a better answer to that question than previously. Colley's argument is that for much of the eighteenth and the first half of the nineteenth centuries, the inhabitants of the newly formed Great Britain (through the parliamentary accession of Scotland in 1707 to the already existing union of England and Wales) saw themselves primarily as Britons and their country as Britain. This did not entail the suppression of other identities based on the previously existing English, Welsh, and Scottish lands, with their various histories, nor of course identities based on region or class. But it meant that on all occasions which called for a mass collective response—the Jacobite threat, the struggles with France, the conflict with the American colonies—the overriding identity was likely to be British rather than any of the other available alternatives.

This then was a national identity of a kind. But it was not a *nationalist* identity, an identity framed in terms of common membership of an ethnic community. Its attachment was primarily institutional—to Church, to Parliament, and, above all, to the Crown, in the shape of the decidedly un-English Hanoverian dynasty that had only recently, amidst much controversy, succeeded to the throne. 'For King and country' was the watchword of this type of national belonging—a nationalism of the state rather than of the people. The other crucial ingredient was religion. The British nation was the Protestant nation. It portrayed itself as the defender of the Protestant faith everywhere, ready to stand against the armed might of Catholic Europe. Formerly represented by Spain, in this period it was France that emerged as the formidable Catholic threat. English, Welsh, and Scottish Protestants—Catholic Ireland as usual being the odd man out—could unite in common denunciation of the reactionary French monarchy and in common plunder of its empire.

So 'Britishness' before 'Englishness', or at least before English nationalism. The English (like the Scots and Welsh) certainly had a sense of their distinctiveness during this period. John Bull was invented (in 1712) for this purpose, and in his successive elaborations his bluff English virtues were contrasted with the mean and treacherous ways of his enemies, especially the French. Englishness was always a handy tool to use against foreigners, including on occasion those, such as the Scots and the Irish, who lived among the English themselves.

But there were limits to this practice and dangers in going too far beyond them. Englishness in this sense did not require the further definition of an exclusive national identity. The circumstances of the time indeed called for quite the opposite. The new Hanoverians, faced with the Jacobite movement, had to do all they could to win Scottish allegiance. Any stress on an English identity would have been counter-productive. The same was true of their position as rulers of an increasingly far-flung overseas empire. It was as British, not English, kings, ruling over British subjects, that they asserted their authority over their colonies in North America and the West Indies.

But the inadequacy of a purely English national identity stood out most clearly in their role—enthusiastically endorsed by the mass of the people—as the protectors and promoters of Protestantism. England might be thought by many, at least among the English, to be the heart of this mission. But to claim this, to emphasize the contribution of a particular partner in the Protestant coalition, would have diminished the grandeur of the task and diluted its missionary quality. England's glory shone the brighter for being reflected in a cause far loftier than the advancement of national self-interest. Like Spain at the time of the Counter-Reformation, or Russia in its conception of itself as 'the third Rome', England's national identity was willingly buried in the service of a missionary cause that was in the fullest sense global. World civilizations do not require anything so puny as national identities. Nationalism is for lesser nations. It is this conviction that underlies the long-standing English disdain for nationalism.

The Moment of 'Englishness'

Sometime towards the end of the nineteenth century, there did begin to emerge something like an English national identity. Why was this? What made it then seem necessary, if not to displace Britishness, at least to develop a firmer sense of Englishness alongside it?

We have to note a marked paradox here. This was the time when Britain reached the height of its influence as a world power—indeed as *the* world power. Its Industrial Revolution—which was a truly British, not simply English, accomplishment—had for the time being given it, as the pioneer, unchallenged pre-eminence. Having lost one empire it had acquired another which, on the eve of the First World War, covered one-fifth of the world's land surface and incorporated a quarter of its population. All this was done under British, not English, auspices. One would surely expect a heightened Britishness, not a newly found Englishness, to thrive under these conditions.

No doubt this occurred as well. Given the prominent role of Scots, Irish, and (to a lesser extent) Welsh in the British Empire, it would have been impossible for it not to do so—though, as Kathryn Tidrick remarks, 'the ideas by which they were consciously guided as imperialists were English in origin', specifically and principally English evangelicalism (Tidrick 1990: 1). Nevertheless, one has simply to record that, whether in tandem or in opposition, there arose at the same time a movement to define more closely what was meant by Englishness—and, with unmistakable intent, to celebrate it.

Of the various possible reasons for this, one was negative. Nineteenth-century developments gradually loosened one of the central planks of Britishness, the idea of the Protestant nation. Partly this was the result of a general European secularization. More particularly, with the rise of Germany and the United States to world prominence, the Catholic threat, especially as represented by France, receded (a development helped by the accession of Ireland to the Union in 1801). Britain's main rivals were now themselves predominantly Protestant. If Britain were still to proclaim its mission in the world, it would increasingly have to do so in secular, not religious, terms.

But probably the most important reason for the rise of English-ness was ideological. The nineteenth century was the age of nationalism, and the latter part of the century saw the new doctrine developed to its most intensive point. Italy and Germany had united around it; the Habsburg and the Ottoman empires were being pulled apart by it. Everywhere on the Continent, and increasingly in the rest of the world, nationalist movements were on the rise. In the United Kingdom itself, Welsh and Scottish nationalism dates from this period, while in the form of 'the Irish question' Irish national-ism threatened, as it still does, to tear the political fabric of the nation apart.

Nationalism at this time had come to be predominantly of the cultural or Herderian kind. As opposed to the older kind, emphasizing common citizenship, cultural nationalism emphasized common ethnicity. The hallmarks of this ethnicity were held to be language, religion, history, and blood or 'race'. These expressed the 'soul' of the nation and every nation, it was felt, must have a soul.

English intellectuals—and it is really only of them we can speak, popular nationalism being as always something of a mystery—responded energetically to this felt need. In language and literary studies, in historiography, fiction, and folklore, there arose what can best be described as a cultural movement to define and, consistent with nationalist practice, celebrate Englishness. England too, the movement seemed to declare, had a soul; and it was a soul different from that of the rest of the kingdom in which for so long it had so unselfconsciously and promiscuously lain.

The lineaments of this movement have from recent studies become reasonably clear, and we can sketch them briefly (see Bur-row 1981; Colls and Dodd 1986; Doyle 1989; Collini 1991; Lucas 1991). Of central importance was the cleaning up of the English language, and the establishment of a 'received', that is, authorita-tive, manner of spelling and speaking English. In the philological studies of the period the English language was purified and purged of its 'regional dialects', and the pronunciation and speech-patterns of the metropolitan south were deemed the national speech model. The great monument to this activity was the *Oxford English Dic-tionary on Historical Principles*—begun, characteristically, by a Scot, James Murray, in 1879. Murray's declared object was to capture 'the genius of the English language', and he presented his undertaking as 'a great national project'. In his *Dictionary* the English language was, for the first time in its history, thoroughly nationalized and standardized.

Literature too was nationalized, in the sense that this period saw the elaboration of a national tradition of literature. Put in more recent terms, this was when the 'canon' of English literature was established. Given the importance of literature, as compared with, say, music, in the national culture, this provided one of the most influential and long-lasting definitions of Englishness. English culture, at its deepest level, is seen as created by a series of great 'national' poets, dramatists, and novelists. Their writing embodies values, whole ways of life, which express the aspirations of the national culture at its best and highest. It is hardly too much to say that English literature came to take on a religious function, far exceeding in importance the vapid Anglicanism that passed for the national religion. Its study and dissemination was conceived in missionary terms (see Baldick 1983).

The definition of a canon of English literature—'a celebratory account of English literary distinctiveness'—has been called by Stefan Collini 'the Whig interpretation of English literature' (Collini 1991: 342–73). It parallels the Whig interpretation of history that celebrates England's political and historical distinctiveness. The markers are, in this case, certain texts, many of the most important of which appeared in the late nineteenth century. Palgrave's *Golden Treasury of English Verse*, whose object was to produce 'a true national anthology', first appeared in 1861, and for long held the field. A somewhat similar function was later fulfilled by Sir Arthur Quiller-Couch's *Oxford Book of English Verse* (1900), which by 1939 had been reprinted twenty times and sold nearly half a million copies. Then there was the 'English Men of Letters' series launched by Macmillan's under the general editorship of John Morley in 1877. The series, writes Collini, 'bore all the marks of a consciously designed national monument' (1991: 355). The selection of writers, from Chaucer to the great Victorian poets and novelists, was meant to illustrate not only the greatness of English literature but its distinctive national qualities. These included sincerity, individuality, concreteness, and a sense of the richness and diversity of life. The implicit contrast was with the formalism and classicism of much continental literature, especially that of France.

As these qualities imply, Romanticism, especially in the form of the Romantic poets, has always ranked high in the national estimation. It indicates the English preference for feeling over intellect, poetry over philosophy, literature and history over social and political thought. It also refers to certain qualities of landscape—not just the rugged mountains of the Lake District associated with the Romantic poets but also the lusher downlands of the south. This was, Alun Howkins (1986) reminds us, the period in which the 'south country' moved into the centre of the national imagination, to some extent displacing the wilder landscape of the earlier part of the century. Gentrified it might be, and ordered to suit the townsman's taste, but still it testified to the enduring hold of the countryside in English life and a persistent anti-urban and even anti-industrial strand in its culture (Wiener 1981). In works such as William Morris's *News from Nowhere* (1890) the southern English countryside was accorded literally utopian status, not simply the locus but the very heart and soul of the good society.

These qualities of the imagination might suggest a certain unworldliness, a poetic flight from the sordid realities of everyday life. While there is an undoubted strain of whimsy in English culture—captured at its best by the Ealing film comedies of the later 1940s—this is matched by an oft-remarked pragmatism and hardheadedness. It was in this period that a certain style of intellectual culture came to be defined as peculiarly and gratifyingly English. English thought, it was claimed, is empirical, utilitarian, concrete, individualist. It is exemplified at its best in such thinkers as Francis Bacon, John Locke, Jeremy Bentham, John Stuart Mill, and Charles Darwin. It is hostile to the abstract and metaphysical cast of continental thought—which, it was further argued, is largely responsible both for its impracticality and for the regrettably extreme and ideological forms of continental politics. It should be noted that this contrast between English and continental thought would have been difficult to draw earlier than the late seventeenth century (despite Bacon), and it remains suspect thereafter as well. Bernard Crick once remarked that though the English like to think of themselves as a nation of shopkeepers, they are really a nation of metaphysical shop-lifters. But in questions of national identity, self-perception is the thing.

In one other area the late nineteenth century produced a powerful current of Englishness. This was in historical consciousness. Effectively this meant the elaboration and intensification of 'the Whig interpretation' of English history, a self-congratulatory myth that portrayed English national development in glowing tones. The elements of this, as described by Herbert Butterfield, were already firmly in place by the end of the seventeenth century. They included the idea of the antiquity and independence of the House of Commons; the 'myth of *Magna Carta*', as the foundation of the liberties of all free-born Englishmen; the belief in a tradition of constitutional rule, limiting monarchy, stretching unbroken from the Middle Ages through to the seventeenth century; and the theory of primitive Teutonic freedom and of the

'Norman Yoke' that had attempted, unsuccessfully, to stifle it (Butterfield 1944: 69).

This classic version of the Whig interpretation of English history represented all these things as having been there, so to speak, all the time. It was a story of ancient and immemorial English freedom that, though it had at times to be defended against attempts to usurp it, had been a constant of English history. What the nineteenth century—building on Burke and the writers of the Scottish Enlightenment—did was to temporalize or historicize this myth. It gave it the form in which it entered the school textbooks and turned into a key element of the English tradition, 'part of the landscape of English life, like our country lanes or our November mists or our historic inns' (Butterfield 1944: 2). In the historical writings of Macaulay, Stubbs, Freeman, Green, and Seeley, English liberties were seen, not as a once-and-for-all achievement or inheritance, but as a story of steady, continuous, and cumulative growth and expansion, broadening out from precedent to precedent. English history was 'a single progressive drama' (Burrow 1981: 295), capable therefore of showing change and improvement. The face of the nation was turned from the past to the future. England was seen as having had a blessed inheritance, allowing it to avoid the fanaticism and bitterness, born of countless revolutions and civil wars, that had disfigured the politics of its continental neighbours. This fortunate legacy had enabled it to become the richest and most powerful country in the world. So she would continue to grow and prosper, the envy and exemplar of other nations.

English Nationalism?

The moment of Englishness at the end of the nineteenth century is not simply a historical marker. It defines, in many ways, the essence of Englishness as this has come to be conceived in the high culture of the nation. Many of the later accounts of 'the English character' or 'the English tradition' drew heavily on it, even while they sought to broaden its base and make it less inward-looking (see, for an example, Stapleton 1994; see also Giles and Middleton 1995).

But the Englishness of the late nineteenth and early twentieth centuries was mostly a cultural definition. It was an affair of poets, novelists, literary critics, philologists, folklorists, and historians. At the level of national politics it was played down, surfacing mainly in occasional pieces and after-dinner speeches (e.g. Stanley Baldwin's

On England, 1926). This was a natural and necessary response to Britain as a world power and the ruler of a world empire.

Other developments in the first half of the twentieth century also muted the political effects of Englishness. Of particular importance was the new labour movement and the rise of the Labour Party. Quite apart from the fact that it was technically international in outlook, the national labour movement was quite unmistakably British, not English. It got its greatest impetus not from England but from its Welsh and Scottish heartlands. It was from industrial Lanarkshire and the steel and mining towns of south Wales, not from London and Manchester, that its greatest leaders came, and where it found its strongest support. The Labour Party and the labour movement arguably linked the parts of the United Kingdom together more comprehensively than any other party or movement and, as with the monarchy, their continued strength depended on maintaining their appeal across ethnic and national lines. This dampened not just English but, perhaps even more, Welsh and Scottish nationalism.

All this began to change in the period after the 1960s. The empire was gone, as was Britain's position as an industrial world power. Lacking the stimulus and the bracing influence—not to mention the profits—of a world role, Britishness capitulated in the face of an assertion, with varying degrees of force, of Scottish, Welsh, and Irish nationalism. England, the core nation, stood exposed, no longer protected by a surrounding carapace of Britishness. The other nations of the United Kingdom began to envisage a rosier future as separate members of the new European Community. England too was forced to consider this prospect and, in the process, to reassess itself and its future identity.

One consequence of the decline of Britishness was a renewed emphasis on Englishness. But now it moved from culture to politics. One might say—cautiously—that something like an English nationalism came into being. There was a new stridency in the utterances. 'New Right' Conservative politicians, starting with Enoch Powell and continuing, in a different vein, with Margaret Thatcher, Norman Tebbit, Michael Portillo, and others, were among the most vocal proponents. They were joined by a group of right-wing historians and publicists such as John Vincent, Jonathan Clarke, Norman Stone, and the 'Bruges Group' opposed to British membership of the European Union. While often they spoke of 'Britain', it was not usually very difficult to read this, as in the past, as a code for 'England'. The former Conservative Prime Minister John Major once memorably evoked the nation in an image composed mainly of village cricket and warm beer—an echo of Baldwin that seemed to exclude not just Welsh, Scots, and Irish but most women, the bulk of the English working class, and the vast majority of the non-white population. He followed this up with the announcement that 'this British nation has a monarchy founded by the Kings of Wessex over eleven hundred years ago' (*The Times*, 24 May 1994)—a view of British history that had the Scots, at the very least, spluttering in their porridge.

It has to be said that such 'Little Englander' views have found an echo among considerable sections of the English population at large—at least if we are to believe their newspapers, or observe their behaviour at football matches. But it has always been clear, at least to outsiders, that Englishness embodied the aspirations and self-images of a particular section of society—for much of the time, those of the dominant upper and upper middle classes. It was their politics, their church, their sports, their manners and ways of speaking, their schools and universities, their view of history, that provided much of the content of 'the national character'. In recent years such a conception has been under assault from a variety of sources—women, workers (or their spokesmen), blacks, gays, and other groups supposedly 'hidden from history'.

The force of the criticism is evident. What is less clear, or less credible, is what are proposed as alternatives. Englishness may be an ideology, but as is well known ideologies tend to diffuse themselves widely in society, touching groups which may be very distant from the centres of power. Monarchy, in so far as it has come to be associated with Englishness rather than Britishness, is one example of this effect. What can compete with such long-standing symbols and sentiments? 'Multiculturalism'? Federalism? 'Europe'? Merely to name them is to be aware of the problems. People may not consciously seek a national identity or even know that they have one, but there are moments in their lives, both individually and collectively, when they seem to need one and to reach for it. Englishness, as it has been handed down and celebrated, is today an embattled concept and practice. It is out of touch with many of the ideas and much of the reality of contemporary British society. But it would be foolish to think that it cannot still generate enthusiasm and mobilize considerable support, at all levels of society. Mrs Thatcher's popularity was one expression of this. That in itself indicates the urgency of the task, but also the difficulty of it.

Further Reading

Butterfield, H. (1944), *The Englishman and his History*, Cambridge: Cambridge University Press. The classic account of the 'Whig interpretation' of English history and its role in the English political tradition.

Colls, R., and Dodd, P. (eds.) (1986), *Englishness: Politics and Culture 1880–1920*, London: Croom Helm. A wide-ranging examination of the 'moment' of Englishness in the late nineteenth century. The essays cover politics, literature, language, and history.

Crick, B. (ed.) (1991), *National Identities*, Oxford: Blackwell. Raises important questions about the political identities of the various parts of the United Kingdom, and their relationship to each other.

Giles, J., and Middleton, T. (eds.) (1995), *Writing Englishness 1900–1950*, London: Routledge. A well-chosen collection of writings on Englishness during this period. Draws upon literature, popular journalism, political speeches, and diaries, as well as more analytical accounts.

Nairn, T. (1994), *The Enchanted Glass: Britain and its Monarchy*, 2nd edn., London: Radius. Far wider than the title suggests, a scintillating account of the national character and culture. Full of fertile thoughts on 'Englishness'.

Newman, G. (1987), *The Rise of English Nationalism: A Cultural History 1740–1830*, London: Weidenfeld & Nicolson. A fascinating and original account of a key period. To be compared with Colley, below, who makes a different case.

References

Alter, P. (1994), *Nationalism*, 2nd ed., London: Edward Arnold.

Baldick, C. (1983), *The Social Mission of English Criticism*, Oxford: Clarendon Press.

Brubaker, R. (1992) *Citizenship and Nationhood in France and Germany*, Cambridge, Mass.: Harvard University Press.

Burrow, J. W. (1981), *A Liberal Descent: Victorian Historians and the English Past*, Cambridge: Cambridge University Press.

Butterfield, H. (1944), *The Englishman and his History*, Cambridge: Cambridge University Press.

Colley, L. (1992), *Britons: Forging the Nation, 1707–1837*, New Haven: Yale University Press.

Collini, S. (1991), *Public Moralists: Political Thought and Intellectual Life in Britain 1850–1930*, Oxford: Clarendon Press.

Colls, R., and Dodd, P. (eds.) (1986), *Englishness: Politics and Culture 1880–1920*, London: Croom Helm.

Crick, B. (ed.) (1991), *National Identities: The Constitution of the United Kingdom*, Oxford: Blackwell.

Doyle, B. (1989), *English and Englishness*, London: Routledge.

Giles, J., and Middleton, T. (eds.) (1995), *Writing Englishness 1900–1950*, London: Routledge.

Greenfeld, L. (1992), *Nationalism: Five Roads to Modernity*, Cambridge, Mass.: Harvard University Press.

Hechter, M. (1975), *Internal Colonialism: The Celtic Fringe in British National Development, 1536–1966*, London: Routledge.

Howkins, A. (1986), 'The Discovery of Rural England', in Colls and Dodd (1986).

Kohn, H. (1940), 'The Genesis of English Nationalism', *Journal of the History of Ideas*, 1.

Lucas, J. (1991), *England and Englishness: Ideas of Nationhood in English Poetry, 1688–1900*, London: Hogarth Press.

Nairn, T (1994), *The Enchanted Glass: Britain and its Monarchy*, 2nd edn., London: Radius.

Newman, G. (1987), *The Rise of English Nationalism: A Cultural History 1740–1830*, London: Weidenfeld & Nicolson.

Stapleton, J. (1994), *Englishness and the Study of Politics: The Social and Political Thought of Ernest Barker*, Cambridge: Cambridge University Press.

Tidrick, K. (1990), *Empire and the English Character*, London: Tauris.

Wiener, Martin J. (1981), *English Culture and the Decline of the Industrial Spirit, 1850–1980*, Cambridge: Cambridge University Press.

Rituals and Representations of Black 'Britishness'

JIM PINES

As well as registering the sense of loss created by globalisation, multiculturalism, European integration and devolution,
the new English nationalism can also stitch together into a
single patchwork what would otherwise be unconnected concerns: the right to raise the flag of St George, to send your
children to a school which teaches pride in English history, to
drink English ale instead of German lager or to see English
football players not outnumbered in the premiership.

(Kundnani 2000: 13)

THE resurgence of St George's Cross during the 1998 World Cup
was significant in terms of ritual expressions of English national
identities. The English flag (with its red cross on a white background) had effectively replaced the more familiar Union Jack (the
British flag) as the dominant emblem of England's presence during
this international sporting occasion. But what was even more striking was the way St George's Cross had also become the symbol of a
shared national allegiance among England fans from different ethnicities and cultural backgrounds during the tournament, both at
home and abroad. The English flag invoked a sense of multicultural
inclusiveness which had not been seen before, and certainly
not seen in relation to the Union Jack, notwithstanding previous
international athletics occasions when black British athletes such as
Linford Christie draped themselves in the Union Jack while doing a
lap of honour.

Indeed, the spectacle of black athletes draping themselves in the Union Jack represented an emotionally charged and ideologically loaded moment in the history of black British representation. It defied all the historical and political connotations usually associated with the British national flag. After all, the Union Jack had become a familiar emblem of the British political far Right, whose flag-waving followers had successfully exploited every public opportunity to brandish their own explicitly white racist sense of British national-ism and national identity. Interestingly, however, there was not the same degree of anxiety expressed when black Welsh hurdler Colin Jackson draped himself in the Welsh national flag, for example. Nor for that matter did it ever appear incongruous, or even slightly controversial in terms of cultural and national identification, when African-American athletes such as Carl Lewis paraded the Stars and Stripes during their victory celebrations on the track. In other words, there appears to be something uniquely problematic about coupling the Union Jack with the idea, let alone the fact, of *black* Britishness, which Paul Gilroy's book title from 1987—*There Ain't No Black in the Union Jack*—neatly encapsulates.

St George's Cross is by no means a neutral emblem of nation-hood, but it does not carry the same uncomfortable connotations generally associated with the Union Jack. Thus, the English flag was able to function—at least during the period of the 1998 World Cup—as a veritable emblem of multicultural inclusiveness and by doing so it succeeded in conveying a relatively progressive image of a multicultural England. It was not uncommon to see, for example, England fans from different ethnicities and cultural backgrounds with the red (or, alternatively, blue) cross painted across their faces and displaying the English flag with a degree of enthusiasm that often looked like good old-fashioned English patriotism. This, surely, represented a unique moment in British or English national identification, in the way that these essentially symbolic or ritual expressions of identity appeared to cut across traditional boundaries of British race and class.

France (the World Cup host nation), the Netherlands, and Eng-land all fielded 'multiracial' teams, which, to varying degrees, was a source of national pride for the respective nations. However, racist grandstanding was still evident on the terraces, for example, where a small but vociferous minority of spectators resorted to familiar racist howls and gestures whenever a black player had possession of the ball. But the overall emphasis in terms of media representation—or, if you like, in terms of public relations—stressed the recognition and acceptance of (ethnic) diversity and inclusiveness within the broader framework of national teams—an emphasis which, of course, ties in with the European Union's vision of the 'New Europe' as well. It is also worth mentioning in this context anecdotal evidence which further suggests that black British fans, in particular, tended to identify more strongly with European 'multiracial' teams—because of a shared sense of history and location (i.e. the politics of diaspora)—than with the Brazilian team, for instance, which in the past was often the focus of 'cultural' and geographical identification, particularly among fans of Caribbean origin.

But this new and apparently more confident image of black Britishness or black Englishness remains an awkward construction nevertheless, partly because of the way that it attempts to play down or elide the unresolved discourses of British race relations and multiculturalism, and partly (perhaps more importantly) because there is little evidence to suggest that this re-invented sense of black Englishness has been able to establish itself as a permanent feature in the contemporary British social, political, and cultural landscape. Indeed, the ubiquitous St George's Cross had already started to lose much of its celebratory multicultural appeal by Euro 2000 two years after the World Cup. The English flag had now become more strongly associated with English football hooliganism, violence, and xenophobia. The scenes of England fans rioting in Brussels, for example, not only provoked a strong sense of national shame, but also refuelled the introspective debate within England itself about what it is to be English in the (post-empire) modern world. As one leading British columnist expressed it, at the time, 'English football has become a threat to England, a curse on football, a menace to the citizens of every country where it's played' (Young 2000: 22).

There is, of course, the danger of overemphasizing the political and cultural significance of these sort of disturbances, given the way international football competitions generally, and not just in relation to England, seem to generate strong feelings of nationalism among certain fans, and the 'moral panic' that inevitably follows whenever such expressions of nationalism spill over into violent confrontation. However, we would still argue that these gladiatorial-like spectacles provide a useful barometer for sensing some of the ways in which cultural and national identities are articulated, reaffirmed, and indeed masqueraded in the face of globalization and the apparent destabilization of nationhood(s). Nationalisms are clearly still strong, and they are evidently on the increase as well. And this raises the awkward question—which we are obliged to ask but which is beyond the scope of this chapter—whether expressions of black Britishness or black Englishness are in any sense coterminous with straightforward British or English nationalism; or indeed whether we need to make a clear distinction between these ritualistic expressions of black Englishness on the one hand, and the so-called 'rise of the Little Englanders' on the other.[1]

The resurgence of St George's Cross is coincidentally linked to the resurgence of a more confident sense of black Britishness or black Englishness, but we would argue that both phenomena can be seen as the culmination of a much wider historical and political process that has been unfolding in Britain in the past two decades—namely, 'the break-up of Britain' and the concomitant emergence of the independent nations comprising the British Isles including England, Scotland, Wales, and Ireland. As Tom Nairn argued, indeed predicted, so eloquently as far back as 1977, this change in the make-up of the British Isles has effectively destabilized the core notion of Britishness itself, with the result that the idea of England and Englishness has been undergoing a fairly radical process of readjustment or reinvention (Nairn 1981). And it is in this sense that we would argue that a revitalized or reinvented conception of England as a nation—existing as it does in relation to the other independent nations comprising the British Isles, as well as in relation to the wider European Union—is now inextricably linked to the kind of inclusive imagery and symbolization that the resurgence of St George's Cross seems to invoke, and that black Britishness, or more accurately black Englishness, is very much part of that process.

Shifting the focus to another realm of cultural production and expression, it is worth re-evaluating the representation of black British identity in black-produced cinematic representation, because here we see some of the ways in which black British cultural practitioners themselves have engaged with questions of cultural identities and (British) national identity. In Horace Ove's film *Pressure* (1975), for example, a British-born black teenager becomes disillusioned and is gradually politicized as he encounters racism and racial discrimination. What is particularly interesting about this representation is the way the film constructs the binary opposition of the teenager's 'black' identity and his 'British' identity—these two identities conflict primarily because of society's inability or unwillingness to recognize the black teenager's right to be treated like any other British-born citizen, irrespective of race or colour. The black teenager's 'identity crisis' is further accentuated by the

1 See Carvel (2000: 4). According to the National Centre for Social Research in its annual survey of social attitudes, reports Carvel, there has been '[a] sharp increase in the number of Little Englanders who do not identify themselves as British and tend towards racist and xenophobic views'. The survey, which was undertaken by John Curtice, of Strathclyde University, and Anthony Heath, of Oxford University, also indicated that '6% of those who described their ethnic origin as black and 7% of those who said they were Asian classified themselves as English, not British. [Whereas] more than a third said they were British, not English.'

attitude of his archetypal first-generation immigrant parents, who consider him to be British and therefore to have the necessary social attributes, advantages, and opportunities that any (white) British-born citizen presumably enjoys. The sense of hope and optimism articulated by the teenager's parents is, of course, an archetypal motif within the immigrant genre, though interestingly it is offset in the film by the teenager's Caribbean-born and politically militant elder brother who constantly chides the teenager about his 'Anglicized' lifestyle and his futile attempts at 'trying to be like the English'.

Pressure does not dismiss outright the notion of black Britishness or Englishness; it does however stress the idea that such a unified sense of cultural identity can only be achieved when the 'black' element in the equation has been secured. Hence the significance of the teenager's identification with the black militant cause at the end of the film. In terms of the representation of British race relations and multiculturalism, *Pressure* thus signalled an important shift in emphasis away from dominant or mainstream discourses of black/immigrant experience which, it should be noted, tended to pathologize this experience in terms of social problems (e.g. the so-called immigrant problem theme), with a greater emphasis on a perspective which stressed instead the way first- and second-generation black people experienced settlement (which the film strongly suggests was often tinged with disappointment), and how second-generation young black people in particular were not accepted as British, despite the fact that they were born in Britain.

Menelik Shabazz's film *Burning an Illusion* (1981) explored the question of black (British) cultural identity along a somewhat different political and cultural trajectory, focusing instead on the idea of 'black' identities being defined from within the black experience or black community itself, as it were. In other words, the mainstream discourses of race relations and multiculturalism do not play a significant part in the film's representation of identity. Thematic emphasis is instead on the question what is it to be 'black in Britain', rather than the quite different question, what is it to be 'black' and 'British' (which is the central theme in *Pressure*)?

Burning an Illusion adopts a more culturalist stance regarding black (cinematic) representation, in the sense that it is concerned primarily with notions of blackness as the defining principle. Moreover, this approach is indicative of the black cultural politics of the late 1970s–early 1980s, during which the emergence of Rastafarian themes and imagery especially played a significant role in the evolution of black popular culture and identity politics in Britain.

This culturalist orientation is expressed in a number of ways in *Burning an Illusion*, but perhaps most strikingly we see it in the film's representation of ethnicity and in the film's stress on a form of black consciousness which has a cultural nationalist sensibility about it.

The idea of black Britishness or black Englishness is certainly present in *Burning an Illusion*, but it is constructed somewhat obliquely in the way that it is linked to notions of social conformity and cosy respectability, that is to say, social attributes or modes of behaviour which the film marks negatively as a form of cultural assimilation and alienation (hence the reference to illusion in the film's title). However, it is worth noting that the young black woman protagonist in *Burning an Illusion* experiences exactly the same kind of conversion or transformation of identity as the black teenager in *Pressure*—in both examples, the main protagonist 'becomes' more politically and culturally aware of his or her presence in the world, and is gradually endowed with a more strident sense of 'black' consciousness, as she or he literally redefines his or her place in society.

Both these landmark films reflect the way an earlier generation of black British cultural practitioners addressed issues of black (British) cultural identity in cinematic representation. However, it is important to stress that both films focused on first- and second-generation black people, for whom (it could be argued) the idea of British or English identification was perhaps marginal, if it had any real relevance at all, given the more pressing need for this generation to secure for themselves a relatively stable presence as homogeneous 'communities', and at a time when anti-black racism was especially rampant in Britain. It is therefore not surprising that both films focus on the idea of difference, and construct narratives that stress black consciousness and oppositional political engagement as the only viable means of securing a more stable cultural identity for the future.

By the mid-1980s a new generation of black cultural film practitioners began to reformulate questions of cultural identity in terms of diaspora, or the politics of location. Black Audio Film Collective's award-winning documentary *Handsworth Songs* (dir. John Akomfrah, 1986) was among the first in the cycle of innovative black British films made during this period which signalled the shift in focus:

[We] used the term 'black' as a component of the diaspora which encompasses a wider social geography, which has a plurality of articulations, of history, politics, languages and cultural forms. [We] are prepared to embrace that kind of definition instead of one where the term 'black' becomes a central organising category of a nationalist discourse, which is precisely the discursive field that [we] wish to move away from in order to explore other avenues. (Gilroy and Pines 1988: 11)

'What this brings into play', Stuart Hall points out, 'is the recognition of the immense diversity and differentiation of the historical and cultural experience of black subjects.' In other words, it marks what Hall has referred to as 'the end of the innocent notion of the essential black subject' (Hall 1989: 28). Black Britishness, therefore, represents a complex set of relations, that is to say, relations which are not necessarily structured as binary oppositions—e.g. black and/or British—but rather relations which are much more subtle and complex in their construction. Though none of the films made during this period of innovative black representation is specifically concerned with questions of black Britishness or black Englishness as such, there is however a sense in which this generation of black British cultural practitioners had succeeded in resolving the 'black and/or British' dichotomy which had framed earlier representations, by shifting the emphasis to notions of diaspora or the politics of location.

This generation had not only found a way of engaging critically with the fact of Britishness, but they had also succeeded in constructing cinematic narratives which addressed some of the more complex ways in which the histories and myths of Britishness intertwined with 'black' or 'diasporic' cultural identities. Titles such as *The Passion of Remembrance* (Maureen Blackwood and Isaac Julien, 1986) and *Dreaming River* (Martina Attille, 1987), to name just two, indicate the move—sometimes expressed in poetic language—away from didactic themes and imagery, towards a much stronger emphasis on, for instance, the role historical and personal memories play in the process of defining one's (cultural) identity. In other words, black (British) cultural identities are not simply sociological phenomena, but they also have important existential aspects to them as well, which the politics of representation has to address.

The cinematic representation of black (British) cultural identity took another turn by the 1990s, notably with Ngozi Onwuhra's hip-hop-inspired *Welcome II the Terrordome* (1994), which reverted to a form of essentialism which Paul Gilroy found 'politically repugnant':

The modest gains of the last 20 years will be placed in jeopardy, through the film's opportunistic, pseudo-political flirtations with racial absolutism and misogyny. Worse still, because so subversive, its incompetence will unleash the laughter of the world against black British cultural activists, just as we seemed to have found a distinctive voice. (Gilroy 1995: 18)

Julian Henrique's quasi-musical *Babymother* (1998), on the other hand, deployed the rich cultural iconography of Jamaican popular culture— patterns of speech, musical expression, dress codes, modes of social interaction, and so on—as a means of exploring the complex social relations within a particular black British community located in West London. It is a hermetically sealed community, however, in which conventional race relations or questions of national identity are completely absent. This representation is interesting in that it re-emphasizes the role played by ethnicity in defining cultural identities (cf. *Burning an Illusion*), but without making it, as it were, a proscriptive or essentialist representation of black (British) experience.

To summarize. This chapter has argued that there is a link between recent expressions of black Britishness or Englishness and the resurgence of St George's Cross, and that these two phenomena have emerged against the backdrop of a broader crisis in British or English national identity, which itself has been precipitated by 'the break-up of Britain' and by England's integration into the European Union. However, we are very wary about pushing this line of argument to the point of implying that St George's Cross has merely been a flag of convenience, or that it has served as an expendable emblem in this postmodern era of multiple identities in which people (so the postmodernist argument goes) are able to manipulate who and what they are at will. Nor are we suggesting that these symbolic expressions of black Englishness or Britishness signal the assimilation of black cultural identities within the broader national identities that are traditionally thought of as British or English. The situation is, no doubt, a lot more complicated.

Indeed, the Stephen Lawrence murder inquiry, along with the subsequent Macpherson Report, have come to represent critical moments in this process of political and cultural change in Britain, not only in terms of highlighting the persistence of racism as such, but also in terms of triggering levels of introspection—that is, an examination of the core institutions that define British society itself—which had never entered into the policy-making equation following previous incidents of racial violence. We would argue that these events, along with the anxieties and misinterpretations which accompanied the publication of the Runnymede Trust Commission on *The Future of Multi-ethnic Britain* (2000)—which some sections of the British media misread as an attack on the very notion of Britishness itself, i.e. that 'British' is a racist term—provide further evidence of the continued insecurity that appears to be attached to British/English national identity.

But returning to the point where this chapter started, there does seem to be a sense in which the resurgence of the English flag represents an attempt to resolve, or at least mediate, albeit in a relatively transient and highly emblematic way, the general crisis in British/English national identity, and the presence of a fourth and fifth generation of young black men and women whose allegiances and identifications are, for better or worse, rooted in a place called England. We would argue further that England itself, perhaps for the first time in its history, has had to face the question—what is it to be English in the post-imperial era?—and that it has had to do so in a more critical, self-reflexive manner than was ever possible, or even likely, in previous times.

This leads us to the relatively optimistic but nonetheless qualified conclusion that there is indeed a cultural and national identity that can be described as black Britishness or black Englishness—and that this identity is coterminous with a reinvented idea of England which has been struggling to (re)define its own sense of national identity and purpose in an increasingly globalized cultural and political economy.

Further Reading

Gilroy, Paul (2000), *Between Camps: Nations, Culture and the Allure of Race*, London: Allen Lane.

Mercer, Kobena (1994), *Welcome to the Jungle: New Positions in Black Cultural Studies*, New York: Routledge.

Owusu, Kwesi (ed.) (2000), *Black British Culture and Society*, London: Routledge.

Sivinandan, A. (1990), *Communities of Resistance*, London: Verso.

Solomos, John, and Back, Les (eds.) (1999), *Theories of Race and Racism*, London: Routledge.

References

Carvel, John (2000), 'The Rise of the Little Englanders', *Guardian*, 28 Nov.

Gilroy, Paul (1987), *'There Ain't No Black in the Union Jack': The Cultural Politics of Race and Nation*, London: Hutchinson.

—— (1995), 'Unwelcome', *Sight and Sound*, 5/2, Feb.

—— and Pines, Jim (1988), 'Handsworth Songs: Audiences/Aesthetics/Independence—Interview with the Black Audio Collective [*sic*], *Framework*, 35.

Hall, Stuart (1989), 'New Ethnicities', in Kobena Mercer (ed.), *Black Film, British Cinema*, London: ICA.

Kundnani, Arun (2000), ' "Stumbling on": Race, Class and England', *Race and Class*, 41/4, June.

Nairn, Tom (1981), *The Break-up of Britain: Crisis and Neo-nationalism*, London: Verso (1st pub. 1977).

Runnymede Trust (2000), *The Future of Multi-ethnic Britain* [Parekh Report], London: Profile Books.

Young, Hugo (2000), 'Banning England would do everyone in football a favour', *Guardian*, 20 June.

British Asian Identities: Something Old, Something Borrowed, Something New

TARIQ
MODOOD

Introduction

OUT of an immigration process which was conceived primarily as the importing of labour to take up jobs in the British economy which white people did not wish to do, there have emerged, for at least some of the migrants and their descendants, new communities capable of and perhaps wanting to maintain themselves as communities. New cultural practices, especially to do with the family and religion, have become a feature of the British landscape; skin colour, identities, place of origin, or cultural community continue to shape the personal lives and relationships of even British-born individuals. The importance of cultural and ethnic differences, however, runs much deeper. Ethnic identity, like gender and sexuality, has become politicized and for some people has become a primary focus of their politics (Young 1990). While not as prominent as in the United States, yet more so than on the European mainland (Baldwin-Edwards and Schain 1994), there is in Britain an ethnic assertiveness, arising out of the feelings of not being respected or of lacking access to public space, consisting of counterposing 'positive' images against traditional or dominant stereotypes. It is a politics of projecting identities in order to challenge existing power relations; of seeking not just toleration for ethnic difference but also public acknowledgement, resources, and representation.

British Asian identities, no less than any other ethnic identities, are not 'pure' or static, but change in new circumstances or by sharing social space with other heritages and influences and the political context. For example, few south Asian migrants thought of themselves as 'Asian' (as opposed to, say, Indian or Pakistani) but in Britain there has emerged an 'Asian' identity based on a hybridic Asianness, rather than, or in addition to, a regional, national, caste, or religious identity derived from one's parents, and sometimes directly influenced by or modelled on forms of 'black pride' and black hip-hop or rap music. More recently, this identity has been disavowed by some Asians in favour of, for example, a Muslim activism and consciousness, especially through the Rushdie affair, giving rise to intense debate about identity and the emergence of a youth which emphasize a British Muslimness and reject ethnicity as un-Islamic (Modood 1990, 1992).

The Fourth Survey

There is now quite a large and stimulating literature on British Asian identities and the processes of racialization (see Further Reading section). What I offer here are some findings from the Fourth National Survey of Ethnic Minorities in Britain, which was undertaken in 1994 and covered many topics besides those of culture and identity, including employment, earnings and income, families, housing, health, and racial harassment.[1] All research methods have their limitations and cannot be substituted for each other; this survey, however, has the potential to offer what small-scale ethnographic studies, armchair theorizing, and political wishful thinking cannot. Crucially, it offers a sense of scale. Amongst Asians, as amongst any group, are diverse and contradictory trends. This survey is a unique data-set which gives some measure of the magnitude and pace of some of the key trends.

Asians and Political Blackness

We found that south Asians, including those born and raised in Britain, strongly associated with their ethnic and family origins; there was very little erosion of group identification down the generations. Despite the various forms of anti-racist politics around a black identity of the last two decades—an identity which politicians and theorists have argued is *the* key post-immigration formation (Modood 1994)—only a fifth of south Asians think of themselves as

1 The survey was based on interviews, of roughly about an hour in length, conducted by ethnically matched interviewers, and offered in five south Asian languages and Chinese as well as English. Over 5,000 persons were interviewed from the following six groups: Caribbeans, Indians, African Asians (people of south Asian descent whose families had spent a generation or more in East Africa), Pakistanis, Bangladeshis, and Chinese. Additionally, nearly 3,000 white people were interviewed, in order to compare the circumstances of the minorities with that of the ethnic majority. Further details on all aspects of the survey are available in Modood et al. (1997).

Tariq Modood

black. This is not an Asian repudiation of 'the essential black sub-ject' in favour of a more nuanced and more pluralized blackness (Hall 1992) but a failure to identify with blackness at all. It has been suggested, however, that the majority of Asians do think of them-selves as 'black', but this cannot be elicited in questioning which is insensitive to the fact that this is an identity which comes alive only in some contexts and not in others, that it is a 'situational identity' (Drury 1990). Others have suggested that it is a political identity forged by working-class Asians through anti-racist and class struggle (Sivanandan 1985), or more found among younger Asians (Rex 1994: 15), and that the opposition to the self-label 'black' is from middle-class Asians (Ratcliffe, 1994: 120) or, alternatively, from Muslims (Husband 1994: 11).

The survey found that for those Asians who think of themselves as black, blackness is not an identity which relates to some but not other contexts, but is perceived to be a fundamental aspect of them-selves (at least in Britain) (Modood et al. 1997: 295–7). This tallies with our development fieldwork in which we found that while only a minority of Asians thought of themselves as 'black', for those who did, this was an important identity, often subsuming all others (Modood et al. 1994: 95).

What was less clear in our development work is that, for some Asian people, not only is 'blackness' compatible with their ethnicity and culture, it is also rooted in their sense of being Asians and/or being treated as Asians, that is to say, as people having a certain physical appearance ('not white') and of being visibly cultural out-siders (wearing a sari, for example). For some Asians, identification with blackness is not just a product of colour-racism, it is also produced by the experience of being made self-conscious about being Asian. This is particularly interesting because it means that even some of those Asians who think of themselves as black do not take the view that skin colour is the attribute of blackness. Rather they think that their cultural attributes are, both in their own eyes and in those of white people, part of their stigmatization, part of their racial identity. This complex understanding of how some south Asians perceive they are 'racialized' is supported by the find-ing that 40 per cent of Asians who said they had experienced racial discrimination in the previous five years believed that the ground of their exclusion was a mixture of race and religion (a further 10 per cent believed it was their religion only) (Modood et al. 1997: 132–3).

An anomaly that emerges from these questions, however, is the discrepancy between the south Asians who thought that white people saw them in terms of skin colour (45 per cent), the Asians who themselves would include skin colour in self-descriptions (30 per cent), and the Asians who thought there were sometimes occasions when they thought of themselves as black (22 per cent). In our preliminary work we found that some south Asians referred to themselves and other south Asians as 'brown' (Modood et al. 1994: 94–5, 99). It may be, therefore, that while most Asians do not see their ethnicity in terms of a 'colour', those who do are as likely to think of themselves as 'brown' as much as 'black'.

Religious Identities

Rather than skin colour, which was prominent in the self-descriptions of Caribbeans, it was religion that was prominent in the self-descriptions of south Asians. This owes as much to a sense of community as to personal faith, but the identification and prioritization of religion is far from just a nominal one. At a time when a third of Britons say they do not have a religion, nearly all south Asians said they have one, and 90 per cent said that religion was of personal importance to them (compared to 13 per cent of whites). While about a quarter of whites attend a place of worship once a month or more, over half of Hindus and seven out of ten Sikhs attend once a month or more and nearly two-thirds of Muslims attend at least once a week. Even amongst the young expressions of commitment were exceptionally high: more than a third of Indians and African Asians, and two-thirds of Pakistani and Bangladeshi 16–34-year-olds said that religion was very important to how they led their lives compared to 5 per cent of whites (though nearly a fifth of Caribbeans took this view). It is clear, therefore, the presence of the new ethnic minorities is not simply changing the character of religion in Britain by diversifying it, but is giving it an importance which is out of step with native trends.

The centrality of religion to the constitution of south Asian communities and ethnic identities can be further illustrated in a number of ways. Very few Asians marry across religious and caste boundaries and most expect that their children will be inducted into their religion. The demand, especially by Muslims, that children be taught and allowed to hold acts of worship in their parents' religion in state schools, and that the state should fund Muslim schools (on the same basis as Christian and Jewish schools currently funded), is a continuing object of political activism and conflict.[1] Religious dress codes that require adherents to wear turbans or headscarves or cover their legs continue to provoke acts of discrimination and

1 The incoming Labour government approved state funding for the first time for a Muslim school in 1997. To date, funding for four Muslim schools has been given.

Tariq Modood

exclusion at schools and workplaces and are the objects of legal rulings (respectively, *Mandala* v. *Dowell Lee* 1983, *Malik* v. *British Home Stores* 1980, and *Shakoor* v. *Anne Gray Associates* 1996; see Poulter 1990). Despite the fact that at least five major south Asian languages are spoken in Britain, and most Asians have some facility in more than one of these languages, each linguistic community is strongly connected to a religious community (Modood et al. 1997: 308–12).

Religion, moreover, is particularly worth exploring in relation to British socialization. For, first, it marks a significant dimension of cultural difference between the migrants and British society. Not only did most of the migrants have a different religion from that of the natives, but all the indications are that they, including the Christians among them, were more religious than the society they were joining. Not only was this likely to have been the case at the time of migration and in the early years of settlement but it is true today. Secondly, one of the major social changes that has taken place in Britain during the lifetime of most Asian settlers has been the decline of indigenous religious observance and faith, and so religion among ethnic minorities is an important test case of the effect of British socialization. Thirdly, generally speaking, most of the cultural practices of migrants and their descendants decline with the length of their stay in the society to which they have migrated. This is usually so with language, dress, arranged marriages, and so on. It is also the case with religion, though perhaps descendants of migrants are more likely to keep alive a distinctive religion rather than a distinctive language (this has certainly been the case with the Jewish and Indian diasporas, for example, though perhaps not with the Chinese diaspora). Rather, what makes religion exceptional is that, if not generally, at least in British society, religion is now strongly correlated with age: the older a Briton is, the more religious they are likely to be. Yet, the longer a migrant has been in Britain the greater the likelihood of a decline in their original culture. So, in the particular case of religion, age, and length of residence in Britain work against each other.

We found, indeed, that while there is not a uniform linear pattern, the more a person's life has been in Britain, the less likely they are to say that religion is very important. Testing for the independent effects of age and length of residence in Britain through an analysis by logistic regression, we found that for Indians and Pakistanis the age and length of residence effects more or less cancel each other out, but among Bangladeshis and African Asians length of residence has about twice the effect that age does. This means that, in the case of the last-mentioned groups, the decline in religion through British socialization is being reversed only partially by age.

New Forms of Ethnicity

Distinctive cultural practices to do with religion, language, marriage, and so on sometimes still command considerable allegiance. The case of religion has already been mentioned. A further example is that nearly all south Asians can understand a community language, and over two-thirds use it with family members younger than themselves. More than half of the married 16–34-year-old Pakistanis and Bangladeshis had had their spouse chosen by their parents. There was, however, a visible decline in participation in distinctive cultural practices across the generations. This was particularly evident amongst younger south Asians who, compared to their elders, are less likely to speak to family members in a south Asian language, regularly attend a place of worship, or have an arranged marriage.

Yet, as has been said, this did not mean that they ceased to identify with their ethnic or racial or religious group. In this respect the survey makes clear what has been implicit in recent 'identity politics'. Ethnic identification is no longer necessarily connected to personal participation in distinctive cultural practices, such as those of language, religion, or dress. Some people expressed an ethnic identification even though they did not participate in distinctive cultural practices. Hence it is fair to say a new conception of ethnic identity has emerged.

Traditionally, ethnic identity has been implicit in distinctive *cultural practices*; this still exists and is the basis of a strong expression of group membership. Additionally, however, an *associational* identity can be seen which takes the form of pride in one's origins, identification with certain group labels, and sometimes a political assertiveness.

The ethnic identities of the second generation may have a weaker component of behavioural difference, but it would be misleading to portray them as weak identities as such. In the last couple of decades the bases of identity-formation have undergone important changes and there has come to be a minority assertiveness. Identity has moved from that which might be unconscious and taken for granted because implicit in distinctive cultural practices to conscious and public projections of identity and the explicit creation and assertion of politicized ethnicities. This is part of a wider socio-political climate which is not confined to race and culture or non-white minorities. Feminism, gay pride, Québécois nationalism, and the revival of Scottishness are some prominent examples of these new identity movements which have come to be an important feature in many countries in which class politics has declined. Identities in this political climate are not implicit and private but are shaped through intellectual, cultural, and political debates and become a feature of public discourse and policies, especially at the level of local or regional government. The identities formed in such processes are fluid and susceptible to change with the political climate, but to think of them as weak is to overlook the pride with which they may be asserted, the intensity with which they may be debated, and their capacity to generate community activism and political campaigns. In any case, what are described here as cultural-practices-based identities and associational identities are not mutually exclusive. They depict ideal types which are usually found, as in the Fourth Survey, in a mixed form. Moreover, a reactive pride identity can generate new cultural practices or revive old ones. Thus a Muslim assertiveness, sometimes a political identity, sometimes a religious revival, sometimes both, is evident in Britain and elsewhere, especially amongst some of the young (Jacobson 1997; Saeed, Blain, and Forbes 1999).

Some of the differences in culture and identity can be partly explained by place of birth, period of residence in Britain, occupational class, or by a combination of these and related factors, but underlying them was an irreducible difference between groups. Easily the strongest influence on south Asians' identity was their age at the time they came to Britain. Getting on for half of those who migrated after they had reached the age of 35 exhibited strong group identity; one-eighth of them were in the 'weak' group (Modood et al. 1997: 334–6). In contrast, half of the south Asians who had been born in Britain were members of the 'weak' behavioural category. An important contrast between groups, perhaps related to the influence of religion, is between African Asians and Indians (about 90 per cent of whom are Sikhs and Hindus), and Pakistanis and Bangladeshis (over 95 per cent of whom are Muslims). On a range of issues to do with religion, arranged marriages, choice of schools, and Asian clothes, the latter group take a consistently more 'conservative' view than the former, even when age on arrival/birth in Britain and economic position are taken into account. The fact that the Pakistanis and Bangladeshis are more likely to come from rural backgrounds, and, in particular, from poorer rural backgrounds, is bound to be relevant, and perhaps also the attitudes and practices in relation to gender roles, marriage, and ties of kinship (Ballard 1990). The sense of 'siege' and 'threat' that some Muslim peoples have historically felt in the context of western colonialism and cultural domination, and to which rural peoples in particular responded through a 'defensive traditionalism', may also be a factor (Modood 1990).

Britishness

A misleading picture would be conveyed if I did not add that besides colour and religion, other ethnic identities too were mentioned by respondents, and indeed, that ethnic/racial/religious identification was of course not universal. For East African Asians, for example, their job was as important an item of self-description as any other.

An equally important point to stress is that the identities discussed here, various as they are, do not necessarily compete with a sense of Britishness. More than two-thirds of Asians said that they felt British, and these proportions were, as one might expect, higher amongst young people and those who had been born in Britain. The majority of respondents had no difficulty with the idea of hyphenated or multiple identities, which accords with our prior study and other research (Hutnik 1991, Modood et al. 1994). But there was evidence of alienation from or a rejection of Britishness. For example, over a quarter of British-born Caribbeans and Asians did not think of themselves as being British. This too accords with our in-depth interviews at the development stage. We found that most of the second generation did think of themselves as mostly but not entirely culturally and socially British. They were not however comfortable with the idea of British being anything more than a legal title; in particular they found it difficult to call themselves 'British' because they felt that the majority of white people did not accept them as British because of their race or cultural background; through hurtful 'jokes', harassment, discrimination, and violence they found their claim to be British was all too often denied (Modood et al. 1994: ch. 6). It should also be borne in mind that 'British' is a problematic and declining feature of identification amongst some white people too, especially the young; always resisted by many Irish in Britain, it is being eclipsed by 'Scottish' in Scotland. Indeed, there seems to be less subjective incompatibility between being British and Pakistani than being British and Scottish.

Group differences of the sort discussed in this chapter used to be regarded by anti-racists as of negligible significance for public policy, for it used to be argued that the important policy goal was eradicating racism and that all the non-white groups in Britain experience the same racism. As the research evidence of differential stereotyping has accumulated over the last decade, the leading theorists discovered what they alleged was a new racism, though the differential stereotyping and treatment of Asians and blacks seems to be as old as the presence of these groups in Britain (Modood 1997). The Fourth Survey strongly supports the contention of differential prejudice targeted at different groups. The survey found that there is now a consensus across all groups that prejudice against Asians is much the highest of any ethnic, racial or religious group; and it is believed by Asian people themselves that the prejudice against Asians is primarily a prejudice against Muslims (Modood et al. 1997: 133–4).

The perception of these groups' cultural practices and the extent to which they are adhered to no doubt is a determinant of the prejudice against them such that the important prejudice in Britain is a cultural racism rather than a straightforward colour-racism. But it would be wrong to assume that groups which are most culturally distinct or culturally conservative are least likely to feel British and vice versa. It has already been mentioned that the Caribbeans, of all non-whites the culturally and socially closest to the white British, had the highest proportion who dismissed identification with Britishness—more than the Pakistanis and the Bangladeshis, the most culturally conservative and separate of these groups. Cultural conservatism does not necessarily consist in simply wanting to be left alone as a community and not making political demands upon the public space, say, in the manner of the Amish in Wisconsin. For example, half of all Muslims wanted state funding for Muslim schools, something which was refused throughout the years of Conservative government and against which there is presumed to be considerable white opposition (not necessarily from committed Christians: the survey found that nominal Christians and agnostics/atheists were more likely to express prejudice against Muslims than committed Christians). The political demands of Muslims such as these are not akin to conscientious objections, to principled exemptions from civic obligations, but—akin to other movements for political multiculturalism—for some degree of Islamicization of the civic. Not for getting the state out of the sphere of cultural identities, but for an inclusion of Muslims into the sphere of state-supported culture.

Yet at the same time, the trend in all groups, however, is away from cultural distinctness and towards cultural mixture and inter-marriage. The trend is not equally strong in the various groups. For example, among the British-born, of those who had a partner, half of Caribbean men, a third of Caribbean women, a fifth of Indian and African Asian men, a tenth of Pakistani and Bangladeshi men, and very few south Asian women had a white partner.

Conclusion

While there is, then, much empirical support for those theorists, such as Stuart Hall, who have emphasized the fluid and hybridic nature of contemporary post-immigration ethnicities in Britain, the suggestion that groups are so internally complex that they have become 'necessary fictions' (Hall 1987: 45; 1992: 254) is much exaggerated. Moreover, the theoretical neglect of the role of religion reflects a bias of theorists of 'difference' that should be urgently remedied (Modood 1998).

Some have argued that the hope for multiculturalism lies in the development of new syncretic and hybrid youth cultures centred on black musical forms like rap and hip hop, and their Asian equivalents (Gilroy 1987). Hybridity or youth, however, cannot be assumed to produce just one kind of cultural formation. The current popularity of the new Islamic identities is indicated by the many Muslim student societies found in British universities and colleges.

The political challenge, I believe, is to reach out for a multi-cultural Britishness that is sensitive to ethnic difference and incorporates a respect for persons as individuals and for the collec-tivities that people have a sense of belonging to. That means a multiculturalism that is happy with hybridity but has space for religious identities. Both hybridity and ethno-religious communities have legitimate claims to be accommodated in political multi-culturalism; they should not be pitted against each other in an either–or fashion as is done all too frequently by the celebrators of British Asian hybridity (e.g. Rushdie 1991; Kureishi 1995) and by some liberal political philosophers (e.g. Waldron 1992). It is fascinat-ing that the incompatible but separately attractive polarities identi-fied by Kureishi amongst Asians are both found in Prime Minister Tony Blair's thinking about Britain. At the start of his premiership, there was a celebration of stylish, creative hedonism (London as a world leader in *couture*, pop music, restaurants, nightclubs and so on), widely referred to as 'Cool Britannia'. Yet he is also identified with a passionate plea to renew the ethical springs of community and to put duty and high-minded responsibility back into citizenship. The making of British Asian identities thus has the potential to influence and be shaped by the remaking of Britishness. What is potentially worrying is the relationship of Asian and other minorities to Englishness. For, while it seems that Asians in Scotland, like other Scots, are thinking of themselves in terms of Scottishness rather than Britishness (Saeed, Blain, and Forbes 1999), in England, where the whole issue of English identity is full of complexity and ambivalence, of implicit superiority and suspicion of nationalism, 'English' has been treated by the new Britons as a closed ethnicity rather than an open nationality. Hence, while many Asians have come to think of themselves as hyphenated Brits, few yet think of themselves as English. If 'British' ceases to be an available option (it has been said that Ulster Loyalists and English non-whites are the last enthusiasts of 'British') then whites and non-whites in England will have to develop a new relationship and common identity or risk losing the open, plural, and hybridic sense of nationality that Britain has started to make possible (Modood 1999).

Further Reading

The following offer a good start on studies of British Asians:

Ballard, R. (ed.) (1994), *Desh Pardesh: The South Asian Presence in Britain*, London: Hurst.

Baumann, G. (1996), *Contesting Culture: Discourses of Identity in Multi-Ethnic London*, Cambridge: Cambridge University Press.

Modood, T., Beishon, S., and **Virdee, S.** (1994), *Changing Ethnic Identities*, London: Policy Studies Institute.

Werbner, P. (1990), *The Migration Process*, Oxford: Berg.

References

Baldwin-Edwards, M., and **Schain, M. A.** (eds.) (1994), 'The Politics of Immigration in Western Europe', *West European Politics*, 17/2.

Ballard, R. (1990), 'Migration and Kinship: The Differential Effect of Marriage Rules on the Process of Punjabi Migration to Britain', in C. Clarke, C. Peach, and S. Vertovec (eds.), *South Asians Overseas*, Cambridge: Cambridge University Press.

Donald, J., and **Rattansi, A.** (eds.) (1992), *'Race', Culture and Difference*, London: Sage.

Drury, B. (1990), 'Blackness: A Situational Identity', paper given at New Issues in Black Politics conference, University of Warwick, 14–16 May.

Gilroy, P. (1987), *'There Ain't No Black in the Union Jack'*, London: Hutchinson.

Hall, S. (1987) 'Minimal Selves', in L. Appignanesi (ed.) *The Real Me: The Question of Identity and Postmodernism*, London: Institute of Contemporary Arts.

—— (1992), 'New Ethnicities', in J. Donald and A. Rattansi (eds.), *'Race', Culture and Difference'*, London: Sage.

Husband, C. (1994), 'General Introduction', in C. Husband (ed.), *A Richer Vision: The Development of Ethnic Minority Media in Western Democracies*, London: UNESCO; Libbey.

Hutnik, N. (1991), *Ethnic Minority Identity: A Social Psychological Perspective*, Oxford: Clarendon Press.

Jacobson, J. (1997), 'Religion and Ethnicity: Dual and Alternative Sources of Identity among Young British Pakistanis', *Ethnic and Racial Studies*, 20/2.

Kureishi, H. (1995), *The Black Album*, London: Faber.

Modood, T. (1990), 'British Asian Muslims and the Rushdie Affair', *Political Quarterly*, 61/2; repr. in Donald and Rattansi (1992).

(1992), *Not Easy Being British: Colour, Culture and Citizenship*, London: Runnymede Trust and Trentham Books.

—— (1994), 'Political Blackness and British Asians', *Sociology*, 28/3.

—— (1997), '"Difference", Cultural Racism and Anti-Racism', in P. Werbner. and T. Modood (eds.) (1997), *Debating Cultural Hybridity: Multi-Cultural Identities and the Politics of Anti-Racism*, London: Zed Books.

—— (1998), 'Anti-Essentialism, Multiculturalism and the "Recognition" of Religious Groups', *Journal of Political Philosophy*, 6/4.

—— (1999), 'New Forms of Britishness: Post-Immigration Ethnicity and Hybridity in Britain', in R. Lentin (ed.) *The Expanding Nation: Towards a Multi-ethnic Ireland*, Proceedings of a Conference held in Trinity College, Dublin.

—— Beishon, S., and Virdee, S. (1994), *Changing Ethnic Identities*, London: Policy Studies Institute.

—— Berthoud, R., Lakey, J., Nazroo, J., Smith, P., Virdee, S., Beishon, S., et al. (1997), *Britain's Ethnic Minorities: Diversity and Disadvantage*, London: Policy Studies Institute.

Poulter, S. (1990), 'Cultural Pluralism and its Limits: A Legal Perspective', in *Britain: A Plural Society*, London: Commission for Racial Equality.

Ratcliffe, P. (ed.) (1996), *Ethnicity in the 1991 Census, iii. Social Geography and Ethnicity in Britain: Geographical Spread, Spatial Concentration and Internal Migration*, London: HMSO.

Rex, J. (1994), 'The Place of Ethnic Mobilisation in West European Democracies', in J. Rex and B. Drury (eds.), *Ethnic Mobilisation in a Multi-cultural Europe*, Aldershot: Avebury.

Rushdie, S. (1991), 'In Good Faith', in S. Rushdie, *Imaginary Homelands*, London: Granta.

Saeed, A., Blain, N., and Forbes, D. (1999), 'New Ethnic and National Questions in Scotland: Post-British Identities among Glasgow Pakistani Teenagers', *Ethnic and Racial Studies*, 22/5.

Sivanandan, A. (1985), 'RAT and the Degradation of the Black Struggle', *Race and Class*, 26/4.

Waldron, J. (1992), 'Minority Cultures and the Cosmopolitan Alternative', *University of Michigan Journal of Law Reform*, 25/3–4.

Young, I. M. (1990), *Justice and the Politics of Difference*, Princeton: Princeton University Press.

5

No Longer 'Ourselves Alone' in Northern Ireland

KEVIN DAVEY

NORTHERN Ireland is a society which has not known the pleasures or pains of hegemony since the early 1960s. The 1998 Good Friday agreement, albeit a milestone in the development of a new settlement, has been based on a very fragile political consensus. In its first two years of operation, the agreement produced no widely shared national or territorial identification, and no force capable of cross-community leadership. Its political representation took the form of a divided Assembly with an unprecedented legitimacy whose longevity was continually in question.

The prospects for a new hegemony depend on whether any new or inclusive cultural and political identifications develop in the space created by the ceasefires and the Good Friday agreement and the degree to which they are articulated or resisted by the traditional political formations currently represented in the new Assembly.

Hegemonic but decidedly non-consensual, unionist rule from partition to the early 1970s was a period of gerrymandered local government. The preferential distribution of housing by unionist councillors was accompanied by a ratepayer franchise and direct discrimination which greatly disadvantaged the poorer Catholic population while facilitating a cross-class unionist identification in the Protestant community.

After the collapse of this regime, and the subsequent proliferation of unionist identifications—reflected in the rising number of political parties seeking to articulate them—direct rule became

Northern Ireland's unreliable substitute for hegemony. Orders in Council and security directives were a painfully ineffective mechanism for managing a divided society, and reduced the space for democratic politics in the north. Nevertheless, the installation of a large military garrison was accompanied by improvements in housing and employment rights for Catholics. One significant outcome was the growth of a new Catholic middle class. Direct rule had many unacknowledged downsides. For example, Northern Ireland not only remained the most economically disadvantaged area in the United Kingdom, it also became an increasingly segregated society. Over half of the population lives in areas more than 90 per cent Protestant or 95 per cent Catholic and 60 per cent of lower-income Protestants and Catholics would not work in a place 'predominantly of the other religion' (Shuttleworth and Shirlow 1996).

A second outcome was two unstable blocs of antagonistic political parties, one nationalist and republican, the other unionist and loyalist, united by counterposed national identifications, religious ambience, and territorialized communities, but nevertheless divided by their class character and varying degrees of commitment or opposition to paramilitary action and power-sharing. Against all expectations, and with the exception of two unionist parties, these were the blocs which concluded the Good Friday agreement with the governments of Britain and Ireland.

How will that agreement, and its subsequent popular endorsement, impact on the hitherto inflexible cultural, political, and spatial identifications which preceded it? Will the result be a strengthening of the political centre ground and a 'new constitutionalism' that engages with civil society rather than with ethnic political agencies (Wilson 1996a)? Will the new Assembly, if it proves to be sustainable, assist the development of a hybrid national identification—both British and Irish, based on liberal rights and cultural realities—in short, a new civic unionism (Porter 1996)? Will nationalist and republican formations begin to acknowledge the diversity within, as well as beyond, the community identifications they construct and regulate? In short, will the old closures and homogenizations of the two traditions be reinforced or dissolved?

The work of Julia Kristeva, a French Lacanian psychoanalyst and theorist of nationalism, is useful here. The challenge facing Northern Ireland is whether the subjectivities produced by the residual identifications of two hitherto counterposed communities can become reflexive 'strangers to themselves', the cultural precondition she identifies for peaceful and pluralist cohabitation with formerly abjected others. Abjection is a process of differentiation and exclusion that Kristeva locates in the construction of individual subjectivities. A closely related process occurs within the act of national identification and it is particularly visible in divided societies like Northern Ireland, where the internal and external menaces that threaten all identifications were externalized and expelled beyond the pale and the peace line, coalescing in abject figures like Taig and Orangeman, planter and terrorist. Following Kristeva, the originating and recoiling subjectivities of Northern Ireland, both individual and collective, must become 'strangers to themselves' if the Good Friday agreement is to succeed in inaugurating a new and 'paradoxical community' in which there is no longer an assumption of homogeneity and in which 'recognition of otherness is a right and a duty' (Kristeva 1993).

A Century of Mutual Abjection

In Northern Ireland representations of national identity, firmly articulated with religious preference, have been polarized, contested, and disseminated into new fields of representation throughout the twentieth century. The unitary notions of community on which they have been based are characterized by fragile and threatened imaginaries. Siege metaphors are 'part of the shared cultural tradition of both Catholic and Protestants in Northern Ireland' (Buckley and Kenney 1995: 97). A Protestant-unionist sense of vulnerability and uncertainty has existed ever since a Home Rule bill passed through the British House of Commons in 1912, and a Catholic-nationalist sense of dismemberment dates from the act of partition in 1921. These anxieties, fears of abjection, and mutual distinctions were sustained on all sides by reference to the territorial claim to the north in articles 2 and 3 of the constitution of the Republic of Ireland, which endured until shortly after the Good Friday agreement, by the practice of direct discrimination, and by fear of violence. The communities which resulted were reaffirmed in the fields of music, sport, language, and territory in a highly politicized bifurcation of cultural and political identifications.

A Catholic struggle for civil rights commenced in the 1960s. Accelerated by the spread of television, which carried egalitarian narratives from black America to Belfast and Derry, it was an unmanageable dynamic within the wider modernization of the north. Forcibly suppressed by the unionist state, it was subsequently rearticulated to older nationalist political projects which had the reunification of Ireland as their objective (Purdie 1990; O'Doherty 1998; O Dochartaigh 1997). Two strategies for the reunification of Ireland—one constitutional, and another involving physical force—were developed by the SDLP and the republican movement respectively. The ensuing violent interaction between the military force of direct rule, paramilitary republicanism, and loyalist death squads reinforced and exacerbated the divisions in the polity, geography, and culture of the north for the next thirty years. Since the late 1960s there have been over 35,000 shooting incidents, almost 10,000 explosions, and more than 3,600 people killed. During this period the old unionist bloc began to fragment, the effect of differing tactical responses to the civil rights and paramilitary challenge, to changing territorial and demographic anxieties, and as a result of the emergence of class divisions in the Protestant community. 'Deindustrialisation . . . threatened a hegemonic unionist bourgeoisie whose assertion of political authority was founded on a paternalistic relationship with working class Protestants' (Shirlow 1997). By contrast, from the mid-1980s, the objectives and strategies of constitutional nationalism and republicanism increasingly converged, despite a fierce difference of opinion on the use of violence—which was, in practice, decreasing in importance, if still capable of atrocity—and periodic outbreaks of electoral competition.

The Troubles not only coincided with the deindustrialization of the north, they helped to accelerate it. Major shipbuilding, textiles, tobacco, and aircraft sectors contracted to the point where today only 20 per cent of the population are employed in manufacturing of any kind. In the first two decades of the recent conflict alone, 70,000 manufacturing jobs were lost, with a particularly heavy impact on the Protestant-unionist community which had long benefited from employment discrimination. The impoverishment of the old trade-based working-class unionist communities led to a partial transformation of the cultural and political identifications reproduced within them, and a growing sense of disconnection from the Protestant middle class (Bruce 1994; McAuley 1994).

The northern workforce is heavily dependent on public sector employment. Almost 40 per cent of those in work are directly employed by the British state, although the figure has begun to fall as a result of the contracting out of public services and the introduction of internal markets. Northern Ireland still has the highest rate of unemployment in the United Kingdom, with a Catholic to Protestant unemployment ratio of 2 : 1 and, in West Belfast, a 46 per cent unemployment rate for Catholic (Bew, Patterson, and Teague 1997).

The reproduction of a society is not just a question of symbolic identifications and distinctions. There are few western societies as attuned to their demographic profile as Northern Ireland. It has an increasingly young population, 25 per cent of which is aged under 15 years of age. Catholics are now 43 per cent of the population and the numbers of Catholic and Protestants are fast approaching balance. Although Protestants remain a territorial majority in Northern Antrim, Down, Armagh, and much of the north-east, they are a minority west of the river Bann and amongst university students. This is having an significant impact on political structures and higher education—and, of course, on the Protestant sense of siege—and it has forced cross-bloc co-operation, particularly in local government. In 1997 Belfast's City Hall briefly fell from unionist control for the first time ever. However, the emergence of Derry's large Catholic majority has been partially tempered by the SDLP's pluralist commitment to the rotation of the post of mayor between all parties and its non-sectarian approach to the development of the city.

In Northern Ireland the codes of cultural and national identity are intensely regulated, asserted, and contested by members of the two blocs as a part of a cultural and political struggle: Orange parades, the use of Gaelic street signs, the flying or unfurling of Irish tricolours and Union Jacks, the creation of new colour-coded stretches of pavement are all occasions of intense political anxiety and reaffirmation of opposed identifications. In the mid-1990s there were major disputes at Queen's University in Belfast following the deletion of the National Anthem from the graduation ceremony and the increasing usage of Gaelic on the campus. Another recent example was the row which followed the introduction of a logo consisting of two figures embracing for a joint marketing initiative intended to promote the island as a tourist venue by the Northern Irish Tourist Board and the Republic's Bord Failte. An accompanying shamrock was deleted in the initial agreement but then restored in the Republic, triggering controversy in the north. A few months later Ulster unionist MP Ken Maginnis hurled two Irish tricolour flags—part of a St Patrick's Day display at Westminster—into the river Thames, stating that they had more to do with the IRA than St Patrick.

The connection between the regulation of the female body and the reproduction of national and political identifications was particularly evident in the tarring and feathering of the young Catholic women who fraternized with British soldiers at dances organized by the British army in the 1970s. These attacks were the work of an absolutist political formation operating a gendered hierarchy and fearful of contamination and social dilution. 'Sexual complicity signalled a form of political ambiguity that republicans were trying to erase' (Aretxaga 1997).The persistence of these defensive and exclusionary practices was evident when Catholic teenager Bernadette Martin was shot dead while sleeping at her Protestant boyfriend's home near Lurgan as recently as July 1997. The control of women is still a shared aspiration of the contrasting, gendered notions of the nation operative in the cultural and political imaginaries of northern paramilitaries. It has delayed the emergence of a women's movement and feminist thinking on the scale common throughout western Europe after the 1960s. It also deters the public expression of non-heterosexual preferences (Nash 1997).

The anxious, self-reassuring practice of abjection, the externalization of the menaces and temptations which are internal and threatening to an identification, is highly visible at the extremes of public discourse. Warnings against fornication with the Roman Whore and the sadism of monks, accompanied by claims that Sinn Fein's membership oath includes a commitment to driving the Protestants like swine into the sea, are commonplace utterances of Ian Paisley and his followers. Equally commonplace in the republican community are colloquialisms like 'Black Bastards' (a reference to the Protestant and unionist Royal Black Institution and its local preceptors which is frequently used to characterize political unionism as a whole) and notions of invasion (used to describe the July 1970 curfew on the Lower Falls Road in Belfast and more recently the most controversial Orange parades). During a tense moment during the marching season of 1997, in which Sinn Fein was attempting to rearticulate the political identifications of Belfast republicans and develop support for the peace process, it was Mo Mowlam who was represented as Pontius Pilate in dissenting murals on the Lower Ormeau Road.

Today the once commonplace distinction between planter and native is rarely invoked by republicans in public. The distinction between Protestant civilizer and native barbarian is also less prominent in Protestant discourse than it used to be. These long-standing oppositions are modulating into an affirmation that the two traditions are both deserving of respect. This end will be difficult to achieve as long as fundamental distinctions and homogenizations still structure thinking about each tradition's identity and contrasted other.

The processes of abjection and racialized distinction at the basis of these residual notions of collective ethnic identity are highly visible at times of intense social conflict. But despite the militarized environment, which still makes identifications alternative to those offered by the main political parties difficult to establish, sustain, and disseminate, these codes can occasionally be unravelled, making the traditional identifications appear strange.

As so often, music scenes generate the best examples. 'Alternative Ulster', 'Suspect Device', 'Barbed Wire Love', and other songs from Belfast indie rock pioneers Stiff Little Fingers vocalized the dissociation of northern youth from the dominant political articulations of the late 1970s. The song 'Green Wogs' also confronted the racialized assumptions of the Anglo-British. However, these are now a distant memory.

A more complicated example is the Bitter Orange Band's album *The Pope's a Darkie*. In many ways it exemplifies a bigoted, cross-generational Protestant sense of racialized superiority and sectarian territoriality, from the title song's association of Catholics with blackness, illiberalism, and hostility to birth control through to the Ulster-affirming Country and Western–reggae hybrid 'This Land is our Land', the designation of non-Protestant areas as 'jungle' in 'Derry Rock', the sexual decadence and moral hypocrisy of Catholicism in 'Blue Nun Blues' and the threat to 'press the button on the twelfth day of July' in 'Six Counties'. But the external menace, signified by nationalist tunes and Afro-Caribbean rhythms, has actually been reintroduced into the music, and licensed as parody— for example in 'Bold Orange Heroes' and 'Sasha Walter's War'. I have watched Protestants at post-parade street parties enjoying these songs and rhythms and have also seen the album generate transgressive laughter and enjoyment in republican homes during an optimistic phase of the peace process. Here perhaps, in such unexpected reversals, are signs of the openness and instability of Catholic and Protestant identifications, and the beginnings of the making strange of oneself that Kristeva's arguments would suggest is necessary for reconciliation in Northern Ireland. One is reminded of that remarkable moment during the peace process in which a coachload of nationalists and unionists, gridlocked for ninety minutes on their way to a White House reception, filled the time with communal singing: 'Gerry Adams joined in, singing the Orange Anthem "The Sash My Father Wore" as loud as the rest' (Sharrock and Devenport 1997: 387). There could be no better or more promising example of the practice of 'paradoxical community'.

The collective memories and narratives of the two blocs are also being reassessed in the fields of history, geography, and popular culture. A promising rethink is under way, particularly amongst a dissident Protestant intelligentsia, which questions the widespread notion of two stable traditions (Hyndman 1996; Boyce and O'Day 1996; Shirlow and McGovern 1997).

Civil society alone cannot be expected to heal political divisions. 'Sport can be an integral element in the creation and exacerbation of political conflict' (Bairner and Sugden 1993). In the case of Northern Ireland, it currently reproduces segregation and political distinction. The Gaelic Athletics Association, which the Orange Order regards as 'the IRA at play', fosters Gaelic football, hurling, and camogie. The Anglo-British sports of cricket and rugby are articulated with Protestantism and unionism. The burning down of a cricket pavilion on Lower Ormeau Road in 1997, a tense zone of Catholic expansion, was a recent consequence of this dynamic. 'A world-sport like football does not transcend national divisions but rather reveals their depth, especially within the working class' (McGarry and O'Leary 1995). Counterposed sectarian affiliations to football teams—Celtic and Rangers, Everton and Liverpool, Ireland and England or Scotland—mobilize and maintain ethnic distinctions, although there is a greater degree of flexibility and openness in relation to the fortunes of the Northern Ireland football team.

The New Opportunity

The late 1990s were a political and cultural watershed for Northern Ireland. They represent a moment in which attempts to change the traditional political identifications and practices of many republicans and unionists began to bear fruit, raising hope and levels of anxiety and generating a defensive contraflow.

In May 1998, after ceasefires by the largest paramilitary organizations, parade route concessions by some Orange lodges and a year of talks, 71 per cent of the population voted for an agreement reached by all but two of Northern Ireland's political parties under the supervision of American Senator George Mitchell, British Prime Minister Tony Blair, and Irish Taoiseach Bertie Ahern. A multi-tiered and non-majoritarian form of governance was endorsed, consisting of a new Northern Irish Assembly based on joint decision-making, a north–south body and a British–Irish council. The deal also included the phased release of paramilitary prisoners, reforms in policing, and the decommissioning of paramilitary weapons. A simultaneous referendum in the Republic agreed to amend articles 2 and 3 of its constitution, laying a unionist ghost and removing a traditional prop of republicanism.

Shortly afterwards, three-quarters of voters elected candidates for the Assembly who were in favour of the deal. But unionism is still in crisis. The UUP took only 21.3 per cent of the vote in the 1998 election, coming second to the SDLP. The UUP's 28 pro-Assembly seats exactly matched the number of unionists opposed to the Good Friday agreement. Serious divisions remain in the unionist community and its parties have proved unable to operate as an alliance. The consensus and stability required for the agreement to stick and for a new hegemony to emerge is far from guaranteed. Amidst growing disputes over decommissioning, the release of prisoners, and contentious Orange parades, journalist David McKittrick suggested that the Assembly might become 'a forum for war by another means' before it had even met. However, this fragmentation of unionism also provides the opportunity for a realignment between constitutional nationalism and pragmatic unionism in the centre ground of politics, based on the converging lifestyles, greater respect for law and order, tolerance of intermarriage, and transnational outlook of the north's middle classes, both Catholic and Protestant.

Although the agreement was a historic turning point, disputes relating to the detailed operation of the institutions of government— as opposed to their perceived incompatibility with entrenched national identifications—are much further down the popular agenda than the actions and reforms expected of politicians. An end to paramilitary violence, the introduction of a bill of rights, and the right to choose integrated education are regarded as more important by both Protestants and Catholics (Irwin 1998).

A major consequence of the replacement of the democratic process with direct rule in 1972 was that national-constitutional demands—through which local leaders formed and maintained counterposed communities—often took priority over popular concerns like employment, health, education, and quality of life issues, over which local politicians have had little influence.

Unionist supremacism, and its successor, direct rule, together choked the space required for a democratic and inclusive politics to emerge. In Northern Ireland universal suffrage for elections to local government, many of whose powers had been transferred to the Northern Ireland Office, has only been in place since 1969. For nearly three decades, government has been remote and unaccountable, legitimized only by unamendable Orders in Council. The mistrust and disengagement from the emaciated political process that resulted now represents a major challenge to those who would like to develop a modern pluralist form of politics. Elected politicians frequently acted as advocates for vested ethnic interests and competing national aspirations. Until the peace process they had little experience of managing resources and brokering partnerships or negotiating priorities. 'They are not forced to consider options, make hard decisions, or weigh financial implications. All of that is largely done for them by ministries and quangos . . . Direct rule has created a system where elected officials promote grievances' (Hazelton 1995). One immediate consequence was that the middle class of both faiths, one reinforced and the other created by the British subvention, withdrew from the political sphere.

A wider scepticism about politics may qualify the legitimacy that opinion polls and voting figures appear to confer on the new settlement. The 'loss of community ownership' of the peace process was a major finding of a cross-community survey of perceptions during 1997. It was widely felt that the initiative had passed from community activists to politicians, ministers, and civil servants. Fearing a stalemate between politicians, the study concluded that 'a parallel and far reaching debate must be taken right to the heart of our two communities' (Hall 1997). Robin Wilson also criticized the early form taken by the talks and peace process: 'in reality the innovation was much less substantial than claimed. Each was marked by a defeatism about political polarisation and a deference towards powerful political and paramilitary organisations. Far from building a "political centre", they entrenched sectarian politics formidably. And neither did anything to redress the unhealthy unbalance where everything is hyper-politicised and nothing is determined within the sphere of civil society' (Wilson 1996b). These observations and warnings still carry great force.

Northern Ireland has an increasingly vibrant civil society of non-governmental, voluntary, and women's organizations, with widely varying degrees of linkage to the dominant political formations. The future of Northern Ireland depends on the quality of the relationship that is established between this milieu and the decision-making processes of the new multi-tiered system of governance.

Kristeva argues that because of modern crises of identity the delegation of power to political parties 'is no longer the most appropriate or efficient representation' (Sichere 1996). She favours the development of forms of power that are 'provisional and stabilising' and 'dispersed and flexible' (Clark and Hulley 1996). In Northern Ireland this would require a modern decentralized pluralism and forms of civic partnership and empowerment that are absent from the political structures which have been established and which have no precedent in the practice of most of the parties involved. The challenge is to develop new forms of political identification and community partnership that will help to revise collective memories of dismemberment, siege, or imminent disappearance.

The residual political formations of the unionist ascendancy, of the era of direct rule, and of historic communities predominantly ordered by their identification with the British or Irish state, may not survive the next phase of the modernization of the north. Northern Ireland in the next five years will be a tense laboratory for many contemporary notions of pluralist politics, deterritorialized national identification, civic nationalism, hyphenated identities, and reflexivity.

A Deterritorialized North, Transatlantic and European

Many accounts of the Troubles emphasize the territorialized nature of the conflict. But the conflict in Northern Ireland has always been a diasporic, even globalized contestation for power and resources.

More than any other part of the United Kingdom, the identifications and forces involved in the region have increasingly been transnational, from Germany's tactical assistance to republicanism during the First World War to the more recent Libyan weapons subsidy, from Dublin's aspirations to reunite the island to European rights legislation, from the psephological calculations of incoming American presidents with an eye on the Irish-American vote to Westminster's changing sensitivity to its fragile 'special relationship' with the USA. The emerging settlement, if it holds, is therefore an integral part of the post-cold War political process, which consists of consolidated regional trading blocs, increasingly diasporic polities, and the transformation of democratic processes by supranational formations and an intensively mediatized western world.

The political identifications of the Irish diaspora in the United States, where 40 million people now claim an Irish ethnicity, have been crucial for nationalists and republicans (Holland 1995: O'Clery 1996; Wilson 1995). They have also impacted on the strategy of the British government. As Bew, Patterson, and Teague point out, in the post-war period 'the high political concerns of its political elite in relation to Ireland shifted from the strategic to the diplomatic: the concern was not to be embarrassed internationally, particularly in the US, by Britain's Northern Ireland involvement' (1997).

Republican articulations were very effective in securing American pressure on Westminster, new policy initiatives, and funds during the early years of the Troubles. Irish Northern Aid was set up in 1970, and the Washington-based Irish National Caucus a few years later. Liberal democratic opinion also went transatlantic. In the mid-1970s John Hume, leader of the SDLP, networked effectively with an influential group known as 'the four horsemen' consisting of Senators Edward Kennedy and Daniel Moynihan, Speaker of the House Tip O'Neill, and New York Governor Hugh Carey (Wilson 1995). The initiative was broadened by the founding of Congressional Friends of Ireland in 1981, which became a successful catalyst for political pressure on London and a political guarantor of the US contribution to the International Fund for Ireland. Transatlantic Irish republicanism was not to be eclipsed, however. 'The hunger strike had the effect of reawakening an Irish American giant,' IRA arms buyer Gerry McGeough told Peter Taylor. 'An Anglophobic one' (Taylor 1997). The combined effect of these initiatives was crucial in securing President Clinton's later and decisive involvement in the peace process.

European integration has also reshaped the structures and discourses of the conflict. Decisions by the European Court placed a check on direct rule. Cross-community and cross-border collaboration to secure European structural development funds has had a political rather than a financial impact. In total, the structural fund spending scheduled for the north in the five years 1994–9 was only £900 million, less than a third of the annual subvention from the British Exchequer. The Republic's membership of the European Union is widely recognized to be a reason for the closer collaboration between Dublin and London on the detail of a settlement from the 1980s onwards.

The European Union was a major arena and social model for the SDLP's John Hume. His claim that it had brought the previously warring neighbours of France and Germany together is known as his 'Single Transferable Speech'. The SDLP actually sought European Union representation in its proposals for joint sovereignty in the north in the early 1990s.

A shared involvement in and affiliation to European institutions is likely to have a weaning and transformative effect on the divergent political identifications mobilized and reproduced in the north. An integrated Europe sensitized to its regions, and based on codified rights of citizenship, might reduce the salience of nation-state-based political identifications and be conducive to the emergence of a pluralist democracy in Ireland (Kearney and Wilson 1994; Democratic Dialogue 1997; Kearney 1997).

Kevin Davey

Meehan and Bew also argue that the European Union embodies processes which will be valuable in Northern Ireland: 'the lessons of its peacemaking origins and the continental tradition of coalitions and alliances, the idea that interdependence is more significant than impregnable borders, and new legal and administrative frameworks for development programmes, particularly cross border ones' (Meehan and Bew 1994).

State and territory are weakening as components of national identification. Young Protestants no longer take the constitutional monarchy as the touchstone of their identification as British (Pollak 1993: 99). Shirlow asserts that it is already the case that the middle classes, 'north and south, increasingly possess a transnationalised identity in which relationships with London, Brussels, Washington and Tokyo predominate over a previously strong association with their respective parts of Ireland' (Shirlow 1997). That is probably a premature claim. But Europeanization may well prepare the ground for more pluralist notions of Irishness and Britishness than are currently enabled, developing the preconditions for Kearney's post-nationalist vision of an Ireland 'beyond unitary sovereignty' (Kearney 1997).

Does this mean that a new and pluralist region, in which Irish Protestants and Catholic Ulstermen co-operate as civic, republican Northern Irish Europeans is now being formed? Not yet. But before it can be identified as a feasible future, or dismissed as a foolish mirage, a number of serious questions have to be answered.

A Series of Hurdles

First, will the comprehensive segregation of the north, a precondition for the transformation of residual identities and sectarian political formations, come to an end? There is an increased level of cross-community interaction in the public sector as a result of fair employment practices. However, the development of integrated education and new integrated housing projects, perhaps with lower rents as an incentive, will probably also be necessary.

A large majority of Protestants and Catholics would like to see an increase in integrated education, although in the past only half of those in favour of the reform were willing to send their children to mixed schools (Gallagher 1993). Although there are now thirty-seven integrated schools in the north, attended by 8,500 pupils, they service only 3 per cent of the school age population. The growth in this sector has been complemented by an increasing number of *gael scoileanna*, attended by 2,000 pupils, where teaching is in the Irish language. In the short term, education is likely to deliver only the message of desegregation, in the form of the Education for Mutual Understanding programme that is required teaching in all schools.

Some modernizing reforms could reinforce the old identifications. A devolution of welfare responsibilities and the diversification of service providers could lead to the development of parallel Catholic and Protestant welfare systems.

Which cultural traditions will be sustained and which transformed in the immediate future? There are roughly 2,500 unionist parades each year, an increase of over 32 per cent since the Anglo-Irish agreement of 1985. Only a few are controversial, mainly where routes pass through areas relinquished by Protestants in a process of suburbanization which has reinforced segregation. Serious attempts at local mediation have reduced the level of conflict as have bans. But it is likely that a number of parades will be converted to static festivals.

Targeting deprivation is a precondition for transforming residual exclusionary identifications, and insuring against the re-emergence of a paramilitary rite of passage for young people. But fair employment legislation, which has only been in place in Northern Ireland for a decade, is viewed with suspicion on all sides. Although workplace discrimination has lessened under direct rule, so have the number of workplaces, particularly for the unskilled or unqualified. Low-income Catholics are sceptical, while Protestants at most levels still perceive equality a threat. They both have rational grounds for disbelief. It could take more than five years of rapid growth to significantly reduce the unemployment disparity of more than 2 to 1 experienced by Catholics (Bew, Patterson, and Teague 1997).

This problem compounds the major economic challenge associated with demilitarization, namely the future of the RUC. The service cannot be sustained in its size or composition. To construct a cross-community police force on a scale appropriate for a modern law-abiding community would require the replacement of 8,500 of the existing Protestant officers with 1,000 new Catholic recruits. An enhanced redundancy progamme is inevitable, with a particularly adverse impact on Protestant employment and incomes which, spread over a long or a short period, will generate anxieties and unsettle the identifications of the unionist community.

Retail, distribution, and increased tourism will of course create new jobs. In 1994, during the first of the two IRA ceasefires during the peace process, Northern Ireland tourism rose by 67 per cent.

Over the next four years £207 million was invested in the tourism infrastructure, resulting in new hotels and ferry improvements. In 1998 Graham Gudgin, director of the Northern Ireland Economic Research Centre (NIERC), expected 'A doubling of Northern Ireland's tourism industry over the next five years, leading to the creation of around 20,000 new jobs'. The Northern Ireland Industrial Development Board expects growth to take place in globally expanding sectors like electronics and telecoms, with a steep rise in tradeable services like software and call centres. But the current thinking is that these will not offset the initial impact of restructuring of the RUC and the Prison Service. Tourism and retail jobs are not based on the same skills or masculine identifications reproduced in the uniformed services. They require a tolerance of difference and openness to cultural modernity. This is just one dimension of the shock that the hybridizing centrifuge of world markets is likely to bring to Northern Ireland's indigenous cultures.

The guns have been laid to one side. Northern Ireland's competing cultural and political identifications, aspirations, and abjections are slowly being reconfigured. A new hegemony may be gestating. But it also appears that Northern Ireland's immediate future, just like its recent past, will be driven not by 'Ourselves Alone', or 'the Protestant people' but by forces originating far outside its still tense borders.

Further Reading

The development of cultural studies is at an early stage in Northern Ireland, emerging from a different disciplinary matrix and with a different trajectory to the rest of the United Kingdom. As a result of the Troubles, many of the best examples are in fact insightful and socially engaged studies in ethnography, conflict resolution, the study of cultural traditions, and liberal and post-Marxist political analysis.

The most important recent studies include: Colin Gahm and Richard Kirkland (eds.), *Ireland and Cultural Theory: The Mechanics of Authenticity* (London: Macmillan, 1999); Brian Graham (ed.), *In Search of Ireland: A Cultural Geography* (London: Routledge, 1997); Neil Jarman, *Material Conflicts: Parades and Visual Displays in Northern Ireland* (Oxford: Berg Publishing Ltd., 1997); Dominic Bryan, *Orange Parades: The Politics of Ritual, Tradition and Control* (London: Pluto Press, 2000); Anthony Buckley, *Symbols in Northern Ireland* (Belfast: Institute of Irish Studies, Queen's University, 1998); and Camille O'Reilly, *The Irish Language in Northern Ireland: The Politics of Culture and Identity* (New York: St Martin's Press, 1999).

Gendered identifications are the focus of Rosemary Sales, *Women Divided: Gender, Religion and Politics in Northern Ireland* (London: Routledge, 1997); Megan Sullivan, *Women in Northern Ireland: Cultural Studies and Material*

Conditions (Gainesville: University Press of Florida, 1999); and Begoña Aret-xaga, *Shattering Silence: Women, Nationalism and Political Subjectivity in Northern Ireland* (Princeton: Princeton University Press, 1997). Youth culture is the subject of Norman Gillespie, Tom Lovett, and Wendy Garner's *Youth Work and Working Class Youth Culture: Rules and Resistance in West Belfast* (Milton Keynes: Open University Press, 1992). The best recent study of racialization in Ulster is Paul Hainsworth (ed.), *Divided Society: Ethnic Minorities and Racism in Northern Ireland* (London: Pluto Press, 1998).

The European context and transformation of the conflict is well presented in James Goodman, *Single Europe, Single Ireland? Uneven Development in Process* (Dublin: Irish Academic Press, 1999).

John Whyte's *Interpreting Northern Ireland* (Oxford: Oxford University Press, 1990) remains the definitive overview of the theoretical debate on the nature of the national conflict in Ireland. Richard Kearney's *Postnationalist Ireland: Politics, Culture, Philosophy* (London: Routledge, 1997) sketches an important route beyond the impasses it describes.

For issues ranging from policing and Orange lodge parades to cross community marriage, the Conflict Archive on the Internet is an invaluable resource. It can be found at *http://www.incore.ulst.ac.uk/*

References

Aretxaga, Begoña (1997), *Shattering Silence: Women, Nationalism and Political Subjectivity in Northern Ireland*, Princeton: Princeton University Press.

Bairner, A., and **Sugden, J.** (1993), *Sport, Sectarianism and Society in a Divided Ireland*, Leicester: Leicester University Press.

Bew, P., Patterson, H., and **Teague, P.** (1997), *Between War and Peace: The Political Future of Northern Ireland*, London: Lawrence & Wishart.

Boyce, G. D., and **O'Day, A.** (1996), *The Making of Modern Irish History: Revisionism and the Revisionist Controversy*, London: Routledge.

Bruce, S. (1994), *The Edge of the Union: The Ulster Loyalist Political Vision*, Oxford: Oxford University Press.

Buckley, A. D., and **Kenney, M. C.** (1995), *Negotiating Identity: Rhetoric, Metaphor and Social Drama in Northern Ireland*, Washington: Smithsonian Institution Press.

Clark, S., and **Hulley, K.** (1996), 'Cultural Strangeness and the Subject in Crisis', in Ross Mitchell Guberman (ed.), *Julia Kristeva: Interviews*, New York: Columbia University Press.

Democratic Dialogue (1997), *Continentally Challenged: Securing Northern Ireland's Place in the European Union*, Report No. 5, Belfast.

Gallagher, A. M. (1993), 'Community Relations', in Peter Stringer and Gillian Robinson (eds.), *Social Attitudes in Northern Ireland: The Third Report*, Belfast: Blackstaff Press.

Hall, M. (1997), *The Death of the 'Peace Process'?*, Island Pamphlets 17, Belfast.

Hazelton, W. A. (1995), 'A Breed Apart? Northern Ireland's MPs at Westminster', *Journal of Legislative Studies*, 1/4

Holland, J. (1995), *The American Connection: US Guns, Money and Influence in Northern Ireland*, London: Viking.

Hyndman, Marilyn (1996), *Further Afield: Journeys from a Protestant Past*, Belfast: Beyond the Pale Publications.

Irwin, C. (1998), 'The Search for Settlement: The People's Choice', *Fortnight Educational*, Feb.

Kearney, R. (1997), *Postnationalist Ireland: Politics, Culture, Philosophy*, London: Routledge

—— and Wilson, R. (1994), 'Northern Ireland's Future as a European Region', *Irish Review* 15, Spring.

Kristeva, Julia (1991), *Strangers to Ourselves*, New York: Columbia University Press.

—— (1993), *Nations without Nationalism*, New York: Columbia University Press.

McAuley, James W. (1994), *The Politics of Identity: A Loyalist Community in Belfast*, Aldershot: Avebury.

McGarry, J., and O'Leary, B. (1995), *Explaining Northern Ireland*, Oxford: Blackwell.

Meehan, E., and Bew, P. (1994), 'Regions and Borders: Controversies in Northern Ireland about the European Union', *European Journal of Public Policy*, 1 / 1.

Nash, Catherine (1997), 'Embodied Irishness: Gender, Sexuality and Irish Identities', in Brian Graham (ed.), *In Search of Ireland: A Cultural Geography*, London: Routledge.

O'Clery, C. (1996), *The Greening of the White House*, Dublin: Gill & Macmillan.

O Dochartaigh, Niall (1997), *From Civil Rights to Armalites: Derry and the Birth of the Irish Troubles*, Cork: Cork University Press.

O'Doherty, Malachi (1998), *The Trouble with Guns: Republican Strategy and the Provisional IRA*, Belfast: Blackstaff Press.

Pollak, A. (1993), *A Citizens' Enquiry: The Opsahl Report on Northern Ireland*, Dublin: Lilliput Press.

Porter, Norman (1996), *Rethinking Unionism: An Alternative Vision for Northern Ireland*, Belfast: Blackstaff Press.

Purdie, Bob (1990), *Politics in the Streets: The Origins of the Civil Rights Movement in Northern Ireland*, Belfast: Blackstaff Press.

Sharrock, David, and Devenport, Mark (1997), *Man of War, Man of Peace? The Unauthorised Biography of Gerry Adams*, Basingstoke: Macmillan.

Shirlow, Peter (1997), 'Class, Materialism and the Fracturing of Traditional Alignments', in Brian Graham (ed.), *In Search of Ireland: A Cultural Geography*, London: Routledge.

—— and McGovern, Mark (1997), *Who are 'the People'?, Unionism, Protestantism and Loyalism in Northern Ireland*, London: Pluto Press.

Shuttleworth, I., and Shirlow, P. (1996), 'Vacancies, Access to Employment and the Unemployed', in E. McLaughlin (ed.), *Policy Aspects of Employment Equality*, Belfast: SACHR.

Sichere, B. (1996), 'Interview: The Old Man and the Wolves', in Ross Mitchell Guberman (ed.), *Julia Kristeva: Interviews*, New York: Columbia University Press.

Taylor, P. (1997), *Provos: The IRA and Sinn Fein*, London: Bloomsbury.

Wilson, A. J. (1995), *Irish America and the Ulster Conflict 1968–1995*, Belfast: Blackstaff Press.

Wilson, Robin (1996a), 'Asking the Right Question', in Democratic Dialogue, *Reconstituting Politics*, Report No. 3, Belfast.

—— (1996b) 'Ten Steps to Reconstituting Politics', in Democratic Dialogue, *Reconstituting Politics*, Report No. 3, Belfast.

Scotland and the Union: Changing Identities in the British State

DAVID
McCRONE

BRITAIN has always been a contradiction in terms. The UK is not Britain is not England, and yet the terms have often been used interchangeably. The argument in this chapter is that this 'fuzziness' (Cohen 1994) is more the result of design than accident, and that for much of the state's history (from 1707, or 1801, or 1921—the three constitutional moments) this fuzzy quality served it well. No longer. The contradictions demand to be resolved, and Scotland, as one of the two key founding partners of the British state, leads the way in their resolution. I will argue, however, that the nationalist challenge from Scotland (and from Wales) is only partly to do with changes in these nations themselves, and is much more concerned with the realignment of Britishness in the late twentieth century.

Defining the State

What is 'Britain'? It is a state-nation masquerading as a nation-state. That is, it was constructed initially in 1707 as a political convenience between England, the senior partner, and Scotland, the junior one. Wales and Ireland were to all intents and purposes under the jurisdiction of England by this time, although the latter was not formally incorporated into the British state until 1801, thus creating the 'United Kingdom' (of Great Britain and Ireland). Britain (I will adopt the term as the usual shorthand for the United Kingdom so as to include Northern Ireland which technically is not on the British mainland) can be considered a 'state-nation' because its political superstructure was grafted onto the civil societies or nations which to a greater or lesser extent remained self-governing in their domestic or 'low' politics. Linda Colley in her book, *Britons: Forging the Nation, 1707–1837* has explored how a new political identity was constructed in these islands. Britain, she says,

> was an invention forged above all by war. Time and time again, war with France brought Britons, whether they hailed from Wales or Scotland or England, into confrontation with an obvious hostile Other and encouraged them to define themselves collectively against it. They defined themselves as Protestants struggling for survival against the world's foremost Catholic power. They defined themselves against the French as they imagined them to be, superstitious, militarist, decadent and unfree. (1992: 5)

The invention of Britishness was forged in the long period of actual and virtual war with France from 1707 until 1837. These were politico-religious wars which acted as an integrating mechanism to forge (in both senses: creating something new, but also something artificial) a state identity, a Britishness 'superimposed over an array of internal differences in response to contact with the Other, and above all in response to conflict with the Other' (Colley 1992: 6). It worked with rather than against the grain of older national identities which were to persist, and even outlast, the later British one.

By referring to Britain as a 'state-nation' we are alluding to this fact that it was a state first, and only later (if at all) a nation. At no times can one seriously consider Britain as a 'nation-state', that is, as a homogeneous cultural grouping which mobilized that homogeneity to become a state. The fact that Britishness sat lightly on top of the constituent nations as a kind of state-identity is the key to understanding state–society relations in the UK (Nairn 1977). The British state was quite unlike later state formations which sought to align political, cultural, and economic structures in the classical form of the 'nation-state'. These formations demanded the lining up of state, nation, and society, and even economy and culture, in such a way that 'national identity' ran through all of these institutions. Being a citizen in these modern states demanded allegiance, and in return the state was made accountable, and its sovereignty limited, often by means of the doctrine of popular rather than Crown/parliamentary sovereignty as in Britain. This is at the root of the claim that the British are actually not 'citizens' of the state at all, but 'subjects' of the Crown.

David McCrone

This, then, is the context in which the Union took place between Scotland on the one hand, and England on the other. With hindsight, we might argue that the only kind of state which allowed the Scots to retain a high degree of civil autonomy was a 'pre-modern' one in which the links between high and low politics were tenuous indeed (Paterson 1994). It is doubtful if the Scots would have agreed to submerge their institutional autonomy into the British state if it actually had been a thoroughly modern and integrationist formation (McCrone 1992).

A related contradiction is that, until 1999, the British state was constitutionally a 'unitary' one with a single legislature at Westminster, yet it is also a multinational state (hence, a 'United Kingdom') in which England, Scotland, Wales, and Northern Ireland forefront their national/territorial identities. With hindsight, we might wonder why a federal constitution did not evolve in these islands to take cognizance of this fact. It almost did, in the late nineteenth century, when Home Rule for Ireland—thereafter 'Home Rule all round'—was on the political agenda, but this possibility was destroyed by the intransigence of the Conservative Party in the House of Commons aided by dissident Liberal 'unionists'. In many respects, however, to the Scots, at least for much of the two centuries after 1707, having a separate legislature in Edinburgh was irrelevant as they had *de facto* autonomy over domestic affairs—notably the 'Holy Trinity' of law, education, and religion—and, after the consolidation of the Scottish Office in 1885, bureaucratic self-government (Brown et al. 1998).

The other obstacle to federalism, then as now, was the sheer demographic size of England which so dominates the UK population (by the 1990s, the English represented 85 per cent), and the English regions showed little—and variable—interest in regional government until the 1990s. Alongside the domination by England lay the seemingly unreconstructed character of the constitution with its doctrine of Crown sovereignty. The unreformed, *ancien régime*-like quality of the British state has been commented upon by many writers. David Marquand, for example, has called the UK an 'unprincipled' society because its state structures are fundamentally deficient. He observes:

Thanks to the upheavals of the 17th century—thanks in particular to the victory of the English landed classes over the Stuart kings—one cannot speak of a 'British state' in the way that one speaks of a 'French state' or in modern times of a 'German state'. The UK is not a state in the continental sense. It is a bundle of islands (including such exotica as the Channel Islands and the Isle of Man which are not even represented at Westminster), acquired at different times by the English crown, and governed in different ways. Its inhabitants are not citizens of a state, with defined rights of citizenship. They are subjects of a monarch, enjoying 'liberties' which their ancestors won from previous monarchs. (1988: 152)

Marquand's point is not that the British state represents an *ancien régime* in a pre-French Revolution sense, but that it is one which suffers from a form of arrested political development. It was a minimal state with a small bureaucracy which was clearly suited to market-driven adjustment in the eighteenth century, but which failed to make the transition to become a 'developmental state' in the late nineteenth century (Marquand 1988, 1993).

How was it that the laissez-faire British state had the doctrine of Crown sovereignty at its core, whereas continental states, which were more interventionist, did not? The answer is that the price for greater state–society integration on the continental model was precisely that it was more accountable to its citizens. Indeed, its population could consider themselves 'citizens', rather than 'subjects of the crown', albeit the Crown in Parliament. In the British case, sovereignty had been transferred from the monarch to Parliament (which became the Crown), but the power of the state remained fairly crude and primitive, and so, it could be argued, accountability mattered less.

Britain simply could not become a 'modern' state like any other without fundamental constitutional change. It had been a 'night-watchman' state post-1707 because it had little option, at least in political terms. Scotland had joined the Union in that year on the basis that it would continue to run its own institutional affairs—its legal, educational, and religious systems, as well as its local government system. This system of 'low politics' could only operate if the British state confined itself to 'high politics'—especially the imperial variety. When Britain lost its empire and when, under pressure of war, it was forced to integrate its institutional and political arrangements the strains eventually began to show.

Who are the British?

One might characterize Britain as essentially an 'empire' state, rather than a 'national' one. We can see this most obviously in the evolution of the concept of British citizenship. If the conventional essence of nationality is 'citizenship', then Britain is an awkward case. The inhabitants of the UK attained citizenship by a legislative sleight of hand under the 1948 Nationality Act as 'citizens of the UK and the colonies'. Prior to 1948 the inhabitants of the British

Isles and the British Empire were formally 'subjects' of the Crown. The 1914 British Nationality and Aliens Act was a consolidation of the law relating to British nationality over the centuries (Goulbourne 1991). This Act did not refer to Britain as a geographical entity; it was perceived in terms of those who owed allegiance to the Crown, reflecting the pre-modern and dynastic origins of the 'Kingdom'.

The post-1945 crisis arose because independent states such as Canada and India wished to redefine citizenship for immigration purposes, and so a separate status was necessary for the remaining inhabitants of the UK. The British government had preferred that people in Commonwealth countries were British subjects first and citizens of individual states second. The legacy was a complex variety of practices. Goulbourne argues that in the post-imperial age the Labour Party sought to encourage a 'traditional', i.e. non-ethnic, definition of 'Britishness' to encompass the Commonwealth while supporting colonial peoples in their liberation struggles. This helps to explain Labour's opposition in the 1960s and 1970s to Scottish and Welsh nationalism as a perceived betrayal of the multinational, non-ethnic identity of Britain. The Conservative Party for its part developed an 'ethnic' definition ('those groups which consider themselves to be British, and also the indigenous and/or white population' (Goulbourne 1991: 245). This can be seen in the 1962 Commonwealth Immigration Act, the 1971 Immigration Act, and the 1981 Nationality Act (which embedded the 'patriality' clause), and was reinforced ideologically under the influence of Enoch Powell and Margaret Thatcher. The politicization of ethnic identity has helped to highlight the racial context of the debate over the last thirty years. The 1981 Patriality Act ushered in the law of blood (*ius sanguinis*) rather than the law of territory (*ius soli*).

This brief overview of how 'Britishness' has come to be redefined in the postcolonial age provides a context for important shifts in national identities within the United Kingdom itself, notably in Scotland (Crick 1995). If British identity is externally fuzzy, so too is its meaning within these islands. Goulbourne argues that until Ireland became a republic in 1948, its citizens remained formal 'subjects' of the British Crown (reinforced by the new republic leaving the Commonwealth a year later). A number of other key confusions remained, notably that between 'Britain' and 'England', a distinction which was, and is, rarely made in the UK's largest country as well as overseas. Anthony Barnett in his book *This Time: Our Constitutional Revolution* (1997) commented:

What is the difference between being English and being British? If you ask a Scot or a Welsh person about their Britishness, the question makes sense to them. They might say that they feel Scots first and British second. Or that they enjoy a dual identity as Welsh-British, with both parts being equal. Or they might say. 'I'm definitely British first'. What they have in common is an understanding that there is a space between their nation and Britain, and they can assess the relationship between the two. The English, however, are more often baffled when asked how they relate their English-ness and Britishness to each other. They often fail to understand how the two can be contrasted at all. It seems like one of those puzzles that others can undo but you can't; Englishness and Britishness seem inseparable. They might prefer to be called one thing rather than the other—and today young people increasingly prefer English to British—but, like two sides of a coin, neither term has an independent existence from the other. (Barnett 1997: 292–3)

Although the Scots and the Welsh worked within a more logical model whereby their national identities were nested in the broader British state identity, the unitary nature of that state seemed to reinforce the equation of Britain and England. In recent years an important debate has started south of the border about whether or not black people can be 'English' rather than simply 'British'. In many ways this is a debate about ethnic (being English by lineage or 'blood') versus civic definitions (being British by residence and citizenship).

The debate north of the border is usually more explicit and seemingly more clear-cut. Broadly speaking, around three-quarters of people living in Scotland opt for 'Scottish' and only one-quarter 'British' if asked to choose. This prioritizing of Scottishness over Britishness is also reflected when a scale is used in survey research asking people to choose from Scottish not British at one end, to British not Scottish at the other (named the Moreno scale after its author (Moreno 1995; Moreno and Arriba 1996). Respondents were asked: 'We are interested to know how people living in [Scotland/Wales/England] see themselves in terms of their nationality. Which of these best reflects how you regard yourself?' (see Table 6.1)

In surveys of this kind, which have been asked since the late 1980s, broadly six in ten opt for either Scottish not British, or more Scottish than British, while only one in ten claim the reverse for Britishness. Nevertheless, well over half of people living in Scotland claim some version of dual nationality, being both Scottish and British, albeit with a clear emphasis on the former. While people in Wales also assert their Welshness over their Britishness, they do so at a lower level than the Scots. The distinction between national and

David McCrone

Table 6.1 National identity by country

Percentage in column	Scotland	Wales	England
X not British	23	13	8
More X than British	38	29	16
Equally X and British	27	26	46
More British than X	4	10	15
British not X	4	15	9
None of these	4	7	6
Sample sizes	882	182	2,551

Notes: X = Scottish/Welsh/English.
Sources: British and Scottish Election Studies 1997; see Brown *et al.* (1968: 2, 3).

state identity is clearly more problematic for the English, and one might interpret their clustering around the 'equally English and British' category as evidence for Barnett's claim that there is a (confusion between the two. The result, in Robin Cohen's words, is that:

British identity shows a general pattern of fragmentation. Multiple axes of identification have meant that Irish, Scots, Welsh and English people, those from the white, black and brown Commonwealth, Americans, English-speakers, Europeans and even 'aliens' have had their lives intersect one with another in overlapping and complex circles of identity-construction and rejection. The shape and edges of British identity are thus historically changing, often vague and, to a degree, malleable—an aspect of the British identity I have called 'a fuzzy frontier'. (1994: 35)

The issues of ethnicity and nationality, then, in the UK are especially 'fuzzy' for reasons outlined above. Britishness is a political identity, roughly equated with citizenship, but as we have seen growing out of a pre-modern prior definition of people as 'subjects' of the Crown, even those who do not live in these islands.

Transforming National Identity

We are now in a position to understand better the challenges to British state power in these islands. To recapitulate: the fuzzy quality of Britishness allowed it to encompass the settler communities in its empire even to the point of awarding 'patrial' status from the 1980s to those who had some ethnic claim to reside here. As the empire was lost, and Britain retrenched to these islands, the contradictions of political identity became more obvious. The Irish question had dogged the British for some time, and by the 1920s, as a result of partition, another part of the British state fell away. The inter-war period also saw the stirrings of modern Scottish and Welsh nationalisms, first in the formation of Plaid Cymru in 1925 and an amalgamated Scottish National Party in 1934. What these political movements were showing was that layers of the British imperium were peeling off, first the white dominions, then the challenge from the Celtic countries.

As Marquand points out, the exhaustion of the Whig imperialist and democratic collectivist visions of British national identity created a vacuum in the 1970s into which 'authoritarian individualism' rushed. Its problem was that, in Marquand's words, 'The state was Britain. The identity was English' (1993: 218). In essence, it was a post-imperial identity, as one of its key prophets Enoch Powell perceived (Marquand 1993: 212). His hostility to immigration from the black Commonwealth lay in recognition that England lay at the core, and that in many respects 'Britain' had come to an end, reinforced by a continuing fuzziness of British 'national' identity. The elision of 'England' and 'Britain' merely masks the issue. We can also relate this to the strongly held opposition to 'Europe' from these Little Englanders. Why swap one empire for another?

By the first half of the twentieth century, British national identity was exposed for what it was—a supra-national identity deriving from an imperial past. Britishness was and is a rather loose rule holding disparate cultures and peoples together, and in this respect there are echoes of its Roman imperial equivalent: 'civis Britannicus sum.' It had been created as an inclusive rather than an exclusive definition under allegiance to the Crown so that all who came under its rule were British subjects whether they liked it or not. While this interpretation had advantages in the imperial era, by the twentieth century it was proving ill adapted to the needs of a modern state.

Scotland in Britain

Where does late twentieth-century Scotland stand in its relationship to the British state? Let us remind ourselves that the Treaty of Union of 1707 was the outcome of a 'marriage of convenience' between Scotland and England. Scotland got access to English markets at home and abroad. England solved its historic irritation with the Scottish–French alliance which was no more. This was a marriage which suited both parties, including the Scots, well for much of its subsequent history. English complaints of 'Scots on the make' were an unwitting acknowledgement of their economic success and political influence out of all proportion to their numbers in the burgeoning empire. That is why, in the middle of the nineteenth century, they could celebrate 'unionist-nationalism' as the apogee of dual identity—Scottish, yes; but British also (Morton 1999). The two were complementary, especially as they stood rooted on the three ideological pillars of unionism, imperialism, and Protestantism.

Warfare had created Britain in the eighteenth and nineteenth centuries, and at first glance it might seem that mass war in the twentieth reinforced Britishness. Dying for one's country dominated the lives of most Britons in the first half of the twentieth century (Stevenson 1984). But it was a two-edged sword. On the one hand, war and its socio-political demands mobilized the population into something resembling a British 'nation-state', but on the other hand, it essentially weakened the capacity of the British state to address the multinational dimensions which were growing more pressing in the second half of the century. The loss of empire, the decline of political influence and waning economic standing highlighted the uneasy marriage which was the Union. Growing secularization had detached most Scots from their politico-religious allegiance to Protestantism. Mass war had temporarily fixed the Scots, with their post-Union attachment to imperialist militarism, into Britishness, but the long peace after 1945 meant that there was little need to fight and die for King and Country, however ambiguous the latter.

To be sure, the post-war creation of the welfare state helped to cement Scotland into a new conception of the Union as a democratic-centralist state. At this point, the Labour Party, which had evolved in Scotland and in Wales as the vehicle for delivering the working classes of these countries into British state citizenship, temporarily gave up its long-standing commitment to Home Rule, and democratic centralism ruled—for a time. The end of the long boom in the early 1970s, coupled with the transformation of Scotland's economy from one dependent on heavy industry founded on imperial markets to a post-industrial one driven by foreign capital and global markets, ushered in a new economic era.

By the late 1970s, the crisis of Labourism coincided with an abortive and half-hearted attempt by the government to introduce a measure of Home Rule in the form of 'devolution'. This was too late, even too little, and was caught up in the incoming Thatcherite revolution which sought to sweep away state dependency and impose rule by markets. This curious amalgam of 'free market, strong state' (Gamble 1988) had a particular impact on Scotland. On the one hand, the Scottish Office, which had been founded in the 1880s and which had turned itself a hundred years later into a Scottish semi-state, was on the front line of the New Right onslaught. In a country which had turned against the Conservatives from the historic highpoint of 1955 when the party won 50 per cent of the popular vote in Scotland, the attack on the state seemed to many to be an attack on the country itself. By 1992, only 25 per cent of Scots were voting Conservative, and five years later, on 17 per cent of the popular vote, no Tory MPs whatsoever remained in Scotland (or in Wales).

The strategy of neo-liberalism and downsizing the state was matched by a revived Conservative nationalism premissed on the ideological and demographic supremacy of England, focused on its southern part (Taylor 1993). With hindsight, we can say that the success of Thatcherism has been to destroy Scottish and Welsh Toryism, thereby reducing Britain to England in political terms. By the time a Labour government was elected in 1997, the die had been cast. Labour's lukewarm and reluctant support for Scottish devolution in the 1970s was turned, by the Thatcher experience, into proto-nationalist championing of a Scottish parliament. Regionalism had become nationalism.

The setting up of a parliament in Scotland, and assemblies in Wales and Northern Ireland, reflects a shift in the politics of identity in these islands. In many respects, what happens in Scotland is the key. Scotland is renegotiating its place in the Union, and even considering whether the 'marriage of convenience' which it represented should hold at all. The Scots had gained considerable economic and political influence within the imperial framework, but that was long gone. The ideological support systems of unionism, imperialism, and Protestantism no longer functioned as they had done. Scotland's economy had been transformed and reoriented towards Europe and a post-imperial world. The new variable geometry of territorial power involving the European Union, the British state, and Scotland was becoming more significant, reflected in the fact that, like the Welsh, Scots saw in Europe a new Union to augment or even replace the older British one. There were few of the English anxieties concerning the loss of political sovereignty in a country which had had to trade off its independent parliament in return for a considerable measure of economic and political benefit. Scots appreciated that sovereignty was no longer, if it ever had been, a zero-sum game (MacCormick 1995).

The New Right challenge to the state had not only amplified

Scottish demands for greater political autonomy and control over their own affairs (something akin to Catalan *autonomisme* in Spain rather than full-blown independence). It also had unwittingly severed the economic sinews of the British state with the privatization of all those companies and corporations with 'British' in their title: gas, telephones, railways, airlines, and so on.

Scots are now more strongly Scottish in their political self-identification than they have ever been. Further, there is now a powerful dialectic between cultural and political nationalism so that they feed off and amplify each other. The population is now stratified by age as regards their national identity so that only those people over 65 who have personal experience of being adults in wartime give any kind of allegiance to being British. Young people, especially those under 30, are much more likely to forefront their Scottishness, and either to express a desire for Home Rule within a reconstituted United Kingdom, or to opt for independence—in Europe. To be Scottish is to define oneself as progressive and forward-looking. Britishness has become, in turn, merely a matter of speaking rather than a matter of weeping (Ascherson 1988).

Conclusion

Will the British Union hold out until its 300th anniversary in 2007? There is a sense in which it can always do so, for during the last hundred years it has entrenched more and more to its core, as first the white dominions gained their independence, and then Ireland left the Union. Scotland and Wales are redefining their relationships to the British state. Whether or not defining the state as *de facto* greater-England constitutes its survival is a matter for debate and conjecture. Whatever the future, we can surely conclude that the 'British' are no longer the people they once were.

Further Reading

Brown, A., McCrone, D., and Paterson L. (1998), *Politics and Society in Scotland*, 2nd edn., London: Macmillan.

Colley, L. (1992), *Britons: Forging the Nation, 1707–1837* New Haven: Yale University Press.

McCrone, D. (1998), *The Sociology of Nationalism: Tomorrow's Ancestors*, London: Routledge.

Nairn, T. (1977) *The Break-up of Britain*, London: New Left Books.

—— (2000), *After Britain*, London: Granta Books.

Paterson, L. (1994), *The Autonomy of Modern Scotland*, Edinburgh: Edinburgh University Press.

References

Ascherson, N. (1988), *Games with Shadows*, London: Hutchinson Radius.

Barnett, A. (1997), *This Time: Our Constitutional Revolution*, London: Vintage.

Brown, A., McCrone, D., and Paterson, L. (1998), *Politics and Society in Scotland*, 2nd edn., London: Macmillan.

Cohen, R. (1994), *Frontiers of Identity: The British and Others*, London: Longman.

Colley, L. (1992), *Britons: Forging the Nation, 1707–1837*, New Haven: Yale University Press.

Crick, B. (1995), 'The Sense of Identity of the Indigenous British', *New Community* 21/2.

Gamble, A. (1988), *The Free Economy and the Strong State*, London: Macmillan.

Goulbourne, H. (1991), *Ethnicity and Nationalism in Post-imperial Britain*, Cambridge: Polity Press.

MacCormick, N. (1995), 'Sovereignty: Myth and Reality', *Scottish Affairs*, 11.

McCrone, D. (1992), *Understanding Scotland: The Sociology of a Stateless Nation*, London: Routledge.

Marquand, D. (1988), *The Unprincipled Society*, London: Fontana.

—— (1993), 'The Twilight of the British State? Henry Dubb versus Sceptred Awe', *Political Quarterly*, 64/2.

Moreno, L. (1995), 'Multiple Ethnoterritorial Concurrence in Spain', *Nationalism and Ethnic Politics*, 1/1.

—— and Arriba, A. (1996), 'Dual Identity in Autonomous Catalonia', *Scottish Affairs*, 17.

Morton, G. (1999), *Unionist Nationalism: Governing Urban Scotland, 1830–1860*, Linton: Tuckwell Press.

Nairn, T. (1977), *The Break-up of Britain*, London: New Left Books.

Paterson, L. (1994), *The Autonomy of Modern Scotland*, Edinburgh: Edinburgh University Press.

Stevenson, J. (1984), *British Society, 1914–45*, Harmondsworth: Penguin.

Taylor, P. (1993), 'The Meaning of the North: England's "Foreign Country" within?', *Political Geography*, 12/2.

7

Welsh Politics in the New Millennium

JOHN OSMOND

WELSH politics in the new millennium will be propelled by the momentum generated by the referendum in 1997. An understanding of the political landscape that awaits us must, therefore, be informed by this event. Equally the 1997 referendum cannot be understood except in the context of the earlier 1979 vote.

The 1997 referendum took place in strikingly different political circumstances from the one held in 1979. It was promoted by a popular Labour government at the beginning rather than at the end of its mandate, and moreover, a government that was anxious for its policy to succeed. There was an effective Labour Yes campaign, led with energy by the then Secretary of State for Wales, Ron Davies. Although there were Welsh Labour backbenchers opposed to the policy, compared with the Labour Vote No campaign in 1979 they lacked coherence and charisma.

However, the changes that took place in Wales between the 1970s and 1990s were the result of deeper forces than those determining the immediate political climate. Most important was a shift in the generations. The Welsh became palpably and self-confidently, indeed patriotically, more Welsh. They were still British, though this was felt less strongly. At the same time they were also becoming European, an identity that, with the Maastricht Treaty, afforded them constitutional citizenship for the first time.

In 1997 the extent to which the Welsh were able to overcome their fears, discover confidence in their Welshness, and support an elected all-Wales institution demonstrated how far Welsh and European citizenship had advanced compared with 1979. This process was reinforced by the experience of the referendum itself and its aftermath. Certainly, the outcome of the first elections to the, significantly termed, *National* Assembly confirmed that a profound shift had taken place in the way Welsh people understand who they are and their place in the world. Britain remains important to the Welsh and in British elections they are likely to vote differently from the way they will vote in Welsh elections. At the same time Britain has changed and continues to change. It no longer provides the essential lens through which Wales and what it means to be Welsh has to be viewed. In any event, as other parts of Britain develop their own institutions and as these evolve within Europe, the meaning of Britain will inevitably be redefined.

So far as Welsh politics and identity are concerned the key reference point is now an autonomous civic institution, embracing Wales as a whole. Welsh identity is no longer to be nationalized within Britain. Nor is it something to be felt primarily as an intensely localized experience, with the Welsh language bearing an undue weight. The National Assembly has opened up a civic space for a truly Welsh politics to occur for the first time.

The 1979 Referendum

In 1979 the 4:1 defeat of the devolution proposal appeared to be the end of the story so far as Wales was concerned. Why, then, did the issue resurface with such renewed force in the 1990s? To answer the question we need to understand the 1979 result, examine the 1997 campaign, and look at what changed in Wales in the intervening eighteen years.

The political circumstances of the 1979 referendum were unfavourable for those arguing for change. An Assembly was being advocated by an unpopular Labour government at the end of its administration. The 'Winter of Discontent' was well under way, with many public sector unions on strike. In a bitterly cold winter, mountains of snow-covered rubbish bags were uncollected and in some areas the dead were left unburied by striking gravediggers.

All of this accentuated an anti-government—anti, that is to say, any government—mood that was particularly strong at the time. Mrs Thatcher's version of Conservatism was in the ascendant, with its rallying cries of 'Roll back the frontiers of the state' and 'Get the government off your back'. Yet here was a proposal for a new tier of democratic governance that opponents could dismiss as more 'bureaucratic government'.

The Labour Party, the supposed supporter of the change, was badly split, with its most articulate and charismatic leaders in Wales leading the anti-devolution campaign. Neil Kinnock, in particular, was building the foundations of his later career as opposition leader on the high profile he achieved as the main spokesman of the No campaign. The Yes forces were divided across the parties, not least in the way they were putting the arguments for change, and found co-operation difficult. The main advocates of an Assembly in 1979 were over-identified with the nationalists, who were then a minority electoral force. This reinforced the claims of those who said devolution was the first step on a 'slippery slope to separatism'.

Why did Wales, unlike Scotland, which faced a broadly similar political climate, reject the assembly? Although an underlying sense of identity is as powerfully felt in Wales, it is less easily expressed in terms of institutions to which an idea of citizenship can be attached. Until now, being Welsh has been much more diffuse and fractured than is the case with being Scottish. There are still, in fact, many different Welsh*nesses*—for some symbolized by the language and the differences between the regions of Wales—rather than a uniting civic sense of Welsh*ness* as such. In the past the Welsh have found it difficult to imagine Wales within an institutional framework, or even as a single entity. Communications in Wales run east to west, along the southern and northern coasts, rather than north to south in a way that would naturally unify the country. Many people in southern Wales have never, or rarely, been to the north, and vice versa. The people of Wales tend to identify most strongly with their valley, town, or village—more accurately expressed in Welsh as *bro* ('one's native region')—rather than a single Welsh entity.

Compared with Scotland, Wales has an underdeveloped national press. The 'national newspaper', the *Western Mail*, hardly circulates in north Wales, while the Liverpool-based *Daily Post* has a weak penetration below a line drawn eastwards from Aberystwyth. Only 13 per cent of Welsh households take a daily morning newspaper published and printed in Wales; in Scotland the figure is 90 per cent.[1] The broadcast media have a greater claim to national coverage, especially BBC Wales. However, the broadcasters are hampered by the many Welsh households that tune into television transmissions from across the border.

Welsh institutions do, of course, exist—most importantly the

1 An analysis of these figures is provided in Institute of Welsh Affairs (1996).

Welsh Office (now incorporated within the National Assembly) and the all-Wales quangos whose number more than doubled to around eighty in the 1980s and 1990s. However, they are relatively recent. The Welsh Office was only established in 1964. The Wales TUC was set up as late as in 1973, and the Welsh Development Agency in 1975. For all these reasons, and certainly in comparison with Scotland, at the time of the 1979 referendum Welsh identity was relatively weak in terms of institutions, and relatively strong in terms of language and a sense of place. Identity markers such as language and locality tend to divide people while institutions held in common are inherently unifying.

Statements made during the 1979 referendum by key opponents within the Labour No campaign illustrate the point. The leader of the Labour No Assembly campaign, Neil Kinnock, was one of the 'Gang of Six' Welsh Labour MPs who opposed their government's policy. A central passage of their manifesto *Facts to Beat Fantasies* (1979) declared:

The view is put forward that Wales has a special identity and urgent needs which make devolution necessary. The Nationalists and the Devolutionists say 'We are a nation, that makes a difference', 'We have a Welsh Office, that makes a difference', 'We have a Wales TUC, that makes a difference' . . . We *are* a nation, proud of our nationality. BUT there is little or no desire for the costs or responsibilities of nation*hood* as the puny voting support for the Nationalists shows. We do not need an Assembly to prove our nationality or our pride. That is a matter of hearts and minds, not bricks, committees and bureaucrats.

Ten years on, one of the shrewdest and most powerful Assembly opponents of the day, Leo Abse, then MP for Pontypool and another member of the 'Gang of Six', recalled:

One of the important strands of Welsh socialism was its anarcho-syndicalist tradition . . . The essential sense of locality; the small pit or forge where all worked, when work was available; the comparative isolation of valley villages or townships; the central role of the local miners' lodge; the cinemas and breweries owned by the miners; and the local health schemes . . . Our allegiance was to the locality and to the world, and nationalist flag-waving, Russian, Welsh or English, was anathema to those of us shaped in such a society. (1989: 173)

The allegiance that Leo Abse strikingly failed to mention was, of course, to Britain, to being British. The Welsh have in the past at any rate felt comfortable with being simultaneously Welsh and British. Here, however, the English have a problem. Is their identity or nationality British in any way that is different from being

English? The keyword is citizenship—a concept outside British constitutional possibilities. In Britain, sovereignty lies with the Crown in Parliament and the people are reduced to subjects. This is the *unitary* state that the opponents of devolution feel is so threatened. What the Scottish Parliament and the National Assembly may achieve is the creation of a *union* state in which its constituent parts are recognized for what they are, separate nations with strong connections, but separate for all that. Leo Abse's generation was unable to contemplate such a change. Instead, it opted in 1979 for subjecthood within a unitary state, together with a Welsh sensibility that was 'sadly slipping away'.

The 1997 Referendum

What could alter so much in the short interval between 1979 and 1997? A key factor was the shift in generations. By 1997 those whose formative experience was the Second World War, the fight against fascism, and the consciousness and then loss of empire had largely passed on. A majority of those who remained were still opposed to devolution, for instance, the figureheads of the Just Say No campaign. The president was 88-year-old Viscount Tonypandy, a former Speaker in the House of Commons, and the campaign was bankrolled by 94-year-old Sir Julian Hodge, a tax exile in Jersey. Among the rising generation were 600,000 people who, in the 1979 referendum, had been too young to vote. To them, the Second World War was as much history as the Napoleonic wars.

In comparison with the Just Say No campaign, the Wales Says Yes campaign was relatively well organized, certainly in comparison with 1979. The sight of Labour, Plaid Cymru, and the Liberal Democrats acting in unison across much of Wales was undoubtedly influential and promoted consensus around the change. It also emphasized that by 1997 Wales had experienced eighteen years of Conservative government. Successive Conservative administrations intensified and dramatized what became known as the democratic deficit. The immediate influence was to change the mood in the Labour Party. In the aftermath of the 1979 referendum devolution was a closed subject at party meetings. But during the Tory years devolution was resurrected as a means of defending Wales from the worst depredations of Conservative policy. Labour leaders began to acknowledge the nationality of Wales in political terms The Caerphilly MP and future Welsh Secretary Ron Davies was an outstanding example. He switched his position on devolution in the immediate aftermath of the 1987 election, the third Labour had lost since 1979. Explaining his decision, Davies recalled

the anguish expressed by an eloquent graffiti artist who painted on a prominent bridge in my constituency, overnight after the 1987 defeat, the slogan 'We voted Labour, we got Thatcher!' I felt the future was bleak. Despite commanding just 29.5 per cent of the Welsh popular vote and majorities in only eight of the 38 Parliamentary constituencies, the Conservatives had won a third consecutive General Election. The Labour Party had performed well in Wales, achieving a 7.5 per cent swing compared to a 2.6 per cent swing in England, and gaining 15 per cent more of the share of the vote in Wales than in the United Kingdom as a whole. If the party had performed as well in England we would have been elected. For me, this represented a crisis of representation. Wales was being denied a voice. (1999: 4)

The excesses of Conservatism under English Welsh Secretaries such as John Redwood and William Hague focused Welsh solidarity. Thatcherite conservatism corrupted a culture of potential citizenship into the culture of individualistic consumerism. This was manifested in the poll tax, the 'opting out' of schools, the internal NHS market, nursery vouchers, and the Lottery, and offended Welsh traditions of community solidarity. In reaction, Welsh voters overwhelmingly rejected the Conservatives in the 1997 general election. Tactical voting in the safest Conservative seats, in particular Clwyd West in the north and Monmouth in the south, meant they failed to return a single member from Wales.

Paradoxically, eighteen years of successive Conservative administrations helped to prepare the ground for devolution on three fronts. First they elaborated the Welsh bureaucratic machine—the existing Welsh state. The powers and budget of the Welsh Office were substantially increased. By 1997 it had full control over every aspect of Welsh education. This involved the creation of two new quangos—the Higher and Further Education Councils for Wales, with a budget between them of some £500 million a year. At this stage, the Welsh Office budget approached £7 billion a year and fuelled Conservative-created quangos such as the Countryside Council for Wales, the Cardiff Bay Development Corporation, the Welsh Language Board, and Tai Cymru—Housing for Wales.

Secondly, the Conservatives reorganized and diminished local government, replacing a two-tier system—the eight counties and thirty-seven districts—with a single tier of twenty-two authorities. At a stroke this removed the 'over-government' argument that had been put with such force in 1979. It also removed the core from Labour's local government power base, the eight counties, which

John Osmond

had been a focus for much of the opposition to devolution in the 1970s.

Thirdly, Conservative support for the Welsh language assisted the removal of the issue from the 1997 devolution debate. In 1979 the language was undoubtedly a disruptive influence. Fears about the domination of the projected Assembly by Welsh speakers were deployed by the No campaigners. Though many of the No campaigners in 1997 were still antagonistic to the Welsh language, they were unable to make political capital from the issue. Ron Davies noted how the transformation in attitudes to the language had changed the tone of Welsh politics:

When I started out as a young councillor in the Rhymney Valley, the Welsh language was a hot potato which aroused angst and ire all over Wales . . . there wasn't much room for neutrality. But now that mode of thinking has been largely abandoned . . . The language is no longer a political football in the way it once was. (*Western Mail*, 2 July 1998)

The rising generations were behind this change, encouraged by the success of S4C, the Welsh Fourth Channel, and the breakthrough of Welsh-language rock groups to English-language audiences. Welsh became associated with modernity rather than a suppressed past. Under pressure, it was the Conservatives who established S4C in 1982 and later the Welsh Language Board. These measures, together with their continued promotion of the language through the education system, did a great deal to depoliticize a debate that had been an important dimension in the defeat of the Assembly proposals in 1979.

Beyond the political changes, the Welsh economy was modernized during the Conservative administration in ways that were conducive to devolution. The old smokestack coal and steel industries were largely replaced by a renaissance in broader-based manufacturing industry, driven by inward investment. These new firms looked to world, and especially European, markets rather than just British ones. By 1997 there were more than 380 overseas companies with substantial investments in Wales, some 170 from continental Europe, 140 from America, and more than 60 from Japan and the Far East (see Jones 1996).

Wales's interface with the British economy and the impact of British institutions was being transformed. By 1997 there was no *British* coal, no *British* steel; not even *British* Rail—instead, Wales had the Great Western Railway. By the early part of the new millennium the Westminster Parliament, the British armed forces, and the British Broadcasting Corporation may be the only public sector bodies holding Britain together—alongside, perhaps, the monarchy. The monarchy has lost swathes of support in the past decade and in the wake of the 1997 referendums the BBC found itself having to defend the integrity of its London-based British news operation, with demands for differentiated news output.

The European dimension was providing more and more of a context for the debate by 1997. Decisions made in Brussels were now having a direct impact in Wales. This was especially the case with changes to the Common Agricultural Policy and the EU structural funds. Acknowledgement that Wales needed to lobby more effectively to ensure its voice was heard came with the establishment in Brussels in 1992 of the Wales European Centre, supported by the Welsh Development Agency, the Welsh local authorities, the University of Wales, and others.

There was a growing awareness that Wales stood to benefit from regional alliances within Europe. Close ties were forged by the Welsh Office with the so-called 'Four Motor' Regions—Baden-Württemberg, Lombardy, Rhône Alpes, and Catalonia, with developing programmes of economic and cultural collaboration and exchanges. A 'Europe of the Regions' was emerging. Representatives from the German, Italian, Spanish, French, and Belgian regions attended meetings of the new Committee of the Regions in Brussels, established under the Maastricht Treaty. Before the establishment of the Scottish Parliament and the Welsh Assembly Britain was the sole large member of the European Union which had no elected regional representatives to participate. In 1997 the regional vision of Europe was challenging Europe of the nation-states and held that provincial autonomy was an essential ingredient of democracy, a view that increasingly permeated the devolution debate in Wales (see Gray and Osmond 1997).

These factors came together at the 1997 referendum to underpin a vision of Wales that needed addressing in a practical, political way. The driving force was the change under way in the Welsh economy during the 1980s and 1990s. Welsh institutions needed to be strengthened in a democratic fashion to capitalize on this process. The Wales CBI had campaigned against devolution in 1979, but adopted a neutral stance in 1997. Business leaders were increasingly uneasy about the prospect of Wales being left behind by a Scottish parliament and the emergence of development agencies in the English regions. During the referendum campaign Welsh Office Minister Peter Hain spoke constantly of this danger, asking: 'Is anybody seriously saying that Wales alone wants to be ruled from Whitehall while everyone else in Britain has more say over the decisions that affect them?' (Hain 1997). The Assembly proposed in 1997 was to have a powerful economic role. By contrast, in 1979, it was envisaged that the Assembly would only govern social policy areas such as education, health, and housing. Control of the Welsh Development Agency was conceded, but overall responsibility for Welsh economic policy would have been left in the hands of the Secretary of State for Wales.

Labour's 1997 policy, outlined in the White Paper *A Voice for Wales*, was published a few months before the referendum. This made clear that the Assembly should inherit the budget and power of the Welsh Office including industry and economic development. Some years previously, in a speech on the future of the Valleys delivered in the Rhondda in November 1992, Ron Davies anticipated this new approach—one that would harness indigenous development and looked to continental Europe for inspiration.

Creating a strong infrastructure demands extensive government intervention and European experience teaches us that public sector/private sector partnership can lead to success. I do not believe, however, that all this can be done by us taking a begging bowl to Westminster. It is something that we can and must do for ourselves, so we must have appropriate structures for local accountability and power. The present regime is thoroughly undemocratic and in the middle of it stands the Welsh Office. For a modern economy we need a modern democracy and this should be based on an elected Welsh Parliament and strengthened local councils. A more democratic and responsive Wales is not only right for democracy, it is also needed for the sake of industry, jobs and regeneration. (quoted Osmond 1995: 87)

By 1997 such arguments sounded like common sense. Yet in terms of the past devolution debate it was a radical break. Welsh citizenship, related to Welsh institutions, was coming to be understood outside the ranks of Plaid Cymru as meaningful and important if Wales was to prosper in the global economy.

Coupled with the other changes since 1979, particularly the movement in generations, the fundamental shift in attitude to the Welsh economy was the most significant development in the devolution politics of the 1990s. Together these factors explained why a Welsh Assembly was now a more realizable objective.

The 'Three Wales Model': Its Limitations and Future

The extremely narrow result in the referendum held on 18 September 1997 was regarded by many in Westminster and Whitehall as indicative of low enthusiasm for change. In fact, it represented a remarkable 30 per cent increase in votes for the Yes side, or a 15 per cent swing, compared with 1979. The more emphatic 2 : 1 majority in the Scottish referendum, held a week earlier, actually produced a smaller swing of 11.5 per cent.

Interpreters of the result insisted that internal divisions had been laid bare in Wales. Half the counties along the western seaboard and in the Valleys voted Yes, while the remaining eleven voted No. This split was not created by the referendum. Rather it reflected an underlying division that stretches far back into Welsh history, arguably to the early Middle Ages when the marcher lordships were created along the border as part of the Norman strategy for containing a troublesome neighbour. The Yes counties contain a higher proportion of people born in Wales and those who most strongly identify themselves as Welsh. In the west and north are the strongholds of the language. The Valley communities, though generally not Welsh-speaking, are nonetheless strongly and distinctively Welsh in terms of their collective experience of the recent industrial past.

In modern times the division between west and east has been accentuated by the press and media. Those areas that voted No by a majority largely coincided with those parts of Wales that can receive English television transmissions, from ITV's Granada in the north to BBC West rather than BBC Wales in the south. It is estimated that some 40 per cent of the Welsh audience are contained within these 'overlap' areas—in north-east Wales, the south-east, and along the border—where there are opportunities to tune in to English rather than Welsh television channels. In the run-up to the 1997 referendum some 30 to 40 per cent of opinion-poll respondents stated their position as 'don't know'. In many cases they literally had not heard the arguments.

The division in Welsh politics highlighted in 1997 had been evident in the 1979 *Welsh Election Study* (Balsom 1985). Fifty-seven per cent of the electorate believed itself to be Welsh, 34 per cent British, 8 per cent English. These proportions varied according to region, resulting in the 'Three Wales Model' which informed much Welsh political and cultural analysis during the 1980s and 1990s. *Y Fro Gymraeg*—the Welsh-speaking heartland—covers north-west and west-central Wales. Here Plaid Cymru sets the political agenda and, if not winning all the electoral contests, largely determines which party does. The second area, dubbed *Welsh Wales*, is made up of the Valleys, defined by the south Wales coalfield. This is Labour's electoral heartland, which dominated Welsh politics for much of the twentieth century. The third and more indistinct area, *British Wales*, consisted of the south-eastern and north-eastern coastal belts, Pembrokeshire ('Little England beyond Wales'), and the regions of mid-Wales bordering England. In 1997 *Y Fro Gymraeg* and *Welsh Wales* together delivered a small majority, the result of close co-operation between Labour and Plaid Cymru.

Yes counties tended to have the highest turn-out figures— Gwynedd, for example, produced a 63.9 per cent Yes vote from a 60 per cent turn-out. The No counties tended to have the lowest turn-out. A 41.1 per cent turnout in Flintshire produced a 61.6 per cent No vote. These statistics tend to correlate with the number of people born in Wales by region. *Welsh Wales* is distinguished by the large numbers of Welsh-born, who account for 84 to 92 per cent of the population. *British Wales* has lower numbers of Welsh-born— especially in constituencies bordering England—varying between 53 and 81 per cent. The population of *Y Fro Gymraeg* is similar to *British Wales* but a higher-than-average turn-out in four of the five Welsh-speaking counties resulted in clear pro-independence support. Across Wales the turn-out was crucial. The relative determination of *Welsh Wales* and *Y Fro Gymraeg* compared to the relative apathy of *British Wales* proved decisive. If the turn-out had been higher in the No counties, such as Flintshire, the outcome may well have been different.

The analysis aligning Welsh identification by region with the votes cast in the 1997 referendum must be qualified. As historian Paul O'Leary has pointed out, a full 39.3 per cent of the Yes votes were cast in the so-called No counties (O'Leary 1998). Support for devolution varied widely across Wales. Twice as many votes were cast in favour of the Assembly in Powys, for example, as in Merthyr Tydfil, yet Powys is depicted as a homogeneous No county on maps of the results. The No counties of Conwy, Wrexham, Pembrokeshire, and Powys had larger Yes votes than the Yes counties of Merthyr, Blaenau Gwent, Anglesey, and Ceredigion. It was votes and not the geographical areas within which they were counted that mattered.

The biggest shift in favour of devolution between 1979 and 1997 took place in *Welsh Wales* and *Y Fro Gymraeg*, though there was a general swing to the Yes side across Wales. Mid-Glamorgan (*Welsh Wales*) saw a 42.5 per cent swing and Gwynedd (*Y Fro Gymraeg*) 49.9 per cent. It can be argued that the borders of the 'Three Wales' defined in 1979 may have shifted over the years. Cardiff and perhaps Newport no longer fit easily within *British Wales*, though plainly they remain separate from the Valleys. Even Pembrokeshire can no longer be categorized, in electoral terms at any rate, within *British Wales*—70 per cent of the population is Welsh-born and 43 per cent voted in favour of the Assembly. Likewise in the north, parts of Denbighshire (the Clwyd West constituency) appear to have become *Y Fro Gymraeg* territory. Wales is becoming a more politically complicated place—a more varied and complex political culture is emerging that defies the analysis of the 1979 *Welsh Election Study*.

The Shift in Generations

How can we account for the very large movement of votes between the referendums in 1979 and 1997? After all, what was on offer was essentially the same. Although an enhanced economic role was envisaged for the Assembly in 1997, few of the electorate were aware of the fine details. Eighteen years may be a long time in politics, but in the history of a nation it is a short period for such a significant movement in voting behaviour to occur.

It should be emphasized that while *British Wales* remained opposed to devolution in 1997, the shift towards the Yes camp was just as pronounced as in the rest of Wales. Although Monmouthshire, for example, voted two to one against the Assembly in 1997, in 1979 it had voted No by a margin of eight to one. The resulting 10,592 votes were to prove crucial in contributing to the overall Welsh majority of just 6,721 (out of the 1,212,117 votes cast).

The movement of opinion across the whole of Wales may be explained by a highly significant generational shift. Arguably this was the most important factor that turned a 4:1 majority against the Assembly in 1979 into the narrow pro-Assembly majority in 1997. A survey of 700 people throughout Wales, within three weeks of the 1997 referendum, underlined the importance of generational factors in determining the way people had voted. Those aged 44 and under voted Yes by a margin of 3:2, while those over 45 voted No by a similar margin.

These figures must be treated with caution when applied to the actual referendum result. The younger age groups failed to vote in much higher proportions than the older. Nonetheless, the generational split reveals a good deal about the changes that took place in Wales between 1979 and 1997 and says as much about the way Britain is perceived as it does about Wales itself. In 1979 the dominant generation had grown up through the Second World War and the nationalized economy and welfare state created in its wake. For this generation, the Second World War was a defining experience personally and collectively. The nationalized industries were hugely influential in the Welsh economy for some forty years. The welfare state, particularly the health service, became embedded in the affections of the Welsh people. These institutions and experiences were distinctively British. For a generation they formed a framework within which Welsh politics and political identity were understood. In 1979 they still determined what really mattered.

Yet in less than two decades this landscape had changed unalterably. For the rising generations the Second World War was history—experienced directly only by their parents. Memories of empire had faded and the nationalized industries were also disappearing from view. In place of British Coal and much of British Steel were multinational manufacturers who enjoyed the relatively cheap and well-educated Welsh labour force and the handy location within the European Union.

Of course, many of the values associated with the previous generation remained. Healthcare free at the point of delivery was representative of a native community solidarity centred around attachment to locality, people, and a shared landscape and culture. But all these things increasingly emphasized what it meant to be Welsh rather than British—a Welshness, moreover, that felt increasingly comfortable within a European embrace. In short, a cognizance of the realities of the Welsh economy, politics, and identity was unfolding. These shifts were reflected in the generational divide in the referendum of September 1997.

The First Elections to the National Assembly

The first elections to the National Assembly in May 1999 provided a further transition in Welsh politics—'the quiet earthquake'. Plaid Cymru emerged for the first time as a significant force in all regions of Wales, and the main opposition party to Labour in the Assembly. There were extraordinary swings of between 25 and 35 per cent to the nationalists in Labour's Valleys heartland.

Plaid Cymru trebled its percentage support compared with the 1997 general election, overwhelmingly at the expense of the Labour Party. The tantalizing question now is whether this shift will mark a permanent change to the Welsh political landscape. Labour suffered from disunity and a poor record in local government, especially in the two Valleys seats it lost to Plaid Cymru—Rhondda and Islwyn. Labour also suffered from the imposition of a leader, Alun Michael, by the London party machine in the face of a clear preference for

Rhodri Morgan expressed by Welsh party activists. These factors contributed to the low turn-out of just 48 per cent, with Labour suffering disproportionately as a result. In contrast, Plaid Cymru mobilized support on an unprecedented scale.

The party was undoubtedly helped by the relative determination of its supporters to turn out and vote. An NOP poll for HTV Wales on the eve of the election suggested that 72 per cent of Plaid Cymru supporters were likely to vote in comparison to between 50 and 53 per cent for the Labour, Conservative, and Liberal Democratic parties. Equally significant were the voting intentions of those who identified themselves as Welsh. Fifty-one per cent said they intended to vote, in comparison to 31 per cent of English identifiers and 45 per cent of British identifiers.

As was the case in the referendum, the determination to turn out and vote amongst those most strongly supporting the Assembly contrasted with a relatively low turn-out amongst those most strongly opposed. Those voters most strongly identifying themselves as Welsh and, even more, supporters of Plaid Cymru were the ones most likely to vote. Plaid Cymru is now the clear second party in Wales, not only in the Assembly itself but also in a majority of the constituencies. In the regional list vote it topped the poll in Carmarthen West, Clwyd West, and Cynon Valley in addition to those it won in the first-past-the-post constituency section. If this pattern continues Plaid Cymru has a real chance to form the Welsh government after the next election in 2003.

The element of proportionality in the new elections reinforced the sense that they were an opportunity for expressing new preferences. The promise of PR encouraged Yes voters in the referendum by assuaging a commonly expressed fear that the Assembly would replicate the dominance of Welsh Labour MPs at Westminster. Without PR Labour would have won an overwhelming number of seats on the basis of less than 40 per cent of the vote. And, despite the shift in votes, the 'quiet earthquake' would not have occurred.

The evidence suggests that the electorate regarded the National Assembly ballot quite differently from Westminster polls. In the run-up to the May 1999 Assembly election the polls consistently showed Plaid Cymru gaining ground. At the same time Labour maintained and in some polls even increased its support when people were asked how they would vote if a Westminster election were being held. The HTV Wales survey, for example, showed a 1.3 per cent increase in Labour support since the 1997 election.

Differential voting between *national* and *regional* tiers of government is common and persistent elsewhere, notably in Canada where Quebec often elects a nationalist (Parti Québécois) administration at home, but regularly votes Liberal in Canadian-wide elections. There seems every reason to suppose that such a pattern may develop in Wales.

A clear message from the May 1999 Assembly elections is that the parties that manage to identify most closely with specifically Welsh concerns tend to do well in a Welsh election. Alongside this, the outcome of the next election, in May 2003, will also depend on how the parties are perceived to have performed during the first term. Here Labour is in the unenviable position of having administrative responsibility for the Welsh government but possessing no overall control in the Assembly.

The referendum, closely followed by the first elections to the National Assembly, undoubtedly gave a new momentum to Welsh politics quite apart from providing an entirely new setting in which it can take place, the new Assembly chamber. An immediate indication was a growing consensus in favour of the constitutional change that had taken place and for further development beyond it. Despite the wafer-thin majority, within a few months most people appeared to be reconciled to the new direction the country had taken. Evidence was provided by a BBC poll in July 1998 which showed that only a relatively small proportion—22 per cent—supported the 'status quo', that is for Wales to continue to be governed by Westminster without an assembly. This compares with pre-referendum figures of around 40 per cent. Equally, an assembly without legislative and tax-varying powers was only supported by 21 per cent, while 38 per cent wished to go further. A substantial number of people in Wales now feel they have embarked on a road that will lead to an increasingly empowered National Assembly, underlining Ron Davies's observation that 'devolution is a process not an event'.

A Question of Identity

People living in Wales consciously or unconsciously can participate in a variety of identities: they can be Welsh, British, European, or, if they are incomers from across the border, they may retain their English identity. More often than not they combine these attachments in varying degrees of intensity. Opinion surveys suggest that those considering themselves Welsh, as opposed to British or English, increased by around 4 per cent between 1979 and 1997, despite key identity markers—numbers of Welsh speakers and those born in Wales—declining slightly (Evans and Trystan 1999: 100).

Forcing people to choose between being Welsh, British, or English does not capture the subtleties of identity, however. This is particularly so given that the meanings attached to identity descriptions such as Welsh and British change over time. What people understood and felt as being *Welsh* and being *British* changed significantly between 1979 and 1997 due to the generational shift that took place in that period. This was conditioned by differing life experiences between the generations and the relative weight they attached to the identities.

Questions of identity are significant because the way they work through in future years will do much to determine the shape of political alignments. This is recognized by all the parties, who endeavour to stress particular interpretations of identity to suit their cause. Labour Party intellectuals argue, for example, that the new devolved institutions in Cardiff and Edinburgh are about creating a new brand of Britishness in which the nationalities of Britain can share a renewed civic consciousness. In the words of Gordon Brown:

to argue that one is either Scottish or British, Welsh or British is to miss what Britishness is all about. Perhaps uniquely in the world, Britain is not just a society of many communities, but also a country of nations—with large, contiguous areas of distinct national heritage . . . Britain is enriched by the strength of all these different cultures. Sometimes they can be noisy; often they're awkward. But what a bland country this would be if all that noise was to fall silent: if Britishness meant we all spoke the same way, with the same accent, inhabiting a single culture. Instead, how strong we can be, enriched by all the range of cultures that live here. Instead of a bland Britain, a Britain buzzing with difference; no longer a state in monochrome but a nation of living colour. (1999)

An alternative view is that the elements and conditions that forged Britain—war, religion, and empire—have either disappeared or lessened in force. Privatization has dealt a mortal blow to the 'nationalized' industries. With their decline, trade unions that mobilized a British working class are pale versions of what they were twenty years ago. Institutions like the armed forces, monarchy, and even the BBC no longer maintain their former unifying role. Parliament has been devolved. The European Union and global economy offer an alternative political and economic context for the Welsh, Scottish, and English nationalities to make their way in the world.

Further Reading

Taylor, Bridget, and **Thomson, Katarina** (eds.) (1999), *Scotland and Wales: Nations Again?*, Cardiff: University of Wales Press.

Fevre, Ralph, and **Thompson, Andrew** (eds.) (1999), *Nation, Identity and Social Theory: Perspectives from Wales*, Cardiff: University of Wales Press.

Balsom, Denis, and **Jones, J. Barry** (eds.) (2000), *Road to the National Assembly for Wales*, Cardiff: University of Wales Press.

Foulkes, David, Jones, J. Barry, and **Wilford, R.** (eds.) (1983), *The Welsh Veto: The Wales Act 1978 and the Referendum*, Cardiff: University of Wales Press.

References

Abse, Leo (1989), *Margaret, Daughter of Beatrice: A Politician's Psycho-biography of Margaret Thatcher*, London: Jonathan Cape.

Balsom, Denis (1985), 'The Three Wales Model', in John Osmond (ed.), *The National Question Again*, Llandysul: Gomer.

Brown, Gordon (1999), 'New Britannia', *Guardian*, 6 May.

Davies, Ron (1999), 'Devolution: A Process Not an Event', *Gregynog Papers*, 2/2, Institute of Welsh Affairs, Feb.

Evans, Geoffrey, and **Trystan, Dafydd** (1999), 'Why was 1997 Different?', in Bridget Taylor and Katarina Thomson (eds.), *Scotland and Wales: Nations Again?*, Cardiff: University of Wales Press.

Gray, Sir John, and **Osmond, John** (1997), *Wales in Europe: The Opportunity Presented by a Welsh Assembly*, Cardiff: Institute of Welsh Affairs, June.

Hain, Peter (1997), speech to IPPR Business Forum in Cardiff, *Western Mail*, 4 June.

Institute of Welsh Affairs (1996), *The Road to the Referendum*, Cardiff, Oct.

Jones, Gareth (1996), *Wales 2010: Three Years On*, Cardiff: Institute of Welsh Affairs, Dec.

Labour No Assembly Campaign (1979), *Facts to Beat Fantasies* (Political Archive, National Library of Wales, Aberystwyth).

O'Leary, Paul (1998), 'Of Devolution, Maps and Divided Mentalities', *Planet*, 127 (Feb.).

Osmond, John (1995), *Welsh Europeans*, Bridgend: Seren.

8

Which Britain? Which England? Which North?

PETER J. TAYLOR

If a dog bites a man in Bond Street, that's news; if a man bites a dog in Chorlton-cum-Hardy or Stoke-on-Trent, that is merely to be expected.

(old Fleet Street dictum; Hopkins 1957: 12)

All geographical locations in England are equal but some are more equal than others.

(Dodd 1986: 4)

The City, the West End and Westminster are the boundaries of opinion-forming Britain.

(Adonis and Pollard 1997: 100)

To focus upon the geographical dimension within British politico-cultural studies is to engage with a number of problematics. On the political side there are simple spatial images such as the 'North–South divide' but once the nuances of culture are added new layers of complexity are created. The result is that the politico-cultural spaces of Britain are confusing both to the British people in general and to those who study their collective quests for identity. In fact we can begin by problematizing the very idea of there being a 'British people'—certainly there is a segment of humanity who have (or will have when they reach the age of 18) the right to vote in United Kingdom general elections, but this state citizenship cannot be translated automatically into a British nation who celebrate their 'Britishness'. In fact British national practices are most conspicuous in the unionist communities of Northern Ireland, the only part of the UK which is geographically outside of the island of Britain!

If not simply British, who are the natives of Great Britain? The reality is that when it comes to defining 'nations' you can pick any number between 1 and 7 to describe the constituent indigenous people(s) of the UK:

- *one nation*—British (imperial and unionist view);
- *two nations*—English and 'Celts' ('Anglo-Saxon' view);
- *three nations*—English, Scottish, and Irish (Scottish view—see Steed (1986));
- *four nations*—English, Welsh, Scottish, and Irish (sometimes denoted WISE as anti-immigrant, extreme white view);
- *five nations*—English, Welsh, Scottish, Ulster unionists, and Irish nationalists (all 'nations' explicitly represented in Parliament, except, of course, the English);
- *six nations*—English, Cornish, Welsh, Scottish, Ulster unionists, and Irish nationalists (the Cornish nationalists have won some local political representation);
- *seven nations*—'Southern' or 'Real' English, 'Northern' English, Cornish, Welsh, Scottish, Ulster unionists, and Irish nationalists (for such a division of the English, see Osmond (1988))

Of course, these various 'nations' have variable contemporary credibility but in the modern cultural maelstrom none can be ignored.

This complex national stratification interacts with the simpler 'North–South' geographical model—which permeates so much popular and scholarly discourse on divisions of Britishness—to generate further conceptional tangles. The Home Counties are the focus point of this spatial configuration in a pattern of nested spaces at four geographical scales: (1) the Home Counties—London's metropolitan region—is formally part of (2) England, which is formally part of (3) Britain, which is formally part of (4) the United Kingdom (was the British Isles, now Great Britain and Northern Ireland). The clarity of this conceptualization is in the identification of the Home Counties as core area; compared to other states it is a particularly comprehensive core, dominant politically, economically, and culturally. However, given our nested spaces, which space is it that the Home Counties are core of—England, Britain, or the United Kingdom? The answer to this question affects what the North is and can seed confusion. For instance, in his chapter entitled 'The North–South Divide in England' Rob Shields (1991) uses the terms 'British North' and 'North of England' interchangeably—his North–South divide map (p. 209) includes Wales but not Scotland in the area shaded as 'British North'. In strictly locational terms, of course, the north of England is 'middle Britain', the area between the English core and Scottish border (Taylor 1993).

Much of the geographical confusion inherent in Britishness stems from a particularly dominant conception of Englishness which Colls and Dodd (1986) have shown was only constructed between 1880 and 1920. In this chapter I explore the question as to whether this century-old, imperial politico-cultural outcome is ripe for revision under contemporary conditions of globalization—is 1980–2020 to be another watershed for Britishness as profound as the imperial one? If this is indeed the case then this is a period of fundamental politico-cultural choice for the citizens of the UK. Hence the argument of this chapter is organized through three questions ordered by geographical scale: which Britain? which England? which North? In the first section I discuss the 'English presumption' which equates just part of Britain with its whole; the second section deals with the 'rural presumption' which idealizes villages as the essential England; and the third section approaches the monolithic presumption which treats 'the North' as a singular and inferior region. Each section concludes with a *fin de siècle* challenge to these 'traditional' positions: devolution, Cool Britannia, and shopping malls respectively. Since this is an argument about choices, the chapter concludes with my own politico-cultural preference in a discussion of which world. Under conditions of contemporary globalization, I promote a very different geography of identity, not territorialist but city-centred in a global and European space of flows.

Before I embark on this questioning there are two important disclaimers I have to make. First, I will not be dealing with the United Kingdom as a whole, clearly the cultural and political issues surrounding the contested location of Northern Ireland in the UK is a distinctive topic in its own right which deserves many more words than I would be able to allocate to it here. Second, as readers may have guessed by my listing of possible 'indigenous nations' above, the multiculturalism consequent upon 'the empire coming to Britain' is not addressed until a final brief discussion of a *fin de siècle* opportunity offered by cosmopolitan cities.

Which Britain? The Land of the English versus Multinational State

England, it has been said, has too much history (Grainger 1986: 12). This intriguing observation makes the English the obverse of Eric Wolf's (1982) description of non-Europeans as 'people without history'. Putting to one side exactly why the English might be in this particular privileged position, we can add a further complicating fact: there is one prominent European people without history—the British! Obviously there is some compensation going on here; the surfeit of English history is in lieu of the lack of British history. It seems the British created the largest empire in the world but somehow failed to create a British history to accompany it. Instead, English history flourished and assumed the mantle of the necessary historical backcloth for imperialism: it was the 'expansion of England' that led to the British Empire. Only recently—since the political rise of non-English nationalisms in the 1970s—has this geographical anomaly been seriously addressed with the beginning of a new school of explicitly 'British history' (Grant and Stringer 1995; Taylor, 1997a). All this is symptomatic of what J. H. Grainger (1986: ch. 4) calls 'the English presumption'.

As the largest component of Britain, especially in population and wealth, England, in many foreign languages and in English itself, is commonly taken to mean the whole of Britain. For instance, on 14 August 1914, newspapers reported 'ENGLAND DECLARES WAR ON GERMANY' (Grainger 1986: 50). This was during the premiership of Viscount Asquith on whose gravestone it states 'Prime Minister of England, 1908–1916'. Actually there has never been a Prime Minister of England; the office of Prime Minister only evolved after England disappeared as an independent political entity through union with Scotland in 1707. It is testament to the power of the English presumption that this early twentieth-century, Scottish-born Prime Minister of the United Kingdom of Great Britain and Ireland could be posthumously celebrated as the political leader of just part of his realm. Of course, such geographical errors are never neutral. The English presumption—in Bernard Crick's (1997: 15) words, treating 'English as the adjectival form of citizenship of the United Kingdom'—turns the Scots, Welsh, and Irish into invisible peoples, hidden by an everyday political lexicon (Haseler 1996: 31).

Formally the relationship between Britain and England is quite straightforward: the former defines a state, the latter one of its constituent nations. In reality, however, the situation is usually confused. One rare piece of evidence on comparative uses of British and English can be found in the 'Britain in Pictures' series (published in the 1930s and 1940s by Collins). In Table 8.1 books are classified by their titles in terms of whether their subject matter is designated as British or English, e.g. *British Sport* and *English Cricket*. Of the original eighty-nine titles, four have no place designation, two refer to London, two to Scotland with one each for Wales and Ireland, leaving seventy-nine divided between Britain and England in the ratio 48 : 31. But the interesting point is that the balance between English and British varies greatly by subject matter. British is more represented in environmental (as an island) and state topics as might be expected but the intriguing area is in cultural matters where the balance is even. Visual and intellectual cultural persons tend to be British, language and artistic cultural persons tend to be English. But the latter is particularly conspicuous with matters pertaining to home: country houses, gardens, garden flowers, at table, and, of course, women and children are all 'English'. Hence. although the people are 'British' in Table 8.1, many of the key traditional attributes for national self-identity are 'English'.

The basis for these British–English distinctions can be found in the historical cultural politics of Britain. With the formation of Great Britain in 1707, the Scots entered the Union as 'north British' but the idea of the English as 'south British' was never a starter. In the eighteenth century the English resisted the use of the name Britain to replace England in international affairs (Colley 1994: ch. 3) but gradually a *modus operandi* evolved whereby Britain became accepted for most foreign purposes—relations with an external Other—but with few or no domestic implications. This remarkable political achievement was made possible because '[t]he British polity refrained from major internal enterprises [and] did not press definitions of identity' (Grainger 1986: 52–3) resulting in a state 'cultural politics' which patronizes the non-English (Crick 1997: 15). That is to say, the English presumption may be insidious but it has remained just what it says it is, a presumption not a dictate.

The result of this cultural politics is a confusing mixture of national identities. Outside England, dual identities have been constructed, so that, for instance, Scottish identity exists alongside British identity; a person may call themselves 'Scottish and British'. But the equivalent phrase 'English and British' has no meaning since, for the English, to be English is to be British (Osmond 1988). This has been called a fused identity and provides the cultural underpinning of the English presumption. This fusion is hardly a conscious adoption; in a recent interview with Richard Hoggart asking him

Table 8.1. What is 'British'? What is 'English'?

British	English
(a) 'Natural' phenomena	
Horses	Weather
Birds	Landscape
Wild flowers	
Wildlife	
Marine life	
Insect life	
Dogs	
Islands	
Trees	
(b) State and state-wide institutions	
Government	Bible
Statesmen	Church
Rebels and reformers	Social services
Trade unions	Education
Seamen	Public schools
Soldiers	
Merchant adventurers	
Battlefields	
Postage stamps	
Universities	
In the air	
Red Cross	
(c) Cultural institutions and practices	
Dramatists	Poets
Romantic artists	Novelists
Portrait painters	Letter writers
Cartoonists	Music
Photographers	Ballet
Historians	At table
Orientalists	Country houses
Philosophers	Gardens
Scientists	Inns
Medicine	Villages
Botanists	Cities and small towns
Journalists	Sporting pictures
Clubs	Water-colour painters
Polar explorers	Cricket
Mountaineers	Pottery and china
Sport	Books
Maps and map-makers	Essayists
Craftsmen	Popular/traditional art
Furniture-makers	Women

Table 8.1. continued

British	English
Drawings	Children
People	Life
(d) Economic practices	
Sea fishermen	Farming
Railways	Rivers and canals
Engineers	
Ports and harbours	

Note that England/Britain is already 'deindustrialized'!

about his identity he admits to being 'puzzled by the difference for an Englishman between Englishness and Britishness' (Anon 1997). If such an outstanding social thinker about England and the English as Hoggart is perplexed, we can begin to appreciate just how deep in English culture the fused identity lies. Many other examples of such confusion could be quoted. Perhaps the most notorious is that of Raphael Samuel (1989) in his monumental survey of patriotism who tells us in the preface of a late decision to change the 'patria' from England to Britain—it is hard to imagine anyone other than an English person not being sure what to call his or her nation (Taylor 1991: 147). We can conclude that there is an important identity divide in Britain, not just in terms of national identities, but also in the manner in which Britishness is handled.

Fin de siècle challenge: devolution. Contemporary constitutional reforms are undermining the English presumption. Devolution to Scotland, Wales, and Northern Ireland provides political identities to their respective cultural distinctive characters. This process is not particularly new: 'Home Rule all round' was part of the Liberal solution to Irish resistance to British incorporation from 1885. The failure of this policy with the establishment of the Irish Free State in 1922 put the issue of Scottish and Welsh political autonomy on the back-burner until the rise of their respective nationalist parties in the 1970s. Ironically the result of devolution is that the English presumption has politically backfired: in the new multinational state only the English have no parliament or assembly of their own; the Scots, Welsh, and Irish MPs in Westminster can vote on many English matters where English MPs cannot reciprocate because power has moved to Edinburgh, Cardiff, and Belfast.

Which England? The Land of Villages versus Political Modernizers

It has not gone unnoticed that the English do not have a 'homeland' as such, rather they have the Home Counties, a corner of the country masquerading as representative of the whole. This reflects the tendency towards exclusiveness in the practices of Englishness (Haseler 1996). Unlike other nationalisms where ideology and actions promote the inclusiveness we call nation-building, English-ness has never been a typical form of national identity because it has been intrinsically linked to class divisions. In this way exclusivity has been central to the formation of Englishness. The classic example is in the use of language where, unlike other nations who use language to unify, English accents are all important to differentiate hierarchically. At the top is RP (received pronunciation, otherwise known as 'posh English' or BBC English), the English spoken by the Home Counties' upper classes who constitute about 3 per cent of the population but wield an exorbitant amount of power (McCrum et. al. 1992: 3–8). This very real association with power means that in England we have language schools to teach English speaking to English people—elocution lessons are sold on the understanding that social and economic advancement depends on how you sound. But it is almost certainly the case that if you need elocution lessons it is too late; real power derives from attending exclusive public schools with their well-trodden pathways into the ancient universities, the guards, and the City. All of this is very class-selective as are the prime summer haunts where the 'English' need to be seen: Royal Ascot, the Henley Regatta, Wimbledon, the Lord's Test, Cowes Week, Epsom Derby Day, and Glyndebourne. These social events are all highly concentrated geographically in the Home Counties, a throwback to the 'Season' when aristocratic fam-ilies visited their London homes. And at the centre of this social whirl is the monarchy residing officially in Buckingham Palace and relaxing at the family home, Windsor Castle. Tom Nairn (1988) calls this world the Crown Heartland, a social realm which is distinct and separate from most of England and the vast majority of the English but, nevertheless, has taken on Englishness as its mantra.

Behind this social structure there is an England of villages, a presumption that everything good about England is rural. This is the great irony of the Englishness constructed a century ago: a rural make-over for the most urbanized country in the world (Howkins 1986). In H. V. Morton's (1927: p. xi) phrase, the English village is still 'the unit of development' behind Britain's greatness,

Peter J. Taylor

the necessary spiritual underpinning of England. This has created a unique national image which excludes most of the people, the non-rural. Furthermore this rural idyll has a specific regional setting: the thatched cottages and village greens are most definitely not in the north of England. For the latter there is the space myth which Shields (1991: ch. 5) has described: excluded England as the 'Land of the Working Class'. industrial, urban, and northern. This was the geographical outcome of the Industrial Revolution being reinterpreted as an historical aberration, quintessentially un-English (Wiener 1981; Taylor 1996).

There is a real sense in which this excluded England is England's Other (Taylor 1993). The exclusive Englishness of the twentieth century has developed precisely to eliminate the dirty, unpalatable working parts of England from influence and power, using class leadership to define the nature of English nationalism to be the very opposite of the experiences of the majority of the English people. This unique national project has therefore succeeded in defining national Self in opposition to an internal national Other. In so doing it has dismissed most of the English as second-rate people living in second-rate places in their own country (Horn 1970: 37–8). From being the land of the future in the mid-nineteenth century (Taylor 1996), the North was relegated to a working adjunct, necessary in war but otherwise to be looked down upon. There is a wonderful example of this in H. V. Morton's (1942) *I Saw Two Englands*. Written to contrast pre-war England with wartime England, the book unintentionally tells us much more about differences in space than of time: it is the geographical differences which most conspicuously define his 'two Englands'. A total of 187 pages are devoted to describing his 1939 summer trip from Kent (as 'Garden of England') in a circle to Northamptonshire (as an 'agricultural shire') via Sussex, Hampshire, Oxfordshire, Bedfordshire, and Huntingdonshire. The monarchy, aristocracy, and church, feature greatly in stories of great buildings used as historical stages for stories of English heroes and heroines. This is the 'pre-war England' which needs saving from foreign invasion. There are 84 pages on his 1939 autumn trip which goes west, and then up through the Midlands to the North. Because of wartime restrictions locations are less precise, but in the west he visits an aircraft factory, a flying school, a naval base and a tank exercise on Salisbury Plain. In the 'dreary, red-brick, industrial Midlands, a region always hideous and deformed' (p. 238) he visits factories making tanks, shells, and anti-aircraft guns. In the 'North country', which is a 'queer country' and found to be 'strange' (p. 251), he visits a munitions factory, a large shipyard, and a fishing port. This is Morton's 'wartime England' inhabited by 'the average provincial' (p. 232) gearing up to protect 'pre-war England' with its surfeit of history. Going into several editions, this popular wartime book put the 'two Englands' firmly into their respective places.

Fin de siècle challenge: 'Cool Britannia'. In a speech in 1993 John Major evoked rural England ('old maids cycling to holy communion through the morning mist') in a way which recalled his prime ministerial predecessor Stanley Baldwin's famous speech on England in 1924 ('the corncrake on a dewy morning') (Paxman 1998: ch. 9). The 1997 election ushered in a new government of self-ascribed modernizers for which the traditional rural presumption had no attraction at all. Instead we have the idea of 'Cool Britannia', the very opposite of traditional, at the cutting edge of new styles and fashions in a high-tech world. This political conflict is reflected in the elimination of hereditary (largely rural landowning) peers in the House of Lords and the plans to abolish hunting by hounds. The fact that the British beef industry could be almost destroyed by incompetent government with hardly a protest while fox-hunters were able to mobilize hundreds of thousands to march through London illustrates the importance of the 'cultural' as opposed to the 'economic' in the construction of the traditional English countryside.

Which North? Inferior Industrial Region versus Cities of Consumption

Following Edward Said's (1978) logic for European construction of the 'Orient', we can identify a southern English construction of the 'North': this was the process whereby industrial Britain was 'northernized' as an inferior place. This external scripting means that 'no coherent "north country" has been invented in its own right: it exists mainly in contrast to southern England' (Paxman 1998: 157). One implication of this is that *regional* political assertion as traditionally conceived may not be the best way of returning cultural dignity to middle Britain. As a regional label, the North (or North-East or North-West) has no meaning except with respect to the rest of England; it is a compass point not a people. It is hardly surprising, therefore, that when questions of regional autonomy or devolution are discussed there is confusion as to exactly what the North refers to geographically. In the 1991 'English Regional Government' debate in the House of Commons, for example, it was the North which dominated proceedings but there was no agreement on such basic matters as where were its boundaries, where was its 'capital city', and whether there was one 'big' North or several 'little' norths (Hansard 1991; Taylor 1993). As these MPs, largely from northern English constituencies, debated, an outsider might well wonder whether there really was such a place as the North.

Within Englishness the North has been constructed as a simple monolithic concept. The North = industry equation drew a curtain across the country and hid the great contemporary variety of land-scapes which make up middle Britain: the Don Valley and the Lake District provide typical contrasts. Of course when the cultural cur-tain was opened to (southern) English visitors they shielded their eyes from the industry and saw only pre-industrial historical sites (Taylor 1991). In his immensely popular *In Search of England*, H. V. Morton (1927; 24 reprints to 1937, and published as a Penguin paperback as late as 1960) purposively 'skirts Black England' (p. 181) in order to see 'the real north' (p. 207) of ancient cities (Chester, Durham, York) and countryside where 'monster towns and cities of the north of England are a mere speck in the amazing greenness of England' (p. 186). But the North is much more than this 'black versus real' English duality. It is largely made up of great nineteenth-century cities which have spent much of the twentieth century trying to come to terms with the decline of their industrial base. This is the real 'real north' as experienced by the vast majority of people who have lived and continue to live in middle Britain, not that 'real north' embodied in the southern search for something comfortably like themselves in an alien land.

It seems to me that any construction of new geographies of identity to challenge 'inferior, monolithic North' must begin with the 'mere specks', the great modern cities of middle Britain which have been the prime geographical victims of traditional twentieth-century Englishness. In this new geographical imagination an amorphous northern region gives way to a land of city regions centred on Manchester, Liverpool, Newcastle, Leeds–Bradford, Sheffield, Hull, Middlesbrough, Preston, and Carlisle. This is a world of 'multiple norths' which derives from the geohistorical development of the area as specialist production complexes during the Industrial Revolution. Each city and its hinterland developed their own industrial character as they supplied the world market with different mixes of manufactures. Blanket designation as the North has not created a new homogeneity: Liverpool is as different from Manchester today as it has ever been. This variety has con-tinued to be recognized in literature and art which focuses upon 'working-class heroes' but it is all lost in the prime image of the North as England's internal 'Other'.

Of course, Englishness was invented precisely to subvert the image of a land of cities. Behind the rural anti-industrialism there lay an antithesis to cities as centres of power and culture. As Paxman (1998: 162) notes: 'Having invented the modern city, not only did the English monied elite recoil in horror, they pretended it had nothing to do with them.' Hence, Paxman goes on to argue, there has been no development in the twentieth century of an 'English urban tradition' (p. 174). He quotes D. H. Lawrence:

The English character has failed to develop the real *urban* side of a man, the civic side. Sienna is a bit of a place, but it is a real city, with citizens intimately connected with the city. Nottingham is a vast place sprawling towards a million, and it is nothing more than an amorphous agglomeration. There *is* no Nottingham, in the sense that there is Sienna. The Englishman is stupidly undeveloped as citizen. (p. 165)

For industrial-Midland Nottingham read any northern town or city. There was, of course, a civic tradition which developed in the cities of industrial Britain—the great Victorian town halls, city parks, and public hospitals remain as monuments to this era—but that was before the rural make-over of England which has dominated the twentieth century.

Seeing middle Britain as a land of cities immediately subverts the space myth of the North as the Land of the Working Class. Cities define functional not homogeneous regions: city regions are socially coherent entities inclusive of all classes, not uniform lower-class ghettos. Hence simplistic North–South divide rhetoric is undermined by the existence of affluent northern city suburbs such as 'comfortable Didsbury' and 'handsome Hallam' (Shields 1991: 239) for the simple reason that all the major cities have their 'little Surreys'—this is how Tynesiders refer to their poshest housing estate, Darras Hall. But the affluence of these cities has reached far beyond these few richest places in functional city regions.

Fin de siècle challenge: consumer modernity. In a recent survey of British shopping centres ranked in terms of turnover, Oxford Street, London, is listed second behind Tyneside's Metro Centre (Hetherington 1996). This triumph for an out-of-town shopping mall is a reflection of the Americanization of British everyday life but it also tells us about the transformation of northern cities (for consumer Newcastle, see Davis 1991). There are other successful malls—Meadowhall and Trafford Centre near Sheffield and Manchester respectively—as well as vibrant shopping centres in Newcastle

(Eldon Square), Leeds (with its 'exclusive' Harvey Nichols men's store), and a redeveloped Manchester (courtesy of the IRA). As consumer modernity has replaced industrial modernity throughout the western world, the old North–South divide looks more and more like a parochial British obsession with an old myth. The contemporary Blairite political project can be interpreted as representing consumers, both north and south.

Which World? Territorialist versus Network Identities

Devolution, Cool Britannia, and shopping malls each in their different ways have recently undermined the image and nature of the Britain, the England, and the North bequeathed by late Victorian and Edwardian forebears. But to understand fully the processes involved in these transformations we need to look outside the bounds of the UK at what is happening in the wider world. The three challenges identified above at this *fin de siècle* are each constituents of wider social forces which have come to be called globalization. A highly integrated world economy combining global production with global consumption based upon global exchange, distribution, and communication has created opportunities for some, difficulties for many, and disasters for the rest. Generally speaking, as part of the core zone of the world economy, the UK has experienced more than its fair share of opportunities. This is most obviously the case for London and the Home Counties.

With New York and Tokyo, the City of London is one of the three great financial centres of the contemporary world economy. Beyond banking and finance there are an additional range of advanced producer services (e.g. accountancy, commercial law) which constitute global cities (Sassen 1991). Working in a global labour market, practitioners and professionals providing global city services have commanded 'global salaries'—levels of pay previously associated only with the 'stars' of that precocious global industry, Hollywood films. There was a time when millionaires were measured by their total assets; today salaries and bonuses adding up to more than a million pounds a year are commonplace in the City. Adonis and Pollard (1997) term these people the new 'Super Class'.

In other countries, the Super Class may be geographically spread as in Germany and the USA within their numerous global or world cities, but in Britain London completely dominates—Adonis and Pollard estimate that 'upwards of three-quarters of the 8,500 top private sector earners' work in or are associated with the City. This concentration of wealth and economic power means that London is probably more dominant in the UK today than even when it was the imperial capital of the largest empire ever constructed (p. 100). However, as before,

Britain beyond the Home Counties does not feature on its collective horizon; yet within that narrow sphere, the size of the Super Class is sufficiently large for it to have equipped itself with a highly developed infra-structure of private schools, hospitals and leisure facilities. (p. 100)

Same pattern but a different process: the Home Counties were the home-base for the British Empire, now they are a home-pad for servicing global capital.

What does this mean for the rest of England and Britain? I have previously argued that there is a sense in which the UK may not be large enough to accommodate both London and England (Taylor 1997b). There are many circumstances where the City of London's global interests might well be at deviance with those of the rest of the country. Are we leading towards the curious situation where the capital city is the enemy within? This is where the North, and indeed England and Britain in general, viewed as a land of many cities, is so important. As the capital city, London was always an exception to the blanket condemnation of things urban within Englishness. After all it was the central place around which the 'Season' unfolded every summer. Globalization thus far has favoured London and Cool Britannia has been a truly metropolitan phenomenon, but the consumer revolution shows that Britain's provincial cities have not been immune to the recent development of a highly integrated world economy. The question is, how can these lower-tier cities of Britain compete with global London?

Most resistance to globalization has been cultural, invoking national particularity against a supposed universal globalism as represented, for instance, by the role of the English language in global media. National political mobilization is typically territorial in nature, using boundaries to resist transnational processes. It seems to me that this spatial strategy is inappropriate for the Britain beyond the Home Counties core. It is not just that there can be little language resistance in the UK (even in the 'Celtic' nations English is easily the majority language) but territorial organization may in fact be intrinsically counter-productive for such a highly urbanized population. Alongside the tradition spaces of territories, globalization promotes new spaces of flows in what Castells (1996) calls a network society. At one level this is a world city network within which a European city network is nested with London at its apex.

And it is at this continental level that the emergence of competition between alternative spatial configurations is occurring as network versus territorial strategies.

This competition is expressed as a choice between a Europe of Regions and a Europe of Cities. It is best illustrated in north-east Spain where Catalonia and Barcelona are embarked on quite different geographical strategies (Morata 1997). After the Catalonian regional government eliminated its major political rival, the Barcelona metropolitan authority, in 1988, the city of Barcelona devised a city-based strategy called the C6 network linking Barcelona to five other cities (Montpellier, Palma de Mallorca, Toulouse, Valencia, and Zaragoza). In contrast Catalonia has set up a western Mediterranean Euro-region, a contiguous cross-border territory including Languedoc-Roussillon and Midi-Pyrénées. The C6 network and the Euro-region are alternative tendencies in the contemporary reshaping of European space (Morata 1997: 297). In general, with the Maastricht Treaty setting up the Committee of Regions the territorialist strategy has a head start over the Euro-cities approach but, in contradiction to this, contemporary forces of globalization would seem to privilege a space of flows in a world city network. The balance between these two forms of space in the reshaping of Europe, and with it Britain, is yet to be decided.

In Britain, this choice of spaces is epitomized by two campaigns for constitutional change: the *City Region Campaign* and the *Campaign for a Northern Assembly*. The former campaigns for a middle layer of government which is city-centred, the latter for an assembly for the official Northern Region. This is a territory defined by central government consisting of the five most northern counties of England. It is not at all clear how any new sense of identity can be developed in an area whose main communality seems to be remoteness from the state officials who defined it (Elcock 1997: 430). The alternative for this area is three city regions (based upon Carlisle, Newcastle, and Middlesbrough) reflecting the spatial organization of the lives of the people who live in the region. My preference for this city solution is based in part from the fact that urbanized Britain developed in a past space of flows defined by free trade and imperialism and declined precisely when designated in territorialist terms as the monolithic North. But the important questions relate to the present and the future.

London is building a position at the apex of a world city network which will include, within the European sector of the world economy, Paris and Frankfurt and possibly one or two other cities such as Milan and Berlin. This apex will not exist at the top of a simple city hierarchy as some have suggested; rather there will be a complex network of niches and layers with cities finding their unique locations in the new information-led world economy. But will the apex cities rule this arrangement in the sense that their interests prevail? With London, Paris, and Berlin aboard, it would seem we could expect little resistance from the three strongest European states. But what of the other cities? London versus Newcastle or Manchester is no contest but co-operation between cities in different strata could well even things up politically. Manchester, Newcastle, and Leeds, with Birmingham, Glasgow, and Edinburgh, might find they had common interest with the likes of Bordeaux and Marseilles, Cologne and Stuttgart, Seville and Valencia, Venice and Turin, and so on, against London and the rest of the apex. Such leagues of cities might create a very new European balance of power in a world space of flows.

Fin de siècle opportunity: cosmopolitan cities. With cities to the fore, cosmopolitan identities can again begin to rival national identities. The world of global cities is also the world of global diasporas leading to multiple layers of identity with state, national, regional, diasporic, and city identities all available. In the case of the English and their British state, the rural English presumption has acted as a geographical exclusion to non-white citizens, concentrated in cities and with no historical link to the idealized English landscape (Kinsman 1995). A multicultural Britain needs to identify with its cities.

Further Reading

Hasseler, S. (1996), *The English Tribe*, London: Macmillan. This provides a comprehensive survey of the peculiarities of the English and their Englishness and emphasizes the need for fundamental political change.

Osmond, J. (1988), *The Divided Kingdom*, London: Constable. With chapters on all the major 'nations' of the UK including the northern English, this volume represents the political and cultural concerns which emanated from the rediscovery of the North–South divide in the 1980s.

Paxman, J. (1998), *The English: A Portrait of a People*, London: Michael Joseph. A comprehensive review of traditional Englishness and its current crisis of identity. Good on the absurdities and contradictions in this most unusual nationalism, the author nevertheless is optimistic for its future.

Shields, R. (1991), *Places on the Margin*, London: Routledge. This important book attempts to locate place at the centre of social theory and uses the 'space-myth' of the North of England as one example to illustrate his thesis.

Taylor, P. J., et. al. (1993), 'Political Geography Debate No. 5: The Break-up of England'; *Political Geography*, 12. This comprises a lead paper on 'the meaning of the North' followed by six comments and reply to provide a variety of views on the position of the North in the UK.

Peter J. Taylor

References

Adonis, A., and **Pollard, S.** (1997), *A Class Act: The Myth of Britain's Classless Society*, London: Hamish Hamilton.

Anon. (1997), 'Just who do you think you are?', *Observer*, 20 July.

Castells, M. (1996), *The Rise of the Network Society*, Oxford: Blackwell.

Colley, L. (1994), *Britons: Forging the Nation, 1707–1837*, London: Pimlico.

Colls, R., and **Dodd, P.** (1986), *Englishness: Politics and Culture 1880–1920*, London: Croom Helm.

Crick, B. (1997), 'The English and the Others', *The Times Higher Education Supplement*, 2 May.

Davis, J. (1991), 'Letter from Tyneside, in the Semiperiphery of the Semicore: A UK Experience', *Review*, 14.

Dodd, P. (1986), 'Englishness and the National Culture', in Colls and Dodd (1986).

Elcock, H. (1997), 'The North of England and the Europe of Regions, or, When is a Region not a Region?', in M. Keating and J. Loughlin (eds.), *The Political Economy of Regionalism*, London: Frank Cass.

Grainger, J. H. (1986), *Patriotisms: Britain 1900–1939*. London: Routledge.

Grant, A., and **Stringer, K. J.** (1995), *'Uniting the Kingdom'? The Making of British History*, London: Routledge.

Hansard (1991), 'Regional Government (England)', *Parliamentary Debates (House of Commons)*, 6 Dec.

Haseler, S. (1996), *The English Tribe: Identity, Nation and Europe*, London: Macmillan.

Hetherington, P. (1996), 'Tyneside Bucks Trend as it "Lives for Today"', *Guardian*, 26 Oct.

Horn, D. (1970), *God is an Englishman*, Sydney: Angus & Robertson.

Hopkins, H. (1957), *England is Rich: A Portrait at Mid-century*, London: Harrap.

Howkins, A. (1986), 'The Discovery of Rural England', in Colls and Dodd (1986).

Kinsman, P. (1995), 'Landscape, Race and National Identity: The Photography of Ingrid Pollard', *Area*, 27.

McCrum, R., Cran, W., and **MacNeil, R.** (1992), *The Story of English*, London: Penguin.

Mackinder, H. (1902), *Britain and the British Seas*, Oxford: Clarendon Press.

Morata, F. (1997), 'The Euro-region and the C-6 Network: The New Politics of Sub-national Co-operation in the Western Mediterranean Area', in M. Keating and J. Loughlin (eds.), *The Political Economy of Regionalism*, London: Frank Cass.

Morton, H. V. (1927), *In Search of England*, London: Methuen.

—— (1942), *I Saw Two Englands*, London: Methuen.

Nairn, T. (1988), *The Enchanted Glass*, London: Radius.

Osmond, J. (1988), *The Divided Kingdom*, London: Constable.

Paxman, J. (1998),*The English: A Portrait of a People*, London: Michael Joseph.

Said, E. (1978), *Orientalism*, London: Routledge.

Samuel, R. (1989), *Patriotism*, London: Routledge.

Sassen, S. (1991), *Global City*, Princeton: Princeton University Press.

Shields, R. (1991), *Places on the Margin*, London: Routledge.

Smith, D. (1989), *North and South*, London: Penguin.

Steed, M. (1986), 'The Core–Periphery Dimension of British Politics', *Political Geography Quarterly*, 5 (Supplement).

Taylor, P. J. (1991), 'The English and their Englishness', *Scottish Geographical Magazine*, 107.

—— (1993), 'The Meaning of the North: England's "Foreign Country" within?', *Political Geography*, 12.

—— (1996), *The Way the Modern World Works*, Chichester: Wiley.

—— (1997a), 'Geographical Correctness', *Progress in Human Geography*, 21.

—— (1997b), 'Is the UK Big Enough for Both London and England?', *Environment and Planning A*, 29.

—— (1999), *Modernities: A Geohistorical Interpretation*, Cambridge: Polity.

Wiener, M. J. (1981), *English Culture and the Decline of the Industrial Spirit, 1850–1980*, Cambridge: Cambridge University Press.

Wolf, E. (1982), *Europe and the People without History*, Berkeley and Los Angeles: University of California Press.

9

Rurality and English Identity

ALUN HOWKINS

ON Thursday, 10 July 1997, a rally of upwards of 100,000 people took place in Hyde Park in London. The purpose of the rally, according to the advertisements placed by the organizers in all the 'quality' newspapers, was 'to fight for the future of the country-side' (*Guardian*, 9 July 1997: 7). However, as the press reports leading up to and following on from the rally and demonstration show, the main focus of this 'defence' was the fear that the new Labour government might ban some field sports, especially fox-hunting. For whatever reason, and by whatever means, support for the rally was organized in rural areas, it was the urban response, and especially the response of the normally unsympathetic left and liberal press, which was so striking. To a person these papers declared, along with John Vidal in the *Guardian*, that the time had come to 'reassess' the issue of fox-hunting, not because it had suddenly become less barbaric, but because it had become a symbol for the rural part of Britain which felt a 'genuine sense of resentment and betrayal' by government and 'the left/green consensus' which was represented in part by the Labour victory in the election of 1 May 1997 (*Guardian*, 9 July 1997: 17).

While the sudden concern for the social conditions in rural areas was entirely laudable, and certainly in Vidal's case genuine, a historical account of the relationship between the 'rural' and the 'national' in this century points to a more complex origin to the great sighs of liberal conscience which greeted the arrival in

London of the Countryside Alliance demonstrators. At its core is a tension, constantly reworked and evolving, between a recognition of the urban nature of England and English society on the one hand, and a wish to preserve what is essentially a cultural fiction that England retains its 'rural' character and that rural essence is at the heart of some 'real' England, on the other.

This tension and its variations are a key part of the cultural history of England in this century. England was, as generations of schoolchildren once learned, the 'first industrial nation'. It was also, by most definitions, the first truly urban nation. In 1851 a narrow majority of the population lived in towns. Continued rural de-population meant that by 1901, 77 per cent of the population lived in urban districts. During the same period the contribution of agri-culture, the main rural industry, to the Gross National Income fell from around 20 per cent to about 6 per cent. Similarly, the numbers employed in the industry fell from just over 2 million men and women to 1.4 million, a decline of about 30 per cent at a time when the population of England and Wales grew by 45 per cent (Mitchell and Deane 1962: 60–6, 363).

What is interesting is that as the twentieth-century progresses these trends start to diverge. The contribution of agriculture to the national product continued to fall to only just above 2 per cent in 1980. The numbers employed in the industry fell likewise; by 1980–1 there were only 57,600 men and women working in agriculture. (Holderness 1985: 170–2). However, from 1911 onwards the decline in the population of the rural districts ceased. This has meant that the proportion of the population living in rural areas was at first stable and then increasing. Between 1971 and 1991 the population of the rural areas increased by nearly 2 million or 17 per cent. (Department of the Environment and MAFF 1995: 13). This means that in the near future, and if present trends continue, we shall have the same distribution of population between the urban and rural in 2001 as we had in 1901, which will make Britain unusual, and possibly unique, in northern Europe.

What this shows is a continuing and growing desire on the part of British, but especially English, men and women to live in the countryside. At its simplest one could argue that this represents a recognition of a reality—country life is better in quality than urban. As Nicci Gerrard the novelist wrote early in 1999.

My version of [London] has undergone a dramatic transformation since having children. I don't think about the quality of night life, but the quality of air . . . I don't want to live near pubs, but near parks. I worry about

Alun Howkins

schools, lorries, syringes in the sandpit, asthma. Health and safety overrule fine food and adult fun. (*Guardian*, 31 Jan. 1999, *Review*: 1)

Yet this is by no means clear to much of the population of Europe, where the urban population continues to grow at the expense of the rural. What this then suggests is that 'country life' or a kind of ruralism has a particular place within recent English history and culture. It is clear that, for example, agriculture has retained a key place in England's cultural self-image, although its economic contribution to Britain's economy is now minute. We can see this beginning at the moment of the industries' nineteenth-century decline. The evidence presented by farmers and many landowners to the two great Royal Commissions on the depression in agriculture in the 1880s and 1890s show the tendency to special pleading in the defence of agriculture as a national 'necessity', both in economic and cultural terms, which was to become more and more clear especially in the years after 1930, and which reached its current apogee in the Countryside Alliance demonstrations of 1997 and 1998. The fact that the 'agriculture' which was being defended was increasingly industrial and commercial in character made (or makes) little difference to those who argued for its essential continuity. A Norfolk farmer of 2,000 acres, by definition an industrial unit, said in the mid-1970s. 'My family have farmed this area for over 300 years. . . . Basically I am a churchman, and I have a feeling of stewardship. One is conscious of the need to discharge adequately one's duty. One has been given a great deal to be responsible for. So I must do things well' (Newby et al. 1978: 333).

In this kind of account the practice of agriculture becomes an essential part of the cultural construction of England The first line of the 1995 government White Paper *Rural England: A Nation Committed to a Living Countryside* reads, 'The enduring character of England is most clearly to be found in the countryside.' Three paragraphs later it continues.

Much of what we most value in the natural scene is the product of farming—hillsides whose beauty is dependent upon grazing, water meadows which need to be used for cattle if they are to be preserved, dry stone wall, hedges and traditional buildings. (Department of the Environment and MAFF 1995: 6)

Here the 'natural' world becomes not the wild and untamed nature of moorland or fen but the farmed landscape of order, thus the 'enduring character of England' rests with her farmers.

Yet it goes deeper than that. The notion that the 'enduring' nature of England is to be found in 'her countryside' clearly transcends the interests of any one group, even farmers. It is, as Patrick Wright has brilliantly written, an appeal to a 'Deep (sic) England'. By this necessarily vague term Wright means, I think, the evocation or even the invention of the idea that within rural England especially there is something, in the view of this invented myth, 'incommunicable' or 'indivisible' in the national heritage. This, it is argued, forms the basis of an appeal which transcends the ideas of essentially elite origins to create a 'stirring and practically-based image of threatened belonging' which extends even to the urban working class (Wright 1995: 87). Deep England with its associated images and metaphors appears to have provided, for the late twentieth century at least, a core of ideas around which appeals to the 'natural' heart of England can be based.

However, changes in notions of the importance of rural life present a historically more complex view, but one within which notions of 'Deep England' have a place. The decline in the importance of agriculture in the national economy was precisely paralleled by a growth in the importance of manufacturing industry and, crucially, by urbanization. Criticism of these changes is, of course, as old as these changes themselves. High Tory and 'radical' criticisms of the 'dehumanizing' effects of factory work and town life abound especially in the period before 1840. However, after that period such criticism tends to decline. The nation, as Peter Mandler notes, 'had come to terms with its urbanity' (Mandler 1997: 160). Yet historical change is seldom linear. While large sections of the elite, and indeed the newly formed working class, celebrated urban life, others, albeit it a minority at first, saw in it new dangers. As Stedman Jones has argued from the 1870s, and particularly after the publication of Andrew Mearn's *The Bitter Cry of Outcast London* in 1884, the problem of the 'city', and especially London, became one of overwhelming concern to a wide range of social observers (Stedman Jones 1971: 16).

The link between the problems of the city and the rural areas was made by Social Darwinist theories of inevitable urban racial degeneration. Put simply these argued that 'natural selection' worked, within a proletarian urban environment, to emphasize what was 'worse' in human development. The products of the city became puny in stature, unable to do hard manual work, and 'devious or cunning' in their attitudes to life. Initially at least these concerns were restricted to a small section of the intellectual elite; however, as Stedman Jones has shown, their importance soon spread well beyond this group.

If the theory of hereditary urban degeneration had been confined to one or two eccentric doctors, there would have been little point in examining it . . . But this was not the case. In the 1880s and 1890s the theory received widespread middle-class support and was given authoritative backing by Booth, Marshall, Longstaff and Llewellyn Smith. (Stedman Jones 1971: 128)

The solutions proposed by these commentators varied enormously and many were constructed within an urban framework; however, a significant group turned to the rural areas for the solution to the problem. At their simplest the arguments centred upon notions of the rural as the 'natural breeding grounds of men'. The city, in contrast, was unnatural, 'and never intended to be the permanent home of men' (Haggard 1899: 466). In this view rural depopulation, a problem which had concerned many agricultural writers from at least the late 1860s, was not merely a problem of the countryside but of the nation as a whole. If city life led to inevitable racial decay, and the countryside was depopulated, the supply of 'good' racial stock would become exhausted, and the 'decay of this country only becomes a matter of time' (Haggard 1899: 466).

The 'rural' response to notions of urban degeneration took many forms ranging from the 'ruralization' of urban life and values via morris dancing for East End working girls, as advocated by Mary Neale in the 1910s, through to wholesale land resettlement via land nationalization and redistribution (Howkins 1986). What they shared in common was a notion of the superiority of rural life over urban. What is more difficult to pinpoint is quite how widespread support for such notions was and how we might relate this to national culture in the form of an essentially rural 'Englishness'.

This question has produced a good deal of debate. On the one side are those, for example the contributors to the collection edited by Robert Colls and Phillip Dodd in 1986 (Colls and Dodd 1986) and Wiener (Wiener 1981), who see ruralism and Englishness as central parts of the cultural construction of twentieth-century Britain. Against them others, most notably W. D. Rubinstein (Rubenstein 1993) and Peter Mandler (Mandler 1997), argue that 'ruralism' and 'Englishness' represent merely a brief moment at the end of nineteenth-century Romanticism, and that 'the shift *towards* a swooning nostalgia for the rural past takes place only among a small, articulate but not necessarily influential *avant-garde* (or rather *derrière-garde*)' (Mandler 1997: 160). In this argument the widespread interest in things rural and in attempts to revive country life as a model for the urban are relatively unimportant compared with other aspects of turn-of-the-century culture which they see as dominantly urban and modernist.

While this view is a valuable corrective to the tendency to see Englishness and ruralism in every early twentieth-century cultural form (Howkins 1995), it simply goes too far. Certainly the most extreme forms of ruralism involving, say, the invention of English national costume or the revival of peasant arts were restricted to a very small number. However to dismiss, for example, the folk-song revival of the 1900s as the province of 'bien-pensant Bohemians and would be squires' (Mandler 1997: 169) ignores the fact that by 1914 the Board of Education—that is, the body responsible for the curriculum development of *every* English state and local authority school—recommended English folk song as the basis of musical teaching. As late as the 1950s the widely used school songbook issued by Penguin, and designed to be used in the new secondary schools of the Butler Education Act, contained a very large body of English folk-song material. How much effect this had is difficult to tell but the exposure of folk song to literally millions cannot be ignored. Further it was at least the early 1940s before the mainstream, as opposed to the avant-garde, of English classical composition freed itself from 'folk song' as the basis of national music (Howkins 1989: 89–99). Further, to dismiss back-to-the-land schemes as cranky or unimportant (or both) after 1900 is seriously to underestimate political interest in the land, and indeed popular demand for land in the form of smallholdings and allotments, as the demand for land by ex-servicemen showed in the years immediately after the Great War. The examples could be multiplied. Although it may be possible to argue that some of the architects of the 1880s and 1890s who espoused the English vernacular style had abandoned it by the 1900s (Mandler 1997: 165–6), this is to ignore that it was precisely at this point that the rural and Tudor models of the ideal English house moved into middle-class taste. Letchworth's middle-class earthly paradise, for example, is dominated by the English vernacular (Jackson 1985: 41). While some sentimental and nostalgic writing about rural England was certainly the taste of none but a few, *Georgian Poetry*, the powerfully, although not exclusively, ruralist and English anthology of new poetry which first appeared in 1911, was widely regarded as the most popular poetry book of its period.

If we can identify the origins of modern ruralist ideology in the years before the Great War and within particular cultural forms, what have they in common? First, despite my belief that even at this point they were much more widespread than others might argue,

Alun Howkins

they remain essentially the possession of a section of the elite. However, the role of that elite in shaping the cultural concerns of the immediate pre-Great War world were fundamental. More importantly, aspects of their ideas were spreading. The early social-ist movement had a profoundly anti-urban streak, and as a result these ideas gained currency among sections of the working-class movement, where they married neatly with an older tradition of radical agrarianism. Further, the quasi-socialist Clarion movement with its cycling and rambling clubs, and the Independent Labour Party's parallel Leader Scouts, pre-date the inter-war hiking craze by twenty years and in many cases formed the basis of working-class rambling and cycling clubs in those years.

Secondly, there was a commonalty of cultural vision associated with these movements which was essentially 'southern'. This linked in with agriculture's insistence on a 'productive' landscape to pro-duce an ideal of rural southern England. This in turn produced a model of an ideal landscape type. It is rolling or dotted with wood-lands, and divided into fields by hedgerows. Its hills are smooth and bare, but not wild or rocky. Its streams and rivers flow rather than rush or tumble. Even more importantly its ideal social structure is the village with its green, pub, and church clustered together, its ideal architecture stone or half-timbered topped with thatch. What is central here is that, even before the First World War, this ideal landscape had ceased to be an exact geographical location and had become instead a set of features by which rural beauty was defined. Hence parts of Shropshire, Suffolk, or even the East Midlands could be included but other parts not. The bringing together, before the Great War, of an elite view of urban and rural decline, a ruralist impulse, and an aesthetic of the southern created an ideal of the countryside which, all too often and all too easily, became 'real' England.

The Great War, with its use of the imagery of the rural in propa-ganda, as well as within the literary and artistic representations of conflict, strengthened the popularity of this ideal view, as did post-war sources as diverse as the search for a plot of land, the Imperial War Graves Commission's debates on the 'English' nature of the war cemeteries, and the dominant image of the war memorial cross on the village green (Winter 1995). A powerful symbolic coming together of many of these elements was the unveiling of the national war memorial to the cyclists killed in the Great War in May 1921 on Meridan Green, the reputed (and then still rural) centre of England. Over 10,000 cyclists from all over the country attended (Lightwood 1928). However, the 'rural' in English culture faced problems in the inter-war years. Those who perhaps ought to have been its natural defenders—the landed elite—seemed in many cases to be more interested in exploiting their lands in whatever way possible. Successive governments in the 1920s showed little interest in the country areas or in agriculture—although that was to change in the 1930s. That decade saw both the first legislation to protect Britain's arable farming and hence its southern landscape, combined with the first town planning legislation which, although weak, enabled some areas, especially in the south and east, to be protected.

Again one looks to the less tangible. In the inter-war period, and from choice, more and more English men and women moved into what were described by the Census as 'rural districts'. Many of these were of course 'suburbs'—by definition hybrids—but railway company slogans like 'Live in Surrey—Free from Worry' or 'Live in Kent and be Content', both over suitably rural images, suggest that although the suburbs lacked squire or perhaps even parson their attraction was at least in part rural. This was reinforced by their architecture—the 'Tudorbethan'. Half-timbering outside was all but universal while grander houses, like those built around the exclusive, and semi-rural, Droveway development in Hove in the 1930s had oak-panelled halls and working inglenook fireplaces. Even those at 'the top' rejected modernism to the extent that the few modernist country houses in Britain were, when built, and were to remain, objects of curiosity rather than admiration (Aslet 1982: 76–83).

The inter-war period saw further changes in the rural areas as sites of recreation—the countryside became a desirable place to play as well as to live. The growth of rambling and cycling clubs, in many working-class areas of London and the south as well as in the more 'classic' proletarian communities of the north, brought tens of thousands of working men and women into the countryside each weekend. The growth of motorcycle and car ownership among the middle class especially in the south created an industry of guidebooks and magazines. The monthly *Morris Owner* took the proud possessor of a new Morris Minor on tours through (especially) southern England, while a guidebook like John Prioleau's *Car and Country* called itself 'a book written for lovers of the open road, and of England, written by one' (Prioleau 1929: p. v). In an age of literary modernism the distinctly un-modernist writings of Kipling (Sussex), Hardy ('Wessex'), Brett Young (Worcestershire), Mary Webb (Worcestershire/Shropshire), Houseman (Shropshire), and Sheila Kaye Smith (Sussex) not only continued to be published but were enormously successful in breeding a tourist industry of their own within their own invented countrysides of the south lands. Clever people in London might read and laugh at Stella Gibbons's inspired parody of country life novels *Cold Comfort Farm* but it sold far fewer copies than the books it satirized.

As in the First World War the Second World War was marked by a mobilization of the identification between Englishness and rural-ism in both elite and popular culture. The examples are legion—from the huge importance of Englishness to the neo-romantic movement in both painting and literature (Mellor 1987), through Frank Newbould's famous series of ABCA posters of rural Britain with the deliberately double meaning slogan, 'It's your country—fight for it now', to the lyrics of two of the war's most popular songs, 'There'll Always Be an England' with its evocation of 'a cottage small | Beside a field of grain' and 'Blue Birds over the White Cliffs of Dover' with its Downland shepherd 'tending his sheep'.

In the post-Second World War period the inter-war tensions re-emerged with the apparent triumph of the urban. Raphael Samuel gives some support to this view in his extraordinary *Theatres of Memory*, where he points out that much popular as well as elite culture in the immediate post-Second World War period was marked by a high degree of 'modernism' and 'urbanism'. It was only really in the late 1960s that what he calls 'neo-vernacular' appeared (or reappeared) as a major cultural force (Samuel 1994: 59–67). However, again there are problems. Modernism and urban-ism did not lead to any desire to stop leaving cities. The 'new' rural housing of the 1950s and 1960s also remains as studiedly 'traditional' as in the 1930s. Even the new towns, taking their cue from the writing of Patrick Abercrombie (who was himself a product of the Englishness of the 1920s), although they contained some blocks of flats, were in general created around the notion of a collection of 'villages' as in Harlow. Culturally the 1950s and 1960s, although fiercely urban in many respects, retain, as in the 1930s, a popular ruralism which found its expression in the enor-mous popularity of the Archers (Laing 1992) and the novels of Miss Reed.

Seen in this historical perspective the centrality of ideas of the rural to the English national culture and identity are much clearer. However, it was not always the same rural. In the inter-war period, as again in the 1950s, different and competing versions of the rural appear, based on class lines or on other criteria. From the 1920s onwards, to some, usually middle-class, defenders of the country 'ideal', the new popular interest in the rural areas was the cuckoo in their nest. Organizations like the impeccably correct (in some ways) Surrey Anti-Litter League fulminated against trippers by car, bike, or on foot who despoiled the countryside not only with their litter, but also with their loud songs and coarse manners. To many in this group the desire of the working-class family to build a wooden hut on a tiny piece of rural England, or the wish of the bank clerk to recreate Tudor life in the 'Tudor Bars' of Slough, was as great a threat to 'their' rural England as electric pylons or arterial roads. In a different way the emergence of a split between 'locals' and 'incomers' so widely studied by rural sociologists since the war, and a key part of the Countryside Alliance appeal in 1997, has produced competing views of the rural.

A greater, but still largely unexplored, challenge might be found in Britain's multicultural identity. The Welsh, the Irish, and the Scots have always been excluded from this English vision, even where elements of their landscapes were appropriated as part of Englishness. This is even more the case, potentially at least, for Britain's Afro-Caribbean or Asian communities. Little has been written about this, but Eve Pollard's remarkable photo essay 'Pastoral Interlude' of 1992 charts the reaction of a Guyanese woman photographer to the 'universal values' of ruralism. For Pollard, who followed in the steps of Wordsworth in the Lakes, the countryside was not a reassuring landscape redolent of deep memory but a threatening and alien land. Her photographs counterpose conventional tourist images of a 'me' figure against a landscape with quotations which ironize and unsettle the viewer/reader (see Taylor 1994). Under a photo of her gazing over a low stone wall into a Lakes landscape she writes:

it's as if the Black experience is only lived within an urban environment. I thought I liked the LAKE DISTRICT, where I wandered lonely as a BLACK face in a sea of white. A visit to the countryside is always accompanied by a feeling of unease, dread. (Pollard 1992)

Yet despite these challenges the continuities of image and ideal are striking throughout this century, and are clearly widely shared. For example the 'special place' afforded to British farming from the Great Depression of the 1880s to the BSE crisis over a hundred years later ensures that anyone who attacks farming, suggests it might by run in a different way, or merely that the huge subsidies might be better spent is instantly dismissed as a crank, a townee, or worst of all some one who does not 'understand' what it is to be English. Conversely to evoke images of what is essentially southern

Alun Howkins

rural England with its village greens, half-timbered pubs, and even red-coated huntsmen is, if the widespread use of these images by advertising directed at the English market is any guide, to add purity, decency, and 'Englishness' to the product or the idea evoked.

Further Reading

This is a subject which is growing and has grown as we move towards devolution and an increasing sense of a nation rediscovering what it might mean to be English. Useful starting points are still, I think, Wiener (1981), Howkins (1986), and Mandler (1997). More recent work can be found in Matless (1998), and several articles by the same author. Taylor (1994) has an interesting way into modern visual representations of landscape, while Mellor (1987) is an accessible way into mid twentieth-century British art and literature—a key period for 'Englishness' and English culture.

References

Aslet, Clive (1982), *The Last Country Houses*, London: Yale University Press.

Colls, Robert, and **Dodd, Phillip** (1986), *Englishness: Politics and Culture, 1880–1920*, London: Croom Helm.

Department of the Environment and Ministry of Agriculture, Fisheries and Food (1995), *Rural England: A Nation Committed to a Living Countryside*, London: HMSO.

Haggard, Sir Henry Rider (1899), *A Farmers Year*, London: Longman Green.

Holderness, B. A. (1985), *British Agriculture since 1945*, Manchester: Manchester University Press.

Howkins, Alun (1986), 'The Discovery of Rural England', in Colls and Dodd (1986).

—— (1989), 'Greensleeves and the Idea of National Music', in Raphael Samuel (ed.), *Patriotism: The Making and Unmaking of British Nation Identity*, iii: *National Fictions*, London: Routledge.

—— (1995), ' "Blue Remembered Hills": Looking Again at Englishness, Ruralism and Nostalgia 1880–1914', paper given at Leeds Centre for Victorian Studies, 17–19 July 1995.

Jackson, Frank (1985), *Sir Raymond Unwin: Architect, Planner, Visionary*, London: Architectural Press.

Laing, Stuart (1992), 'Images of the Rural in Popular Culture 1750–1990', in Brian Short (ed.), *The English Rural Community: Image and Analysis*, Cambridge: Cambridge University Press.

Lightwood, James T. (1928), *The Cyclists' Touring Club*, London: CTC.

Mandler, Peter (1997), 'Against "Englishness": English Culture and the Limits to Rural Nostalgia 1850–1940', *Transactions of the Royal Historical Society*, 6th ser. 7.

Matless, David (1998), *Landscape and Englishness*, London: Reaktion.

Mellor, David (ed.) (1987), *A Paradise Lost: The Neo-Romantic Imagination in Britain 1935–55*, London: Lund Humphries.

Mitchell, B. J., and **Deane, Phyllis** (1962), *Abstract of British Historical Statistics*, Cambridge: Cambridge University Press.

Newby, Howard, Bell, Colin, Rose, David, and **Saunders, Peter** (1978), *Property, Paternalism and Power*, London: Hutchinson.

Pollard, Eve (1992), 'Pastoral Interlude', *TEN.8*, 2/3.

Prioleau, John (1929), *Car and Country*, London: Dent.

Rubenstein, W. D. (1993), *Capitalism, Culture and Industrial Decline in Britain, 1750–1990*, London: Routledge.

Samuel, Raphael (1994), *Theatres of Memory*, London: Verso.

Stedman Jones, Gareth (1971), *Outcast London*, Oxford: Oxford University Press.

Taylor, John (1994), *A Dream of England: Landscape, Photography and the Tourist's Imagination*, Manchester: Manchester University Press.

Wiener, Martin J. (1981), *English Culture and the Decline of the Industrial Spirit, 1850–1980*, Cambridge: Cambridge University Press.

Winter, Jay (1995), *Sites of Memory: Sites of Mourning*, Cambridge: Cambridge University Press.

Wright, Patrick (1985), *On Living in an Old Country: The National Past in Contemporary Britain*, London: Verso.

Britain, America, and Europe

BILL SCHWARZ

In most conventional maps of the world Britain is still placed in a prominent position: not plumb in the centre—that would smack too much of unwarranted grandeur—but prominent nonetheless. Perspective and consequent distortion tend also to make Britain look unduly large; if not exactly equal in size to Australia, for example, then at least not dwarfed by it either. And for long it has been a unified *Atlantic* ocean which appears to structure the world, while most world maps split the Pacific in two, concealing the degree to which North America is both a Pacific power and only a stepping-stone (across the Bering Strait) from the land-mass of Asia. Needless to say, such cartographies are not innocent.

There was a time, in the late Middle Ages, when England, Scotland, and Wales (identifiable territories by the eleventh century) were conspicuously marginal to the power centres of Europe, which were then concentrated around the Mediterranean. Britain truly was an offfshore backwater of Europe. The rise of the maritime economies—initially associated with Portugal, Spain, and the Netherlands—marked a critical transformation, drawing the Americas, Africa, and Asia into a globally organized European system. The centre of economic gravity shifted away from the Mediterranean to the Atlantic. Britain's rise to power, in turn, was inseparable from its position as an Atlantic nation. From the sixteenth century the island story (Elizabeth, the Armada, Drake, and so on) became one of the founding frontier myths of the English nation—as powerful for the English as the western has been for the non-indigenous citizens of the USA—articulating in symbolic terms the palpable reality of Britain's maritime prestige, notwithstanding the fact, of course, that to imagine England as an island requires some tampering with geographical imperatives. So long as the Atlantic economies held their position, Britain's global, and hence cartographic, prominence was secured.

Centres, clearly, are as much imaginative and political as they are geographical constructs. This holds for the internal geographies of the nation-state as it does for global structures. The symbolic centre of Britain, in turn, is far removed from its geographical centre, however that might be determined. Traditionally, the convergent centre for the nation's signposts—the point from which all distances to and from London are calculated—is a tiny spot in what (since 1820) has been Trafalgar Square. As if to emphasize the degree to which Cromwell's republican interregnum in the 1640s was an aberration, this symbolic centre was (and is) marked by a statue of Charles I, the one sovereign whom the British people, through the will of Parliament, have deemed fit for public execution. The contentions which arose from this national landmark are now forgotten—the statue itself barely visible due to the volume of traffic which surrounds it. Parliament, suitably attuned to the cash nexus, sold the statue to be melted down: instead, it was (in a wonderful gesture, anticipating an entire genre of magical realism) furtively buried, and resurrected after the restoration of Charles II. It now stands facing the place in Whitehall where Charles I met his death. These morbid associations notwithstanding, one old guide-book declares that 'if you look at it with an honest eye, you must admit the king looks singularly well-dined, almost debonair' (Piper 1964: 94). That this symbolic centre should be located in Trafalgar Square is fitting.

For in the square, in 1842, an enormous column was constructed, devoted to the memory of Lord Nelson, who after all figures pre-eminently in the various dramas of the island story. Nelson himself stands some three times the height of the actual human being represented, the column itself more than 167 feet high. His sea-battles are depicted around the base of the column, cast from gun-metal captured at his naval victories. Added some quarter of a century later were the four vast bronze lions. This is monumental history with a vengeance. Henceforth Trafalgar Square served to remind the nation's populace, and later generations of tourists, of the historic defeat of Britain's continental foes.

By the end of the seventeenth century, Portugal and Holland

had ceased to be serious maritime and economic rivals to the British. The eighteenth century witnessed a prolonged, recurring, global struggle between the three dominating European powers: Spain, France, and Britain. The wars were fought in Europe itself, and on the seas of the world. The principal theatres of engagement, however, were in the Indian subcontinent and in North America. As the great imperialist historian J. R. Seeley noted, in the eighteenth century 'the history of England is not in England but in America and Asia' (Seeley 1883: 109). The final defeat of the French and of the Spanish at the Battle of Trafalgar in October 1805 opened the moment of Britain's supremacy in Europe, the dominating factor in nineteenth-century diplomacy, and marked too Britain's future dominance in India. That the symbolic centre of the nation should commemorate this moment is entirely appropriate.

Evidence of these monumental commemorations of Britain's past greatness is still scattered throughout the world, in Calcutta, for example, or in the entire *raison d'être* of New Delhi. By the time of Trafalgar, Britain's American possessions rested only with Canada and with sections of the Caribbean. The British colonies in the north secured their independence, as did—some fifty years later— the Spanish colonies in the south. Even so, the linguistic and cultural affinities between Britain and the United States were to constitute a potent political influence long after the USA had been founded, while in the south, the sheer dynamism of British manufacturing and trade effectively transformed the new Latin republics (and Brazil) into informal spheres of the British Empire. Today, in the north of the American continent, atop the Heights of Abraham in Quebec City, there stands a memorial to General Wolfe and his troops who seized the city from the French in 1759. At the other end of the continent, just outside the central station in Buenos Aires a red-brick clock-tower was constructed in the early years of this century, funded by Argentine business leaders to mark their respect and gratitude to Britain. These are appropriate symbols for the various modes of British expansion in the Americas. Equally, the fact that the Buenos Aires clock-tower has fallen into decrepitude, the home now of dispossessed young children destroying their brains on glue, may also be suggestive—not only of the war of 1982, but in larger terms, indicating the demise of the Atlantic economy in which both Argentina and Britain, through the nineteenth century and much of the twentieth, were inextricably bound. Through the long hegemony of the white Atlantic nations, from the sixteenth to the twentieth centuries, Britain—both in historical reality and symbolically—occupied a strategic, central position in this larger frame.

For all Britain's cosmopolitanism, relations with continental Europe have always been more mediated than those with America or with the empire, the maritime dimensions of the British nation-state always tempting Britons to view themselves as marginal Europeans, with greater things on their mind than their parochial continental neighbours. Through the nineteenth century, during the height of Britain's global power, diplomatic objectives for the Continent were simple enough, organized to ensure that no single European power predominated. The rise of Germany, in the heart of Europe, challenged this equilibrium, and eventually proved a contributing factor in Britain's declaration of war in 1914. Britain and its allies destroyed Germany in 1918, and did so again in 1945—when the country was divided into two, partly as a means to ensure its continued subordination. Only in the latter decades of the twentieth century—with Germany once more established as the most powerful European nation—have the British been forced to negotiate with their European neighbours on terms by no means their own. Even the most unsentimental political leaders in Britain, habituated perhaps unconsciously to the historic centring of their nation, have not found this a comfortable situation.

These long histories are active in the contemporary epoch. Despite appearances, in our own modern times these profound historical durations and even their monumental iconographies, have not completely melted down: like Le Sueur's statue of Charles I, they never quite go away, and one never knows when next they will be resurrected. To bring things closer historically we might cite, for example, the case of Winston Churchill at the Conservative Party conference in Llandudno in 1948. In the days before flip-charts and spin, he informed his audience that he wished that he had been supplied with blackboard and chalk the better to illustrate his theme. He wanted to communicate his conviction that Great Britain lay at the centre of three defining concentric circles: the empire, the anglophone Atlantic world, and Europe. In diplomatic, strategic, and cultural terms, this really was to position Britain in the centre of the world. In part, such scheming represented the folly of an aged man, born and brought up in the Victorian world. But arguably, much that happens in the public world is produced by the follies of aged men: there is no reason to suppose that Churchill's dreams were simply his alone, the product of an individual pathology. Far from it: even when the formal properties of monumental histories diminish, their traces still remain present.

In order to understand Britain's contemporary relations to Europe and to America it is necessary to have a historical sense of the rise and fall of the Atlantic epoch: in this context, the (relative) decline of Britain can be located. And so too the consequent *decentring* of Britain and the British. It is this which—currently—is decisive.

The myths of all nations play upon the ancient and the modern. This is a dialectic which needs to be resolved in the national imaginary, and it is always in a state of irresolution. In the British case, in the 1960s and again in the 1980s, much has been heard of the modernity of British culture, and of the breaks with the (imperial) past. Yet the formal structures of the official nation, centred on Westminster, seem to remain peculiarly immune to the forces of modernity. For all the hype of the modern it is still the case that, in some essential aspects, Britain is an old country.

To say this means, in part, that culturally and mythically Britain is deeply centred: it is a nation which knows its place. There are various aspects to this. First, in a commonsensical historical explanation, Britain as a nation-state was formed in the early phase of European modernization, and thus has chronology on its side. Second, in so far as the British nation-state has been organized symbolically by the ethnic codes of its core internal nation—of England—one can also say that, ideologically, the myths of the unitary British state are those which play upon the archaic and the ancestral. In the more extreme versions of these myths, Britain is less a historical formation than one divined by nature: its history is coeval with landscape, territory, and coastline, evolving slowly from the mulch of organic progress. Third, the historical continuities which compose the culture of the British are pronounced, especially compared to their continental European neighbours. Not only has Britain (within its own borders) largely escaped the worst catastrophes of modernity, at the same time relations between the three constituent nations and the overarching state have been relatively stable. (It may be worth recalling that Cromwell's republican interlude, and the attendant civil war, survive in popular memory as a conflict between hedonists and killjoys. No central European could construct their past in this manner.) One need only contrast this history, for example, to that of Poland: not only has the configuration of Poland adopted many different territorial forms in the modern period, but for the nineteenth century the Polish nation-state disappeared altogether, allowing Poland to be lived peculiarly intensely within the imagination. There *was* no other Poland except in people's dreams. For good reason, native British culture—in the grander scheme of things—has been regarded as relatively benign, insulated from the traumas which have burned through the history of other comparable modern nations in Europe; to put this in a homely vernacular, unlike the Poles the inhabitants of Britain have always (or mostly) known where their nation is. It has not been moved in the night. The relative absence of historic rupture—its seeming permanence—gives some credence to the experience of national continuity, and can legitimize the myth of a peculiarly ancient, peculiarly providential, nation.

The relations of Scotland and Wales to the British nation-state have always been complex, and cannot be subsumed in the catch-all of a lived Englishness. Even those Scots or Welsh most drawn to London, and most sympathetic to the strategic objectives of a unitary British civilization, have still most often thought of themselves as Scots or Welsh. In contemporary times, when the break-up of Britain remains a possible political occurrence, the disengagement from England and its culture is palpably more intense. This represents, in part, the continuing decline of Britain, and the continuing contraction of England and of English hegemony. But yet the creation of the British nation-state was as much a symbolic issue as a matter merely of technical statecraft. If affiliation to the subordinated nations of the new state provided a centrifugal tendency—pulling away from the centre—affiliation to the overriding civilization of the British Empire produced, on the contrary, a centripetal tendency—pulling those in the further orbits of the nation-state toward the centre. Such contrary processes can be found, almost by definition, in any multinational state. They can occur simultaneously, even within the same person. But in so far as it is possible to name the symbolic imperative which represented the centripetal tendencies of the British state, the ethnic codes of England (as opposed to subscription to English *nationalism*) are powerful contenders. Not only has English ethnicity been profoundly centred: it has been profoundly *centring*, an active element in the wider configuration of British civilization.

This is an urgent contemporary issue. The end of empire; the continuing nationalist conflicts in Northern Ireland; the incipient uncoupling of Scotland and Wales; and the ethnic recomposition of England itself, all have conspired to transform the historic legacy of a (largely) uncontested dominance of what the British state is, or should be, which—under the formal banner of unionism—has been in place since the 1920s. But this is not a matter simply internal to Britain. There are two aspects of the consequent decentring of Britain and the British which I am going to follow here. For convenience I shall discuss one of these in relation to Europe, the other to America. The first turns on the question of national sovereignty; the second on the relations between mass culture and civilization. They are not as distant as they might at first seem.

Even though there may be contemporary Conservatives who might be doubtful of the fact, Winston Churchill was a European idealist, looking to a time when Britain would be part of some kind of united European confederation of nations. After all, in the terrible days of June 1940, it was Churchill himself who advocated most strenuously the unification of France and the United Kingdom, such that 'France and Great Britain shall no longer be two nations, but one Franco-British Union' (Churchill 1985: 183), and proposing that common citizenship be established. It was the French, not the British, who scuppered the plan. But however strong Churchill's sympathies for closer political union with Europe, it was always the empire and the USA which were upper-most in his mind. In this he was not unusual: in the 1940s and 1950s there was barely anyone amongst the political classes who pressed for unity with Europe at the expense either of the empire or of the 'special relationship' with the USA. So as France and Germany slowly began to move to various schemes for co-operation through the 1950s, at every stage Britain was reluctant to intervene. It was only at the end of the decade, and into the 1960s, that through a very small group in the British cabinet in conjunction, on the one hand, with the White House and the US embassy in London and, on the other, with a handful of key technocrats in the civil service, the change in policy towards Europe was effected. Essentially, the impetus which propelled this cadre to shift position was a matter of state rather than of nation: it had more to do with markets and prosperity than it did with the less tangible issues of civilization, despite an accompanying rhetoric—proclaiming a new era of culture—which was of stupendous banality. Indeed, since the 1960s the European question in British politics has indicated a growing cleavage between state and nation. Although, when put to the test, those in favour of closer integration with Europe have managed to win the numerical advantage, the passions of those hostile to Europe have been the more intense in delineating a popular politics.

Suspicion of Europe has been most powerfully articulated in terms of the threat to sovereignty. It has never been entirely clear, within the hurly-burly of daily political strife, what this means. Various facets of sovereignty seem to have been conceded in the past, without dire results, nor even with much debate. When pressed, opponents of Europe insist that to pass further legal powers to Brussels would undermine the peculiarly British system of the indivisible authority of the Crown, acting through Parliament. It is this system—in which the will of Parliament ineluctably transubstantiates into the will of the Crown and, more to the point, in which the Crown is the people—which those committed to 'the British way' believe to be most in danger. For the British system of the Crown in Parliament is conceptually distinct from other democratic systems in which sovereignty lies with the people, and is delegated to their chosen rulers.

This is an issue which is revealed most fully in relation to Europe. Further political integration of Britain into the European Union offers no guarantee that this system of sovereignty would be overhauled. Despite the populist rhetoric of both Mrs Thatcher, when she was Prime Minister, and Mr Blair, the unitary, *absolutist* form of constitutionalism favoured by political leaders in Westminster remains—to date—intact. Such a faith demonstrates the degree to which those long durations can still be active in the present. To say this is not simply to evoke a political history (for here we can see Mrs Thatcher and Mr Blair yoked together), for it has as much to do with an *ethnic* system and the structuring of an entire political culture. The seemingly permanent identity between nation, state, territory, and language has bequeathed an intoxicating history, in which every part of public and civic life is dependent on the other. To tamper with one is to tamper with a peculiarly providential history. It is difficult in Britain to think of the political system—the state—without *also* seeing it as being hugely overdetermined by the idea of a particular civilization and by a deeply rooted call upon ethnic belonging. The imbrication of state and civil society in Britain, working through the medium of ethnicity, has been powerful. In such a situation sovereignty is not only a question of politics, it carries too—as the Irish, erstwhile Whig, Edmund Burke was the first to appreciate—a metaphysical resonance.

Such is the political system of an old country. Popular anxieties about a European future are not easily overridden by the rational calculus of an easy or formal pluralism. They mark one index of the continuing decentring of the British. But given the degree to which conceptions of politics and conceptions of civilization move along the same circuits of ethnicity, each confirming the other, in different parts of the national culture the principles at stake remain remarkably constant. The inhabitants of continental Europe speak English (don't the British know it), but invariably not as their mother tongue. Relative lack of direct engagement with the cultures of the nations of continental Europe is a reminder of the parochialism of the British. But with the USA, the nation where mass culture *happens*, the relations are of a different order.

Traditionally—until the 1960s, satire, and Carnaby Street—British culture was known for its ancestral virtues. For outsiders, this was a matter both for mimicry and respect, often intertwined. From the late nineteenth century, there were many prominent intellectuals who came to Britain—despite their ambivalence—precisely because it was where they believed culture was at its most assured, at its most *located*. Henry James, a native American, provides one of the earliest, and one of the sharpest, instances. He was sceptical about the potential of America to produce a civilization. He had high regard for the putative verities of the—spatial and temporal—locatedness of British culture. And he was sufficiently outside the customs of the British to be unnerved by what he revered, a situation it would seem which constituted *his* pleasures of exile. James, a product of a self-consciously new country, came to be obsessed by 'that quiet and comfortable sense of the absolute' enjoyed by the English (James 1967: 142).

The reverse of this was that the native protagonists of the old country spent much time and effort decrying the barbarities of the new country—of the USA especially. This is a constant theme in the established intellectual life of Britain for very nearly a century. From the 1880s to the 1950s it is very difficult to find exceptions, in any political quarter. Mass America represented a peculiarly intense transgression of what culture was. There were many British intellectuals, of course, who participated in the pleasures of American popular culture, just as the populism of American mass culture had wide appeal even at the moment it was being traduced morally or intellectually. As much as in the case of Henry James, the ambivalence in play could not have been more pronounced. But even so, the point stands: in this long historical period, as part of the substratum of the common sense of British intellectual culture, the belief predominated that Britain represented culture and 'the past', while America represented no more than the market and the lowest form of modernity.

Such dichotomies, of course, generate all manner of upheavals, even at the moment when the frontier marking one from the other is being put in place. 'Lowest forms of modernity' held an intrinsic appeal, especially to a population located culturally (for example) by the ethnically bounded programming of the BBC. In the 1960s, it really does seem as if, in a complex cultural transformation, mass culture did break into, and rearrange, the traditional authority of the national culture, across every sphere. This phase of mass culture coincided with the breaking apart of nation and state in the British nation-state. Alongside decolonization, immigration, the move to Europe, and the internal decomposition of the unitary state—the very stuff of conventional histories—the arena of mass culture, in which these transformations were lived, was critical. The demarcations between high and low, old and new, could never quite carry the same authority again. For a nation which had invested so assiduously in the prerequisites of the culture of the past, the impact of Americanized mass culture did much, as conservatives of all stripes had feared, to dislocate the native culture of the British.

One manifestation of this dislocation in the native culture, given the concerns of this volume, needs to be emphasized. It was British cultural studies itself. In the larger frame, one can suggest that cultural studies in Britain developed as an effect of the decentring of the British, and of the growing fissures between nation and state. If Henry James (in all his captivating ambivalence) revered the *location* of the British, then later generations of cultural studies iconoclasts, from the 1960s onwards, became attached to the political and aesthetic possibilities of the dislocations of the British: to what was essentially hybrid in the seeming purity of the national culture. Much of this intellectual battle took place in the arena of Americanized mass culture, and much of it was conducted—with spirit— by exiles from the Americas, from Europe, and from the erstwhile colonies who found themselves congregating on the margins of the native British culture.

Conceptually, the intellectual break inaugurated by British cultural studies in the 1950s and 1960s has a long and complex history, which cannot detain us here. One point, though, is pertinent. In 1932, Q. D. Leavis (married, as it happened, to a Polish immigrant, the renowned literary and cultural critic F. R. Leavis) wrote a startling book with the title *Fiction and the Reading Public* (Leavis 1984). Her argument turned on a fierce denunciation of mass culture, suggesting that a culture driven by the market broke the capacities for individuals to discriminate rationally between those cultural artefacts which were of ethical or human value, and those which were mere dross. In this argument, the ethnic givens of British life constituted the principal axis by which her attack was mounted. What was unusual, however, was that its object of analysis (the forms of mass culture) and its methodologies anticipated closely the future mainstream of cultural studies—though drawing quite contrary conclusions. A quarter of a century later Richard Hoggart's *The Uses of Literacy* (1972)—in similar mode—can be said to have inaugurated cultural studies in its serious anthropological attention to the lived cultures of the people, yet at the same time its uncompromising critique of Americanized culture was fuelled by sympathy for the very locatedness, in place and time, of a distinctly native, British folk culture. For this reason, *The Uses of Literacy* truly is a text 'of the break'. It was some years before more nuanced approaches to the impact of American culture in Britain began to take shape, in which the inherent nativism of much inherited cultural analysis began to be opened out. (See especially Hebdige 1988 and Worpole 1983.) In a strange conjunction in the early 1960s high European culture fused with American mass culture—evident not only in British cultural theory but in, for example, the predilection of art-house cinemas of the time to show French New Wave films alongside the schlock of US B-movies—to serve as yet another index of the dissolution of a native British culture which knew its place.

This is a long way from the frontier myths of the British, and from the rise of an Atlantic Britain in which the absolutes of British culture could thrive. The historical process was always fractured, always dissonant, and always unfinished. Maybe though, from our own historical vantage point, we can see these histories somewhat more clearly than hitherto. And this in turn may derive, precisely, from the decentring of the British. The maps have been turned around, or upside down—at least symbolically. The lines of authority, from the centre to the margins, are now less forceful. Britain begins to look a little more like it looked before the Atlantic economies rose to prominence: a little archipelago off north-western Europe.

The recent imaginative reconstitution of the Atlantic as an active theatre of black civilizations demonstrates the degree to which the predominating historical narratives (which have been in place, let's say, since the island stories of the sixteenth century) have been interrupted and relocated as a result of other stories intervening. To situate Britain as a component of the black Atlantic allows us to see its culture with new eyes. Lines of connection emerge which do much to decentre the British and to confirm (modestly enough, one might have thought) that their civilization, far from being uniquely providential, is simply the product—like any other—of a chaotic, profane history.

A microscopic indication of these cultural shifts not only shows the manner in which the historical centring of Britain is ending (for this is obvious enough), but also suggests that—inside the cultures of the white Atlantic nations—other stories were all the while incubating. It reminds us too of the power of *unseen* histories. One story concerns T. S. Eliot, a North American whose anxieties about his own national culture—and his consequent admiration for the British—redramatized the earlier concerns of Henry James. The story is told by the Barbadian Kamau Brathwaite:

For those of us who really made the breakthrough, it was Eliot's actual voice—or rather his recorded voice, property of the British Council (Barbados)—reading 'Preludes', 'The Love Song of J. Alfred Prufrock', *The Waste Land* and late the *Four Quartets*— not the texts—that turned us on. In that dry deadpan delivery, the 'riddims' of St Louis (though we didn't know the source then) were stark and clear for those of us who at the same time were listening to the dislocations of Bird, Dizzy, and Klook. And it is interesting that, on the whole, the establishment could not stand Eliot's voice—and far less jazz. (Brathwaite 1993: 23)

The long durations which make up the history of the British are not only those most visibly commemorated in the official institutions of the national culture.

But it is not only Britain which is having to contend with the vicissitudes of a declining Atlantic-centred history, white or black. As the axis of power shifts globally, and the civilizations of the Pacific displace those of the Atlantic, the gravitational centre of American life imperceptibly shifts from the east coast to the west coast, confirming Hegel's predictions that the movement of history is from east to west. Fifty years ago, Churchill could assume with confidence not only that the axis of power turned on the Atlantic, but that America essentially was an Atlantic power. The 'special relationship' between the USA and the United Kingdom, which Churchill and every British Prime Minister since have been desperate to invoke, could only have any reality in so far as the USA was positioned as the hegemonic Atlantic power. Yet this is a situation which no longer pertains with anything like the force of half a century ago. Seattle and San Francisco (and Vancouver in Canada) are not only economically and culturally dynamic in a way which the older cities on the eastern seaboard are not, they are also becoming integrated into a new Pacific matrix, more proximate in their economic imperatives to comparable Asian Pacific cities than to the historic Atlantic nations. Indeed, these American cities are significantly demographically 'Asian' (and Los Angeles significantly demographically Hispanic) in a manner which suggests that the classic nineteenth-century model of the integrated nation-state, of which Britain proved such a masterly exponent, is itself history. The *locations* of peoples, territories, and languages—demarcated and kept in place by historic frontiers—have only ever existed in the dreams of the nation-builders. In the late twentieth century, pressures from within and without the nation-state suggest the degree to which this is now a model of civilization inherited from the past. In the imagination of Winston Churchill, America would simply have ceased to exist if confronted by such ethnic turmoil. For this veteran imperialist Australia appeared—as its founding constitutional documents averred—to be the authentic country of the white man: and yet today there are substantial numbers of Australians, some of whom are the white grandchildren of the nation's founders, who are consciously reinventing Australia as an Asian nation. In such a global scenario, old postcolonial Britain moves off the map. After all, even a good portion of Hollywood—once the master-sign of all that historic British culture was not—is now owned by Sony. In such a world all the maps need to be rethought, not least the ones which place Britain in the centre of things.

Further Reading

Colley, L. (1992), *Britons: Forging the Nation, 1707–1837*, New Haven: Yale University Press. A cracking account of the formation of the British nation.

Hall, S. (1991), 'Old and New Identities, Old and New Ethnicities', in A. King (ed.), *Culture, Globalization and the World-System*, London: Macmillan. An enlightening exploration of the relations between globalization and the imaginative reworkings of ethnic identity.

Kearney, H. (1989), *The British Isles: A History of Four Nations*, Cambridge: Cambridge University Press. One of the first histories to take seriously the multinational dimensions of the British nation-state.

Nairn, T. (1981), *The Break-up of Britain: Crisis and Neo-nationalism*, London: Verso. A classic, prescient discussion of the growing crisis of the United Kingdom.

References

Brathwaite, K. (1993), *Roots*, Ann Arbor: University of Michigan Press.

Churchill, W. (1985), *The Second World War*, ii: *Their Finest Hour*, Harmondsworth: Penguin.

Hebdige, D. (1988), *Hiding in the Light*, London: Comedia.

Hoggart, R. (1972), *The Uses of Literacy*, Harmondsworth: Penguin.

James, H. (1967), *Hawthorne*, London: Macmillan.

Leavis, Q. (1984), *Fiction and the Reading Public*, Harmondsworth: Penguin.

Piper, D. (1964), *The Companion Guide to London*, London: Collins.

Seeley, J. (1883), *The Expansion of England: Two Courses of Lectures*, London.

Worpole, K. (1983), *Dockers and Detectives*, London: Verso.

Section II

When Will We Be Modern? Culture, Tradition, and Heritage

Introduction

THE articles in this section all address the contradictory dynamics
set up by the interplay between the forces of modernity, traditionalism, and heritage which remain at the heart of contemporary British culture. Addressing one of the most recalcitrant forms of these
traditionalisms, Linda Mugglestone traces the long historical roots
which lie behind the association of 'Proper English' with the particular variety of the language spoken by a socially privileged and
culturally powerful minority. As she demonstrates, this privileged
form of speech was initially associated with the language of the
royal court and later with the metropolitan elite on a broader scale.
At the same time all other regionally based forms of the language—
in accent or dialect—have always been taken to signify some lack of
intelligence on their speakers' part and correspondingly associated
with various forms of social inferiority. In more recent times, as
witnessed in the debates provoked by the work of Basil Bernstein
and William Labov in the 1970s, the association of prestigious
forms of speech with middle-class or white speakers, and the
corresponding classification of working-class and black forms of
speech and language as in one way or another deficient, has
remained a staple focus of educational debate. Clearly, as she notes,
the question of what is to count as 'Proper English' is hard to
disentangle from the question of who the 'Proper English' are to be
defined as socially. The metalanguage of prescriptivism enshrined
in the notion that schools should function as a remedy for the

'infections' of dialect and other debased forms of speech is still with us. The hysteria which motivates this position is well captured when Mugglestone quotes Norman Tebbit's outburst to the effect that 'maintaining standards' is ultimately all of a piece. In an extraordinary moment of rhetorical overdrive, Tebbit claims that if teachers fail to teach 'proper' spelling and punctuation, so that 'good English is no better than bad English'—then, once such symbolic standards have fallen, 'there's no imperative to stay out of crime'. The continuing mutual inscription of conservative and reactionary forms of politics and language in contemporary British culture could hardly be better exemplified.

However, if the politics of language displays very significant continuities over a long historical period, there are nonetheless some crucial areas of British cultural life which display significant change. As Steve Bruce points out in his survey of contemporary religious cultures, not so long ago, the state Church provided a basic Christian vocabulary which imposed its contours on the cultural life of the nation—to this extent members of the nation lived inside a common religious culture. From a position where the Christianity of the state Church dominated many aspects of social life we now see, not only a general decline in religiosity and churchgoing among the (white) population at large, but also its redistribution, partly along ethnic lines. Thus we see the decline of (principally white) Protestantism, the rise of (predominantly black) Pentecostalism and (predominantly Asian) forms of Islam. Bruce offers striking evidence of their religion now being a much more central part of their lives for contemporary Britain's ethnic minorities than for its white majority population. For the latter, the place of religion in their lives has shifted from being a taken for granted common framework of understandings and cultural reference to being just another form of voluntary association for a small minority— alongside the growing number of those who subscribe to the various eclectic forms of 'New Age' mysticism. As Bruce notes, the contours of Britain's religious history are different in important ways from that of the Catholic countries of Europe. Here secularization has not taken the form of principled anticlericalism so much as a mode of indifference which pays lip-service to religious iconography (a white church wedding if possible, for good form's sake; perhaps a church school for the children as a bulwark against the chaotic decline of the public educational system) without retaining any significant investment in the Christian faith itself.

If religion has been historically one key element of British cultural tradition another has, of course, been the monarchy. David

Chaney is concerned in his analysis of the contemporary 'mediated monarchy' to explore how and why this phenomenon has survived into the era of modernity in this country. Chaney's argument is that the British monarchy has undergone a fundamental transformation from being a form of feudal privilege to becoming a mediated form of international celebrity. This transformation, which recreates the monarchy as the pro-filmic dimension of the 'royal soap opera' as a popular phenomenon, has to be understood within the overall dynamics of the mediated international economy of symbolic prestige. Chaney situates his analysis within the broader framework of an approach that would see the 'reinvention of traditions' as a defensive response to the destabilizing flux of modernity. His concern is with understanding how monarchy has been reinvented as one particular form of celebrity for the modern era—so that, as he puts it, 'tradition is redramatised as mass entertainment for a global audience'. Of course, as he observes, the price of this transformative accommodation is always high, and sometimes fatal, as in the case of Princess Diana. It is not simply that the monarchy inevitably suffers a loss of deference as the price of the new forms of mediated intimacy that it enjoys with its subject-consumers. The mediated machinery of publicity (from *Hello* magazine to the BBC's *Panorama* 'Interview Special') has its own demands, which often produce sharp and contradictory clashes of needs and interest with the royal celebrities whom it now makes all the more 'available' to their publics ('Go on, just one more shot love . . . how about a smile then?'). When monarchy takes the form of celebrity, it necessarily falls prey to the travails of commercially orchestrated forms of popularity.

In his analysis of British royalty as but one (if distinct and particular) form of contemporary celebrity culture, Nick Couldry goes further than does Chaney in his analysis—by starting from the phenomenon of mediated celebrity itself, rather than treating the mediation of the monarchy as a 'late twist in royalty's long-term history'. For Couldry, the question is what distinguishes royalty among the various forms of media celebrity—including those who are simply 'famous for being famous'. His particular focus is on the development of mediated forms of royal populism which involve carefully constructed and choreographed performances (or embodiments) of ordinariness. This was the style (once described as 'populism in trainers') principally associated with Princess Diana, the 'People's Princess' in Tony Blair's posthumous eulogy—who managed to produce an image of herself as more 'ordinary', and thus more in touch with popular feeling, than the rest of the royals.

In this complex process of the public ventriloquizing of the 'ordinary' by those who are (by definition and by birth) the most extraordinary members of the nation, Couldry argues that we see an attempt at the 're-enchantment' of the monarchy informed by the public relations techniques of contemporary celebrity culture. As he notes, Diana's populist style of public self-presentation has now been picked up by her son Prince William ('Wills' in the discourse of the tabloids), as evidenced in the well-known photograph of him as 'just another supporter' of the England football team, wearing his Union Jack waistcoat under his Eton jacket. Clearly, whatever other dangers it faces, the successful management of its mediation is central to the monarchy's future.

Turning from the question of the tenacity and adaptability of established cultural forms to that of the explicit formulation of cultural policies in the political arena, Ken Worpole demonstrates the enormous continuities visible in the public subsidy of the metropolitan elite arts throughout the post-war period in Britain. As he observes, on coming to power 'The "New" Labour Party made various proclamations of its newness' and of that of its notional product 'New Britain'. Thus the Department of National Heritage's name was changed to that of the Department of Culture, Media, and Sport—'as a symbol that we mean to look forward not back', in Tony Blair's words at the time. However, Worpole rightly argues, despite these cosmetic changes, one can still trace strong continuities in government cultural policy which go back at least to the post-war settlement of 1945. Still, now just as then, the lion's share of cultural funding is distributed within a metropolitan-based elite world of privileged 'National/Royal' institutions which serve up a diet of 'official' High Culture (highly conventionalized forms of opera, ballet, etc.) which has little to do with most people's lives. Sadly, as Worpole demonstrates, the same remains true of the much-trumpeted Lottery funding which was supposed to address new needs in new ways; most of its funding also goes to capital funding of projects close to the heart of the traditional metropolitan cultural elite. Worpole's depressing conclusion is that, beyond the familial linkages of patrimony (from Herbert Morrison to Peter Mandelson) which tie the Millennium Experience back to the Festival of Britain of 1951, cultural policy in Britain has moved on hardly at all in the last fifty years, despite the transformation of the cultural industries in this country, as elsewhere, during that period.

The highly symbolic moment in which the Department of National Heritage, set up by Mrs Thatcher to promote a Conservative vision of national identity, was renamed by the incoming New Labour government in 1997 is also scrutinized in Andrew Higson's account of the involvement of Britain's film and television industries in the production and selling of 'heritage'. It may well be that these cultural industries are increasingly central to the economy of Labour's 'New Britain'. However, as Higson argues, a key part of what they still produce and sell (especially for export) is precisely 'heritage'—films and programmes (from *Chariots of Fire* to *Pride and Prejudice* and *The Remains of the Day*) which focus on the glories of the British past and specifically on a pre-technological, ruralist, aristocratic cultural tradition. As Chaney argues in relation to the monarchy (and as Higson notes here in relation to the recent rush of 'royal' films), all these institutions and trappings of tradition are now inevitably caught up in the mechanics of the global media marketplace. In these circumstances, as Higson puts it, the national heritage is now being busily reinvented by the audio-visual industries in a highly entrepreneurial spirit. The landscapes and narratives of British (or perhaps more properly, English) tradition and privilege represented in these 'period' costume dramas, with their lavish displays of picturesque country house settings, function in close tandem with the operation of the National Trust and English Heritage to promote forms of cultural tourism, as whole areas of countryside ('Thomas Hardy's Dorset') are rebranded so as better to attract visitors who wish to see the sites featured in these films. Higson also returns us to the conundrum explicated by Mugglestone in relation to 'Proper English'. If these are the 'quality' films and programmes on which the reputation of Britain's TV and film industries increasingly rests, they are also forms of representation which focus, by and large, on those who traditionally have been defined in social terms as 'the Quality'—the privileged white elite of the Home Counties. The question thus remains as to whose heritage is being represented here, however profitable and prestigious its international representation may be for its producers.

John Corner begins by rightly reminding us of the sheer extent of the social and cultural transformation wrought by the coming of television, before turning to address what he sees as the central tensions and dynamics of the current television industry. In the first place here he identifies the tension between what he calls television's functions as 'knowledge machine' and as 'pleasure machine'. If the first has its roots in the long shadow of Reithian conceptions of public service broadcasting which historically preceded and institutionally framed the arrival of commercial television in this country, the latter is now equally vital to any understanding of television's role in contemporary cultural life. In this respect Corner argues that television displays a simultaneous dynamic of both centripetal and centrifugal forces, as it both documents, draws in, ingests, and then rapidly recirculates in mediated form the different elements of regional and national culture. It is in this dynamic that television constructs not only the 'official' but also the 'private' life of the nation and thereby creates a 'parallel social universe'. In this latter respect Corner also points to the centrality of representations of the 'ordinary' on British television, whether in the big soap operas such as *Coronation Street* and *EastEnders* (which contrast so strongly with US-made 'glamour soaps'), in the workplace-based fictional forms (hospital- and police-based series) of TV drama, in sitcom, or in the new programme strands (Access/DIY programming, docu-soaps, talk shows) which increasingly feature 'ordinary people' as the stars of their own show. Here we have one of the key processes through which the nation is constituted as it is 'reflected' back to itself—although, of course, as Corner notes, all these forms of national television face an increasingly uncertain future in a world of proliferating of channel choice, under the impact of deregulation, digitalization, and the growth of satellite and cable delivery systems.

In his chapter on contemporary popular music, David Hesmondhalgh explores the role of a variety of different musical styles and elements in the production of British culture over the last decade. He takes as his starting point the debates engendered by the rise of 'Britpop' in the 1990s, as represented by bands such as Suede, Blur, and Oasis. Here Hesmondhalgh points to the way in which Britpop emerged fairly explicitly as an anti-American (and, to a lesser extent, anti-European) sensibility, dedicated to the celebration of a specifically British musical tradition. This distinctive tradition, its proponents claimed, stretched back through Ian Dury and the Beatles to the days of music-hall and was characterized by a now self-conscious mobilization of particularly 'British' themes and styles. As he notes, there was a profound irony in the spokesmen of these supposedly 'alternative' cultural institutions (the 'indie' labels from which Britpop initially emerged) articulating such a conservative definition of the 'essential character' of British music. For Hesmondhalgh it is crucial that against the essentialist (if not racist) 'Little Englandism' of the Britpop movement we set other musics, which were not so readily recoupable within the 'rebranding Britain' exercise which attempted to articulate Britpop (along with 'young British art') to the image of 'Cool Britannia'. In doing this Hesmondhalgh points to the crucial role of the electronic dance music which developed out of the rave/trance culture of the period to transform itself into drum and bass and its various musical cousins. The key point about these musics, in Hesmondhalgh's argument, is that they were both multicultural in practice, avowedly cosmopolitan, and 'placeless', having no investment in anti-Americanism or anti-Europeanism in the way that Britpop did. It was for these reasons, he argues, that it was in these areas of musical development, rather than in what was in effect the white cultural movement of Britpop, that what he calls 'two-tone' and hybrid cultural sensibilities could be better developed. In some of their later manifestations, Hesmondhalgh argues, these musics also serve in part to give expression to what he calls 'the dark side' of British urban cultural experience in this period—in a way one does not find in other musical forms—and certainly not in the celebratory mode of Britpop.

In her analysis of the rise of the young British artists (yBas) Rosemary Betterton focuses on the paradoxes which surround it. The yBas can be argued to be the bastard children of Thatcherism, in so far as the collapse of public funding for the arts both forced their greater reliance on the private market and thus moved them more fully into the realm of marketing, hype, and spectacular consumption—and in so far as the emerging artists themselves were forced into a professionalized and entrepreneurial mode of self-promotion at a very early stage in their careers (cf. the trajectory of Damien Hirst for the classic case). As Betterton notes, the contradictions in play here are profound, as the art market and the sphere of commercial consumption have undergone new forms of realignment. Taking the case of the *Sensation* show of 1997 Betterton demonstrates the complex two-way trade involved as the new generation of yBas had their aesthetic status confirmed by association with the Royal Academy, just as that venerable institution attempted to 'rebrand' itself (in the phrase of the times) as modern, cool, and hip by virtue of its association with the yBas. And of course, in the background was the Svengali of the Great Show, Charles Saatchi, wizard of hype, playing the markets for all they were worth. On the terrain of media visibility (the key to commercial success) the worlds of marketing and art have increasingly moved into symbiosis—witness the increasing significance of the Channel 4-sponsored annual Turner Prize ('the art world's Britpop awards', according to Matthew Collings) or the role of tabloid press outrage in creating the 'buzz' about the original *Sensation* show at the RA. However, for Betterton more than this is at stake: she argues that what we can see in all of this—represented emblematically perhaps in the work of Sarah Lucas—is the condensation of a complex process of both cultural and economic change. If the yBa movement invokes kitsch in order to shock (contrary to Clement Greenberg's classic analysis) then, Betterton argues, Lucas's parodies of misogynistic 'laddism' also encode the profound shift in the balance of gender relations consequent upon the collapse of traditionally masculine spheres of productive employment in the national economy and the correlative rise of the traditionally feminine spheres of service and consumption. If the new and much-heralded 'creative industries' offer some shocking imagery, that may be because we live in shocking times.

In approaching contemporary British literary fiction, Bernard Sharratt poses the question of how the 'condition of England' novel might possibly be written in our times. As he notes, the novels of the key nineteenth-century authors were replete with 'representative dilemmas, typical figures and emblematic events', whereas nowadays it seems the key issue is precisely that of diversity and fragmentation of identity—to an extent that makes any project of providing an overview which might map the new 'multicultural geography' of Britain deeply problematic. Sharratt asks whether in fact we confront a simply 'unimaginable diversity and complexity' both of 'symbolic ethnicities' and of cultural forms based on continuing divisions of class, region, or gender. As he observes, mere miscellany itself offers no form and any catalogue of the hyphenated forms of Britishness still requires some overall framework or grid of connectedness within which to situate each element and its relation to the others. Sharratt's delicate survey of the attempts made by writers from different cultural backgrounds (from Hanif Kureishi to Irvine Welsh) to articulate the specificities of their own communities is instructive in the way it highlights the difficulties of recognizing (and validating) other forms of ordinariness than one's own and the dangers of falling back into a hermetically sealed space of cultural memory. As he argues, ultimately, it is a question of finding forms of representation adequate to a situation in which many people live within a shared physical location or 'common ground', under common constraints, in an inherited form of coexistence and daily contact, but with little conscious or deliberate sense of connection. From this perspective, as he puts it, 'the nation state seems more a condition of mutual dependence than any common culture'. It is perhaps the forms of that mutuality which constitute the agenda for the next round of 'condition of England' novels.

11

'Proper English' and the Politics of Standard Speech

LYNDA
MUGGLESTONE

LANGUAGE constitutes the 'best *prima-facie* evidence of general culture', stated the nineteenth-century writer William Phyfe (1885: p. v), readily illustrating the extent to which language and its variations are embedded in both society and the cultural constructions (and perceptions) of its speakers. Indeed, as he continued, 'on this account it appeals to all, since there is no one so wholly indifferent to the estimate formed of his social position, and who, in consequence, would not cultivate those arts that are at once the criteria of social standing and the stepping stones to a more liberal culture'. It is these intersections of language, class, culture, and society which this chapter will explore, looking at the rise of a standard in English, and the legacies which this has brought in terms of the interpretation of regional, social, and individual difference in language use. As Phyfe's words already illustrate, a standard variety, rather than merely acting as a neutral and non-localized means of national communication, tends instead to assimilate other, more controversial, images within its stated norms. Notions of class, culture, status, and even intelligence are regularly assumed to be reflected in its forms, and in the 'proper' ability to deploy them. Presented as 'the common Tye of society' by Locke, language, and specifically a standard variety of language, can, as we shall see, often constitute instead a source of division and discord, marginalizing some speakers even as it legitimizes—and privileges—others.

Assumptions about the cultural value of language (and, more

significantly, about the cultural value of different language varieties) are in fact pervasive. Even in the Middle Ages, comments about French and English—then both used in England, alongside Latin too—commonly refer to attendant socio-cultural correlates. 'Gentilmens children' spoke French, observed Ranulph Higden in the fourteenth century, making the socio-linguistic consequences of this still clearer in his description of those 'vplondissh men' who 'counter fete & likene hem selfe to gentilmen & arn besy to speke frenssh for to be more sette by'. Regional varieties of English could partake in similarly evaluative processes as Higden also confirms: 'Some vse strange wlaffing chitering harrying garryng & grisbyting . . . alle the langages of the northumbres & specially at york is so sharp slitting frottyng & vnshappe that we sothern men may vnneth vunderstande that langage.'

Such early notions of language and disadvantage, here phrased in terms of both aesthetic demerit and unintelligibility, lay the foundations for what was to become a fundamental contrast in cultural constructions of language and language use. The validation which Higden offers to southern above northern usage, further confirmed by the presence of the court ('by cause that the kyngis of englond . . . duelle more in the south contrey than in ye north contre'), already, for example, indicates the potential location of a 'standard'—and of its converse. As the nineteenth-century writer on language (and theologian) William Enfield later stressed moreover, 'A standard is that by which we ascertain the value of things of the same kind' (1809: 5), and 'value', seen from a variety of perspectives, does indeed come to be a dominant concern in discussions of standardization. In terms of English and its varieties, notions of hierarchy embedded in culture and social value almost inevitably surround the rise of a standard (and those with facility in its forms), bringing in their wake corresponding notions of a socially as well as linguistically constructed 'non-standard'. The emergence of a standard variety around London in fifteenth-century England was, in consequence, rapidly accompanied by shifting perceptions regarding its superior status, even though such a standard was essentially arbitrary in origin, dependent upon non-linguistic factors such as the location of court and capital, and on Caxton's decision to establish his printing press at Westminster, thereby disseminating one public and printed variety of London English over the country. Other varieties of English increasingly coming to be perceived as dysfunctional, it was this variety alone which was to take both cultural and linguistic precedence; as the writer on language John Hart notes in 1570, this alone is 'the flower of the English tongue'. Regionally marked dialects conversely come to connote ill-educated rusticity so that, in Shakespeare's *King Lear* for example, Edgar, son of the Earl of Gloucester, is able to assume Kentish forms as an effective social as well as linguistic disguise in the course of the play. Later writers such as the eighteenth-century lexicographer and elocutionist Thomas Sheridan, make the consequences of such shifts still more explicit, articulating a set of unequivocal socio-cultural equations which explicitly locate disadvantage in usage which transgresses the stated norms of 'standard' speech. As he points out, 'all other dialects, are sure marks, either of a provincial, rustic, pedantic, or mechanic education; and therefore have some degree of disgrace attached to them' (1762: 30). In contrast, a 'proper' assimilation to the 'standard' can operate as a social testimony, 'a sort of proof that a person has kept good company'.

Such attitudes are, of course, strikingly at odds with the linguistic truism that all language varieties are equal, and that all constitute equally good rule-governed systems. Standardization, however, is not merely a linguistic process, tracing the rise of one originally localized variety alone into a mode of national communication. It also constitutes a social process, with the resulting standard functioning as a social—and cultural—institution. As the words of Sheridan and Hart affirm, it can in addition be recognized as an ideology, generating a set of beliefs which readily extend to speakers as well as speech. Apparent in the cultural marginalization of other coexisting varieties, standardization is thus peculiarly double-edged, legitimizing one variety and delegitimizing others to the extent that, by dint of the non-localized status it assumes, the standard variety popularly comes to be seen as 'the language' in itself. Displacing other varieties from the public, written, and culturally statusful forms which they too once enjoyed, the rise of the standard serves moreover as a hegemonic process which valorizes one set of linguistic features alone, often (at least in terms of popular socio-cultural assumptions) being seen by extension as empowering those with command over them. As modern sociolinguistic studies have confirmed, speakers betraying regional (and thereby 'non-standard') markers in their speech may indeed score highly in subjective assessments of their friendliness and approachability. It is nevertheless those speakers who conform to the nonlocalized requisites of the 'standard' who are regularly assumed to be more intelligent and more self-confident, more authoritative and more powerful. Notions of an essentially subjective inequality are, in such ways, regularly mapped onto differences in language use as complex games of identity politics come to be played around the nuances of speech, and the presence or absence of non-standard features such as a double negative or dropped [h]. In the realms of language attitudes, linguistic commonplaces about the fundamental equality of all linguistic systems tend, as this suggests, to be replaced by firm beliefs in a linguistic hierarchy with marked socio-cultural associations. 'Are, then, all provincial dialects equally good?', as the essayist and philosopher James Beattie queried rhetorically in 1788. His answer was illuminating:

By no means. Of accent, as well as of spelling, syntax, and idiom, there is a standard in every polite nation. And, in all these particulars, the example of approved authors, and the practices of those, who, by their rank, education, and way of life, have had the best opportunities to know men and manners, and domestick and foreign literature, ought undoubtedly to give the law. (1788: 92)

Formulations of a standard, as this illustrates, can thus display a clear alliance between notions of 'best English' and 'best speakers' in ways which may prove problematic both culturally and linguistically. Apparent in George Puttenham's sixteenth-century constructions of a socio-linguistic model for the aspiring writer ('neither shall he follow the speach of a craftes man or carter, or other of the inferiour sort . . . But he shall follow generally the better brought vp sort . . . men ciuill and graciously behavioured and bred' (1589: 120)), it is, however, in the late eighteenth and nineteenth centuries that such conceptions receive particularly explicit discussion. It was at this time that the concerns of codification became particularly prominent in issues of linguistic standardization, as writers on the language often sought to specify invariable (and frequently arbitrary) rules by which the 'best' language and, by extension, the 'best' speakers might be known. Split infinitives, prepositions in final position, double comparatives, or constructions such as *different to* (as opposed to the 'proper' *different from*) all owe their highly negative proscription to this period, in spite of their longevity within the realities of usage. Cultural ideals of order, regularity, and analogy informed the need for their 'correction' (double comparatives such as 'more nicer' were thought to be 'illogical' while the cultural hegemony which Latin as supremely 'learned' language could still exert similarly brought its own influence to bear in these matters—infinitives, for instance, could not be split in Latin, a premiss thence erroneously extended to English). That such specified norms contained an attendant set of socio-cultural and class-based meanings is likewise made increasingly clear. Knowledge of the 'proper' norms of Latin itself imaged forth notions of elite culture, while 'talking proper' in the wider sense emerged as a significant cultural ideal (see Mugglestone 1997). Dialectics of culture and class, 'educatedness' and ignorance, came to exert their own hegemonic persuasions in the attempt to impose a single form of speech upon the nation and its speakers, with consequences which cannot be distanced to the past.

Accounts of language (both then and now) thus tend to be far from socially or culturally neutral in the specifications of a standard which they seek to encode. Though linguistic usage—what speakers actually say—must, descriptively, constitute the language *per se*, the normative versions of 'usage' which appear in the prescriptive texts of the eighteenth and nineteenth centuries are, as a result, themselves often constructed in ways redolent of cultural and class formation. Notions that only the 'vulgar' and 'ignorant' drop [h]s, end sentences with prepositions, or use double superlatives led to the emergence of a series of socio-linguistic stereotypes, further reinforced of course by the fictions of writers such as Charles Dickens. 'Manners is manners, but still your elth's your elth,' states the blacksmith Joe Gargery, his markers of non-standard English made plain for all to see. 'Joe is a dear good fellow . . . but he is rather backward in some things. For instance . . . In his learning and manners,' his nephew Pip avers, his contrastive propriety of grammar and phoneme standing as a clear indication of the 'great expectations' of the title in more ways than one. Such patterns echo the paradigm set out by the eighteenth-century theologian and scholar George Campbell, for instance, whose definition of 'proper' language offers a quite literal privileging of the forms recommended for general use: 'the language, properly so called, is found current, especially in the upper and the middle ranks, over the whole British empire' (1766: i. 334). In the history of a standard, and of attitudes to it, such class-based constructions of 'the language properly so called' are by no means rare. Benjamin Smart's nineteenth-century works on pronunciation, to give one further example, readily exhibit a similar focus so that 'a *good* pronunciation' is 'the use of these elements exactly where the custom of *good* (that is *well-bred*) society places them' (1836: p. xi), a definition accompanied by a particularly extensive set of socially and culturally constructed epithets. 'Well-bred society', 'the mouth of a well-educated Londoner', and 'metropolitan usage among educated speakers' all appear in specifications of the 'best speech', in marked contradistinction to the 'vulgar negligence' given as typifying 'a vulgar mouth'.

As both Campbell and Smart confirm, such images can create

powerful and pervasive fictions of usage which readily correlate extralinguistic and intralinguistic, irrespective of the facts of language in which, for example, a marked disjunction tends to exist between the real flexibility of standard English as actually deployed—even by the so-called 'best speakers'—and these rather more rigid myths of correctness which tend to surround notions of 'standard' use. Apparent even today in popular attitudes to non-standard grammar so that speakers using double negation ('I didn't not do it') can—erroneously—be interpreted as being intellectually disadvantaged rather than simply using a different (if non-standard) grammatical rule, it is in the realms of pronunciation where such subjective equations perhaps become particularly transparent. Regularly presented as the most immediate signifier of cultural status ('what can reflect more on a person's reputation for learning, than to find him unable to pronounce without propriety and elocution?', as the eighteenth-century grammarian James Buchanan (1757: p. vii) demanded), it is again the non-localized but clearly minority 'standard' which is often depicted, and perceived, as a marker of superior cultivation, creating binary images of those who speak 'without an accent'—though it is, in reality, impossible to do so—and of those whose accents still betray their regional (and social) origins. While the regional forms of the latter are, in the rhetoric of standardization, constructed as dysfunctional and deficient, assimilation to a non-localized 'received pronunciation' is, on the contrary, commonly framed with quite different intimations of socio-cultural superiority. As Phyfe (1885: p. v) hence categorically declared, 'It is certain that nothing marks more quickly a person's mental and social status than his practice in this regard.'

Such connotative fictions of 'standard' and 'non-standard', and the cultural divide which they come to embody, can be endorsed in ways which have far-reaching effects. Encoding what Joseph (1987: 4) has termed 'the cognitive fallacy', regionally and socially marked 'errors' in pronunciation such as [h]-dropping were, for instance, placed under the heading of 'Defective Intelligence' in the popular nineteenth-century schoolbooks of John Gill (see Gill 1857), their tenets instilled in generations of schoolchildren and teachers. The 1921 Newbolt Report on 'The Teaching of English in England' was still more explicit in the cultural (and entirely ideological) manipulations it brought to bear upon notions of linguistic variation. 'The great difficulty of teachers in Elementary Schools in many districts is that they have to fight against the powerful influence of evil habits of speech contracted in home and street,' its authors asserted (Newbolt Report 1921: 59): 'the teachers' struggle is thus not with ignorance but with a perverted power.' 'Standard' speech, they claim, conversely makes children into 'articulate and civilised human beings', where cultivation of speech acts as a ready signifier of culture in the wider sense too, a 'refinement of speech which, in a subtle manner, is an index to the mind, and helps to place it beyond the reach of vulgarity of thought and action' (1921: 67). As in its eighteenth-century predecessors—though here endorsed in the form of governmental proclamation—the fundamental text disturbingly remains the same.

As Ronald Carter rightly points out (1995: 123), 'nationally, in Britain at least, proper English is a social view of who the proper English are'. In consequence, though standardization as linguistic process does confer unquestionable advantages, not least in the development of non-localized linguistic norms of communication (especially in the written language), in other respects, and particularly in the role of standardization as socially oriented ideology, communication can conversely become a symbol of division in which difference—as in Smart and the Newbolt Report—may be constructed as deviance, polarizing notions of 'educated' and 'vulgar', 'cultured' and 'negligent'. Images of insiders and outsiders, of exclusivity—and corresponding exclusion—indeed frequently dominate prescriptive iterations of the need to assimilate 'standard' speech. Johnson's *Dictionary* (1755: C1ᵛ), for example, makes the politics of socio-linguistic exclusion overt in its rejection of mercantile diction from its pages: 'Nor are all words which are not found in the vocabulary, to be lamented as omissions. Of the laborious and mercantile part of the people, the diction is in great measure casual and mutable . . . [which] therefore must be suffered to perish with other things unworthy of preservation.' Dryden's *Dufresnoy* reflected a similar position with reference to English grammar: 'we make a countryman dumb, whom we will not allow to speak but by the rules of *grammar*.' Such comments polarize usage around 'language' and 'non-language', norm and deviation, in which regional and lower-status forms (and those who use them) are relentlessly construed as 'other'.

Prevalent images of the 'standard' as social symbol, conflating both social peers and linguistic exemplars in the drive to inculcate the stated norms of speech, can hence expose a more dangerous side of a form of speech which, in prescriptive rhetoric, was ostensibly to unite the realm. Just as standardization was often constructed as linguistic remedy, offering a cure for dialectal 'infection' through the hegemonies of standard speech, so too can it be presented as a social remedy, potentially solving the ills of a divided nation by conferring the same speech (and attendant socio-cultural values) upon all. In what can thus seem paradoxically skewed forms of representation, discussions of standardization (with the pressure on all sections of society to adopt the language of the statusful upper echelons) hence regularly deploy images of the greater social and cultural cohesion which thereby might be achieved—while simultaneously being phrased in highly loaded forms of language explicitly directed against those forms of speech (and their speakers) which, as yet, evidently failed to conform to the designated proprieties of 'good' speech. The Newbolt Report, as we have seen, is unambiguously marked by this approach, regional difference being constructed as perversity while articulacy is located only in those with competence in the forms of 'standard' speech. Fundamentally, however, the tenets remain those expressed by Sheridan in the late eighteenth century, as in his conviction that differences of pronunciation emphasized diversity rather than ordered harmony, confirming and consolidating 'odious distinctions within the people'. Altruism, egalitarianism, and prescription blended—at least ostensibly—in Sheridan's linguistic crusade to enfranchise all within the community of standard speech. As he demanded in his paean to the virtues of standardization: 'Would it not greatly contribute to put an end to the odious distinctions kept up between subjects of the same king, if a way were opened up by which the attainment of the English tongue in all its purity, both in point of phraseology and pronunciation, might be rendered easy to all inhabitants of his Majesty's dominions?' (1780: A2ᵛ).

The utopia of a realm rendered harmonious by means of a standardized and uniform speech was one to which nineteenth-century writers also often returned. In an era preoccupied by the class divide of Disraeli's 'two nations', it was an image which inevitably proved evocative, leading Francis Newman (1869: 16) to depict England as 'a nation which desires to eliminate vulgar provincial pronunciation, to educate and refine its people' and thereby 'get rid of plebeianism, and fuse the orders of society into harmony'. The phonetician Henry Sweet (1877: 196) made a similar point: 'When a firm control of pronunciation has thus been acquired, provincialisms and vulgarisms will at last be entirely eliminated and some of the most important barriers between the different classes of society will thus be abolished.' The ideal of standardization becomes one in which differences are transcended, and divisions healed. It is this which most explicitly lies behind the visions of education as standardizing force deployed in the Newbolt Report, whereby the prescription of one invariant language for all would create 'a bond of union between classes . . . the right kind of national pride':

We believe that such an education . . . would have important social, as well as personal, results; it would have a unifying tendency . . . If the teaching of the language were properly and universally provided for, the difference between educated and uneducated speech, which at present causes so much prejudice and difficulty of intercourse on both sides, would gradually disappear. (1921: 21–2)

The metalanguage of prescriptivism, as such examples indicate, can display remarkable continuities. Nevertheless, for all their longevity, the weaknesses within such utopian visions are clear, evident in Newman's socio-cultural equations which simultaneously eradicate 'plebeianism' and the 'provincial' (hence presumably eliminating the lower orders of society altogether), and equally transparent in the images of unintelligibility and ugliness which accompany Sheridan's exhortations for all to assimilate to 'standard' speech (1780: A2^r): 'would [it] not contribute much to the ease and politeness of society . . . if all gentlemen . . . should be able to express their thoughts clearly . . . [in] utterance so regulated, so as not to give pain to the understanding, or offence to the ears of their auditors.' In such instances, social and linguistic ideologies fuse, prescribing a 'unity' achieved not merely by imposing one form of speech on all, but also by imposing a single—and monolithic—set of cultural values which firmly deny the legitimacy of all other modes of speech. Society in these terms appears as unidimensional rather than pluralistic, monolithic in its aims and ideals and its images of culture and cohesiveness. Dismissing as 'ignorance' those forms of speech which reveal other (non-elite) forms of identity, such assumptions adhere to a doctrine of change through hegemony which 'presupposes that the prestige forms will be recognised as such and thus desired by the group that does not yet have them' (Crowley 1996: 179). As a still variable modern English (particularly in its spoken forms) nevertheless suggests, notions that a standard would eliminate 'odious distinction' in the populace by means of an 'equal' speech for all were doomed to remain unrealized—not least since these particular constructions of socio-linguistic utopia—and indeed 'equality' *per se*—have, in effect, some distinctly dystopian aspects. What for one person is 'talking proper' will, for another, be 'talking posh', denying aspects of identity and social cohesion fundamental to other, but equally legitimate, constructions of self. Interpreting allegiance to different socio-linguistic markers in terms of uniform 'failure' is similarly problematic, as a number of educational studies have stressed (see, for example, Trudgill 1975).

The fact that such proscriptive assessments (and attendant images of 'failure') have, in the history of standard English, commonly also extended to Scottish and Irish speakers (as well as to those who adhered to linguistic signals of still wider ethnic origins) is, in this, perhaps especially telling. Prescriptive assertions of the symbolic—and national—significance of one 'standard' for all, for instance, often presented adherence to these language varieties as equally deleterious to constructions of 'proper' culture. 'By Provincials is meant all British subjects, whether inhabitants of Scotland, Ireland, Wales, the several counties of England, or the city of London, who speak a corrupt dialect of the English tongue,' stated Sheridan (1762: 2), setting out explicit recommendations for the remedy of such 'corruption'. His contemporary Sylvester Douglas writes eloquently of the damaging effects of a Scottish accent in an era increasingly sensitized to the culturally laden forms of 'standard' English speech: 'there are, I believe, few natives of North-Britain . . . that have not learned by experience the disadvantages which accompany their idiom and pronunciation' (1991: 99). Other writers reflect a similar position. The Scot James Buchanan writes his *British Grammar* (1762) to disseminate the 'best English' to the 'Schools of Great Britain and Ireland'; his *Linguae Britannicae vera Pronunciatio* (1757) is illuminatingly glossed as 'a New *English* Dictionary' on the title page. Elphinston's *Propriety Ascertained in her Picture* (1786: i. 6) locates 'propriety' only in 'the language ov London', devoting the second volume to 'systematizing Scotticisms, and evvery deviation from Inglish purity'. Smart (1836: p. xl) offers parallel proscriptions in a section dealing with 'Vulgar and Rustic, Provincial and Foreign Habits', urging speakers to combat 'deficiencies . . . grating on polite ears'. Though Sheridan was himself Irish, while Buchanan and Beattie, Douglas and Elphinston, were Scots, it is these who (among many others) affirm the ideology of 'standard' and 'non-standard' in these contexts too, delineating, as Elphinston notes, the binarisms of 'Inglish Truith' against the 'false' forms of Scottish and Irish, and making the cultural hegemony of a standard particularly explicit in the process. That such binary articulations of 'right' and 'wrong', 'standard' and 'other', are not limited to the past is moreover illuminatingly revealed in twentieth-century attitudes to Black English Vernacular (BEV), not least in its frequent stigmatization as a non-language redolent of cognitive deficiency in educational contexts (see Labov 1972; Whiteman 1980).

As recent socio-linguistic work on BEV has confirmed, language is, in reality, a social symbol of significantly greater complexity than is suggested in accounts of language which endorse a standard at the expense of all other forms of speech. Precisely aligned with speaker variables such as age, class, gender, and ethnicity, its variations reveal much more than the popular binary schema of 'cultivation' and 'ignorance', 'refinement' and 'vulgarity'. Instead, language as socio-cultural symbol is itself pluralist, imaging forth notions of belonging and birth which can run counter to the stated 'standard', but which are nonetheless equally significant in cultural terms. The socio-linguistic research of Peter Trudgill in Norwich (1974; 1983: 169–85) provides a case in point. Investigating the usage of stated 'prestige' variables such as the use of [ɪŋ] in words such as *walking* [wɔːkɪŋ], his findings clearly reveal that although 'dropping the g' (*walkin'*) may indeed act as shibboleth in popular cultural constructions of 'educated' usage, it is nevertheless the *absence* rather than the presence of [ɪŋ] which, for a considerable number of speakers, continues to constitute the preferred form. In fact, in . subjective reaction tests where speakers are asked to identify the forms of speech they *think* they use (in contradistinction to empirical evidence on which forms are actually used), men in Trudgill's study tended to indicate that their use of [ɪn] was lower (and hence their use of 'non-standard' forms such as 'walkin' higher) than, in reality, they could be proved to be. It was not that articulating words such as *walking* as [wɔːkɪŋ] was not recognized as prestigious, but more that other vernacular, and covert, forms of prestige were, in this instance and in others, given precedence in the role of language as social symbol, signifying aspects of local cohesion and vernacular culture which, in the traditional paradigms of standardization, are habitually ignored. It is, of course, factors such as these, here given additional credence through empirical investigation, which clarify the failure of the doctrine of change though hegemony.

Features of language use such as those explored in Trudgill's research are of course by no means rare. They do, however, serve to reveal the politicization which can lie at the heart of notions of a standard speech for all in the history of English. 'No one set of cultural practices is inherently superior,' notes Carter (1995: 32), and the same is true of language, in spite of the socio-cultural manipulations regularly practised in its name, endorsing notions of 'language' and 'non-language', norm and deviation, in a rhetoric of standardization which empowers some and disempowers others in conventional constructions of its use. In reality, as already indicated, even the 'standard' is far more variable than is habitually assumed, subject to flux and change, its features often remote (even in its written forms) from the fictive proprieties deemed to characterize its 'best' usage. Though spelling may indeed have stabilized to a greater degree, certain features popularly stigmatized as 'non-standard' remain prominent, even in 'proper' English. Split infinitives occur naturally and unexceptionably; similarly, constructions such as *the book whose pages I tore* with *whose* plus inanimate antecedent are, as Joseph (1987) confirms, on the increase. In the realities of standard English in use, prescriptive proprieties of *who* and *whom* can likewise be conspicuous by their absence except in contexts of marked formality, even if more traditionally inclined writers such as John Honey would, as a result, like to see 'explicit teaching' on this and other points where 'correctness' appears to be on the decline (1997: 133).

'Proper English', in both spoken and written forms, thus remains a prominent social and cultural construct, departures from its use still regularly construed in ways which map intralinguistic onto extralinguistic, linguistic stereotypes onto socio-cultural ones, regardless of the flaws which such stereotyping may hold. The cultural fictions which surround popular notions of a standard, in spite of its somewhat more complex linguistic reality, hence remain healthy. Candidates scoring the highest grades in the GCSE English exams of 1993 were, for instance, censured for their evident 'uneducatedness' if they dropped their [h]s, suggesting that the subjective import of certain linguistic variables could, on occasion, still (disturbingly) be capable of transcending objective assessments of achievement. Similarly Lord Tebbit's outburst on linguistic degeneration in 1985 (cited in Carter 1995: 149) reveals a ready (and symbolic) equation with other, seemingly inseparable, forms of decline:

we've allowed so many standards to slip . . . teachers weren't bothering to teach kids how to spell and punctuate properly . . . if you allow standards to slip to the stage where good English is no better than bad English . . . all those things cause people to have no standards at all, and once you lose standards there's no imperative to stay out of crime.

Standards in linguistic terms are, it seems, seldom recognized for what they are. Or as Colin McCabe (1990: 7) has rightly averred: 'complaints about standards are rarely just that. In the case of English they are never just that.'

Further Reading

Crowley, T. (1989), *The Politics of Discourse: The Standard Language Question in British Cultural Debate*, London: Macmillan. An extremely valuable analysis of notions of standardization and associated socio-cultural premisses.

Joseph, J. E. (1987), *Eloquence and Power: The Rise of Language Standards and Standard Languages*, New York: Blackwell. A useful and well-researched study of the theory and practice of standard languages and varieties.

Honey, J. (1997), *Language is Power: The Story of Standard English and its Enemies*, London: Faber & Faber. A controversial and spirited attack on liberal educational and linguistic policies on English in education and elsewhere.

Milroy, J., and **Milroy, L.** (1991), *Authority in Language: Investigating Language Prescription and Standardization*, London: Routledge. A detailed account of prescriptive notions of correctness in prevalent assumptions about standard English and its teaching.

Mugglestone, L. (1997), *Talking Proper: The Rise of Accent as Social Symbol*, Oxford: Clarendon Press. An examination of shifting language attitudes towards pronunciation in England, particularly concerning correlations with culture, class, gender, and education.

References

Beattie, J. (1788), *The Theory of Language*, London: W. Strahan, T. Cadell, & W. Creech.

Buchanan, J. (1757), *Linguae Britannicae vera Pronunciatio*, London: A. Millar.

—— (1762), *The British Grammar*, London: A. Millar.

Campbell, G. (1766), *The Philosophy of Rhetoric*, 2 vols., London: W. Strahan & T. Cadell.

Carter, R. (1995), *Keywords in Language and Literacy*, London: Routledge.

Crowley, T. (1996), *Language in History: Theories and Texts*, London: Routledge.

Douglas, S. (1991), *A Treatise on the Provincial Dialect of Scotland*, ed. C. Jones, Edinburgh: Edinburgh University Press (1st pub. 1799).

Elphinston, J. (1786), *Propriety Ascertained in her Picture*, 2 vols., London: Jon Walter.

Enfield, W. (1809), *A Familiar Treatise on Rhetoric*, London: B. Crosby.

Gill, J. (1857), *Introductory Text-Book to School Education, Method and Management*, London: Longman, Green, Longman, Roberts, & Green.

Hart, J. (1570), *A Methode or Comfortable Beginning for all Vnlearned*, London: Henrie Dobson.

Honey, J. (1997), *Language is Power: The Story of Standard English and its Enemies*, London: Faber & Faber.

Johnson, S. (1755), *A Dictionary of the English Language*, London: W. Strahan.

Joseph, J. E. (1987), *Eloquence and Power: The Rise of Language Standards and Standard Languages*, New York: Blackwell.

Labov, W. (1972), *Language in the Inner City: Studies in the Black English Vernacular*, Philadelphia: University of Pennsylvania Press.

McCabe, C. (1990), 'Language, Literature, Identity: Reflections on the Cox Report', *Critical Quarterly*, 32.

Mugglestone, L. (1997), *Talking Proper: The Rise of Accent as Social Symbol*, Oxford: Clarendon Press.

Newbolt Report (1921), *The Teaching of English in England: Being the Report of a Departmental Committee Appointed by the President of the Board of Education to Enquire into the Position of English in the Educational System of England*, London: HMSO.

Newman, F. W. (1869), *Orthoëpy: Or, a Simple Mode of Accenting English*, London: Trübner & Co.

Phyfe, W. (1885), *How Should I Pronounce? Or the Art of Correct Pronunciation*, London: G. P. Puttnam's Sons.

Puttenham, G. (1589), *The Arte of English Poesie*, London: Richard Field.

Sheridan, T. (1762), *A Course of Lectures on Elocution*, London: W. Strahan.

—— (1780), *A General Dictionary of the English Language*, London: W. Strahan.

Smart, B. H. (1836), *Walker Remodelled: A New Critical Pronouncing Dictionary*, London: T. Cadell.

Sweet, H. (1877), *A Primer of Phonetics*, Oxford: Clarendon Press.

Trudgill, P. (1974), *The Social Differentiation of English in Norwich*, Cambridge: Cambridge University Press.

—— (1975), *Accent, Dialect and the School*, London: Edward Arnold.

—— (1983), *On Dialect: Social and Geographical Perspectives*, Oxford: Basil Blackwell.

Whiteman, M. F. (ed.) (1980) *Reactions to Ann Arbor: Vernacular Black English and Education*, Arlington, Va.: Center for Applied Linguistics.

12

Religious Culture in Contemporary Britain

STEVE BRUCE

Introduction

In November 1996, the sale of a church property in Reading completed a fascinating chain. The Oxford Road congregation of Methodists, who were uniting with the West Reading congregation, held their last service before selling their Victorian church to the Church of God Worldwide Mission Pentecostal Church, which previously met round the corner in Waylen Street. The Pentecostal premises were sold to the Bangladeshi Association for use as a community centre (*Reading Weekend Post*, 22 Nov. 1996). In that one property deal one has three of the main features of the religious life of modern Britain: the decline of the Protestant denominations which had dominated the nineteenth century, the rise of loosely federated Pentecostal churches (recruiting primarily from black communities), and the establishment of non-Christian institutions.

The Decline of Traditional Christianity

This century had seen a steady decline in the popularity and importance of the Christian churches. In 1900, just over a quarter of Britons were church members; now it is about 10 per cent. The national census of church attendance conducted in 1851 showed at least a third of the population went to church; now 14 per cent of

Scots, 12 per cent of the Welsh, and 9 per cent of the English attend church (Bruce 1996a). The decline of the churches can be more dramatically illustrated from the number of professionals they employ. Between 1900 and 1984, the number of Church of England clergy was halved. At the start of the century there were 3,600 ministers in the various Presbyterian churches in Scotland. In 1990 there were only 1,500. Although new institutional expressions of Christianity have been created (notably in the independent congregations often called 'house churches') these come nowhere near to compensating for the losses sustained by the major organizations.

As they have declined, the national British churches have changed. In the Middle Ages, religion was not a matter for individuals but for the whole country. A single Church, drawing its income mainly from the ownership of land, performed religious services on behalf of the entire nation. Through its network of parish churches, the state Church dominated every aspect of social life. Babies were christened, children were baptized, young couples were married, and the dead were buried. The calendar of the Church mirrored the agricultural seasons. Although most people were not what we would now describe as enthusiastic Christians, well versed in the details of the faith, they participated in the Church's religious glossing of their lives and were sufficiently convinced of the existence of heaven and hell, and of the Church's power over which of those would be their destination, to accept the basically Christian contours which the Church imposed on their lives.

What distinguishes the United Kingdom from most modern European states is its multinational character. Instead of one state church, at times in its recent history it has had four. The Church of Scotland was Presbyterian while the Church of England (which was at times also the Church of Ireland and the Church in Wales) was Episcopalian. Most people attended those state churches but there were minorities outside the religious establishment. There were Roman Catholics, who continued in the faith that had been displaced when Britain became Protestant. In Ireland, they were the majority; in England, Wales, and Scotland, a small minority. There were also increasingly large numbers of Protestants who rejected the state churches in favour of more radical Protestant sects. These later grew into the great Nonconformist denominations that, in their evangelical theology and in styles of worship, gave the dominant tone to the Victorian era. Religious affiliation became one dimension of division within the United Kingdom. Against the English centre, Scots (and Ulster people of Scots descent) asserted their

Presbyterianism, the Irish their Catholicism, the Welsh their Methodism.

For all that British Christians were divided into competing organizations, the shared evangelicalism that pervaded most of them in the last half of the nineteenth century created a common religious culture that was an important part of the British identity. That culture was earnest and serious. It promoted temperance and self-reliance. It was democratic. It proliferated voluntary associations for 'good works' which became the model for the trade union movement, for workers' insurance associations, and for educational institutes. Churches proliferated adjuncts such as choral societies, brass bands, youth groups, and sporting associations. Evangelical self-confidence was one of the engines of the great British imperial project. Not just the missionaries but many of the soldiers, engineers, traders, planters, teachers, doctors, and administrators who went out to the colonies were driven by the belief that they had a mission to civilize, educate, convert, and moralize the world.

The decline of the British Empire coincided with the decline of the British churches and a gradual turning to the national religions for a source of social identity. In the nineteenth century, the reality of the minority status of the Episcopalian churches of Ireland and Wales was recognized and they were 'disestablished'. Although Britain still has state churches in Scotland and England, the real value of legal establishment has gone. Although it retains some nominal influence, Parliament gradually gave up its control of church business. The land taxes which had funded the churches were capitalized and the funds given to the churches to manage. As membership has declined the Church of England and the Church of Scotland have had to come to terms with no longer representing the people but being just voluntary associations for the small numbers of people who wish to be associated with them.

This has produced a curious situation. Many people who are not active supporters of the national churches still feel that they have a right to their offices for baptisms, weddings, and funerals. Although the number using religion for these rites of passage has declined, it remains higher than church membership or attendance: a fact that many of the clergy resent. Even more deeply resented is the desire of many non-churchgoers to have the churches fixed in amber. It is ironic that schemes designed to adapt the national churches to their new reduced circumstances are often most bitterly opposed by those whose absence from the churches has created the straitened circumstances. The English have a nostalgic attachment to their great cathedrals and expect to be able to hear choirs singing Latin masses at Christmas but complain when cathedrals introduce charges to fund their enormous maintenance costs and maintain their choir schools. They have a nostalgic attachment to a Constablesque vision of Anglo-Saxon church towers rising up from fields of corn and mourn the closure of parish churches which they never attend. Though similarly distant from the strong personal attachment to their religion which characterized their grandparents, the Scots and Welsh (especially in contexts of arguments with the English and in particular the Westminster government) remain fond of asserting their radical Protestant traditions as proof of ethnic superiority.

Notwithstanding their evolution from state churches to denominations, the Churches of England and Scotland are still expected periodically to represent the conscience of their nations. They provide ceremonial salad dressing for such occasions as the state opening of Parliament and coronations. They are also regularly called upon by political leaders (and, bizarrely, by editors of prurient tabloid newspapers) to provide a lead on matters of morality. Frequently, conservative commentators and politicians follow some observation about rising crime, the decline in the popularity of marriage, the increase in the rate of illegitimate births, and other supposed indices of moral and social decline by asserting that the churches have failed to give a moral lead. To their credit church leaders have usually refused to play their allotted role. While they have often repeated basic Christian principles, they have also questioned both their right to tell non-Christians what to do and the likely effect of them so doing.

Religion and Ethnicity

The above picture of decline and nostalgia needs to be qualified with a number of important cases of religious identity and culture remaining important because it continues to serve a variety of important social functions. The 1989 census of church attendance which showed the English norm to be around 10 per cent also showed that 17 per cent of Afro-Caribbeans attended church. Where the typical churchgoer tends to be elderly and female, the 'black' British who regularly worshipped were much more representative of the black community at large. A recent study of ethnic minorities asked people to respond to the proposition 'Religion is very important to how I live my life.' The percentages who agreed were as follows: Chinese—11 per cent; white—13; Caribbean—34;

African Asian—43; Indian—47; Pakistani—73; and Bangladeshi—76 per cent (Modood 1997).

Ken Pryce's *Endless Pressure* offers an excellent description of life among one group of black Pentecostalists in Bristol which makes clear the appeals of a radically puritanical evangelical Protestantism for an ethnic minority population which still struggles against deprivation and discrimination. 'If one cannot accept society or be aggressive towards it with a view to reforming it, then one can devalue the significance of this world by withdrawing from it in a community of like-minded individuals and projecting one's hopes into a supernatural and other-worldly Kingdom' (Pryce 1979: 221). But Pentecostalism does more than provide the promise of supernatural rewards to compensate for the lack of reward in this life. It also offers an ethical code and a character which assist survival and social mobility. The 'saints' do not drink, smoke, take drugs, or gamble. They do not dress in flash clothes or drive extravagant cars. Sexual relations are only permitted in the context of traditional marriage. As an alternative to the drugs and dance hall culture that is popular with young black men, such puritanism is highly adaptive. So too is the character which Pentecostalism promotes. Saints are supposed to be temperate, diligent, loyal, hard-working, and cheerful. Although the religion stresses individual responsibility for one's destination in the next life and one's fortunes in this, the individuals form a tight-knit and strongly supportive community.

The role of religion in maintaining community is also central to the life of the ethnic minorities from the Indian subcontinent. However, there are structural constraints that prevent such an influence providing a model for a reinvigoration of British religious life generally. The social mores of the minority communities that provide almost all of Britain's Muslims, Sikhs, Buddhists, and Hindus are such that traditional practice isolates the believers from the wider society. For example, attitudes to gender roles tend to keep those women who remain orthodox in their religion separate from the wider society. The cultural distance between these newly imported minority religions and a largely secular but still vaguely Protestant society is such that the preservation of the former from the evils of the latter has been achieved by the erection of considerable social barriers.

The other great exception to the picture of a largely secular society is Northern Ireland. Though both have declined in the last two decades, church membership and church attendance are still far more common in Northern Ireland than in the rest of the UK. The Northern Ireland conflict is not about religion. It is a struggle for

political power of two ethnic groups with incompatible constitutional aspirations. Most Catholic nationalists in Ulster wish to
break the links with Great Britain and complete the project of Irish
nationalism with the reunification of the entire country as a sovereign independent Irish republic. Most non-Catholics (and some
Catholics) wish to remain part of the United Kingdom. However,
though the conflict is not about religion, religion plays a fundamental part. It identifies the two contending groups, it figures
prominently in their histories, and it is frequently used by each side
to justify positive self-images and negative views of the other.
Although Catholic and Protestant church leaders have worked hard
to distinguish their religious values from the political agendas
of their respective peoples and have frequently denounced the
violence of political extremists, Catholic priests and Protestant
clergymen still endorse the political programmes of their people
and the second largest unionist party—Ian Paisley's Democratic
Unionists—draws much of its strength and support from its close
ties with evangelical Protestantism (Bruce 1988).

This survival of a close link between religion, ethnic identity, and
political conflict has an ironic consequence. It is read by the rest of
the United Kingdom as an example of what happens when people
take religion too seriously. We have handled religious diversity (and
cultural diversity more generally) by drawing a clear distinction
between the public and the private. We permit people great liberty
to entertain whatever culture they wish in their private lives but
heavily constrain the exercise of religiously inspired values in the
public arena. To go back to the debate about declining moral standards, what we wish to encourage in public life are only the most
general ethical consequences of a conservative religion, not the
religion itself. This creates a problem dealing with any religious
group which insists that life cannot be so compartmentalized and
that its religious culture must affect every aspect of life. Thus we
place gender equality before any religious culture which wishes to
maintain clearly distinguished gender roles outside the narrow confines of the home. We place free speech above religious injunctions
against blasphemy. Although any well-informed discussion of Islam
would recognize that the radical fundamentalism found in Iran is
not typical even of conservative forms of Muslim religion, the general perception is that any religio-ethnic group which does not
confine its religion to the domestic hearth and the leisure sphere is
dangerous. Similarly any group which reminds us of the historically
undeniable link between evangelical Protestantism and British identity (especially if it insists that Protestantism is still a source of

superior social mores) is dismissed as threatening to bring Ulster's problems to the streets of Great Britain.

Social Influence of Religious Ideas

The Catholic countries of France, Spain, Portugal, and Italy divided over religion. A powerful single church generated an equally powerful consciously anticlerical opposition. It is no accident that those countries are also the ones which this century have produced the most powerful communist parties. The religious diversity of the United Kingdom meant that those who opposed the close ties between the established churches and the ruling class could produce sects and denominations better suited to their own interests and to their vision of the world. Radicals and reformers might oppose the particular privileges of the state churches without becoming alienated from religion itself. Hence secularization in Britain has taken the form, not of strong and principled opposition to the churches or to religion in general, but of indifference. A religious society has been replaced not by a self-consciously secular one but by a society which pays occasional lip-service to Christianity and by a culture in which people still claim attachment to religious ideas and beliefs.

Social surveys repeatedly show that the number of people who describe themselves as religious or claim to believe in God is vastly greater than the numbers who take part in any shared activity derived from, or intended to maintain and spread, such beliefs. However, such surveys also show that such beliefs are becoming increasing amorphous and increasingly distant from the orthodox Christian faith which once informed them. For example, among those who do not go to church but who claim to believe in God, the formulation 'higher power' has overtaken the more traditional image of God as a person. Though many people believe that there is something after death, the Christian notions of heaven and hell have been replaced by some idea of reincarnation (Gill et al. 1998).

What we are seeing here is the gradual expenditure of cultural capital. The Christian churches had an enormous impact on every aspect of our culture. At the very least, Protestant Christianity provided a basic vocabulary. Phrases from the Tyndale translation of the Bible, the Book of Common Prayer, the Shorter Catechism, and the great Victorian hymns became firmly embedded in our language: 'Rock of ages', 'abide with me', 'dust to dust, ashes to ashes'. The words of 'Jerusalem' still resonate. But because it is not reinforced by contemporary religious commitment, that cultural heritage is a wasting asset. Most people now in their fifties went to Sunday School, attended church (if irregularly) as children, took part in specifically Christian acts of school worship, and were familiar with the common Protestant hymns. I now teach university students (still drawn largely from that class which has the greatest involvement with organized religion) who have little or no knowledge of Christianity.

Socio-Moral Crusades

In the countries of the former Soviet Union or Yugoslavia, indeed in most parts of the world, religion is intimately bound up with ethnic or national identity. I have suggested that, nostalgic attachment apart, this remains so in Britain only for recently migrant ethnic minorities and for the people of Northern Ireland. The United States provides a model of a very different sort of link between religion and public life: religion as a source of contentious socio-moral values.

The Christian Right in America is a powerful movement which has not succeeded in imposing what televangelist and founder of the Moral Majority Jerry Falwell called 'our shared Judeo-Christian values' on the public life of the United States, but it has provided a powerful challenge to pro-abortion legislation, to the movement for gay and women's rights, to textbooks which teach evolutionary models of the origins of species, and to attempts to enforce a rigorous secularism on public institutions such as schools and colleges. Attempts by conservative Christians in Britain to promote similar socio-moral crusades have utterly failed. Even abortion has not raised political temperatures. In the United States, anti-abortion campaigners have been able to drive abortion clinics out of business with sustained picketing and medical staff involved in abortions have been murdered. Such protests are almost unknown in Britain. In the 1997 general election, the Pro-Life Party fielded the more than fifty candidates necessary to win entitlement to party political broadcasts. Despite considerable publicity, the pro-lifers won on average just 0.64 per cent of the vote in the English seats they contested and 1.5 per cent of the vote in the nine Scottish seats they fought. The better result in Scotland is almost certainly a consequence of targeting constituencies with large numbers of Catholics, but even that figure left the party very firmly in the world of the Monster Raving Loony Party, esoteric varieties of Marxism, and anti-road-building protesters. Indeed in some English seats the Monster Raving Loony Party polled better than the Pro-Life Party.

Cultural Bricolage

The greatest innovation in modern religious culture has been the growth of interest in what Paul Heelas (1996) calls 'self-religions'. The new religious movements of the late 1960s can be divided into two camps. Movements such as Hare Krishna, the Divine Light Mission, and the Moonies, although novel to the West, were quite traditional in the sense of being 'world-rejecting'. They were puritanical in their morals and encouraged people to distance themselves from this world in preparation for the next. But there were also movements such as Scientology and Transcendental Meditation (or TM) which were largely concerned with making people more effective in this world. Although it had its origins in Hindu mysticism, TM advertises itself in this country as a technique 'which relaxes, revitalises and recharges your energy to get more out of life. It leaves you feeling positive, alert and clear with the calmness and inner commitment to tackle life with enthusiasm. . . . A simple technique to develop your true potential. It requires no belief or change in lifestyle' (advertisement in the *Herald*, 17 February 1995).

A number of tendencies have combined to form a milieu of 'New Age' religion. The decline of traditional cultures has encouraged a narcissistic individualism which places the 'self' at the centre of our concerns. Increasing cultural diversity has led to a general relativism, not just in matters of taste or morals but even in matters of fact. We no longer expect there to be one single authoritative truth; instead there is what works for you and what works for me. Many of what were originally secular psychotherapies have become increasingly spiritual. Many eastern religions have been borrowed and turned into personal therapies for self-improvement and self-actualization.

Although there is enormous diversity in New Age religion, there are shared characteristics. At the centre lies the idea that 'God' is no longer an external authority but is to be found within us all. Spirituality is no longer found through subordinating oneself to some external authority and serving him but by getting in touch with your true feelings, your inner self, the still voice within, and the like.

Although most of the particular organizations that promote New Age beliefs and therapies would like to attract adherents, followers, and members, most New Agers defy these expectations and instead construct their own packages by sampling a wide range of alternatives. Knowledge of the future might be sought through the use of Tarot cards and astrological readings. Mastery over the present might be sought through witchcraft rituals. Greater self-understanding might be acquired by attending est, Scientology, or Insight courses. The seeker after physical improvement might dabble with Bachian flower remedies, Shiatsu massage, crystal therapy, and iridology. Greater spiritual enlightenment might be sought by reading books of wisdom 'channelled' from the spirits of long-dead spiritual masters. The operating principles of this milieu are eclecticism and narcissism.

Although New Age spirituality is popular, its overall social impact is limited. First it is limited in, and hence by, its appeal: those attracted are almost all university-educated middle classes working in the caring professions and the arts. Second it is limited by the very nature of the change it promotes. Often New Age beliefs and therapies do no more than offer people a new vocabulary for talking about themselves and allow them to feel better about their circumstances. To an outsider they often seem more about coming to terms with one's life and world than about changing either. Indeed, as the TM advert says: 'no change of belief or lifestyle is required.' A banker who becomes a Scientologist or who is trained in est does not cease to be a banker or even become a different kind of banker; he just becomes a better-adjusted and more efficient banker. Even in personal life, there seems little positive change. The enlightened leaders of the Findhorn Community (the oldest and most popular of western European New Age centres) seem no better at ordering their personal lives and social relations than the rest of us (Bruce 1998).

Third, New Age spirituality is constrained by the relativism which lies at its heart. Victorian evangelicals could claim a mandate to convert the world to their beliefs and, along the way, to change the world into a more humane and Christian place. Religion that places the final authority within each person allows no mandate for arguing, for conversion, or for reordering the world.

In summary, what is most significant about the New Age is not its departure from the prevailing ideas and ethos of the surrounding culture. Though it presents itself as 'alternative' and counter-cultural, it actually exemplifies the prevailing ideas of our age: it is profoundly individualistic, inward-looking, privatized, and consumerist.

Conclusion

Protestantism was once a central part of British culture and British identity. Particularly in the Victorian era, a generalized evangelicalism was profoundly influential in both the specific sense that it inspired social and political changes (such as the ending of child labour and slavery) and in the general sense that it provided a bank of values and a sense of social superiority. Religion also informed the identities of the constituent parts of the British Isles. On those occasions when the Welsh, the Scots, or the Irish concentrated on what distinguished them from the English, their distinctive variants of Christianity were a vital resource. Though the decline of Empire has opened the way for the break-up of Britain into its constituent parts, religion has played very little part in recent reassertions of regional autonomy. In arguing for devolution the Scots and the Welsh have accompanied the case for greater democratic accountability and greater efficiency by vague assertions of cultural difference but religious affiliation has played little part in those cultural differences, for the simple reason that, Northern Ireland apart, the United Kingdom is now a very largely secular society.

For many of us, orthodox religion is now associated with problems. Religion is the violent politics of Northern Ireland, arguments about the rights of ethnic minorities, and death threats against authors who offend Iranian mullahs. In news reports from distant places, ethnic religion is what inspires Bosnian Serbs, Croats, and Muslims to slaughter each other. Voluntary association religion (if taken too seriously) leads to doctors being murdered by anti-abortionists. All of this reinforces the British preference for religion to be confined to the private hearth and not taken too seriously.

Further Reading

Bruce, Steve (1995), *Religion in Modern Britain*, Oxford: Oxford University Press.

Davie, Grace (1994), *Religion in Britain since 1945: Believing without Belonging*, Oxford: Blackwell.

Heelas, Paul (1996), *The New Age Movement*, Oxford: Blackwell.

References

Bruce, Steve (1988), *God Save Ulster: The Religion and Politics of Paisleyism*, Oxford: Oxford University Press.

Bruce, Steve (1996a), 'Religion in Britain at the Close of the 20th Century: A Challenge to the Silver Lining Perspective', *Journal of Contemporary Religion*, 11.

—— (1996b), *Religion in the Modern World*, Oxford: Oxford University Press.

—— (1998), 'New Age Authenticity and Social Roles: Good Intentions and Bad Sociology', *Journal of Contemporary Religion*, 13.

Gill, Robin, Hadaway, C. Kirk, and Marler, Penny Long (1998), 'Is Religious Belief Declining in Britain?', *Journal for the Scientific Study of Religion*, 37.

Heelas, Paul (1996), *The New Age Movement*, Oxford: Basil Blackwell.

Modood, Tariq (1997), *Ethnic Minorities in Britain: Diversity and Disadvantage*, London: Policy Studies Institute.

Pryce, Ken (1979), *Endless Pressure*, Harmondsworth: Penguin.

The Mediated Monarchy

DAVID CHANEY

Introduction

IT is easy to be surprised by the continued existence and indeed the popularity of the royal family. It seems an anachronistic institution in the politics of mass society. While it is clear that in the early modern period the role of the monarchy as a focus for the central-ization of state power in the transition from feudalism was vitally important, with the development of the democratic institutions of bourgeois public life the monarchy should have been irredeemably tainted with the now illegitimate privileges of caste society. Thus indeed in many European countries the forcible overthrow of a social structure focused on monarchical rule was seen to be an essential step in the struggle for modernization and the mobiliza-tion of popular enthusiasm for national citizenship. And yet in Britain the royal family has survived the twentieth century and in doing so seemingly survived transitions within the representations of status in democratic politics. It has certainly remained at the heart of national political institutions, and it has clearly become a staple of popular cultural entertainment. Indeed royal narratives have come to constitute one of the more significant televisual genres.

At the time of writing the ways in which the royal family as an institution combines authority and legitimacy are no longer self-evidently successful. This is not to say that there is a strong republican current in contemporary Britain, but that in becoming celebrities (and, unwillingly, spawning Diana, a global figure who has become one of the great mythological icons of the twentieth century (Richards et al. 1999)), the members of the family have been adapting to the demands of a new cultural environment less successfully than in the previous transitions they have managed before. In this chapter I shall discuss some aspects of how and why the British royals have shifted from symbolizing feudal privilege to become international celebrities. The story is relevant to a collection of British cultural studies both because it illustrates the importance of representations of tradition in constituting contemporary social identity, and because it illuminates important distinctions between status and power in the cultural politics of late modernity.

Although the focus of my chapter will be on imperfect adaptation by the British royal family in the later twentieth century, I will not follow one interpretation of the significance of this story. This is that the royals, lying at the heart of a network of hereditary privilege which includes the parliamentary second chamber as well as the disproportionate power of the landowning classes, symbolize a curious deformation of modernization in British history: what has been called the incomplete or unfinished character of the bourgeois revolution in Britain (Nairn 1988). While I am sympathetic to the need for a broader account of the continued salience of hereditary privilege in the changing formations of British social structure, in the space available I shall concentrate on the modes of adaptation by the royal family to the public culture of democratic politics. The royal family has come to constitute a cultural form that in the British context has interestingly struggled more or less successfully with the dynamics of symbolic prestige.

The British royal family are unusual celebrities in that their fame is displayed in the performance of public duties, ritual occasions, that occasionally become international 'media events' (Dayan and Katz 1992), as well as news about personal lives. In both aspects it seems that they have been genuinely popular with the mass audiences of global, not just British, media. By genuinely popular I mean: that people are interested in reading or watching stories about their doings; that within the cast of what has been called the only soap opera to be, however loosely, based in reality there are heroes and villains whose popular identity is continuously evolving; and that the narratives of family dynamics are taken to be, with all the qualifications I shall subsequently introduce, relevant to everyday conceptions of both personal and more importantly collective social identity. The plethora of stories about the British royals as news, magazine features, and television programmes, etc., is not just about them as a collection of individuals but is also a sort of mirror in which competing versions of Britishness as well as everyday gendered and family identities are overlappingly articulated. It is in these dynamics of identity by performers and audiences that the real interest in the British royals lies.

The Invention of Tradition

When investigating the transformation of institutional symbolism in modernization it is necessary to see change as a process developing through time. The first step here is to recognize that change has to be made sense of by social actors while it is happening. It is in this respect that the concept of the invention of tradition has proved particularly useful (Hobsbawm and Ranger 1983). In their introduction to the collection of essays under this title Hobsbawm and Ranger argue that it is as a response to the constant change and innovation of modernity that actors have sought to frame change in the forms and rituals of tradition. It seems that the changes generating new institutions, such as mass education or the politics of mass democracy, could be effectively legitimized through being given a factitious historical cast; that is, through inventing traditions to give order, cohesion, and legitimacy to new social practices. These traditions dramatize and formalize through ceremonial repetition the necessarily vague and abstract values and identities of new sorts of imagined communities. They thus give the appearance of tangible form to the idea of a collective memory, and thereby reassuringly locate novelty in a social continuity that transcends the limitations of personal experience.

Although in this original form the concept of the invention of tradition was seen as primarily a functional response to change and, relatedly, seen as being particularly salient to the period of establishment of modernization it does not have to be restricted in these ways. It can rather be seen as a more general feature of the simulations of modernity working to dramatize institutional identity (Chaney 1993), and to provide a mythological terrain on which new cultural identities can be enacted (for a description of some instances of a quest for authenticity amongst suburban residents as distinctive ways of inventing cultural traditions, see Chaney 1997). The notion of tradition can therefore be used very loosely but it is also clearly relevant to an institution such as the monarchy in Britain which claims an unbroken link to antiquity (traditions can also of course be invented for such monarchical innovations and short-lived dynasties as the shahs of Persia). In the British case the fact that there has been a monarch occupying the throne for the great majority of the last thousand years, and they have been, however loosely, related by some sort of family tie to each other is not in doubt. This does not mean, however, that the rituals and public ceremonials of the royal family have remained unchanged during this period; indeed it can be argued that the traditions of monarchical performance have been substantially invented and reinvented during the modern era.

One of the contributions to the collection edited by Hobsbawm and Ranger is such a study of the changing cultural form of the monarchy. Cannadine suggests that the history of the British monarchy since 1820 should be divided into four phases. In the first, roughly 1820–75, the monarch was head of a social elite rather than the nation and the rituals of royalty were the defensive displays of a beleaguered class. In the second, 1877–1918, the nationalistic displays of a monarch designed to transcend social conflict and symbolize integration while lacking any real power began to be invented. In the third phase, 1918–53, this basis of ceremonial nationalism was built upon and consolidated using the full weight of the new mass media of press and radio to impress working-class audiences and symbolize a triumphant imperialism vis-à-vis other European powers. In the final phase, from the coronation of Elizabeth II to the present day, the invented traditions of a symbolic monarchy were combined with the intimate address that television has increasingly made possible to transform the monarchy into media celebrities.

Cannadine has given us a framework within which we can begin to see how and why an emphasis upon monarchical tradition facilitated change, how it 'was not so much despite, as because of, the continuity in style and circumstance, that the "meaning," of royal ritual altered once more' (1983: 150). In the emphasis upon meanings of rituals we are explicitly being asked to treat the monarchy as a cultural performance, that is an imaginative articulation, through in this case spectacular performances (and an increasingly pervasive intertextual public commentary) of symbolic identity. While Cannadine is correct to emphasize the significance of changing media of performance he does assume that the transition to televisual status makes all performers celebrities in an equivalently unproblematic way. The monarch's subjects, initially at least the British people, have gradually become an audience rather than the awestruck onlookers of a traditional crowd. The combination of selected items from a repertoire of historical imagery allied with a formalization of address and shows of deference might all suggest that the basis of monarchical privilege essentially persists but in order to grasp change we need to be more sensitive to the dynamics of spectacular dramatization (on changing meanings of spectacle see Chaney 1993: ch. 2).

The Show of Majesty

In the nature of things the monarchy symbolizes awesome power and monarchs are frequently treated as being imbued with sacred qualities as well as being able to pursue boundless indulgence (on the forms and meanings of some pre-industrial rituals of royalty see Cannadine and Price 1987). In the modern era, however, processes of bureaucratization and secularization have inevitably meant that royal authority has been diffused. And yet if the institution is to continue to have any validity some aspects of the aura of sacred status have to be maintained—the members of the institution have to be treated with a deference and a formality that signals their status. The implications of these demands work at a number of levels from the trivial to the serious. For example, it has jokingly been pointed out that the Queen must think the world permanently smells of new paint because wherever she goes somebody has recently refurbished it in her honour; more seriously, the members of the royal family have been expected to exemplify conservative moral standards because they symbolize national 'traditions'. I will go on to suggest that in the news rhetoric of an era of mass culture it has become increasingly difficult for all public figures to control their presentation, and particularly to find ways of controlling the image of the actors of the royal family to show them to be always acting as moral exemplars.

I have spoken of the monarchy becoming a cultural form because as an institution it has over the last hundred years been centrally located at the level of image and representation. More precisely one can say that as the substance of power has been taken over by bureaucratic agencies so the spectacular representation of national identity has become more salient. The best way of conceptualizing a cultural form is as a distinctive vocabulary or medium of expression. This vocabulary will combine the facilities of its medium with the codes and conventions of articulation that have developed in a particular production setting.

These resources both technical and expressive will be used to tell certain sorts of stories or engage in particular modes of representation. So it follows that one way of characterizing the distinctiveness of particular cultural forms is through the sorts of stories or narratives that typify it. But a concentration on content (unwrapping layers of meaning through the interaction of form and content) is insufficient as it neglects at least two other key dimensions—these are the characteristic modes of production that make performances possible and the characteristic ways in which audiences participate in performance (there is a fuller account of my use of a notion of cultural form in Chaney 1994: ch. 4). The particular concern of this chapter is how the audiences for the monarchy have come to view or interact with a particular mode of symbolic leadership when it is made available through media of mass communication.

The narratives of who the royal family are, how they represent British values and way of life, and how they are the envy of other less fortunate nations have been told and embellished through media presentations (on the nature of national pride in the distinctiveness of the British royalty see Billig 1992: ch. 2). This is not to say that the monarchy is merely the product of an ideological consensus which has functioned as a form of social glue. Rather it is important to recognize that those who have been responsible for trying to invent and generally steer the presentation of symbolic leaders have had a fraught relationship with media of mass communication, which they have seen as a necessary friend but also simultaneously a very dangerous enemy. There has therefore been a constant interaction between those who control the royal image (on manipulation of the royal images see Pearson 1986), and working journalists. While both sides have usually tried to anticipate what they see as audience expectations while following journalistic norms of a good story, shifting patterns of cultural discourse have meant that 'the story' of the royals has never been homogeneous or entirely consistent. More generally, one can say that the tension between the quasi-mythic status of a semi-sacred institution and the intensive interest in all aspects of the lives of media celebrities has created incompatible narrative demands.

One can say then that the existence of media of mass communication has been essential for the dramatization and popularization of royal spectacle. Events such as births, deaths, weddings, anniversaries—the biographical round of any family—have been able to be combined with institutional celebrations such as honouring war dead and opening new sessions of the legislature to project the royal family as somehow enshrining national identity. But at the same time the very force of media demands constantly to observe national figures means that it has become impossible to maintain a façade of royalty as purely public figures. The intertextual commentary on public celebrities, plus the drive in news discourse to personalize public activities (Chaney 1993: ch. 4), has overwhelmed distinctions between public and private spheres for such figures. This is a process that has been particularly problematic in terms of how mass publics have been allowed to perceive royal figures—the terms upon which we are being invited to identify them as public figures. The remainder of this section will address this aspect of participation in public identity before returning to more general issues of royal narratives more directly.

What is meant by the notion of participation in media presentations of royal lives, the third theme in the characterization of the monarchy as a cultural form, is the ways in which the public has become an audience for the monarchy. This issue is important because media presentation means that the defining distance between a royal personage and their subjects is shrunk and made to appear more intimate. An early illustration of what is involved here comes in the contemporary study by Mass Observation of the coronation of George VI in 1937 (Jennings and Madge 1937; on this study and media presentations of national rituals more generally see Chaney 1986a). Let me pick out one detail here, which is concerned with how people heard radio broadcasts of the coronation (the first time such an event had been broadcast on the radio). Ordinary citizens in pubs and other public places were suddenly confronted with a form of vicarious participation in national ritual. Unsurprisingly contemporary observers reported that people did not know how to comport themselves. Should they stand up or even stand to attention? Should men remove their hats as a sign of respect and should the informal radio audience group behave as though they were members of the crowd physically present?

These issues are at one level trivial but at another significant because they point to how a new form of public drama was being created, how a new type of citizenship was being articulated. It is important to note that the coronation in 1937 was seen as a possible turning point because the previous heir apparent had just renounced his throne to marry a woman who was divorced and therefore unacceptable in the eyes of the Church of England. There was therefore a crisis of legitimacy for the monarchy and consequently an unprecedented amount of effort by opinion leaders and other influentials was invested in generating public interest in and sympathy for the new King. By the time the King crowned in 1937 had died and his daughter was in her turn being crowned

(1953) another new mass medium, television, was gaining a national audience. Once again a new form of public access posed questions about the relationship between monarch and subjects.

In this case the issues were initially crystallized by concerns over the role of television in filming the ceremony of crowning. At a particularly sacred moment the monarch being crowned retires (into what Turner would call a liminal space) and re-emerges clothed in new ceremonial robes. This transformation is largely invisible to the dignitaries present in the Abbey but could be made available to a mass audience through television. A number of influential people were greatly exercised at the time as to the propriety of in effect democratizing sacred ritual for impersonal media audiences. Part of the perceived problem was again that the ways in which they watched could not be controlled so it was thought to be likely that solemn ritual would be trivialized by becoming part of domestic entertainment. Eventually the 'modernizers' won the battle by arguing that popular affection for the new monarch could best be ensured by humanizing the new monarch and national ritual—giving the royal family 'human interest'. In effect an important precedent was created by the argument that tradition had to be redramatized as mass entertainment that was ultimately available to a global audience (the staging of the coronation is more fully discussed in Chaney 1986b).

The effect of the successful televising of such a significant national ritual as the crowning of a new monarch was profound in three ways. First, it established television as the pre-eminent element in representations of national life. Secondly, it established the royal family as a narrative resource, almost a genre, for the new medium. Thirdly, it seemed to inaugurate a successful adaptation of a traditional institution to the conditions of late modernity. These consequences have not, however, combined very happily, as a symbolic institution (a spectacle of collective identity) has had to be restaged to the demands of public entertainment for privatized audiences. That is, the price of broadening public interest in the members of the royal family and showing them as 'ordinary folks' much like anyone else in the mass audience was that they became secular celebrities no longer entitled to automatic deference or to be shielded from the intrusive gaze of the common people. The inevitable consequence is that the royals have been familiarized—it is now commonplace for them to referred to by their first names or even (sometimes abusive) nicknames in popular media.

There has therefore developed a curious new form of public intimacy with the British royal family. The constant attention of diverse media means that the mass audience is aware of the most private doings of individuals. In this process the characterization of individuals as, for example, heroes, victims, villains, or fools is quickly accomplished and becomes part of the stock of everyday knowledge bandied about in pub, workplace, and the home. The career of 'Fergie', Duchess of York, who has moved effortlessly from romantic princess to public buffoon is a cautionary tale of the perils of celebrity-hood (although her afterlife as b-list television celebrity confirms the conclusion that you need never fall into complete obscurity). The majesty and mystique of royalty has therefore been made paradoxical—both continually emphasized through formal roles and punctured through intimate personalization (to give but one example, the publication of a letter from the heir to the throne in which he confesses a wish to become his mistress' tampon signals an unprecedented degree of intimate revelation).

Billig's fascinating study of everyday talk about the royal family (1992) is germane to the general issue of celebrity status. Billig argues that for the audience thrust into this quasi-intimate relationship with their symbolic rulers the revelations are not straightforwardly discrediting. It is rather that this relationship is part of a wider shift in public discourse: 'It is a theme of this book that the mockery and lack of deference [of the Royals] . . . represent contemporary ideological forms by which the unprivileged accept their position of ordinariness' (1992: 14). In this account the audience is only too aware of how the monarchy is mediated to them through imagery of staged occasions and intimate revelations. They are aware of being manipulated through spectacle but accept it as a distinct form of public life and entertainment. Cynically aware of an ineluctable role distance between performers and public personae the audience seem to be able to work with images and representation existing in an infinite regress from which there is no escape to 'reality'. Billig suggests that in their sophistication of appropriation and participation the mass audience anticipate the theoretical fascination with simulation in postmodern culture; for the audience: 'The majesty is accepted as display—it is an image. It is all the more real, rather than less real, for being such' (1992: 72).

Billig's study was of course undertaken before the career of Princess Diana had moved from romantic marriage to betrayed wife, unhappy lover, and ultimately tragic martyr. As I have noted, Diana transcended the symbolic status provided by the traditional institution to become a global star (and therefore deserves a separate study in her own right, particularly in relation to her death; see Kear and Steinberg 1999). As such a mythological figure it is easy to say that she is/was anachronistic in relation to the traditions this British institution is meant to represent. It is, however, true that the failure of the institution adequately to dramatize an appropriate grief at her death both illustrated the demands of televisual identity (critics and defenders of the royal family at this time quarrelled over whether the appropriate script for public mourning was that of national institution or 'conventional' family), and seriously threatened the viability of the monarchy itself. The crisis passed and it maybe that the eventual transition to a new monarch will be successfully staged, but it is unquestionable that the tortured life of Diana, Princess of Wales, robbed the royal family of much their legitimacy as a symbolic institution. They may well initially have successfully adapted to the demands of new modes of celebrity status but it is also at least likely that they will be eventually sacrificed on the altar of dramatic verisimilitude. What I mean by this is that their failure to conform to the sentimental codes of soap opera (see below) may condemn them as irrelevant to the public culture of the new millennium (discussed more fully in Chaney forthcoming).

Celebrity Status

Amongst the many modes of self-congratulatory guff that crowd public discourse in Britain about how good British institutions are, one of the most frequently reiterated themes is the unique virtues of the British royal family. Rather than take the myths of tradition combined with modernity at face value I hope to have shown that the cultural form of the monarchy is only uncertainly adapting to the demands of its media status. At its most effective the stories the royals articulate constitute an ideology of rapprochement between public and private lives; between the privileges of celebrity life and the mundanity of the domestic settings in which they are observed. It is an ideology that makes sense of a type of public sphere that has developed in an era of mass television and tabloid journalism (on ideology in mass communication more generally see Thompson 1990). Brunt has forcefully summarized a more critical view of the ideological function of the monarchy (1992), but her account solely stresses an ideological deception that impedes rational self-government (and in that sense retains Habermas's hopes for the public sphere rather than Scannell's reformulation of the idea 1989).

In contrast I see the ideology of the monarchy as more complex than just deception.

In order to grasp this complexity it may be helpful to link the story of the monarchy with the narrative ideologies of other televisual genres such as the continuous serial and the crime series, and thus see it as an important element in reconstituting public life. I mentioned earlier the idea that the multitudinous stories concerning the British royal family can be seen as cumulatively analogous to the interweaving narratives of a continuous serial or soap opera (Coward 1983 was one of the first to develop this analogy). The advantage of the analogy is that it brings out how royal stories tend to concentrate on interpersonal tensions, rather than issues of structural tension; it also helps to bring out how characters as essentially wooden and two-dimensional as many members of the royal family can still command public interest. Above all continuous serials can be said to privatize public life—more or less representative settings and characters are explored through the perspective of private experience (the literature on this genre is now quite extensive).

Of course the analogy cannot be pushed too far—there is no master script or narrative for the monarchy, who are subject to real political pressures—but the current treatment of the royal family does significantly blur public and private distinctions. Meant in a different way, this is one of the familiar objections to media 'intrusion'—that is, that the media should respect a distinction between public and private lives: usually leading to a further corollary that, because they do not, celebrities can be seen to be victims rather than successes (an approach unsurprisingly popular with celebrities themselves). These objections suggest harking back to a more deferential mode of representation and are misplaced because they assume that public roles can be defined and restricted to formal settings. The public drama of family life in public settings and private experience is the story. In the constant shifting between the show of performance and what has been necessary for its production the narrative of the royal family constitutes for us an imagery of public life; it reflexively articulates the nature of collective life.

Other themes in media, particularly televisual, discourse that seem to me to work in equivalent ways are stories about contemporary politics and what Sparks has called the 'drama of crime' (1992). Television stories about 'real life' trade upon, and of course reinforce, the audiences' sophisticated grasp that institutionalized settings have to be staged and managed through interpersonal interaction. In addition to this sociological sense which allows everyone a degree of identification with people in alien settings, these stories also have distinctive narrative emphases that character- ize distinctions between genres. In relation to the royal family three emphases that come through critical commentaries as well as ordinary responses in studies such as Billig's are: how historical symbolism offers a degree of stability and identity for institutional order that is, quite often grudgingly, admired and appreciated; that the romance of family life is particularly salient to female audiences and in this sensibility the royal family reinforce gendered identities; and that the pomp and privileges of symbolic leadership can be ambivalently appropriated in ways that confirm the satisfactions of the ordinariness of everyday life. These emphases help to flesh out the ideology of the mediated monarchy.

Further Reading

Billig, M. (1992), *Talking of the Royal Family*, London: Routledge.

Chaney, D. (1993), *Fictions of Collective Life: Public Drama in Late-Modern Culture*, London: Routledge.

Kear, A., and **Steinberg, D. L.** (eds) (1999), *Mourning Diana: Nation, Culture and Performance*, London: Routledge.

References

Billig, M. (1992), *Talking of the Royal Family*, London: Routledge.

Brunt, R. (1992), 'A "Divine Gift to Inspire"? Popular Cultural Representation, Nationhood and the British Monarchy', in D. Strinati and S. Wagg (eds.), *'Come on Down'? Popular Media Culture in Postwar Britain*, London: Routledge.

Cannadine, D. (1983), 'The Context, Performance and Meaning of Ritual: The British Monarchy and the "invention of tradition" *c*.1820–1977', in Hobsbawm and Ranger (1983).

—— and **Price, S.** (eds.) (1987), *Rituals of Royalty: Power and Ceremonial in Traditional Societies*, Cambridge: Cambridge University Press.

Chaney, D. (1986*a*), 'The Symbolic Form of Ritual in Mass Communication', in P. Golding et al. (eds.), *Communicating Politics: Mass Communications and the Political Process*, Leicester: Leicester University Press.

—— (1986*b*), 'A Symbolic Mirror of Ourselves: Civic Ritual in Mass Society', in R. Collins et al. (eds.), *Media, Culture and Society: A Critical Reader*, London: Sage.

—— (1993), *Fictions of Collective Life: Public Drama in Late-Modern Culture*, London: Routledge.

—— (1994), *The Cultural Turn*, London: Routledge.

—— (1997), 'Authenticity and Suburbia', in S. Westwood and J. Williams (eds.), *Imagining Cities: Scripts, Signs, Memory*, London: Routledge.

—— (forthcoming 2001), *Cultural Change and Everyday Life*, London: Macmillan.

Coward, R. (1983), *Female Desire*, London: Paladin.

Dayan, Daniel, and Katz, Elihu (1992), *Media Events: The Live Broadcasting of History*, Cambridge, Mass.: Harvard University Press.

Habermas, Jürgen (1989), *The Structual Transformation of the Public Sphere: An Inquiry into a Category of Bourgeois Society*, Cambridge: Polity.

Hobsbawm, E., and Ranger, T. (eds.) (1983), *The Invention of Tradition*, Cambridge: Cambridge University Press.

Jennings, H., and Madge, C. (1937), *May 12, Mass Observation Day Survey*, London: Faber.

Kear, A., and Steinberg, D. L. (eds.) (1999), *Mourning Diana: Nation, Culture and Performance*, London: Routledge.

Nairn, T. (1988), *The Enchanted Glass: Britain and its Monarchy*, London: Radius.

Pearson, J. (1986), *The Ultimate Family: The Making of the Royal House of Windsor*, London: Michael Joseph.

Richards, J., Wilson, S., and Woodhead, L. (eds.) (1999), *Diana: The Making of a Media Saint*, London: I. B. Tauris.

Scannell, P. (1989), 'Public Service Broadcasting and Modern Public Life', *Media, Culture & Society*, 11/2.

Simmonds, D. (1984), *Princess Di, the National Dish: The Making of a Media Star*, London: Pluto Press.

Sparks, R. (1992), *Television and the Drama of Crime: Moral Tales and the Place of Crime in Public Life*, Buckingham: Open University Press.

Thompson, John B. (1990), *Ideology and Modern Culture: Critical Social Theory in the Era of Mass Communication*, Cambridge: Polity.

14

Everyday Royal Celebrity

NICK COULDRY

THE mediated monarchy, like mediated politics, is now a well-established topic for academic study. One approach to each area is to argue that the media have amplified, or provided a new tool for the promotion of, our already existing collective fictions (Chaney 1993) of royalty or politics but without altering their fundamentals. Alternatively, you can argue, as I will, that the media have altered, perhaps distorted, the very basis of royalty and politics. (Although I will concentrate on royalty—British royalty—the two questions of the mediation of royalty and politics are connected.) Whereas the first approach regards mediation as a late twist in royalty's long-term history, the second starts instead from the process of mediation itself, as a general phenomenon, and explores how it is worked out in the specific example of royalty. I will not try to arbitrate as to the ultimate value of these two approaches, only to push the second approach a stage or two further. My starting premiss is that all elements in the monarchy (not only the performance of royalty and the circulation of representations about it, but also the consumption of royalty)[1] are primarily mediated, which certainly makes for complexity in analysing the historical surfaces that result.

Some of the difficulties can be illustrated by looking briefly at the development of Tom Nairn's celebrated analysis of the British monarchy in *The Enchanted Glass* (1994). Its first edition (1988) can be placed firmly in the first approach to the mediated monarchy. As

1 If the television 'audience' is empirically elusive, yet continually constructed as 'fact' by the television industry (Ang 1991), so too is the royal 'audience' a production of the various sectors of the royalty industry. Which is not to say that royalty has no one watching it, only that we have to be very cautious about claims to speak for it. This is a variant on the general problem of 'public opinion': Pollock (1976); Bourdieu (1990).

a primarily political analysis of the developing relationship of the British monarchy to the structure of the British state and social hierarchy, it treats the monarchy's obvious celebritization as a side-show: 'in Britain at least, the Queen and her family are never merely stars, or celebrities. They possess . . . an element of mystique whose glamour is in the end far greater than that of any media personality' (from 1st edition, in 1994: 27). He argued that, for all its paradoxes, the British royal family was a successful adaptation to modernity which managed to hold the social hierarchy in place, symbolically, even if the conditions under which it did so now included becoming media celebrities as well.

By the second edition (or at least its new introduction) Nairn's argument had changed, although in one crucial respect it remained unresolved. Given the fall in popularity of British royalty as an institution in the early 1990s, he wrote in 1994 that 'the old mirror-image has shattered and the glamour of "Britain" has effaced itself. However, no other convincing image yet presents itself to the formerly enchanted' (1994: p. xix). Not only does Nairn leave open how this crisis will be resolved, but he does not comment on whether the celebritization of British royalty had anything to do with generating this crisis (rather he looks in another direction, to contradictions within Thatcherism (1994: p. xxiii)). Nairn makes no comment on the ultimate royal celebrity of the 1990s, Princess Diana, and her possible role in that crisis, a role that became easier to see from the mid-1990s onwards. In his first edition, when discussing royal attire, he had commented on the *untypical* (and *temporary*) impact of Diana on royalty's distance from general fashion: Diana's rejection of what Nairn wittily calls 'the permanent effigy-look' (in 1994: 31), in favour of an attempt at being fashionable (1994: 32). But, as we will see, it may be Diana's merging with the fashion world that proved the more lasting change. I comment later on Prince William's continuation in this direction.

Should we, then, in view of late 1990s opinion polls that suggested a revival in royalty's popularity after Princess Diana's death, adjust Nairn's original argument again, and claim a *re*-enchantment of the British monarchy's 'mirror' to the nation? It is too early to reach such a conclusion, but we can surmise that, to the extent that such a re-enchantment is under way, it is likely to be at the price of transforming the residual political associations of British royalty ever more into the coinage of celebrity. From the perspective of the start of the new century, Nairn's 1988 reading of the monarchy in terms of a 'moral-spiritual authority' that operates above celebrity and above the process of mediation looks increasingly implausible. At least that will be the wider implication of my argument.

'Famous for Being Famous'?

Nairn dismisses the idea of British royalty as 'just celebrities' (1994: 35) on the grounds that royal, unlike simple media, celebrity involves membership of a genuinely exceptional category. To be royal, you must enter by birth (or by marriage) the nation's first family, the apex of Britain's social hierarchy. For Nairn this exceptional status makes any thoroughgoing royal populism self-defeating. As he puts it ironically:

A kind of moral-spiritual authority is at stake which allows—indeed, prescribes—visits to the lower regions and enthusiasms for the denizens, but absolutely prohibits going native. There is simply no long-term way of keeping a foot in both camps. (1994: 33)

Underlying Nairn's argument is a sharp distinction between the type of personal authority which royalty involves and that which can be derived from mere media fame. Certainly there is a difference to be explained. Royal celebrities are not just *any* celebrity (Nairn, of course, even in the first edition, does not dispute that British royalty are celebrities).

This difference can be expressed in structural terms. Royalty have a very different type of pre-eminence from most celebrities, relative to the system through which they acquire celebrity status. Whereas many, although not all, other celebrities are celebrities by virtue of taking part in an industry which generates an endless stream of celebrity positions of varying ranks, with their occupants changing at varying speeds, royalty means occupying the highest level of a hierarchy above the rest of society, in most circumstances for life. Royalty, by definition, have no rivals for their status, since they occupy the apex of a whole social system; whereas media stars merely pass through a particular region of the media system. It is no surprise therefore that an Aids victim, reflecting on what Princess Diana's visit to the London Lighthouse project had meant to him, saw a category difference between her and even the most famous film star: 'Because she was so high-profile, no one could ever do as much for Aids acceptance. Even when Elizabeth Taylor visited us, it felt like an anti-climax in comparison' (quoted *Daily Mail*, 12 Feb. 2000: 24).

That, however, does not exempt royalty from contradictions

similar to those which affect celebrity status, particular the tensions between their ordinariness and their extraordinariness. The point surely is not that royalty is entirely separate from the general conditions of celebrity, but that in royal celebrity *two*, not one, hierarchies of social exclusion coincide. Royalty are exceptional by virtue of their position in both a social hierarchy and a media hierarchy (cf. Couldry 2000 on the 'symbolic hierarchy of the media frame'). It is clearly wrong to collapse the two hierarchies into one in their case, but equally, given that they continually intersect in the celebrity 'world', why assume in advance that the 'authority' (in Nairn's term) of royalty will always be grasped by its subjects as separate from, and in a sense superior to, general media celebrity? This is perhaps what the first approach to mediated monarchy requires, but it involves making more general assumptions about the continuation of political and social authority, and its insulation from processes of mediation; yet this is precisely what is in issue. At the very least, we need empirical research into people's actual sense of the priorities between different forms of social and symbolic authority.

Clearly, Nairn is right to deny that royalty are *merely* 'famous for being famous' (nor are most celebrities: that is part of the point of what we might call the 'celebrity system'), but the authority of royalty is not hermetically sealed from other contests over social and symbolic authority, particularly those in the media arena. The anthropologist Maurice Bloch makes an analogous point in discussing ancient royal ritual in Madagascar, long pre-dating modern media:

In order to understand royal symbolism it is necessary to stress the relationship of the practices and concepts governing royal life *and those governing the life of ordinary people*; only in this way will we be able to understand the emotional and political power of these [royal] rituals for those who witness them. (Bloch 1987: 272, added emphasis)

We cannot, in other words, understand the resonance that claims to transcendent authority have, unless we understand how they are embedded in, and in part generated from, the symbolism of everyday life. In contemporary societies, however, even this relationship—between the royal and the 'ordinary'—is negotiated, primarily through the media. It is worth therefore exploring further how royal celebrity is involved in the contradiction between ordinariness and extraordinariness which characterizes all celebrity.

'Populism in Trainers'

The phrase 'populism in trainers' is taken from a press article written in the aftermath of Princess Diana's death (Grove 1997: 10), the reference obviously being to new forms of public mourning by non-royalty, and their supposed political significance. But it was not long before royal iconography involved royals *themselves* wearing trainers in public: for example, in a photo reproduced in the *Sun*'s 'Royal Souvenir Edition' for Prince William's 18th birthday, of him emerging from a car after a driving lesson (*Sun*, 17 June 2000: 9; Fig. 14.1). Prince William, in replies to Press Association questions for his 18th birthday, insisted that he prefers 'casual wear' (ibid.); by contrast with his Eton uniform no doubt, but by contrast also with the curious definition of casual wear (tie, kilt, and sporran) often adopted by his father.

Hardly more subtly, William (or his press team) decided to make

Fig. 14.1 Prince William emerges from a car after a driving lesson.
Sun, 17 June 2000. © UK Press.

him available for the *Sun*'s front page for that special edition, sporting under his Eton long-tailed jacket a Union Jack waistcoat (with a radio mike clipped onto it). The publication date (although a few days before Prince William's birthday) coincided with England's crucial Euro 2000 football match against Germany. Hence the headline and byline: 'HEIR WE GO . . . Footy-mad Wills cheers England.' The waistcoat itself had sewn onto it the words 'Groovy Baby'. As the *Sun* explained, this was the 'catchphrase of his movie hero Austin Power—. . . and let's hope we all feel like that after tonight's result!' Whose populism are we talking about now?

The combination of the uniform of Britain's most elite public school with a Union Jack waistcoat (seemingly artlessly personalized with Prince William's own homage to one of the most popular films of 1999) fits, in a curious way, Nairn's description of earlier royal dress as 'totemic exhibitionism' (1994: 31), but hardly his other term 'anti-chic'. Prince William, unlike his mother, is not 'a fashion-conscious [Prince] who cannot wear fashionable clothes' (as a 1980s commentary on Princess Diana put it, quoted Nairn 1994: 32). Prince William, on the contrary, can both wear fashionable clothes off duty and adapt his formal clothes for fashionable, indeed directly populist, ends. As the 2000 series of royal birthday photos hardly avoided suggesting, and the *Sun* insisted, he is 'the pin-up Prince' (*Sun*, 17 June 2000: 3), dressed not for respect, but for admiration, even if a few notches short of a new royal dandy (like the pre-coronation Edward VII). This is everyday royal populism, able to turn everyday fashion into an extraordinary, even if contradictory, icon of ordinary allegiances.

This iconic clothing has to be placed in the context of conflicts between 'ordinariness' and 'extraordinariness' for royalty and celebrity generally. A central paradox of film stars, indeed of all celebrities, is that to varying degrees they are 'ordinary' underneath their 'extraordinariness' (Dyer 1998: 43; cf. Couldry 2000: 94–7). Particularly paradoxical is the television 'personality', who (in most people's eyes) has few distinguishing features apart from the fact (hardly trivial, however) that he or she is on television. Typical soap opera celebrities are perhaps the most paradoxical of all because their media role is to *play* 'ordinary people' (often with a disguise of their real-life class position: Couldry 2000: 103).

The British monarchy, since at least the early twentieth century, has presented itself as an 'ordinary' family (Davies 1999: 143), but the tensions associated with this self-image reached a climax with Princess Diana's 1990s claim to be *more* 'ordinary' than the rest of the royal family. Whereas, as Nairn (1994: 22) argues, the royal family had before been popularly imagined as on 'our' side against the 'them' of the 'system' (the political side of the state), Diana projected this difference onto a conflict within the royal family itself, at least from her famous *Panorama* interview onwards. Diana, as so many posthumous tributes claimed, was the 'real' royal (although in fact only royal by marriage) because she was more 'ordinary' than the (in fact real, since hereditary, royals) who had lost touch with 'ordinary people'. Prince William has with the help of his advisers sought to turn the performance of 'ordinariness' back into an asset for the royal family as a whole.

Underlying the differences between royal and other celebrity, I suggest, is a parallel structure, summarized diagrammatically in Fig. 14.2. In royal celebrity, two social and symbolic hierarchies intersect, since British royals are both the apex of a social hierarchy and (because of the particular way they enter the celebrity field) a rare, elite type of media celebrity, with global reach. The ordinary/ extraordinary paradox is, in fact, not so much distinctive of celebrity *per se*, as of *all* hierarchies. It is because media celebrity is part of a wider symbolic hierarchy between media and ordinary (i.e.

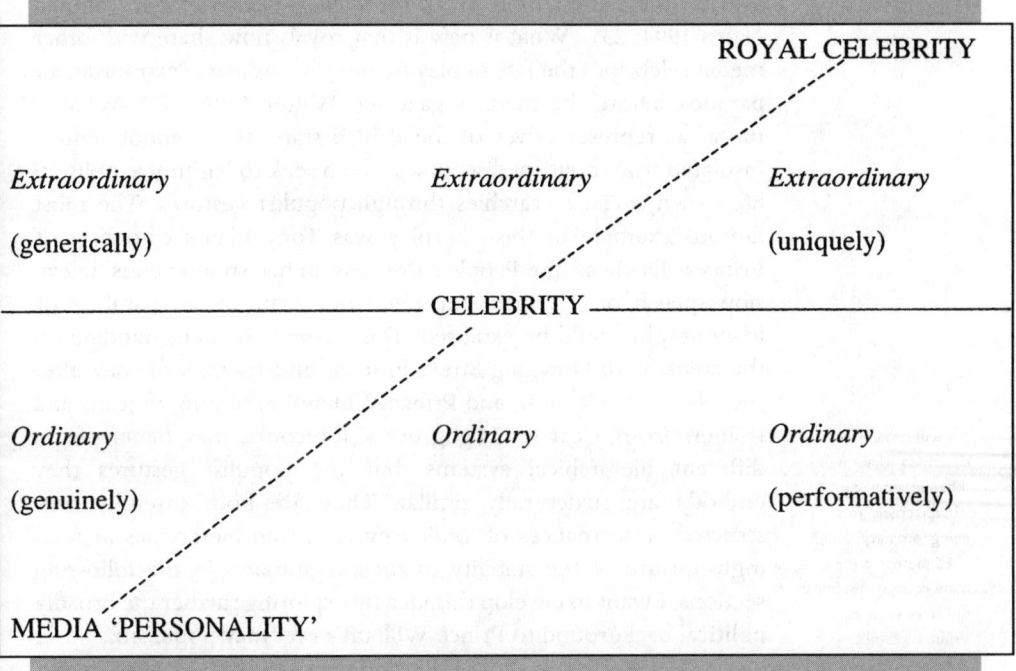

Fig. 14.2

non-media) 'worlds' (Couldry 2000: ch. 3) that media star, celebrity, and 'personality' are each contradictory positions: extraordinary (by virtue of their place in the media world), yet also ordinary. Royalty exhibit the same paradox, not because they are celebrities, but because they are the apex of a hierarchy: the discovery of their ordinariness 'after all' is part of what legitimizes the inequality from which they benefit. As Michael Billig in his brilliant study of talk about British royalty (1992: 82) puts it, when discussing the apparently status-effacing magic of meeting royalty: 'differences of status seem to disappear from such moments of myth. But here is the illusion, the mystification, or the forgetfulness. The inequalities must persist, in order to make those desired moments of equality so magical,' and therefore, we might add, so effective as legitimizations. A socially legitimized hierarchy must, as Maurice Bloch (1987) suggests, *connect* the extraordinary to the ordinary.

British royalty, not in spite of but because of the actual social exclusiveness which underlies their position, are the most extraordinary embodiment of ordinariness. The particular paradox is not entirely new, since it was that old apologist of empire John Buchan who wrote that the King 'while lifted far above the nation, should also be the nation itself in its most characteristic form' (quoted Nairn 1994: 23).[2] What is new is that royals now share with other media celebrities the fate of playing out this ordinary/extraordinary paradox before the media's gaze (cf. Walter 1999: 277). What is more, as representatives of the British state, they cannot remain insulated from political discourses which seek to legitimize political life's own social hierarchies through populist gestures. The most famous example of this interplay was Tony Blair's co-option of Princess Diana as 'the People's Princess' in his 'spontaneous' television speech on 1 September 1997. But many other parallels of iconography could be explored: Tony Blair's children, standing on the steps of 10 Downing Street in jeans and trainers the day after the May 1997 election, and Prince William, emerging in jeans and trainers from a car on Highgrove's[3] forecourt, may benefit from different hierarchical systems, but the populist gestures they embody are structurally similar. They are both carefully constructed performances of 'ordinariness' within hierarchies increasingly unsure of the stability of their legitimacy. In the following sections, I want to develop this idea by exploring further the broadly political background to Prince William's everyday populism.

2 I will come back shortly to what might differentiate being 'characteristic' from being 'ordinary'.
3 Highgrove is the main country residence of Prince Charles, William's father.

Celebrity and Inequality

There are two ways one could pursue this. One would involve analysing the detailed narratives associated with, and projected onto, contemporary British royalty—for example, the image of 'rebellious royalty' projected so successfully onto Princess Diana and in a more muted and controlled fashion onto her son.[4] Instead, however, I want to explore how far a more abstract, structural argument can be taken. Both celebrity and royalty are hierarchies based on social exclusion that need to project themselves as inclusive, and their main means of self-projection are the media. By thinking about the tensions which this involves, can we advance our understanding of the recent history of Britain's mediated monarchy?

That celebrity is part of a social hierarchy rests upon the fact which the media industries are compelled to deny: that most people *are* excluded from direct participation in media production, even if the reasons and justifications for this exclusion are hardly the subject of open public debate. Indeed, as I have argued elsewhere, the spatial segregation of most people from the processes of media production contributes to the legitimization of the concentration of symbolic power in media institutions (Couldry 2000: 52–5). This is an argument, essentially, about the ideological implications of spatial organization (Lefebvre 1990; Debord 1983), which I cannot pursue here, although it has a detailed bearing on the spatial tensions around celebrity, including royal celebrity (Couldry 1999). There is a distance, and I would argue an implicit hierarchy, between those 'in' or 'on' the media and those not. This remains true, even if, as Richard Dyer (1998: 42) classically argued, media celebrity, such as film stardom, is associated with a wider ideology of social mobility, the 'myth of success'. Indeed, it is this underlying inequality that gives spice to that myth: 'you too can become exceptional, in spite of everything . . .'

If, however, royalty shares with wider celebrity some features (such as their normal physical remoteness from audiences, except at staged moments of 'access'), there are others that royalty cannot share. Royal celebrity cannot, *without much further work*, reproduce the 'myth of success', precisely because it is the one type of 'success' which for almost everyone is in principle impossible—for ever and from birth. Indeed, it might be argued, royalty is one of the wider structures of inequality which makes the myth of 'ordinary' celebrity so resonant with meaning.

Britain in the 1990s, however, saw one royal, Princess Diana,

4 For a particularly interesting exploration of the coincidence in Diana of wider narratives around self-help and the contradictions of 1990s femininity, see Blackman (1999). For a useful insistence that royalty offer a discursive space whose *multiple* uses cannot be reduced to one simple message, see McGuigan (2000).

develop her celebrity into a curious variant of the myth of success, and this (leaving aside the details of the symbolic work involved: on which, see Blackman 1999) was related to her unusual structural position within the royal hierarchy: a member by marriage only, a failure in her royal duties from the perspective of the hereditary members (or most of them), and a rebel.

There are a number of interesting connections to be made here. First, there must be some connection (although it is difficult to say exactly what) between the unstable support for royalty in 1990s Britain and the wider fall in allegiance towards the British political system (and of course many other countries' political systems as well). Political alienation, and its connections with the mediation of politics, is an important and growing debate (Eliasoph 1998; Morley 1999; Buckingham 2000), to which there is no space to add here, except to mention that 1990s Britain also saw the rise of new forms of protest in public space (Couldry 2000: part III) which in some respects resembled the public actions in the weeks after Princess Diana's death. This is an unexpected connection across the political terrain that I have explored in detail elsewhere (Couldry forthcoming).

A second, although highly speculative, connection is to Manuel Castells's (1997) diagnosis of the growing structural conflict at the heart of contemporary social and economic organization: the absolute divide, and opposition between the interests of 'the network' and the interests of the individual. The network is the framework through which capital, information, and profits flow, routed through certain key nodes, but moving nonetheless without reference to local claims. By contrast, the individual's main site of identity-construction remains the local place (which is rarely of any consequence to the network). As Richard Sennett (1999) has powerfully argued for the specific case of white-collar workers, there is a growing crisis in individuals' capacity to tell convincing narratives of how, and where, they belong, and how what they do makes wider sense.

Princess Diana, paradoxically, may have signified, for some at least, an analogous conflict between individual and system, her enemy being the unyielding face of royal tradition. She was admired for her professionalism, for her ability to go on working and performing in public, in spite of her personal turmoil behind the scenes, but also for the explicit challenge she made to formalities of royal protocol and a perceived failure of royal tradition to connect (cf. Gibson 1999). There are of course many celebrity stories which resonate with wider problems of loss of connection and alienation. But if, in the case of Diana, royal celebrity could have projected onto it a wider anti-systemic *cri de cœur*, then the connections of royalty's shifting 'moral-spiritual authority' (Nairn 1994: 33) to today's wider shifts in political and social cohesion (the long-term 'politics' of alienation from formal politics) may be complex indeed.

Conclusion

Some caution is necessary, of course: the nation is not a text, and we need more extensive empirical research into changing attitudes to British royalty, and perhaps also British politics (Michael Billig's work derives from the late 1980s and early 1990s). On the face of it, however, there is evidence for a shift towards a new, mediated form of royal populism: a regular performance of 'ordinariness', which is quite different from a formal attempt to condense the 'character-istics' of the nation in gestures, dress, and talk (the John Buchan version of representative monarchy). Everyday royal populism rests on at least some members of the royal family[5] regularly showing (at greater or lesser cost to themselves) that they are, really and in spite of everything, 'like us'.

This form of royal populism reflects the forms of celebrity as a wider phenomenon and its usual contradiction between ordinari-ness and extraordinariness. The resonances of royal celebrity in Britain may also be related, at least as a defensive reaction, to a wider alienation from the state and its various political forms. Royal performances of ordinariness may even have a continuing role (I hesitate to say 'function'!) as 'access-points' where certain key values can be reasserted and trust in the wider social system 'reem-bedded' (Giddens 1990). We can attempt such a reading of the *Daily Mail's* article 'Diana: The Legacy of Love' from which I have already quoted (12 Feb. 2000: 24–5); there people who had met Princess Diana remembered their meetings with Diana as encounters with her compassion, caring, love, and so on. There is no need to trivialize these reflections on royalty, since they relate to wider shifts in the public sphere and the incorporation of emotional claims previously excluded from notions of politics (McGuigan 2000; Stevenson 1997).

The contemporary mediated monarchy may, then, from one per-spective be engaged in some such form of social 'repair', although that does not mean that such performances are successful. As Keith Thomas (1971: 205–6) noted many years ago, the evidence for

5 This is not to deny of course that old forms of royal 'anti-chic' are dead; they may even be claimed as fashionable, at least from a 'foreign' perspective. An example, as I write, is the *Guardian's* front-page news story 'Wowing them in Pastels and Pearls' about Italian fashion designers' reaction to the Queen's outfits on a recent state visit to Italy (*Guardian*, 20 October 2000: p. 1).

disbelief and scepticism is even harder to assess than that for belief. This may be particularly true for societies whose reference points for belief are provided primarily by media narratives, including the media's claims about what the nation does (or does not) believe. If so, it is all the more important to explore, as I have tried to do, what it means to say that our monarchy and politics are mediated. The long-term implications for our wider theories of both have not yet, I suspect, been fully appreciated.

Further Reading

Couldry, Nick (2000), *The Place of Media Power: Pilgrims and Witnesses of the Media Age*, London: Routledge: ch. 3.

Gabler, Neal (2000), *Life: The Movie—How Entertainment Conquered Reality*, New York: Vintage. An interesting comparison with celebrity in the USA.

Nairn, Tom (1994), *The Enchanted Glass: Britain and its Monarchy*, 2nd edn., London: Verso.

References

Ang, Ien (1991), *Desperately Seeking the Audience*, London: Routledge.

Billig, Michael (1992), *Talking of the Royal Family*, London: Routledge.

Blackman, Lisa (1999), 'An Extraordinary Life: The Legacy of an Ambivalence', *New Formations*, 36.

Bloch, Maurice (1987), 'The Ritual of the Royal Bath in Madagascar: The Dissolution of Death, Birth and Fertility into Authority', in D. Cannadine and S. Price (eds.), *Rituals of Royalty: Power and Ceremonial in Traditional Societies*, Cambridge: Cambridge University Press.

Bourdieu, Pierre (1990), 'Opinion Polls: A "Science" without the Scientist', in *In Other Words: Essays towards a Reflexive Sociology*, Cambridge: Polity Press.

Buckingham, David (2000), *The Making of Citizens*, London: Routledge.

Castells, Manuel (1997), *The Power of Identity*, Oxford: Blackwell.

Chaney, David (1993), *Fictions of Collective Life*, London: Routledge.

Couldry, Nick (1999), 'Remembering Diana: The Geography of Celebrity and the Politics of Lack', *New Formations*, 36.

—— (2000), *The Place of Media Power: Pilgrims and Witnesses of the Media Age*, London: Routledge.

—— (forthcoming), 'The Umbrella Man: Crossing a Landscape of Speech and Silence', *European Journal of Cultural Studies*.

Davies, Jude (1999), 'Princess: Diana, Femininity and the Royal', *New Formations*, 36.

Debord, Guy (1983), *The Society of the Spectacle*, Detroit: Black & Red.

Dyer, Richard (1998), *Stars* 2nd edn., London: BFI.

Eliasoph, Nina (1998), *Avoiding Politics: How Americans Produce Apathy in Everyday Life*. Cambridge: Cambridge University Press.

Gibson, Mark (1999), 'The Temporality of Democracy: The Long Revolution and Diana, Princess of Wales', *New Formations*, 36.

Giddens, Anthony (1990), *The Consequences of Modernity*, Cambridge: Polity.

Grove, Valerie (1997), 'A Triumph for Populism in Trainers', *The Times*, 6 Sept. 1997.

Lefebvre, Henri (1990), *The Production of Space*, Oxford: Blackwell.

McGuigan, Jim (2000), 'British Identity and "The People's Princess"', *Sociological Review*, 48/1.

Morley, David (1999), 'Finding out about the World from Television News: Some Difficulties', in J. Gripsrud (ed.), *Television and Common Knowledge*, London: Routledge.

Nairn, Tom (1994), *The Enchanted Glass: Britain and its Monarchy*, 2nd edn., London: Verso (1st pub. 1988).

Pollock, Friedrich (1976), 'Empirical Research into Public Opinion', in P. Connerton (ed.), *Critical Sociology*, Harmondsworth: Penguin (1st pub. 1955).

Sennett, Richard (1999), *The Corrosion of Character: The Personal Consequences of Work in the New Capitalism*, New York: W. W. Norton & Company.

Stevenson, Nick (1997), 'Media, Ethics and Morality', in J. McGuigan (ed.), *Cultural Methodologies*, London: Sage.

Thomas, Keith (1971), *Religion and the Decline of Magic*, Harmondsworth: Penguin.

Walter, Tony (1999), 'And the Consequence Was . . .', in T. Walter (ed.), *The Mourning for Diana*, Oxford: Berg.

15

Cartels and Lotteries: Heritage and Cultural Policy in Britain

KEN WORPOLE

I'm sure a trip in a time machine to 1851 would re-awaken a hatred for the over-dressed pretensions of Victoriana. To it, and to the rat-infested ruins created by the war, the clarity of the South Bank in 1951 came like a bite of lemon at half-time.

(Aldiss 1976: 177)

In July 1997, following the May general election victory of New Labour, the Department of National Heritage was renamed the Department of Culture, Media, and Sport, 'a symbol that we mean to look forward, not back', said the Prime Minister, Tony Blair, announcing the change (Blair 1997). This apparently decisive shift from the cultural politics of conservation to the cultural politics of modernity was however achieved with little apparent organizational change. The Arts Council of England remained intact (though somewhat scaled down), as did the Crafts Council, the Regional Arts Boards, the Sports Council, the British Film Institute (though this body changed more than most others), and most of the other administrative bodies which channel public funds into sports and cultural organizations. Meanwhile, local authorities throughout the UK continued to cut leisure and amenity budgets (from which most local arts, libraries, parks, and sports are funded), as they had done before the election.

The one area where the new Labour government announced significant policy changes concerned the Lottery, though in doing this it was picking on an easy target, as there was no entrenched establishment in place to defend a historic cultural remit. The Prime Minister publicly backed the proposed—and controversial—Millennium Exhibition at Greenwich (despite the misgivings of the majority of cabinet members) and appointed a close ally, Peter Mandelson, to bring the project to fruition. A White Paper, *The People's Lottery*, was quickly produced in July 1997 which proposed that, in addition to the existing five distributing bodies (Arts, Sports, Heritage, Charities, and Millennium), an additional body be established, the 'New Opportunities Fund', to be focused on health, education, and environmental projects, including the establishment of NESTA (a 'National Endowment for Science, Technology, and the Arts'). The new government also announced a Creative Industries Task Force made up of high-profile entrepreneurs such as Richard Branson, Alan McGee, and Paul Smith, who were to be the 'ambassadors for the New Britain'. Lottery income allowed the new Prime Minister to appear to be setting sail for the new country, with the holds stacked with gold (in reality the windfall of a massive form of regressive, voluntary taxation), while making few if any changes to the parameters of cultural policy in Britain, which have been largely unchallenged since the political and cultural settlement of 1945.

In this chapter I want to chart the trends, continuities, and policy assumptions (generally more implicit than explicit) of public cultural policy in Britain, principally England, since 1945, with particular reference to three main institutional initiatives—the Arts Council, the National Lottery, and the millennium celebrations—concluding with a summary of some related, though no less important, debates which have arisen over cultural policy in the intervening years.

The Arts Council

The story of the intrigues and cultural power games surrounding the setting up of the Arts Council in 1945 has been well described at length elsewhere (Hewison 1981; Hutchinson 1982; see also McGuigan 1996 and Mulgan and Worpole 1986). Briefly, the wartime CEMA (Council for the Encouragement of Music and the Arts), whose brief had been to organize morale-boosting national tours by theatrical and musical companies (in the spirit of 'Let the People Sing!'), was replaced in 1945 by the newly formed Arts Council under the proposed chairmanship of Lord Keynes. CEMA's success had resulted from a judicious mix of amateur and professional performances, putting on shows in factories, church halls, military camps, and doing so with no initial set of fixed cultural assumptions about high or low, or appropriate and inappropriate settings for cultural performance. Within months of the establishment of the Arts Council, Lord Keynes, who was already chairman of Covent Garden Opera (soon to be a major beneficiary of Arts Council spending, a breathtaking example of what Arts Council chronicler Robert Hutchinson aptly described as allowing the mice to distribute the cheese), was strongly associated with the decision to cut the Council's links with the amateur, participatory traditions of CEMA, causing a rift with Vaughan Williams, who had long been an advocate of the folk music tradition.

It was later decided that the logic of its anti-amateur ethos meant that the English Folk Song and Dance Society, for example, was more appropriately funded by the Sports Council, folk music and dance being taught at the knee rather than in the seminar room. The disdain for the self-taught tradition has hardly ever wavered in the corridors of official culture, whether in respect of music, dance, literature, the visual arts or crafts. This has resulted more recently in some very difficult cultural confrontations with ethnic minority communities where oral traditions of music and literature, as well as craft traditions in the visual arts, are still much stronger and vital, though well beyond the cultural comprehension of those who have been brought up in a canonical, 'selective tradition'. A recent study of the social impact of the arts, *Use or Ornament?*, has added more weight to the argument that popular participation in arts activities can benefit individuals and communities in significant ways, but one should never underestimate the power of the professionals to marginalize such arguments, and carry on regardless (Matarasso 1997).

In much the same spirit Keynes also thought that the main business of the Arts Council was investing in buildings, principally theatres, art galleries, and concert halls, for 'if with state aid the material frame can be constructed the public and the artists will do the rest between them' (cited in Hutchinson 1982: 96). The preoccupation with the bricks and mortar of culture—in its heroic mode with new architecture and grand openings, in its everyday mode with the problems of the burgeoning costs of staffing and maintenance—has since been a continuing issue, now to be compounded by Lottery money that is required to be spent as capital investment rather than revenue. In August 1997, the Green Room, an experimental theatre in Manchester, had to close soon after spending a £750,000 Lottery grant on its premises, because it could not cope with the increased revenue costs. 'We needed the building, but the lottery money went to builders and plumbers—we didn't get it,' said the artistic director, at the time of its (temporary) closure (Ward 1997). Some years ago I interviewed a well-known Liverpool playwright who told me that the city's principal theatre spent more on maintaining the central heating boiler than it did on commissioning new plays. The dull reality of much public cultural policy is that more time is spent discussing leaking roofs and drains than is spent arguing about aesthetics.

The *bal de masque*, or comedy of identities, at which the first chairman of the Arts Council could preside over the giving of a major grant to the Covent Garden Opera House, of which he was also chairman, set a precedent for future patterns of funding. In an almost exact parallel, fifty years later, Lord Chadlington, chair of the Arts Council's Lottery Awards Panel, presided over a £78 million grant to the Royal Opera House, of which he became chairman shortly after (Cumming 1997). The relations between donor and recipient, giver and given, adviser and advisee, possess a circularity that is at times breathtakingly unashamed. Those outside the magic circle are seriously disadvantaged when it comes to securing attention, let alone funding. While certain rules of probity and etiquette are observed by all Arts Council panels—advisers with a financial interest in an application are obliged to leave the room during the relevant discussions—the levels of personal familiarity, of sheer cultural presence, combined with the fact that all minutes are private and all grant panels are held in camera, together produce what Raymond Williams once called 'the mellow dusk', in which a degree of discreet exchanges, understandings, and unspoken covenants preserve a cultural continuity and hegemony that remains difficult to disrupt or challenge.

Yet even in this benign nomenclature, panel members themselves have only limited powers, since the largest grants come down to them as *obiter dicta*. A recent Arts Council music panel member described how, 'during my years on the music panel, when the music budget was around £30 million, £23 million was earmarked for the Royal Opera House and the English National Opera. Not by the panel, though. Not only did the panel not get to discuss these two beneficiaries, they were even banned from discussing the ban' (Cork 1997). Public controversies over the funding of opera, particularly the Royal Opera House, are now as much a part of the small change of English cultural life as are debates about the cost of supporting the royal family.

In a sense the Arts Council presents an easy target for the cultural critic. Most of its money is earmarked for a small number of 'National' or 'Royal' institutions (the two are easily elided) based in London, and its organizational ethos and board membership are set up precisely for this purpose: defending the national/metropolitan interest. Until the appointment of businessman Gerry Robinson in 1998, the previous three chairmen of the Arts Council, Sir William Rees-Mogg, Lord Palumbo, and Lord Gowrie, had all been self-proclaimed members of the Conservative Party. It is significant that, for example, when the much-trumpeted 1984 policy document *The Glory of the Garden* called for savings, 'all but one million of the six million pounds to be found by the cutting of organisations actually came from the cutting of regional companies' (Hutchinson 1982: 255). Today the London 'interest' is always paramount, a far cry from the strength of regional identities and cultures in the nineteenth century, so persuasively described in Krishan Kumar's 1981 essay on 'The Nationalization of British Culture' (Kumar 1981).

The large mainstream grants could easily, and more properly, come direct from the government's own cultural department, but the arm's length principle conveniently allows politicians to pretend that the many and inevitable controversies about funding are nothing to do with them. At the time of writing, the new government seemed to be continuing with this convenient pretence.[1] While occasionally deferring to other discourses of arts and cultural policy—the need to support an avant-garde, the role of the arts as a critical practice, the rise of the cultural industries as the dominant forms of cultural production and representation—in essence the Arts Council's role has been to support and sustain a mainstream, largely metropolitan, pre-electronic, grand live performance culture, whether it is Sibelius at the Barbican, Shakespeare at the Royal National Theatre, Kiri Te Kanawa at Covent Garden, or Britten at the Wigmore Hall. It is what Hewison describes as the 'official culture, a celebration of the country's power to sustain cultural activity and tradition, yet empty of significance beyond that' (Hewison 1997). It remains largely irrelevant to the changing meanings, cultures, and patterns of many, if not most, people's lives.

The Lottery

Lottery funding has also been characterized by the same metropolitan, self-electing, establishment processes too. Of the five 'distributing bodies', only the Millennium Commission and the

1 The recent tortuous history of the 'arm's-length' principle is given by former Arts Council Secretary-General Anthony Everitt, in *Financial Times*, 8 Nov. 1997.

Charities Board were entirely new creations; arts, sports, and heritage money were respectively given to the existing Arts Council, Sports Council, and Heritage Memorial Fund to administer. It is extraordinary how so much money, some £1.5 billion a year, could be left to a number of small committees of non-elected people to distribute, given how often elected local authorities have come under attack for errors of judgement in the provision of even the tiniest of grants.

The Millennium Commission, the Arts Council, and the Heritage Lottery Fund all operate within the same general constraints (with the exception of the Charities Board) in that they can only award grants for capital expenditure. The geographical, social, and cultural distribution of the grants has naturally been subject to intense scrutiny, and while it is early years yet—with the exception of the Millennium Commission, due to wind up by 2002—many of the old patterns of metropolitan, patrician administration have emerged. As a summary of spending to date noted,

Bias towards London in grant-making was even more pronounced last year [1996] than in 1995 . . . The charities and sports boards are praised for taking steps to ensure a more even spread of grants. Recognising that the heritage and arts boards face more difficulty in helping disadvantaged areas . . . they should therefore make greater effort to do so. But they have in fact done less.[2]

The big national cultural institutions—the Tate Gallery, the Royal Opera House—have received large Arts Council awards. The Millennium Commission chose London as the site for the big festival, despite what appeared to some to be the stronger argument for Birmingham. Heritage awards have, by definition, largely gone to the preservation of historic artefacts, monuments, landscapes, buildings, principally taking advice from already existing bodies such as English Heritage which has always had a cultural agenda of its own. The 'People's Lottery', as the Labour Party have rather opportunistically called it, has more often than not been awarded to projects and institutions close to the hearts of a metropolitan elite.

An interesting anomaly in all this has been the environmental cause. There were a very large number of national and regional environmental projects which applied—successfully—for funds from the Millennium Commission. Yet now that is due to close, there is the extraordinary situation in which one of the most important and popular lottery causes finds itself without a dedicated distribution body. Such projects usually had very strong regional, often geographically marginal, identities, typically

2 Review of the National Lottery Yearbook published by the Directory of Social Change, Guardian, 15 Apr. 1997.

Ken Worpole

involving the restoration of canal networks, coastal paths, landscaping ex-industrial sites, national cycle networks, and creating new community forests, and it is these that the London decision-makers have chosen to let wither on the vine.

The Millennium Festival

Aware of public dissatisfaction with some of the 'good causes' to which Lottery funding was being directed, the Labour Party proposed a sixth 'Good Cause'. The emphasis in the NESTA proposal on promoting young artistic and scientific talent was very much of a piece with the Labour Party's self-promotion as the party of 'the new'. 'New Labour' and 'New Britain' were the key watchwords of the 1997 election campaign, and the changes which resulted from Lottery spending were largely to do with the promotion of British talent and British creativity, and were accompanied by a widely broadcast rhetoric around the new fund, as well as the Millennium Festival itself. There was much talk of 'the new Britain', 'this British success story', of 'selling Britain', of giving 'our visitors a strong sense of Britain's energy as soon as they arrive here', which almost precisely echoed that of the 1951 Festival of Britain, when an earlier Labour government decided to celebrate Britain's (and by implication its government's) achievements in telling 'one continuous, interwoven story of British contributions to world civilisation in the arts of the people' (Banham and Hillier 1976: 8).

Central to both old and new visions was the iconic role of design. Ironically this was also Margaret Thatcher's favourite—possibly only—aesthetic cause. The Council of Industrial Design was centrally involved in the planning of the 1951 Festival, which was substantially used to showcase the work of a new generation of young designers, and there were explicit intentions to emulate the internationally successful 1930 Stockholm Exhibition which catapulted Swedish architecture and design (but also, as importantly, Swedish social democracy and its more equally distributed high standards of living) onto the world stage. The Millennium Experience created a series of Millennium Awards for product design. However, the idea that design alone can re-energize, remoralize, and even reindustrialize a nation seemed to signify the triumph of aesthetics over politics. The millennium proposals showed little of that deeper commitment to the integration of the social with the aesthetic represented by the Arts and Crafts movement, for example, or the Bauhaus in its early days, where social concerns and design concerns were strongly interwoven.[3] The fact that the separate Zones in the Millennium Dome were each to be commercially sponsored did not augur well for any great civic revelation to emerge triumphant.

The parallels established between the 1951 Festival of Britain and the rhetoric surrounding the 'Millennium Experience' underlined that Labour had learned very little that was either genuinely new, or politically radical, in the intervening fifty years, other than to put out more flags. What is most sobering is that having been in opposition for so many years, in a period in which large-scale processes of political realignment and rethinking were going on in economic and social policy, Labour's cultural policy remained largely untouched by similar transformations. Labour's 1997 election cultural manifesto *Create the Future: A Strategy for Cultural Policy, Arts and the Creative Economy* managed to squeeze every technocratic buzzword into the title, but inside was prefaced by a very old-fashioned morally improving epigram by Ruskin—'A person who every day looks upon a beautiful picture, reads a page from some good book, and hears a beautiful piece of music will soon become a transformed person—one born again' (Labour Party 1997).

Cultural Studies and Cultural Policy

It is ironic that Labour's inability to sketch out the skeleton of a coherent cultural policy during its two decades of opposition coincided with the proliferation of cultural studies within the universities and intellectual journals. This says much about the territorial divisions which continue to exist between cultural studies and cultural policy, an issue recently raised by Tony Bennett, Jim McGuigan, and Tom Steele among others (Bennett 1998; McGuigan 1996; Steele 1997), and one which now will not go away (see also Greenhalgh 1998). The many new ways in which we are now required to think about identity, about lifestyles, about media impacts, about ethnic and gender relations, and all the nuances of Gramscian and postmodern cultural relations of power in modern post-industrial societies, often informed by work in cultural studies, has produced very little in the way of new public policy imperatives. The imbalance between the rich, theoretical world of cultural theory and the impoverished world of cultural policy has never been clearer.

Yet cultural policy is deeply and publicly problematic, even if along fairly simplistic lines, often framed in popular discourse as

3 Reyner Banham's essay 'The Style' in Banham and Hillier (1976) provides an instructive list of cultural borrowings represented in the 1951 Festival 'style', while being a thoroughly enjoyable essay on post-war European aesthetics in its own right.

public subsidy to opera for the toffs at the expense of hospitals for the sick, or millions of pounds of public money paid for dead carcasses or piles of bricks, while there are leaking roofs at the local public library, It was, significantly, the Millennium Festival which provided the very first stumbling block for the new government, which had otherwise enjoyed a well-tempered media honeymoon. Despite the pretence of considering other possible sites for the great Millennium Festival, it was self-evident to many that it was always going to be in London. Indeed not just London but specific-ally on the south bank of the river Thames, which occupies a special place in the English geography of pleasure as a result of its association with Chaucerian culture, the Vauxhall Pleasure Gar-dens, the Crystal Palace, the Old Kent Road, the populism of the Old Vic, as well as a long historical identification with criminality and prostitution.

Other cities and other regions resented this *fait accompli*. People were also aghast at the estimated cost—at least £750 million—going to a site and a set of buildings that not only might prove temporary, but also seemed to have no self-evident spiritual or social meaning. 'What exactly are we celebrating?' people asked. One architectural journalist described the proposed Millennium Dome as 'like build-ing Canterbury Cathedral without having invented Christianity first'. Suddenly all the old historic cultural tensions came into play again: metropolitan bias, a preference for spending money on build-ings rather than people, and having a cultural programme without a cultural policy; all these elements, and many others, fitted into a familiar pattern.

In another ghostly echo, the politician appointed to take charge of the Millennium Festival, Peter Mandelson, was the grandson of the 1951 'Lord Festival', Herbert Morrison, and both were, unusually, cabinet ministers without any departmental responsi-bilities. Even the design of the Millennium Dome by the Richard Rogers Partnership made clear architectural references back to the 1951 Dome of Discovery. The 1951 Festival was criticized at the time for its lack of internationalist outlook, particularly at a time of post-war European reconstruction, and in its final form was little more than a British trade festival with an exhibition of arts thrown in. A decision was even made to ban foreign foodstuffs from the South Bank restaurants and cafeterias (Banham and Hillier 1976: 35). Criticism for its lack of internationalism has already been voiced about the Millennium Experience proposals. A strong sense of history repeating itself, but with a reversal of the Hegelian edict—in this case, first comedy, then tragedy—proved in the final outcome to be entirely apposite. It was a complete political and cultural disaster.

At least the organizers of the 1951 event sought to tap into older traditions of pleasure and popular taste. In addition to the Waterloo site, the Festival of Britain also took up a major site at Battersea Park with the establishment of the Pleasure Gardens, elements of which remain even today. If the Dome of Discovery, the arts and crafts exhibitions, and the demonstrations of milk-separating machines and nylon processing at Festival Gardens were worthy if sometimes rather dull, the emphasis at Battersea was on *fun*—a word which the distinguished historian Johans Huizinga in his magisterial study of play said could only be found in English: no other European language had an equivalent (Huizinga 1949). The Battersea Park Pleasure Gardens were not quite an afterthought, but as work progressed, the main organizer, Gerald Barry, 'was finding the South Bank rather clinical for his tastes. Architects and the scientists seemed to be running away with it. He wanted a place where people could relax and have fun—elegant fun. Remembering the old pleasure gardens at Vauxhall he decided we'd have a Festival Gardens. Battersea Park, then given over to allotments and a cricket pitch, was to be the site' (Banham and Hillier 1976: 118).

The reference back to the Vauxhall Pleasure Gardens is particularly interesting. As Mark Girouard and others have often pointed out, it was the English who invented the *passeggiata* or the social promenade, as well as the night-time pleasure gardens (where in park surroundings one could enjoy music perfomances, concerts, theatricals, food, and drink in an atmosphere of heightened sexual anticipation), yet with the rise of Methodism in the nineteenth century and with the greater control over public space and public life which Nonconformist local government increasingly exerted, these traditions were effectively quashed.[4] This suspicion of pleasure remains endemic to the Labour tradition. One of the most astute people who saw the possibilities for a different kind of English culture represented by the success of the Battersea model was the theatre director Joan Littlewood. In her recent autobiography she described the (abortive) plans for the 'Fun Palace' which were intended to build on the success of the Battersea experiment.

In London we are going to create a university of the streets—not a gracious park, but a foretaste of the pleasures of the future . . . In the music area—by day, instruments available, free instruction, recordings for everyone, classical, folk, jazz, pop, disc libraries—by night jam sessions and festivals, poetry and dance. In the science playground—lecture demonstrations, supported by teaching films, closed-circuit television and working

4 A new study of 18th-century life and culture, Brewer 1997, devotes several pages to the extraordinary range of entertainments offered in the London pleasure gardens, and their very wide social range of clientele.

Ken Worpole

models, at night an agora or Kaffeeklatsch where the Socrates, Abelards, Mermaid poets, the wandering scholars of the future—the mystics, sceptics and sophists—can dispute till dawn . . . But the essence of the place will be informality—nothing obligatory—anything goes. There will be no permanent structures. Nothing to last more than ten years, some things not even ten days: no concrete stadia, stained and cracking, no legacy of noble contemporary architecture, quickly dating.

With informality goes flexibility. The 'areas' that have been listed are not segregated enclosures. The whole plan is open, but on many levels. So the greatest pleasure of traditional parks is preserved—the pleasure of strolling casually, looking at one or other of these areas or (if this is preferred) settling down to several hours of work-play. (Littlewood 1994: 704)

This was not just a programme or prototype for a park; it was also the prototype of a different kind of society. Littlewood had also recruited some distinguished and energetic supporters to her cause. The architect principally associated with Littlewood's vision, Cedric Price, still in practice, remains an outsider to New Labour's favoured architectural circle. Yet very recently Rem Koolhaas, now perhaps one of the most influential architects on the world scene, cited Price as one of his mentors (Hayward Gallery 1999). This was one of those rare moments when a door of radical opportunity opens—and it was quickly slammed shut, by the Labour Party's ingrained puritanism and Weberian institutionalist mentality. Fun? The English were in the process of disinventing a tradition. Yet even today you can go to Skansen Park in Stockholm, or Tivoli Gardens in Copenhagen, where learned museums are located adjacent to swingboat parks and ferris wheels, where symphony orchestras alternate with dance bands in both open and indoor concert halls, where educational parties are taken to demonstration lectures on traditional farming methods, where expensive restaurants and sandwich kiosks stand alongside each other, and where pristine gardens are laid out adjacent to boating ponds, and still people seem able to accommodate to this inter-mix of the educational, the recreational, and the carnivalesque without any undue cultural stress and enervation, or loss of social control.

The Never-Ending Story

The continuities of policy and practice in the past fifty years of national cultural policy have been far greater than any processes of development or change. Yet the cultural lives and identities of the

British people have undergone staggering transformations, few of which have been reflected in the definitions and funding patterns of 'culture' at an institutional level.

There have been occasional and tentative explorations of new areas of policy such as community arts, cultural diversity (one of the many changing phrases used to indicate an engagement with ethnic minority cultural traditions), with architecture and public art, with the new electronic media, with the commercial cultural industries, but these have been sporadic forays or cultural sorties which have largely returned empty-handed. The Labour Party, out of power for most of the time, has shown rather increasing interest in the cultural industries, but more as examples of exportable products than as signifiers of changing relationships of power and cultural meaning. The new bonds between Labour politicians and architects such as Sir Richard Rogers, and designers such as Paul Smith, indicate some tentative movement towards a more contemporary understanding of style and public cultures.

The key understanding, that new cultural forms and breakthroughs in cultural production and dissemination mostly start by taking subcultural or oppositional forms, which ought to strike a chord with Labour's political origins, is strongly resisted. New Labour is culturally very conservative, its puritan tendencies still deeply ingrained, as we saw in March 1998 when Education Minister David Blunkett called for a withdrawal of public funding for Mark Ravenhill's highly successful play *Shopping and Fucking*, at the very same time that Culture Minister Chris Smith was endorsing a British Council European tour. The artistic currents and subcultures that have in the past two decades produced musicians such as Steve Williamson, Kathryn Tickell, Steve Martland, Massive Attack, filmmakers such as Sally Potter and the Quay Brothers, writers such as John Berger, Angela Carter, Jenny Diski, Carol Anne Duffy, Irvine Welsh, theatre ensembles such as Théâtre de Complicité, photographers such as Martin Parr and Chris Killip, visual artists such as Rachel Whiteread, Tony Cragg, Andy Goldsworthy, fashion designers such as Vivienne Westwood and John Galliano, and architectural practices such as Future Systems, all of which have successfully read the times and tried to shape the Zeitgeist, largely remain beyond the reach of the official cultural gaze.

Yet no one can avoid the rather difficult truth that cultural innovation and creativity happens in spite of official cultural policies rather than as a result of them. This was demonstrated, surely, in the strange symbiosis between the excesses of the Thatcher years with their overtly hostile attitude towards 'subsidized culture' and the international success and esteem of very many forms of British culture, particularly in writing and the visual arts, a lot of which grew out of or were related to the drug and rave scene. All those who take an interest in public cultural policy need to think hard about this. It is not enough simply to stand back and admire the way in which new cultural movements and identities struggle into being. On the other hand, how and where to intervene with public funding remains a difficult issue. Yet given capitalism's inherent logic, which is to incorporate, commodify, and globalize all forms of cultural production, support for emergent, independent production and distribution surely remains one of the key areas of intervention. London may have had its day. With the emergence of the Regional Development Agencies already happening, allied to regional parliaments and possibly incorporating the existing Regional Arts Boards, the development of what in architectural circles is now being described as 'critical regionalism' seems likely to be a more considered cultural response to the globalization of the imaginary.

Further Reading

Bennett, Tony (1998), *Culture: A Reformer's Science*, London: Sage.

Hewison, Robert (1995), *Culture and Consensus: England, Art and Politics since 1940*, London: Methuen.

Hutchinson, Robert (1982), *The Politics of the Arts Council*, London: Sinclair Browne.

Kelly, Owen (1984), *Community, Art and the State*, London: Comedia.

McGuigan, Jim (1996), *Culture and the Public Sphere*, London: Routledge.

Matarasso, François (1997), *Use or Ornament? The Social Impact of Participation in the Arts*, London: Comedia.

Mulgan, Geoff, and **Worpole, Ken** (1986), *Saturday Night or Sunday Morning? From Arts to Industry: New Forms of Cultural Policy*, London: Comedia.

Owusu, Kwesi (1986), *The Struggle for Black Arts in Britain*, London: Comedia.

Williams, Raymond (1965), *The Long Revolution*, Harmondsworth: Penguin.

Worpole, Ken (2000), *Here Comes the Sun: Architecture and Public Space in 20th Century European Culture*, London: Reaktion.

References

Aldiss, Brian (1976), 'A Monument to the Future', in Mary Banham and Bevis Hillier (eds.), *A Tonic to the Nation: The Festival of Britain 1951*, London: Thames & Hudson.

Banham, Mary, and **Hillier, Bevis** (1976), *A Tonic to the Nation: The Festival of Britain 1951*, London: Thames & Hudson.

Bennett, Tony (1998), *Culture: A Reformer's Science*, London: Sage.

Blair, Tony (1997), 'Britain can Remake it', *Guardian*, 22 July.

Brewer, John (1997), *The Pleasures of the Imagination: English Culture in the Eighteenth Centure*, London: Harper Collins.

Cork, Conrad (1997), *New Statesman*, 8 Aug.

Cumming, Laura (1997), 'Nobody Loves the Arts Council', *New Statesman*, 25 July.

Greenhalgh, Liz (1998), *Arts Policy to Creative Industries*, Media International Australia incorporating *Culture and Policy*, 87, May.

Haywood Gallery (1999), *Cities on the Move*, Exhibition Catalogue edited by Fiona Bradley, London.

Hewison, Robert (1981), *In Anger: Culture in the Cold War 1945–60*, London: Weidenfeld & Nicolson.

—— (1995) *Culture & Consensus: England, Art and Politics since 1940*, London: Methuen.

—— (1997), 'At Last, a Government that isn't Shy of Talking about Culture', *New Statesman*, 1 Aug.

Huizinga, Johans (1949), *Homo Ludens: A Study of the Play-Element in Culture*, London: Routledge Kegan Paul.

Hutchinson, Robert (1982), *The Politics of the Arts Council*, London: Sinclair Browne.

Kumar, Krishan (1981), 'The Nationalization of British Culture', in Stanley Hoffman and Paschalis Kitromolides (eds.), *Culture and Society in Contemporary Europe*, London: Allen & Unwin.

Labour Party (1997), *Create the Future: A Strategy for Cultural Policy, Arts and the Creative Economy*, London.

Littlewood, Joan (1994), *Joan's Book*, London: Methuen.

McGuigan, Jim (1996), *Culture and the Public Sphere*, London: Routledge.

Matarasso, François (1997), *Use or Ornament? The Social Impact of Participation in the Arts*, London: Comedia.

Mulgan, Geoff, and **Worpole, Ken** (1986), *Saturday Night or Sunday Morning? From Arts to Industry: New Forms of Cultural Policy*, London: Comedia.

Steele, Tom (1997), *The Emergence of Cultural Studies 1945–65*, London: Lawrence & Wishart.

Ward, David (1997), 'Windfall brings down Curtain', *Guardian*, 14 Aug.

Heritage Cinema and Television

ANDREW
HIGSON

SINCE the late 1970s, the term 'heritage' and the particular relation to the past that it implies have become central to the debate about national identity. Despite the efforts to 'rebrand' Britain and the emergence of 'Cool Britannia' in the late 1990s, the construction of English national identity remains profoundly dependent on the recovery of heritage, the insertion of the present into the miasma of tradition. The idea of nationhood of course has both a temporal and a spatial dimension, a historical and a geographical dimension. The national heritage is thus articulated as both exemplary narrative and traditional landscape (Daniels 1993: 4–7). In recent years, that heritage has become increasingly commodified and now takes the form of artefacts, images, and experiences that can be sold in the marketplace. Central among those images are the heritage film and television's classic serial (and its more recent variants such as the mini-series). These quality period dramas play a crucial role in the process of imagining nationhood, telling symbolic stories of class, gender, ethnicity, and identity, clothing them in elegant costumes, and staging them in the most picturesque landscapes and houses of the Old Country.

The contemporary fascination with period drama, and especially costume drama about the English upper classes, can be traced back to 1981, when *Brideshead Revisited* and *Chariots of Fire* caught the imagination of audiences, critics, and awards ceremonies. Granada TV's *Brideshead Revisited* was a lavish serialized adaptation of

Evelyn Waugh's lament about the decline of the English country house, its values, and its inhabitants. The serial was taken up as the embodiment of all that was best in British television. Its quality was visible in the casting, the adaptation, the locations and interiors, and the slow, expansive unfolding of the narrative: 'the truth is that *Brideshead Revisited* looks like the nearest thing to perfection that the television serial has managed in its entire history. It is an immense achievement' (Dunkley 1981). An enormous box-office success, *Chariots of Fire* also stirred up patriotic sentiments with its 1920s-set drama about class, ethnicity, and national identity:

It puts you in direct touch with sentiments so long un-expressed publicly that you wonder if they ever existed—love of country, fear of God, loyalty to the team, unselfish pursuit of honour, becoming modesty in victory, and that doesn't by any means exhaust the list. I'd add it is a wholly English film . . . if that didn't seem in the circumstances like boastful bad form. (Walker 1981)

Since 1981, British cinema and television have spawned several cycles of similar drama, many of them adaptations of canonical English literature (unlike *Chariots*, which was from an original screenplay). Among the most prominent is the cycle of films produced in Britain by Merchant–Ivory. These include the E. M. Forster adaptations *A Room with a View* (1986), *Maurice* (1987), and *Howards End* (1992), as well as their adaptation of a much more recent novel dealing with similar issues of class, inheritance, and national identity, Kazuo Ishiguro's *The Remains of the Day* (1993). These films are celebrated for their tasteful, soft-edged pictorial recreations of the Edwardian past—and, in *Remains*, the country house lifestyle of the mid-twentieth century. As the *Washington Post* put it, 'if Merchant [and] Ivory . . . have anything to do with it, there'll always be an England' (Kempley 1992: D8). Adaptations of Forster's novels in themselves constitute another cycle, with a further two films produced in the mid-1980s by other directors, David Lean's *A Passage to India* (1985) and Charles Sturridge's *Where Angels Fear to Tread* (1991). *A Passage to India* was also part of what was dubbed 'the Raj revival' in the mid-1980s (Rushdie 1984). Other texts in this cycle exposing imperialist fantasies of national identity include the highly successful fourteen-part television serial *The Jewel in the Crown* (1984), and another serialized adaptation, *The Far Pavilions* (1984). More recent films about the English abroad include *White Mischief* (1987), *Enchanted April* (1991), and *The English Patient* (1996).

In the 1990s, two other canonical authors replaced Forster: Jane Austen and Thomas Hardy. There is a long tradition of serialized adaptations of Austen's novels on British television, including *Pride and Prejudice* (1980) and *Mansfield Park* (1983). Austenmania really hit the screens in the mid-1990s, however, with the Emma Thompson-scripted film version of *Sense and Sensibility* (1995), and the enormously successful six-part BBC serialization of *Pride and Prejudice* (1995), written by Andrew Davies. Davies also wrote a feature-length version of *Emma* (1996) for ITV. A big-screen version of *Emma*, starring Gwyneth Paltrow, appeared the same year, as did *Persuasion*, a BBC single drama (on the Austen boom, see Ballaster 1996; Sales 1996: 227–39; and Pidduck 1998). In 2000, a very racy version of *Mansfield Park* worried some guardians of the literary heritage (see Mullan 2000). Hardy was author of the moment in the late 1990s, with film versions of *Jude* (1996), and *The Woodlanders* (1997), and television serial versions of *Far from the Madding Crowd* and *Tess of the d'Urbervilles* (both 1998). The television serial that revived the tradition of the costume drama on the BBC in the 1990s was from another Davies script: the 1994 adaptation of George Eliot's *Middlemarch*.

Other adaptations which deserve a mention, but which do not necessarily fit into any of the above cycles, include versions of Waugh's *A Handful of Dust* (1987), Henry James's *The Wings of the Dove* (1997), and two Virginia Woolf novels, *Orlando* (1992) and *Mrs Dalloway* (1998). There have also of course been numerous adaptations of the work of Shakespeare and Dickens. The literary connection figures again in a series of bio-pics, including *Shadowlands* (1994, about C. S. Lewis), *Tom and Viv* (1994, about T. S. Eliot's relationship with his wife), *Carrington* (1995, which features Lytton Strachey), *Wilde* (1997, about Oscar Wilde), and *Shakespeare in Love* (1999, a comic version of an imagined moment in Shakespeare's life).

One could also trace across the 1980s and 1990s a range of moving image appropriations of the royal family, including various live broadcasts of weddings, jubilees, and funerals, but also fictionalized filmic accounts of the royal heritage, such as *Elizabeth* (1998), *The Madness of King George* (1995), and *Mrs Brown* (1997), about Queen Victoria's relationship with her servant John Brown. It is noteworthy that a screening of *Emma* was slotted into the television schedule sensitively reorganized on the day of the funeral of Diana, Princess of Wales, in September 1997. This tasteful though not always reverential period drama, about a charismatic but insecure and less than perfect young upper-class heroine moving uncertainly towards a fairy tale romantic closure, provided the happy ending that Diana's fairy tale did not have. That it did so with the cultural authority of Jane Austen meant that it could be deemed safe in the context of what many saw as a day of national mourning.

What is to be gained by grouping together such a diverse set of films and television programmes, and therefore marginalizing other British products of the same period? First, it is worth noting how important these genres of cinema and television are in ensuring the reputation for quality in British moving-image media. The classic serial and other reverential adaptations of canonical literature have long been one of the cornerstones of the public service broadcasting schedule. In a similar way, literary adaptations and 'tasteful' period dramas, along with the documentary-realist tradition, have held pride of place in the debates about what constitutes British national cinema. The aura of art and quality around heritage drama affords it a special place in the contemporary national culture. Not simply national culture, however, for British heritage films and television programmes are frequently sold in export markets. Many of the television programmes and series mentioned have had an airing on America's PBS channel, and have been bought by other broadcasters around the world. Many of the films mentioned have had an art-house release overseas, or have been otherwise promoted to 'discerning' international audiences. As such, the films and television programmes operate as cultural ambassadors, promoting certain images of Englishness.

This, then, is a second reason for grouping together the films and television programmes cited above. In one way or another, they all articulate a version of the national heritage that contributes to a core English identity. This does not necessarily mean that all audiences read these texts in this way; it simply means that it is *possible* to read them in this way (and certainly many have). Such texts frequently articulate a pre-technological, ruralist, and aristocratic heritage. Some explore the tension between ruralist tradition and the modernity of the city and technology; some are concerned less with the aristocracy than with the sensibility of the bourgeoisie, the officer class, and gentlefolk. But taken together, there remains an overwhelming concern with the landscapes and narratives of British, or, more properly, English, tradition and privilege.

Even if these films and television programmes articulate a version of the English national heritage, it would be difficult to argue that they are uniquely English products. In today's global cultural economy, it is rare to find a film or television programme that is not designed for both domestic and export markets, and which is not therefore funded from a variety of sources or created by a multinational team. *Howards End*, for instance, described by one reviewer as 'an instant national treasure . . . a country-house classic . . . an immediate part of the British heritage' (Hutchinson 1992: 39), received substantial funding from Japan and the United States. Its production team was equally cosmopolitan: it was directed by an American, produced by an Indian, and scripted by a woman of Polish extraction. *Sense and Sensibility*, while similarly populated with the cream of English actors (Emma Thompson, Kate Winslet, Hugh Grant, et al.), was funded by Columbia Pictures and directed by the Taiwanese-American Ang Lee. Shekhar Kapur, an Indian director, made *Elizabeth*, while the Australian actress Cate Blanchett played the part of the iconic Virgin Queen. In this respect, heritage films are no different from most other recent 'British' films, in that they are thoroughly dependent on American funding and specialized distribution in the hugely lucrative American market. If critics use such films and television programmes to define a national cinema and television distinct from the culture and economy of Hollywood, they do so only by ignoring their dependence on that culture and economy.

We must therefore come to terms with the fact that what may seem to be a national representation is in reality an international mythology—that is, a story and characters that are assumed to have meaning, significance, and poignancy for international audiences. Perhaps this simply underlines rather more obviously the constructed nature of representations of the English national past and English identity. Indeed, in this context of transnational production and consumption, it is possible to discern a tension in the films and television programmes themselves between a pure and distinctive version of Englishness and a much more hybrid and transgressive sense of cross-cultural identity. The geography of national heritage, the 'pure', 'traditional' England it is possible to read in many of these texts, is often carefully constructed by the film- and programme-makers, stitched together from a variety of locations and interiors which masquerade as the real thing with the help of modern technology and imitation fabrics and materials. The task is very often to construct a place that pre-dates the Americanization of English culture. In fact, America is a constant and often ironic reference point in the dialogue of these texts, some of which address the very issue of Americanization. In *Chariots of Fire*, for instance, Englishness is specifically set against the modernity of America; in *The Remains of the Day*, the traditions of the stately home at the heart of the narrative are eroded when it is bought by an American.

Acting is always about masquerade, of course, but when key

English figures are played by American or Australian actors such as Gwyneth Paltrow or Cate Blanchett, the very slipperiness and inconstancy of identity is brought to the fore. In some films and television programmes, identity is thematized as a tirelessly shifting sandscape, a collage of overlapping fragments that can be put together in all manner of ways. In *Chariots of Fire*, the 'purest' Englishman is from Lithuanian Jewish stock; in *Howards End*, the embodiment of England, Margaret Schlegel, is Anglo-German. Cross-dressing similarly confuses identity in *Orlando*, *Carrington*, and *Shakespeare in Love*.

This instability is held in check by the overwhelming concern to reproduce heritage landscapes and narratives with the appropriate degree of authenticity. While most of the films and television programmes cited above are presented as fiction, it is a fiction that the producers will often try to ensure has as strong a realist effect as possible. The discourse of authenticity is central to the promotion of these texts, in terms of both the 'faithfulness' of adaptations to their source novels, and the 'correctness' of the period settings, fashions, interior designs, and artefacts. Even as self-consciously irreverential a film as *Elizabeth* still made some claims to historical authenticity. The periods reproduced are also limited. Many of the films and television programmes are set in the latter decades of the nineteenth century or the early decades of the twentieth century, a crucial period in the formation of the dominant modern version of English national identity. The Austen adaptations were set much earlier, in the Regency period, *Elizabeth* and *Shakespeare in Love* earlier still, in the Elizabethan period. Both periods are frequently appropriated as key moments in and vital representations of the national heritage.

A third reason for grouping these various films and television programmes together is that, for all their differences, collectively they play a crucial role as part of the larger heritage industry. The emphasis on spectacularly picturesque landscapes and fine old buildings, and the public interest thereby generated, dovetails neatly with the work of heritage bodies like the National Trust and English Heritage. As a reviewer for the *Sunday Telegraph* suggested of the 1995 *Pride and Prejudice* adaptation, it was like 'a lovely day out in some National Trust property' (1 Oct. 1995, quoted in Sales 1996: 237–8). Websites and books about the making of particular films and television programmes will often detail the locations used in period dramas, and visits to those locations will often increase dramatically (see Rice and Saunders 1996; Sargeant 2000). Cinema and television drama promote a form of cultural tourism which overlaps with the work of bodies like the English Tourist Board, and their creation of brand images such as Thomas Hardy's Dorset, 1066 Country in East Sussex, and Constable Country in Suffolk. In the summer of 1999, the British Tourist Authority produced an official 'Movie Map', more than a quarter of a million copies of which were sent to travel agencies in North America, the Far East, Australia, and Europe (Wintour 1999). The purpose was to encourage tourists to visit British sites that have featured in films. While films with historical settings were by no means the only films to appear on the map, half of the 1990s films featured did in fact have pre-Second World War period settings. A whole range of other formal and informal tie-ins, cross-promotions, spin-offs, and chance juxtapositions encourage the public to consume much more than simply a film or a television programme. Publishers bring out new editions of adapted books, or create the book of the film or television series; clothes stores such as Laura Ashley exploit period costume fashions; upmarket lifestyle magazines promote period properties, interior designs, furnishings and fabrics; and food outlets offer traditional fayre.

Period food, fashion, fabrics, and furnishings are crucial elements of the *mise-en-scène* of heritage cinema and television, and they are displayed to best advantage by the characteristic aesthetic organization of these texts. The formal similarities between these films and television programmes thus provide a fourth reason for grouping them together. Heritage cinema is typically slow moving and episodic, lacking the fast pace and dynamic energy of the mainstream American action film. This enables the films to focus much more on character, and on the visual splendour and period richness of the settings. Art and costume design and choice of locations are vital features of the heritage film, and camerawork and staging will frequently make space for the display of landscape, architecture, interior decor, and costumes. Television's classic serials, period mini-series, and one-off costume dramas will often work with the same formal strategies. The long-running serial of course can afford to open out its narratives even further, to put its stories together even more episodically. The emphasis on character rather than action in the television adaptation of canonical literature will often go hand in hand with an emphasis on dialogue, on the reproduction of the source novel's prose. Serials like the early 1980s adaptations of *Pride and Prejudice* and *Mansfield Park* are littered with scenes of characters walking through verdant heritage landscapes, or standing in front of elegantly cluttered museum interiors, quoting chunks of Austen.

The limited range of period landscapes, buildings, and props on display gives a very reductive view of English heritage. The aesthetics of display however often seem to suggest that this reductive view is both real and desirable. At the same time, the narratives which many of these heritage dramas relate are often much more radical, questioning the desirability of the lifestyle of those who inhabit these spaces. This creates a tension between the visual work and the narrative work of these dramas. Visually, the impression is that England is a wonderful place of tradition and privilege; narratively, on so many occasions, that place is in disarray, the traditions are exposed as repressive, and privilege revealed as exploitation. Where the narrative often encourages a critique of privilege and tradition, the visuals seem too often to invite a nostalgic delight in the images of wealth and antiquity.

I have inevitably overstated this tension between narrative and image and others will read the same texts differently. The *mise-en-scène* of these films and television programmes is undoubtedly also used in a functional way to indicate character traits and sensibilities, thus working in tandem with the narrative movement of the texts. Some critics have argued that in more recent work, the aesthetics of display has been displaced by a much more narratively functional *mise-en-scène* (Sales 1996: 237–8). Some have argued that, as the heritage cycle has developed, so its later entrants are much more knowing, even parodic, of the conventions established by their predecessors: their makers are only too aware of the conventions and are willing to play with them. In particular, they are less chaste about sexual activity. Thus Roger Sales (1996: 238), discussing the 1995 television adaptation of *Pride and Prejudice*, charts a shift from 'a much more serious and reverential manner' in previous adaptations to a camp and frivolous emphasis on the 'period bosom' and Darcy's tight-fitting trousers. Claire Monk (1995a: 33) similarly notes 'a deep self-consciousness about how the past is represented' and a concern with 'transgressive sexual politics' in what she calls 'post-heritage films' like *Orlando* and *Carrington*. But, as she goes on to note, 'paradoxically the post-heritage films revel in the visual pleasures of heritage, even as they seem to distance themselves'. Pamela Church Gibson (2000) argues that costume dramas such as *Persuasion* and *Jude* are deliberately anti-nostalgic in their refusal to fetishize the past. The broad farce, the slapstick, the wordplay, and the sex scenes of *Shakespeare in Love* are certainly far more populist than the polite comedy of manners of *A Room with a View*. The overtly stylized camerawork and fast cutting of *Elizabeth*, its conspiracy thriller narrative, and its scenes of torture and murder, make it clear that new audiences are being addressed by later entrants in the heritage cycle.

As these qualifications suggest, if there are advantages in grouping together this body of films and television programmes under the rubric of heritage cinema and television, there are also some disadvantages. First, can we really assume that all these texts work in the same way in terms of how they represent national history? I suggested above that it is possible to see in all of them an articulation of core national heritage values, but that it is also possible to see in them a tension between a pure national identity and a more hybrid cultural formation. We can take this discrepancy further if we cast it in terms of reception. For if some audiences embrace these films and television programmes as heritage products, others embrace them for very different reasons. It makes eminent sense to see the films as charming, but also often quite challenging romances, for instance. As some critics have argued, what I and others have called the heritage film could equally be classed as a modern variant of the woman's picture, while the classic serial on television may be seen as soap opera in period costume. The protagonists around whom many of the films and programmes cited above revolve are quite often strong-willed, independent women, and it is their interests, outlooks, and desires that are explored (Dyer 1994; Monk 1995a, 1995b; Higson 1996).

Audiences who read the texts in these ways may simply not consider them in terms of debates about heritage, tradition, and the national past. The relative popularity of such texts does not necessarily indicate that audiences are buying into a fantasy of the national past, or an international mythology of Englishness. It may on the contrary be the case that audiences are engaging with the films and television programmes as dramas of romance, desire, and sexual politics. It is worth recording that if one of the promotional discourses circulating around the films and television programmes listed above is precisely the discourse of heritage and authenticity, another equally strong discourse is that of youthful romance. So often, the key promotional image for these films and television programmes features the attractive, youthful male or female lead— or, better still, the male and female leads engaged in an intimate embrace. Of course, they appear in period costume, and, of course, behind them is a heritage landscape or period property, but these are to some extent simply the trappings of romance.

A third problem with my definition of 'heritage' concerns its reductiveness. Some audiences clearly do regard such texts as dealing with the national past, and many of those texts do engage with pre-technological, ruralist, and aristocratic traditions. But there are also many other heritages with which audiences, consumers, and historians of all types engage. As Raphael Samuel (1994) has argued, heritage culture is neither a new phenomenon, nor an exclusively elite or conservative practice, nor indeed one that can be reduced to the terms of consumerism. People engage with the past in many different ways. Considerable amounts of energy are invested in the active exploration of, for instance, local heritages, working-class heritages, industrial heritages, and the heritages of diasporic communities who have found a home in Britain. It is worth noting, however, that, as Stephen Daniels (1993: 4) puts it, while 'this has involved the restoration of alternative versions of English heritage, some . . . like parish pride, may overlap uncomfortably with conservative versions'.

To identify as heritage drama a body of films and television programmes of dubious national identity, offering a limited set of representations, is clearly to beg the question of whose heritage is being circulated. In a multicultural society, there are many, often contradictory traditions competing for attention; yet so-called heritage cinema and television would seem to focus primarily on the traditions of the privileged, white, Anglo-Saxon community who inhabit lavish properties in a semi-rural southern England, within striking distance of the metropolitan seat of power. On the one hand, for many, this is not a national culture, but a much more specific class-bound culture. On the other hand, the arguments of Samuel and others notwithstanding, this culture, this set of traditions, is overwhelmingly presented as embodying the *national* past. Audiences who engage with these representations must in some degree negotiate their ideas of England and Englishness in relation to these representations. This does not mean that all audiences who engage with these representations automatically buy into a particular mythology of nationhood; but if they do not, then they must actively resist such representations and seek to create an alternative mythology.

Such a stance is not entirely at odds with the narrative work of the various films under discussion (though not necessarily the television dramas). If, on the one hand, these texts seem to privilege a very limited social stratum, on the other hand, almost all of them can be read as liberal dramas of social transgression. So many of them seem to be about reaching across the boundaries of class, ethnicity, gender, and sexuality, offering a vision of a more inclusive, democratic, even multicultural England (Higson 1993, 1996). Thus in *Chariots of Fire*, aristocracy gives way to meritocracy. In *Howards*

End, the ultimate inheritor of the house that symbolizes traditional England is the illegitimate son of the lower middle-class Leonard Bast and the upper middle-class, Anglo-German Helen Schlegel. In *Maurice*, *Carrington*, and *Mrs Dalloway*, there are central and charismatic lesbian and gay relationships. In *Maurice* and *The Wings of the Dove*, the central relationships also transgress class boundaries.

The final problem with the effort to define 'heritage' as a key term in the national vocabulary is that the moment of heritage may have passed. One of the legacies of the Thatcher years was a government department designed to create and maintain the infrastructure necessary to promote a conservative vision of national identity: the Department of National Heritage. Under Tony Blair, that office became the Department of Culture, Media, and Sport. The election of New Labour in 1997 coincided with the displacement of the heritage industry by the mythology of 'Cool Britannia' and the celebration of the apparent youthful energy of the contemporary design, fashion, music, and film industries. In the words of a headline in the *Sunday Telegraph*, 'Heritage is a thing of the past' (Powell 1998). Except of course that the term 'Cool Britannia' is itself a pastiche of an icon at the centre of heritage culture. In any case, the culture of 'Cool Britannia' frequently reworks the heritage of the 1960s and 'Swinging London'. Again, tradition and modernity walk hand in hand; again the national heritage is reinvented in an enterprising manner.

Further Reading

Church Gibson, P. (2000), 'Fewer Weddings and More Funerals: Changes in the Heritage Film', in R. Murphy (ed.), *British Cinema of the 90s*, London: BFI. A succinct and insightful survey of developments in the 1990s.

Corner, J., and **Harvey, S.** (eds.) (1991), *Enterprise and Heritage: Crosscurrents of National Culture*, London: Routledge. A useful collection of essays looking at the heritage business, including cinema and television, in the Thatcher years.

Hewison, R. (1987), *The Heritage Industry*, London: Methuen. The standard version of the argument that our relationship to the past has been commodified.

Higson, A. (1993), 'Re-presenting the National Past: Nostalgia and Pastiche in the Heritage Film', in L. Friedman (ed.), *Fires Were Started: British Cinema and Thatcherism*, Minneapolis: University of Minnesota Press and London: UCL Press.

—— (1996), 'The Heritage Film and British Cinema', in A. Higson (ed.), *Dissolving Views: Key Writings on British Cinema*, London: Cassell.

—— (2002, forthcoming), *English Heritage, English Cinema*, Oxford: Oxford

University Press. In these three publications, I examine the heritage film in much more detail than I have been able to here.

Hill, J. (1999), *British Cinema of the 1980s*, Oxford: Clarendon Press. A good survey of British cinema in the 1980s, a section of which is devoted to representations of the past.

References

Ballaster, R. (1996), 'Adapting Jane Austen', *English Review*, Sept.

Church Gibson, P. (2000), 'Fewer Weddings and More Funerals: Changes in the Heritage Film', in R. Murphy (ed.), *British Cinema of the 90s*, London: BFI.

Daniels, S. (1993), *Fields of Vision: Landscape Imagery and National Identity in England and the United States*, Cambridge: Polity Press.

Dunkley, C. (1981), review of *Brideshead Revisited*, *Financial Times*, 14 Oct.

Dyer, R. (1994), 'Feeling English', *Sight and Sound*, NS 4/3.

Higson, A. (1993), 'Re-presenting the National Past: Nostalgia and Pastiche in the Heritage Film', in L. Friedman (ed.), *Fires Were Started: British Cinema and Thatcherism*, Minneapolis: University of Minnesota Press and London: UCL Press.

—— (1996), 'The Heritage Film and British Cinema', in A. Higson (ed.), *Dissolving Views: Key Writings on British Cinema*, London: Cassell.

Hutchinson, T. (1992), review of *Howards End*, *Mail on Sunday*, 3 May.

Kempley, R. (1992), '*Howards End*: Resplendent Return to Forster's England', *Washington Post*, 24 Apr.

Monk, C. (1995a), 'Sexuality and the Heritage', *Sight and Sound*, NS 5/10.

—— (1995b), 'The British Heritage Film and its Critics', *Critical Survey*, 7/2.

Mullan, J. (2000), 'Fanny's Novel Predicament', *Guardian*, 28 Mar.

Pidduck, J. (1998), 'Of Windows and Country Walks: Frames of Space and Movement in 1990s Austen Adaptations', *Screen*, 39/4.

Powell, K. (1998), 'Heritage is a Thing of the Past', *Sunday Telegraph* (*Sunday Review* section), 10 May.

Rice, J., and **Saunders, C.** (1996), 'Consuming *Middlemarch*: The Construction and Consumption of Nostalgia in Stamford', in D. Cartmell, I. Q. Hunter, H. Kaye, and I. Whelehan (eds.), *Pulping Fictions: Consuming Culture across the Literature/Media Divide*, London: Pluto Press.

Rushdie, S. (1984), 'Outside the Whale', *Granta*, 11.

Sales, R. (1996), *Jane Austen and Representations of Regency England*, rev. edn., London: Routledge.

Samuel, R. (1994), *Theatres of Memory*, London: Verso.

Sargeant, A. (2000), 'Making and Selling Heritage Culture: Style and Authenticity in Historical Fictions on Film and Television', in J. Ashby and A. Higson (eds.), *British Cinema, Past and Present*. London: Routledge.

Walker, A. (1981), 'Britain back on the Tracks', *New Standard*, 2 Apr.

Wintour, P. (1999), 'Now You've Seen the Film, Don't Miss the Location', *Observer*, 13 June.

17

Television and Culture: Duties and Pleasures

JOHN CORNER

IN Britain, as in many other countries, television has become a central ingredient of everyday life and an indispensable factor in the organization of polity, society, and culture. The sheer scale of operation of television services, their reach and variety, coupled with the distinctive properties of a medium able to present high-definition moving colour images and quality sound reproduction to home viewers, mixing recorded material with live transmission, has over forty-five years or so brought about huge changes in the nature of popular culture and the idea of 'home entertainment'. In ways which are often awkward and complex to assess it has formed a new symbolic matrix, reconfiguring the relationship between the public, the private, between the official and the popular, between the local, the national and the international.

British society is a thoroughly 'mediatized' society in which very few social processes occur entirely free of a media element and many interconnect substantially with mediation as both resource and publicity. There are dangers for those who assume too simplistic and direct an idea of cultural influence on the basis of this fact, but it is also possible for the pervasive nature of the new symbolic environment to be underestimated.

All societies with developed television systems have evolved a distinctive discourse of 'duties' and 'pleasures' surrounding the medium. The precise terminology used differs greatly and so do the relationships struck between the two, but it is incontrovertibly the case that television is both a major agency of public communications, a primary means of knowledge, and at the same time a great source of diversion and entertainment. Most of the key debates about national television systems have hinged on the relationship between television as 'knowledge machine' and as 'pleasure machine'. One would not expect to find such a tension at work in cinema, for example, since cinema is established as a matter of commercially organized private choice in relation primarily to pleasure. In the British press, a tension of a comparable kind can be discerned, but this is still largely displayed across the division between 'quality' and 'popular' newspapers and is finally regarded as a matter of individual market choices not of public policy.

Television, Culture, and Everyday Life

Before looking in more detail at how the British system is organized and how it is changing I want to open up a little further the general question of television, culture, and everyday life. In previous writing, I have pursued the idea that television is a device which acts, culturally, both centripetally and centrifugally. Centripetally, it is involved in a virtually continuous, selective ingestion of ingredients from the wider culture—drawing from fashion, magazines, films, music, sports, embedded elements of local and regional culture, occupational and leisure subcultures, shifting attitudes, emerging values. It then gives to these a transformed, television presence (perhaps in a new show, a new presenter, a new advert, a new series idea, a new studio set, or a new treatment). Television lives partly by its alertness to what is 'happening' in culture and therefore what might achieve contemporary resonance on the screen, preferably just slightly ahead of its full realization in the culture at large but, if not this, then certainly with little delay. Its own economics of competitive novelty and rapid content-exhaustion rates encourage this surveillance, reinforcing that 'hunter-gatherer' voracity which producers of television typically display.

In what I think is best seen as a separate but related phase, television works centrifugally too. It projects out to the widest edges of the culture its own mix of original and reworked cultural experience (attitudes, jokes, styles, personalities, looks, situations, types, ways of speaking). In Britain, this projection remains strong enough to ensure that it will take only a few weeks for certain 'new' people, shows, catch-lines, great successes, and utter flops to become woven, however temporarily, into great stretches of national cultural life, sometimes crossing class, gender, and age differences with a surprising speed. The popular press in Britain often reinforces this sense of television as still a 'national cultural stage', a focus for gossip as well as for anxieties about national values. Acting as a massive cultural producer and distributor, of part original and part reworked material, television sets the terms for much subsequent non-televisual cultural practice.

In this kind of double pump-action, circulating and recirculating the 'national', there has recently been an increasing element of the 'international'. Of course, with any articulation of the national, implications about that which lies beyond national boundaries are always present, just as the construction of the 'television national' itself will take place in relationship to tensions and power relationships obtaining between the different groups which make up a nation. It is worth pointing out here, too, that very few if any other cultural agencies can work at the level and reach of national television in their culturally constitutive activities. Television, then, should be seen to be at least as much a shaper as a reflector of national culture.

In its culturally formative activities, helping significantly to construct not only the 'official' life of the nation but also its private, popular pleasures (its jokes as well as its heritage), British television has displayed two characteristics which any student of it should note. First of all, it has shown strong national self-consciousness and confidence, a characteristic predicated largely on the imperialist history of many British cultural institutions and one which has been particularly important in defining the 'British' against the 'American' in television (the relationship here still being the key one for many national television systems, often organized from a position of economic and cultural subordination). Secondly, and relatedly, it was for a very long time institutionalized as a *public service* television system in which consequences for the national culture were not just the by-product of a commercially profitable transaction between producers, advertisers, and viewers but *were the primary corporate goals of the system*. This has given to British television a wholly distinctive set of protocols about 'duties' (responsibilities, standards, missions to inform, requirement to educate, etc.) and also about 'pleasures' (tastes, brow-levels, the dangers of 'triviality', etc.). These protocols have proved a mixed blessing, combining for some time, on the one hand, a genuine impulse to foster excellence, widen accessibility, and discourage exploitation with, on the other, metropolitan, class-based taste preferences shot through with disdain for the 'ordinary' and sometimes hankering after 'standards' with a punitive, schoolmasterly zeal (for argument about the nature and consequence of 'public service' ideals in British broadcasting, see Scannell 1989). Although much has changed in the last few years, British television is still marked by the way in which a discourse about public values and 'quality' (a key term of connection between duties and pleasures) uneasily coexists with an increasing market imperative and a strong market version of the popular.

The Institutional Basis of British Television

Television in Britain has a cultural profile essentially inherited from radio broadcasting, set up in the 1920s as an 'embassy of national culture' by its first director-general, Sir John Reith. The Reithian legacy is more complex than is sometimes assumed (see Scannell and Cardiff 1991) but in its initial formation it employed broadcasting as an instrument of national cultural development (of 'improvement') in a manner which has a continuing presence in the way the British talk about television (and especially about the BBC) whatever the dilution it has undergone.

From the start of British television services after the war until 1955, a key period in the establishing of television as a medium of both public knowledge and popular entertainment, the BBC ran its single-channel service as a monopoly. With the advent of Independent Television (ITV), a regionally based commercial network, viewers not only had a choice of channel but also the option of a more regionally flavoured schedule. It is possible to overstate the real differences between the two services, but ITV, necessarily, had not only to reflect aspects of regional culture but also, in the search for advertising-attractive audiences, to explore the possibilities of 'the popular', specifically working-class pleasures and interests, more thoroughly than the BBC had generally felt inclined to do. That this sometimes shaded into 'populism' (the exploitation of assumed 'popular tastes' for maximum market advantage with little real regard for popular cultural life itself) is undoubtedly true, but the opening out of regional and social class representations (voices, images, concerns, entertainments) which followed the breaking of the BBC monopoly is, nevertheless, one of the most significant phases in British post-war cultural history.

It is important to note here that the ITV network was, from its inception, regulated as a 'public service' system by an Independent Television Authority, a public body whose powers drew criticism from those who had championed a model driven by unfettered market competition. So, in a very British way, the commercial version of the 'popular' was at least partially framed by a prior, 'public' ethos. However, ITV's developing impact upon the looks and sounds of British television soon caused the BBC's own versions of British cultural life to be rethought in many areas of programming—particularly popular drama, documentary, and situation comedy—often with results which won both popularity and critical acclaim.

The launch of the BBC's second national television channel, BBC2, in 1964 was also a significant development in television's contribution to national cultural life. The initial idea was to increase the scope for 'experimental programmes' and to provide a range of serious and sometimes minority-interest material which it was getting increasingly awkward to carry on the Corporation's existing single channel. Although it had initial difficulties, the new channel quite quickly established itself as carrying a schedule of programmes from which, selectively, all viewers could benefit and gain pleasure (a documentary series, *The Great War*, mixing archive film with oral testimony about the 1914–18 war, was its first big success in establishing itself with the national audience).

It was not until 1982 that the 'duopoly' of the BBC's two channels and the ITV network was broken by the arrival of Channel 4. To a certain extent a development of those ideas about television's role in 'serious' culture (factual and fictional) which were behind BBC2, Channel 4 nevertheless represented a much more radical approach. It was predicated on a strong sense of Britain as a pluralist and multicultural society in which dominant notions of national broadcasting were becoming inadequate to the real patterns of demography, of cultural choice, and of everyday life. By adopting a 'publisher' model, commissioning programmes from a range of providers some of which were very small companies, and by operating as a protected 'public' operation *within* the advertising-supported ITV network (an arrangement ended in the mid-1990s), Channel 4 sought to open up and diversify British broadcasting, partially disestablishing it from the big institutions. On the whole, its history throughout the 1980s and most of the 1990s is one of significant cultural development in the use of the medium for both information and entertainment, including the bringing of a much sharper awareness of European and international culture to British viewers. Much discussed, it has undoubtedly made a major contribution to the present cultural identity of British television. Its initial mode of organization was an imaginative, hybridized solution to conflicting imperatives within a television system having to resituate itself in relation to both changed public values and market structures.

This is the broad character of a 'national television'—inclusive, pluralist, but still concerned with an encompassing unity and with the holding together within the schedule of diverse programme types—which is now undergoing rapid change as the terrestrial grouping of four well-established channels is steadily joined by the range of new channels made available to viewers. These are arriving either by direct satellite reception, by the new cable systems which have been introduced into many regions, or, more recently, by the introduction of a digital technology which will massively increase multi-channel capacity as well as accelerate the convergence with computer-based home applications, bringing interactivity and a new directness of demand-led supply. Indeed, the proliferation of 'channel choice' within the deregulatory climate initially established by the Conservative government in the late 1980s as the optimum linkage of new technology and commercial profit is such that the launching of a terrestrial Channel 5 in 1997 (with a small budget, an uncertain identity, and a nervously qualified credo—'modern but mainstream') created minimal cultural impact. Although there is widespread recognition of the amount of low-quality, 'fillers and repeats' material currently on offer through cable (considerably qualifying the extent to which 'choice' can be seen simply in terms of number of channels), movie channels in particular have made substantial inroads, reinforcing an effect starting in the 1980s with the use of the screen for hired video playback. The shift to digital, which includes terrestrial channels (begun in 1999), will complicate the market pattern even further and require strategies for winning viewers to what may turn out to be radically changed routines and forms of television use.

The next few years will be watershed ones, as the scale and nature of shifts in viewing patterns and the character of the digital experience as a feature of popular culture become clearer. A new pattern of regulation will emerge, one having to take account of the multimedia settings of television and the increasing requirement to recognize that the delivery systems of the medium and its various types of content need separate consideration as the older, unified models of production and distribution no longer define the national industry.

Programme Culture

I now want to turn from the system to the programmes themselves. Given a high degree of international styling in 1990s television, with the continued, strong influence of US formats, what kind of national television aesthetic, with what kind of embedding in specific cultural and social relations, does British television show today?

One of the first areas which deserve attention is the British strand of soap opera, not only because of the huge, ratings-topping audiences which these draw and their increasing frequency (once, by convention, weekly, now sometimes daily) but also because of the distinctive social and aesthetic perspectives within which most of them frame their fictions. *Coronation Street*, starting on ITV in 1962, was the first major popular series drama in Britain to base its appeal in the routine life of a small group of residents within an 'ordinary' community (rather than, say, focusing on a particular family). It mixed the appeal of domestic melodrama with a distinctively British version of social realism, an attempt to use drama as a way of not only giving pleasure but also exploring the changed circumstances of working-class life. Since then, there have been many kinds of soap series, but currently the three big British-produced programmes are *Coronation Street* (ITV), *EastEnders* (BBC), and *Brookside* (Channel 4), the last two starting in the 1980s. All three employ distinctive recipes for presenting 'ordinary' life on the screen, centring on domestic and neighbourhood relationships though not entirely neglecting the shaping factors of workplace. In this, they contrast strongly with the US 'glamour soaps' of the 1970s and 1980s (classically, *Dallas* and *Dynasty*) in which the lives of the rich and elite provided the dramatic milieu. They are to be compared more with the Australian series *Neighbours* and *Home and Away* which have done extremely well in Britain, probably as a result of the way they mix the resonant values of 'ordinary community' (in a decidedly more upbeat version than their British equivalents) with the exoticism of almost perpetual sunshine.

Indeed, as I noted above, the British soaps, although they have all been subject to extensive overhaul in recent years, have to be understood in terms of a particular, national version of 'community'. This version is grounded in a broad set of cultural meanings surrounding locality, social class, wealth, and family. In particular, it strongly foregrounds the various roles, problems, and capacities of women in a way which much 'serious' as well as 'popular' drama has failed to do. Community is partly sentimentalized in all three principal British soaps, but their distinctive vein of realism has kept them alert to changes and to the newer kinds of problem faced in ordinary living. Although they inevitably depend upon a degree of fictive distortion, an intensification of character and plot, for their appeal, their range of social reportage is wide and often perceptive. Any analysis of the British popular television experience needs to start with an appraisal of their mundane rhythms and the 'parallel social universe' they offer to many viewers (see Geraghty 1991).

A concurrent development with the soaps but one also taking strong bearings from the tradition of British social documentary is that of 'workplace' drama. Here, the distinctive line of British police series (from the 1950s *Dixon of Dock Green* and the 1960s *Z Cars* through to *The Bill* in the 1980s and beyond) stands out, reflecting 'public' and 'private' aspects in a varying but distinctive mix in which crime is mostly a far less important ingredient than working relationships at the police station. Similarly, in British hospital drama, a strong vein of documentary commentary on political and social contexts and institutional difficulties is often to be found, nowhere more so than in the long-running achievements of the BBC's *Casualty*. Perhaps the most recent success in this broad area has been ITV's *London's Burning*, about a particular crew at a London fire station. This series, in its scripting, acting, and location shooting, combines some of the developed documentary strengths with the dramatic satisfactions of understated 'ordinariness' (the routines of work within the rhythms of living) central to the British television experience.

Situation comedy, a genre increasingly internationalized in its formats, also takes strong national inflections. Sitcom has produced some of the 'classics' of British television and, despite the competition from US imports, has proved to be successfully reworkable for 1990s contexts, particularly by the BBC. For instance, *One Foot in the Grave* (BBC) explored the domestic experience of retirement and elderliness but got comic energy from the irritability and caustic critical disposition of its central character. *Men Behaving Badly* (BBC) put a farcical twist on new styles of the 'masculine' in which assertion and display (principally around beer, sport, and sex) hid doubt and anxiety. Set in a shared household (two men, two women), its comedy was nicely judged in its mix of gendered appeals and gender-model questioning. *Absolutely Fabulous* (BBC) was much more exotic, taking two wealthy women in the world of fashion and advertising and playing their extravagance and excess off against a serious and sensible daughter, whose firmly post-hippy disapproval of her mother's wild lifestyle both inverted the normal terms of parent–child comedy and provided a strong line of empathy with younger viewers. One of my own favourites from the mid-1990s was *The Brittas Empire* (BBC), which portrayed the bizarrely incompetent activities of the manager (Mr Brittas) of a local leisure centre. With its stable team of centre workers, *Brittas* developed the appeal and energy of the best ensemble comedies. It also served as a commentary on the new managerialism afflicting British culture, with its distinctive language of corporate aspiration, relentless efficiency gains, and the setting of regular targets and goals.

These series are merely a selection from a far larger range of programmes but they show not only the importance of comedy to the social identity of national television but also some of the ways in which that national identity is reflected, reinforced, subverted, and reworked in popular comic forms.

There are three other broad areas of generic development which I think it useful to comment on here. The first is the rise of a wholly new kind of 'access' programme occasioned by the domestic avail-ability of camcorder technology. This has been dubbed 'DIY televi-sion' and it is likely to increase in the range of its formats and its cultural impact. At one end of the scale, there is the screening of viewers' video clips within a light entertainment presentation, now an international recipe. Here, the 'mishaps' format (for instance, *You've Been Framed* (ITV), *Caught in the Act* (BBC)) has been a pre-dictable (and cheap) success. But the BBC series *Video Diaries*, intro-duced in the early 1990s, broke new ground by giving full slots over to programmes commissioned from members of the public, shot on VHS, and given professional post-production. A new system of looks and sounds—by turns confessional, polemical, socially investigatory, and ethnographic—emerged from this series and some of the work which followed. Although it is possible to see signs of the assimilation and dilution of this development within mainstream television (the 'amateur' input then recruited to profes-sional and commercial ends; the very awkwardness turned into another self-conscious 'style'), fresh, engaging, and sometimes pro-ductively shocking kinds of image, encounter, and talk were allowed to come through onto the screen.

A related but more controversial strand of programming appeared in the late 1990s with the enormous success of the 'docu-soaps' across all terrestrial channels. Essentially a modification of the well-established 'fly-on-the-wall' approach to documentary, docusoaps typically presented sustained observational portrayals of ordinary work and ordinary leisure with a strong element both of self-conscious performance on the part of the 'principal characters' and of editorial selection to ensure good levels of dramatic continuity and on-screen incident. With their confidence in packaging versions of the everyday within a free-style mixing of artifice and realism put primarily to the purposes of entertainment, the docusoaps perhaps came closer than any other form to characterizing the 'market-demotic' tendency of British television at the end of the decade.

Another form showing this tendency was the newer kind of talk programming. Taking their cue from US series like *The Oprah Winfrey Show*, a whole new set of British talk shows, mostly screened in daytime schedules, have brought ordinary people together in a studio to talk about selected problems. The talk is a mix of testimony, confession, debate, and perhaps sharp personal exchange. It is regulated by a host whose own performance is required to mix various elements of planning and spontaneity. The problems aired vary from the acutely personal to the broadly public, although with an increasing emphasis on the revelatory, disclosing possibilities of the former. In the late 1990s, some British talk shows started to shift a little more towards the model of US programmes like *The Jerry Springer Show*, where a clear division between talkers and audience is indicated and more than a touch of the 'freak show' is often apparent. The ordinary experience and frank speaking which the shows offer have been seen by some writers to mark a significant shift in television culture towards less constrained, and indeed less masculinized, modes of public expression, quite apart from the extension of topics for public debate. However, other commentators have detected a fundamental exploitation and triviality in the whole development, particularly as the shift towards more sensational kinds of disclosure by 'guests' has become established (see Livingstone and Lunt 1994 for a detailed study of the earlier formats).

Conclusions

In the last few decades, television in Britain has spread out from the evening across the whole day and night. Daytime schedules, always likely to seem makeweight in comparison with primetime, have nevertheless received more strategic attention and have sometimes produced formats for subsequent primetime development. The talk shows noted above are one part of this, the rise of a whole new range of 'lifestyle' series, providing novel (sometimes game-show-based) ways of responding to, and further stimulating, viewer interest in such activities as cooking, gardening, and interior decoration is another.

The new infrastructure and production dynamics of British television will inevitably introduce a more diluted and fragmented form of the 'national' on the screen and in viewing experience, although the significant shift will only come when there is a major move away from the main national services for *other* than sport and films. A radical dispersal of viewing across different channels for news services would certainly signal a crucial change, as would one for new comedy and drama. At the moment, much cable, satellite, and (so far) digital provision is, in effect, a vast recycling machine, with a low level of new production. This may change. What of the European or more broadly international dimension? Ironically, it was only in the early days of the new cable services that capacity allowed a number of European channels to be offered to subscribers. With the arrival of more entertainment and special interest services, many systems are now restricted to just one or two if any European channels. It is possible to argue that, increasingly and far from what was once predicted, a sense of the 'European' within the new distribution systems will be heavily mediated via domestically originated material, with the US cultural presence still the next most significant.

Over its fifty-year history, British television's version of a 'national culture' has mixed a sensitivity to the variety of the nation and a real concern both for quality and for equality with good measures of complacency and culpable blind spots (for instance, its failure properly to address minority ethnic groupings in Britain has only just begun to be corrected). New energies, new talents, and new voices will certainly benefit from its reconfiguration and from the hybridized and original forms which are being generated through structural change. However, if underlying this turbulence there is a greater systemic commitment to commercial profit, then it is hard to see how this will help television either in substantially increasing its range or quality of pleasures or in fulfilling those duties which it is still important for the quality of national public life that it recognizes. This is a challenge not only for programme-makers but for regulatory systems, which will have to combine sanctions and encouragements in imaginative new ways if they are to be effective within the emerging technological and commercial dynamics.

Further Reading

Corner, J. (1995), *Television Form and Public Address*, London: Arnold. A review of television aesthetics in relation to debates about 'public communication', with an emphasis on British conventions in news, documentary, and advertising.

—— (ed.) (1991), *Popular Television in Britain: Studies in Cultural History*, London: British Film Institute. This volume brings together a number of articles exploring the early history and development of British television, giving particular attention to generic formation and selected programmes.

Hood, S. (ed.) (1994), *Behind the Screens*, London: Lawrence & Wishart. A collection of essays on the restructuring of British television in the early 1990s, mixing historical account with evaluative commentary.

Morley, D. (1992), *Television, Audiences and Cultural Studies*, London: Routledge. This volume brings together aspects of the author's research into British television audiences during the late 1970s and 1980s and gives a good sense of the complexity of television's impact upon national 'everyday life'.

References

Geraghty, C. (1991), *Women and Soap Opera*, Cambridge: Polity.

Livingstone, S., and **Lunt, P.** (1994), *Talk on Television*, London: Routledge.

Scannell, P. (1989), 'Public Service Broadcasting and Modern Public Life', *Media, Culture and Society*, 11/2.

—— and **Cardiff, D.** (1991), *The Social History of British Broadcasting*, i, Oxford: Blackwell.

18

British Popular Music and National Identity

DAVID
HESMONDHALGH

ONE of the reasons that popular music is so interesting is that musicians, listeners, and journalists often engage in intense battles over what sounds mean. Debates about Britishness in popular music in the 1990s throw intriguing light on recent concerns about cultural identity, by showing how identity is understood and struggled over in the everyday creation and interpretation of popular culture.

In recent years, British popular music has undergone radical change. For a long time, British rock was at the centre of international popular culture. The Beatles and other 1960s British beat musicians were lucky: their arrival on the national stage coincided with an intensified globalization of the entertainment industry, led by US corporations and usually conducted in the English language. Many talented and not-so-talented British rock musicians in the 1960s and 1970s had their records and images exported across the Atlantic and around much of the world. And when punk attempted to revolutionize rock from within in the late 1970s, once again, many of the key musicians were British, although their sales were minuscule compared with those of their forerunners. Rock, however much it connected with the attitudes and feelings of a generation of youth across the world, was fundamentally an Anglo-American phenomenon, and Britain was an equal partner in this formation.

Nowadays, even though rock still sells, it is no longer the

dominant force in popular music that it was in the 1960s and 1970s. And British popular music, which was always more diverse than might have appeared on the basis of its global rock superstars, can certainly no longer be equated with rock. A short chapter such as this could not hope to cover in adequate detail the full range of popular music being produced and consumed in Britain. As in most countries of the world, there is enormous diversity. Instead, I want to focus here on those recent genres (and debates about them) in which tensions about contemporary British national identity have been most strikingly played out. Since the end of the classic rock era in the 1980s, two genres have emerged as the most written-about and argued-over categories of British popular music: first, a mutated version of rock, mediated through punk, known as 'alternative' pop or rock in many countries, but often called *indie* in the UK (because, at one time, it was usually made and distributed by independent companies); and secondly, *electronic dance music*, which has fundamentally transformed the politics of popular music in much of Europe. But I also want to discuss important developments in what, for shorthand, I will call *black British music*, as the children of Caribbean, Asian, and African migrants to Britain have adapted to and transformed British popular culture in the late twentieth century.

Popular music is more than mere entertainment. It is a means by which people affirm, create, and nurture their individual identities (Frith 1996 is an important attempt to understand these complex processes). But music is often also the basis of *struggles* over social and collective identity. For example, we are often attracted to music made by social groups that we do not belong to, in order to express solidarity with that group and/or to reaffirm our difference from those apparently similar to ourselves (see Born and Hesmondhalgh 2000). Such identity-work may be unconscious or semi-conscious, in that what we are initially drawn to is a pleasurable, exciting sound and look rather than a set of meanings which we have already worked out in advance. But perhaps because the meaning of music is so hard to work out, popular music is surrounded by enormous amounts of written and spoken commentary, in the media and in ordinary, everyday interactions between people. And here music's remarkable ability to unite and divide people becomes manifest in fraught, explicit debates over the political meanings of records, stars, and genres.

This is what happened in Britain in the 1990s, when the indie genre became associated with an attempt to identify a supposedly distinctive national tradition of popular music. Musicians, listeners,

David Hesmondhalgh

and writers emphasized a continuity in British popular music from the late 1960s to the 1990s, a lineage of rock creativity which to them suggested 'alternative' forms of British identity, less conformist and complacent than those embodied in older, traditional forms, or in Thatcherism. Electronic dance music, on the other hand, was interpreted by many commentators as a much more appropriate representative of new British identities, as reflective and constitutive of a more hedonistic, less puritanical country, one connected to a network of global flows of culture. What, then, were the politics of such battles over British identity through popular music? What do they have to say about the way that Britishness is understood in and through contemporary popular culture?

Indie Music and the Britpop Debates

In September 1992, the *New Musical Express* (*NME*), for two decades Britain's most influential rock magazine, published an article on the then great white hopes of indie, Suede, headlined 'The Brettish Movement'. This was an unfortunate but deliberate pun on the name of the group's singer (Brett Anderson) and one of the UK's leading neo-Nazi factions, the British Movement. Suede (and their interviewer, the prominent music journalist Stuart Maconie) were determined to resist what they perceived as the Europeanization and Americanization of British culture. Brett Anderson explained: 'Suede are a reaction to endless hours of watching Europe on *Top of the Pops*. . . . It pisses me off immensely that America has kidnapped British music. . . . All great British pop artists from the Beatles to the Fall have celebrated Britain in some way' (*New Musical Express*, 5 Sept. 1992).

A patriotic snowball began to roll. In April 1993, the music magazine *Select* acclaimed a new generation of British indie bands by putting a picture of Brett Anderson against a Union Jack background on its cover and headlining the issue, 'Yanks Go Home!'—a reference to the domination at the time by US bands such as Nirvana of the UK alternative rock/indie constituency. In 1994, for the first time in years, a new crop of British rock bands achieved significant sales, and the term 'Britpop' began to be used widely in the music press. A number of features in the music press (such as *Melody Maker*'s special feature on Britpop, 22 July 1995) identified a tradition of 'distinctively British' pop with recurring themes, such as: an intense interest in style (1960s mod bands such as The Who, 1970s glam rock acts, punk, the New Romantics, Pulp's Jarvis

Cocker); modes of performance which stress androgyny and/or sexual ambivalence (David Bowie, Annie Lennox, Morrissey, Brian Molko); and oddball, eccentric characters, seemingly derived from the music-hall tradition (to be found in the Beatles, the Kinks, Ian Dury, Blur). Britpop came to wider prominence when it became the focus of conflicts between different types of Britishness (though, as so often, this was elided with Englishness). In 1995, PR agents built up a 'battle' between the two leading indie bands of the period, as each vied for the top of the charts with their new singles. Oasis were portrayed as northern English and authentic, Blur as southern English and ironic. In the summer's slow news months, 'Britpop' spread to national consciousness via the popular press and TV news.

The term Britpop has caused some confusion. The term was generated within one particular genre—indie/alternative rock—to describe a tradition of Britishness in popular music, and then it was applied to a number of contemporary acts within that genre. Many of the bands labelled as 'Britpop', such as Blur, echoed the sentiments of the music-press journalists who invented and disseminated the term regarding what constituted 'distinctively British' popular music. Nevertheless, Britpop was never, in any sense, a *movement* with common artistic aims. Nor can Britpop usefully be thought of as a musical *genre*: a distinctive set of conventions for musical production and consumption never crystallized around the word. Having made records which drew on the supposedly 'British' traditions they identified, bands such as Blur moved on to other styles. Britpop is best understood, instead, as a *discourse*: a group of utterances and statements that have a significant role in organizing understanding of the social realm. And what Britpop discourse did was to construct a tradition of quintessentially British and/or English music that distorted and simplified British musical culture.

It is important to separate out debates about the aesthetic merits of those indie records and acts (temporarily) labelled 'Britpop' from the political implications of Britpop discourse. Aesthetic debates about British indie in the 1990s, especially 'Britpop', mainly concerned whether or not it was aesthetically regressive. Indie's over-reliance on pastiche and on reference backwards to the canon of British rock made it uninteresting and unoriginal to many observers drawn to other genres (see Hesmondhalgh 1999 for a fuller discussion of indie). My main interest here though is, as I have said, not with such aesthetic debates but with the politics of Britpop discourse's implicit anxiety and conservatism about British national identity, and also the ironic fact that such discourse was initially produced amongst purportedly 'alternative' popular cultural institutions. Britpop echoed anxieties elsewhere, amongst educationalists, political leaders, and public commentators, about the fragmentation of national identity. But precisely because it came from within the realm of alternative popular culture, Britpop discourse arguably had a more powerful effect in reaffirming nationalism than the tired complaints of more respectable public figures.

In what ways did Britpop resonate with debates about identity in British political culture more generally? Its latent conservatism was made manifest when the xenophobic, ultra-right wing of the British Conservative Party took up the notion of a distinctive national character in Britain's popular music. The faction's leading figure, John Redwood MP, wrote in the *Guardian* (20 Mar. 1996) that the Britpop bands were a sign that there was still 'a lively cultural heart ticking away in the UK'. Britpop discourse was easily mobilized to support the opinion of Redwood and his fellow Conservative opponents of British-European integration that increasing links with Europe were a threat to British culture, rather than a complement to it. Britpop was also frequently referred to by those on the left concerned to 'rebrand' the UK, to promote British economic prosperity by associating its trading activities with a new, upbeat, vibrant identity, in contrast with the post-imperial pessimism and understatement which marked much of post-war popular culture in Britain (e.g. Leonard 1997; Mulgan 1997). In this respect, Britpop was linked to British success in fine art and fashion design. What the indie journalists and the centre-left think tanks associated with rebranding Britain had in common was a desire to think about Britishness in new ways, to challenge those forms of national identity which had previously been dominant, and to enable an expanded and modernized sense of British identity. And the nationalism of the actual Britpop bands and journalists should not be exaggerated. As Martin Cloonan (1997: 53, 55) notes, even Suede and Blur were ambivalent about Britishness/Englishness: they satirized and criticized aspects of national culture, while celebrating an interest in it. But somehow, in the attempt to hijack notions of tradition and continuity for more progressive ends, some of the most exciting and interesting developments in British popular music culture got left out of the story that Britpop discourse told, with implicitly conservative results.

For there is a fine line between, on the one hand, the identification of recurring themes in a particular national culture, and on the other a celebration of certain traditions as embodying *the essential character* of a national popular music. Talk of distinctive national lineages of cultural expression (such as F. R. Leavis on the 'great tradition' in English literature) has nearly always served the purpose of flattening the diverse range of regional and national cultures within Britain into smooth homogeneity. There are three main ways in which Britpop discourse failed to recognize, and served to downplay, the complexity and multiplicity of 1990s British culture. First, there was a constant slippage between Englishness and Britishness, and the presentation of a notion of Englishness that marginalized regional variation within England itself. Second, Britpop implicitly equated Britishness with *white* Englishness: nearly all the acts and records in its canon were white. This downplayed how, since the 1950s, successive waves of immigration into the UK from its former colonies and elsewhere have created a more complex and diverse British culture than that represented by the Beatles–Kinks–Smiths–Blur lineage. Third, Britpop denied the tendency of cultures to mix, blend, and borrow. British rock culture was forged, after all, out of a dialogue with American music—often black American music. The Britpop history of rock saw British musical identity as not forged out of a cosmopolitan interaction with other cultures, but as made up of a limited number of essential national characteristics and musical traditions. The problem, then, was not so much the fact that Britpop discourse valued music which looked and listened backwards into history (most musics do, in different ways) but that by constructing a simplistic, linear account of tradition, it left so much interesting British music and so many other alternative forms of social identity out of the picture.

Electronic Dance Music

At the very time that these debates were taking place, transformations in club culture were, according to many people, making the notion of indie as a symbol of British creative tradition outdated and inappropriate. Most popular music has some sort of relation to dancing; but 'dance music' as a term in Britain has come to mean electronic music, with an insistent (though not necessarily repetitive) beat, designed mainly for dancing to in clubs. In the USA, such music has had relatively little impact on popular music culture (though see the next section for remarks on hip hop) but in Europe electronic dance music was the most debated form of the 1990s. Some saw it, at least for a while, as a utopian subculture, which offered the possibility of a society based on pleasure and mutual respect and which was in the vanguard of innovation in sound texture and rhythm. Others heard it as moronic machine music, designed to keep the masses passive.

The recent importance of dance music culture partly derives from the long-standing centrality of the dance club in the lives of British youth, a factor which is difficult to convey to outsiders. In the UK, the club is the site of adolescent rites of passage towards adolescent independence; and also a mythical place where the limits of the puritanical aspects of British culture can be explored. By contrast, in the USA, as Sarah Thornton (1995: 16–17) points out, the car is the focus of teenage transition; and in continental Europe, clubs tend to be merely another place to socialize. The special status of the dance club in British musical life enormously intensified in the late 1980s and early 1990s, because of a number of factors which coalesced to form what is often referred to as the *rave* or *acid house* phenomenon. First of all, club culture became hip amongst some students and the slightly older cosmopolitan middle class, in part through coverage in the 'style press' (such as *The Face* and *ID*). By 1986, parties held in spaces outside the city centres where dance clubs were usually based had become very fashionable. Warehouses and Spanish holiday resorts were the main examples, but some alternative dance clubs such as Manchester's Hacienda also gained coverage. Secondly, the drug Ecstasy came into these spaces. Ecstasy gave its users a sense of uninhibited euphoria; and coverage in the style press gave indications of how to behave in response, based on a neo-hippy ethic of love and peace. Thirdly, a new influx of music was being picked up by these hipper clubs, as post-punk and reggae began to decline as the most favoured music there. The new sounds were at first made by black Americans, and were then picked up by European musicians. Dancing grew wilder as DJs became increasingly adventurous in mixing tracks, making the point at which a new record was played harder to locate, and encouraging dancers to keep on dancing and dancing. Fourthly, press coverage of police clampdowns on illegally organized parties encouraged British youth to identify the new dance culture with rebellion and danger (see Collin 1997 for an account of some of these developments). It is worth noting, though, that in spite of these significant changes, the dance clubs most people attended—town centre venues—actually played pop music from the charts rather than the innovative new dance sounds being acclaimed by many commentators.

Most significantly for our purposes here, dance music culture came to be perceived as *cosmopolitan*, as a reflection of a more complex set of international cultural flows. This was partly because dance music culture seemed *placeless*, for a number of reasons: the initial lack of video and live-appearance promotion, because dance scenes tended to value the anonymity of performers highly, and because discussion of dance music tended not to concern the geographical origins of records, acts, and styles, as often happens with rock. This placelessness contrasted with the strong sense that rock music was very much an Anglo-American form: the centrality of rock in British musical life from the 1950s reflected an era when American popular culture offered fantasies of another kind of life, a different mode of pleasure (see Chambers 1985).

If rock was Anglo-American, dance music culture was readable as the hybrid product of flows between Europe, the United States, and, as we shall see, the Caribbean. This reading was possible for a number of reasons. Post-house dance music derived its inspiration from black American appropriations of European electronic music (most famously, the German band Kraftwerk). The production and consumption of British dance music are oriented towards Europe rather than the other side of the Atlantic. The lack of emphasis on words in dance music has meant that European artists have been able to compete on more equal terms with Britons whereas, outside the dance music world, there is still immense snobbery amongst many British journalists, musicians, and fans about European popular music. (In rock, pop and rap markets, it remains almost impossible for, say, Swedish, Spanish, or Greek singers to have their music heard widely in the UK unless they sing in English.) Finally, the independent companies at the core of the British dance music industry operate mainly within European networks. Such links suggest that the new electronic dance music was a phenomenon that worked to counteract the parochialism which famously marks much of Britain's island culture. Because of these factors, dance music was felt, by many of its enthusiasts, to be open, *hard to place*, defiant of the very notion that you are, or should be, defined by where you are from.

Another impact of the new dance music culture on the everyday working-out of British national identity was that it made the goal of utopian hedonism widespread, in contrast to the long-standing influence of puritanism and utilitarianism on British culture. Many dance clubs were joyless places in the early 1980s, full of stiff, reluctant dancers. For many young men and women, they were merely places to extend drinking time beyond that allowed by Britain's absurd licensing laws, which demand that pubs finish serving alcohol at 11 p.m. Many clubbers testify that, after the changes in dance culture in the late 1980s, discussed above, there was a new atmosphere in the best of these clubs, making them places where, in Jason Toynbee's words, 'mutuality was at a premium' and where there was a utopian sense of 'what democracy might be like if everyone wanted to help everyone else have a good time' (Toynbee 2000: 150). It is too cynically high-handed to say that this was mass delusion. And it is too simplistic to say, as some ex-clubbers do, that the euphoria of the early 1990s club scene was merely the result of a supply of good Ecstasy, before drug dealers started cutting it to increase their profits. Yet at the same time that these exciting innovations were taking place, Britpop discourse was ignoring them.

Once again, I want to make it clear that my aim here is not to argue that any one form of recent UK popular music is aesthetically superior to another. But it might be worth pointing to some mistaken assumptions about dance music, in order to strengthen my argument that it represented an enrichment of British musical culture marginalized by Britpop discourse. One fallacy is the idea that, because dance music is usually composed and recorded through the use of computers, it involves less musical skill than the playing of other musical forms. In fact, like playing the guitar, programming can be done well or badly. Another mistaken assumption is that the rhythms of dance music are more repetitive than those of rock. In fact, because of the need to produce danceable polyrhythms, the reverse often applies. Rock and pop's aesthetics focus on voice and melody, on the well-constructed song based around the chorus and solo. Electronic dance music is based on looser formal structures, even where it is clear we are still hearing a song. Musically, the main interest is *texture*, on innovations in the soundscape of the musical track. So, in important ways, dance music is not necessarily inferior to rock; it merely adheres to a different understanding of what makes for a successful piece of music. (For a more detailed discussion of electronic dance music, see Toynbee 2000.)

Black British Music

If an excessive focus on rock marginalizes important developments in dance music culture, it does even greater symbolic violence to the musical cultures of African-Caribbean and Asian Britons, which have largely eschewed rock (though one of the most interesting developments in indie in the late 1990s was the subversion by British Asian musicians, such as Cornershop, of this assumption). Few major black artists have developed in Britain, in spite of the centrality of music-making in black British culture, whereas in the USA, popular music has been one of the main ways in which the culture of African-Americans has reached a wider public. Black British music's lack of prestige is partly explained by the fact that the most important black music form of the last twenty years, hip hop, has been almost entirely dominated by US musicians. But it is also because other musical forms very popular amongst black audiences have been neglected to the point of dismissal by white audiences, often as a result of the decisions and choices of industry and media gatekeepers. This is true, for example, both of bhangra, popular amongst some British-Asian audiences, and of the (often US-produced) soul and R&B sounds that thrive in British-Caribbean communities. It is quite common for people who read the British music press regularly, and who consider themselves to have a deep and broad knowledge of contemporary popular music, to be completely unfamiliar with the biggest names in these genres. Black British artists may have success with soul/R&B singles, but few record companies have provided the level of investment necessary to maintain careers across a series of albums.

These conditions reflect long histories of racism. Nevertheless, from the 1960s to the 1980s, much of the music designated as 'dance music' in the UK was generally made by black musicians, whether American, British, or from the Caribbean. British cities have never been as segregated as their US counterparts, and there have been examples of rich cultural exchange and dialogue (see Back 1996 for a fine study of these issues) as well as of appropriation and exploitation. Paul Gilroy has written eloquently about the role of black expressive culture in British life:

There is, of course, no contradiction between making use of black culture and loathing real live black people, yet the informal, long-term processes through which different groups have negotiated each other have intermittently created a 'two-tone' sensibility which celebrates its hybrid origins and has provided a significant opposition to 'common-sense' racialism. (Gilroy 1993: 35)

Music has been a particularly important element in this 'two-tone' sensibility. Gilroy's use of this term is a reference to a musical moment/movement in the late 1970s when racially integrated groups drew on ska, the Jamaican music loved by some of the most racist sections of working-class youth, to promote (through frenetic dancing, rather than worthy preaching) racial interaction and harmony. Revealingly, this moment was almost completely ignored in Britpop discourse's reconstruction of musical history.

Also ignored was a significant 1990s example of an interracial British music of black origin, jungle. A fusion of elements of hip hop, techno, and Caribbean popular music aesthetics, it represented a key development in electronic dance music, because it drew attention to the *racialization* of dance spaces. In the new dance music culture of the 1990s, described above, there was significant racial integration at parties and amongst musicians. But many black and Asian musicians soon came to feel that the rave scene was a 'white thing'. In house and techno music, a pounding, regular 'four on the floor' rhythm was usually the focal point; other rhythms were combined with it to create polyrhythms to engage the upper body in dancing. Some house records, though, borrowed *breakbeats* from hip hop records. Breakbeats are the parts of 1970s and early 1980s funk and disco records where all the other instrumentation drops out. Hip hop was partly based on taking these sections and, by spinning the record back in live performance or by looping the breakbeat in recording, maintaining the rhythmic excitement. Increasingly in the early 1990s, certain clubs—especially those with a mainly black audience—began to focus on breakbeats. This was partly because it was easier to sample and loop them than to programme a computer with a new rhythm, but it was also because it was exciting and, significantly, because it sounded hip-hop-derived (and therefore was coded as 'black'). A sound developed called *ardkore techno*, but the music, the clubs, and the pirate radio stations that popularized the genre were ignored by the dance and rock press. By 1993, in the light of coverage by *Melody Maker*'s Simon Reynolds, the music press and national media picked up on the scene, by then called jungle (by 1995, it was also called 'drum and bass', more or less interchangeably). In jungle/drum and bass, electronic dance music's placeless, hybrid cosmopolitanism came to a peak, and became associated with a critical multiculturalism. For jungle/drum and bass derived its inspiration from black musical traditions and practices. These included the focus on breakbeats from records made by African-Americans; the use, borrowed from Jamaica, of specially created, ultra-rare 'dubplate' recordings by DJs; and the Caribbean use of an MC to talk over the playing of the records. Yet this was a thoroughly interracial music, produced and consumed by black and white Britons alike, and by British-Asian musicians, for so long excluded from the British musical public sphere. Some of these British-Asian musicians achieved recognition for work which fused samples from, for example, Indian film music with breakbeats, in the process refusing the idea that Asian cultures should be valued for their 'purity' and tradition (see Sharma et al. 1996 for debates on new Asian dance music).

Jungle's interraciality was not easily assimilable into a cosy multiculturalism, however. Its hard edge defied indie's bubbly optimism. In spite of movements to legitimize jungle/drum and bass by developing 'intelligent' and 'progressive' versions, the sound of jungle was often menacing and out of control, reflecting the dark side of dance music culture's close relationship with psycho-tropic drugs and the psychic costs of living on the margins of an increasingly prosperous society, but one marred by inequality and lovelessness. At times, there was a horror-film aesthetic at work—samples of disembodied voices culled from the virtual memory-banks cried for help and expressed appalling fears. This was in very sharp contrast to the happy euphoria of rave and indeed to the upbeat nostalgia of much 1990s indie. If, as seems likely, the 1990s will be portrayed retrospectively as a time of "British spring" (Mulgan 1997), of optimism and cultural resurgence, then many of the most interesting jungle recordings might serve as useful reminders of how simplistic such history-by-decades can be.

The significance of Britpop discourse was that it resonated with anxieties, particularly *English* ones, about the loss of a secure national identity in an era of transnational flows of cultures and peoples, and of increasing political and economic ties with Europe. In other words, Britpop can be seen as a defensive reaction against globalization. But its construction of a tradition of distinctive Brit-ish rock sits uneasily with certain features of popular music as a medium of communication. Compared with other mass media such as radio, television, and the press, late twentieth-century popu-lar music has been relatively autonomous of the processes by which nation-states have created and reinforced national identity. While some music was experienced nationally through these other media, music tends to evade location. The mobility of musical commod-ities, the tendency of musicians to borrow from each other, and the fragmented, localized nature of much musical consumption make it difficult to identify popular music as characteristic of a particular place. This does not mean that pop always has liberating effects, that it always works to untie identities from localities. It does suggest, though, how unwise it is to think that any one par-ticular genre can crystallize the massive array of histories, artefacts, attitudes, and feelings that make up the many different forms of national identity available in contemporary Britain. Rock has appar-ently made it possible to think of Britain as a less fusty, colonial nation than it once was. But attempts to identify a distinctive Britishness purely through rock and its indie descendants, as in Britpop, only serve to marginalize some of the most important and

David Hesmondhalgh

revealing ways in which popular culture is being transformed and reinvented.

Further Reading

Two British rock journalists, Simon Frith and Jon Savage, have played a fundamental part in helping to remove rock from its pedestal as, supposedly, the only form of popular music worth considering seriously. They did so mainly by deconstructing rock's disdainful attitude towards pop. This is particularly apparent in Frith's collection of journalism *Music for Pleasure* (Cambridge: Polity, 1988) and his *Art into Pop* (London: Methuen, 1987), co-written with Howard Horne, which is a history of British pop's debt to the art school. For two decades, Frith has been the English-speaking world's leading popular music academic—his *Sound Effects* (London: Constable, 1983) and *Performing Rites* (Oxford: Oxford University Press, 1996) are also strongly recommended. Jon Savage's work includes the definitive history of punk, *England's Dreaming* (London: Faber & Faber, 1991); a collection of his journalism, *Time Travel* (London: Chatto & Windus, 1996); and an anthology co-edited with Hanif Kureishi, *The Faber Book of Pop* (London: Faber & Faber, 1995), which serves as a history of pop music culture since the 1940s, viewed from a mainly British perspective.

Simon Reynolds's magnificent *Energy Flash: A Journey through Rave Music and Dance Culture* (London: Picador, 1998) is an intelligent and detailed history of dance music culture (and it comes with an excellent CD compilation of electronic dance music). Matthew Collin's *Altered State* (London: Serpent's Tail, 1998) is also very good on the same subject, although it is less insightful about the music itself. Sarah Thornton's *Club Cultures* (Cambridge: Polity, 1995) is the best academic study of dance music culture. Much of Paul Gilroy's *Small Acts* (London: Serpent's Tail, 1993) and some of the chapters in his *The Black Atlantic* (London: Verso, 1993) brilliantly demonstrate how black music in Britain, North America, and the Caribbean has been based on cultural exchange and interaction between the diasporic populations of these countries.

The best attempt to identify distinctive themes and treatments in English (not British) pop music (and in literature, film, and art) is Michael Bracewell's *England is Mine: Pop Life in Albion from Wilde to Goldie* (London: HarperCollins, 1997), which is full of wonderful insight and which does not simplify the diversity in English cultural life. The best book about 1990s British popular music (though it deals with US examples too) is the music journalist Ben Thompson's witty *Seven Years of Plenty: A Handbook of Irrefutable Pop Greatness 1991–1998* (London: Gollancz, 1998).

For details on some of the enormous range of music which there was no space for me to consider in this chapter, I recommend the journal *Popular Music*, published by Cambridge University Press since 1981, and the Open University book series *Popular Music in Britain* (much of it now sadly out of print). Andrew Blake's *The Land without Music: Music, Culture and Society in Twentieth-Century Britain* (Manchester: Manchester University Press, 1998) covers a very wide range and usefully draws attention to neglected traditions such as light music, folk, and British jazz. Finally, Richard Middleton's two chapters in Stephen Banfield (ed.), *The Blackwell History of Music in Britain*, vi:

The Twentieth Century (Oxford: Blackwell, 1995), 'The Rock Revolution' and 'The "Problem" of Popular Music' provide superb musicological analysis and contextualization of rock and other forms of British popular music.

References

Back, L. (1996), *New Ethnicities and Urban Cultures*, London: UCL Press.

Born, G., and **Hesmondhalgh, D.** (2000), *Western Music and its Others: Difference, Representation and Appropriation in Music*, Berkeley and Los Angeles: University of California Press.

Chambers, I. (1985), *Urban Rhythms: Pop Music and Popular Culture*, Basingstoke: Macmillan.

Cloonan, M. (1997), 'State of the Nation: "Englishness", Pop and Politics in the mid-1990s', *Popular Music and Society*, 21/2.

Collin, M., with contributions by J. Godfrey (1997), *Altered State: The Story of Ecstasy Culture and Acid House*, London: Serpent's Tail (rev. edn. 1998).

Frith, S. (1996), *Performing Rites: On the Value of Popular Music*, Oxford: Oxford University Press.

Gilroy, P. (1993), *Small Acts: Thoughts on the Politics of Black Cultures*, London: Serpent's Tail.

Hesmondhalgh, D. (1999), 'Indie: The Institutional Politics and Aesthetics of a Popular Music Genre', *Cultural Studies*, 13/1.

Leonard, M. (1997), *Britain: Renewing our Identity*, London: Demos.

Mulgan, G. (1997), *The British Spring*, London: Demos.

Sharma, S., Hutnyk, J., and **Sharma, A.** (1996), *Dis-Orienting Rhythms: The Politics of the New Asian Dance Music*, London: Zed Books.

Thornton, S. (1995), *Club Cultures: Music, Media and Subcultural Capital*, Cambridge: Polity.

Toynbee, J. (2000), 'Dance Music: Business as Usual or Heaven on Earth?', in *Making Popular Music: Musicians, Creativity and Institutions*, London: Arnold.

'Young British Art' in the 1990s

ROSEMARY
BETTERTON

19

In April 1998 the London auction house Christies held a major sale of recent work which, for the first time in their saleroom history, was promoted under the banner of 'contemporary' art. It filled a warehouse in newly fashionable Clerkenwell with works by, amongst others, British artists Damien Hirst, Gary Hume, and Sarah Lucas, who had come to attention a decade before in Hirst's legendary curated exhibition *Freeze*, held in the London Docklands. Later in the same year, Charles Saatchi sold off part of his private collection of art which had played a pivotal role in establishing a group identity for these artists in the early 1990s through a series of exhibitions at his North London gallery entitled *Young British Artists*. By 1992, an emergent artistic formation had already been identified—more by propinquity than shared style—as *the* New British Art. Often controversial, frequently courting publicity, and deliberately populist in its address, the institutionalization of this group of British artists within the international art world was so rapid and so complete that questions were repeatedly raised in the 1990s about the degree of critical opposition they represented to previously established art practices. In less than ten years from graduation, many young British artists had moved from alternative exhibition spaces to major public and institutional acclaim. Between

This piece has previously appeared as 'Undutiful Daughters: Avant-Gardism and Gendered Consumption in Recent British Art' and is reprinted with permission from the publishers of *Visual Culture in Britain*, 1/1, ed. Ysanne Holt (Aldershot: Ashgate, 2000).

'Young British Art' 287

1992 and 1999, Grenville Davey, Rachel Whiteread, Damien Hirst, Gillian Wearing, Chris Ofili, and Steve McQueen had won six of the annual Turner Prize awards and Hirst, Whiteread, and Hume had been selected to represent Britain in the Venice Biennale. Christie's Contemporary Art sale represented the final accolade bestowed on them by the art world—their entry into saleroom history.

The history of recent British art is, of course, much more diverse and multi-faceted than the meteoric rise of one grouping of artists implies; nevertheless, their success did point to the crucial connection between new art and the operation of the market which was characteristic of the 1990s. The paradoxical status of recent art in Britain was a consequence of a realignment between new art and the sphere of cultural consumption, a shift that made it possible for it to be represented as 'subversive' and yet rapidly assimilated to the art market. One significant aspect of this new alignment, frequently noted but rarely analysed in depth, was the unprecedented visibility of a new generation of women artists. Here, I will focus on work from the 1990s by Tracy Emin and Sarah Lucas, whose aesthetic strategies drew explicitly on gendered identities offered within mass culture, but implicitly on a reworking of sexual politics in art from the 1970s and 1980s. While the two women are often represented together in accounts of the young British artists (yBas), I suggest that their work addresses the politics of identity and class in very different ways. This suggests a reading of recent British art as less homogeneous and more indebted to earlier histories than its many promoters and detractors suggest.

Sensation, Saatchi, and the Shaping of New British Art
IT'S AN ARTRAGE (*Sun*, 26 June 1997)

The uneasy marriage between avant-garde shock and commodity consumption was perfectly encapsulated in the exhibition *Sensation: Young British Artists from the Saatchi Collection*, held at the Royal Academy of Arts in 1997. Unlike the Turner Prize shortlist and British entries to the Venice Biennale which were sponsored by the Tate Gallery and the British Council, *Sensation* represented the final acceptance of the new art by the 'old' artistic establishment. Curated and installed by the collection's owner, Charles Saatchi, and sponsored by Christies and *Time Out*, the London listings magazine, the high profile of *Sensation* was guaranteed. But it was the extraordinary degree of media attention the show received before and after its opening that attracted over 300,000 visitors in the three-month period of the exhibition. This attention was generated by the RA's own publicity which deliberately played on the 'sensational' nature of the work and was fuelled by the press furore and subsequent public resignation of several Royal Academicians over the inclusion of Marcus Harvey's *Myra*, a painting in which he used a child's handprints to recreate the notorious photo-portrait of the child murderer Myra Hindley. The work was defaced soon after the show opened and subsequently rehung, flanked by uniformed attendants and accompanied by a barrage of tabloid headlines: 'EXHIBITED BY THE ROYAL ACADEMY IN THE SO-CALLED NAME OF ART. DEFACED BY THE PEOPLE IN THE NAME OF COMMON DECENCY' (*Mirror*, 22 Sept. 1997).

This manufactured moral outrage echoed a recurrent response to modern art from Manet's *Olympia*, shown in the Paris Salon of 1865, to Carl Andre's *Equivalent VIII* (the 'Tate Bricks') in 1976. What seemed to produce the most extreme press responses to *Sensation* was the apparent transgression of the boundaries between subjects deemed valid for mass media coverage—sex, crime, violence, and child abuse—and those perceived to be within the domain of the arts. Yet in many ways this was a category mistake, a failure to grasp the unwritten rules of the art world, which define new art precisely in terms of risk and innovation; while this might offend popular taste, it tests the limits of rather than subverts the cultural mainstream. This position was perfectly summed up by show's other curator, the secretary to the Royal Academy, Norman Rosenthal, who, while repeating the familiar mantra that 'the chief task of new art is to disturb', nevertheless asserted that 'contemporary art is a club worth joining' (Royal Academy of Arts 1997: 10–11). *Sensation* thus served a dual purpose: it gave recognition to artists seeking confirmation as major players in the 'club' and street credibility to the Royal Academy, reinventing itself as daring and innovative (as well as seeking financial stability) at the end of the century. The precise limits of the RA's risk-taking were perhaps demonstrated not so much by the inclusion of *Myra*, as by the timid exclusion of under-18s from the room containing Jake and Dinos Chapman's overtly sexed child mannequins. The continuing notoriety of *Sensation* was guaranteed in 1999 by the intervention of Mayor Rudolf Giuliani of New York, who threatened to withdraw funding from the Brooklyn Museum of Art where the exhibition was being shown. His objection to Chris Ofili's depiction of the Virgin Mary with elephant dung balls was on the grounds of its offence to Catholic belief and—in a curious reprise of the *Myra* incident—an aggrieved member of the public assaulted the painting, which was withdrawn from the exhibition.

While its promoters presented the sensational aspect of the work as a radical attitude to 'real life' (Royal Academy of Arts 1997: 10), critics divided between those who acclaimed the show as an important event and those who dismissed it as a new form of academicism. Both fêted and vilified in the media, the critical reception of *Sensation* finally enshrined young British artists as contemporary cultural icons. Like the destructive behaviour of rock stars, the extreme content of the work and their licence to 'shock' was taken to be evidence of their subversive status. But if contemporary art is a form of 'permitted disorder' (Crow 1996: 19), then the question of who 'permits' and the degree of repressive tolerance allowed is pertinent. The rhetoric of *Sensation*, which attempted to place a diverse group of artists as a homogeneous 'generation' within a history of twentieth-century artistic transgression, disguised both the complexity of its formation and real differences between the works of art shown. If we examine the integral relationship of Brit art to particular forms of exhibition and distribution, we can identify the institutional conditions that underpinned its success in the 1990s.

In their polemical analysis of British arts policy, *Saturday Night or Sunday Morning? From the Arts to Industry: New Forms of Cultural Policy*, Ken Worpole and Geoff Mulgan asked who was doing most to shape British culture. Their answer was unequivocal: private enterprise as represented by Benetton, Virgin, or Saatchi rather than the 'Tudor cottage' of the state-subsidized arts, was the determining influence on British cultural life (Mulgan and Worpole 1986: 9). A decade later and the changes they had identified in the mid-1980s had resulted in the virtual collapse of boundaries between public and private sectors of the arts. Under pressure of ideologies of entrepreneurship advocated by the Thatcher government throughout the 1980s and the impact of economic recession in the early 1990s, public arts funding was cut in real terms and private sources of funding were increasingly sought. In his complementary roles as patron, collector, and dealer in the new art, Charles Saatchi was in a unique position not only to usurp the role of public institutions in promoting new art forms to audiences through his private gallery, but also to influence the collecting policies of public institutions themselves. In 1999, Saatchi donated 100 of his own works of art to the Arts Council Collection; probably the act of an astute dealer rather than an altruist at a time when prices for much of the work were falling. Perhaps equally significant, as the co-founder of the most successful and politically influential advertising agency in Britain in the 1980s, Saatchi helped to usher in a new model for the scale and marketing of art, renewing the explicit links between art and entrepreneurship which had long been mystified within modernist ideologies of the artist.

As critic Lynne Cooke commented, 'geographical proximity, peer group familiarity, and shared cultural contexts' provided conditions for the emergence of a group identity amongst young London-based artists who were 'very knowing . . . highly educated and very sophisticated' (Renton and Gilllick 1991: 39). While the material effects of the recession in the late 1980s had diminished the contemporary art market, as a result of collapsing property prices relatively cheap studio and exhibition space became available mainly in East and South London. Paradoxically, the effect was both to professionalize young artists who were forced to market themselves, and to provide a platform for new and experimental work in artist-run collectives like Bank and City Racing. As well as opening up alternative spaces for exhibition, following Hirst's 'seminal' example, artists used sponsorship and effective publicity to gain access to an established art scene. The rapidity with which many Goldsmiths College students, for example, moved from graduation to public exhibitions and private dealer shows was symptomatic of their ambition to succeed *within* the terms of the art market. The outcome of this promotion of a network of connections between London-based artists, art schools, key curators, collectors, and dealers, was to ensure the visibility of the few and, by definition, to exclude the rest. Successful regional artists like Willie Doherty in Belfast, international artists based in Britain such as Shirazeh Houshiary, and British African and Asian artists of the same generation like Lubaina Himid and Lesley Sanderson challenge the hegemony of a national art which attributes specific value to a narrowly conceived 'British' identity. Their absence from the ranks of the yBas—with the notable exceptions of Mona Hatoum, Steve McQueen, Chris Ofili, and Yinka Shonibare—reinforced an image of the new British art as predominantly white and London-based in its cultural reference.

Undoubtedly, the media also played a crucial role in this selective promotion of 'stars'. The annual competition of the Turner Prize, transformed into 'the artworld's Britpop awards' (Collings 1997: 66) by Channel 4 television, increased the monetary value and profile, if not the public acceptability, of contemporary art. But, if not all the publicity was good, it kept artists in view, somewhere between chefs and fashion designers in their celebrity status and commercial

Table 19.1. Goldsmiths College graduates, 1982–1995: selected group exhibitions

Date of graduation	Artist	Exhibitions
BA Fine Art		
1982	Julian Opie	B
	Lisa Milroy	B
1983	John Frankland	C
1985	Grenville Davey	A, B, D
1986	Marcus Harvey	D, E
	Richard Patterson	A, E
1987	Fiona Rae	A, B, D, E
	Sarah Lucas	A, D, E
1988	Michael Landy	A, E
	Bridget Smith	C
	Ian Davenport	A, B
	Anya Gallacio	A, C
1989	Damien Hirst	A, C, D, E
	Gary Hume	A, B, C, D, E
	Abigail Lane	A, D
	Simon Patterson	A, E
	Matt Collishaw	A, C, E
	Angus Fairhurst	A
1990	Gillian Wearing	C, E
	Sam Taylor Wood	D, E
1992	Jonathan Parsons	E
1993	Ceal Floyer	C
	Steve McQueen	C
	Michael Maloney	E
	Jason Martin	E
1994	Adam Chodzko	E
1995	Peter Davies	E
MA Fine Art		
1985	Mark Wallinger	C, D, E
1987	Cathy de Monchaux	B
1988	Jordan Baseman	C
	Caroline Russell	B
1990	Catherine Yass	C
1991	Yinka Shonibare	E
1992	Jane and Louise Wilson	C
	Glenn Brown	D, E
	Brad Lochore	D
	Stephen Murphy	D
	Caroline Weidle	D

Key to exhibitions:
A: *Freeze*, 1988, London.
B: *British Art Show 3*, 1990, Glasgow, Leeds, London.
C: *British Art Show 4*, 1995, Manchester, Edinburgh, Cardiff.
D: *Young British Artists I–IV*, 1992–6, Saatchi Gallery, London.
E: *Sensation: Young British Artists from the Saatchi Collection*, 1997, Royal Academy, London.

Table 19.2. Goldsmiths College graduates, 1982–1995: first solo exhibition at a London gallery

Date of graduation	Artist	Gallery	Date of exhibition
BA Fine Art			
1982	Julian Opie	Lisson	1983
	Lisa Milroy	Nicola Jacobs	1984
1983	John Frankland	Hales Gallery	1993
1985	Grenville Davey	Lisson	1987
1986	Marcus Harvey	White Cube	no date
	Richard Patterson	Anthony D'Offay	1995
1987	Fiona Rae	Waddington	1988
	Sarah Lucas	City Racing	1992
1988	Michael Landy	Karsten Schubert	1989
	Ian Davenport	Waddington	1990
	Anya Gallacio	Karsten Schubert	1991
	Bridget Smith	Entwhistle Contemporary	1995
1989	Gary Hume	Karsten Schubert	1989
	Matt Collishaw	Karsten Schubert	1990
	Craig Wood	Laure Genillard	1990
	Damien Hirst	ICA	1991
	Angus Fairhurst	Karsten Schubert	1991
	Abigail Lane	ICA	1995
1990	Gillian Wearing	Interim Art	1994
	Sam Taylor Wood	The Showroom	1994
1992	Jonathan Parsons	Richard Salmon	1996
1993	Michael Maloney	Karsten Schubert	1996
MA Fine Art			
1985	Mark Wallinger	Anthony Reynolds	1992
1986	Simon Linke	Lisson	1987
1987	Cathy de Monchaux	Laure Genillard	1990
1988	Caroline Russell	Anthony Reynolds	1988
	Jordan Baseman	Alternative Arts	1991
1989	Perry Roberts	Laure Genillard	1989
1990	Catherine Yass	Laure Genillard	1992
1991	Yinka Shonibare	Stephen Friedman	1997
1992	Jane and Louise Wilson	Lisson	1992
	Glenn Brown	Karsten Schubert	1995

potential. While it has been argued that increased visibility does not necessarily correspond to an expanded audience for the arts (Garnett 1998), there is evidence to suggest that the audience for the visual arts was indeed increasing in the last decade. For example, visitor numbers to the Tate Gallery, host to the Turner Prize, rose from 1 million a year in 1989/90 to 2.8 million in 1994/5 and the new TateModern has proved to be both a popular and critical success (*Cultural Trends* (1995), 42). The mythical status of the avant-garde in twentieth-century art had itself become a means of promotion, its shock tactics commodified as fashion. Subcultural and cutting-edge aesthetics became marketable assets for an audience which was far more likely to come across Hirst, Emin, or Lucas in the pages of style magazines like *ID* or *The Face* than in the art press. One effect of this increased visibility was the creation of a wider and younger audience for contemporary art used to a crossover between street 'cool' and commodity consumption, between aspects of an alternative culture and the commercial market. The more accessible language of art practices which drew on the rhetorics of advertising and the tabloid press, sexual slang and kitsch aesthetics, both itself reproduced and was a self-conscious response to these changing patterns of cultural consumption.

Gendered Identities and Cultural Consumption

It is a truism to say that artists who were born in the 1960s and grew up in the 1970s received unparalleled exposure to television, video, magazines, and the tabloid press, but critical writing on art has paid little attention to the implications for the construction of artistic identity of these subjective, and usually gendered, pleasures of consumption. If contemporary art now asserts its continuity with, rather than difference from, pop music, football, or fashion, it is because artistic identities are increasingly formed within a common sphere of consumption. As younger consumers look to cultural artefacts as markers of their identity, so artists of the same generation increasingly define their artistic subjectivity in terms of a shared consumption of mass culture. This blurring of the lines between forms of artistic production and mass consumption is partly what underpins practices like those of Gillian Wearing which mimic the voyeuristic pleasures of 'docusoaps' while claiming the status of uniquely authored artworks. Recent British art plays with this contradiction between concepts of uniqueness and authenticity, traditionally the hallmarks of art, and the transitory and reproduceable characteristics of the cultural industries. This perhaps accounts for the fact that it was simultaneously attacked for being too conceptual *and* too consumerist.

John Roberts has suggested that one key change in the art of the 1990s was its 'loss of guilt in front of popular culture' (Roberts

1996: 30). He argues that the 'bad behaviour' of the young British artists—'playing dumb, shouting ARSE and taking your knickers down' (p. 29)—should be read neither as apolitical, nor as merely infantile, but as a celebration of aesthetically despised categories of popular language and culture in deliberate reaction to theory-led, deconstructive art practices of the 1980s. Rather than deconstructing forms of popular culture from a critical distance, these artists go out and 'live' them, identifying positively with the values of mass culture: 'there is a way of reading the new art, then, as a generation moving the critique of representation out of the domain of academic reference onto the "street"' (p. 30). This distinction might aptly be drawn between an artist like Mary Kelly whose work during the 1980s engaged in a critical practice of deconstruction, and Tracy Emin whose work draws on affective experiences largely shaped within mass culture. While Kelly brings the cultural codes of femininity into view in order to develop a sustained critique of them, Emin's work deploys the feminine subject as her central material to very different ends. If Kelly's work explores the cultural and political dilemma of being a middle class woman in middle age, Tracy Emin's work inhabits a different gendered territory of female adolescence and her struggle to establish her identity as a working-class girl growing up in Margate in the 1970s. But significantly, whereas Kelly sought strategically to distance the viewer from identification with the autobiographical content of her work, Emin insistently adopts a confessional mode in which she herself is the 'star' of her own narrative.

It is conventional critical wisdom to see younger 'Bad Girls' like Emin at the opposite end of the artistic spectrum from Kelly, one of the leading practitioners of British feminist art. This opposition is constructed in part as generational—Kelly was born in 1941, Emin in 1963—but more especially as one between feminism and post-feminism, a position which argues that the feminist political project is either achieved or irrelevant to women. For example, Roberts suggests that Emin's work is a 'proletarian-philistine reflex against '80s feminist propriety about the body' and further that 'embracing the overtly pornographic and confessional have become a means of releasing women's sexuality from the comforts of a "progressive eroticism" into an angry voluptuousness' [sic] (p. 38). Within the sexual politics of the 1990s, of New Lads and Ladettes, not only men but women are licensed to behave badly and talk dirty. By positioning Emin's work as a 'reflex' against a negative stereotype of feminist political correctness, Roberts resists a more complex reading of her work within the context of previous women's art practices (as well as conflating the differently gendered genres of pornography and confession). But Emin is consciously engaged in sexual politics, albeit of an individualized kind, and her kind of gender-identity-based work would be impossible without an awareness of feminist 'foremothers'.

The highly mediated procedures involved in Emin recreating her own life narratives as 'art' is seldom recognized by critics, who are happy to take her word for it when she, somewhat disingenuously, describes this confessional art as the 'truth'. This misrepresents and disguises the complexity of Emin's relationship to her source materials, just as she does herself. While Emin frequently uses images, objects, and materials from her own life to tackle taboo subjects such as rape and abortion, her work consciously reworks her 'life story' as a set of narratives and fantasies. It is perhaps significant in this context that her main material is derived from the period of her life before she became an artist: that of her childhood, adolescence, and early adult sexuality. The highly verbal (and vocal) characteristics of Emin's work suggest loss, a gap that is repeatedly filled with words, evident for example in the video pieces where her voice insistently retells stories of growing up as a sexually active— and abused—child in Margate. Emin's *Everybody I've Ever Slept With: 1963–1995* (Fig. 19.1), although read by many critics as an assertion of 'in yer face' female sexuality, painstakingly inscribed all her sleeping partners through an appliquéd litany of lovers, friends, family, including her aborted fetus, on the inside walls of a tent. The experience of viewing the work, which can only be seen fully by peering inside the cramped interior, suggests that the audience is being offered an experience of self-revelation which may be intimate or intrusive depending on your viewpoint. Joan Smith has made a distinction between 'truth' and 'autobiography', suggesting that current self-revelation by many women artists is not so much a form of exhibitionism, as a 'counter aesthetic', a conscious reclaiming of female identity and sexuality in what she calls 'a transgressive voyeurism of the self' (*Guardian*, 24 Feb: 1998). In this sense, Emin's work is autobiography; a purposeful reconstruction of her past as a set of stories rather than the 'truth'. But the degree of its transgression seems less if we read it not only within the context of fine art, but within an increasingly confessional culture in which women in particular are incited to reveal their intimate selves on TV. As we have learnt, the confessional genre of talk shows is in actual fact complexly crafted to convey artless self-exposure. The 'artfulness' of Emin's work is to present itself in a similar way so as to convey an unmediated intimacy.

Fig. 19.1 Tracy Emin's *Everybody I've Ever Slept With: 1963–1995.*
© Tracy Emin, courtesy Sadie Coles HQ, London.

The connection between a feminized genre of daytime television catering primarily for women and Emin's work becomes stronger if we look at her aesthetic techniques. She consistently uses genres and techniques historically gendered, albeit not exclusively, as feminine, such as embroidery and patchwork, handwritten diaries, self-portraiture, and autobiography. Emin's work establishes a visual dialogue which derives from specifically gendered experience and is rendered through an unrefined aesthetic. Her work typically explores sexual rather than domestic oppression with an emphasis on the representation of female subjectivity and a first person mode of address. But, although Emin's aesthetic strategies bear a marked resemblance to earlier feminist art, there are key differences in their practice and politics. Feminist artists in the 1970s subverted the conventions of art in order to challenge the myth of individual genius and to assert a collective female experience and aesthetic lineage in opposition to established, male-dominated art practices. Emin's positioning of herself as an anti-intellectual, bohemian artist mystifies these antecedents, reproducing the surface gestures of previous work without transforming them. As Katy Deepwell commented, the transgressions in work such as this can be seen to come from 'libertarian individualism, rather than a liberationist politics' (Deepwell 1997: 56). Breaking down the boundaries between art and life still does produce different meanings for women from those for men—not least because women's lives continue to have different status and meaning ascribed to them—but what in the 1970s was a radical collective challenge to masculine formalism ceases to have the same effect when performed again by an individual woman artist in the different art world and cultural context of the 1990s. If daytime 'talk shows' distantly echo the procedures of early women's consciousness-raising groups which encouraged women to 'speak' their oppression, they do so in the interest of emotional voyeurism. Emin's confessional artworks equally simulate earlier feminist practices, but within the changed context of sexual consumption in the 1990s. For an artist such as Emin to represent herself as sexed and specific may provoke, but does not necessarily pose any opposition to pre-existing gendered assumptions about art.

Continuing in her earlier vein of self-exposure, Emin's exhibition for the 1999 Turner Prize consisted of her unmade bed complete with stained sheets and empty vodka bottles. No longer an interpretation of her life, it was a direct trace in which the gap between art and life had been short-circuited. Emin freely acknowledges her own success to be part of a wider confessional culture in which everyone can tell their own story, the more excessive the better. That such deeply feminized forms of expression are so popular may point to a space opened up by the current demise of feminism as a political ideology and its recuperation through forms of cultural representation. For the subject of confession, the process of purging can be cathartic, but by representing her bed as a substitute for her self, Emin did not open up a critical distance between her subjectivity and its signification. Like the daytime chat show, Emin's work does not transform the sexual politics it lays bare.

As Andreas Huyssen demonstrated in his analysis of the relation between modernism and mass culture, mass culture has been persistently feminized in avant-garde writings as 'Modernism's "Other"' (Huyssen 1986). Since the mid-nineteenth century, the relations between production and consumption within the capitalist economy have been gendered. When mapped onto art, this gendered split was reproduced as a division between the male creator (producer) and the woman artist (a second-order creativity linked to her domestic role as decorator and consumer). As more women entered the art world, Huyssen suggested this gendering device would become obsolete, but the destabilization of gender roles has foregrounded questions of artistic identity in new ways. If gender identities *are* shifting, this may be seen as part of a wider process of 'feminization' in society in which the traditionally male sphere of production has lost value while the importance of the spheres of service and consumption, historically classed as female, has increased. This process is, of course, experienced unequally and unevenly. In Britain, it is white working-class men who have above all lost the economic power identified with production. As contemporary art differentiates itself from modernism by embracing mass culture, it also becomes linked to the 'feminine' sphere of consumption. This may account in part for the 'new laddishness' of so many young male British artists and their identification with masculine working-class culture, which can be understood not so much as transgression, but as a defensive posture, a disavowal of their entry into newly feminized territory. That young working-class masculinity has itself come to be viewed as transgressive in Britain is evident from the current moral panic over young men's failure to be socialized into education, work, fatherhood—and football.

In this context, Sarah Lucas is interesting. Through her chosen identity as 'one of the lads', she paradoxically exposes that classed masculine identity as a construction. Unlike Tracy Emin's claim to 'truth', Lucas's aggressive performance of masculinity in self-portraits and photographs is more like a masquerade in the sense that Joan Riviere used it (Riviere 1986). But Lucas upturns Riviere's formulation in which the 'masculine' woman masquerades 'in a feminine guise' in order to avert the reprisals if she were found to possess male power. Lucas mimics an excessive masculinity in a way that destabilizes that power and exposes it as fantasy in a doubling effect which implies gender transitivity rather than fixity. In one photographic self-portrait, Lucas's masculine pose and 'hard man' stare apes aggressive masculinity while, at the same time, her parodic fried egg 'breasts' undermine it. And, if we read that transgressive masculinity as defensive when adopted by the male *artist*, her work of mimicry as a woman artist is doubly undoing. The repetitive phallic references in her work—exploding beer cans, clenched cigarette, razor-tipped boots—deliberately parody male sexual performance and push it to an extreme in a way that challenges the cultural meanings ascribed to a 'woman' artist.

Lucas's work has been read as ambivalent in its reference to heterosexist male culture. What do we make of an art practice that consciously mimics misogynist pleasures of consumption? Should we see it as exploiting the contradictions within and between fine art and mass media to critical purpose or, conversely, complicit with both, as having your artistic cake and eating it? Lucas herself is ambiguous: 'I use sexist attitudes because they are there to be used. I get strength from them' (Kent 1994: 58). One of her early works from 1991 consists solely of handwritten alphabetical lists of obscene terms for the male and female genitals, thereby revealing our anatomical obsession. In a series of large-scale reproductions of the pages of *Sunday Sport*, Lucas mirrors the misogyny of tabloid culture and its gross exploitation of women as sexual objects, evoking a world of routine, emotionally numbing, sexual objectification. But, by exaggerating it to a scale much larger than life, the represented female body becomes literally obscene; the sexual abject. If, as Lynda Nead has argued, the female nude in high art functioned traditionally to contain and regulate female sexuality, thus rendering it an object of beauty, Lucas breaks that aesthetic code by using sexual slang (Nead 1992). In her best-known work, *Two Fried Eggs and a Kebab*, 1992 (Fig. 19.2), the reclining nude is reduced to a crude sexual pun. The exotic location of a Matisse *Odalisque* is replaced by the banality of a kitchen table, junk food marking out the woman's breasts and genitalia. The routine domestic objects serve to fix the work within the immediate currency of social experience, and yet its careful making—the kebab is set into the hollowed surface of the table, the fried eggs are replaced regularly in their greasy stains—emphasize its signification as an art object. Similarly, *Au Naturel*, 1994 (Fig. 19.3), suggests a parody of traditional still life paintings with their phallic candlesticks and ripe fruit. In a critical juxtaposition between the title and a deliberately junk aesthetic, the symbolic sexual discourse within high art traditions is laid bare. The soiled and sagging mattress with two melons and a bucket, a cucumber and two oranges, exposes the poverty of sexual expression in popular language that high art has, traditionally, sought to transcend. Her work therefore offers a double commentary on sexual discourses within high art and low culture, both of which reduce the female body to an assemblage of parts.

Sarah Kent, one of the few critics in the 1990s to locate Lucas within a gendered as well as a class context, suggested that she acts as an 'aesthetic terrorist pillaging mainstream culture.' (Kent 1994: 58). The shock tactics involved in translating the obscene into art conciously mimic earlier avant-garde artists like Marcel Duchamp.

Fig. 19.2 Sarah Lucas, *Two Fried Eggs and a Kebab*.
© Sarah Lucas, courtesy Sadie Coles HQ, London.

Like Duchamp, Lucas insists on the aesthetic indifference of her found objects—'they are there to be used'—and similar acts of choice, as well as humour, characterize the deliberate provocation of her work. Peter Burger has described this repeated gestural operation of art practice as the 'neo-avant-garde', arguing that an authentic avant-garde is critical not only of practices of art, but of the social relations in which art is embedded (Burger 1984). If Lucas's work is read as a critical commentary on the sexual politics embedded in both fine art and mass culture, it can be seen as operating in a critical relationship to both traditions. But her refusal to ascribe political meaning to her own work neutralizes its effect, allowing it to be easily incorporated within the Bad Girl image of Brit art. What is suppressed within this rhetoric of indifference is precisely the critical connection that can be made between her visual practices and the broader project of reconceiving and

Fig. 19.3 Sarah Lucas, *Au Naturel*.
© Sarah Lucas, courtesy Sadie Coles HQ, London.

reinscribing the body within representation which artists like Mary Kelly initiated in the 1970s and 1980s.

Whereas both Emin and Lucas can be seen to engage with a sexual politics, I have suggested that they do so in very different ways. Emin's autobiographical mode confirms a trope of the feminine as hysteric evident in the current cult for confessional television, while Lucas's mimicry and destabilization of the masculine masquerade seems to perform a more radical act of subversion. The contradictory positioning of both artists between the politics of feminism and a depoliticized post-feminism and between modernist shock and postmodern irony is typical of the ambivalent status adopted by many of the young British artists in the 1990s. The content and form of their work was often disturbing and challenging, yet their silence or indifference to its meaning effectively defuses—or confuses—theoretical and critical analysis. Critical responses to the new British art have polarized between those who claimed it was genuinely subversive of the status quo (Roberts 1996), and those who argued that its intimate relation to the art market led to an inevitable institutional absorption (Bickers 1995). But this either/or is too simplistic: it is precisely the refusal by the artists to be pinned down that was their defining characteristic. Both knowing and anti-intellectual, emulating mass culture yet claiming the status of art, fascinated with the kitsch of consumer society while buying into the art market, recent British art subverted the authority of a received national culture in the name of populism, but showed in its formation how closely it depended on the institutional structures of the art world. These critical and curatorial paradigms created the myth of a homogeneous generation of artists born fully fledged in reaction to previous art, following the familiar trope of avant-gardist revolt. Ironically, the very success of many of the artists lay in their unabashed self-promotion and willingness to exploit the mass media, underpinned by the support of key institutions, critics, dealers, and collectors. From this perspective, the modernist model of avant-garde rebellion is not an appropriate model for the position of the artist in late twentieth-century Britain, but a rather brief aberration in the generally close relations between art and commerce within British cultural life. Perhaps it is not so surprising in this context that the bad girls and boys of Brit Art were briefly co-opted by New Labour into the project of cultural regeneration of a 'Creative Britain'. It will be interesting to see whether artists like Hirst and Hume, Emin and Lucas, now in their late thirties, can escape the Saatchi-inspired framing myth and claim their own histories.

Further Reading

The critical debate over the status and significance of recent British art has been mainly conducted through British journals including *Art Monthly*, *New Left Review*, and *Third Text*. Key articles and books are listed below.

References

Bickers, P. (1995), *The Brit Pack: Contemporary British Art, the View from Abroad*, Manchester: Cornerhouse.
Burger, P. (1984), *Theory of the Avant-Garde*, Manchester: Manchester University Press.
Collings, M. (1997), *Blimey! From Bohemia to Britpop: The London Art World from Francis Bacon to Damien Hirst*, Cambridge: 21 Publishing Ltd.

Crow, T. (1996), *Modern Art in the Common Culture*, London: Yale University Press.

Deepwell, K. (1997), 'Bad Girls? Feminist Identity Politics in the 1990s', in J. Steyn (ed.), *Other than Identity: The Subject, Politics and Art*, Manchester: Manchester University Press.

Garnett, R. (1998), 'Britpopism and the Populist Gesture', in D. McCorquodale, N. Siderlin, and J. Stallabrass (eds.), *Occupational Hazard: Critical Writing on British Art*, London: Black Dog Press.

Huyssen, A. (1986), *After the Great Divide: Modernism, Mass Culture and Postmodernism*, London: Macmillan.

Kent, S. (1994), *Shark Infested Waters: The Saatchi Collection of British Art in the 1990s*, London: Thames & Hudson.

McCorquodale, D., Siderlin, N., and Stallabrass, J. (eds.) (1998), *Occupational Hazard: Critical Writing on Recent British Art*, London: Black Dog Press.

Mulgan, G., and Worpole, K. (1986), *Saturday Night or Sunday Morning? From Arts to Industry: New Forms of Cultural Policy*, London: Comedia.

Nead, L. (1992), *The Female Nude: Art, Obscenity and Sexuality*, London: Routledge.

Policy Studies Institute (1995), *Cultural Trends*, London: PSI.

Renton, A., and Gillick, L. (eds.) (1991), *Technique Anglaise: Current Trends in British Art*, London: Thames & Hudson.

Riviere, J. (1986), 'Womanliness as Masquerade', in V. Burgin et al. (eds.), *Formations of Fantasy*, London: Methuen.

Roberts, J. (1996), 'Mad for It! Philistinism, the Everyday and the New British Art', *Third Text*, 35.

Royal Academy (1997), *Sensation: Young British Artists from the Saatchi Collection*, London: Royal Academy of Arts.

Stallabrass, J. (2000), *High Art Lite*, London: Verso.

20

Writing Britains

BERNARD
SHARRATT

NINETEENTH-century British novelists seem, with hindsight, to have had little difficulty choosing a focus of concern, a topic on which to hang their imaginative enquiries into the 'condition of England'. Jane Austen's poised probings of the convergence of classes, finances, and sensibilities through marriage negotiations, George Eliot's provincial cross-sections, Dickens's entrepreneurs and debtors, railways and law cases, Thackeray's social vanities, Trollope's parsonages and cathedral closes, Hardy's determined destinies—all these can appear to have traced the contours of a once shared history, through representative dilemmas, typical figures, emblematic events. The governess and the doubting vicar, the thrusting politician and the autodidact, could come together in a panorama of an apparently common Britain.

But what representative focus for imagining being 'British' is now available? Some would claim the obvious primary concern as differentiation and diversity, ethnic and cultural. Contemporary Asian-British novelist Hanif Kureishi emphatically asserts, against George Orwell's complacent 1941 sketch-map of the 'British character', that

[Orwell's] tolerant, gentle British whites have no idea . . . of the violence, hostility and contempt directed against black people every day by state and individual alike in this land . . . . it is major adjustments to British society that have to be made. . . . I stress that it is the British who have to make these adjustments. It is the British, the white British, who have to learn that being British isn't what it was. (Kureishi 1986: 37–8)

But Kureishi himself suggests the too easy notion that only white British have to make such adjustments, side-stepping the problem that the several varieties of non-white British may also have to extend their own notion of 'British' to include a larger complexity. 'Britain's multicultural demography', writes one critic, comprises 'not merely "symbolic ethnicity", the quaint or passing display of cultural wares in "Asian" Leicester, "Bengali" Whitechapel, "Chinese" Liverpool or "Arab" Kensington. A necessary and always deeply threaded, historicity underwrites each' (Lee 1995: 72). A roll-call of 'typical' characters in a contemporary condition of Britain novel might feel constrained to include not only English, Welsh, Irish, Scottish but also Polish, Egyptian, Jewish, Cypriot, Italian, Chinese, Caribbean, Nigerian, Kenyan, Indian, Pakistani, Sri Lankan, Australian, New Zealand, Canadian, American, Maltese, Turkish, Zimbabwean, South African, Falklander. . . . Nor are ethnic or hybrid identities necessarily the primary focus, given other continuing diversities of class, region, age, gender. A nineteenth-century novelist, returning and surveying, might well regard the received forms as crumbling into unmanageable diversity and complexity.

Yet mere miscellany offers no form. To justify any social grouping or fictional cast as 'British', however hyphenated, requires some shared framework or apparatus, of overlapping history or common culture. Raymond Williams, a novelist who described himself as a Welsh European, once commented:

When we hear the word 'culture', some of us reach for our fancy dress. Real life is home, family and a job; wages and prices; politics and crisis. Culture, then, is for high days and holidays: not an ordinary gear but an overdrive. So if you say 'Welsh culture' what do you think of? Of bara brith and the Eisteddfod? Of choirs and Cardiff Arms Park? Of love spoons and englynion? Of the national costume and the rampant red dragon? All these things are here, if at different levels and in different ways. But over and above them is another culture. Not the alien Saxon, who belongs, in truth, with the fancy dress. Not even, in any simple way, the alien or at least different English. Taking culture in its full sense you would be speaking of something quite different: of a way of life determined by the National Coal Board, the British Steel Corporation, the Milk Marketing Board, the Co-op and Marks and Spencers, the BBC, the Labour Party, the EEC, NATO. But that's not Welsh culture. Maybe, maybe not. It's how and where most people in Wales are living, and in relation to which most meanings and values are in practice found . . . And if we have shared these things with others, that sharpens the question. Where is it now, this Wales. Where is the real identity, the real culture? (Williams 1989: 99)

Williams was a founding figure in British cultural studies but also wrote several ambitious novels deeply shaped by a political as well as aesthetic commitment to attempted totalization, to grasping in imagination and analysis a whole social formation. His early work can stand for a form of the novel still in deep continuity with those nineteenth-century procedures and solutions. The focus of *Border Country* (1960) is the continuing ramifications of an intensely local conflict within the wider 1926 General Strike. *Second Generation* (1964) uses the city of Oxford to embody cultural and political contrasts between middle-class academia and Cowley factory life. In *The Fight for Manod* (1979) the establishment of a new town in Wales focuses not only relations and conflicts within Wales but European-wide economic policies, procedures, and priorities. For though Williams might be claimed as a Welsh novelist his own emphasis upon a shared 'culture' (in that larger sense) took him conceptually and imaginatively beyond the familiar but problematic boundaries of 'nation' or 'state' and their accompanying assumptions.

His extraordinary final set of novels, *People of the Black Mountains* (1989, 1990), stretches both the received fictional form and our sense of historical continuity and identity. The novel uses a loose framing narrative to layer brief episodic tales upon one minutely mapped area of what is now the border between Wales and England. It is one of the few novels to be read with an Ordinance Survey map to hand: every path, cairn, and ruin holds a story. This exact local attention organizes an enormous temporal sweep, beginning with neolithic cave communities and moving through several thousand years of imagined histories to break off, with Williams's premature death in 1988, only into the fifteenth century. Unlike the reader, however, the successive generations of inhabitants of this small local terrain are aware of their predecessors only, if at all, as legend, hearsay, distorted folk memories. What is emblematic here is the construction of a shared, inherited, coexistence and several kinds of mutual dependence but with no consciously acknowledged and continuing identity across the discontinuities, opacities, and partial ignorance. The nation-state is relativized by the sheer sweep of the novel merely to a historically recent, and temporary, construction of identity.

Several related problems lurk as we move to the more recent generation of novelists. The diversity reflected on the shelves of any adequate bookshop questions whether any contemporary fictions can appropriately imagine an overarching culture within which such multiple differences operate, or whether the new range simply offers enclosed cultural self-presentations more akin to 'fancy dress' or symbolic ethnicity. Moreover, in so far as much of contemporary Britain's multicultural diversity stems from a previous imperial sway, there is also the problem of an asymmetrical relation to an apparently shared history: each ex-colony's relation to that global history was connected to the metropolitan power but not necessarily shared in any specific way with those other histories. This is also an aspect of that question side-stepped by Kureishi: how the several communities within the UK relate not just to the dominant ethos but also to each other. Reading each other's fiction may be part of that wider exploration.

Andrew Cowan's novel *Common Ground* (1996) echoes, not least in its title, Williams's own concerns with the ordinary shape of a whole social experience. Its England would be widely recognizable among a certain class of reader, focused as it is through a year in the lives of a dissatisfied geography teacher and a community arts worker living on the semi-blighted edge of an anonymous town, their mundane miserableness shaped by a tight income and a new baby, by rain and waiting for buses, by National Childbirth Trust exercises and reluctant DIY. Cowan's common ground is a sour but not unbearable territory of casual street and playground violence, of vandalized cars and TV-noisy neighbours. The novel offers a downbeat climax in the official violence of bailiffs and police as a campaign to save a local common from a bypass is defeated. Here that nineteenth-century metaphor for devastating change, the railway, has been replaced by the motorway, as the spreading city seeps into a changing countryside, with the transport system itself now as much a lived area as the nineteenth-century parlour. Cowan takes the struggle against the encroaching motorway as the focus for his concerns and characters, most of them deliberately low key and unheroic. The overall tone is self-deprecatingly stoic, a touch away from grim humour. One ironic strand includes a global gesture as the narrative interleaves letters to a brother travelling the worldwide tourist trails, through India, Singapore, Thailand, Guatemala. But neither local nor global strand yields much illumination, transformation, or achievement, only a resisting resignation. This structure of feeling may indeed be familiar and representative of a glum middle England, but it registers only a limited awareness of a terrain outside its specific concerns: the community focused round this common ground contains, for example, few non-white faces.

Timothy Mo's *Sour Sweet* (1982) is a very similar novel of ordinary depressed urban living, in its depiction of an unremarkable family struggling to make a living and bring up the next generation, avoiding all officialdom in the form of even tax returns or driving licences, establishing a bearable living without, it seems, much claim to significance. But Mo's family is immigrant Hong Kong Chinese and the family's life centres on a Chinese takeaway, an established feature of the English landscape but still alien territory for most English readers. In that sense the novel opens up an unknown aspect, a glimpse backstage. Sartre once commented on his own temptation as a novelist always to diverge from telling the tale of his central characters to recounting the lives of all those they encounter; he instanced the waiter who serves his hero in a restaurant. Mo's Mr Chen begins the novel as an anonymous Soho waiter and is only catapulted into the takeaway business by an involuntary debt-entanglement with a Triad gangster gang. The Triad plot allows glimpses into an underworld even less familiar than the kitchen of a Soho restaurant or a high street takeaway, but also operates as exotic fancy dress: Mo's Chinese community can too easily be filtered through reader's lenses borrowed from Kung Fu or James Bond movies, even though Mo deliberately presents the Triads as themselves just another fairly mundane family business, seeking profit maximization, product diversification, and modernization, a banal multinational corporation that happens to be overtly criminal. In this novel it is the non-Chinese who are marginalized, almost all encounters outside that community restricted to the cursory relations of a passing customer. In that respect its horizons are as restricted as those of Cowan's allegedly common ground.

Hanif Kureishi's film *My Beautiful Launderette* (1985) deploys a parallel device in relation to the Pakistani community in England, again allowing a glimpse behind a familiar high street façade, this time the Asian-owned launderette. Direct global links come through the central character's extended family relations with Karachi-based wealth and privilege, which emphasizes a business resourcefulness bordering on ruthlessness and an element of sub-criminal dealings which risks highlighting those aspects of the Pakistani community which reinforce white readers' stereotypes. That the relation between the main Asian character and his white lover is homosexual in effect keeps the issue of interracial conflict unexpectedly marginal. In Kureishi's novel *The Black Album* (1995) the viewpoint is that of a British Pakistani generation familiar with interracial sex and violence, and this novel does overtly overlap cultural communities, as white, black, and Asian groupings occasionally collide and collaborate. However, the dominant cast of Muslim fundamentalist vigilantes and drug-dealing petty gangsters again verges into caricature. The narrative tone of comic confidant hovers between the assurance of a voice articulating a community to those outside it and the anxiousness of someone uncertain of being accepted within it. That the publication of Salman Rushdie's controversial novel *The Satanic Verses* (1988) is used to date the action acknowledges a wider unease at the community's possible reaction to Kureishi's own novel, including its semi-parody of Rushdie's alleged blasphemy when Kureishi's protagonist rewrites the entrusted verses of a guru.

The device of extended family relations deployed by both Mo and Kureishi allows a historical as well as a geographical reach. The autobiographical first novels of second-generation writers often include encounters with or memories of an earlier generation's perspective upon a previous homeland and a past imperial history. Some novels may also attempt a direct novelizing of a national history prior to a British re-location. Thus Abdulrazak Gurnah's outstanding *Memory of Departure* (1987) gives vivid glimpses of an East African childhood while his *Paradise* (1994) layers several aspects of East African history into a vividly representative experience. In Fred D'Aguiar's *The Longest Memory* (1994) a complex plantation tale unfolds, with its marvellous interplay of perspectives upon the relation of unknown half-brothers across divisions of skin and the slave/free divide. Ben Okri's *Famished Road* (1991) gives a broad panorama of Nigerian history while A. Sivanandan's *When Memory Dies* (1997) attempts a major novel of Sri Lanka. These variously incorporated histories, precisely through their density and their specificity to one community, highlight the genuine difficulty of combining the global dimension of one community with an adequate awareness of the equally specific but very different cultural inheritances of other communities.

An interesting example is David Dabydeen's *The Intended* (1991), which opens with the overtly encompassing device of a multicultural school group:

It was the regrouping of the Asian diaspora in a South London schoolground. Shaz, of Pakistani parents, was born in Britain, had never travelled to the sub-continent, could barely speak a word of Urdu and had never seen the interior of a mosque. Nasim was more authentically Muslim, a believer by upbringing, fluent in his ancestral language and devoted to family. Patel was of Hindu stock, could speak Gudjerati . . . I was an Indian West-Indian Guyanese, the most mixed-up of the lot. There we were together in our school blazers and ties and grey trousers, but the only real hint of our shared Asian-ness was the brownness of our skins. Even that was not uniform. Patel was Aryan, tall, fair-skinned, crisp and cared-for in appearance. . . . Shaz was stoutly built, shabbily dressed and extremely black; Nasim, slim, was two shades darker than Patel and two shades less immaculate. I, the medium to dark brown West-Indian, was merely clumsy in my schoolclothes. (Dabydeen 1991: 5)

But though this multicultural group begins almost as a collective protagonist, the narrative 'I' begins to separate out, partly as each character grows into a differentiated adulthood but also, and significantly, as that first person viewpoint is deepened and particularized by memories of Guyana:

And truly she was old, her African face sprouting hairs between the cracks, like a golden-apple seed. She was as old as the village, old as the huge tamarind tree, heavy with fruit, that cast a broad shadow over one side of the yard which her father planted when she was a child, and as black as the trench water in which every day of her life she dipped her bucket and took to the house to wash pans, scrub floors, bathe children. Auntie Jessica brought a handful of plums and gave them to me. 'Tek some to Englan and when you see white man give him and say you Auntie Clarice send him gift from she back garden in Albion Village, Berbice, Guyana, South America, all the way across the Ocean, you hear, and that he and he race must be kind to you and we, for all body on dis earth is one God's people, not true?' . . . She reached into her bosom, searched about, pulled out a handkerchief knotted at one end which she untied to reveal a five-dollar note creased and humid from being saved up for weeks. She kissed me and put the money in my pocket. As I turned to go she called out a final riddle: 'you is we, remember you is we.' (Dabydeen 1991: 39)

None of the others in Dabydeen's carefully differentiated cast is awarded a parallel dimension of memory and cultural specificity. Indeed the novel acknowledges this thinness in its blatant symbol of inadequate global awareness: Battersea Fun Fair's artificial 'World Tour' where three of the characters converge. Moreover the intended of the title, the white English girlfriend, also remains entirely two-dimensional, without convincing cultural presence of her own, another fantasy of relation. There are no rich memories of England to resonate with those of Guyana.

Part of the difficulty is to know what would count as an appropriate parallel within Britain to these charged and ambivalent memories of overseas imperial dispossession and alternative cultural awareness. The British working class has itself rarely been given that kind of articulation in British fiction, despite several sagas of working-class nostalgia (Catherine Cookson, Roy Hattersley, Katie Anderson). Contemporary working-class experience has found some recent articulation, but within a myopic concentration on such 1990s fashions as football or ecstasy novels.

John King's *The Football Factory* (1996), for example, offers another behind-the-scenes glimpse, this time into the violence-ridden life of football thugs. The novel is shaped round football games, home and away, the central concern of a Chelsea supporters' subculture defined by 'getting pissed, shagging a bird and kicking the fuck out of' other thugs and, where possible, the police, thought of as just another firm of thugs. The dominant mood is utter frustration, endless aggression, mindlessness—yet the text itself is articulately littered with politically correct sentiments and parables. The central strand of repeated match violence alternates with episodic tales incorporating other aspects of footballing culture, including an elderly supporter who punches two young neo-Nazis for abusing a Pakistani family, and an England supporter who ventures beyond away-game travel to find an alternative life in India and Australia. Encounters with black and Asian are predictably violent but the emphasis is not primarily racist, since a black thug is easily accommodated into the Chelsea 'firm'. What remains curious but also symptomatic is the mode of address, combining an assumption of hooligan insiderness with a presumption of impeccably liberal sentiments in the intended reader. Like Kureishi, King seems uneasily to speak for but not to the community he depicts.

King acknowledges a debt to Irvine Welsh's work, most widely known through the film version of *Trainspotting* (1993), which also portrays from within another clearly defined subcultural territory in which violence, drugs, and sex are a way of death in life. The primary focus of these novels of housing estates, rave clubs, and street dealing is an age group rather than a regional or ethnic identity. Welsh is one of a wave of new writers, however, who choose to speak both for and to a generation which allows outsiders to eavesdrop only semi-comprehendingly since the accent and vocabulary remain deliberately enclosed. *Disco Biscuits*, edited by Sarah Champion (1997), presents reports from the chemical generation's battlefront, both social and psychological. The prose tends towards streams of syntaxless semi-consciousness from characters who have little perspective outside or even upon their own drug-fuelled lives of sex, sweat, noise, daze, movement, within a social environment summed up by, for example, Ben Graham's deliberate clichés:

This is a skint and dangerous neighbourhood. Flats are regularly broken into or torched; passing cars are pelted with stones; drunken strays at midnight are waylaid with baseball bats and Stanley knives. The pubs are grim, functional alehouses where giros are cashed in return for a few hours of welcome oblivion. Where a desperate middle-aged blues band pound away in the corner, and a hollow-eyed housewife screams vainly at her man to come home while he still has money to put food on the table. Sometimes, cliches are all you have left. Another cliche—where there's poverty, fear and desperation, that's where we go to buy our drugs. (Champion 1997: 164)

This is a last-days mentality, expressed in appropriately hollow poetic prose, and the relation between the restricted horizons of these novels of youth subcultures and that of, say, Martin Amis's *The Information* (1995), set in an equally self-regarding and culturally enclosed metropolitan literary world, is depressingly close.

Yet if these are mutually unaware and restricted local cultures what could possibly claim the status of the majority culture? Meera Syal's heroine, the Indian-Derbyshire lass of *Anita and Me* (1996), has no doubt: her ambition of assimilation is defined as being allowed to eat fish and chips and to watch television soaps, both pleasures deeply frowned upon by her respectable immigrant parents. Yet though watching TV does indeed provide the most widely shared cultural framework for most people in Britain, including television adaptations of those sprawling nineteenth-century novels, and soaps in particular more successfully portray a composite multicultural society than most novels, it is rare for a novelist actually to acknowledge that centrality. A comic counter-example is Toby Litt's *Adventures in Capitalism* (1996), which features characters who, for example, attempt to believe and obey all television adverts or who write letters to the characters in those adverts. Litt's Britain is one where all social experience is filtered through publicity images, consumerist enticements, and advertising jingles. His fiction remains, correspondingly, fragmentary.

Julian Barnes's *England, England* (1998) takes the more ambitious step of imagining an England wholly transformed into such a media-shaped construction. Its central plot concerns a megalomaniacal billionaire who buys up or replicates every well-known tourist attraction and relocates it to the Isle of Wight, now a commercially owned statelet and renamed England, England. In a parodic variation on Williams's device in *Black Mountains* Barnes situates Stonehenge, Windsor Castle, Manchester United football club, the Houses of Parliament, Buckingham Palace (including its redeployed royals) all within walking distance of each other, so that tourists need no longer endure the actuality of travel in the real England to sample Devon teas, London taxis, Cotswold cottages, and the Changing of the Guard in the compass of a single theme park. The satire turns partly upon the reader's uneasy sense that England has already been so transformed, but Barnes's own counter-vision of a post-industrial Britain offering a regressive utopia is wholly uncompelling. It may well be that any contemporary attempt to capture and focus the 'condition of England' in such a traditional fictional form can itself only offer a form of cultural nostalgia and tourism

Geoff Ryman's extraordinary *253* (1998) was, however, originally published as a hyperfiction on the Internet, which allowed the possibility of deploying devices reminiscent of both Williams's strategy and Sartre's dilemma. Here a London tube-train provides the physically shared terrain, complete with maps and diagrams. Seven tube carriages carry a total of 253 passengers, each of whom is given one page of 253 words, comprising a brief description of their outward appearance (as they might be seen by other passengers), some biographical information, and an inward account of what each is currently wishing, dreaming, hoping, planning. This overall device allows a plausibly wide roll-call of identities and backgrounds, preoccupations and destinies, to be literally juxtaposed while the hypertext links allow the reader-browser to explore multiple interwoven connections not apparent even to the travellers themselves: some passengers are related, about to meet, once knew each other, work for the same firm, are travelling to the same exhibition, will take each other's places, etc. The usual small incidents of commuter travel create momentary trivial encounters and interactions while, as readers, we gradually realize that these lives are also shaped by larger forces beyond the perception of each, including the fact that this train will soon crash. Ryman's work successfully, and humorously, captures the real diversity of urban Britain with its oddly optimistic mode of contemporary coexistence, a combination of mild curiosity about and deliberate semi-ignorance of others, a structure of feeling precisely shaped and regularly reinforced by commuter travel. It is encouragingly characteristic of that sensibility that we reassure ourselves that most of 253's passengers will get off before the crash actually comes, to survive and continue their apparently independent but repeatedly interconnected lives.

From Raymond Williams to Geoff Ryman there may be a certain continuity of theme: a recognition of people as living within a shared physical location under common constraints yet with little conscious or deliberate connection, a common ground but little actually held in common. Yet neither total indifference nor only intolerance; a daily contact, an inherited coexistence. Like the planet itself, on this perspective, the nation-state seems more a condition of mutual dependence than any common culture. It is then hardly surprising that contemporary novelists' various attempts at imagining a Britain or writing the experience of some fragment of it may not share any overarching cultural frame or even a common audience, but merely a publishing apparatus, also in decline. Before we attach too much significance to their efforts we should perhaps remind ourselves that, after all, before the award of the 1998 Booker Prize the eventual winner had sold barely a thousand copies, and that was more than the rest of the short-list put together.

Further Reading

Ashcroft, W., Griffiths, G., and **Tiffin, H.** (eds.), (1989), *The Empire Writes Back: Theory and Practice in Post-colonial Literatures*, London: Routledge. A seminal collection of critical essays.

Bassnett, Susan (ed.) (1997), *Studying British Culture: An Introduction*, London: Routledge. Includes essays on fictional maps of Britain by David Punter and on teaching West Indian literature by David Dabydeen.

Bell, Ian A. (ed.) (1995), *Peripheral Visions: Images of Nationhood in Contemporary British Fiction*, Cardiff: University of Wales Press. Combines statements by practitioners with critical essays on writing in Scotland, Wales, Ireland, the north-east, Cornwall. Contributors include Glenn Patterson, William Owen Roberts, and Ken Worpole.

Lee, A. Robert (ed.) (1995), *Other Britain, Other British: Contemporary Multi-cultural Fiction*, London: Pluto Press. Useful collection of essays on post-colonial and immigrant writing in Britain, including Lamming, Selvon, Emecheta, Rushdie, Naipaul, Kureishi, Ishiguro. Contributors include Abdulrazak Gurnah and Louis James.

References

Novels

Amis, Martin (1995), *The Information*, London: Flamingo.

Atkinson, Kate (1995), *Behind the Scenes at the Museum*, London: Doubleday.

Barnes, Julian (1998), *England, England*, London: Jonathan Cape.

Champion, Sarah (ed.) (1997), *Disco Biscuits*, London: Hodder & Stoughton.

Cowan, Andrew (1996), *Common Ground*, London: Michael Joseph.

Dabydeen, David (1991), *The Intended*, London: Secker & Warburg.

D'Aguiar, Fred (1994), *The Longest Memory*, London: Chatto & Windus.

Gurnah, Abdulrazak (1987), *Memory of Departure*, London: Jonathan Cape.

—— (1994), *Paradise*, London: Hamish Hamilton.

Hattersley, Roy (1990), *The Maker's Mark*, London: Macmillan.

King, John (1996), *The Football Factory*, London: Jonathan Cape.

Kureishi, Hanif (1995), *The Black Album*, London: Faber & Faber.

Litt, Toby (1996), *Adventures in Capitalism*, London: Martin Secker & Warburg.

Mo, Timothy (1982), *Sour Sweet*, London: Andre Deutsch.

Okri, Ben (1991), *The Famished Road*, London: Jonathan Cape.

Rushdie, Salman (1988), *The Satanic Verses*, London: Viking Press.

Ryman, Geoff (1998), *253 : the print remix*, London: Flamingo.
—— *http://www.ryman-novel.com.*
Sivanandan, A. (1997), *When Memory Dies*, London: Arcadia Books.
Syal, Meera (1996), *Anita and Me*, London: Flamingo.
Welsh, Irvine (1993), *Trainspotting*, London: Martin Secker & Warburg.
Williams, Raymond (1960), *Border Country*, London: Chatto & Windus.
—— (1964), *Second Generation*, London: Chatto & Windus.
—— (1979), *The Fight for Manod*, London: Chatto & Windus.
—— (1989), *People of the Black Mountains*, i: *The Beginning*, London: Chatto & Windus.
—— (1990), *People of the Black Mountains*, ii: *The Eggs of the Eagle*, London: Chatto & Windus.

Other Works

Lee, A. Robert (ed.) (1995), *Other Britain, Other British: Contemporary Multicultural Fiction*, London: Pluto Press.
Kureishi, Hanif (1986), *My Beautiful Launderette and The Rainbow Sign*, London: Faber & Faber.
Williams, Raymond (1989), 'Welsh Culture', BBC Radio 3 talk, 27 Sept. 1975, published in Williams, *Resources of Hope*, London: Verso.

Section III

In the Place of Britishness? Lifestyles, Subcultures, and Cultural Politics

Introduction

THIS section begins with Philip Crang and Peter Jackson's analysis of what is happening with consumer culture in Britain, in the context particularly of new global markets. What, they ask, is the relation now between global and local dynamics? They detect a certain erosion of older models of identity, involving what is often an aestheticization of the exotic and colourful—it involves a negotiation between the old national identities and the new cultural forces associated with multiculturalism. The increasing familiarity with global consumer culture may provoke a certain defensiveness—as has been the case for many decades with the British stance towards American culture. There may be certain anxieties about the preservation of an imagined authentic national culture (which Crang and Jackson argue has never been all that authentic, anyway). In the end, however, it is suggested that British culture can no longer be defined in terms of narrowly defined national boundaries. What globalization has given rise to is, potentially at least, a new, more accommodating and open-ended, kind of Britishness.

Linda McDowell is concerned with the changing status and meaning of work in British culture. She identifies a new polarization, over the last twenty years, between those who have been excluded from the national (and global) economy—and who now live in what have been called 'third spaces' and 'fourth worlds'—and those who have benefited from the growth of the new service sectors, and particularly financial services. Through the course of deindustrialization in the British economy, McDowell argues, we have seen the progressive erosion of a familiar kind of collectivist work identity—one that had distinctive gender, class, and also regional dimensions. What have now become more salient are new kinds of (post-industrial) work culture and ethos, associated with the new—flexible and precarious—service industries. One significant development has involved an increasing emphasis on personal (i.e. non-collectivist) attributes and attitudes, in what may be regarded as a culturalization of the workplace. McDowell also places great importance on the feminization of the workforce. And what she draws attention to here are the consequences that this development has had for male culture and masculine identity. What she observes is a powerful reassertion of masculine values and machismo lifestyles, particularly in the new global businesses (here her argument also connects with Sean Nixon's later in this section).

Developing McDowell's analysis of the feminization of the workforce, the changing position of young women is the focus of Angela McRobbie's chapter, in which she argues that they represent a crucial 'metaphor for change' in our times, just as other groups have done in previous periods ('youth' more generally, in the 1960s, for example). The combination of the culture of 'girl power' and the new emphasis on women at work, in the context of the overall 'feminization' of the economy, places young women in a crucial position. McRobbie argues that we see here a confluence of the commercial discourse of market liberalism with New Labour's form of 'governmentality' which both focus on new forms of female 'success' in education and in the marketplace to produce young women as 'newly remapped entities'. She argues that young women in Britain today have to be understood as the daughters both of Thatcherism and of feminism, but that their position is increasingly being articulated through a depoliticized form of neo-liberal market feminism. The limits of this discourse are McRobbie's principal concern and she argues that the much vaunted new 'meritocratic' avenues of educational and marketplace 'success' are in fact only open, in reality, to a privileged minority of young women, while remaining largely closed to the daughters of the poor, the disadvantaged, and, in particular, many ethnic minorities. She foresees the emergence of new forms of social division— between the majority of less well-off 'ordinary women' with few educational qualifications, working in poorly paid part-time jobs while simultaneously still performing the traditional feminine domestic roles, and an elite of highly educated, affluent, often childless women in full-time careers. From a cultural perspective, she argues, this emerging division, along lines of both class and ethnicity, is already being articulated as one between the 'good girls' who do well at school and go on to a successful career and the (often implicitly racialized) 'bad girls' from poor backgrounds, who leave school unqualified and become teenage mothers—the new scapegoats of our moralistic times. As McRobbie notes, what we see here is the emergence of a moralistic discourse (often articulated to neo-Darwinism) which, while celebrating success, punishes failure as a matter of individual weakness. McRobbie's hope is that out of the all too evident limitations of this prevailing discourse, we may yet see the emergence of a new and revitalized form of contemporary feminism which is more sensitive to these issues.

With Sean Nixon's chapter, we move from new forms of femininity to the question of (young) masculinity in contemporary Britain. Nixon offers a historical overview of style magazines—like the *Face*, *Arena*, and *GQ*—in which new models of masculine identity have been manufactured. What he identifies are successive attempts to link masculinity, no longer primarily to the world of work, but now increasingly to the world of consumption. And what he argues is that there have been peculiarly British ways of linking male identity to the world of consumerism. The 1980s was a critical period in which the prevailing image was that of the so-called 'new man'. This was a style that sought to balance masculinity with a certain softness and sensuality, resulting in an ambivalent, and also more 'multicultural', masculinity—an image that perhaps had certain emancipatory possibilities with respect to dominant ideologies of manhood. In the early 1990s, however, this image was displaced by the image of the so-called 'new lad'. With the 'new lad', Nixon explains, a new machismo was reintroduced into male lifestyle culture—thus, for example, the world of football became a key reference point. In concluding his narrative, Nixon points to the great difficulty of reinventing masculine heterosexual scripts in contemporary Britain—old models still exert a powerful hold over the masculine imagination.

Developing the theme of gender and sexual identities further, Ken Plummer examines questions of lifestyle and identity in British society, with reference to gay and lesbian cultures. Whilst homosexuals had no visibility in the cultural world through much of the twentieth century ('British culture could be approached through [the] culture of the closet'), Plummer argues, it is now the case that 'gayness' is everywhere; it is an integral part of the British cultural scene. He identifies a number of significant developments—what he calls 'symbolic moments'—in the progressive demarginalization of gay culture in Britain. First, there was the moment of the Wolfenden Report in 1957, which sanctioned homosexual acts (between consenting adults) in the private sphere, whilst still denying public acceptance of gay culture. Then, with the development of the Gay Liberation Front, in the early 1970s, there arose a new initiative to bring gay issues out into the open, through public demonstrations and campaigning. A third defining moment was associated with recognition of HIV/Aids in the early 1980s, which gave the gay community increasing social prominence, bringing at the same time a new, more professional political style to its political activism. Plummer's fourth symbolic moment came with the implementation of section 28 of the Local Government Act, in 1988, involving both a new attack on gay and lesbian culture and a new revitalization of gay communities. The gay community still defines itself according to long-established cultural reference points—associated with cultural suppression—as a minority or marginal or dissident culture. But Plummer identifies important transformations associated with the mainstreaming of gay culture in Britain. What has become more apparent, he argues, is the diversity of gay cultures, reflecting such factors as the class and ethnic identities of gays—it is a diversification that 'may be seen as expressing a mirror image of the wider and dominant cultures'. What has also been occurring has been a shift from political activism towards a new involvement of gays in market and consumer identities (a development that Angela McRobbie also identifies with respect to feminism).

In his discussion of British sporting culture, Alan Tomlinson rightly emphasizes the historical prominence of sport in British cultural identity (or identities), arguing that sport is one of the privileged sites for exploring the trajectory of Britishness. He sets out from a consideration of the nineteenth-century significance of (national) sports, mobilized in the cause of athleticism, character-building, and moral rectitude. Throughout the course of the twentieth century, this particular national project has been eroded by a set of developments associated primarily with consumerism. We have seen the massive transformation of sport into a consumer spectacle, particularly through its televisual commodification. More recently, sport has also become more and more related to questions of lifestyle and personal identity, connected to new gender and ethnic styles, and to a new politics of the body. Making a similar point to Crang and Jackson, Tomlinson also argues that the new commercial imperatives are following an ever more global logic. The new transnational cultural forces have considerably challenged the old national basis of sporting culture in Britain.

The last set of chapters in this section is concerned with questions of public space and citizenship in contemporary British society. In his contribution, David Sibley is concerned with the control of space, focusing particularly on the countryside, which he regards as a place of significant conflict now. From a historical perspective, he considers how the forces of control and surveillance have been mobilized against successive Gypsy migrations and movements—how the supposed order of the countryside has been defended against what are imagined to be the disruptive influence of nomadic Roma populations. And he links this long historical persecution to the recent imposition of controls on New Age Travellers. This latter exercise of state control has involved the British state in managing the movement and mobility of young people especially—whether they be involved in the new lifestyle of rave gatherings or in the new politics of eco-radicalism and hunt sabotage. Here Sibley particularly emphasizes the significance of the 1994 Criminal Justice and Public Order Act, which he regards as the main instrument now of movement management. Whilst some commentators have seen this political-legal mobilization as an offensive of the New Right, Sibley regards it—rightly in our view—as a reflex of the 'political class' as a whole—as militant under New Labour as under previous Conservative administrations. At its heart is a systematic offensive, on behalf of sedentary culture, directed against the perceived threat of mobile/fluid cultural forces—forces that seem to transgress (English?) norms of cultural order and stability. An offensive against the environmentalists at Manchester Airport, against the New Age Travellers at Stonehenge, against Roma 'asylum-seekers' in the infamous 'Dover'. It is about who belongs in contemporary Britain, and who does not. In some respects, Sibley argues, the controls introduced by the Criminal Justice Act have been highly effective in containing alternative cultures in Britain today. But he also points to new alliances and sympathies that have brought surprising forms of support for oppositional movements and cultures—the boundaries between classes, ethnic groups, generations, and geographical zones are more complex than we might sometimes be led to think.

In her chapter—which picks up on themes developed by David Sibley, and also on the discussion of English ruralism by Alun Howkins in Part I—Linda Merricks considers the development of animal rights and enviromentalist activism in British society. First, she provides a context, showing how, from the early nineteenth century, environmental interests (vegetarianism, the protection of animals) were driven by an agenda of moral reform. Interestingly, she also links nineteenth-century vegetarianism to the growing cosmopolitanism of British urban culture (as a consequence of migrations from Europe). Merricks then goes on to look, in more detail, at developments since the 1960s, when what she calls the new naturism began to take off in Britain. This involved a shift from an agenda of moral reform to one of social and political transformation in the domain of nature. The new agenda, according to Merricks, combined personal politics with green ideas and youth counter-cultural energies. On the one hand, it was a question of personal and lifestyle development, becoming more in tune with the 'natural order', and often involving a reaction against middle-class cultures (by middle-class young people). This was commonly associated with new forms of alternative enterprise and consumerism (Cranks, Infinity Foods). On the other hand, it may involve a more overt and confrontational political articulation. The new naturism has also given rise to the idea of a 'community of resistance', characterized by an anti-authoritarian ethos, and involved in direct action on behalf of its causes (hunt sabotage, animal liberation, protest against new motorways, and so on). Merricks notes that, whilst the core of activists is a small minority, the causes that they fight for have gained a wide support across British society. She also observes that this new counter-culture is involved in a reclamation of Englishness—the ideal of 'Albion' that it champions connects to the marginalized but important tradition of the Levellers and Diggers.

Graham Murdock begins his chapter on new media culture in Britain by also invoking the tradition of dissent in English society—in this case the opposition to the enclosures movement. Murdock is concerned with the history of public space and common culture in Britain, and, therefore, by necessity, with the powerful forces that have stood in the way of the creation of a genuinely public and common culture. His argument (which invokes the spirit of E. P. Thompson) is that these counter-democratic forces have worked through a logic of enclosure—first the enclosure of physical spaces, and then, in the twentieth century, the enclosure of media and communications spaces, what Murdock calls 'electronic commons'. The chapter considers the case of British broadcasting culture, exploring what has stood in the way of its functioning as a democratic public sphere. In one respect, Murdock argues, it has been disabled by the elitist ethos of Arnoldian and then Reithian cultural paternalism. But even more significant have been the consequences of accelerating commercialization, and the corporate enclosure of media space—a development in which audiences have been regarded as markets, rather than moral communities. Murdock then turns his concern to the new communications technology of the Internet, considering its potential for a democratic communicative culture. Will we now see enclosure in cyberspace, he asks? Or are there possibilities of building a digital commons? In reflecting on the possibilities for contesting the potential enclosure of the Internet, Murdock suggests that the BBC might be given a new role, that it may be possible to mobilize its public service tradition to underpin public culture in the new media order.

Finally in this section, Stephen Driver and Luke Martell consider the interventions of New Labour in the matter of national culture and identity. For the party, under Tony Blair, has sought very actively to counter what it regards as Tory traditionalism and insularity, and to create a new, more 'modern' and more open, spirit in British culture. To counter the old insularity of Little Englandism, there has been a conscious attempt to encourage a greater internationalism. And to counter the weight of tradition and the past, an emphasis has been put on youth and the idea of Britain as a 'young country'. The national ethos is connected to new post-industrial economy—information, services, design, cultural industries—through the idea of 'creative Britain'. There has been a very conscious attempt, Driver and Martell suggest, to reposition Britain in the context of the new global order (a development that Peter Taylor comments on positively in Section I). In some respects, this cultural modernization has had positive consequences, providing certain new possibilities for transforming the national identity in more enlightened directions. But it is also apparent that the whole exercise has been one of identity engineering and image management—and we have quickly come to see how thin and insubstantial some of the projected images—'Cool Britannia', for example—have actually been. Driver and Martell also point to some of the contradictions in the New Labour discourse, suggesting that the discourses of the old nationalism may be just below the surface of the new modern rhetoric—there in the discourse on community and the new patriotism. In the context of devolution they detect an anxiety in New Labour, worries about the dangers of fragmentation, and a consequent concern with cultural and political cohesion. And, whilst there has been a readiness to engage with the logic of globalization (albeit passively and unquestioningly), there also remains a commitment to conservative and 'traditional' social values.

21

Geographies of Consumption

PHILIP CRANG

PETER JACKSON

Introduction

LIKE all national cultures, 'British culture' is a highly elusive concept, its boundaries increasingly porous, its content hard to define. Rather than trying to resolve these difficulties in the abstract, this chapter attempts to take one particular perspective on the unstable, shifting character of contemporary British culture, arguing that cultural identities are increasingly defined through the multiple geographies of consumption, at a range of scales from the global to the local. Geographies of production remain important, of course, though fewer and fewer people can rely on the assumption of a 'job for life' around which their own and their family's identity can be securely built. As work-based production cultures have been destabilized by successive rounds of industrial restructuring, with increasing job insecurity, the 'feminization' of the workforce, the rise of temporary contracts and other 'flexible' working practices, so have other bases of identity and identification come to the fore. This chapter examines the significance of one such set of processes, defined here in terms of geographies of consumption, for establishing the contours of contemporary 'British culture'.

After years of neglect, when production dominated the intellectual agenda, consumption studies have flourished during the 1980s and 1990s, coinciding with a boom in consumer spending. While many on the Left were suspicious of this apparent sea change, fearing an abandonment of traditional commitments to organized labour and a capitulation to the logic of the market, the field has now settled down to more considered analysis and reflection (Mort 1989; Miller 1995). Earlier work, following cultural theorists like Walter Benjamin and Jean Baudrillard, has now been supplemented by more historically and geographically grounded empirical work. Old oppositions between consumption and production, between pessimistic readings of the consumer-as-dupe and optimistic readings of heroic consumer resistance, have been transcended.

Consumption is increasingly understood as a social process that can be traced backwards into the social relations of production and forwards into cycles of use and reuse (Miller 1987; Jackson 1993). In comparison to North American literatures, in British work there is less emphasis on the rarefied world of 'lifestyle shopping' and postmodern culture (Shields 1992; Featherstone 1991), with their apparent fixation on spectacular mega-malls and other sites of 'heroic consumption' (Ley and Olds 1988; Pred 1991). Attempts to theorize the relationship between consumption and identity are increasingly focusing on more mundane sites of everyday consumption such as homes (Silverstone and Hirsch 1992; Jackson and Moores 1995), high streets (Fyfe 1998), and shopping centres (Wrigley and Lowe 1996; Miller et al. 1998). A greater diversity of consumption venues are also being attended to: in work on so-called alternative shopping sites, such as charity shops, thrift stores, car boot sales, and factory outlets (Gregson and Crewe 1994; Crewe and Gregson 1998); in the analysis of the urban and suburban milieux of consumption cultures (Mort 1996; Silverstone 1997); and in studies that explore a range of consumption practices other than shopping, from tourism (Urry 1995) to eating out (Finkelstein 1989; Warde 1997) or clubbing (Thornton 1995; Malbon 1997, 1999).

This chapter argues that charting the multiple *geographies of consumption* is a valuable way of extending these debates. Building on the broader interest in questions of space and place within cultural studies (cf. Carter et al. 1993), it develops an argument about consumption by drawing on three such geographies. The first of these concerns the variety of *local sites* in which consumption both takes and makes place. Including sites as diverse as homes, shopping centres, restaurants, and nightclubs, these are the arenas within which consumers and the consumed come together. They mark consumption practices with distinctive forms of (co-)presence and social interaction between both people and things. They embody a range of different but not unrelated consuming ethoses, from domesticity to sociality, from civil inattention to hospitality and communality. In consequence, *where* people consume is part of *what* they are consuming (Bell and Valentine 1997).

As well as comprising such situationally specific coming-togethers, the geographies of consumption are also characterized by absence and distance. Local sites of consumption can only exist through *global networks* of commodity production and provision. So, for example, consuming a meal in a British home is highly local, with particular consuming bodies inhabiting a particular domestic context, but it also depends on increasingly globalized 'systems of food provision' (Fine and Leopold 1993). Think of a fairly typical (though, to help our example, rather large) British breakfast of grapefruit, cornflakes, toast, and tea. This meal can only happen through a huge amount of provisioning work, not only by house-hold members planning, organizing, and doing food shopping according to gendered divisions of labour (De Vault 1991) but also throughout the food system, in the production, supply, and promo-tion of grapefruits, sugar, cornflakes (not to mention cornflake boxes), bread, butters and low-fat spreads, tea and tea bags, and milk. Not only that, but this breakfast also depends on the industrial manufacture and promotion of kitchen equipment: fridges, toasters, microwaves maybe, as well as cutlery, crockery, and kit-chen furniture. And it is embedded within complex circuits of culinary knowledge, to the extent that even this simple meal relies on past tuition in how to prepare and eat a grapefruit (at one time a novel and 'exotic' addition to the British diet), a knowledge of how to make a refreshing cup of tea, and understandings of what consti-tutes a proper breakfast, which in turn require an engagement with wider discourses on both health (what to eat for breakfast) and family life (how breakfast should be eaten). It should be apparent then, to quote David Harvey, that this very local act of consumption comprises not only 'sensuous and interpersonal contact' but also 'the obligation and material connection that exists between [con-sumers] . . . and the millions of other people who had . . . a direct and indirect role in putting breakfast on the table this morning' (Harvey 1993: 15). Recognizing this, ethical consumer organizations work to position these obligations and connections more centrally within consumer cultures.

This leads to the third geography of consumption: the *imagina-tive geographies* of commodity culture. As the didactic activities of ethical consumption groups show, consumption is not only made up of (geographical) sites and networks of provision, it also involves (geographical) knowledges about these settings and origins. The meaningful nature of consumption comes in part from this ability to constitute both our local places of belonging (our home, our shopping centre, our favourite restaurant) and our fantasies of elsewhere and otherness (in Britain recurrent motifs include the 'American', the 'Italian', the 'exotic', and the 'ethnic'). These commodified constructions of otherness have been the subject of a growing range of studies, examining advertising (Richards 1990; Goss 1993; McClintock 1995), the geographical theming of consumption sites (Lash and Urry 1994; Gottdiener 1997), and the wider associations of commodities with (dis)placed cultural origins (Crang 1996).

This chapter interweaves these three geographies of consumption—the local setting, the global commodity system, and the imaginative geographies of each—around the concept of scale (Smith 1993), encompassing the global and the local. Rather than arguing that one scale is increasingly subordinate to the other, however, we emphasize the interpenetration of the global and the local (cf. Morley 1992). We begin by arguing that our understanding of the global needs to be localized. We then reverse the logic to suggest that local contexts of consumption need to be broadened out to the wider scales of the nation and the world. Exploring these global-local geographies of consumption allows us to challenge some dominant ways of thinking about the world of consumption and to propose some alternatives to the received wisdom. In brief, we argue that contemporary consumption is not dominated by processes of homogenization and disorientation, in which placed identities are being obliterated or, by being mediated, made less authentic. Nor, we suggest, is contemporary consumption marked by increasing individuation, where the postmodern self is engaged in a desperate search for identity through ever more extravagant acts of self-indulgence. For the majority of people, most of the time, contemporary consumption is still dominated by domestic concerns, governed by traditional social bonds of obligation and reciprocity, and set predominantly within a family or friendship-group context. The geographies of consumption described here are characterized neither by creeping global sameness nor by hyper-individualized differentiation. Rather, consumption is profoundly contextual, embedded in the particular spaces, times, and social relations that constitute contemporary British culture; but this contextuality is itself constituted from the materials and imaginations of far-flung commodity systems.

Localizing the Global?

The spectre of a singular, global consumer culture sweeping away the distinctive traits and landscapes of British cultural identity has long haunted commentaries on the geographies of consumption. For some, this is a matter of a monolithic global capitalism, comprising 'a powerful culture which overwhelms local and regional experience . . . breaking down the old geography of society and culture' (Peet 1967: 176). More often, though, this global consumer culture has been located rather more specifically in terms of a pervasive and invasive Americanization (see Hebdige 1988). Perhaps the most recent echoes of this are to be found in various local resistances to the opening of American-identified franchises, such as McDonald's, especially in areas where some local residents seek to preserve what they see as a distinctively British local built environment. In Hampstead, North London, for example, McDonald's gained planning permission in 1993 for an outlet only by agreeing to modify their usual restaurant frontage into a more 'genteel' form (Massey 1995).

However, it has become increasingly apparent that British consumers' reactions to 'Americanization' are in fact locally variable and specific. As both Dick Hebdige and Iain Chambers have demonstrated, whilst for some it is seen as a threatening trend, for many British people, especially youthful consumers, 'America' has served to represent the possibility of escaping the traditions and institutions of British life. It has signalled 'a more extensive and imaginative sense of the possible' (Chambers 1990: 42). Marie Gillespie's study of the relations between consumption and ethnicity for young Punjabi Londoners in Southall provides an example of this (Gillespie 1995). Asking about attitudes to TV adverts, Gillespie was struck by the use of America as a symbolic space that allowed these consumers to achieve one of their primary consumption aims, 'being cool'. For them, American products escaped both Britishnesss, with its connotations of cultural exclusion, and Indianness, with its parental associations and, until recently, largely uncool positioning within British youth cultures. The transnational fantasy communities to be found in something like a Coca-Cola advert offered these youngsters an alternative; a resonant utopia allowing identifications with ethoses of style and freedom, an identificatory space far less loaded and susceptible to racist devaluation than consumer products and adverts more directly aimed at British-Asian consumers. So, when it came to soft drinks, it was Coke, rather than Rubicon (a producer of 'exotic' canned drinks based on mango juice and other 'tropical' flavours such as passion-fruit), that was seen as possessing the imaginative geographies that matched the syncretic cultural aims of the young-sters Gillespie researched, as they attempted 'to achieve equality and recognition in British society without affronting their parental values' (1995: 5).

Thus, even (and perhaps especially) for archetypically global products such as Coca-Cola, consumption is locally specific, bound up with variable imaginative geographies. Whilst in Southall, West London, Coke might be treated as a marker of the imagined free-doms of Americanized transnational youth culture, this is not so everywhere. In Trinidad, for example, its consumption is radically different, as it is combined with rum and positioned as a local Trini 'black sweet drink' (Miller 1997). But it is not just the fact that American consumer products are positioned according to different imaginative geographies in different places (see also Webster 1988) that problematizes any equation of consumption with the flatten-ing out of culturally significant geographic difference. It is also the fact that this difference is increasingly a logic to be found at the very heart of British consumption. Geographical difference is pro-duced within consumer culture. It is not seen as a barrier to it. For example, the internationalization of commodity supply chains has become the basis for a host of promotional commentaries that celebrate the 'world showcase' of cultures they produce. And as Jonathan Rutherford has argued: 'cultural difference _sells_' (1990: 11). Food is exemplary of this trend, with British culinary culture characterized (by food providers and writers) less by some indigenous essence than by its cosmopolitan character, its provi-sion of the 'world on a plate' (Arce and Marsden 1993; Cook and Crang 1996).

At an abstract level, this suggests that notions of local difference are not just external to commodity culture, something to be worked and reworked. Rather, commodity culture is intimately involved in the production of difference itself (cf. Grossberg 1995). At a more practical level, though, the crucial issue is what sorts of cultural and geographical difference are being constructed within British consumer cultures? What kinds of multicultural imaginaries underlie this commodified production of a world of difference? How is Britishness being (re)fashioned? These are questions that past research on the imaginative geographies of British culinary culture has explicitly addressed (see, for example, Cook et al. 1999) but our current research on 'commodity culture and South Asian transnationality', working jointly with Claire Dwyer and

Suman Prinjha, is looking to extend such concerns through an examination of the syncretic corporate and commodity identities being constructed, circulated, and consumed through British Asian products in the food and clothing sectors.

Of course, there are no simple answers to these questions about the multicultural politics of British commodity and consumer cultures. However, it is possible to draw out two rather different possibilities. The first, and more depressing, is that these landscapes of cosmopolitan consumption produce difference in such a way as to reinforce static and exclusionary senses of Britishness. Take, for instance, the following anecdote from the tabloid newspaper, the *Daily Star*. Under the heading 'Korma out for a Meal', this item reported on the popularity of 'Indian' restaurants and takeaways amongst British consumers ('curry lovers have sparked an eating out boom in Britain'). At the same time, however, its notion of Britishness was extremely narrow as, in the very next sentence, it reported that 'just 26% [of those dining out] chose British restaurants' (*Daily Star*, 5 Dec. 1995). Indian restaurants are a popular British pastime, it seems, but not British themselves. The logic here is all too clear. Indianness is something white British people may enjoy consuming, but that does not make it, or the British-Asian restaurateurs and waiting staff who embody it, culturally British. Difference is appreciated and enjoyed, at least when it comes to food, but it also distances those to whom it is applied.

Nonetheless, there are other geographies lurking in these cosmopolitan consumptions. However much retailers and consumers organize the world into neat cultural spaces—as, for example, in the supermarket shelves organized into 'Indian', 'Oriental', 'Italian', and 'Tex-Mex' sections to maximize product visibility and legibility (see Cook et al. 2000)—other more connected geographies keep emerging. Take curry. It is a fabrication produced through histories of British colonialism in South Asia, just as much as India itself is (Narayan 1995). Taken from the Tamil word 'kari', curry was developed by the British as a generalized signifier for a range of local masalas. It was, in turn, converted into a material form via the British invention of curry powder. Curry is thoroughly British, and its Britishness is thoroughly outward-looking, dependent on transnational connections. In fact, the same is true of a host of foods that are seen as mundanely British. For example, Stuart Hall has pointed out how the British 'cup of tea' is both a symbol of national identity, and yet, of course, not simply British:

Because they don't grow it in Lancashire, you know. Not a single tea plantation exists within the United Kingdom . . . Where does it come from? Ceylon-Sri Lanka, India. That is the outside history that is inside the history of the English. There is no English history without that other history . . . People like me who came to England in the 1950s [from the West Indies] have been there for centuries; symbolically, we have been there for centuries . . . I am the sugar at the bottom of the English cup of tea. I am the sweet tooth, the sugar plantations that rotted generations of English children's teeth. There are thousands of others . . . that are . . . the cup of tea itself. (Hall 1991: 48–9)

The quintessentially English 'cuppa' is the product of Britain's global history. Its ingredients still depend upon globally extended commodity networks. Constructions of a separate, spectating Britishness, gazing onto and sampling a diverse world, are always being troubled by these interconnected transnational geographies of their own ingredients.

Globalizing the Local?

So far we have established that the global geographies of British consumption do not signal the end of local differences. In part this is because global commodities are encountered and used by consumers in distinctive local settings. But it also reflects the fact that understandings of local difference are increasingly something that commodity systems set out to produce. Now, concentrating in particular on shopping as a social practice (cf. Falk and Campbell 1997), we turn this argument on its head by suggesting that local contexts of consumption and local consumption practices involve much wider social networks and contexts, expanding outwards from the neighbourhood to the nation and ultimately to the world.

The argument is relatively easy to make for certain class fractions such as those who have access to the necessary economic and cultural capital to immerse themselves in the world showcase of goods and to enjoy 'a little taste of something more exotic' (May 1996a). Recent research in Stoke Newington, in North London, shows that the neighbourhood is home to an unusually high concentration of residents from what Jon May (following Ley 1994) calls the 'new cultural class' (artists, designers, and other media professionals). Such residents, May argues (following Bourdieu 1989), use their taste for exotic food as a way of marking out social and cultural distinctions. As one of his informants enthuses:

I just love it. I love it because it's different—a little taste of something more exotic . . . Most days I might have an Indian meal, or a Thai meal or a Chinese meal, or a vegetarian take-away, or pasta. I never just have a cheese omelette, never, it's boring. (May 1996a: 61)

It is probably no great surprise that members of these groups are prone to engage in what bell hooks disparagingly calls 'eating the Other' (hooks 1992), whereby commodity culture provides an opportunity to consume the products of various different ethnicities but in a highly contrived and controlled way, strictly on the consumer's own terms. It is by 'eating the Other', hooks asserts, that one asserts one's power and privilege. Sharon Zukin (1995) uses a similar culinary metaphor—'domestication by cappuccino'—to refer to the process whereby consumers aestheticize the fearful object of their desire. Members of this 'new cultural class' refer to a highly selective reading of the area's historic past (Wright 1985) and to its ethnic diversity as welcome aspects of a 'world of difference' which they encounter and attempt to contain on their own terms. The desire for difference, May argues, is powerfully aestheticized:

Stoke Newington, and Stoke Newington Church Street in particular, is the new arcadia, a space beyond the hustle and bustle of city life and the more expensive house prices of other gentrified neighbourhoods. Rather than a curse, the relative isolation guaranteed by the lack of a tube [underground train] link, for example, has been embraced and the almost rustic feel afforded by such isolation extends beyond the public iconography of Church Street (with its churches, parks and overgrown Gothic cemetery) to the interiors of these new residents' homes. The stark functionalism of the 1970s is out; stripped pines, dyed wood, comfy sofas (and, if one can afford it, an Aga) are in. (May 1996b: 202)

The aestheticization of difference is best conveyed in the residents' own words, as in this extract from 'Alex' (a graphic designer in his mid-thirties who moved to the area about ten years ago):

Coming through Church Street you've got that glorious shot of church spires and the trees and the park, and all that . . . it's a real sort of postcardy thing. The only thing that's missing is the cricket pitch . . . It's very sort of Englishy . . . And, er, I mean I'm English and I do like England's Englishness I suppose . . . So, whilst I accept, you know, multi-cultural society and stuff like that, I probably wouldn't if Stoke Newington became sort of radically Muslim in its feel—then I probably wouldn't feel that comfortable living here anymore, you know? (May 1996b: 203)

As Alex's references to 'Englishness' and 'radically Muslim' suggest, such a visual aesthetic quickly spills over into racialized forms of social exclusion. For other residents, such as 'Dorian' (another graphic designer, in her thirties, who moved to Stoke Newington when she found she could not afford the higher prices of Islington), part of the area's appeal is its ethnic diversity which makes it feel 'kind of sharp':

It has a feeling of variety, of variety in class and colour and therefore a slight feeling of alternativeness, because there are lots of little cultures—lots of gay little cultures—which feel fairly safe in terms of violence . . . I like the fact that there are lots of races—as long as they don't make too much noise . . . [it's] slight bohemian, slightly off beat, and I like that very much. (May 1996b: 208)

Other cultures can be commodified and safely consumed, Dorian implies, provided that the threat of violence is contained and provided that the different 'races' don't get out of hand.

While these arguments about the aestheticization of difference might be expected to apply to very specific class fractions in particular parts of gentrifying inner London, further research suggests that similar arguments can be applied more widely, constituting a key part of Britain's changing consumer cultures. In a comparative study of shopping in Brent Cross and Wood Green in North London, Miller et al. (1998) provide evidence of the wider material and imaginative geographies on which apparently local consumer cultures now draw and of their often highly racialized character. The argument can be made in terms of specific commodities but also in terms of wider discourses about the significance of the domestic in an increasingly globalized world.

In a series of focus group discussions, residents in the Wood Green study frequently drew a contrast between familiar 'local' products and what they regarded as inherently inferior products from further afield. Their fondness for a 'good old cup of tea, roast beef and all that', for 'pure linen', and for other British goods from 'nice quality shops' was regularly contrasted with the alleged shoddiness of imported goods ('it's rubbish today: Taiwan, Hong Kong, Jamaica'), with the 'stinking cooking' that they attributed to the area's recent immigrants, and to 'foreign muck' generally ('you get stuff from all over the world these days . . . you don't know where they're grown'). Ignoring the fact that archetypally 'British' commodities like tea and sugar are imported from abroad (as discussed above), they draw, instead, on a set of discourses about cleanliness and purity, defiled by the allegedly dirty and polluting influence of foreign cultures. These discourses have a long history in Britain's imperial past as demonstrated by Anne McClintock's (1995) work on the 'commodity racism' of nineteenth-century advertising (for Pears's soap and other products) which demonstrates how the mass marketing of Empire was refigured in Britain as part of a reinvented cult of domesticity.

Similar discourses are reproduced in Wood Green, where focus group participants regularly argued that 'it was good years ago, but it's not anymore'. The differences are attributed to the racialized nature of recent neighbourhood change, following post-war immigration from the New Commonwealth, related to a wider discourse of national decline: 'it's altered, hasn't it? I mean England, hasn't it? It's all altered. It's multiracial isn't it, after all, you get all kinds' (Wood Green focus group). In this light, purpose-built shopping centres (of which Brent Cross was the first in Britain) provide middle-class consumers with a controlled environment in which to shop, a sanitized version of the high street, where the risks of random encounters with racialized Others are reduced to manageable proportions. As such, shopping malls can be interpreted as representing a kind of 'domestication' (through privatization, surveillance, and control) of the public spaces formerly associated with the high street (Jackson 1998).

In more suburban areas, such as Brent Cross, the racialized nature of consumption discourses is apparently more muted but emerges in a slightly different form. Here, the emphasis is on the family as a positive alternative to a generalized (but still clearly racialized) sense of Otherness. Shopping centres like Brent Cross market themselves as 'family environments', suitable for 'family shopping'. Research shows, however, that while the family continues to provide the dominant context for most consumption decisions, very few people actually shop as families and those who do so would prefer to shop on their own or with friends (Holbrook and Jackson 1996). Around 70 per cent of the 600 people interviewed at Brent Cross and Wood Green usually went shopping on their own and fewer than 5 per cent shopped with children or other family members. Pedestrian counts (based on over 900 observations) confirmed that family groups were a minority of those observed (29 per cent at Brent Cross, 22 per cent at Wood Green). People's preferences were equally unequivocal with nearly 70 per cent ranking shopping on their own as their first preference, less than 1 per cent preferring to shop with other family members, 2–3 per cent with their children, and 6–7 per cent with their spouse or partner (Miller et al. 1998). The paradox of 'family shopping' being undertaken by very few actual families is resolved once it is realized that 'family' serves as a kind of mutually accepted metaphor for the comfort, warmth, and security that is still attributed to family life, despite all the evidence that many contemporary British families differ markedly from this idealized image.

The examples in this section confirm that 'local' consumption practices involving the purchase of apparently local products extend rapidly outwards into wider networks of international commodity production. Making sense of these practices, consumers draw on a much wider set of discourses that link the neighbourhood to the nation, through popular understandings of the racialized nature of neighbourhood change and narratives of national decline. In this sense, our understanding of the local needs 'globalizing' at least as much as our understanding of the global needs to be 'localized'.

Conclusion

Working both from the global to the local and from the local to the global, this chapter has developed three main arguments about the geographies of British consumption. First, we have argued that, rather than promoting an individualized engagement with a locally invariable consumer culture, British consumption is characterized by the production of highly variable local identities. Our second suggestion has been that these personal and collective identities are often characterized by socially differentiated (racialized, classed, and gendered) senses of separation and controlled engagement, constructing a consuming subject with the power to sample a commodified world of difference. Lurking within consumption, however, are other geographies of connection and fabrication that work to undermine this sense of separation and to challenge its exhibitionary logic. Finally, we have shown how senses of personal and local consumption identities are interwoven with, and depend on, understandings of larger geographies, such that the appeal of a neighbourhood, or something as mundane as a shopping centre, is bound up with conceptions of Britishness and Britain's place in the world.

Exactly what kinds of 'Britishness' are being fashioned through these locally situated yet increasingly globalized consumption processes is (in quite positive ways we think) an open question. Britishness can no longer be defined (if it ever could be) as restricted within narrowly defined national boundaries. Rather, we have argued, it is being fashioned via an active engagement with an increasingly globalized range of products, forged within increasingly diverse local contexts. While some commentators have lamented this vision of increasing 'multiculturalism', or dismissed it as

Philip Crang and Peter Jackson

a mere creation of the marketplace ('the united colours of capitalism'), the sense of Britishness that it implies potentially has an open-endedness that many will prefer to more established and exclusionary ideas of a settled national identity.

This chapter draws on material from three ESRC-funded projects in which we have been and are still involved: 'Eating Places: The Provision of Geographical Food Differentiations' (R000236408, Phil Crang with Ian Cook and Mark Thorpe); 'Consumption and Identity: An Ethnography of Two North London Shopping Centres' (R00023443, Peter Jackson with Daniel Miller, Nigel Thrift, Michael Rowlands, and Bev Holbrook); and 'Commodity Culture and South Asian Transnationality' (L214252031, Phil Crang, Peter Jackson, and Claire Dwyer with Suman Prinjha). We acknowledge the financial support of ESRC and the intellectual support of our fellow researchers. In addition, Phil would like to thank UCL's 'all consuming' graduate students—Ben Malbon, Tracey Bedford, Martin Cox, and Sam Holland—for ongoing inspirations.

Further Reading

Bell, D., and **Valentine, G.** (1997), *Consuming Geographies: You Are Where You Eat*, London: Routledge. An overview of the geographies of consumption, ranging from the body to the globe, all worked through the example of food.

Jackson, P. (2000), 'Cultures of Difference', in V. Gardiner and H. Matthews (eds.), *The Changing Geography of the United Kingdom*, 3rd edn., London: Routledge. Discusses the UK's changing cultural geography, the commodification of cultural difference, and the contested nature of British multiculturalism.

Lury, C. (1996), *Consumer Culture*, Cambridge: Polity Press. An introductory account of recent debates in consumption studies, written primarily for an undergraduate audience.

Mackay, H. (ed.) (1997), *Consumption and Everyday Life*, London: Sage. An accessible review of recent debates about consumption, produced by an inter-disciplinary team for the Open University.

Miller, D. (ed.) (1995), *Acknowledging Consumption*, London: Routledge. A comprehensive, multidisciplinary review of recent consumption studies.

References

Arce, A., and **Marsden, T.** (1993), 'The Social Construction of International Food: A New Research Agenda', *Economic Geography*, 69.

Bell, D., and **Valentine, G.** (1997), *Consuming Geographies: You Are Where You Eat*, London: Routledge.

Bourdieu, P. (1989), *Distinction: A Social Critique of the Judgement of Taste*, London: Routledge & Kegan Paul.

Carter, E., Donald, J., and **Squires, J.** (eds.) (1993), *Space and Place: Theories of Identity and Location*, London: Lawrence & Wishart.

Chambers, I. (1990), *Border Dialogues: Journeys in Postmodernity*, London: Routledge.

Cook, I., and Crang, P. (1996), 'The World on a Plate: Culinary Culture, Displacement and Geographical Knowledges', *Journal of Material Culture*, 1.

—— —— and Thorpe, M. (1999), 'Eating into Britishness: Multicultural Imaginaries and the Identity Politics of Food', in S. Rosencil and J. Seymour (eds.), *Practising Identities*, London: Macmillan.

—— —— —— (2000), 'Regions to be Cheerful', in I. Cook, D. Crouch, S. Naylor, and J. Ryan (eds.), *Cultural Turns/Geographical Turns*, Harlow: Pearson Education.

Crang, P. (1996), 'Displacement, Consumption, and Identity', *Environment and Planning A*, 28.

Crewe, L., and Gregson, N. (1998), 'Tales of the Unexpected: Exploring Car Boot Sales as Marginal Spaces of Consumption', *Transactions, Institute of British Geographers*, 23.

De Vault, M. (1991), *Feeding the Family: The Social Organisation of Caring and Gendered Work*, Chicago: University of Chicago Press.

Falk, P., and Campbell, C. (eds.) (1997), *The Shopping Experience*, London: Sage.

Featherstone, M. (1991), *Consumer Culture and Postmodernism*, London: Sage.

Fine, B., and Leopold, E. (1993), *The World of Consumption*, London: Routledge.

Finkelstein, J. (1989), *Dining Out: A Sociology of Modern Manners*, London: Polity.

Fyfe, N. R. (ed.) (1998), *Images of the Street*, London: Routledge.

Gillespie, M. (1995), *Television, Ethnicity and Cultural Change*, London: Routledge.

Goss, J. (1993), 'Placing the Market and Marketing Place: Tourist Advertising of the Hawaiian Islands, 1972–92', *Environment and Planning D: Society and Space*, 11.

Gottdiener, M. (1997), *The Theming of America: Dreams, Visions and Commercial Spaces*, Boulder, Colo.: Westview Press.

Gregson, N., and Crewe, L. (1994), 'Beyond the High Street and the Mall: Car Boot Fairs and the New Geographies of Consumption in the 1990s', *Area*, 26.

Grossberg, L. (1995), 'The Space of Culture, the Power of Space', in I. Chambers and L. Curti (eds.), *The Post-colonial Question: Common Skies, Divided Horizons*, London: Routledge.

Hall, S. (1991), 'Old and New Identities, Old and New Ethnicities', in A. D. King (ed.), *Culture, Globalization and the World-System*, London: Macmillan.

Harvey, D. (1993), 'From Space to Place and Back Again: Reflections on the Condition of Postmodernity', in J. Bird et al. (eds.), *Mapping the Futures: Local Cultures, Global Change*, London: Routledge.

Hebdige, D. (1988), 'Towards a Cartography of Taste 1935–62', in *Hiding in the Light: On Images and Things*, London: Comedia.

Holbrook, B., and Jackson, P. (1996), 'The Social Milieux of Two North London Shopping Centres', *Geoforum*, 27.

hooks, b. (1992), *Black Looks: Race and Representation*, London: Turnaround.

Jackson, P. (1993), 'Towards a Cultural Politics of Consumption', in J. Bird et al. (eds.), *Mapping the Futures: Local Cultures, Global Change*, London: Routledge.

—— (1998), 'Domesticating the Street: The Contested Spaces of the High Street and the Mall', in N. R. Fyfe (ed.), *Images of the Street*, London: Routledge.

Jackson, S., and Moores, S. (eds.) (1995), *The Politics of Domestic Consumption: Critical Readings*, London; Harvester Wheatsheaf.

Lash, S., and Urry, J. (1994), *Economies of Signs and Space*, London: Sage.

Ley, D. (1994), 'Gentrification and the New Middle Class', *Environment and Planning D: Society and Space*, 12.

—— and Olds, K. (1988), 'Landscape as Spectacle: World's Fairs and the Culture of Heroic Consumption', *Environment and Planning D: Society and Space*, 6.

McClintock, A. (1995), *Imperial Leather: Race, Gender and Sexuality in the Colonial Contest*, London: Routledge.

Malbon, B. (1997), 'Clubbing: Consumption, Identity and the Spatial Practices of Every-Night Life', in T. Skelton and G. Valentine (eds.), *Cool Places*, London: Routledge.

—— (1999), *Clubbing*, London: Routledge.

Massey, D. (1995), 'The Conceptualization of Place', in D. Massey and P. Jess (eds.), *A Place in the World? Places, Cultures and Globalization*, Oxford: Oxford University Press.

May, J. (1996a), '"A Little Taste of Something More Exotic": The Imaginative Geographies of Everyday Life', *Geography*, 81.

—— (1996b), 'Globalization and the Politics of Place: Place and Identity in an Inner London Neighbourhood', *Transactions, Institute of British Geographers*, 21.

Miller, D. (1987), *Material Culture and Mass Consumption*, Oxford: Basil Blackwell.

—— (ed.) (1995), *Acknowledging Consumption*, London: Routledge.

—— (1997), 'Coca Cola: A Black Sweet Drink from Trinidad', in D. Miller (ed.), *Material Cultures*, London: UCL Press.

—— Jackson, P., Thrift, N., Holbrook, B., and Rowlands, M. (1998), *Shopping, Place and Identity*, London: Routledge.

Morley, D. (1992), 'Where the Global Meets the Local: Notes from the Sitting-Room', in *Television, Audiences and Cultural Studies*. London: Routledge.

Mort, F. (1989), 'The Politics of Consumption', in S. Hall and M. Jacques (eds.), *New Times: The Changing Face of Politics in the 1990s*, London: Lawrence & Wishart.

—— (1996), *Cultures of Consumption*, London: Routledge.

Narayan, U. (1995), 'Eating Cultures: Incorporation, Identity and Indian Food', *Social Identities*, 1.

Peet, R. (1986), 'The Destruction of Regional Cultures', in R. J. Johnston and P. J. Taylor (eds.), *A World in Crisis?* Oxford: Blackwell.

Pred, A. (1991), 'Spectacular Articulations of Modernity: The Stockholm Exhibition of 1897', *Geografiska Annaler*, 73B.

Richards, T. (1990), *The Commodity Culture of Victorian England: Advertising and Spectacle, 1851–1914*, London: Verso.

Rutherford, J. (ed.) (1990), *Identity: Community, Culture, Difference*, London: Lawrence & Wishart.

Shields, R. (ed.) (1992), *Lifestyle Shopping: The Subject of Consumption*, London: Routledge.

Silverstone, R. (ed.) (1997), *Visions of Suburbia*, London: Routledge.

Silverstone, R. and Hirsch, E. (eds.) (1992), *Consuming Technologies: Media and Information in Domestic Spaces*, London: Routledge.

Smith, N. (1993), 'Homeless/Global: Scaling Places', in J. Bird et al. (eds.), *Mapping the Futures: Local Cultures, Global Change*, London: Routledge.

Thornton, S. (1995), *Club Cultures*, Cambridge: Polity Press.

Urry, J. (1995), *Consuming Places*, London: Routledge.

Warde, A. (1997), *Consumption, Food and Taste*, London: Sage.

Webster, D. (1988), *Looka Yonder! The Imaginary America of Populist Culture*, London: Comedia.

Wright, P. (1985), *On Living in an Old Country: The National Past in Contemporary Britain*, London: Verso.

Wrigley, N., and Lowe, M. (eds.) (1996), *Retailing, Consumption and Capital: Towards the New Retail Geography*, London: Longman.

Zukin, S. (1995), *The Cultures of Cities*, Oxford: Basil Blackwell.

Changing Cultures of Work: Employment, Gender, and Lifestyle

LINDA
McDOWELL

THE nature of academic and policy debates about waged work (and with an apology and acknowledgement of feminist critiques of the definition of work, I shall restrict myself in this chapter to waged work) have undergone a remarkable transformation over the last thirty or so years. In the 1960s and at the beginning of the 1970s, after three decades of economic growth and expansion, a new era seemed to be dawning when the prospect of greater leisure time and a wider range of opportunities to fill it seemed within the reach of a larger and larger proportion of the working population of Britain. Almost thirty years later, at the end of the century, a sullen *fin de siècle* anxiety and a new set of concerns about waged work—about its nature, necessity, distribution, certainty, and rewards—dominate both academic literature and more popular or accessible articles on the financial pages of the daily broadsheets. Work—or rather waged labour—is no longer the central certainty and key element of individual identity that it once was for working- and middle-class men, for waged work was a quintessentially masculine affair in the main, but is now a more uncertain, contingent or casual, impermanent and discontinuous activity shared among larger numbers of people in the new times of New Labour. And perhaps surprisingly, in the 1990s, a decade in which growing inequalities in the distribution of and rewards for waged labour have become noticeably more evident, there seems to have been a shift from the more material aspects of work to a focus on its cultural aspects. As Martin Jacques argued in an introduction to an interview with Stuart Hall, the British sociologist who perhaps has made the greatest contribution to analyses of cultural change in contemporary Britain: 'The word culture is now ubiquitous. From politics to business, from lifestyle to the media, everyone talks about culture. Together with business it is the new language of our times' (Jacques 1997: 9). Hall made the point, in his interview, that the contemporary use of the term culture seems to date from some time in the late 1950s or early 1960s as cultural critics attempted to capture the post-war changes that had transformed British society:

When Raymond Williams and Richard Hoggart tried to give a description of the changes taking place in British society, they found that 'culture' was the privileged term in which to describe those changes. This rather vague word 'culture' captured how attitudes, values, ways of life, forms of relationships, the structures of meaning that people use to interpret what is going on in their lives, had been transformed. The prewar cultural order had been changed by the democratisation of the war, the decline of deference, Americanisation, the birth of mass consumption and the coming of television. (Hall in Jacques 1997: 9)

Several decades later, a further set of social and economic changes means that the significance and nature of culture has again been transformed. As Hall noted, since the 1960s, the rapid pace of technological change, the attitudes and values that regulate social and sexual life, definitions of masculine and feminine identities, the challenges to the literary canon and other forms of 'high culture', among other changes, have produced both cultural democratization and greater uncertainty and unpredictability in British society.

This periodization—of two distinguishable sets of social changes, albeit working out rather unevenly—also maps onto changes in the workplace and is a helpful way to think about the changing cultures of waged work and their relationship to and impact on gender relations. In the post-war decades of economic growth— approximately from the end of the Second World War to the shock of oil price rises in 1973, a particular set of cultural assumptions about waged work were dominant. These included the expectation of lifetime work for men, the centrality of waged work in the social construction of male identity and the expectation of rising incomes for the majority of households supported by a male breadwinner. The political corollary was the dominance of masculinized and class-based forms of organization. From the early 1970s many of these certainties have unravelled. For the few, new forms of work have brought high financial rewards and social status, whereas for

Linda McDowell

many more people, especially working-class men, the collapse of heavy industries and the associated geographical regions into obsolescence has brought unemployment and poverty in its wake. While numerically greater employment opportunities have opened up for working-class women, many of these jobs are poorly paid and offered on a discontinuous basis. Indeed at both ends of the labour market, greater uncertainty about continuous employment is a corollary of the often-praised 'flexibility' that purportedly characterized the British economy in the late 1990s. For growing numbers of middle-class men, work has become a less certain affair, as middle management is 'delayered' and privatization dismembers organizations, so that tasks once undertaken within an organization are now provided on contract. Even parts of the civil service, for example—once the apotheosis of safe but certain employment—have been 'contracted out'.

Representing Work

Reflecting the current interest in popular culture, it is interesting that, in a recent comment on the changing nature of male employment, Freedland (1997) illustrated his argument by comparing two situation comedies shown on British television. He suggested that Alan Partridge was for the 1990s what Reggie Perrin was for the 1970s.

Perrin was the ultimate corporate man, a time-serving middle manager in a middle ranking company. For years he deferred to his boss and dutifully filled his place in the hierarchy. He kept the same office, the same secretary and the same seat on the 8.16 train to Waterloo. His problem was ennui, his dream escape from the rat race. Twenty years later, and job security like that is a thing of the past. Alan Partridge is the chronic freelance, a man who meets the new top dog at the BBC and asks not for a job, but for a six-month contract. He does not work in a firm but owns his own small company: Peartree Productions. When Partridge fails to get his desperately desired second series, he has to choose between giving up his Rover 800 or sacking all his employees; he fires the lot—over the speaker phone.

The *kind* [original emphasis] of work Britain does has also changed since Perrin's day. He was with a company that actually made things: Sunshine Desserts. Partridge is in that most 90s of industries: the media. Indeed the shift from manufacturing to service is one of the themes of the Alan Partridge programme. Much is made of petrol station mini-marts, courtesy hot-towels and hotels that boast a '24-hour carvery' . . .

Historians should find all this quite useful. Like the union stoppages and drinks cabinets of Reginald Perrin, the mobile phones, theme-park heritage sites and corporate videos of Alan Partridge make a pretty effective time capsule. Future students anxious to know about the rise of the flexible market, the shift from manufacturing to service industry and the breakdown of family life in Britain could do a lot worse than to sit down and watch Alan Partridge. (Freedland 1997: 19)

What Freedland has not captured, however, in his comparison is the parallel world of the working woman, as exemplified perhaps by the tough world of women professional employees like Inspector Jane Tennison, in the television police procedural series *Prime Suspect*.

The feminization of many parts of the labour market has been one of the most noticeable changes in the second half of the twentieth century. Partly a corollary of the shift from manufacturing to a services-dominated economy, and associated with downsizing, delayering, disinvestment, deregulation, and flexibility (and other euphemisms that capture the shift to a neo-liberal economic regime in the final two decades of the twentieth century), there seem to have been partial gains for women in the labour market at the expense of men. I shall suggest in the conclusion, however, that for working-class women and for the households of which they are part the gains are perhaps more illusory than they at first appear. The growing feminization of the labour market has led to an interesting debate about the growing 'redundancy' of boys and men, paralleled by an apparent crisis in schools as women are not only becoming numerically dominant in the labour market (a statistical dominance briefly achieved in September 1997 (11,248 million women to 11,236 million men) but then overturned in the next month's employment figures) but are also outperforming boys in school-leaving examinations and have recently become the majority among university entrants (McConville 1998; Weiner et al. 1996). This refocusing of concern for men in the search for equal opportunities at work is an astonishing—and not entirely justified—change of emphasis.

In the sections that follow, I want to examine briefly the nature and consequences of the changing structure of employment opportunities, especially the gendered nature of the changes, first sketching in the outline of the world we have lost—Reggie Perrin's world—and then looking in more detail at the changing culture of work in post-1970s Britain. The unifying theme is the emphasis on the links between work and identity, whether the focus is on the identity of collectivities or individuals. Questions about what work means or stands for, about workplace cultures, what it is like in different workplaces, and what sort of people are comfortable there/constructed there will be addressed.

The World We Have Lost

In 1955, Great Britain—once, and perhaps at that time still, the 'workshop of the world'—was the most highly industrialized nation the capitalist world has ever seen 'Never before, nor since, in any capitalist country, at any time, has industrial employment been significantly more important than it was in Britain in 1955' (Rowthorn 1986: 3–4). Perhaps the most noticeable feature of the economy at that time, apart from the male dominance of manufacturing employment, was its regional differentiation. A narrow range of industrial activities dominated each regional economy, associated with strong regional class differences which were reflected in distinct cultural patterns. Thus as Anthony Giddens argued, 'In class society, spatial division is a major feature of class differentiation . . . one of the most important features of the spatial division of class is the sedimentation of divergent regional "class cultures" over time' (Giddens 1979: 18).

As E. P. Thompson and Raymond Williams, among others, documented, common experiences in the workplace in localities dominated by a single or small number of economic activities were embodied in 'local traditions, value systems, ideas and institutional forms' (Thompson 1980: 9), creating a spatially specific local class culture, which Williams referred to as a 'structure of feeling'. Williams noted in particular the importance of solidaristic class cultures in those areas dominated by male-employing heavy industrial work and their role in left-wing politics, but, as Doreen Massey and I argued, these same local class cultures are also often both paternalistic and masculinist (McDowell and Massey 1984).

As economic growth created rising standards of living throughout the 1950s and 1960s—at least for men employed in secure and relatively well-paid industrial work and for their families—a challenge to the apparent communal or solidaristic culture of the traditional working class was identified by industrial sociologists. In a study of car workers in Luton, for example, Goldthorpe et al. (1969) identified a distinctly new version of masculinity. Compared to the working-class men 'up North', a domesticated and privatized, newly embourgeoised working class seemed to be emerging in the south-east, personified by these Luton car workers. These men, interested in becoming home owners and in the acquisition of the newly available range of consumer durables, were assumed to be individualized, constructing their self-identity in the arena of consumption as much as through productive relations and so less prone to take class-based action. But, as so often, they challenged the newly minted sociological generalizations about the decline of workplace-based militancy by striking, just as the book by Goldthorpe and his team about their changing culture became well known.

But what is without doubt is that the significance of manufacturing employment, especially for men, is now greatly reduced. The local economies of those types of areas dominated by a single large employer have been strangled by economic restructuring and changing global patterns of manufacturing production, leading to high levels of unemployment, poverty and social isolation. Large numbers of young people in these areas may never have been employed and growing numbers of older people, but men especially, have come to a premature end of their working lives. So marked are the spatial inequalities in employment prospects and life chances in contemporary Britain that commentators have suggested both old industrial villages and inner areas of industrial conurbations are now distinct or separate worlds, with as much in common with the poor of the third world as the prosperous parts of Britain. Indeed the common sociological terminology used to refer to these areas reflects this: either third spaces or fourth worlds.

Third Spaces or Fourth Worlds

The concept of a third space has been used in particular to refer to those rural industrial areas that once relied on male employment in mining. Thus, in a study of twentieth-century Scotland, Harvie identified the specific problems of

an unlovely 'third Scotland' sprawled from South Ayrshire to Fife . . . old industrial settlements that ought to have been evacuated and demolished . . . isolated, ignored, lacking city facilities or country traditions—even lacking the attention of sociologists. (Harvie 1981: 66)

Daniel Wight (1993) partially remedied this lack by a detailed ethnographic study of one such industrial village, focusing on whether and how men maintained their sense of self-respect, social networks, and cultural traditions in the absence of work. Interestingly Wight argued that 'Cauldmoss'—a pseudonym—still retained (in the early 1980s when he undertook his research) aspects of those regional class cultures that personified industrial villages in their more prosperous times in the 1950s and 1960s.

The striking cultural similarities between the northern English working class—as described, for instance, by Dennis et al (1956)—and the inhabitants of Cauldmoss illustrate how much more important their common experience as an industrial proletariat has been in shaping their culture than have national characteristics. (Wight 1993: 2–3)

Wight reminds his fellow sociologists that their own cultural assumptions or standpoint have perhaps been overly influential in the identification of widespread cultural change.

Indeed the recent concern with postmodernism amongst many sociologists illustrates how the theoretical interests that arise from the metropolitan subculture in which most social scientists live can prompt debates largely irrelevant to other sections of the population. According to Simmel's analysis of modernity (Frisby 1985), Cauldmoss is, in many respects, pre-modern. (Wight 1993: 3)

As Wight demonstrated in the close-knit lowland village where he worked, unemployed men were able to retain their sense of self-worth despite their loss of work and reliance on welfare payments. As Wight indicates by his title, these men are still 'workers, not wasters'.

The term fourth world has been used by urban sociologist Manuel Castells (1997) to refer to the concentration of economically and socially marginalized populations into the inner areas of large cities. These areas are less homogeneous, socially and ethnically, than old industrial villages and are often marked by a distinctive oppositional culture that has developed in reaction to exclusion from mainstream society, often through racism as well as economic decline. In these areas street culture offers young people, in particular, an alternative forum to the workplace for the development of personal autonomy and self-respect. Forms of creative and oppositional street culture, based around personal style, fashion, music, and dance, sometimes distinguish these areas. Ironically, mainstream society often co-opts these oppositional styles and sells them back as pop culture (Skelton and Valentine 1997). But this optimistic view of the cultural creativity of inner city residents is countered by the real poverty in these areas, where, also ironically, the very styles that are celebrated by consumer capitalism may exclude the residents from what employment opportunities there are. Their hair, looks, and bodily style are seen as inappropriate for the type of service sector work that is available (Bourgois 1995). And, as I show in a later section, an alternative reaction to unemployment is the search for self-respect through various more or less criminal activities.

Reshaping the World of Work

At the end of the twentieth century, not only has the nature of work changed—the majority of workers in Britain no longer earn their living in the manufacturing sector but in service occupations—but employment opportunities have been redistributed over time and space and between people.

One of the features of current patterns of employment in Britain is its uneven distribution: too many people work very long hours whereas others have only casual or part time employment or no work at all. Unlike the French government who are attempting to tackle the maldistribution of employment by introducing a 35-hour working week, Britain is still characterized by long working hours for many people in full-time work. The British work the longest hours in Europe, an average 44.7 hours a week, and this seems to be combined with growing evidence of stress and work-related illnesses. Indeed, occupational psychologist Cary Cooper has recently argued that anxiety about job insecurity is partly responsible for long hours, leading to a new phenomenon that he has termed presenteeism. In the individual achievement-oriented environment of private and privatized workplaces, people are afraid to be the first to leave work in case they are seen as lacking commitment. Perhaps one of the most noticeable changes in the culture of contemporary organizations is a dominant emphasis on personal attributes and attitudes as an essential ingredient for success. As Paul du Gay (1996a) concluded from a survey of management practices:

In recent years, people working in large organizations are very likely to have found themselves exposed to 'cultural change' programmes as part of attempts to make enterprises more efficient, effective and profitable. . . .

A cursory inspection of any number of recent management texts reveals the primacy accorded to 'culture' in governing contemporary organizational life. In this literature 'culture' is accorded a privileged position because it is seen to structure the way people think, feel and act in organisations. The problem is one of changing 'norms', 'attitudes' and 'values' so that people are enabled to make the right and necessary contribution to the success of the organization for which they work. (du Gay 1996a: 151)

Schoenberger's (1997) study of the mismatch between managers' cultural assumptions in large US corporations and the 'realities' of global restructuring is a salutary illustration of the limitations of a reliance on getting attitudes and values 'right'.

Perhaps the most widely discussed change in employment patterns, however, is its redistribution between men and women. Women's entry into the labour market has risen steadily over recent decades. Since 1979, for example, when Mrs Thatcher became Prime Minister (but not of course because of her), the number of women in employment has risen by 23 per cent while the number of men in employment has fallen by 16 per cent: partly a reflection of the corresponding rise of the service sector. The feminization of bottom-end, often part-time and poorly paid, service positions has been well documented (Game and Pringle 1984; McDowell 1989; Walby 1988, 1997). These are the types of jobs in which the naturalization of 'feminine' attributes—caring, empathy, docility—is often given as the reason why these jobs are defined as 'women's work' and concomitantly under-remunerated. However, women are also successfully competing for professional positions, partly as a consequence of their rising educational capital. In an analysis of national trends, the London Chamber of Commerce reported at the end of 1997 that of the 450,000 professional jobs created between 1981 and 1996, 69 per cent had gone to women. In London, professional women had been more successful in entering formerly male-dominated professions like law and accountancy, and were also successful at an earlier age than their female counterparts elsewhere in the country, as well as better educated and better paid. Despite this evident success, though, full-time women employees, as a group, are still paid 20 per cent less than men as a group, an average that conceals wide differences between occupations. In the financial services sector, for example, the pay gap is actually widening at present, where women earn only 54 per cent of average male earnings as they tend to be confined to the lowest-paying grades in the sector. Even when women are promoted to managerial positions, they earn considerably less than men: 63 per cent in 1993 according to figures collected by the banking union, Bifu. This is partly a reflection of restructuring where middle management positions formerly occupied by men are stripped out and women in supervisory roles are reclassified as managers, without a resultant rise in earnings (Crompton and Sanderson 1994; Halford and Savage 1995). The financial services sector is a key part of the economy of Greater London, where investment banking rather than retail banking is dominant. Despite women's general success in Greater London, in banking, earning differentials are still evident between men and women, even when comparisons are made within employment categories. In the sector as a whole, just as in retail banking, women are predominant in the lowest grades (McDowell and Court 1994).

As the economy moves inexorably away from masculinized 'smokestack' jobs towards a services-dominated economy, opportunities for poorly qualified men, in particular, are disappearing. For many commentators this is connected to the recently identified crisis of masculinity (Hearn 1998; Phillips 1993; Weiner et al. 1996; Williams 1998) in which men apparently feel either increasingly powerless and redundant in the face of contemporary economic and social changes which draw on a rhetoric of femininity or respond by constructing an exaggerated version of irresponsible masculine behaviour, often referred to as 'New Laddism' or, in another reference to a popular late 1990s television serial, 'Men behaving badly'. I want to examine this latter phenomenon in three occupations.

Butch Culture: 'Fast' Money/Clean Data/Fast Cars

Despite assertions in contemporary management texts that workplace cultures are becoming increasingly feminized, I want to emphasize the continuing, and indeed deepening, dominance of masculinized values in different sectors of the economy in the 1980s and 1990s. The examples are drawn from the financial services sector, high-tech industries, and the police service. In all areas, perhaps especially in the 1980s, the correlates of hegemonic masculinity were highly valued attributes of workplace performance. In an economy dominated by deregulation and risk-taking, traditional British caution seemed to be flung to the winds in a country which became, in the words of Beatrix Campbell, 'reckless, butch and dangerous' (1993: 3). In the City of London, for example, the pursuit of profit led to brutal takeover bids and asset stripping and, with deregulation, the more obvious flouting of traditional standards of behaviour based on a 'gentleman's word'. Indeed, the City of London became notorious for the number of financial scandals that were uncovered in the decade following 'Big Bang' (that is, the explosion of deregulation that followed the 1984 Financial Services Act). Blue Arrow, the Guinness scandal, the collapse of the Bank of Commerce and Credit International, financial irregularities at the European Bank for Reconstruction, Nick Leeson's efforts in bankrupting Barings—then one of the longest established and most establishment banks in the City—the list grew ever longer as what were rather dismissively termed 'American practices' changed the culture of the City (Budd and Whimster 1992; McDowell 1997; McRae and Cairncross 1991; Leyshon and Thrift 1996).

In these years of fast money and financial scandal, the heroes of the City were the young men—traders, dealers, analysts, and corporate bankers—who could create the fastest deal and turn in the highest profits. In my own research work in three then British-owned banks in the City in the first half of the 1990s (McDowell 1997) I found that the exaggerated version of machismo only partly parodied in Michael Lewis's documentation of his career in Salomon Brothers (Lewis 1989) was a substantially accurate version of the culture of banking, especially in the fast-moving world of the trading and dealing rooms. Here, in a carnivalesque atmosphere, exaggerated versions of men behaving badly were acceptable modes of everyday social interactions in the workplace. Often unbuttoned and in shirtsleeves, men (and these occupations remain almost entirely male dominated) shouted, sweated, bawled into phones, indulged in forms of verbal and visual sexual denigration of women—both in general and of their few female colleagues and greater numbers of female support workers—as well as in schoolboyish antics and pranks (see McDowell 1997: esp. ch. 7 for more details). Women were excluded by being constructed as too frail and powerless to deal with the essential rough and tumble of this world. The best performers were, as Lewis emphasized, 'savages' and 'beasts', the 'big swinging dicks' of the financial 'jungle'.

In studies of traders and dealers the physical and bodily aspects of masculinity that dominated their workplaces are emphasized rather than the more cerebral and disembodied intellectual powers of rational deduction that is the alternative social construct of masculinity that is highly valued in the workplace. In bureaucratic or scientific occupations it is brain rather than brawn that tends to be valued, although in an astute comment Bob Connell (1995) has noted how computers are marketed to men in battleship colours and with names such as Powerbook and PowerMac. In a study of high-technology industries, Doreen Massey (1995, 1997) showed how the association of disembodied rationality with embodied men was used to exclude women from the high-paying, high-tech, 'boys with toys' work in the sunrise industries in Cambridge's Science Park. In a city long used to the idea of cerebral masculinity (the absent-minded professor is always male (and even in 1998 although publicly announcing its commitment to an equal opportunities policy this ancient university has only managed to appoint 15 women to the 300 or so chairs in the institution), new science-based high-tech jobs are constructed as masculinist and occupied in the main by men.

Reflecting on the research and development sections in Science Park high-tech firms, Massey (1997) notes that these 'are places of "science". They are places of Reason, not emotion. And—reflecting this—they are separated off, specialised, defended. They are also "masculine" spaces, not in the sense that it is mainly men who work here, but in the sense that their construction as spaces embodies the elite, separated, masculine concept of reason dominant in the West' (p. 27).

The third example of masculinity at work is not from the high-paid new professions of 'new' Britain but instead the police force, where 'no nonsense' is tolerated in a celebration of 'zero tolerance' of less than law-abiding behaviour. Under progressively (probably the wrong word) tougher Home Secretaries, civil liberties have been eroded and the numbers and status of the police have increased in recent years. The police force is, however, an occupation where traditional masculine traits—brute force and violence in particular—are part of the job, at least for the police on the streets. In the last few years in Great Britain, a number of notorious cases of gender discrimination and sexual harassment have become public—from the case taken by Alison Holford, then a deputy chief constable of a regional police force, against discriminatory promotion procedures to a more recent case in 1998 of harassment of women officers in Yorkshire in bizarre initiation ceremonies. In jobs which are constructed as masculine and, in the main, carried out by men, resentment against the entry of women is common. As Martin (1980), in a study of police work in the United States, has noted:

For blue collar men whose jobs often do not provide high incomes or great social prestige, other aspects of the work, including certain 'manly' features take on enormous importance as a means through which they confirm their sex-role identity. Work that entails responsibility, control, use of a skill, initiative and which permits the use of strength and/or physical agility characteristic of males is highly valued not only for its own sake but for its symbolic significance. Similarly, working in an 'all-male' environment reinforces the notion that they are doing 'men's work' and is a highly prized fringe benefit of a job. (1980: 89, also quoted in McElhinny 1994: 161)

If women move into these jobs, it is seen as a reduction in their status and in the social worth of the men who do them. This partially explains, but does not excuse, the explicit and more covert cultural attitudes and rites that make life for the minority of women in male-dominated occupations so difficult, whether they are jobs that emphasize masculinity as physicality—in the forces, for example, or masculinity as rationality—the two previous examples.

In her book *Goliath* Beatrix Campbell (1993) has drawn out the similarities between the 'hard men' in the police force and the 'bad lads' on the street that they are set to catch and control. Both groups, Campbell argues, celebrate through their attitudes and behaviour a particular form of masculine identity in which material possessions, money, speed, status, and domination of women are part of a valorized sense of self. For the police, these assets and assumptions are constructed through work. For 'the lads', they are acquired illegally through involvement in, usually, relatively minor crimes such as petty theft, vandalism, and TWOCing (taking a car without consent). The parallels between the two groups of young men become clearest in car chases in which both groups indulge their love of cars and of speed: one illegally, the other legally, but in both cases too often with fatal consequences for the participants and for bystanders. These cultural attributes of masculinity—once perhaps relevant in the world of male camaraderie that developed doing dangerous manual work—now disqualify young men from the service sector jobs that are often all that is available, which demand 'docile bodies' and subservient attitudes towards clients and customers (see Leidner's (1993) study of fast food for example, or du Gay's (1996b) work on fashion retail outlets).

From Welfare to Workfare

The associations between declining labour market opportunities and high unemployment especially for working-class men and various forms of unacceptable behaviour from truanting during school-age years to involvement in street crime, have become part of the recent construction of the crisis in masculinity. In what seems to be a surprising lack of serious analysis of the consequences of economic restructuring in Britain, changing global patterns of industrial investment, ownership, and production, and the current moves in Britain towards a polarized economy, dominated by poorly paid and casual employment (Mcdonald's is now a major employer in the UK, for example; and the largest concentration of trade union members are now employees of the supermarket chain Tesco), the new Labour government has announced a number of measures through which it hopes to resolve this apparent crisis and to redress the lack of opportunities facing young men and, to a lesser extent, young women. Committed to tight fiscal policies and public spending restraints, the government is determined to shift the emphasis in the support available for the unemployed from dependency on welfare benefits, apparently regarding lack of employment as a personal failing rather than a structural and cyclical factor.

In a belief that labour market participation is the singular way to achieve self-respect and independence for all adults, seemingly irrespective of their obligations and abilities, a workfare programme, termed the New Deal, with its explicit reference to Roosevelt's inter-war reconstruction programme in the United States, was introduced in 1998. From January, initially in twelve pilot areas, young unemployed people between 18 and 25 are required to pass through a 'gateway' involving up to four months' specialist advice before having to take up one of four 'options' or face losing their eligibility for state benefits. The options are a subsidized full- or part-time private sector job for an initial six-month period, full-time education, or employment either in the voluntary sector or with an environmental task force, also for a limited programme, although the hope is that this required short-term participation might lead to further paid work.

While young working-class women are not entirely free from the adverse impact of economic change (as I noted above, the shift to feminized service sector jobs, albeit often casualized and poorly paid, has meant that they have not been so seriously affected as young men), their response to their inability to achieve self-respect and adult status through labour market participation is often different from that of men's: rather than participation in youth gangs and street life or in illegal activities (although some women do: see Wilkinson and Mulgan 1995), young women may seek to find fulfilment in early motherhood. In her comparison of young mothers from different backgrounds and ethnic groups, Phoenix (1991) found that the common thread that united all the young women whom she interviewed was their disillusion with and rejection of low-paid work. In what appears to be a singularly vindictive move, the government announced in late 1998 its intention to 'encourage' these women to seek employment by insisting on their participation in the New Deal programme, with a penalty of loss of benefits. As this policy is to be introduced before a new network of childcare facilities is up and running, it is hard to understand how the living standards of single mothers will be significantly enhanced by entry into poorly paid work.

Conclusions

At the end of the twentieth century, just as it was fifty years ago, waged work is regarded as the central element in individual and collective worth. Full employment is seen as a desirable economic objective and labour market participation as a requirement and an obligation of good citizenship. Debates in the intervening decades—a more distant one about the 'problem of leisure' or more recent assertions about the declining centrality of work and the search for identity and fulfilment through consumption—now seem like irrelevant curiosities in the face of this singular insistence on labour market participation as an indicator of social worth. And yet, the nature of the British economy has been so fundamentally transformed that the certainties of the 1950s—full employment in full time and lifetime for men, while the majority of women supported the participation of these 'breadwinners' by work in the home—also seem like historical curiosities. It is now the expectation that men and women should and must work to provide for the vicissitudes of lifetime change. But waged employment for many has become less certain, temporary, and interrupted, and often poorly paid. Where once a working-class man might be able to support a partner and their children on a single wage, many households have to depend on the wages of two or more household members to reach the same standard of living (McDowell 1991). One consequence of women's entry into the labour market has been to increase income inequalities, as many women are among the lowest-paid workers. A related consequence is less time for leisure or family obligations, for voluntary work and communal participation (Hochschild 1997). For the growing number of households where nobody is in waged work, living standards have fallen, with the result that Britain is now a more unequal society than it was half a century ago. Clearly, any nostalgic notion of a return to the 1950s is out of the question—and there is no intended implication that, for women at least, the social and economic changes of the last fifty years have been without advantages; this is not the case—but equally clearly a radical rethinking of how to alter the nature, distribution, and rewards from waged work to achieve greater social justice is urgently required. The so-called New Deal for workers seems far from this.

Finally, to return to popular representations of work in the media, it is interesting to note that the centrality of work is also reflected in contemporary soap operas and television dramas. As Matthew Sweet (1999) spotted at the beginning of June 1999, 'every firstrun British drama on the box this week has a well-qualified high-achiever as its star. . . . our heroes now all have careers, uniforms and pension schemes. They get fringe benefits. They pay the NI contributions' (p. 6). Doctors, lawyers, vets, pathologists, photojournalists now dominate prime time. Heroes and heroines may still be maverick individuals, as in the old days, but in the new world of New Labour in the end they get the results that reinforce their professional expertise and keep their jobs. So, the contemporary centrality of work is reflected in more than policy shifts. It dominates popular representations too, reinforcing the exclusion of those without work or trapped in insecure employment.

Further Reading

There has been an explosion of interest in the changing nature of work and employment, the culture of organizations, and the implications of restructuring for identity in the last few years. An interesting recent account of the changing nature of work in the UK is the book by Zygmunt Bauman *Work Consumption and the New Poor* (Buckingham: Open University Press, 1998), where he argues that well-paid work is increasingly an aestheticized and desirable activity, albeit one that depends on total commitment, whereas the poor are trapped in casualized and often intermittent work that increasingly has no meaning. Richard Sennett has also addressed the connections between employment and local cultures in his chapter 'Growth and Failure: The New Political Economy and its Culture' in the volume edited by Mike Featherstone and Scott Lash, *Spaces of Culture* (London: Sage, 1999). Both authors, however, neglect the significance of the transformation of gender divisions of labour and it may be that Sennett falls into the metropolitan trap identified by Wight. Good contemporary surveys of changes in the British labour market include Mark Cully, Stephen Woodland, Andrew O'Reilly, and Gill Dix's *Britain at Work* (London: Routledge, 1999) and Paul Gregg and Jonathon Wadsworth's *The State of Working Britain* (Manchester: Manchester University Press, 1999). John Hass and Ruth Holliday's *Organization/Representation* (London: Sage, 1998) is an interesting collection of essays about the representation of work and organizations in popular culture.

References

Bourgois, P. (1995), *In Search of Respect*, Cambridge, Cambridge University Press.
Budd, L., and Whimster, S. (eds.) (1992) *Global Finance and Urban Living*, London: Routledge.
Campbell, B. (1993), *Goliath: Britain's Dangerous Places*, London, Methuen.
Castells, M. (1997), *The Information Age*, ii: *The Power of Identity*, Oxford: Blackwells.
Connell, R. (1995), *Masculinities*, Oxford, Blackwell.

Crompton, R., and **Sanderson, K.** (1994), 'The Gendered Restructuring of Employment in the Finance Sector', in A. Scott, (ed.), *Gender Segregation and Social Change*, Oxford: Oxford University Press.

Dennis, N., Henriques, F., and **Slaughter, C.** (1956), *Coal is our Life*, London: Eyre & Spottiswood.

du Gay, P. (1996a), 'Organizing Identity: Entrepreneurial Governance and Public Management', in P. du Gay and S. Hall (eds.), *Questions of Cultural Identity*, London: Sage.

—— (1996b), *Consumption and Identity at Work*, London: Sage.

Freedland, J. (1997), 'Alan Partridge—our Man of the 90s', *Guardian*, 10 Dec.

Frisby, D. (1985), 'Georg Simmel: First Sociologist of Modernity', *Theory, Culture and Society*, 2.

Game, A., and **Pringle, R.** (1984), *Gender at Work* London: Pluto.

Giddens, A. (1979), *Central Problems in Class Theory*, London: Macmillan.

Goldthorpe, J., et al. (1969), *The Affluent Worker in the Class Structure*, Cambridge: Cambridge University Press.

Halford, S., and **Savage, M.** (1995), 'Restructuring Organisations, Changing People: Gender and Restructuring in Local Government and Banking', *Work, Employment and Society*, 9.

Harvie, C. (ed.) (1981), *No Gods and Precious Few Heroes: Scotland 1914–1980*, London: Edward Arnold.

Hearn, J. (1998), 'Troubled Masculinities in Social Policy Discourses: Young Men', in J. Popay, J. Hearn, and J. Edwards (eds.), *Men, Gender Divisions and Welfare*, London: Routledge.

Hochschild, A. (1997), *The Time Bind*, New York: Metropolitan Books.

Jacques, M. (1997), interview with Stuart Hall, *New Statesman*, 14 Nov.

Leidner, R. (1993) *Fast Food, Fast Talk*, Berkeley and Los Angeles: University of California Press.

Lewis, M. (1989), *Liar's Poker: Two Cities, True Greed*, London: Hodder & Stoughton.

Leyshon, A., and **Thrift, N.** (1996), *Money/Space*, London: Routledge.

McConville, B. (1998), *The State They're in: Young People in Britain Today*, Leicester: Youth Work Press.

McDowell, L. (1989), 'Gender Divisions', in C. Hamnett, L. McDowell, and P. Sarre (eds.), *The Changing Social Structure*, London: Hodder & Stoughton.

—— (1991), 'Life without Father and Ford: The New Gender Order of Post-Fordism', *Transactions, Institute of British Geographers*, 16.

—— (1997), *Capital Culture: Gender at Work in the City*, London: Blackwell.

—— and **Court, G.** (1994), 'Gender Divisions of Labour in the PostFordist Economy: The Maintenance of Occupational Sex Segregation in the Financial Services Sector', *Environment and Planning* A 26.

—— and **Massey, D.** (1984), 'A Woman's Place?', in D. Massey and J. Allen (eds.) *Geography Matters!*, Cambridge: Cambridge University Press.

McElhinny, B. (1994), 'An Economy of Affect: Objectivity, Masculinity and the Gendering of Police Work', in A. Cornwall and N. Lindisfarne (eds.), *Dislocating Masculinity*, London: Routledge.

McRae, A., and **Cairncross, F.** (1991), *Capital City: London as a Financial Centre*, London: Methuen.

Martin, S. (1980), *Breaking and Entering: Policewomen on Patrol*, Berkeley and Los Angeles: University of California Press.

Changing Cultures of Work

Massey, D. (1995), 'Masculinity, Dualisms and High Technology', *Transactions, Institute of British Geographers*, 20.

—— (1997), 'Economic/Non-economic', in R. Lee and J. Wills (eds.), *Geographies of Economies*, London: Arnold.

Phillips, A. (1993), *The Trouble with Boys: Parenting the Men of the Future*, London: Pandora.

Phoenix, A. (1991), *Young Mothers?*, Cambridge: Polity.

Rowthorn, B. (1986), 'Deindustrialisation in Britain', in R. Martin and B. Rowthorn (eds.), *The Geography of Deindustrialisation*, London: Macmillan.

Schoenberger, E. (1997), *The Cultural Crisis of the Firm*, Oxford: Blackwell.

Skelton, T., and **Valentine, G.** (eds.) (1997) *Cool Place: Geographies of Youth Cultures*, London: Routledge.

Sweet, M. (1999), 'Office Heroics', *Guardian 2*, 2 June.

Thompson, E. P. (1980), *The Making of the English Working Class*, Harmondsworth: Penguin.

Walby, S. (1988), *Gender Segregation at Work*, Milton Keynes: Open University Press.

—— (1997), *Gender Transformations*, London: Routledge.

Weiner, G., Arnot, M., and **David, M.** (1996), 'Is the Future Female? Female Success, Male Disadvantage and Changing Gender Patterns in Education', in A. H. Halsey, P. Brown, and H. Lauder (eds.), *Education, Economy and Society*, Oxford: Oxford University Press.

Wight, D. (1993), *Workers not Wasters: Masculine Respectability, Consumption and Unemployment in Central Scotland*, Edinburgh: Edinburgh University Press.

Wilkinson, H., and **Mulgan, G.** (1995), *Freedom's Children*, London, Demos.

Williams, F. (1998) 'Troubled Masculinities in Social Policy Discourses: Fatherhood', in J. Popay, J. Hearn, and J. Edwards (eds.), *Men, Gender Divisions and Welfare*, London: Routledge.

Good Girls, Bad Girls? Female Success and the New Meritocracy

ANGELA
McROBBIE

THIS chapter argues that since New Labour came to power in May 1997 young women have become a 'metaphor for social change' and that in this capacity they are charged with the not insignificant task of, in effect, delivering the new meritocracy by means of 'female achievement'. This phrase 'metaphor for social change' intentionally echoes Hall et al. writing over twenty years ago and describing the position occupied by 'youth' (Hall and Jefferson 1976). For Hall et al. it was implicitly young working-class males who appeared to embody, to politicians, journalists, and electorate alike, the turmoil of the post-war years. They were the subject of concern for the social problems they gave rise to, they also bore the brunt of changing labour market requirements, and they came to be associated with all the anxieties of consumerism. In what might be understood as an almost magical reversal we now see young women occupy this same symbolic space. 'Girls', including their bodies, their labour power, and their social behaviour are now the subject of governmentality to an unprecedented degree. They have become 'newly re-mapped entities' (Riley 1988). Until now it is impossible to imagine any Prime Minister in the post-war years considering that the self-image of teenage girls in relation to body weight was sufficiently important for him or her to make a statement to this effect. But on the week starting 10 April 2000 Tony Blair confirmed the importance of the report presented by Minister of Women Tessa Jowell. She had said, 'I am concerned that girls may not be fulfilling their potential because of their lack of confidence about themselves' (*www.10 Downing Street Newsroom* 10 Apr. 2000). Jowell went on to announce the setting up of a young women's summit on body image and weight to be held in July 2000. The initiative was the result of research carried out at Exeter University which showed that, from a sample of 37,500 girls between the ages of 12 and 15, 57.5 per cent were on diets.

Two other main points will also be argued here, first that meritocratic female success in so far as it exists or will exist in the next few years has to be understood within the broader context of the increasing triumphalism of global neo-liberalism and its associated values. Thus a significant proportion of young women are positioned to become standard bearers for the new economy, as creators of wealth. This aspiration is applauded in the UK popular media especially in women's magazines and in the right-wing newspapers such as the *Daily Mail*. Success takes on a distinctively gendered, indeed feminized, form in these media spaces. It ranges from celebrating 'girl power' and discussing women's rights, and from encouraging 'blondes who will do anything for fame' to advising women on investment portfolios and profiling top-earning women chief executives (Cole 1998). The rewards for the girls who compete hard enough to get to the top are wealth, financial independence from men, and glamour and good looks (in that these can now be acquired through a vast range of beauty goods and services including cosmetic surgery). The prize in other words is to become what I have elsewhere labelled a 'TV blonde' (McRobbie 2000*a*). The prevalence of these embodiments of womanhood and the constellation of attributes and behaviours upon which they depend mark the presence of a new normativity, a consistent set of injunctions about 'how to be' for young women. The convergence of governmental and commercial discourses points to a new disciplinarity cast in terms of the drive for money and power.

These young women are not only the daughters of Thatcherism (although she herself had little to say about women or girls), but also of feminism. Feminism has struggled to produce at least some of these (unanticipated) outcomes. It has played a key role in education, managing to overturn, in a period of less than twenty years, systematic underachievement and under-representation. It represents a continual point of reference for young women in Britain today, even as it is repudiated by them (Walter 1999). It is also as though elements from the old 1970s triumvirate of liberal feminism, (equal opportunities) radical feminism (against male violence), and socialist feminism (equal pay, anti-feminization of poverty) have been selectively drawn on by New Labour, allowing them to come up with a new and more energetic liberal feminism (although the f word is never mentioned) which can in turn and without any noticeable difficulty slide into becoming 'neo-liberal feminism'. The advantage of New Labour's commitment to women, and especially to young women, to the business world is that it appears to be shorn of any recognizable feminist features. The government aims to produce a generation of women whose commitment to earning a living and accumulating assets is taken for granted, a mark of female identity, a distinguishing feature of gender.

What remains uncertain is the outcome of these new pathways for young women. The new meritocracy does not promise equality of outcome, which in turn raises the question of those young women who continue to get left behind, girls from poorer backgrounds or who are disadvantaged in other ways. If ruthless female individualism prevails, then it might also come up against its own limits. This, I would hazard a guess, will occur at that point when in their thirties these new young women either decide to have children, or, as is increasingly common, decide not to have them. This is not to posit a kind of gender essentialism around maternity or indeed avoidance of maternity. Instead it is to argue that so burdened with this mission to embody all the values of the new prosperous and classless society, indeed to embody a new kind of citizenship, young women will surely buckle under the pressures of having to deindividualize and prioritize the needs of others through having children, or else they will surely suffer psychologically for having to invent new ways of being women without having children. There is also another more likely scenario, which is that many young women will find themselves in average-earning households where they are breadwinners and they are still charged with caring for others in the domestic field, i.e. their own children, their partners if they have one, and possibly their elderly parents.[1] Totally unprepared for this by the culture of individualism and the ideology of success, there is the chance that new forms of feminist sociality might emerge.

In School and at Work

It has become commonplace to comment on the 'great leap forward' undertaken by girls in education. This is where the 'metaphor for social change' really kicks in. They outperform boys in most

1 In Fay Weldon's 1997 novel *Big Women* which was dramatized by Tariq Ali and broadcast on Channel 4, the main character is a young woman called Saffron who seeks vengeance on feminism and on her mother's suicide by becoming a cool Thatcherite editor of a glossy women's magazine. She ends up making a lot of money, living at home, and supporting her alcoholic father and her jobless brother.

school subjects, are rapidly gaining ground in the sciences and in mathematics, and in traditionally male subject areas on degree courses at university such as law and medicine the number of girls is now edging over 50 per cent. Education has long been recognized as the most effective vehicle for social mobility.

In recent years the possession of a degree qualification has become one of the most reliable guarantors of an above-average income. With New Labour committed to creating a new and more genuinely open meritocracy (knowing that in the past class advantage had a much greater impact than ability and 'merit' in shaping educational outcomes) and with the government's triple focus on education, youth, and specifically on young women, then there should be no doubt that it is through educational success that the future independence and prosperity of girls will be grounded.[2] However, the idea of a smooth path to achievement for a determined and ambitious population of young women might be a politician's ideal and an advertiser's fantasy (as the latter group look to future disposable income), but to the sociologist it is vitally important to describe the unevenness of changes such as those of girls in education, and also to delineate those features which are not just a matter of pockets of residual failure, but which are and remain endemic to the whole educational system: instances where 'plus ça change'.

Nor is this still a straightforward matter of 'residual' class differences among young women, or for that matter ethnic disadvantage. These are not simply anachronisms which, with some further support from government, will soon be ironed out. Rather they are pervasive conditions where traditional disadvantages now combine with the downside effects of new and less predictable fluidities of opportunity. There are also many respects in which boys and girls can share the same disadvantages. The outcome of these are gender-specific, but equally dismal. The Thatcher years saw a shift of responsibility for young people from the state back to the privatized sphere of the family. For those who did not have the good fortune of a happy home life and who were either forced to leave home or found themselves 'in care' the opportunities to gain even the most minimal of qualifications have dramatically decreased. Benefit changes, and the removal of access to housing subsidy, have pushed disadvantaged young people if not onto the streets then noticeably into poverty. Research shows that young people leaving care do so with on average no qualifications whatsoever and that the majority of girls leaving care at 16 are pregnant within months.

2 The slogan 'Education, education, education' played a key role in New Labour's election campaign 1997. The commitment to youth was visible first in Blair's Young Country speech (Blair 1997) and then in the ill-fated Cool Britannia episode which attempted to promote young British creative talent internationally. For a savage lampoon of Blair's 'youthism' see Nairn (2000). For the focus on young women see www.10 Downing Street Newsroom Jan.–Apr. 2000.

Angela McRobbie

But even for young people who live at home but in low-income families the (English and Welsh) highly specialized A-level route to university remains virtually impossible. The involvement of parents in supervising evening homework, the purchase of textbooks, the know-how of university application procedures, leaves young people who cannot rely on these resources entirely dependent on the goodwill and commitment of teachers. But the quality of education and indeed of teachers varies widely and as sociologists for many years have demonstrated good schools tend to exist in affluent areas. This marks just one point in a field of deeply unequal opportunities. But this single point becomes joined up with others to form a predictable curve. For example, good schools which get the best results tend to channel their students to the best universities, which as it happens tends to be those favoured by employers. Even after graduation young people who can rely on parental support (including all the necessities for job interviews including clothes and travel) can more easily survive the early years of low income by staying at home, until they move into the higher-income bracket for which they are destined. For these 'gilded youths', and especially for girls who are now seen by employers as 'the most desirable workers of all', the new global economy promises a wealth of opportunities (Franks 1999 quoted by Segal 1999). These are the girls who will be able to buy their own flats and decide in their thirties whether or not to have children (with or without a partner, since there is less moral disapproval if there is plenty of money to afford it). And it is precisely this new way of being young and female which has led sociologists to predict new social divisions (and thus potential antagonisms) within the female population. For example Roger Penn suggests that a new bifurcation will emerge between 'ordinary women' who will have children and work part-time, and the estimated 20 per cent of young women born in 1975 who will remain childless, a decision which in turn correlates with higher levels of education with the effect that 'childlessness is a rapidly increasing phenomenon in Britain' (Penn 2000).

The majority of young women do not have these opportunities to become high wage earners, and although there is no doubt that their chances for earning a decent living are indeed rising, the obstacles they still have to overcome are formidable. The best account of the sheer difficulties to succeed confronted by young black women in school remains the ethnographic study by Safia Mirza. In one, by no means unrepresentative, school in South London, Mirza showed how the girls themselves and their parents were determined to gain good qualifications, but in this respect their desires were not just frustrated by poor-quality schooling but actively blocked by racist teachers who attributed to the girls 'cultural differences' which as they saw it were antithetical to success. This school system consistently underestimated the abilities of the girls and paid scant attention to the importance of preparing them for examinations (Mirza 1992). Mirza showed how the girls adopted strategies to succeed against the assumptions and the practices of the teachers, for instance they would not choose subjects or options taken by teachers whom they perceived to be openly racist and prejudicial in their treatment of the pupils. The chances of gaining the right qualifications for a good university in this environment were tiny, and if the girls did stay on for higher education they would need to depend on the sector which accepts candidates with much lower passes. Fortunately such colleges and universities do exist, but as indicated above they are not favoured by employers. This case shows the dangers of accepting at face value the high achievement of girls; it also highlights the errors in assuming that in terms of underachievement, it is only boys who now constitute a problem. Finally it reveals the pernicious nature of racial discrimination in the educational system and its deleterious impact on males and females alike.

If the groundwork for reversing sex role stereotyping in schooling was carried out by feminist academics engaged in this subject from the mid-1970s onwards, the issue of the continuing discrepancy in income between men and women has been recently addressed by government. This focus on young women presumably stems from the expectation that it might well be easier to narrow the pay gap between young people entering the labour market now, than to attempt to bring the incomes of middle-aged women closer to (if not equal to) their male counterparts. But this attention by government is also a sign of their determination to create a new category of 'women as workers'. In the week starting 21 February 2000 the government website (*www.10 Downing Street Newsroom*) commented at length on how women are undervalued in the workplace. The results of a study carried out at the London School of Economics by Katherine Rake showed that 'a woman leaving school with no qualifications foregoes nearly £200,000 over a lifetime . . . with GCSEs there is a loss of £250,000 while women with degrees and professional qualifications lose £143,000 simply by being female'. This study compared typical women from three different categories of work with their male counterparts. Tessa Jowell concluded that 'girls achieve equally well as boys at school but clearly this does not translate to the same opportunities in the workplace . . . we are determined to see women properly rewarded and able to reach their full potential'. The report concludes that 'different women need different kinds of support'.

There are two points which can be drawn from this concern to eradicate pay differentials. The first is that the education and work couplet represents on New Labour's behalf what might be described as a new settlement for young women. By so firmly taking on board this feat of social engineering the present government could be described as attempting to invent a new female subjectivity, a population of 'good girls' who will do well at school, go on to get good jobs, and from then on juggle the demands of home and work alike but with more help and support from government than has ever been the case in the past. This contract with women is a bold attempt to secure the consent of women to New Labour's agenda in years to come. However, it is not an invitation for them to become active political subjects, nor is there any suggestion that feminist values of campaigning and self-organization, sisterhood, support, solidarity, or childcare sharing have any place in this new contract. Although the above report concludes that different solutions will need to be sought for different women, no specific invitation is issued to black women to tackle the discrimination they still experience in the workplace, nor to Asian women and girls who still find themselves limited in job opportunities, nor to those without academic qualifications trapped within the lowest-paid and least protected sectors of manufacturing (Phizacklea 1992). Instead this is a New Labour managerialist solution, an appeal to women to be assured that they are in good hands and that their needs will be looked after at a political level as long as they play their role in the new world of work.

It would be churlish and dishonest to deny the many strengths of this new initiative. Many policies currently being implemented echo earlier feminist demands. Others are of overall benefit to men and women alike, for example the minimum wage. But there is also a seeming depoliticization of women's issues as they are made compatible with and reconciled with the needs of capital. By this means the ranks of the 'good girls' will become the 'docile subjects' of the new governmentality. This also leaves unanswered the requirements of the employers. How can 'we' be assured of their co-operation with this plan for women? As I have recently argued, in run-down parts of the country and in regions where private enterprise is loath to reinvest, the only means by which employment can be created is through the public sector, even though this goes against the grain of current government thinking (McRobbie

2000*b*). Thus it could be argued that the new work ethic for young women is as much a moral imperative, requiring a readiness and willingness to work, and a high degree of self-reliance, as it is a full-blown employment policy.

But there is one other point which emphasizes the scale and breadth of this social transformation. The fact that young women are now being told that they must make their own money for life and that indeed their lifetime earnings should be equal to those of men marks an incredible departure from tradition. At present, the life earnings of women over 50 in the UK are barely more than a pittance. Poverty is most acute among old and divorced or widowed women, it is endemic among old working-class women. It is they who can be seen in supermarkets as soon as they get their pensions dropping just a few cheap items of food into their baskets. The assumption has been until now that women's needs would be looked after by a husband. The scramble to marry was consequently as urgent for middle-class girls as it was for their infinitely less well-educated working-class counterparts. And now (this very week) we have government announcements featuring Tessa Jowell yet again on the BBC Radio 4 *Today* programme (17 Apr. 2000) proposing that girls should be discouraged from going into hairdressing because of its lifetime low-pay levels. In short the transition for women from economic dependence to full independence is a seismic shift; for the first time young women across the social classes and from different ethnic backgrounds are being told by government, 'earn your own living and do not rely on a husband/partner to support you'.

Bad Girls: Sex, the Body, and Neo-Individualism

Who are the bad girls in New Labour thinking? If it is agreed that a good deal of the socio-economic manœuvrings described above have the fundamental objective of dramatically lowering the cost of social security, then it is the teenage mother who remains emblematic of cost in this respect. But 'she' is not part of a dwindling group of unfortunate young women, she instead is part of a growing band of determined girls whose capacity for motherhood is the best way of drawing on their limited resources. This is because teenage mothers come largely, indeed almost exclusively, from extremely disadvantaged communities which have been experiencing for some time the impact of joblessness. While the rise in birth rate for this social category is hardly exponential (despite the tabloid headlines), the danger such activity poses to government lies not just in dependency on state benefit but in the threat to family values and in the moral failings of these girls who embark on motherhood without sufficient thought for their own economic well-being or that of the child.[3] Having a child in these circumstances horrifies government because of the future costs it must bear in supporting the mother into reasonably well-paid work, helping her also with childcare, and then providing sufficient state support for the child or children to make them job-ready in years to come. Hence the priority placed by the Social Exclusion Unit and the Women's Unit and the enormous efforts made by them to tackle this problem.

In fact these girls symbolize the scale of the changes and expectations affecting young women at the bottom end of the social hierarchy in Britain today. As various feminists, myself included, have argued, the girls who get pregnant in their teens are largely drawn from low-income groups where women have never expected to earn anything more than minimum part-time earnings (Phoenix 1991; McRobbie 2000c). This group have inevitably acted opportunistically in economic circumstances which have never favoured them. During twenty-five years of high unemployment (1975–2000) poor single parents were 'better off' on benefit than in part-time work. In addition young women recognized that there was no status, indeed no identity, for an unemployed woman in such communities if she was not a mother. Hence the spate of teenage pregnancies in the various areas which writers like myself and Phoenix observed through this period. Like the chronically high levels of drug abuse in these same regions, early motherhood is simply the response by bodily means of a population abandoned as all industry moves out, and the state enters into a programme of reducing benefits and support.

The present government therefore sees attending to this issue as a priority. Wary of antagonizing the anti-abortion lobby and of upsetting those who argue for traditional family values, it must embark on a course of recommending easy access to birth control to girls who are having sex at a young age and terminations for those who get pregnant. The extent to which New Labour is actively pursuing these ends is testimony to their positioning of girls at the centre stage of social policy. This is a matter of population management. If they get it right there are real gains to be made. Hence the summits, day conferences, and commissions on this subject involving crucially the editors of the girls' magazines, experts on family planning, psychologists, sociologists, and a range

3 UK birth rates are 30 births for every 1,000 girls between 15 and 19 compared to 8 in Spain, 7 in France, 4 in the Netherlands, as reported in the *Guardian*, 24 Mar. 1999, G2: 8.

of academics from other disciplines.[4] While there are many issues which might be discussed further in this regard (for example the effects on the health and well-being of girls put on the pill at 13), I want to conclude this section by arguing that the designation of 'bad girls' put on those poor and disadvantaged girls who become young mothers has much wider social and disciplinary consequences. It can lead to a new divide (along the lines of class and ethnicity) among young women, between the morally flawed who have pursued this course and thus do not possess the footloose and fancy-free requirements of the new flexible labour market, and the 'TV blondes' who can present themselves flawless to the recruitment agencies (and who in addition can spend all their wages on themselves, further improving their market position). In bodily terms there is a world of difference between the groomed, 'toned', and immaculately dressed 20-something and her counterpart who has a baby. Hence the disincentive to give birth can be made through recourse to feminine success in terms of 'slim blondeness' while the image of the young mother prominent in the tabloids is of an unkempt, overweight, 'slovenly', and prematurely aged girl with her baby in a pushchair.

The extent to which this discourse can be pushed in the direction of a kind of neo-right eugenics can be seen in an article in the left-wing weekly the *New Statesman* by columnist (and self-proclaimed archetypal 30-something girl-about-town) Christina Odone (Odone 2000). Drawing on a report published by the right-wing think tank the Family Policy Studies Centre she writes, 'teenage single mothers are fast becoming the biggest social group giving birth'. This, she claims, is a frightening thought to the middle classes because it means that 'top range women . . . prefer to leave reproduction to the second eleven'. She continues 'a bump . . . risks becoming as clear a proof of a working class background as the fag hanging from someone's lips'. This will produce, she argues, a 'society made up of mediocrities', a 'poor quality world' because a teenage mother produces 'a socially autistic adult with little expectation and even less talent'. Of course, the reader of this piece of neo-Darwinianism might be expected to interpret this column ironically, since Odone dabbles in the style of self-mockery associated with any number of 'post-feminist' young women journalists.

Ironic or not, the article first demonstrates the social acceptability (editorially at least) of New Right thinking within the orbit of New Labour, second it reveals the neo-individualism of the ambitious young woman journalist who trades empathy for and understanding of her disadvantaged 'sisters' for the cheap thrills of

4 The government is quietly supporting the setting up of school-based clinics for birth control advice and access to the 'morning after pill'.

Angela McRobbie

shocking left and feminist points of faith as a career bid to get herself in front of the TV spotlights as 'controversial' (in this case as a brunette 'TV blonde').[5] Third, if we were to rid Odone's implicit coding of working class with white and introduce instead into her article the category of young black women who become pregnant, then the full force of her hostile, New Right, and socially conservative values would be apparent. This then is the concluding argument here, that sliding into place almost unnoticed and on the backs of the new concern with young women in political debate is a New Right vocabulary which celebrates female success in the marketplace, which punishes failure as individual weakness, and which boldly advocates competitive individualism as the mark of modern young womanhood. This discourse appeals to young women by connecting success in work with traditional success in body and appearance. Indeed the former promises to lead to the latter, since a good job brings girls into the heartland of consumer culture and all its bodily benefits. In this context there is no excuse not to look good.

This scenario is both politically unpleasant and deeply disappointing to feminists. It is not my usual mission as an academic to be the bearer of such bad news. But it is difficult to withhold a form of concern which is actually counter to the anxiety of government. This after all is frequently the role of sociology. For example we might ask what are the values which the so-called successful young women will embrace and draw on other than those of acquiring wealth and access to consumer culture? Where does rampant neo-individualism lead for girls? If it means ruthlessly trampling on others and disregarding social and political concerns for the goals of self-advance and personal gain, then are we not observing the rejuvenation of the New Right spearheaded by young women but located within the wide and welcoming embrace of New Labour? Unused to sharing anything more than the next round of cocktails, how will these young women surrender their time and attention to the needs of children, how will they learn the importance of female solidarity and sisterhood when such values have been so ridiculed as quaintly feminist?[6] And if they have no children and are also disappointed with men where might we expect any connection to the social good to spring from? Will we simply see the birth of a new female business elite? In delivering politics for women while at the same time discouraging women from being political New Labour is adopting a 'corporate managerialist' strategy aimed at keeping business happy while being seen to do good things for young women (Barnett 1998). It is also protecting itself from political

5 This author had the dubious honour of appearing in the same current affairs programme as Ms Odone, who is a regular on such slots. On this occasion the discussion was trust in the medical establishment and women's health. Not surprisingly perhaps Christina Odone advocated an anti-feminist position, suggesting that 'we' should not lose our trust in figures of authority. BBC2, *Newsnight*, 4 Feb. 2000.
6 Re cocktails see *Guardian*, 19 Apr. 2000: 9, report by Datamonitor indicating that 'British women are hitting the bottle as never before'.

dissent, since overtly feminist participation by young women might upset its own applecart of electoral success. Living without feminism is therefore part of the new settlement, but on the longer term it may prove fatal. Thus this chapter concludes by asking the question under what conditions does feminism become, once again, a political necessity?

Further Reading

Brooks, Ann (1997), *Post-feminisms: Feminism, Cultural Theory, Cultural Forms*, London: Routledge.

Douglas, Susan J. (1994), *Where the Girls Are: Growing up Female with the Mass Media*, London: Penguin.

Furlong, Andy, and Cartmel, Fred (1997), *Young People and Social Change: Individuation and Risk in Late Modernity*, Milton Keynes: Open University Press.

Hollows, Joanne (2000), *Feminism, Femininity and Popular Culture*, Manchester: Manchester University Press.

Walby, Sylvia (1997), *Gender Transformations*, London: Routledge.

References

Barnett, A. (1998), 'All Power to the Citizens', *Marxism Today*, Nov.–Dec.

Blair, T. (1996), *New Britain: My Vision of a Young Country*, London: Fourth Estate.

Cole, A. (1998), 'Blondes Who Will Do Anything for Fame', *Daily Mail*, 11 Dec. 1998.

Franks, S. (1999), *Having None of It: Women, Men and the Future of Work*, London: Granta.

Hall, S., and Jefferson, R. (eds.) (1976), *Resistance through Rituals*, London: Hutchinson.

McRobbie, A. (2000*a*), 'Feminism v the TV Blondes', inaugural lecture, Goldsmiths College, London.

—— (2000*b*), 'Feminism and the Third Way', *Feminist Review*, Spring, 64.

—— (2000*c*), *Feminism and Youth Culture*, 2nd edn., Basingstoke: Macmillan.

Mirza, H. Safia (1992), *Young Female and Black*, London: Routledge.

Nairn, T. (2000), *After Britain: New Labour and the Return of Scotland*, London: Granta.

Odone, C. (2000), 'If High Flyers Refuse to be Mums, We Shall Rear Mediocrities', *New Statesman*, 3 Apr.

Penn, R. (2000), 'Some Conjectures', *Sociology*, 34/1.

Phoenix, A. (1991), *Young Mothers?*, Cambridge: Polity Press.

Phizacklea, A. (1992), *Unpacking the Fashion Industry*, London: Routledge.

Riley, D. (1988), '*Am I That Name?*' *Feminism and the Category of 'Women' in History*, Basingstoke: Macmillan.

Segal, L. (1999), *Why Feminism?*, Cambridge: Polity Press.

Walter, N. (1999), *The New Feminism*, London: Virago.

Resignifying Masculinity: From 'New Man' to 'New Lad'

SEAN NIXON

In November 1988, Grey, the London-based advertising agency, produced a new television advert for Beechams' Brylcreem. The advert supported the launch of an extensive new range of Brylcreem products (including mousse, gel, and aftershave) and built on earlier press and television work which Grey had produced for Beechams following their winning of the account in 1985. In doing so, the advert aimed to extend the repositioning of the brand as an essential purchase for stylish young men and so reverse its near terminal decline in sales (*Campaign*, 11 Nov. 1988: 3).

The advert was set in a barber's shop, amidst the traditional paraphernalia of masculine grooming. Its narrative was based around a young man being wet shaved by the barber. In dramatically lit gloom, we see the shaving cream being applied, the razor being used, and the barber massaging the model's temples and then pulling a hot flannel over his face to complete the grooming. Throughout this ritual, which is shot in rapid close-ups, the model is narcissistically absorbed in the care he is receiving. His self-absorption is highlighted by the fact that the process of shaving is shot in such quick edits to a thunderous soundtrack. We glimpse a flame, the razor against his face, a razor being sharpened on leather, and the steaming flannel being pulled across his face. In all of this the model remains self-absorbed until he spins round at the end to face us in a challenging look to camera.

The advert was high on drama and atmosphere and exemplified

the kinds of creative advertising for which a number of the newer London-based agencies were gaining a strong reputation during this period. It is, however, the coding of masculinity in the advert which makes it pertinent to my concerns here. This coding was largely carried through the casting and styling of the advert's star, the 26-year-old Corsican model Jean-Ange Chiapinini. His 'look' combined strong masculine features with elements of softness or sensuality. Thus strong chin, nose, and jaw-line were mixed with very glossy hair, dark seamless skin, and full lips. In addition, the lighting of the advert worked to signify further the elements of sensuality, whilst the use of close-ups gave an intensity to the relationship between the model and the viewer. Codings of this sort, however, were not unique to the Brylcreem adverts. In fact, across three connected consumer markets in the UK—those of menswear, grooming and toiletries, and consumer magazines—there was a proliferation in the mid–late 1980s of imagery of this sort. This imagery was distinguished not only by its mixing of both softness and hardness in the facial characteristics of its models and by the intensity of the spectatorial look at them, but also by the recurrence of other physical features—notably, developed chest, arm, and upper-body muscles. Significantly, the surface of these men's bodies was also, often, displayed.

The circulation of these codings—already condensed, by the end of 1986, in the figure of the 'new man'—was identified by many commentators (both popular and academic) as being exemplary of some wider decisive shift in representations of masculinity; a shift which was throwing up new images of the British male (Melly 1986; Lyttle and Kennedy 1986; Moore 1987; Jones 1988; Rutherford 1988; Chapman 1988). Frank Mort, in his essay 'Boy's Own: Masculinity, Style and Popular Culture' (Mort 1988), offered the most sustained argument about the cultural significance of this 'new man' imagery. He argued that what marked out the imagery was the way it offered a new, more sexualized representation of the male body in ways which drew on codings traditionally associated with representations of femininity within consumer culture. He also suggested that the imagery resisted the assertion of a fixed or true sense of maleness in its styling of appearance. The significance of this for Mort was that such codings pointed the way to a radically different version of masculinity; one characterized by a more self-conscious sense of maleness. He developed his argument about the significance of the 'new man' imagery through a particular conceptualization of the problem of masculinity; a conceptualization rooted within the injunctions of contemporary sexual politics to problematize

Sean Nixon

dominant and exclusive forms of masculinity and heterosexuality. Drawing upon an argument put forward by Rosalind Coward and Maria Black, Mort argued that at the heart of the contemporary problem of masculinity were a set of discursive practices which positioned the masculine as the social norm; that is, as embodying the human or universal experience. For Mort, these unmarked positions (which Coward and Black specify in relation to discourses of citizenship, the law, anthropology, and sexuality (Coward and Black 1981: 83)), made it possible for men not to recognize the problem of their masculinity for women or to take responsibility for it. His central contention about the 'new man' imagery was that it precisely spoke to men 'through their gender—as a community of men' (Mort 1988: 212). In other words, he saw the new codings as making it possible for men to live out their masculinity in more provisional, gendered terms. This lay at the root of the ruptural potential of the profusion of the 'new man' imagery for him.

In this chapter, I want to return to the 'new man' imagery produced in the mid- to late 1980s and to the arguments about its cultural significance. In the first part of the chapter, I want—in a fairly summary fashion—to set out my reading of the novelty and distinctiveness of the imagery produced between 1984 and 1990; the period, I argue, when a distinctive regime of 'new man' imagery was developed and consolidated. In the second part of the chapter, I want to address developments since the end of 1990 in the men's markets associated with the 'new man'. These developments—particularly in magazine culture—both cast illuminating retrospective light over the earlier moment and point to ongoing shifts in popular codings of masculinity within these fields of commercial culture. As we will see, at the heart of them is the formation of another new masculine subject—the 'new lad'.

Taken together, the phenomenon of both the 'new man' and the 'new lad' point to a peculiarly British settlement in the way groups of young (and youngish) men were invited to participate in more intensified forms of style and lifestyle consumption. The 'new man' and the 'new lad', then, I want to contend, represent distinct cultural scripts through which the link between masculinity and these forms of individual consumption was established and which worked to circumvent the previous problem of British men being labelled outlandish or homosexual if they were concerned about the cut of their clothes or the gloss of their skin. Thus, while the circulation of the codings of masculinity which I discuss in this chapter formed part of a shift in which the consumption patterns of groups of men were brought closer to those of some of their continental European and North American counterparts, it did so in a peculiarly British way, signifiying peculiarly British masculinities.

The Specificity of the 'New Man'

Perhaps the most immediately striking aspect of the 'new man' imagery was its proliferation across a range of commercial sites. I have already suggested that these were principally linked to three key consumer markets in the UK—menswear, grooming and toiletries, and consumer magazines. What this meant, however, was that the imagery appeared in more than one place. We find it not only in television and press advertising, but also in shop windows and shop displays, on posters and postcards, and in magazine fashion photography and magazine features. Grasping this aspect of the 'new man' imagery—its constitution as a distinctive regime of representation—forms the first step in beginning to understand its specificity. In emphasizing the multiple sites across which the 'new man' codings signified, however, I also want to suggest that one of these sites—popular magazines for men—occupied a particularly privileged position. This privileged position derived both from the fact that the magazines—pre-eminently Wagadon's style magazine the *Face*, its men's general interest magazine *Arena*, and Conde Nast's general male title *GQ*—were the cultural form responsible for carrying the greatest volume of these new representations, and also because it was within the magazine's fashion photography that the new codings of masculinity first appeared and were most extensively elaborated. Given the centrality of the magazine fashion photography to the regime of 'new man' imagery, I want to use an analysis of it as a way of carrying more general points about the distinctiveness of the 'new man' codings.

The first point to note about the magazine fashion photography is that it circulated more than one set of 'new man' codings. What we find, in fact, in the magazines' fashion spreads are a range of codings which share a loose family resemblance. Across this range of codings three 'looks' were particularly important. These were the 'Buffalo' look associated with the stylist Ray Petri, an Italian-influenced look, and a version of Edwardian Englishness. Of the three 'looks' Petri's 'Buffalo' stylings were the most disruptive of the established conventions of men's fashion photography. He produced the stylings regularly on the pages of the *Face* between 1983 and 1987. The stylings were built around a close group of models and associates. 'Buffalo', in fact, was very much a 'family affair' (as a headline to one of Petri's stylings once put it) characterized by the regular casting of 'Buffalo's' familiar faces. This was no accident, as Petri identified casting as the essential element in defining the 'Buffalo' look.

Away from the established catwalks, Petri's stylings drew on and helped shape a distinctive repetoire of urban style. Most famously his styling of the MA-1 flight jacket turned the item into an essential element in 'tough', metropolitan street style. Testifying to Petri's influence, the *Face*, in its review of 1989, suggested, 'Who could argue that the combination of MA-1 flight jacket, Levis 501s and Dr. Martens is the urban uniform of the decade?' (*Face*, 1/100 (1988): 50).

The fashion styled by Petri asserted a tough, muscular masculinity that drew tangentially on the representational genres of 1950s body-building and boxing portraiture. In line with the often ambiguous and ironic tone of the *Face*'s journalism, Petri's 'Buffalo' look knowingly played on this 'simpler' and fixed sense of masculinity. References to this pre-permissive manliness were spliced with the contemporary paraphernalia of style to carve out a striking and distinctive repertoire of codings of masculinity.

The choice of models was central to the shaping of the 'Buffalo' look. Young-looking—boyish even—black, light black, and southern European men dominated Petri's spreads, invoking the ethnic and racial mix of metropolitan cities in Britain—particularly London. They were also markedly groomed to emphasize the sensuality of their features (such as glossy hair, dark shining skin, mouths). This boyish softness, however, was counterpoised by the strong, well-defined features of these men and their developed physiques. The combination of these elements produced an ambivalent masculinity; one which mixed softness and sensuality with a harder, assertive masculinity.

A similar mixture of 'soft' and 'hard' was coded in the Italian-influenced look. This was a 'look' which, whilst not exclusive to him, was also developed by Petri in his early work for the *Face*'s sister magazine *Arena*. It played heavily on a set of motifs and symbols of Italianness, mediated in part through the signs of Italian-Americaness. Figuring prominently in this was the casting of archetypally Italian-looking men. Thus, a dark skin tone, strong features, and a marked sensuality were prominent amongst the models. These features were combined with both other physical characteristics (such as strong chins and noses) and the connotations of the bravado and swagger of an Italian 'macho' to produce the play of 'soft' and 'hard'.

The casting of the models in the Edwardian Englishness spreads—which were strongly represented on the pages of GQ—gave less scope for the coding of this form of masculine sensuality, though it was still present. The models all had pale white skin, with lighter hair and softer features than the Italian-looking models who featured in the Italian 'look' and 'Buffalo' stylings. The styling of the hair, however, was particularly important to the coding of the 'Edwardian Englishness' look'. It was cropped at the sides and back, but left long enough on top to be pushed back. Slightly dressed with hair grease, the weight of the hair on top was also cut to flop forward. This combined the Romantic associations of long hair with the connotations of the masculine discipline and civilized neatness of the 'short back and sides'.

Across all three of the 'looks', the choice and styling of the clothing coded an assertive masculinity. This was one which often emphasized a broad-shouldered and solid body shape. There were significant differences between each of the 'looks', however, in relation to the codes of menswear. The deliberate jumbling of the conventions of menswear in the 'Buffalo' stylings—especially the mixture of tough outerwear with camp accessories—produced some sexually ambivalent codings. In the Italian-influenced look the choice and styling of the clothes, however, was less disruptive of the conventions of menswear than that styled by Petri under the 'Buffalo' label. The 'Edwardian Englishness' stylings on the other hand drew very deliberately on a nostalgic (and conservative) version of menswear and sanctioned less display of the surface of the body.

A common feature of the fashion spreads in which each of the three 'looks' were produced was the intensity of the framing of the models. Through the cropping and placing of the image on the page, the reader's eye was brought close up to the models. This intensity generated by the framing of the model formed one part of the distinctive coding of spectatorship across the imagery. Although these forms of spectatorship were complex, at their most interesting they sanctioned forms of looking which had historically been the prerogative of gay men. In other words, each of the three 'looks'—but most especially Petri's 'Buffalo' stylings—invited the imagined male reader of the magazines to look at men coded as both openly sensual and highly masculine. This look was coded without its homosexuality being pathologized or—it has also to be said—clearly fixed. So, at their most ruptural, what was distinctive about the new codings of masculinity was not—*pace* Mort—their self-consciously gendered address to men, but that they constituted a representational space for the display of masculine sensuality and the coding of sexual ambivalence in the look. In carving out this space, the fashion photography—and the 'new man' imagery in general—resignified the relations between gay and straight-identified men through the codes of style and consumer spectator-ship. In doing so it extended a space for an ambivalent masculine sexual identity which had precedents within the metropolitan con-tours of post-war British popular culture—most spectacularly, within mod subculture in the 1960s, amongst soul boys and Bowie fans in the 1970s, and within the experimentations of 'Blitz' culture and 'New Pop' in the early 1980s. Much harder to read, however, was its significance for relations between men and women. Women occupied a marginal position within this imagery. It was this mar-ginality of women in the regime of 'new man' representations which begin to be targeted by commercial practitioners concerned to delimit the ambivalences thrown up by the imagery.

The Rise of the 'New Lad'

Developments since the end of 1990 in the men's markets associ-ated with style and individual consumption have underlined the specificity of the moment of representation associated with the 'new man'. At the heart of these developments has been the explicit ambition—most clearly articulated within magazine culture—to establish a break with the figure of the 'new man' and an attempt to close down the space of sexual ambivalence associated with it. The publisher Conde Nast's decision to introduce a new editorial mix into GQ in January 1991 (backed up by a high-profile advertising campaign) offered the hardest version of this explicit backlash against the 'new man' within magazine publishing. With un-disguised relish, Conde Nast's publicity proclaimed, 'GQ is proud to announce that the New Man has officially been laid to rest (if indeed he ever drew breath). The 90s man knows who he is, what he wants and where he's going, and he's not afraid to say so. And yes, he still wants to get laid' (Conde Nast press release, Jan. 1991). Figuring strongly in this new editorial approach was the introduc-tion of what was rather euphemistically called 'glamour' in the trade. By this publishers meant the inclusion of sexualized visual representations of women as a main feature in the magazines and an accompanying sexual scrutiny of women in editorial pieces. The introduction of these features marked the more assertive articula-tion of a post-permissive masculine heterosexual script which had been evident in a less strident form within GQ from its launch in the UK in 1988.

Editorial changes, however, were not unique to GQ. Arena also reworked its editorial mix at this time. Its new approach was strongly signalled in its Winter 1990/1 issue which featured a woman on the cover of the magazine for the first time. The cover star was the model Tatjana Patitz, one of the women featured in the issue's main story 'Girls! Girls! Girls! Arena's 100 favourite women (and twenty belles from hell!)'. The piece drew upon a regular feature called 'Women we Love' from the American magazine Esquire, and offered a 'celebration' of women within cinema, comedy, fashion, music, the literary world, and sport. Unsurprisingly, the feature largely revolved around a scrutiny of the women's physical 'looks', though the tone of the written text was informed by Arena's trademark irony and witty irreverence. Thus, in the category 'Word Up, literary spectacles', Jeanette Winterson's entry was accompanied by the line 'What's it with her and fruit', whilst Marge Simpson, the fictional cartoon character from The Simpsons, featured in the 'Women etc, Lest We forget' category together with the line 'Homer, are you blind'.

Accompanying these developments in its editorial, Arena, self-reflexive as ever, offered a cultural analysis of the new masculine identity which it saw its new editorial mix as being addressed to. This was the figure of the 'new lad'. For Sean O'Hagan, author of the piece, the 'new lad' was 'a rather schizoid fellow. He aspires to New Man status when he's with women, but reverts to old man type when he's out with the boys' (Arena, 27, Spring/Summer (1991): 23) For O'Hagan, the 'new lad' was a culturally and generationally specific identity:

he tends to be part of the thirtysomething generation—educated, stylish, more often than not well groomed and totally in tune with the shifting codes of contemporary culture . . . [H]e is well versed in the language, and protocol, of post-feminist discourse and he will never ever, even after a few post-prandial brandies, slip into Sid the Sexist mode like a regular (Jack the) lad might. (Arena, 27, Spring/Summer (1991): 22)

As with GQ's editorial rethink, Arena's address to the 'new lad' marked the more confident articulation of the sexual scripts already established in the magazine and instituted a deepening of its celebration—shot through, in this instance, with Arena's particular avant-garde metropolitanism—of the shared culture of young(ish) heterosexual masculinity and its updated post-permissive scripts of 'cars, girls, sport and booze'.

These editorial rethinks were also accompanied by shifts in the visual codes of masculinity which appeared in the magazines—particularly, within the magazine fashion photography. Three shifts were particularly noteworthy. The first, and perhaps most important, was the less intense framing of masculinity within the images. The second was the decline in the display of masculine sensuality which came largely through changes in casting. The third shift was the display of a harder musculature amongst the models. It is important to state that none of these shifts amounted to a dramatic change in the visual codes of masculinity produced within the magazines. Nonetheless, in the context of the changes in the magazines' editorial material, they did mark the pulling away from the more ambivalent display of masculine sensuality sanctioned in the period 1984–90.

The refocusing of the format of the general interest men's magazines from the end of 1990 around a new target consumer suggested their repositioning in relation to wider formations of masculinity and masculine culture. This was a repositioning driven, like those commercial initiatives around the 'new man', by calculations about shifts in the lived culture of groups of men. The repositioning of GQ and Arena, however, was given further impetus by the launch of IPC's Loaded in March 1994. Its rapid success in terms of circulation figures has transformed the men's magazine sector and associated fields (such as advertising to young men). In particular, it has pushed to new heights of excess the articulation of a post-permissive heterosexual script of 'cars, girls, sport and booze' across the expanding sector of men's magazines. Loaded's founding myth is instructive in understanding its distinctiveness. As Adam Black of the magazine recounted it, 'The idea of Loaded came about at a Leeds vs Barcelona match [. . . James Brown and Tim Southwell, co-founders] saw the match and when they came out into the street afterwards, they thought: "we should make a magazine to replicate this feeling of euphoria" ' (Independent, 26 Apr. 1997: 17).

The story points to the centrality of football culture to the magazine and explains the subsequent predominance of young footballers as exemplary figures on the pages of Loaded. It is these young men who articulate the upfront—often, it seems, wildly dangerous—hedonism celebrated by the magazine and its class-specific version of the good life in which beer and sex go with BMWs. The women who figure in the magazine's version of the good life echo the (working-) class-specific connotations of the 'new lad' script promoted by Loaded. Typified by tabloid stars like Kathy

Resignifying Masculinity

Lloyd and Jo Guest, they are accessible and familiar objects of desire; more girls next door than distant stars. *Loaded*, in this sense, has little truck with haughty or more quirky beauties—Uma Thurman notwithstanding.

At the same time the magazine also celebrates underachievement and juvenility; it aspires to be anti-aspirational. Slumming it, slobbing out, and generally being—in its favourite phrase—'too pissed to bother' are characteristic *Loaded* postures. These attributes were given a distinctly ethnic gloss in one of the regular features in the magazine, 'Greatest Living Englishman'. This celebrated various reprobates and examplars of a certain tradition of British eccentricity, bloody-mindedness, and waywardness. A good deal of this cult of excess and juvenility in *Loaded* is bravado and front, deliberately designed to rub up against more respectable or dynamic masculine scripts. There is also a sense that these postures are performed tongue in cheek—this is, after all, the magazine subtitled 'for men who should know better'. *Loaded* can certainly be read as a magazine for middle-class or lower middle-class young men—like its first editor James Brown—playing at being working-class lads. The magazine's impact, however, has been phenomenal. As I have already suggested, it has pushed *GQ* and *Arena* (together with *Esquire* and *FHM*) further into the use of more explicitly sexualized representations of women and clearly encouraged *Penthouse*, the hardy perennial of the soft-porn market, to relaunch as a style magazine. Furthermore, so-called *Loaded* ladspeak has also been excitedly taken up—to be enjoyed as well as disparaged—by the broadsheet press and by other sectors of the media like advertising agencies. Certainly, *Loaded* ladspeak has encouraged those advertising agencies addressing young men to take into account its expressive idiom. Saatchi & Saatchi's advert for Club 18–30 which led with the copy 'Beaver Espania' and Jo Tanner's and Viv Walsh's advert for the Great Frog Jewellers which concluded with the line 'if you don't like our jewellery fuck-off', most notably, testify to this. These developments have not gone unchallenged in advertising, though they have also generated some prissy responses. As the consultant and cultural critic Peter York put it, 'The new Loaded ladspeak advertising reduces refinement and daintiness in public life' (*Campaign*, 23 July 1996: 3).

Loaded's success and the earlier shifts initiated by *GQ* and *Arena* shed illuminating retrospective light on the cultural significance of the visual codes associated with the 'new man' which I summarized earlier. They underline the novelty I detailed and the importance, as I have argued on a number of occasions, of the space of masculine sexual ambivalence opened up in this moment of representation. There are other lessons, however, which we can derive from the emergence of the 'new lad' within magazine culture. The first is that the 'new lad' is a post-'new man' phenomenon. By this I mean that many of the elements of the 'new lad' were already in place within the representation of the 'new man' (most clearly within magazine culture). This included not only the sexual scripts I have referenced already, but also the persistence of the more elaborated codes of style and individual consumption for men associated with the 'new man'. Secondly, though the language of 'glamour' developed within the magazines certainly marked the confident articulation of an updated post-permissive masculine heterosexual script, it needs to be set in the context of the contemporaneous appropriation of highly feminine and sexualized femininities by young women within magazine culture and beyond. Thus, the use of the term 'babe' to signify a certain kind of femininity was both deployed within the men's magazines as well as appearing in young women's culture as a term positively laid claim to by groups of women. This suggests that to understand fully the significance of these new languages of masculinity and sexual identity we need to situate them within the wider field of gender relations. Such an exercise would also reveal that the 'new lad' has not been the only new masculine identity to emerge in relation to these consumer markets since 1990. The publisher Northern Shell Plc's attempt to address explicitly a mixed male readership of both gay and straight-identified men in its magazine *Attitude* built upon the space of sexual ambivalence opened up by the 'new man'. In particular, *Attitude*'s attempt to mobilize the identity of 'strays'—'straight men who act and think gay or at least hang out with gay men' (as the *Guardian* rather clumsily put it)—was unthinkable without the impact of the 'new man' on magazine culture. Likewise the emergence of queer as a term of self-identification adopted by groups of gay men can be partly attributed to a more entrenched articulation of difference and postioning in relation to the blurring of gay and straight signified by the more ruptural versions of the 'new man'. As such, then, the 'new lad' is one of a number of outcomes within popular representations of masculinity which have followed the emergence of the 'new man'.

Perhaps, however, the most important lesson of the emergence of representations of the 'new lad' in relation to the images I began with concerns the way it points up the difficulty of reinventing masculine heterosexual scripts. This relates to a clear limit position within the shifts in masculinity associated with the 'new man'.

Thus, while the moral language of anti-sexism associated with the sexual politics of the new social movements clearly impacted on the debates about the 'new man' (putting a limited block on the more trenchant sexualized scrutiny of women within magazine publishing, for example) no alternative sexual scripts were fully elaborated. The most interesting development within magazine culture, as I suggested earlier, was *Arena*'s deployment of irony to establish a critical distance from these sexual scripts. However, because no new heterosexual scripts were articulated—scripts that were both sexy and anti-sexist—the opportunity for established scripts to reemerge was always left open. The 'new lad' represents the return of that particular repressed.

There is one final point to make about both the 'new man' and 'new lad' representations which I have been discussing. This concerns the assertion I made at the outset concerning the ethnic particularity of these masculine scripts. It is clear that both the 'new man' and the 'new lad' constituted codings of masculinity in which ethnic meanings also figured strongly. In the case of the more interesting 'new man' codings—notably Petri's 'street style' look—these took up and gave shape to the ethnic and racial mixing celebrated within certain strands of British popular culture. With the 'new lad', on the other hand, a recurrent theme—particularly in *Loaded*—concerned the link between these new scripts of masculinity and the ambiguous, reinvogorated forms of British nationalism condensed in other cultural phenomena such as Britpop and Cool Britannia. Both codings of British ethnicity were important, however, in rooting the shifting codes of masculinity thrown up by the commercial initiatives to expand style and lifestyle consumption amongst British men. They helped to give peculiarly British shape to the resignifying of masculinity within popular cultural forms over the last fifteen years.

Further Reading

Chapman, R., and **Rutherford, J.** (1988), *Male Order: Unwrapping Masculinity*, London: Lawrence & Wishart. A collection of essays exploring the changes in masculinity, including three essays on the 'new man' phenomena.

Mort, F. (1996), *Cultures of Consumption, Masculinities and Social Space in Late Twentieth Century Britain*, London: Routledge. Builds on and refines his earlier 'Boy's Own' essay and contains further discussion of consumption and social space.

Nixon, S. (1996), *Hard Looks: Masculinities, Spectatorship and Contemporary Consumption*, London: UCL Press. Develops in more detail some of the arguments presented here, including attending to advertising and the menswear industry, as well as magazine culture.

Segal, L. (1990), *Slow Motion: Changing Masculinities, Changing Men*, London: Virago. A review of the secondary literature on masculinity, including a discussion of changes associated with the 'new man'.

References

Chapman, R. (1988), 'The Great Pretender: Variations on the New Man Theme', in R. Chapman and J. Rutherford, *Male Order: Unwrapping Masculinity*, London: Lawrence & Wishart.

Coward, R., and Black, M. (1981), 'Linguistic, Social and Sexual Relations: A Review of Dale Spender's Man-Made Language', *Screen Education*, Spring.

Jones, M. (1988), 'We'll Make a Man of You', *Campaign*, 19 Feb. 1988.

Lyttle, J., and Kennedy, B. (1986), 'Wolf in Chic Clothing', *City Limits*, 4–11 Dec.

Melly, G. (1986), 'Why the Tables have Turned on Macho Males', *Campaign*, 18 July 1986.

Moore, S. (1987), 'Target Man', *New Socialist*, Jan. 1987: 4–5

Mort, F. (1988), 'Boy's Own: Masculinity, Style and Popular Culture', in R. Chapman and J. Rutherford, *Male Order: Unwrapping Masculinity*, London: Lawrence & Wishart.

Rutherford, J. (1988), 'Who's that Man?', in R. Chapman and J. Rutherford, *Male Order: Unwrapping Masculinity*, London: Lawrence & Wishart.

Gay Cultures/Straight Borders

KEN PLUMMER

> An understanding of virtually any aspect of modern Western culture must be, not merely incomplete, but damaged in its central substance to the degree that it does not incorporate a critical analysis of modern homo/heterosexual definition.
>
> (Sedgwick 1991: 206)

BEING gay[1] in Britain (as in most of the western world) has been potentially to live life on culture borders: of gender, sexuality, lifestyle, and identity. And until roughly thirty years ago, the borders of gayness were strongly drawn: they were a major (if tacit) organizing feature of British culture. Indeed, I came of age—and 'came out'— in a world where male homosexuality was a crime, a sickness, and a pathology and where the norms regulating gender and sexuality were clearly drawn. What it was to be a man or a woman; what it was to 'have sex'; and who it was permissible to marry were unambiguously clear and sharply defined. Sexual cultures were minimal and hermetically sealed into heterosexuality and familism. What little gay culture might have existed was strictly taboo and pushed to the extreme borders of society. Homosexuals had absolutely no place and no existence in a cultural world (see Westwood 1952; Weeks 1990).

And yet, by the start of the twenty-first century, 'gayness' had come out from this underground and blossomed into a cornucopia of new lifestyles and cultures. It had crossed borders and come to

1 Which term to use
poses formidable
problems. I use 'gay'
here to mean to include
lesbian, bisexual, queer,
homosexual, and the
like. I am fully aware
that they are indeed
different, and to use a
different word would
provide a different story.
I use 'gay' because of
my generation and
history: all words have
their problems.

permeate wider cultures: cabinet ministers became openly gay, television mainstreamed gay programmes (from *Queer as Folk* to *Graham Norton*), and Elton John, superstar, could arrive openly at Princess Diana's funeral with his boyfriend. For those who would wish to look, gay culture is now everywhere to be seen. From being 'the love that dared not speak its name' it has now become a veritable Tower of Babel. It is part of British culture!

Crossing the Borders: The Making of Modern Gay Cultures

How did this come about? Although a much longer history of gay cultures in Britain could be written, I sense four formative, 'symbolic moments' in the post-war period. The Wolfenden Report of 1957 (the result of a commission set up in 1954 after several 'homosexual scandals') established a framework for moral discourse in Britain, arguing for a public space controlled by law and a private space which was not the law's business. Stuart Hall has identified this as 'Wolfenden's double taxonomy: toward stricter penalty and control, towards greater freedom and leniency: together the two elements in a single strategy' (Hall 1980: 14). Ultimately, Wolfenden's proposals came to be enshrined in the Sexual Offences Act 1967, which started decriminalizing homosexuality in England and Wales (but later in Scotland, 1980, and Northern Ireland, 1982). What Wolfenden so clearly reinforced was the culture of the closet. For whilst homosexual acts between consenting adults were no longer illegal, this was only so in private places between two consenting adults. The division of a public and private space was central to this, leaving the stigma of the past still hanging over homosexuality and keeping it a crime in many situations. For most gay men and indeed lesbians (who were not directly touched by the law), this still meant that their lives would be conducted in the closet. Gay cultures have been deeply shaped by this: unable or unwilling—in the main—to tell friends, families, or workmates, the culture of homosexuality has remained one of passing and hiding (Wolfenden Report 1957; Hall 1980; Jeffery-Poulter 1991).

The first 'chink' in this closet appears with the foundation of the Gay Liberation Front, established in October 1970 at the London School of Economics (LSE). Riddled with internal conflicts, it had a short life—effectively dead by 1973. Yet it achieved much: a manifesto; the first large, visible, and public demonstrations by gays; the first large non-commercial dances (initially at the LSE in December 1970); a proliferation of pamphlets (*With Downcast Gays, The*

Anti-psychiatry Group), and a broadsheet (*Come Together*). With slogans, badges, and marches, it raised public awareness of homosexuality in a way that simply had not happened before. It made 'coming out' a major political process at the forefront of gay politics. The tightly policed margins of the past were starting to be punctured. 'Gay was good', and a new visible culture was in the making (Walters 1980; Weeks 1990; Power 1995).

A third defining moment occurs between 1981 and 1986 with the gradual recognition of HIV/Aids. This catastrophic pandemic was another calamity for British gay life (as throughout the world) and it brought chronic illness, early death, and tragic bereavement for many disproportionately young men. But, in an ironic twist, it also brought a major revitalization to a slumbering gay movement and it brought 'gayness' sharply into mainstream focus. Initially through the establishing of the Terence Higgins Trust (THT) in 1982 (by friends of the first British gay man to die with Aids), it got its first government grant of £35,000 in 1985 (King 1993: 208–16). As it became a leading campaign body, it brought a different and more mainstream style of gay politics, one which had to be more professional, more informed, angry but responsible, and capable of working with government and other professionals as part of the Aids industry. It was a cunning moment of assimilation: the margins being further weakened. And from the THT came Crusaid, Body Positive, Positively Women, Blackliners, Mainliners, Frontliners, London Lighthouse. In a most curious paradox, Aids brought benefits to the gay community in making it more visible and making its 'leaders' more professional: they were now actually sitting down and talking to government officials. The borders were moving again (Davies et al. 1993).

A fourth moment came when section 28 of the Local Government Act became law on 24 May 1988. This controversial bill stipulated that a local authority should not intentionally promote homosexuality or teach the acceptability of homosexuality as a 'pretended family relationship' (Colvin and Hawksley 1989; Wilson 1995). It instantly became a rallying cry for the gay movement, symbolizing the disaffection from 'Thatcherism', which had increasingly been marking out not just an economic conservatism, but a moralistic pro-family agenda. Harking back to the 'permissive' era of Roy Jenkins and 1960s Labour, the Tories had been looking for a return to 'basic, family, traditional values'. Whilst they did not have an explicit policy of sexual regulation, Thatcher's 'familism' pervaded all; the initiatives on sexual politics had during the 1980s largely passed to the political Right (cf. Durham 1991). Thatcher herself critically remarked that 'children who need to be taught to respect traditional moral values are being taught that they have an inalienable right to be gay' (Jeffery-Poulter 1991: 218). So whilst section 28 was the immediate cause of the new protest, it was generated by a strong sense of bad times for gays. More: it could also be seen as linked to the arrival of a new generation—a post-GLF grouping who had come of age in the twenty years since the passing of the Sexual Offences Act: young radicals (and professionals) with not much concern for history and the past, just wanting change and wanting it straightaway. This new revitalized movement is generally seen as a 'watershed in the struggle for gay equality' (Jeffery-Poulter 1991: 234), and as 'the coming of age of the gay and lesbian movement' (*Capital Gay*, 18 Mar. 1988). This is another irony: at the very moment when lesbians and gays were seemingly most under attack, a new revitalized community appeared. The borders by now were becoming weaker and weaker, as gays and lesbians moved into many public spaces, and claimed cultures of their own.

Shaping the Cultures: Taboo, Gender, Desire, and Identity

Even as gay culture has become more and more mainstream, it remains deeply shaped by four boundaries which it has to cross over. In the past, these boundaries were almost uncrossable: today, they have shifted. But they are still there and they give an elementary shape to the way gay cultures work. They help organize the ways of life that can be identified as gay.

The first border highlights taboo. Homophobia, heterosexism, stigmatized difference, marginality—all lead many gay lives to evolve strategies of passing and hiding—a splitting strategy of being 'in' or 'out'. It leads to gay cultures being—to varying degrees—*cultures of the closet*. British culture could be approached through this metaphor of the closet—with most people hiding their identities through the development of a repertoire of concealment and passing strategies. It is a theme which haunts gay life: from 'bunburying' (inventing fictional friends to ease a deception) in Oscar Wilde's *The Importance of Being Earnest*, to the first major British film about gays—*Victim* (1962), where blackmail is a major concern. But its mirror image—'coming out'—becomes more and more significant through the last decades of the century. It is the key to GLF in 1970, where 'coming out' may be seen as its most crucial political dimension; and it turns into a major political debate during the 1990s when the issue of 'outing' famous but closeted gays becomes an increasing concern. Yet even though, at the turn of the century, very substantial numbers of gays and lesbians are 'out', it is still the case that the culture is heavily closeted. Many are only 'out' within the organized 'scene' or to a few friends: remaining closeted at school and from family, workplace, and strangers. Taboo and the closet remain major features of gay life (cf. Sedgwick 1991; Seidman et al. 1999).

Secondly, homosexuality sits on the borders of gender, rendering it as *cultures of campness, drag, and gender irony*. Clear gender roles, presumed heterosexuality, the centrality of 'familism'; all these lead many gay lives to evolve an ironic code for living on what may be seen as the gender borders. It is to be found everywhere in gay culture: in the popularity of 'drag' within gay circles; in the role playing of (some) lesbians into 'butch and femme' (O'Sullivan 1999); in the effeminacy of many gay men during the 1950s which turns by the 1970s into a 'masculinist, macho clone'—exemplified by the Village People—and, in the 1990s, the emergence of a rough-trade skinhead look as a popular style (Healy 1996); in the championing of bisexual culture (Bi-Academic Intervention, 1997). It is also seen in the strong strain of campness running through it. In early days, for instance, it was present in the *Carry On* films, radio programmes like *Round the Horn*, TV comedies like *Are You Being Served*; and in stars like the late Kenneth Williams and Frankie Howard, continued through Julian Clary and Graham Norton (Howes 1993; Simpson 1994). It was present at early GLF meetings with the 'radical faeries'; and it continues today in the 'politics of queer': where bisexuality, transgender politics, and gender bending are prominent.

Third, homosexuality contrasts with the dominant heterosexual order, rendering it also as *cultures of dissident desire*. Whereas the dominant culture presumes a heterosexual coitus, everything about gay life does not. Gay desire speaks of masturbation, anal sex, oral sex, fetishes, pornography, cybersex, sadomasochism—of a world full of sexual possibilities outside the so-called conventional. Some of this helps organize key features of the gay world—bars, magazines and literature, dress and dress codes—and much of it seeps out, so to speak, into the wider culture through safer sex campaigns, advertising, and fashion. Certain spaces of gay culture create a heightened sexual sensibilty—in dress, in looks, in cruising. And there are dense areas of 'hot sex' and 'raunch': telephone sex lines, porn, hustling, clothing fetishes, back rooms, leather, fisting, rimming, dyke balling. Thus, for instance, one 'hot topic' within lesbian and gay life over the past twenty years has been SM: it has become well organized in the male gay world; it has split the women's movement in many directions. It led to stormy debates when the London Lesbian and Gay Centre was established; and it hit the public headlines in 1992 when 'Operation Spanner' involved the police arresting a group of gay sadomasochists who were subsequently found guilty and sent to prison (although an appeal was made to the European Court of Human Rights). Ironically, again, this certainly increased its visibility—and possibly its practice. And it should be clear that this is not just a male world: though lesbians remain sharply divided over this, many celebrate the rise of the 'new dildocracy', with explicit sex magazines such as *Quim*, radical—often SM—lesbian photographers such as Della Grace and Tessa Boffin, and sex radical groups such as PUSSY (Perverts Undermining State Scrutiny) (cf. Healy 1996). And again some of it is taken over into heterosexual worlds, making such concerns more visible. Indeed, in part we may see the homosexualization of heterosexual culture (cf. Altman 1982).

Despite these heightened cultures of eroticism within gay cultures, they should not be overstated. In one of the major studies of gay men's sexual behaviour in Britain, the authors conclude that 'among very many respondents there is a clear preference for a small number of fairly unremarkable acts' (Davies et al. 1993: 105). Masturbation is the most common by far (but of least interest to health professionals) whilst anal intercourse turns out to be not that common at all (though of greatest interest to health professionals!). Nevertheless, it is the extremes that attract attention and it is these which render parts of gay cultures as sexual outlaws, transgressors, and radicals.

A fourth shaping feature of gay culture is the issue of identity, creating *cultures of gay identification*. Indeed, gay identity has been at the core of gay culture in the recent past, though there are some signs this is changing. Identities structure borders—of who is in and who is out—and help provide a history of one's past, a sense of being different from others in the present, along with a possible guide to the future. And the process of telling the story of a gay identity is one of the key organizing narratives of modern gay life (Plummer 1995). Three main issues surround this. One highlights the ways gay identities are built up—looking at the various stages a man or woman may pass through in 'going gay'. Often this is a move from a simple confusion and shame to a full-blown and positive sense of self. A second concern is the politics of identity—the ways in which the very category of 'being gay or lesbian' may be linked to the lesbian and gay movement and turned into a challenging political category around which mobilization may take place. In a key way, this is exactly what took place in the UK between the emergence of the radical GLF in 1970 and the huge rallies protesting against section 28 in 1987. A sexual identity became a political one. But most recently a third issue no longer sees the importance of the gay identity and attempts to deconstruct it. This is the day of the 'pomo homo' or the postmodern 'queer'— who rejects strong identities as being built on a binary system of gay/straight; and seeks instead to challenge such 'essentialist' categorizations through a transgressive sexual politics. Once again, we are in the land of the 'bisexual imagination' and the transgender queer.

Moving the Borders: Diversification in Modern Gay Cultures

The march from Wolfenden through GLF and HIV to section 28 may be seen as a gay culture assembling itself around various borders, creating in effect the most visible forms of gay life in Britain. This is evidenced by those hugely symbolic rallying events of gay culture Gay Pride Marches. When they started in 1972 in London, they attracted only 2,000 people: by the 1990s a quarter of a million took to the streets. From small beginnings, large cultures have grown.

But they are *cultures* and not *a culture*. Like all lived cultures, they are never coherent, stable, and fixed but always in shifting process, inchoate ambiguity, and full of dialectical tension and contradiction. They are composed of a multiplicity of social worlds which interpenetrate each other (often, these days, globally); and they are deeply embedded in the dynamics of inequality and social division, profoundly patterned by class, ethnicity, gender, age, disablement, and the like. Just as social exclusion works its way through dominant worlds, so too gay cultures consistently get depicted as white, middle class, young and beautiful (as a glance at any of the main UK British gay magazines would reveal and as the popular television series *Queer as Folk* strongly suggests). Yet gay cultures themselves generate their own borders and margins. Thus class, age, and ethnic borders structure divides within gay cultures. The life worlds of the Elton John super-rich are at extreme odds with those of a gay underclass of unemployed and homeless. The situation of an ageing, wealthy, closeted Cambridge 'don' can hardly be compared with the situation of a young, black, lesbian care assistant raising her child and working long hours for little pay in a nursing home. In many ways, working-class gays and lesbians have been consistently marginalized in gay communities: patterns of wealth—and patterns of consumption—differ sharply across gay lives and the lifecycle. Yet somehow gay culture itself is most frequently represented as white, male, middle class. In this it reflects a dominant class strategy: to reproduce the existing order as if it were middle class. The relation of gay cultures to class cultures has been seriously under-explored, and it is a dynamic tension within gay culture.

There is, then, no one gay culture but a multiplicity of such cultures. And a danger is that many commentators, journalists, gay people, and gay politicos speak only for small fragments of it. Only some voices are ever heard. There is, I believe, a vast network of gay and lesbian experiences involving several million people, and largely hidden from sight, which involves friendship networks, partnerships, isolates, and 'casual experimenters'. It constitutes a huge underbelly of gay life in Britain today. It is little discussed.

But what could be called the 'gay scene' is very different: it is this which gets the attention. It is much more visible, usually youthful, predominantly white and middle class, relatively 'out', and heavily male, though women are more prominent now than in the past. It includes such institutions as gay media, bars and clubs, health clubs, tourism, political activism, cruising grounds, community support services, and most recently cyberspaces. A look through the pages of *Gay Times* will soon provide a sense of the range of cultures on offer.[2] The gay media itself has moved from its humble but radical origins in *Gay News* (in 1972) through the creation of a 'free press' distributed through bars and meeting places during the 1980s (*Capital Gay*, *The Pink Paper*, *Boyz*) and on to the mass circulation in the 1990s of *Shebang*, *Diva*, *Attitude*, *Phase*: glossy, glitzy and nowhere near so directly political as their predecessors (cf. Burston and Richardson 1995). The quintessential institutions of gay life are the bars, and they come in many forms: dyke bars, dance bars, coffee bars, tea dance bars, pick up bars, drag bars, strip bars, piano bars, sleaze bars, back room bars, SM bars, fetish bars, 'rent' bars, hotel bars. Alongside these are gay and lesbian groups for all: Jewish, Irish, Welsh, Cypriots, Turkish, Black, and Asian; for swimming, cricket, running, scuba diving, sailing, walking, badminton, cycling, squash, mountaineering, volleyball, and football; for the deaf, the blind, the disabled; for the young, the student, the old, the parent; for the Christian, the Catholic, the Christian Scientist, the pagan, the humanist, the spiritualist; for barristers, firemen, librarians, and accountants; for choirs and the arts; for bridge, classic cars, and real

2 What follows is a selection of items listed in the *Gay Times* Guide section, 20 Mar. 1998: 119–21.

ale drinkers. And along with all these come the cultures of self-help social worlds: from a vast network of HIV/Aids care, switchboards, drop-ins, counselling, befriending, 'pink counselling', and specialist groups like those for homeless teenagers, bisexuals, family and friends, legal worries, bereavement, parenting. There are also academic worlds—a growing range of books and courses which establish Lesbian and Gay Studies as an academic discipline (cf. Plummer 1992; Wilton 1995; Medhurst and Munt 1997); along with a string of political groupings: from radical queers in Outrage to the assimilationist and professional lobby in Stonewall (see Plummer 1999, where I discuss these splits). And in the midst of all this are the newly emerging cyberqueers, where the 'web' becomes an increasingly important way of communicating across global gay communities (cf. Wakeford 1997).

With so much going on, the diversity of gay cultures may be seen as expressing a mirror image of the wider and dominant cultures. There is no space here to analyse all this, except to note two key recent trends: the push towards growing urbanization—the creation of queer spaces such as 'the Village' in Manchester and 'Soho' in London (Quilley 1997; Whittle 1994)—and the trend towards a gay consumerism and a massive commercialization (Field 1995: ch. 4). Many of the radical ideals of the earlier gay movement (which was often 'left based' and produced magazines like *Gay Left*) now get swamped in a world of 'Gay Lifestyle Events (the Ideal Homo)', Gay business organizations, 'Boyz culture', and 'Lipstick Lesbians'. To look at the 150-page glossy full-colour catalogue of *Gay Pride 96* is to enter an apolitical world of clubbing, Calvin Kleins, Mr Gay UK, designer beers, body piercing, kitchen styles, dream houses, gay holidays, gay marriages, themed parties, suntan products, gyms for the body beautiful, antiques, flash cars, internets, financial services, dance, video, and media of all forms; and all this sandwiched between ads for Benetton, Eyeworks, Virgin Vodka, Mercury, Buffalo Boots, and American Express! With this, gay cultures have come a long way from the margins. As Chris Woods remarks in an analysis of all this: 'The politically active in the community have been marginalised in the interest of profit' (Woods 1995: 45), and it has led to the 'Anti-Gay' Movement within gay culture itself, which decries the visible shallowness of much contemporary gay culture (Simpson 1996; cf. Sinfield 1998).

One might end by noting that, while the borders demarcating straight and gay cultures have shifted in recent years, nonetheless, there are those who seek to maintain and police them. In May 1999, right in the heart of the Gay Village in Soho and right in the heart of a gay pub, a bomb went off, killing three and seriously injuring many. The bombing was part of a wider series of bomb attacks, by a seriously disturbed man with far-right links, who also targeted the Asian community in East London and the black population in Brixton. In the wake of the bombing what became evident was the wide support available for the gay community from the 'straight' community. The tragic incident highlighted the continuing double bind within which British gay cultures find themselves. Gay cultures have travelled a long way in the past century; but although they have shifted borders in this process, they still remain firmly on them.

Further Reading

The classic history of early gay life in the UK is contained in Jeffrey Weeks's *Coming Out: Homosexual Politics in Britain from the Nineteenth Century to the Present*, and it is updated in a 1990 revision (London: Quartet Books). A lively inventory of gay culture can be found in Keith Howes's hugely entertaining *Broadcasting It: An Encyclopedia of Homosexuality on Film, Radio and TV in the UK 1923–1993* (London: Cassell, 1993). The sociology of homosexuality is well represented in Peter Nardi and Beth Schneider's edited collection *Social Perspectives on Gay and Lesbian Studies* (London: Routledge, 1998). A good introduction to Queer Studies in the UK is to be found in Andy Middleton and Sally R. Munt (eds.), *Lesbian and Gay Studies: A Critical Introduction* (London: Cassell, 1997).

References

Bristow, Joseph, and **Wilson, Aneglia R.** (eds.) (1993), *Activating Theory: Lesbians, Gay, Bisexual Politics*, London: Lawrence & Wishart.

Burston, Paul, and **Richardson, Colin** (1995), *A Queer Romance: Lesbians, Gay Men and Popular Culture*, London: Routledge.

Colvin, Madeleine, and **Hawksley, Jane** (1989), *Section 28: A Practical Guide to the Law and its Implications*, London: National Council for Civil Liberties.

Cooper, Davina (1994), *Sexing the City*, London: Rivers Oram Press.

Davies, Peter, Hickson, Ford, Weatherburn, Peter, and **Hunt, Andrew** (1993), *Sex, Gay Men and AIDS*, London: Falmer Press.

Altman, Dennis (1982), *The Homosexualization of America: The Americanization of the Homosexual*, New York: St Martin's Press.

Durham, Martin (1991), *Sex and Politics: The Family and Morality in the Thatcher Years*, London: Macmillan.

Edge, Simon (1995), *With Friends Like These: Marxism and Gay Politics*, London: Cassell.

Epstein, Debbie, Johnson, R., and **Steinberg, D.** (2000), 'Twice Told Tales: Transformation, Recuperation and Emergence in the Age of Consent Debates', *Sexualities*, 3/1.

Evans, David (1993), *Sexual Citizenship*, London: Routledge.

Field, Nicola (1995), *Over the Rainbow: Money, Class and Homophobia*, London: Pluto Press.

Hall, Stuart (1980), 'Reformism and the Legislation of Consent', in National Deviancy Conference (eds.), *Permissiveness and Control: The Fate of the Sixties Legislation*, London: Macmillan.

Healy, Murray (1996), *Gay Skins: Class, Masculinity and Queer Appropriation*, London: Cassell.

Howes, Keith (1993), *Broadcasting It*, London: Cassell.

Jeffery-Poulter, Stephen (1991), *Peers, Queers and Commons: The Struggle for Gay Law Reform from 1950 to the Present*, London: Routledge.

Jeffreys, Sheila (1990), *Anticlimax: A Feminist Perspective on Sexual Liberation*. London: Women's Press.

King, Edward, (1993), *Safety in Numbers*, London: Cassell.

McIntosh, Mary (1997), 'Class', in Medhurst and Munt (1997).

Medhurst, Andy, and **Munt, Sally R.** (eds.) (1997), *Lesbian and Gay Studies: A Critical Introduction*, London: Cassell

O'Sullivan, Sue (1999), 'I Don't Want You Anymore: Butch/Femme Disappointments', *Sexualities*, 2/4.

Plummer, Ken (ed.) (1992), 'Speaking its Name: Inventing a Lesbian and Gay Studies', in K. Plummer (ed.), *Modern Homosexualities: Fragments of Lesbian and Gay Experience*, London: Routledge.

—— (1995), *Telling Sexual Stories: Power, Change and Social Worlds*, London: Routledge.

—— (1999), 'The Lesbian and Gay Movement in the UK 1965–1995: Schisms, Solidarities and Social Worlds', in Barry Adam, Jan Willem Duyvendak, and André Krouwel (eds.), *Gay and Lesbian Movements since the 1960's*, Philadelphia: Temple University Press.

Power, Lisa (1995), *No Bath But Plenty of Bubbles*. London: Cassell.

Quilley, Stephen (1997), 'Constructing Manchester's "New Urban Village": Gay Space in the Entrepreneurial City', in G. Ingram, A. Bouthillette, and Y. Rettered (eds.), *Queers in Space: Communities/Public Places/Sites of Resistance*, Seattle: Washington Bay Press.

Sedgwick, Eve Kasofsky (1991), *Epistemology of the Closet*, London: Harvester Wheatsheaf.

Seidman, Steven, Meeks, C., and **Traschen, F.** (1999), 'Beyond the Closet?' *Sexualities*, 2/1.

Simpson, Mark (1994), *Male Impersonators*, London: Cassell.

—— (ed.) (1996), *Anti-Gay*, London: Cassell.

Sinfield, Alan (1998), *Gay and After*, London: Serpent's Tail.

Smith, Anna Marie (1994), *New Right Discourse on Race and Sexuality: Britain 1968–1990*, Cambridge: Cambridge University Press.

Wakeford, Nina (1997), 'Cyberqueer', in Medhurst and Munt (1997).

Walters, Aubrey (ed.) (1980), *Come Together: The Years of Gay Liberation (1970–1973)*, London: GMP.

Weeks, Jeffrey (1990), *Coming Out: Homosexual Politics in Britain from the Nineteenth Century to the Present*, 2nd edn., London: Quartet Books.

Westwood, Gordon (1952), *Society and the Homosexual*, London: Gollancz.

Whittle, Stephen (ed.) (1994), *The Margins of the City: Gay Men's Urban Lives*, Aldershot: Ashgate Publishing.

Wilkinson, Sue (1996), 'Bisexuality as Backlash', in L. Harne and E. Miller, *All the Rage: Reasserting Radical Lesbian Feminism*, London: Women's Press.

Wilson, Angelia R. (ed.) (1995), *A Simple Matter of Justice: Theorising Lesbian and Gay Politics* London: Cassell.

Wilton, Tamsin (1995), *Lesbian Studies: Setting an Agenda*, London: Routledge.
Wolfenden Report (1957), *Report of the Departmental Committee on Homosexual Offences and Prostitution*, London: HMSO, Cmnd. 247.
Woods, Chris (1995), *State of the Queer Nation: A Critique of Gay and Lesbian Politics in 1990's Britain*, London: Cassell.

Sport, Leisure, and Style

ALAN
TOMLINSON

Introduction

T. S. Eliot recognized, in the late 1940s in his famous formulation of English culture, the importance of sport in any list of 'the characteristic activities and interests of a people: Derby Day, Henley Regatta, Cowes, the twelfth of August, a cup final, the dog races, the pin table, the dart board, Wensleydale cheese, boiled cabbage cut into sections, beetroot in vinegar, nineteenth-century Gothic churches and the music of Elgar' (1962: 31). Indeed, the Caribbean intellectual and critic C. L. R. James asserted that 'cricket and football were the greatest cultural influences in nineteenth-century Britain, leaving far behind Tennyson's poems, Beardsley's drawings and the concerts of the Philharmonic society. These filled space in print but not in minds' (James 1994: 64). Sport has long had prominence in English (and British) culture, and the ways in which it has changed can be read as symptomatic of key changes in the social and cultural life of Britain; sport as a moral site for the making of national and sometimes regional identity has been equalled and in many respects exceeded in importance by sport and leisure consumerism as a source for the expression of new cultural identities (Veblen 1953). In this chapter the cultural and political legacy of sport and athleticism is examined; the aestheticization and commodification of the sporting body reviewed; and the ascendancy of sporting style over the older claimed values of sport discussed in relation to issues of access and identity.

Sport, Athleticism, and Cultural Change

The roots of athleticism in Britain were planted in the nineteenth-century public schools (Girouard 1981: ch. 11; Holt 1990; Hargreaves 1986), in which an 'ideology of athleticism'—'a complex of ideas and feelings deliberately and carefully created through ritual and symbol' (Mangan 1981: 6)—was established. This was based upon the belief of physical educators within the public schools that physical education and sport would cultivate physical and moral courage, loyalty and co-operation, the capacity to act fairly and take defeat well, and the ability to command and obey (Mangan 1981: 9). Such beliefs reverberated far beyond the playing fields and gymnasia of the institutions themselves, based as they were in wider theories of cultural reproduction which claimed competitive sport both as ethical, and as morally transferable to the world beyond the playing field (McIntosh 1979: 27).

The public schools therefore developed sport as a vehicle for the transmission of moral values to newly educated generations of upper-class and middle-class males. Testimony to the longevity of this process is found in the reminiscences of English cricket commentator Brian Johnstone (Johnstone 1990: 1), echoing classic Edwardian beliefs (see Dobbs 1973: 28) in the character-forming benefits of the game. There is a clear manifesto here for the production of a disciplined individual living by a socially acceptable behavioural code and acting according to a desired set of moral values. Such a view of sport was also held by Conservative Prime Minister, prominent Scottish landowner, Cambridge philosopher, and golf enthusiast A. J. Balfour. Balfour's triangular social circuit comprised Westminster and the elite social circles of London; weekends in grand houses within easy reach of London; and excursions, particularly in parliamentary recesses, and at North Berwick (close to the England–Scotland border), to small hotels or accommodation near his favourite golf courses: 'He remembered his golfing holidays as the happiest hours of his life' (Ridley and Percy 1992: 37), and his enthusiasm helped golf become fashionable. Balfour could write in 1899 of how golf could provide the pleasures of both exercise and nature, rooted in his 'firm conviction . . . that there is no public interest of greater importance than the public interest of providing healthy means of recreation for all classes in the community' (Balfour 1912: 276). Sports and recreation in state schools in the first half of the twentieth century also reflected such principles of rational recreation, seeing sport as both moral improvement and social discipline. In 1928, for instance, the Sheffield Corporation

Alan Tomlinson

Physical Training Department could state that 'manly vigorous play in healthy surroundings [is] the antidote to cramped home and school conditions; is the preventive treatment of ailments'; and could make boys fitter for industrial life (Fishwick 1989: 4). Mangan (1986) has demonstrated how such beliefs were also framed in a universalist imperialist sense, good English games being seen as important dimensions of the remit of missionaries in the colonies, and useful for the taming of the indigenous cultural practices of conquered native populations. The taming presence of the muscled white body has persisted in representational depictions of the white man's role and impact in the colonial context: 'the built body and the imperial enterprise are analogous . . . The built white male body and colonial enterprise act as mirrors of each other, and both, even as they display the white man's magnificent corporeality, tell of the spirit within' (Dyer 1997: 165).

The transformation of this traditional sports culture was accomplished, particularly from the mid-twentieth century onwards, under the influence of the expanding media profile of sport, accompanying new forms of finance and economy underpinning the culture of elite professional sports, and concomitant forms of spectating. Whannel has referred to this as 'a period of transformation which constitutes a remaking of British sport' (Whannel 1986: 129; 1992). Television and sponsorship have produced a cultural transformation whereby 'the traditional, amateur, benevolent paternalism of sport's organisation came under pressure from entrepreneurial interests as the contradiction between sport's financially deprived organisations and its commercial potential widened' (Whannel 1986: 130). Traditional organizations of sport were undemocratic and elitist, particularly in class, gender, and ethnic terms, yet dedicated in a voluntarist way to service and resource distribution. An opportunistic entrepreneurialism brought more money into selected sports, and, from the earliest days of professionalism in sports such as football and Rugby League in the north-west of England in particular, released its meritocratic and democratic potential. This—as with any significant cultural shift—did not of course happen overnight. It is interesting to observe the survival of some sports, for instance, from the very early industrial period into the later twentieth century. Two such sports highlighted by Holt (1990: 67) are knur-and-spell (also known as tipping, or poor man's golf) in the north of England (Tomlinson 1992); and the Celtic sport of hurling (also known as shinty) in the Scottish Highlands (Whitson 1983). But these survived very much in residual (Williams 1977) terms, out of step with what Bourdieu (1989: 310

and 311) sees as the 'ethical retooling' of the 'new bourgeoisie'; and a world away from the 'mobile privatization' (Williams 1974, 1983; Philips and Tomlinson 1992: 16–17) so characteristic of the new consumer culture. Emergent forms of consumerism and market forces increasingly determined the shape of sports (Mason 1989).

By the last years of the twentieth century the traditional culture of athleticism, in which amateurs could effortlessly aspire to gold at low-profile Olympic Games, was long gone. British athletics had experienced its boom years in the early days of professionalism, television revenue, and significant sponsorship in the 1980s, only to overpay top athletes in non-competitive races, to reallocate huge and scarcely accounted for cash sums, and for its main federation to be declared bankrupt in 1997. In football, the English Premier League clubs, on the basis of Sky Television revenues and energetic marketing and merchandizing of club-branded products and paraphernalia, were wealthier than ever before. Top clubs, in the wake of a European judgment in the famous Jean-Marc Bosman case (which made national leagues' contract and transfer regulations obsolete), redistributed unprecedentedly high sums in players' and coaches' wages to a galaxy of foreign as well as home-grown stars; and a handful of Premier clubs followed up the France '98 World Cup with secret negotiations with a consortium seeking to establish a pay-per-view European super league, with no relegation from or promotion to it. The European body UEFA responded by expanding its Champions League format still more, whilst the world body FIFA launched its plans for a world club championship that would inevitably disrupt domestic schedules (drawing Manchester United into the politics of England's 2006 World Cup bid). Sport—a century earlier in its amateur, athleticist form a source for moral preachings and experiments in character-building (Almond 1893; Ensor 1898)—was now a significant player in the global leisure and cultural industries. Some old motifs persisted—the Conservative government of John Major proposed a sports policy (*Raising the Game*, see Department of National Heritage 1995) which could have come straight out of the files of nineteenth-century apologists of the empire, in its stress upon the values of traditional team games and its concern for the expression of national identity. Major's Sports Minister Ian Sproat could write, in January 1994, of his claimed 'revolution' in school sports, that aerobics or rambling were not part of the solution to the country's sporting needs: 'I want team games properly organized, competitive team games, preferably those sports *we* invented such as soccer, rugby, hockey, cricket and netball (my italics)' (cited in Holt and Tomlinson 1994:

452). New Labour confirmed sport's raised political profile, pointing to how 'art, sport and leisure are vital to our quality of life and
the renewal of our economy', and 'central to the task of recreating
the sense of community, identity and civic pride that should define
our country' (Labour Party 1997: 30). To this end, New Labour
reaffirmed school sports as 'the foundation', and committed
'full-backing to the bid to host the 2006 football World Cup in
England' (ibid.), despite the realpolitik of European and world football organization (Sugden and Tomlinson 1998: 121–4). Away from
the rhetoric of the politicians, the pedagogic ideals of the physical
educators, and the stadiums of the elite, sport's profile within the
wider cultural and leisure industries was becoming more prominent, linked to lifestyle choices and the articulation of various
dimensions of identity and style. This was especially true of black
youth cultures, in which sport and sporting style beyond just the
mainstream sports contributed to 'the plurality of black cultural
expression as it is lived and experienced through social interaction',
the 'black leisure sphere . . . a site for the creative contestation
between the individual and the collective' (Alexander 1996: 105 and
106). Hoberman's (1997: 44) reminder in the US context that 'sport
and music are the two great theaters of black style' is echoed in
British research. Back (1996: 225) has argued that dialogues between
and across black musical traditions and innovations have produced
'new intermezzo cultures' which have had widespread influence
across both black and white leisure practices. Around youth leisure
and style, McRobbie claims, it is necessary 'to pay greater attention
to the space of inter-racial, interactive experience and to explore the
processes of hostility, fascination and desire which penetrate and
shape the nature of these encounters' (1994: 188).

Style in Contemporary British Sport and Leisure Cultures

Style, for Ewen (1990: 43), has at least three important roles—as
self, society, and information—in contemporary consumer society:
first, as a 'critical factor in definitions of the self'; second, in the
institutional images through which we understand society; and
third, as 'a basic form of information within our society'. As old
sports have been modernized, and new sports and physical activities
marketed, sport's profile as a source for the expression of personal
and cultural identity has increased. Sports themselves, as cultural
forms and social institutions, have presented themselves in ways
increasingly concerned with a recognizable style—in top-class

football, the corporate logo of the UEFA Champions League or the logo or brand of the shirt sponsor now dominant over and above the traditional club crest or badge. And sport has been reinvented as style in organs of popular communication, from the broadcast media through to the newer print media of the glossy and ruthlessly niched magazine market.

Sport and leisure practices, cultures and choices are statements of selfhood and identity, whether at an individual or more collective level. As such, they represent what Poirier (citing primarily literary examples) sees as a 'remarkable opportunity' for human beings: 'the release of energy into measured explorations of human potentialities . . . one way, at least, of defining "the performing self"' (Poirier 1971: p. xiii). Basketball in the USA in the 1990s has been linked to the visual culture of the music video, and hailed as, 'like music, a cultural venue heavy on history and substance' (Boyd 1997: 117 and 127).

The phenomenal success of the Arsenal football fan and writer Nick Hornby, in his confessional account of his 'fan's life', *Fever Pitch*, offers a performance angle on the spectating self. This publishing phenomenon has found its way onto the revolving bookshelves across the airport shops of the world, and spawned a mass of imitative initiatives in which sport is linked to personal issues of selfhood, sexuality, and status, and more public issues of community, collective identity, and nostalgia. Backlashes inevitably follow successes such as Hornby's, and critic Boyd Tonkin regrets the 'self-lacerating' Hornby hero, and the passionless and 'flat two-dimensional space' in which such a character moves, even in the representation of 'sporting monomania' in *Fever Pitch* (Tonkin 1998: 49). But the book struck a remarkably resonant chord in 1990s popular culture, in which social and personal crises and inadequacies could now be catalogued and linked to previously unfashionable forms of public culture such as football. Alongside, even before, the revelations and death of Diana, Princess of Wales, Hornby's book signalled a new respectability and popularity for the confessional search for self and authentic identity. For Hornby, the fortunes of a former Arsenal player could 'take on a shamanistic quality' (Hornby 1992: 123), in which the player is portrayed as the priest-like presence who in an earlier, easier time could ensure that the gods were smiling upon Hornby and his lovelife. What a mere few years before would have been received as toe-curlingly uncool was the harbinger of a style which blended a newly popular and respectable football culture—way beyond the old boundaries of unreflexive and repressive masculinity—with an emerging rhetoric of Cool Britannia. In 1994 David Baddiel, co-author of the English football anthem 'Three Lions' two summers later for the Euro '96 event, wrote of 'intellectuals coming out of the closet . . . singing, crying and clutching copies of *Fever Pitch* because they feel safe, at last admitting' their attraction to the game (cited in King 1995: 309). Haynes (1995: 113–14) comments that despite the wide impact of the book, Hornby's memoir is essentially constitutive of a male identity. But it is the vulnerability of that male identity that echoes throughout *Fever Pitch*. It is the fragility of cultural and sexual identity—and football culture as part resolution to this, in the search for authenticity—that dominates the obsessional Hornby narrative, and accounts for the breadth of its impact. It also followed on from the tears of Paul Gascoigne during the 1990 World Cup in Italy, commissioned 'in response to the new cultural position of football . . . which the media conglomerates had a major role and interest in creating' (King 1995: 307; on *Fever Pitch*, see pp. 296–9). *Fever Pitch*, and other forms of sport and leisure writing and initiatives, opened up wider markets for newly stylized forms of sport and leisure consumption.

Style as self. A performing self has embodied the intensifying connectedness of sport and style in an expanding culture of consumerism. The obvious focus for such developments has been the body (Scott and Morgan 1993; Shilling 1993; Featherstone and Turner 1995: 6). 'Being in the world in the 1990s', comments Hall (1998: 40), 'requires, more than hitherto, a styling of the self, a settlement in and with one's own body.' Hargreaves has pointed to the significance of the body in consumer culture and sports culture, in their shared 'capacity to accommodate the body meaningfully in the constitution of the normal individual' (1987: 150). Increasingly, this 'normal individual' is far from homogeneous, in a global consumer culture in which a 'Black Atlantic world' establishes 'the popularity of a figure like Michael Jordan in lives of British youth, regardless of his American "origins"' (Andrews et al. 1996: 448).

The rise in popularity of activities such as keep-fit and aerobics, heralded as health-based initiatives but quite as much to do with fashion and image, has been striking in the last quarter of the twentieth century. This was true for both men and women, though more radical and important for women, as traditional patterns continued to characterize their levels and modes of involvement in sport. Even in new sports like windsurfing, it was 'privileged women who had the opportunity to gain access to the culture' (Wheaton and Tomlinson 1998: 270). In the 1980s women's participation in outdoor sports remained very much lower than men's, and actually fell through the mid-1980s. Women were, though, participating in higher numbers in those sports which could be undertaken in the safety and comfort of an indoor venue, and which provided both health and self-image benefits (Sports Council and Women's Sports Foundation 1992). The overlap of the cultural and the fashion industries, and the sports culture, made aerobics the most prominent growth sport for women. But participation in such activities brought with it too contradictions and tensions: the aerobics class may be a safe haven, but also renders the body vulnerable to the gaze of others (Flintoff et al. 1995: 98 and 99). The sporting body can be marginalized or appropriated by the dominant culture, as the sculptured body of the physically empowered woman can be either labelled as threatening, or constructed as sexually desirable and an object of the male gaze (Hargreaves 1994: 160–2; Willis 1982; Tomlinson 1997). The muscled black body, too, in populist mass media, has been widely depicted as one or other of the stereotyped images of sexually attractive but threatening beast, or comic joker, as Carrington's work on black British sportsmen Frank Bruno (boxing) and Linford Christie (athletics) has so vividly shown (Carrington 1998, 2000).

The body as vehicle for the expression of the self has in turn spawned a wide range of activity accessories and fashion aids: the leotard, the trainer/sports shoe, the jogging suit, leggings, sweatshirts and sweatbands, toiletries, bags, lotions, soft drinks. In an increasingly fierce global market any pause in growth is pause for gloom for the expansionist cultural industries. In November 1997 the jeans manufacturer Levi Strauss announced that it was to close eleven factories, due to disappointing sales. The trainer market, it was feared, would follow suit. Paul Fireman, chairman of Reebok, could warn of a 'consumer rebellion' against the most expensively marketed brands, such as his own and those of rivals Nike and Adidas (Crowe 1998: 24). But at the same time as US sales growth had halved in the period 1996 to 1997, demand in the UK remained high, accounting for 18 per cent of all shoe sales. Particular target markets were women, and fashion-conscious youth. A BMRB (British Market Research Bureau) survey of over 6,000 young people in 1993, zooming in on the consumer potential of around 9 million 7–19-year-olds, calculated that they were directly involved in £8 million of disposable income, and indirectly involved in still greater levels of expenditure. Of the 7–10-year-olds, 44 per cent of parents could still choose the child's newest trainers. Less than 1 in 4 of children aged 11–14 permitted the parents to choose. Only 1 in 20 of parents of 15–19-year-olds made this choice. The pubescent, adolescent, and young adult punter expressed not only an increasing autonomy of choice, in the brand of newest trainer bought, but a statement about acceptable style. These are huge markets, tied up in 'global commodity chains' and worldwide marketing strategies stressing consumer choice and style: sports products as 'an important and visible symbol of social status and identity', in 'the construction of a world of symbols, ideas and values' (Korzeniewicz 1994: 249 and 251; see, too, Wilson 1996). Nike sold itself, in the 1970s and 1980s, as 'hipness, irreverence, individualism, narcissism, self-improvement, gender equality, racial equality, competitiveness, and health' (Korzeniewicz 1994: 258). Despite downturn in growth, Nike continued to be a model: Robert Louis-Dreyfus, power behind the resurgence of Adidas, concentrating on clothing above the foot, noted in 1997 that 'all I did was borrow what Nike and Reebok were doing' (Sawyer 1998: 17).

Style statements through sport are inextricably linked with processes of commodity production and the strategies of the consumer industries. Although all products are in turn appropriated by the consumer in a ceaseless cycle of what Willis (1990) has labelled a 'grounded aesthetic', and can inform an 'aestheticization of everyday life' and 'suggest romantic authenticity and emotional fulfilment in narcissistically pleasing oneself' (Featherstone 1990: 17 and 19), it would be misleading to downplay the sheer *constructedness* of the consumed commodity. Sport as personal style, in terms of the accoutrements of sports fashion and apparel—replica football shirts and keep-fit outfits, as well as shoes—must be understood as realizing the goals and strategies of the production industries, quite as much as fuelling the fantasies and shaping the identities of the particular consumer.

Style as society/institutional images. A sport style can be seen in the institutional images through which we understand society, and the rapid spread of sponsorship and logos in the sites of sport and on the bodies of sports people. A Reebok advertisement of the mid-1990s, placing Manchester United 1960s legends Sir Bobby Charlton and George Best on either side of contemporary starlet Ryan Giggs, is revealing of these changes. Unadorned plain shirts boasting neither club logo nor sponsor's name are worn by the legends: Giggs's shirt foregrounds the sponsor, Sharp, and gives prominence too to the club crest/logo, the latter having emerged as the corporate identity of the lucrative multi-million pound industry that the Manchester United Football Club had become (Routledge 1995: 7). This was confirmed when in September 1998 Rupert Murdoch's

Sky company's bid to buy Manchester United, for £634 million, was accepted. That the Monopolies and Mergers Commission blocked this bid early the following year—on the grounds of conflict of interests, and protection of the balance of the English football industry and culture—was testimony to the high profile of sport and its status as a cultural industry. Such issues would not simply go away, as Granada's July 1999 deal with Liverpool Football Club demonstrated, generating £20 million for the club to attract top players, but raising further questions about the conflict of interests in the involvement of the media in the sports culture. The 'golden triangle' of sport, sponsor, and television, mediated by the marketing visionary, has done much to change the culture of contemporary football, with the European footballing body taking the lead in some of these developments (Sugden and Tomlinson 1998: 94–9). Such an emerging political economy of sport has dramatically reshaped some of the historical sport landscapes of Britain. Derby Football Club's old Baseball Ground was laid to rest and succeeded by the pristine Pride Park; Bolton Wanderers' new ground, replacing their long-established base Burnden Park, was emblematic of such changes—the new Reebok Stadium rising as testimony to the expanding contribution of sport to the integrated interests of the culture and leisure industries.

Whatever the cultural meaning of a style, the culture and leisure industries are adept at maximizing profit and institutionalizing symbolic meanings, in what Mercer (1994: 125) calls a 'postmodern melee of semiotic appropriation and countervalorization' between consumers and producers. He sees black hairstyles as commodified in ways parallel to 'the commodification of electro and hip hop, break-dancing and sportswear chic' (ibid.).

Style as information. An established but revamped prominence of sport—and particularly football—is also evident in style's role as a form of information in society. The sport sections of quality newspapers in Britain were expanded greatly in the 1990s, and new media players battled for broadcasting rights against such providers as the BBC—with particular success in the case of satellite broadcasters such as Sky. As such forms of coverage increased—including panel shows, documentary features, and chat shows as well as action coverage and review—the expanded print outlets offered commentaries on screen commentaries and features, in a solipsistic merry-go-round of increasingly superficial sports information, usually foregrounding gossip over analysis, glossy style over interpretative substance. Also of interest, in the context of the success of new young adult males' magazine markets, was the place of sport in the pages, preoccupations, and discourses of magazines such as *Loaded* and *GQ*.

The November 1997 edition of *Loaded*, for instance, featured several sport items alongside its usual mix of sex, laddish bravado, film, rock, and fashion coverage. These covered baseball in New York City, the magazine's new sponsorship deal with lower-division football club Barnet, and a feature on the suave doyen of football commentary on the BBC, Alan Hansen: 'As TV pundits go, they don't come much hipper or cooler than the boy Hansen' (p. 84), and Hansen was reported as one of the most sexually desired (by women viewers) TV presenters (p. 88). In its sport coverage shorts at the end of the magazine, alongside the football features, lay a piece on the world windsurfing championships in Brighton. In *FHM* (November 1997) the main sport-related story was of survival on a climbing expedition on Everest; but the main sport-based feature was a 'Snowboard Special', covering thirty-four pages, integrated with advertisements for clothes and equipment, and just a page or two before 'FHM FASHION the biggest and best fashion section for men'. Sport is presented as style and fashion in such magazines, the outdoor and active sporting body of the male juxtaposed by the magazine's consistent presentation of the unclothed passive female body, particularly in the issue's 'lingerie special': 'the silkworm's finest work, modelled by a batch of knee-weakeningly attractive celebrity women', for twenty-seven pages of poses and accompanying puffs or spoofs. In its November 1997 edition *GQ* also featured lingerie—'the sexiest women's underwear you should be stealing from washing lines this season'—with Manchester United footballer Roy Keane the main sports figure in the features section; and cricketer Nasser Hussain featured in a competition item in the style section. An individualization of sport as style blended here with a conception of masculinity prioritizing sexual pleasures and voyeurism. Framed within the glossy production values of the remarkably successful men's magazines of the later 1990s, such developments drew upon a variety of cultural sources, most fully embodied in the *GQ* offshoot title, *GQ Active: Health, Fitness and Sport for Men*.

In *GQ Active*, sexual and sporting problems are seen as one and the same thing. 'Are you tough enough? Our karate work-out could save your life' is a front-cover byline lying alongside 'How to pull a young girl and seduce an older woman', and 'Sexual Amnesia—can you remember who you did last night?' A cover-page footer announces further treats: 'Pumping iron with the King of Tonga'; 'We play around with Europe's No. 1 golfer'; 'The latest in Aids medicine'; 'Ten most remote places in Britain'. The crouching male at the centre of these bylines is clad in trainers and tracksuit bottoms, with a 'Ready, Steady, Go! A better life starts here' message blazoned across his legs, but could be wearing a James Bond polo-neck rather than an athletics vest. His crouch is the springing pose of the sprinter. Surrounded by these how-to bylines addressing sexual and sporting prowess, the invitation is clear: spring into action a superior sporting and sexual animal. Inside the magazine, features cover the pin-striped suit of boxer Evander Holyfield, haircut styles, the psychological potential of 'extreme sports' ('scaring yourself stupid and coming out unscathed clearly has a direct line to transcendental bliss', p. 46), and various angles on snowboarding, gym workouts, golf, and travel. Advertisements for personal health aids—sweat rash avoiders, body fat monitoring devices—alternate with fashion and equipment features, all the components of the package on the whole indistinguishable in style and format. *GQ Active* takes to its extreme the fusion of sport as style, in an information-based how-to manual for the resculpting of the public and performing self.

Conclusion

Sport and leisure are revealing topics for cultural analysis, and for understanding some central aspects of British society and culture; for they are public and personal sites for the articulation of identity at a variety of levels. As sport has been developed more and more integrally with the wider cultural industries, it has provided an expanding range of sources for the expression of personal and individualized identities as well as traditional, more collective identities. The primary influence in this process has been the penetration of the market into *both* the public and private spaces of contemporary culture. As Braverman puts it, capitalist production reaches into the most private of spheres, effecting the transformation by capitalism of 'all of society into a gigantic marketplace'. Corporate institutions have, he asserts, 'transformed every means of entertainment and "sport" into a production process for the enlargement of capital' (Braverman 1974: 278). Sport embodies the successful expansion and penetration of the universal market, and lies in fascinating tension with traditional British conceptions such as fair play. Sport both reflects and generates negotiated forms of British and intra-British identity.

Sport and the manifestations of modern sport style express two elements central to consumer culture (Slater 1997; Tomlinson 1990).

They can provide authentic opportunities for the formulation of self and the display of social identity. Broadened lifestyle and consumer choices in contemporary Britain are testimony to this. But they are also (almost always) the object of 'strategic action by dominating institutions' (Slater 1997: 31) astutely and calculatingly concerned with the economic competition and forms of productive organization which fuel and promote those opportunities. Thus cinema viewing and football spectating are reshaped towards new family audiences, and more and more niche markets around race, age, and gender are targeted by the leisure industries. As Adorno (1967: 81) once put it: 'Modern sports . . . train men all the more inexorably to serve the machine. Hence sports belong to the realm of unfreedom, no matter where they are organized,' and such realms and organizational forms are dominated by the imperatives of the culture industries. At the same time sport in contemporary Britain can contribute—at least, for those with the available resources, access, and means—to a sense of the potential remaking of the self; and public sport forms such as spectatorship provide, however fleetingly, a prominent forum for the expression of collective identity. Sport can show how a 'culture has turned', as Hall (1998: 43) puts it—black faces visible and prominent in soccer, but on the field of play rather than in the boardroom—and how this can impact on 'the culture of sport where the nation's myths and meanings are fabricated' (ibid.). If the traditional model of sport spoke to a claimed national identity in the countries of the United Kingdom, sport and leisure have become a source, often rooted in a new consumerism, for the articulation of new cultural identities. Sport's Janus face encapsulates the contradictions of the contemporary cultural world and British culture itself, speaking as it continually (and sometimes simultaneously) does to old certainties and new possibilities.

I am grateful to the editors of this volume for their pithy and constructive responses to an earlier draft; and to Dr Ben Carrington, Sport and Leisure Cultures, University of Brighton, for a constructively critical response to that draft, and for references on youth culture and race.

Further Reading

Holt, R. (1990), *Sport and the British: A Modern History*, Oxford: Oxford University Press. This authoritative book identifies continuities as well as breaks in the history of British sport throughout the nineteenth and twentieth centuries.

Hargreaves, Jennifer (1994), *Sporting Females: Critical Issues in the History and Sociology of Women's Sports*, London: Routledge. This study demonstrates the deep-rootedness of patriarchal influences in sport, but shows too how sport has been a progressive force in some spheres of women's experience.

Mangan, J. A. (1981), *Athleticism in the Victorian and Edwardian Public School: The Emergence and Consolidation of an Educational Ideology*, Cambridge: Cambridge University Press. This study describes vividly the class and masculinist character of the formative period in the development of British team games.

Tomlinson, A. (ed.) (1990), *Consumption, Identity and Style: Marketing, Meanings and the Packaging of Pleasure*, London: Routledge. This collection outlines central themes in studying leisure within consumer culture, and includes focused case-study analyses of the constructedness of selected cultural forms.

Whannel, G. (1992), *Fields in Vision: Television Sport and Cultural Transformation*, London: Routledge. This study traces key shifts in the character, values, and impact of sports broadcasting, and the media's relationship to sponsors within the new political economy of sport.

References

Adorno, T. W. (1967), *Prisms*, London: Neville Spearman.

Alexander, C. E. (1996), *The Art of Being Black: The Creation of Black British Youth Identities*, Oxford: Clarendon Press.

Almond, H. H. (1893), 'Football as a Moral Agent', *Nineteenth Century*, 34, Dec.

Andrews, D. L., Carrington, B., Mazur, Z., and Jackson, S. J. (1996), 'Jordanscapes: A Preliminary Analysis of the Global Popular', *Sociology of Sport Journal*, 13/4.

Back, L. (1996), ' "Inglan, Nice up!": Black Music, Autonomy and the Cultural Intermezzo', in *New Ethnicities and Urban Culture: Racisms and Multiculture in Young Lives*, London: UCL Press.

Balfour, A. J. (1912), *Arthur James Balfour as Philosopher and Thinker: A Collection of the More Important and Interesting Passages in his Non-political Writings, Speeches and Addresses 1879–1912*, selected and arranged by Wilfrid M. Short, London: Longmans, Green & Co.

BMRB International (British Market Research Bureau) (1993), *Youth TGI 1993*, London: BMRB.

Bourdieu, P. (1989), *Distinction: A Social Critique of the Judgement of Taste*, London: Routledge & Kegan Paul.

Boyd, T. (1997), 'True to the Game: Basketball as the Embodiment of Blackness in Contemporary Popular Culture', in *Am I Black Enough for you? Popular Culture from the 'Hood and Beyond*, Bloomington: Indiana University Press.

Braverman, H. (1974), *Labour and Monopoly Capital: The Degradation of Work in the Twentieth Century*, New York: Monthly Review Press.

Carrington, B. (1998), 'Deconstructing Bodily Narratives of "Animalism" and "Athleticism": "Race", Gender and Sexualization of the Black Male Sporting Body', paper presented at the 14th World Congress of Sociology, Montreal, Canada, 16 July–1 August.

—— (2000), 'Double Consciousness and the Black British Athlete', in K. Owusu (ed.), *Black British Culture and Society: A Reader*, London: Routledge.

Crowe, R. (1998), 'Boom in Trainers Wanes', *Guardian*, Saturday, 7 Feb. 24.

Department of National Heritage (1995), *Raising the Game*, London: Department of National Heritage.

Dobbs, B. (1973), *Edwardians at Play: Sport 1890–1914*, London: Pelham Books.

Dyer, R. (1997), *White*, London: Routledge.

Eliot, T. S. (1962), *Notes towards the Definition of Culture*, London: Faber & Faber (1st pub. 1948).

Ensor, E. (1898), 'The Football Madness', *Contemporary Review*, Nov.

Ewen, S. (1990), 'Marketing Dreams: The Political Elements of Style', in A. Tomlinson (ed.), *Consumption, Identity and Style: Marketing, Meanings and the Packaging of Pleasure*, London: Routledge.

Featherstone, M. (1990), 'Perspectives on Consumer Culture', *Sociology*, 24/1, Feb.

—— and Turner, B. S. (1995), 'Body & Society: An Introduction', *Body & Society*, 1/1, Mar.

Fishwick, N. (1989), *English Football and Society, 1910–1950*, Manchester: Manchester University Press.

Flintoff, A., Scraton, S., and Bramham, P. (1995), 'Stepping into Aerobics?', in G. McFee, W, Murphy, and G. Whannel (eds.), *Leisure Cultures: Values, Genders, Lifestyles*, Brighton: Leisure Studies Association, Publication No. 54: 93–104.

Girouard, M. (1981), *The Return to Camelot: Chivalry and the English Gentleman*, New Haven: Yale University Press.

Hall, S. (1998), 'Aspiration and Attitude . . . Reflections on Black Britain in the Nineties', *New Formations: A Journal of Culture/Theory/Politics*, 33, Spring: 38–46.

Hargreaves, Jennifer (1994), *Sporting Females: Critical Issues in the History and Sociology of Women's Sports*, London: Routledge.

Hargreaves, John (1986), *Sport, Power and Culture: A Social and Historical Analysis of Popular Sports in Britain*, Cambridge: Polity Press.

—— (1987), 'The Body, Sport and Power Relations', in J. Horne, D. Jary, and A. Tomlinson (eds.), *Sport, Leisure and Social Relations*, Sociological Review Monograph 33, London: Routledge: 139–59.

Haynes, R. (1995), *The Football Imagination: The Rise of Football Fanzine Culture*, Aldershot: Arena/Ashgate Publishing Ltd.

Hoberman, J. (1997), *Darwin's Athletes: How Sport has Damaged Black America and Preserved the Myth of Race*, Boston: Houghton Mifflin Company.

Holt, R. (1990), *Sport and the British: A Modern History*, Oxford: Oxford University Press.

—— and Tomlinson, A. (1994), 'Sport and Leisure', in D. Kavanagh and A. Seldon (eds.), *The Major Effect*, London: Macmillan.

Hornby, N. (1992), *Fever Pitch*, London: Victor Gollancz Ltd.

James, C. L. R. (1964), *Beyond a Boundary*, London: Stanley Paul.

Johnstone, B. (1990), *It's Been a Piece of Cake: A Tribute to my Favourite Test Cricketers*, London: Mandarin.

King, A. (1995), 'The New Football Consumption', unpublished Ph.D. thesis, Department of Sociology, University of Salford.

Korzeniewicz, M. (1994), 'Commodity Chains and Marketing Strategies: Nike and the Global Athletic Footwear Industry', in G. Gereffi and M. Korzeniewicz (eds.), *Commodity Chains and Global Capitalism*, Westwood, Conn.: Greenwood Press.

Labour Party (1997), *New Labour: Because Britain Deserves Better*, London: Labour Party.

McIntosh, P. (1979), *Fair Play: Ethics in Sport and Education*, London: Heinemann.

McRobbie, A. (1994), 'Different, Youthful, Subjectivities: Towards a Cultural Sociology of Youth', in *Postmodernism and Popular Culture*, London: Routledge.

Mangan, J. A. (1981), *Athleticism in the Victorian and Edwardian Public School: The Emergence and Consolidation of an Educational Ideology*, Cambridge: Cambridge University Press.

—— (1986), *The Games Ethic and Imperialism: Aspects of the Diffusion of an Ideal*, London: Viking.

Mason, T. (ed.) (1989), *Sport in Britain: A Social History*, Cambridge: Cambridge University Press.

Mercer, K. (1994), 'Black Hair/Style Politics', in *Welcome to the Jungle: New Positions in Black Cultural Studies*, New York: Routledge.

Philips, D., and **Tomlinson, A.** (1992), 'Homeward Bound: Leisure, Popular Culture and Consumer Capitalism', in D. Strinati and S. Wagg (eds.), *Come on Down? Popular Media Culture in Post-war Britain*, London: Routledge.

Poirier, R. (1971), *The Performing Self*, London: Chatto & Windus.

Ridley, J., and **Percy, C.** (eds.) (1992), *The Letters of Arthur Balfour and Lady Elcho 1885–1917*, London: Hamish Hamilton.

Routledge, M. (1995), ' "Visible, Tangible and All-Embracing": A Study into the Football Identity', unpublished BA (Hons.) dissertation, Graphic Design, University of Brighton.

Sawyer, M. (1998), 'Not just a Pose: It's not Working out', *Observer Life*, 3 May.

Scott, S., and **Morgan, D.** (eds.) (1993), *Body Matters: Essays in the Sociology of the Body*, London: Falmer Press.

Shilling, C. (1993), *The Body and Social Theory*, London: Sage.

Slater, D. (1997), *Consumer Culture and Modernity*, Cambridge: Polity Press.

Sports Council and Women's Sports Foundation (1992), *Women and Sport: The Information Pack*, London: Sports Council.

Sugden, J., and **Tomlinson, A.** (1998), *FIFA and the Contest for World Football: Who Rules the People's Game?*, Cambridge: Polity Press.

Tomlinson, A. (1990), 'Consumer Culture and the Aura of the Commodity', in A. Tomlinson (ed.), *Consumption, Identity and Style: Marketing, Meanings and the Packaging of Pleasure*, London: Routledge.

—— (1992), 'Shifting Patterns of Working-Class Leisure: The Case of Knur-and-Spell', *Sociology of Sport Journal*, 9/2, June.

—— (1997), 'Ideologies of Physicality, Masculinity and Femininity: Comments on *Roy of the Rovers* and the Women's Fitness Boom', in A. Tomlinson (ed.), *Gender, Sport and Leisure: Continuities and Challenges*, Aachen: Meyer & Meyer.

Tonkin, B. (1998), 'No sex, Please, we're British: Nice Blokes and Good Girls Behaving Slightly Naughtily', *ism: Independent Saturday Magazine*, 9 May.

Veblen, T. (1953), *The Theory of the Leisure Class: An Economic Study of Institutions*, New York: Mentor.

Whannel, G. (1986), 'The Unholy Alliance: Notes on Television and the Remaking of British Sport 1965–1985', *Leisure Studies*, 5/2, May.

—— (1992), *Fields in Vision: Television Sport and Cultural Transformation*, London: Routledge.

Wheaton, B., and **Tomlinson, A.** (1998), 'The Changing Gender Order in Sport? The Case of Windsurfing Subcultures', *Journal of Sport and Social Issues*, 22/3, Aug.

Whitson, D. (1983), 'Pressures on Regional Games in a Dominant Metropolitan Culture: The Case of Shinty', *Leisure Studies*, 3/2, May.

Williams, R. (1974), *Television: Technology and Cultural Form*, London: Fontana Collins.

—— (1977), 'Dominant, Residual, and Emergent', in *Marxism and Literature*, Oxford: Oxford University Press.

—— (1983), *Towards 2,000*, London: Chatto & Windus.

Willis, P. (1982), 'Women in Sport in Ideology', in Jennifer Hargreaves (ed.), *Sport, Culture and Ideology*, London: Routledge & Kegan Paul.

—— (1990), *Common Culture: Symbolic Work at Play in the Everyday Cultures of the Young* (with Simon Jones, Joyce Canaan and Geoff Hurd), Milton Keynes: Open University Press.

Wilson, B. (1996), '"It's Gotta be the shoes": Youth, Race and Sneaker Commercials', *Sociology of Sport Journal*, 13/4.

27

The Control of Space: Travellers, Youth, and Drug Cultures

DAVID SIBLEY

Introduction

THE British countryside, often represented as a space of stability and harmonious social relations, is also a site of social conflict. In this chapter, I will examine some recent tensions in English and Welsh rural areas which arise from the juxtaposition of different cultures. Part of the problem is concerned with mobility and fixity, with movements of people who do not fit into the ordered world of the dominant members of the sedentary rural population. It is an instance of the ancient conflict between the nomadic and the sedentary. However, the conflict is also, to some extent, generational, one concerned with the threats posed by youth cultures to the established order. Nomadism and youth culture intersect and both generate panics in the larger society, but their social significance is not identical. Some people, Gypsies or Roma, Irish and Scottish Travellers, spend a life on the road or, since the introduction of legal restrictions on travelling, one largely contained on sites for Travellers. Others may become Travellers when young, opting for an alternative to a settled existence, although these New or New Age Travellers may, in the longer term, represent an addition to established nomadic traditions in Britain. The latter are a particular target for abuse, however, because they are not seen as legitimate, not 'real' Travellers. Movement is also a part of youth cultures and I am particularly concerned in this essay with movements into the countryside for gatherings, festivals, and musical events, ephemeral movements which may trigger strong reactions from the settled population.

These conflicts are a part of a larger story, one concerned with the state's attempts to restrict access to particular places, to control movements over space as a tactic of policing dissident and troublesome minorities, and even to eliminate those who threaten an avowedly stable and harmonious society. This raises questions about who does have a legitimate place in British society, who should control territory in locales like the English countryside, and what constitutes an acceptable identity. In thinking about belonging and not belonging, who 'belongs' where, other spaces, cities and the nation, are implicated. These issues came to a head with the introduction of legislation to control movements into the English and Welsh countrysides in the public order sections of the Criminal Justice and Public Order Act, which became law in 1994. This legislation is the principal subject of the chapter but, to provide a meaningful context for a discussion of the Act, I will first consider the people affected by the law and their historical relationship to the spaces which are implicated in the legislation.

Old Travelling

The Gypsy diaspora reached the British Isles in the early sixteenth century. The first recorded presence of Gypsies in Scotland was in 1505 and in England in 1514 (Fraser 1992: 113). Undoubtedly, Gypsies would have been an addition to an existing indigenous population of nomads, pedlars, migrant labourers, and entertainers, for example—but Gypsies soon became a particular target for control and repression. Fear of the nomad was compounded by a fear of an exotic 'Other', versed in the magic arts. The first Act in England to prohibit further immigration of Gypsies, on the grounds that they had been guilty of fortune telling, deceit, and theft, was passed in 1530. This was one of a series of exclusionary measures introduced in western European countries, often accompanied by harsh penalties 'for being a Gypsy', including transportation and execution (Liegeois 1986).

The policing of Gypsy migrations and settlement has continued to concern both central and local government to the present day. Although the city, until the early twentieth century, could apparently absorb Gypsy families (Sibley 1981), in rural areas the illegal occupation of land and an association of Gypsies with dirt and contagious disease ensured continuous harassment (Mayall 1988). There was an ambivalence in the larger society's response to Gypsies, however. Contrary to their representation as a malign and polluting presence, they were portrayed as having a natural place in the countryside. They were romanticized, particularly in the nineteenth century by writers like George Borrow, as an exotic people, close to or at one with nature, untrammelled by the routines and disciplines of industrial society. This romantic image was drawn on by some Members of Parliament in debates on Moveable Dwellings Bills in 1908 and 1911 and the admiration and envy of politicians may have weakened attempts to enact controls over movement and settlement at the national level although, as Mayall points out, local efforts to evict Gypsies were frequent in the late nineteenth century. Although the parliamentary debates in 1908 and 1911 did not lead to effective legislation, they marked a concern by the state to institute spatial controls. In fact, there was no national strategy for the control of nomadism until the 1968 Caravan Sites Act, part 2 of which was concerned with Gypsies. From 1970 until 1994, when the legislation was repealed in the Criminal Justice and Public Order Act, local authorities in England and Wales were required to provide sites for Gypsies and other Travellers 'residing in or resorting to' their areas. While the measures were introduced, ostensibly, to allow Gypsies to continue their traditional (nomadic) way of life (Sibley 1981: ch. 9), in practice the Act led to greater control and surveillance of Travellers. Where, to the satisfaction of the Home Office, enough sites had been provided, local authorities were granted designation, which gave them powers to evict any families not accommodated on official sites. Designation had serious consequences, for the more nomadic groups, particularly Irish Travellers, were neither recognized as 'residing in' nor 'resorting to' most local authority areas frequently enough to warrant site provision. The sites themselves were effectively sites of surveillance, supervised by wardens who were usually not Gypsies and subject to rules which had an adverse affect on Gypsy culture. Traditional work, like scrap metal sorting, was generally prohibited on sites as were fires, and it was difficult for extended family groups to position their caravans in proximity to each other. Thus, from the Gypsies' perspective, sites were often rather alien territories.

The recent history of the state's response to Gypsies indicates clearly the continuing desire to impose controls on a people whose lifestyle violates dominant ideas about land use and spatial order. Much of the negative argument about Gypsies has been based on stereotyped representations of criminal and antisocial nomads.

Many Gypsies are not nomadic and their criminality is primarily a consequence of legislation which curtails their traditional economic activities and migrations. However, it is easier to gain support for the policing of space if the threats are exaggerated.

New Travelling

Indigenous nomads have appeared at various times in the past, particularly in times of crisis. Many Scottish Travellers, for example, probably became nomadic in response to the Highland clearances in the eighteenth century. Similarly, New Age Travellers have been recognizable as a nomadic or semi-nomadic minority in Britain since the early 1970s when legislation to evict squatters became more effective. However, this was also a period when a hybrid, anti-materialist culture emerged, variously informed by mysticism, ecology, communitarian principles, and anarchism. One manifestation of this was the revival of horse fairs in East Anglia which provided a focus for new ecological movements. Another was the articulation of a national festival circuit, including Stonehenge and the Green Moon Festival at Nenthead in Cumbria. These were primarily the creations of New Travellers, known initially as the Peace Convoy. Partly to get away from the materialism of urban life but also because of the practical difficulties of finding somewhere to stop, New Traveller culture is primarily a rural one, although some are found among the urban homeless and in city squats. As one Traveller put it: 'Whereas in the early eighties it was mostly alternative-y type people who picked an alternative lifestyle, now it's people who are basically fucked off with the city' (Lowe and Shaw 1993: 240–1). As Lowe and Shaw's ethnography demonstrates, New Age Travellers are a disparate group. The ascription covers settled communities, like Tipi Valley in Dyfed, south Wales, one which consciously adopted the style of North American Plains Indians, as well as semi-nomadic groups living in converted buses and trailers. Some have a strong consciousness of politics and history, like the English Dongas who 'see themselves as indigenous Englanders, recovering and celebrating pre-Christian traditions of the land' (McKay 1996: 134) and gain inspiration from the Diggers and the Levellers of the English Civil War. Their eco-radicalism was a particular feature of the protest against the construction of the M3 motorway at Twyford Down in Hampshire in 1992. Different identities were clearly of little interest to the popular press which amplified the deviance of New Age Travellers during the 1980s. The size and mobility of Traveller groups, their 'invasions' of cherished heritage sites like Stonehenge, and associations with drugs and alcohol were emphasized. A single event in 1985, the 'Battle of the Beanfield', signalled a less tolerant attitude on the part of the state towards New Travellers. As one Traveller recalled: 'The Beanfield was a big turning point for everyone, I think. They'd place an injunction on a few named people, banning them from going within five miles of Stonehenge, but really I think it was set up from way back; a deliberate plan to give everyone a good hiding and decommission [the Peace Convoy]' (Lowe and Shaw 1993: 70). The spatial control of nomads, which had become more systematic with the implementation of part 2 of the 1968 Caravan Sites Act, now became more intensive. A model for restricting movement and thus hampering protests had been provided by the policing of the National Union of Coalminers' strike in 1984/5. Following the 1994 Act, the police had the job of making life difficult for any group of nomads.

Transgressive Youth

A third element in the creation of contested rural space in the 1980s and 1990s was the demonization of young people who occasionally travel from the city into the country to attend a rave (although there are also, presumably, rural youth who participate in these events). There is nothing peculiarly rural about raves, however. McKay (1996) traces the history of raves from the Roundhouse in Camden Town, London, and other venues in the capital, to Manchester, Blackburn, and Ibiza, and from LSD (acid) in the 1960s to Ecstasy and other designer drugs in the 1990s. Rural raves are certainly a part of the scene and these events are akin to free festivals: 'These rave events are generally compressed in time—lasting a long night rather than a long weekend or solstice week—but with the familiar use of squatting as challenge to rural land ownership, some drug selling to finance things, some moving around the country, that the festival and related traveller scene displayed' (McKay 1996: 120).

It is the geography of raves which appears to have most concerned politicians. The unpredictable movement of young people, supposedly from the city into the country, is constructed as a transgression. Ravers, their drugs, and their music 'belong' in the city and, more particularly, in the inner city. Raves bring an alien culture into rural space. As with New Age Travellers, it is the assumed fluidity and placelessness of the culture which creates anxieties.

What is accepted as proper in the English countryside is violated and the threat is more potent when those claiming space for non-conforming cultural practices are young.

In Geoffrey Pearson's 'history of respectable fears' (1983), it is striking how often the alleged violence of young people, usually working-class youth, is described by those who uphold 'true British values' as alien, from somewhere else: 'At the heart of the matter stands the un-British crime of violence, its supposedly alien presence asserting itself time and time again in "new" and unparalleled forms; the lawlessness of "street arabs" in the 1840s; the ungentlemanly garotters of the 1860s; the degenerate "unEnglish" Hooligan of the 1890s . . . the "foreign" importations of street crime by black muggers' (Pearson 1983: 209). Elsewhere (p. 13), Pearson refers to a speaker at the 1958 Tory Party conference who talked of a sudden increase in crime and brutality 'which is so foreign to our nature and our country'. So, violence, and particularly that attributed to young men, is something alien, the work of 'street arabs' (Oriental), hooligans (Irish), and so on. The moral panics surrounding these deviant groups are manufactured by referring to a supposedly tranquil past. In a more recent manifestation of bourgeois *angst*, troublesome ravers disturb a tranquil space, the English and Welsh countryside. They belong in the cosmopolitan city, with its drugs and violence, as if there was no rural drugs problem and there were no disturbances in small market towns on Saturday nights. This imagined geography of the rural highlights the deviance of other cultures and the threat from without. The proper place of deviant youth, however, is now in the city rather than beyond national boundaries.

Hunters and Saboteurs

The last element of the problem, as it was constructed in the parliamentary debates on the Criminal Justice and Public Order Bill, is the hunt saboteur issue. This touches on something of great symbolic importance to those sections of the rural population who see themselves as custodians of the countryside. Fox-hunting, in particular, is represented by the hunting lobby as an essential part of country life, an ethically defensible way of controlling fox numbers which also provides employment and contributes to a sense of community. Hunting verges on the sacred. Those who challenge this view, who argue that hunting foxes with hounds is a cruel sport and who take direct action against it, have also been portrayed as young, urban, and criminal. Thus, in a memorable contribution to the debate on the Criminal Justice Bill, the Conservative member Sir Cranley Onslow made the following observation on hunt saboteurs:

It is a disgrace that organized violence, deliberate provocation and physical assaults on people and animals have become an accepted way of life for a militant section of urban society. The saboteur movement has its roots not in the countryside but in the towns. Anyone who has seen busloads of Millwall supporters brought in to disrupt a hunt knows exactly what I am talking about.

In this world-view, saboteurs are barely distinguishable from ravers and Travellers. All are pariahs in the eyes of those who uphold what they see as the true values of 'the rural community'. This perception of who belongs and who does not have a legitimate place in the countryside resulted in the law's net being spread widely, to include all Travellers, hunt saboteurs, ravers, and, possibly unintentionally, a disparate group of environmental protesters.

The Countryside, the State and New Right Politics

The sentiments expressed by politicians intent on limiting access to the countryside and expelling troublesome minorities might be taken as a symptom of New Right politics. As Gamble (1988: 58) has characterized the New Right position on dissent: 'The coercive power of the state should be used against the most visible agents of chaos and disorder—strikers, criminals, demonstrators and vandals. Public order and essential services should be maintained at all costs.' Freedom, then, is circumscribed. While the state celebrates market freedoms, it sees coercion and intimidation as legitimate measures in its efforts to stifle challenges to the market economy. In Gamble's terms, this is the 'strong state', cherished by the New Right.

Crouch and Marquand (1989: p. viii), however, have argued that this strategy is not the preserve of the New Right but a long-established tendency of the 'political class' in Britain. It is certainly the case that the Labour government which came to power in 1997 is as concerned as the previous administration with control of the social uses of public space. Current (March 2000) panics, fuelled by government ministers and their opposition shadows, about 'aggressive' begging by Roma (Gypsy) refugees from south-eastern Europe and their 'abuse' of children by carrying them while begging on the street, and government responses to youth crime, including local curfews for young children, demonstrate a deep anxiety about the use of public space by the marginalized. I think we have to distinguish here between mainstream protest movements, like the Campaign for Nuclear Disarmament, which was allowed to organize demonstrations, given space and time in the centres of power (although demonstrations were heavily policed), and protests by groups relegated by those in power to the edge of society, like young people involved in squatter movements. The latter, like New Age Travellers and Gypsies, threaten the cohesion of society through their appropriation of space, and they explicitly reject many mainstream values. While governments have grudgingly tolerated mainstream campaigners, they have been consistently antagonistic towards nomadic groups and others who have challenged dominant ideas about property and settlement. Harassment and eviction of Gypsies, for example, was as big a problem in the 1960s, under both Conservative and Labour governments, as in the 1980s and 1990s, and it continues to be an issue under the new Labour administration which has done nothing to restore the limited protection which nomads enjoyed before the 1994 Criminal Justice and Public Order Act. Interestingly, however, the judiciary has been a source of some support for Gypsies and other Travellers (see below).

The recent history of the state's response to Travellers, ravers, and environmental protesters seems to indicate the existence of a boundary crisis (Erikson 1966), the sort that appears periodically when 'a group's uncertainty about itself is resolved in ritualistic confrontations between the deviant and the community's official agents' (Erikson, cited by Cohen 1972: 192), rather than being a manifestation of some new political ideology. John Major's tirade against New Age Travellers at the 1992 Tory Party conference— 'Not in this age; not in any age'—was probably more about galvanizing support in the party's rural constituency than implementing a well-thought-out New Right programme of coercion but the state's actions against nomads and other transgressive minorities have had serious material consequences for those affected. I will now discuss some of the clauses in the public order sections of the 1994 Act because this is still the main instrument of movement control.

The Criminal Justice and Public Order Act

Whatever the broader significance of this Act, which became law in England and Wales in January 1994, the public order clauses do represent an interesting exercise in policing space. As the then Home Secretary, Michael Howard, claimed, '[the public order section] contains important measures designed to tackle the destruction and distress caused mainly to rural communities by trespassers. Local communities should not have to put up with, or even fear the prospect of, mass invasions by those who selfishly gather, regardless of the rights of others.' The fear of movement, invasions from elsewhere, to which 'local, rural communities' were subject was clearly a central issue. It was necessary to make the lives of the invaders less secure by criminalizing their activities or even their presence in the countryside.

The principal move against nomads was to repeal part 2 of the 1968 Caravan Sites Act, which obliged local authorities to provide sites for Travellers. At the same time, the Act repealed section 70 of the Local Government, Planning, and Land Act 1980, which empowered central government to pay the capital costs of site development. This left roughly half the families counted in the government's own six-monthly census of Traveller caravans without a legal stopping place. Gypsies and others are now expected to apply for planning permission for a site and to pay the construction costs. The insecurity resulting from the repeal of these Acts is compounded by stronger laws of trespass. According to section 45 (1), 'if the senior police officer present at the scene [believes] that two or more persons are residing on land and are present there with the common purpose of residing there for *any period* and . . . those persons have between them six or more vehicles on the land', the officer can direct them to leave. If they do not, or return within three months, they are liable to a fine or three months' imprisonment. If they are arrested under section 45, the police are given powers under section 46 to confiscate their vehicles, effectively rendering them homeless.

The other groups targeted in the Act were 'disruptive trespassers', that is, according to section 52 (1), 'people who trespass on land in the open air and, in relation to any lawful activity which people are engaging in, or are about to engage in, on that or adjoining land in the open air [do] there anything which is intended by [them] to have the effect of intimidating those persons or any of them so as to deter them or any of them from engaging in that activity'. This vague wording, describing actions which are termed 'aggravated trespass', is coupled with the granting of police powers of arrest, 'on reasonable suspicion', without a warrant. A person does not have to be in the act of disrupting a lawful activity to commit an offence. A police officer needs only to be satisfied that someone 'intends to commit' such an offence. Hunt saboteurs are clearly the main target of this clause but a range of environmental protesters could also commit a criminal offence by their actions.

Apart from identifying illegal acts and likely perpetrators, the public order clauses of the Act are concerned with controlling the movements of those who pose a threat to 'the rural community'. Legal powers become available to exclude or expel nomads, ravers, and protesters from rural space. Remarkably, the Act includes measures designed specifically to discourage travel to raves, a kind of movement perceived as large-scale, unpredictable, and primarily a movement from urban to rural areas. Under section 47, a police officer of at least the rank of superintendent is given the power to direct people to leave the land 'if he reasonably believes that ten or more persons, present on the land in the open air, are waiting for [a rave] to begin'. This section also allows for the creation of an exclusion zone, an area within a 5-mile radius of a site where the police believe that a rave might take place. Within this zone, a police constable may stop a person and order them not to proceed in the direction of the suspected gathering. This is precisely the kind of policing which was employed during the 1984–5 miners' strike to prevent secondary picketing. Here, it is applied to a kind of musical event which may well prove ephemeral.

Apart from the measures introduced to discourage settlement, New Age Travellers are also affected by the prohibition of 'trespassory assemblies', which would include those festivals on the Traveller circuit. These are gatherings which, under section 55, are (a) 'likely to be held without the permission of the occupier of the land or [to be conducted] in such a way as to exceed the limits of any permission' or (b) (i) to 'cause serious disruption to the life of a community' or (ii) to cause serious damage to land, buildings, or property of historical, architectural, archaeological, or scientific importance. All these likelihoods have to be assessed by a senior police officer.

These restrictions on movement and the staging of events in the countryside by people who did not belong to the Conservative government's imagined rural community provide a clear demonstration of the strong state in action. There was little opposition to the measures in the House of Commons and the bill became law without modification, suggesting a broad consensus about the marginal, transgressive, and deviant quality of the groups the public order legislation was supposed to affect.

David Sibley

Strange Alliances

In some respects, the controls introduced by the Criminal Justice Act have been effective. Free outdoor raves have been almost extinguished and police have used their new powers to confiscate sound systems and arrest the organizers. In the place of spontaneous gatherings, there are now a few licensed events, like Tribal Gathering, a huge annual dance weekend. As Garth Cartwright (*Guardian*, 27 May 1997: 18) asked: 'What's the point of legal raves? No dodging cops, no squatting in fields. Above all, no stories to tell your mates.' The essentially transgressive nature of innovative youth culture is lost.

With no systematic recording of evictions, it is difficult to know what effect the legislation has had on Travellers, although there have been some significant challenges to the Act. In 1995 an eviction order on a group of New Age Travellers in East Sussex was quashed on the grounds that the local authority had failed to take account of the primary need for shelter and a modicum of security (*Guardian*, 1 Sept. 1995). In 1999 a judge ruled against Cheltenham Borough Council, which had refused a booking of council premises by a Gypsy woman for her daughter's wedding reception (*Smith v. Cheltenham Borough Council*, Bristol County Court, Apr. 1999). According to the judge: 'The truth is that as soon as the word "gypsy" appears assumptions are made that large numbers will descend and cause trouble.' Finding that the women had been racially discriminated against, he suggested that the way they had been treated by the police and the council was 'in complete contrast to the way in which, for example, the organisers of the Hunt Ball, an event known to pose serious risks of disorder, were treated' (*Travellers' Times*, 2000: 3). It is still safe to assume, however, that nomads are pariahs in British society.

The attempt by the former Conservative administration to represent environmental protesters as another group of troublesome urban youth certainly failed. It is notable that members of the rural middle class, whom the Tory government would have claimed as its own, have supported environmental activists, for example, in opposing the new runway at Manchester Airport, and have joined protests against live animal exports (including the late Lord Clarke). In these cases, the new legal powers have not been used or they have proved ineffective. Britain's most celebrated environmental protester, Swampy, briefly had a high media profile and appeared on the BBC comedy quiz *Have I Got News for You*. Tunnelling became respectable. The alliance of some of the rural middle class and activists suggests that the former now perceive the threats to their rural sanctuary to come from large-scale developments in the countryside, from capital and the state, rather than from young environmental protesters, whose deviance was amplified by the government in making its case for the public order clauses of the 1994 Act. Clearly. there is no simple opposition between a rural middle-class and transgressive urban youth cultures.

Conclusion

Recent moves by the state against dissident and deviant minorities echo previous conflicts over space, between generations, and between sedentary and nomadic people. The Criminal Justice and Public Order Act does not seem to me to be a manœuvre peculiar to the New Right although it could be argued that the current Labour government occupies the same position on the political spectrum as the New Right on these issues. The conflict between the settled society and nomads is an enduring one and the spatial control of Gypsies has been a national policy objective at least since 1970. New Age Travellers constitute a relatively new pariah group but they are only filling the role previously occupied by Irish Travellers, who are generally more nomadic and, thus, more disturbing than English and Welsh Gypsies. Youth culture is a periodic source of anxiety. In Stanley Cohen's now familiar litany of moral panics, Teddy boys, mods and rockers, and punks were on the leading edge of style, occupying a position similar to that of ravers, although these earlier folk devils were not seen to warrant legislation. Recent environmental protests are in a tradition of protest and activism going back to Gerrard Winstanley and many have involved a fairly broad 'left' coalition, like the opposition to cruise missiles in the 1980s, which involved both tracking missile movements through rural England, by young activists, and socially more inclusive street demonstrations.

What brought a fairly disparate set of nonconformists and protesters together in the 1990s was the last Conservative government's attempt to erect a strong boundary around its imagined rural constituency, thus creating a problem of transgression and criminalization. New Labour has produced another reaction through its promise to legislate against traditional country sports, particularly fox-hunting. The government has been challenged by the Countryside Alliance, another loose coalition which promotes myths about 'real country people' and rural tradition. The idea of a pure and homogeneous countryside which is reflected in the 1994 legislation and the Countryside Alliance's resistance to change also resonates with earlier attempts to resist social and spatial change, like the establishment's reaction to the movement of the urban working class to plotlands in rural areas in the 1920s. Significantly, what surface in these conflicts are questions about English identity and who belongs and does not belong where (particularly who belongs in the countryside). These arguments about belonging have been very much bound up with questions of class and ethnicity. Thus, recent measures taken by central government to affect the social composition of the countryside are not exceptional. They echo long-standing anxieties about social class and space.

The postures and actions of New Labour indicate a continuation of Tory practices in a wider programme of territorial controls which are directed also at the street, where the homeless, beggars, and some children are represented as dangerously transgressive, and at national boundaries, which represent the first defence against demonized beggars from the Balkans. However, in recent attempts to defend some mythical English countryside, British governments have failed to recognize that social and moral values cannot be sorted simply by class, by race, by generations, or geography.

Further Reading

Cooper, D. (1998), *Governing out of Order: Space, Law and the Politics of Belonging*, London: Rivers Oram. An illuminating collection of case-studies dealing with contested spaces in England and Wales and the positions of the legislature and the judiciary in power relations affecting territorial claims.

Lowe, R., and Shaw, W. (1993), *Travellers: Voices of the New Age Nomads*, London: Fourth Estate. A useful ethnography, demonstrating the diverse origins of New Age Travellers.

McKay, G. (1996), *Senseless Acts of Beauty: Cultures of Resistance since the Sixties*, London: Verso. An excellent, well-illustrated account of the British counterculture by an anarchist.

References

Cohen, S. (1972), *Folk Devils and Moral Panics*, London: MacGibbon and Kee.

Cooper, D. (1998), *Governing out of Order: Space, Law and the Politics of Belonging*, London: Rivers Oram.

Crouch, C., and Marquand, D. (eds.) (1989), *The New Centralism*, Oxford: Basil Blackwell.

Erikson, K. (1966), *Wayward Puritans*, New York, Wiley.

Fraser, A. (1992), *The Gypsies*, Oxford: Basil Blackwell.

Gamble, A. (1988), *The Free Economy and the Strong State*, Basingstoke: Macmillan.

Liegeois, J.-P. (1986), *Gypsies: An Illustrated History*, London: Al Saqi Books.

Lowe, R., and Shaw, W. (1993), *Travellers: Voices of the New Age Nomads*, London: Fourth Estate.

McKay, G. (1996), *Senseless Acts of Beauty: Cultures of Resistance since the Sixties*, London: Verso.

Mayall, D. (1988), *Gypsy-Travellers in Nineteenth Century Society*, Cambridge: Cambridge University Press.

Pearson, G. (1983), *Hooligan: A History of Respectable Fears*, London: Macmillan.

Sibley, D. (1981), *Outsiders in Urban Societies*, Oxford: Basil Blackwell.

Travellers' Times, Newsletter of the Traveller Law Research Unit, Cardiff Law School.

Green Politics: Animal Rights, Vegetarianism, and Naturism

LINDA
MERRICKS

28

AT the end of the Second World War the elements of British society which make up the title of this section would barely have merited a mention in a study of British culture except as the interests of the eccentric. Vegetarianism and animal rights were the concerns of a minority. Organic farming was the preserve of cranks and notions of environmental damage and preservation, while present in British society, were largely restricted to 'protecting' the countryside from large-scale industrial and urban incursions and the still small-scale work of the National Trust.

Yet in the years since the late 1960s these movements have come, in the views of some at least, to constitute not merely a major socio-cultural phenomena but the basis of a 'new politics'. In order to understand this transformation, though, we need a much longer historical account of change. The relationship of human beings to animals has exercised philosophers and other writers in Britain since the Tudors. Biblical scholars were concerned with the story of Creation as presented in Genesis, and the results of their concerns impacted on everyday life in a society where all education and promises of salvation came from the Church. The generally accepted version as summarized by Keith Thomas (Thomas 1983) was that, before the biblical Fall, humans had lived in harmony with animals, and probably ate no meat. However, after the Fall, the fight for existence became more difficult, plants were no longer provided by a munificent God, and animals needed subduing. A result of this was the human ascendancy over animals from which the doctrine of ultimate power over those animals could be deduced. By the time of the Old Testament, humans were carnivorous and no rules of behaviour in the Bible questioned the eating of meat.

Although, as Joan Thirsk (Thirsk 1997) has shown, there have been well-attested cases of vegetarianism in Britain dating from the 1690s, it was only in the eighteenth century that questions about the morality of using animals as food were raised. Although there were concerns about the matter, and a shift in cooking to well-done—and therefore apparently not 'bloody'—food has been observed by some writers, little impact on the majority of the population can be discovered until the late nineteenth century; the decision to eat no meat as part of the normal diet was one taken by a very small minority who believed in the benefits to their health of a non-meat diet. The Vegetarian Society was founded in 1847 but it was not until the 1880s and 1890s that there were any signs of a popular movement. At this time, lectures were given, books appeared and a number of vegetarian restaurants were opened, of which twenty-nine were found in London. During the same period organizations like the Humanitarian League also began to link vegetarianism with issues of animal welfare as well as with diet—a move which was to have considerable significance in the later twentieth century (Kean 1995).

Although this wave of vegetarianism had little lasting effect on the British diet it had three main areas in common with the post-Second World War experience. First was the coincidence of changes in eating habits with a more cosmopolitan society. The major areas in which vegetarianism were found were within the large cities, where immigrants had brought southern European patterns based on salads and fruits to a Britain still wedded to an ideal of roast beef. Second was an early recognition of the ecological imperatives of vegetarianism. Anne Kingsford, vice-president of the Vegetarian Society, 'saw vegetarian diets as a way of feeding large numbers of people on less land, of providing work, and reducing imports' (Thirsk 1997: 201). Finally, vegetarianism, as Hilda Kean shows, was especially followed by women—again something repeated in the late twentieth century (Kean 1995).

Throughout this period, there developed a parallel concern for the welfare of animals. During the first half of the nineteenth century, England was seen as 'the hell of dumb animals', where 'the continual and wanton persecution of birds [and animals]' was commented on. Even Queen Victoria, in 1868, gave as her opinion that 'the English are inclined to be more cruel to animals than some other civilised nations are'. Despite this, a humane movement was growing which led to the founding of the Society for the Prevention of Cruelty to Animals in 1824. Throughout the nineteenth century a number of new organizations were formed to provide support for animals and there were eight national organizations by the turn of the century. These movements should be seen within a wide movement for social reform during the period, but they also demonstrate a shift in attitudes to animals. The Victorian sentimentality was extended to kittens and birds as well as children, and 'man's' duty was to protect the weak, increasingly seen to include animals. There was, however, no question that animals were in any sense equal to humans. They were protected because they were subordinate. As a result, meat eating continued to be an acceptable part of animal protection, so long as no excess cruelty was used in the farming or slaughter of the animals (see Ritvo 1987).

Between the 1900s and the 1960s the well-established organizations seemed able to cope with both animal welfare and diet issues and only nine new organizations were founded in the first sixty years of this century. Probably the most influential of these, in the long term at least, was the Soil Association. Founded in 1946 by Lady Eve Balfour, it grew out of pre-war 'humus-farming', the belief that only natural products should be used to fertilize the soil. The SA also inherited a liberal dose of pre-war 'crank' ideas about the magical nature of the soil and remained a fringe organization until the 1980s, tainted with gibes about 'muck and mysticism'.

However, after the mid-1960s many of these older organizations began to seem too traditional for a new generation, and, between 1960 and the mid-1980s, fourteen national, loosely environmental organizations were created (Garner 1993: 42). Alongside, and probably greater than, the increase in number of national organizations has been the foundation of local groups, with perhaps 300 in existence by the early 1990s. Finally, and most difficult to quantify, is support from the general public who do not belong to any group but share general or specific aims. While the numbers here cannot be given, the strength of this kind of feeling reveals itself in consumer pressure, as in the furore over the Body Shop's 'No Testing on Animals' claim which initially backfired but soon resulted in all major supermarket chains making the same claims for ranges of cosmetic and other products.

Reasons for these increases in what we might loosely call 'environmental' groups are relatively straightforward. The nineteenth-century movements, as I have said, tended to be set within a wider attempt at moral reform, while the post-1960s ones reflect the growth of environmental consciousness. Since the 1960s, questions about human duties to preserve nature and the relationship of humans to nature have been growing. According to David Pepper, the Green movement has reformulated the conventional value that humans are separate from nature (so that nature 'can and should be exploited and dominated for human benefit' and that the laws of nature, or scientific laws, should be used to exploit nature) in favour of insisting that humans are part of nature; that nature must be protected and respected for itself, regardless of its value to humans; and that the laws of nature like the carrying capacity of the earth must be obeyed, even when they mean limits on human behaviour (Pepper 1996: 11). From here, theorizing about the welfare of animals amongst philosophers, social scientists, and environmentalists has led to arguments about animals' rights as opposed to animal welfare. This movement is well described by Garner. He distinguishes a 'continuum of views graduated in order of the moral recognition their exponents consider we ought to accord to animals'. These move from those who would argue that animals have no moral status, through the orthodoxy that they have some moral status but are inferior to humans. Garner again divides these into those who argue that although animals are sentient they lack any significant interest and those who say that while animals have an interest in not suffering, this can and should be overridden to promote the greater good of humans, who are truly autonomous. Finally there are those challenges to the orthodoxy based on animal rights of some kind (Garner 1993: 10).

A number of philosophers have, since the 1970s, argued these issues in some detail, and their roots can be seen in 1960s liberation politics. They can be seen to occupy two very different positions. The first, and in many ways still most important of these was Peter Singer, whose *Animal Liberation*, published in 1975 (Singer 1975), remains a key text. Extremely crudely Singer argues that the degree of sentiency in animals in the avoidance of pain and hunger should count as much as the comparable interests as humans. To deny this is akin to denying the specific claims of, for example, women or blacks (sexism and racism) and is therefore 'speciesism'. However Singer, in the last analysis, does concede that there might be situations where animals' rights are subordinate to the needs (and rights) of humans. This possibility is denied by Tom Regan in *All that Dwell Therein* (Regan 1982) and *The Case for Animal Rights* (Regan 1988); the second of the two contemporary positions on animal rights. Regan argues that if a creature has a life of its own then that creature possesses rights akin to 'civil' rights. Such a creature also has intrinsic value, and is worth dignity and deserves respect. The logic of Regan's position, which he does not deny, would be the end of animal husbandry in any recognizable form.

These arguments were in large part a response to the first signs of serious, provable disturbances in the natural world which had an impact outside the minority cultures of vegetarianism and organic farming. The publication of Rachel Carson's *Silent Spring* in England in 1963 (Carson 1963) raised concern about the effects of the widely used pesticide DDT on the food chain. A year later, *Animal Machines* by Ruth Harrison (Harrison 1964) went some way to revealing the realities of the new production methods which lay behind both the increased quantities and low prices of meat. These works spread the unease already felt by a minority of the population about the food we eat to a much wider public.

More important though were the growing links in the 1960s between 'natural' life styles and the youth counter-culture. In 1945, as we have seen, vegetarians were a tiny minority of the population with only 100,000 people registered as such for rationing. The immediate post-war growth was slow, but by the late 1970s the number calling themselves vegetarians reached nearly a million. But in the next two decades growth was enormous and the number of vegetarians doubled from just over a million in 1980 to 2.5 million (4.3 per cent of the population). More significant still was that the largest increase was among young middle-class men and women.

To these young men and women food represented a part of both a rebellion against the middle-class families in which most of them had grown up and a positive assertion of a new and more 'spiritual' life associated with sometimes naive notions of a more natural and harmonious world. When, for instance, the Krishna Consciousness movement opened its London restaurant in the late 1960s it combined eastern spirituality with the Beatles (who in part financed it), outlandish clothes, and 'pure' food free from any animal content. The final blow was that it did not charge—unless the customer wanted to pay—a perfect combination of rebellion and rejection for 1960s youth. However, it quickly moved outside the sometime exclusive world of West London. Peter Dedman, founder of Infinity Wholefoods in Brighton, an enormously successful business, began with catering at the first Glastonbury Festival. 'It was all brown rice and vegetable. The main thing was that it had to be cheap, and you had to be able to churn out huge quantities of cheap and healthy food' (Hardyment 1995: 164).

Youth counter-culture transformed vegetarianism from the preserve of a few odd characters eating nut cutlets in 'healthy' restaurants to something approaching a mass movement, at least among the young. The success of fashionable health food restaurants and shops like Cranks and Infinity Foods marked the change from personal idiosyncrasy to acceptance of whole food into, if not the mainstream, then a highly visible position. However, it did more than that. If 'conversion' to vegetarianism was for many, or even most, a fashionable and even temporary phase, to some it represented a statement about the whole of their personal politics.

To trace this movement in terms of 'mass support' as a whole is extremely difficult. For most the change was an intensely personal one, often having an almost religious sense of discovery and self-discovery leading to personal solutions. Some simply 'dropped out', or to use a more fashionable term 'downsized'. Small is beautiful became the slogan, as those who could left their jobs to aim for a new lifestyle in the countryside. In families or larger groups they headed for the west of Britain, especially the Welsh hills, where land was cheap. Their motives were simple and understandable. They wanted to escape the pressures and pollution of twentieth-century urban life and headed instead for the rural. The price of an average London house easily bought an alternative rural idyll: a house with enough land to grow fruit and vegetables for the group; to have hens running around for eggs; possibly goats for milk and cheese; even a sheep for wool. No more meat full of hormones, vegetables covered in pesticides and herbicides, fruit ripened artificially, most of all, no more factory farming. By conviction, and for economy, most self-sufficiency amateurs were vegetarian; meat is both difficult and expensive to produce on a very small scale. In this world human endeavour would provide food and clothing for all, what could not be grown could be exchanged, and, of course, all agriculture was organic. An essential part of the dream was the organic family. Away from the attractions of television and street culture the family would rediscover itself, all would work together for the good of all. Even the smallest child could be allocated tasks which it could usefully fulfil. This is the ideal presented by the guru John Seymour in his writings and it sounded extraordinarily attractive (Seymour and Seymour 1973). In this view, to know which chicken produced the breakfast egg, to have watched fruit ripen before jam- or wine-making, became a statement of personal and even political fulfilment. Some communes went even further than this and declared communistic lifestyles in which all was held in common, the larger initial investment and continuing larger group facilitating an easier life for all. However, for those accustomed to urban life the necessary slow pace of rural life came hard. Beyond all this was the hard economic reality of the twentieth century and many found self-sufficiency an unattainable dream. For the few the solution was presented with some ease—write an account of the whole process and live off the proceeds. This was the tip of the 'hippy capitalist' iceberg. Organizations, like Brighton's Infinity Foods, managed to make a successful business from the lifestyle politics. For most though, as the small ads in magazines like *Resurgence* show, with their holidays on organic smallholdings, circle dancing classes, and aromatherapy, it was the converted preaching to the converted.

To others conversion meant extending the logic of the personal is political into action. Upon 'conversion' these individuals, if they joined any kind of organization, joined one that was likely to be transient, localized, and often underground. However, even given these problems, we can sketch in an outline of political change. The first element was the growth in interest and concern for animal welfare. At one level refusal to eat the flesh of animals is obviously a response to the killing of animals, but this did not necessarily mean, before the 1960s at least, that any connection was made between 'cruelty' to animals and not eating them. The membership of the RSPCA was, until the 1960s, hugely greater than the number of vegetarians, for example. What seems to have happened is that the growth in alternative lifestyles led to a wider awareness of the kinds of arguments early ecologists were, and had been, making about the relationship between people and the 'natural' world. To this new generation, schooled in CND and the anti-Vietnam War movements, the 'peaceful' methods adopted by generations of animal welfare activists seemed worthless and outdated.

What began to emerge in the 1970s as a result of these initially personal/political decisions was a complex (and heady) mixture. It is difficult to separate the constituents of this brew since many of them do not fit with older categories of political or social analysis. What we see in what I will call 'naturism' is a combination of personal politics, green ideas, and youth counter-culture. Added to this is the central notion, derived originally from the late 1960s, of non-violent direct action. This began as simply a 'method' of protest; however, the peace camps of the 1980s, and especially the women's camp at Greenham Common, changed the definitions. As George McKay writes (1996):

Direct action has developed physical obstruction and intervention to combine an oppositional impulse with a positive effort at community organisation. The aim is to produce the kind of situation witnessed at . . . Claremont Road in East London [the protest against the M11 extension], 'a community of resistance', a form of communal protest honed from a jumble of live experience and faith.

The notion of a 'community of resistance' with its own codes, cultures, and ways of life is central to the new naturism. At one level its origins lie in the wish to 'drop out' already referred to, but the key difference was the notion that resistance was no longer simply a matter of 'sorting out your head' but of confronting authority. The origins of this, in turn, lie in 'politicization' of the free festival movement of the 1970s, by increasing opposition from the authorities including the police. This culminated in the notorious 'Battle of the Beanfield' in 1985 where the police, having driven the group of New Age Travellers off the roads around Stonehenge, moved into arrest some and to (apparently) disable their vehicles, with a level of force that many, even some who had accepted the demonization of the Peace Convoy, found completely unacceptable.

The free festivals movement gave to the new naturism not only the key element of a community of resistance but also its link with music and 'fun'. *SchNEWS*, the news-sheet published by the Brighton group Justice, gives a weekly listing under the title 'Party and Protest' which includes illegal free festivals, progressive gigs, as well as appeals for support and announcements of meetings and demonstrations. However, other elements which are less tangible came from the 1970s movement. The 'cultural' side of the free festivals movement, especially as expressed in 'Fairs of Albion' held across Norfolk and Suffolk during the 1970s, had a profoundly romantic view of the countryside. A compound of Tolkien, Blake, English folk music, and a ragbag of vaguely mystical thoughts about nature, it found its expression in the notion of 'Albion'. Deliberately taken from Blake, via the 'Albion Free State', a London hippy collective of the early 1970s, the notion of Albion gave the land and the countryside of England a particular significance. This notion was not however simply nostalgic—at least for some. As McKay writes, 'whatever politics functions here in the early 1970s is a politics of rejection of technology, a contribution to a hippie organic ideal through a parody of history' (McKay 1996: 38).

Alongside the growth in notions of 'cultural and community resistance' and the gradual politicization of the festival culture other changes were taking place which were to have considerable significance to the full-blown emergence of 'naturism' in the 1990s. These were mainly centred around animal rights, and especially the growth of much more politically active and violent groups around opposition to hunting (hunt saboteurs) and the use of animals for scientific experiment (the Animal Liberation Front). Again both groups emerged out of an impatience with the constitutional methods used by long-established organizations like the League against Cruel Sports, various anti–vivisection groups, and the RSPCA.

However, it was the issue of roads which brought these groups together, especially around the campaign to prevent the building of an M3 extension through Twyford Down near Winchester in 1992. A campaign had been started by local groups and by Friends of the Earth. In March 1992 a new element entered the picture— the Dongas. The Dongas grew out of what McKay sees as 'the deep dissatisfaction felt with the established environmental pressure groups of the time' (McKay 1996: 136). However they also built, sometimes consciously and sometimes unconsciously, on an existing if diffuse set of ideas. Their methods came from Greenham, hunt sabbing, and even the ALF. Their notions of lifestyle came from the free festivals, fairs, and the New Age Travellers; their politics from a perceived failure of conventional methods made worse by the defeats of the 1980s when even the strongest, the miners, seemed unable to survive government attack. Their beliefs were rooted in deep ecology, animal rights, and vegetarianism.

Despite the failure of the Dongas and others to prevent the building of the M3, or for that matter the M11 extension in East London or the Newbury bypass, the impact of their protests has been huge. By the summer of 1997 more people knew who 'Swampy', a young road protester, was, than knew who was Home Secretary. However, this was only the most visible sign of what appeared to be a much larger change. At Twyford Down and at Newbury the press confronted the unlikely phenomenon of 'county' England alongside dreadlocked eco-warriors. This was to be more striking still at the protests against live animal exports in southern and eastern England in 1994–5. Here, unlike earlier protests, the movement was able to claim at least temporary victories. By the spring of 1995, although the government had not banned shipments, all major ferry companies had stopped carrying live animals.

It could be argued that despite its high profile 'born-again naturism' is a limited or minority phenomenon. If one means the hard core this is certainly true; however, there are more general shifts which suggest that this hard core is simply the 'advance guard' of much broader changes. The question of food, for example, in both a negative and positive sense, had become a major political/cultural issue since the late 1970s. Doubts about factory farming were at first centred around the production of battery eggs and broiler chickens, which combined inhumane conditions with an increased risk of salmonella poisoning. The debate intensified when the full implications of the cattle disease BSE began to be realized in the spring of 1995. Similarly concern, coming first from Carson's early 1960s (Carson 1963) attack on DDT but continuing through to the 1990s with worries about the genetic modification of plants, spread anxieties about the safety of food products even to fruit and vegetables.

Positively, as I have already suggested, one response to this was the huge growth in the number of vegetarians since the early 1970s. However, it was not simply that the numbers who refused to eat meat grew but that general patterns of consumption changed. As Alan Warde has shown, what he calls 'menu pluralism', with ever larger groups eating vegetarian dishes as part of normal diet, had grown enormously, a fact recognized by the growth of vegetarian menus in mainstream cooking and women's magazine features (Warde 1997: 48–88). A parallel movement can be seen in the very widespread public support locally and nationally for the demonstrations against live animal exports (Howkins and Merricks 1996) and roads (Howkins and Merricks 1997).

A final element in relation to the more general appeal of these movements arises from their concern with the land, the 'natural' world, and ironically with Englishness, although a version of that far removed from its usual manifestations. As Linda Grant wrote of these 'new movements' in the *Guardian* in the summer of 1995 (*Guardian*, 3 June 1995):

There is a sense of a reclaiming of Englishness, a harking back to the radical protest movements of the English Civil War, the Diggers and the Levellers . . . At some protests one spies the extraordinary sight of the Union Jack, wrenched away at last from the hands of the British National Party and reworked as the Union Jill in rainbow colours.

With its mixture of animal rights, defence of the English landscape, and simple life personal politics, sometimes the new naturism looks very like earlier movements, and not only movements of the 'Left'. Yet problems remain in evaluating these diverse component parts in terms of conventional analysis. The work of Ted Benton and Simon Redfern (Benton and Redfern 1996) has suggested they mark a distinctive shift in the field of politics, bringing in new constituencies and new issues. But less than five years after Benton wrote, at the height of the live animal exports campaign, this judgement looks premature. That does not mean no change has taken place. In 1999, within weeks of the lowest turn-out ever recorded in a parliamentary election, something in the region of 8,000–10,000 representatives of the new politics took over the City of London. Their posters, their costumes, and their 'party and protest' politics bore all the hallmarks of the underground politics of the 1980s and 1990s. They were brought there through the Web. This unlikely mixture of technology and Albion, of tribalism and the Internet, suggests that any analysis which dismisses this group does so at its peril.

References

This bibliography refers only to works cited directly in the text. The published literature is now enormous. Readers wanting further information should consult the bibliographies in these and other works.

Benton, Ted, and **Redfern, Simon** (1996), 'The Politics of Animal Rights: Where is the Left?', *New Left Review*, 215.

Carson, R. (1963), *Silent Spring*, Harmondsworth: Penguin.

Garner, R. (1993), *Animals, Politics and Morality*, Manchester: Manchester University Press.

Hardyment, C. (1995), *Slice of Life: The British Way of Eating since 1945*, London: BBC Books.

Harrison, R. (1964), *Animal Machines*, London: Vincent Stuart.

Howkins, A., and **Merricks, L.** (1996), 'Dewy Eyed Veal Calves. Middle Class Opinion and Live Animal Exports 1970–1995', unpublished paper.

—— —— (1997), 'Not in my Back Yard: Public Opinion and Road Protest', unpublished paper.

Kean, H. (1995), 'The "Smooth Cool Men of Science": The Feminist and Socialist Response to Vivisection', *History Workshop Journal*, 40.

McKay, G. (1996), *Senseless Acts of Beauty: Cultures of Resistance since the Sixties*, London: Verso.

Pepper, D. (1996), *Modern Environmentalism*, London: Routledge.

Regan, T. (1982), *All That Dwell Therein: Animal Rights and Environmental Ethics*, Berkeley and Los Angeles: University of California Press.

—— (1988), *The Case for Animal Rights*, Berkeley and Los Angeles: University of California Press.

Ritvo, H. (1987), *The Animal Estate: The English and Other Creatures in the Victorian Age*, Cambridge, Mass.: Harvard University Press.

SchNEWS round—the Inside Story from the Direct Action Frontline, issues 51–100.

Seymour, J. and **S.** (1973), *Self-Sufficiency: The Science and Art of Producing and Preserving your own Food*, London: Faber.

Singer, P. (1983), *Animal Liberation: Towards an End to Man's Inhumanity to Animals*, Wellingborough: Thorsons.

Thirsk, J. (1997), *Alternative Agriculture: A History from the Black Death to the Present Day*, Oxford: Oxford University Press.

Thomas, K. (1983), *Man and the Natural World: Changing Attitudes in England 1500–1800*, London: Allen Lane.

Warde, A. (1997), *Consumption, Food and Taste: Culinary Antinomies and Commodity Culture*, London: Sage.

29

Against Enclosure: Rethinking the Cultural Commons

GRAHAM
MURDOCK

Contested Commons

> Let's suffer no encroachment upon our Lane to be,
> But to repel such Tyranny let's ever now agree
> (anti-enclosure ballad from Nottingham;
> quoted in Thompson 1991: 125)

IN 1794, six men dressed in black descended from a coach and set about tearing down the fences that the Duke of Bedford had erected around Streatham Common in South London. It was a small incident with large implications. 'London . . . would have no parks today' if people had not reasserted their right to use historic common land and opposed its conversion into private property (Thompson 1991: 125). These, and similar acts of local resistance up and down the country, were the closing skirmishes in a guerrilla war against land enclosure that had stretched over several centuries. By 1794, with three-quarters of England successfully fenced off (Wordie 1983: 488), it was clear that the major battle had been lost. The local economies that the commons had supported through customary rights to graze animals and gather firewood and gleanings had already been displaced by an intensive system of capitalist agriculture.

This process had begun in the 1500s under the Tudors, when landlords, often backed by an Act of Parliament, bought up land that had been communally worked for generations and converted it into pastures for intensive sheep farming to service the burgeoning textile industry. The officially appointed Commissioners descended on villages with account books in hand, parcelling out the commons into 'neat orderly rectangles, each with a separate owner', cancelling all past relationships and mutual obligations and replacing reciprocity with hourly wages (Rifkin 1998: 40–1). Villagers had become labourers.

The 'No Trespassing' notices did not put an end to struggles over access. Rural families, many subsisting on pitifully low wages, continued to supplement their diet by poaching game and fish and scrumping fruit from orchards, and the historic footpaths and rights of way were still used, with or without the consent of the landowners whose property they crossed. Nor were conflicts confined to the countryside. Disputes over what constituted public space and how it should be used were a constant feature of life in the industrial cities. Demands for privacy and propriety were continually pitched against popular claims, from local arguments over rowdyism in the streets to incidents with a more general resonance.

The ribbon of royal parks that stretched from St James's at the back of Whitehall to Hyde Park was a particular bone of contention. In 1774, Queen Caroline had erected a fence around Kensington Gardens with servants 'placed at the different entrances to prevent persons meanly clad from going into' it (quoted in Porter 1994: 173). Hyde Park, which Charles I had given to the people in 1637, though open formally, was used almost exclusively by the fashionable and well-to do, who rode out along Rotten Row in the mornings and took the air in their carriages around 'The Ring' on summer evenings. The tension between *de jure* openness and *de facto* closure came to a head in 1866 with the affair of the railings.

That year, an electoral Reform Bill, which would have significantly extended the right to vote, was defeated, prompting demonstrations around the country. In London, the Reform League announced their intention of marching to Hyde Park and holding a protest rally. Though nominally open to the public, the Park was still widely 'regarded by middle-class Londoners as a pleasure garden set aside for themselves and their families . . . and the notion of mass meetings being held there filled them with disgust and alarm' (Dover Wilson 1966: p. xxvi). On the day of the rally, the marchers arrived to find the gates closed on the orders of the Home Secretary. Part of the crowd refused to accept this, pulled down a section of the railings and entered the Park, trampling flower beds in the process. Although no one was hurt, 'respectable' opinion was appalled at this invasion of 'roughs'. As a later commentator noted, 'it is scarcely too much to say that the fall of the Park railings did for England in July 1866 what the fall of the Bastille did for France in July 1789' (Dover Wilson 1966: p. xxvi). Matthew Arnold, the eldest son of the reforming public school headmaster Thomas Arnold, gave powerful voice to establishment fears in his influential book *Culture and Anarchy*, published three years later. In a passage that conjures up images of a monster emerging from the mud at the bottom of a deep lake he presented the destruction of the railings as proof positive that 'the working class which, raw and half-developed, has long lain half-hidden' had now issued 'from its hiding place' and claimed its right of 'meeting where it likes, bawling what it likes, breaking what it likes' (Arnold 1966: 105). Left unchecked he saw this assertiveness leading inevitably to bloody class war and he urged those in power to help head-off this cataclysm by supporting the 'great men of culture' in their efforts at 'making prevail' and 'carrying from one end of society to the other, the best knowledge, the best ideas' (Arnold 1966: 70).

He was not the first to see the diffusion of common knowledge and shared cultural experience as a way of healing social divisions. As Sir Robert Peel had argued, in the 1830s, the principal reason to build a national art gallery, open to everyone, in the heart of London was 'to cement the bonds of union between the richer and poorer orders of the state so that each can take pleasure in the same great things' (quoted in MacGregor 1997: 36). This impulse steadily gathered momentum as the century wore on and produced an array of cultural sites—museums, libraries, educational institutions—open to all and paid for out of philanthropy and the public purse. The profits from the Great Exhibition of 1851 were used to begin building a cluster of public museums in Kensington on the south side of Hyde Park. The Victoria and Albert was started on almost immediately, in the 1850s, followed by the Natural History (1873–81) and the Science Museum (1907). New art galleries joined the National Gallery, with the opening of the National Portrait Gallery in 1856, and the Tate Gallery (funded by the sugar magnate Sir Henry Tate) in 1897. These structures were part of an unashamedly paternalistic project. It set out to promote a highly selective definition of the cultural commons whilst displacing more open and contested understandings of common culture. As Raymond Williams rightly insisted, 'a common culture is one which is continuously remade and redefined by the collective practice of its members, not one in which values framed by the few are taken over and passively lived by the many. For this he prefers the term "culture in common"' (Eagleton 2000: 119). Its organizers reserved the right to define what counted as 'great things' or useful knowledge and to arrange their classification and display. The ordinary people who entered these new symbolic spaces did so as guests invited to a cultural feast prepared in kitchens hidden from view. As Arnold's telling phrase 'making prevail' suggests, creating this new 'culture in common' was as much an act of aggression as a gesture of goodwill. It required shared cultural spaces to be cleared of all unapproved structures and unregulated activities and called for the censor's blue pencil and the policeman's truncheon as well as the civil servant's planning skills and the missionary's ardour. It also assumed command over central systems of communication.

As Oxford Professor of Poetry and a long-serving schools' inspector, Arnold thought mostly in terms of institutionalized education and the promotion of literature. But by the time *Culture and Anarchy* appeared, more prescient observers had already begun to argue that a cultural commons capable of meeting contemporary conditions might be better organized around forms of communication based on electrical flows rather than printing plates.

Electric Affinities

On 10 June 1837, William IV had signed the patent giving William Forthergill Cooke and Charles Wheatstone the rights to a version of the electric telegraph. However, their coding system for messages proved cumbersome and was eventually displaced by the simple language of dots and dashes devised by the American Samuel Morse. In the spring of 1844, when he successfully sent the message, 'What hath God wrought?' the 40 miles from the Supreme Court in Washington to a receiving station in Baltimore, his contemporaries were in no doubt that he had ushered in a revolution. Sentiments previously communicated by letters, parcels, or bouquets of flowers could now be translated into his digital code and sent as pulses down the great network of wires that snaked out across the landscape. Communication was uncoupled from transportation. It no longer mattered if the wheels came off the coach, or a rock fall blocked the road. Telegraphic messages could pass almost instantaneously over rough terrain and through inclement weather. The tyranny of distance had been defeated. The inhospitable spaces that had kept people apart were filled with a continual electric traffic.

The telegraph held out the promise that the social ties broken by migration and diaspora could be repaired and a new, more inclusive, sense of fraternity forged. It seemed to offer the prospect of a collective conversation to which everyone could contribute. The *American Telegraph Magazine* greeted the idea of building this new, and thoroughly modern, cultural commons with undisguised enthusiasm, claiming that 'nearly all our vast and widespread populations [will be] bound together . . . by a Telegraph and Lightening-like affinity of intelligence and sympathy, that renders us emphatically "ONE PEOPLE" everywhere' (quoted in Czitrom 1982: 10).

But this democratic impetus was at odds with the telegraph's pivotal role in providing a communicative infrastructure for corporate capital and the bureacratized state. As the *National Telegraph Review and Operator's Companion* noted in 1853, just seven years after the medium's launch; 'At its very birth, the . . . system became the handmaiden of commerce' (quoted in Standage 1998: 154). Economic and political interests decided which points would be connected and which left unserved, and set the price of sending messages at a level that most ordinary people could only contemplate using in dire emergencies or on special occasions. As a letter to the London *Times* complained in 1851, the telegraph was 'a means of communication available only to the rich' (quoted in Morus 1996: 371). The telegraphic commons had been comprehensively enclosed. In 1899 the British Tory Prime Minister Lord Salisbury told the Institution of Electrical Engineers that the telegraph had 'assembled all mankind upon one great plane, where they can see everything that is done, and hear everything that is said, and judge of every policy that is pursued at the very moment those events take place' (quoted in Morus 1996: 339). He saw no need to mention that these capacities were less the common possession of 'mankind' than the property of governments, financial institutions, and the rapidly expanding news agencies. By then it was taken for granted.

Faced with this corporate annexation observers began to look for an alternative space in which to pursue the utopian ideal of a common culture. Many fixed on the emerging technology of the telephone and later of wireless which Marconi had demonstrated in 1896. Many early enthusiasts of the telephone saw it primarily as a device for distributing music and news rather than relaying private conversations. As the London magazine *Nature* noted in 1876, 'by paying a subscription to an enterprising individual who will, no doubt, come forward to work this vein, we can have from him a waltz, a quadrille, or a gallop just as we desire' (quoted in Briggs 1977: 43). Entrepreneurs in London did come forward with an 'eletrophone' service that offered relays of music but it was not as popular as they had hoped. Founded in 1894, the Electrophone Company had only 47 subscribers at the end of its first year of operations and only 600 at the end of its first decade. The Budapest Messenger (Telephon Hirmondo) launched the previous year was rather more successful. Within five years it was delivering a daily service of news, music, and talk to 6,000 subscribers in and around Budapest. It was conceived and run as a vertical distribution network. Subscribers could access the programming but they could not talk to each other. It was still operating in 1918 though in a much diminished state. As late as 1922, when radio broadcasting was already becoming the preferred medium of mass dissemination, commentators in other major markets could still envisage the 'radiotelephone' making 'our ordinary home or office telephone receivers also our broadcasting receivers' (Frost 1922: 9).

Radio's displacement of the telephone as the mass broadcasting medium of preference was accompanied by the collapse of early enthusiasts' hopes for the medium's capacity for two-way communication. They had assumed that because radio waves travelled through the atmosphere, a natural resource held in common, wireless communication would not be commandeered by private interests or confined to particular routes. And since the contacts made were immaterial and did not rely on physical connections, they would be infinitely mobile and flexible, allowing people to speak and listen across huge distances. This euphoric dream of a new kind of cultural commons is nicely caught in this American account from 1923; 'Here we have sat in the little back room in a home in Indiana, and, with not even a wire extending beyond the lot, have heard the boys talking all over America . . . and a great chorus of others we did not stop to identify. . . . It is great step out of the every-day into the sublime' (quoted in Sconce 1998: 217).

In the corridors of power, however, there was mounting concern over this unregulated mobility of contact. What appeared to enthusiasts as a marvellous release from geographical and social boundaries appeared to governments as both chaotic and dangerous. The widespread social unrest that followed the end of the First World War in the major capitalist countries resurrected longstanding fears of popular disruption and revolution which were further fuelled by the Bolshevik seizure of power in Russia. Against this background, governments in the new mass democracies were convinced that radio's mobilizing potential must be harnessed to the task of rational reconstruction and national unity. They justified concerted intervention by arguing that the usable part of the electromagnetic spectrum was a scarce resource that could only accommodate a limited number of channels before signals interfered with each other, creating chaos in essential services. The right to broadcast had to be carefully regulated. This argument prevailed. Transmission capacity was removed from standard radio sets and the horizontal networks of radio enthusiasts were replaced by vertical systems distributing programming from a central point. Users became listeners.

Broadcasting and Communality

Broadcasting's consolidation in the 1920s coincided with the emergence of two great formations—mass democracy and mass consumption—offering different conceptions of a reconstructed cultural commons.

With the granting of the vote to women, 'citizen' finally became a universally available identity in Britain. For the first time, every adult was promised the right to participate fully and equally in social and economic life and to help shape its future forms, together with a responsibility to contribute to building a sense of communality based on respect for the diversity of moral codes and ways of life generated by a complex and continually shifting social order. This new social contract was underwritten by the expectation that the resources needed to support it would be forthcoming. Some of these were material; an adequate lifetime income, healthcare, personal safety, and access to transport. But others were cultural. We can identify four basic cultural resources for citizenship: information; knowledge; representation; and participation.

The ideal of active citizenship presupposes a universal right to know what is happening in the world and why. More particularly it insists on people's right to know what the governmental and business organizations with significant power over their life chances and choices are doing and what options of action and change critics are proposing. Information by itself, however, does not equip people with the resources they need to take well-grounded decisions in their own lives or considered positions on issues of public policy. They also require access to the frameworks of analysis and interpretation that link biographies to histories, connect events to underlying processes, and tease out the causes of present conditions, together with access to criteria of judgement that enable them to adjudicate between competing accounts and explanations. At the same time, complex conceptions of citizenship recognize that because people participate in social life in and through a plurality of identities, they have a right to see the variety of their lives and aspirations represented in the central spaces of public culture, together with a right to contribute to creating these representations; to become cultural producers as well as consumers.

This vision of a cultural commons built around universal citizenship found itself, from the outset, competing with an alternative conception grounded in the emerging mass consumer system. In this parallel world, people were encouraged to think of themselves not as members of moral and political communities with a responsibility to respect other people's needs and identities but as actors in the marketplace whose necessities and desires could be met by a proliferating array of commodities. It constructed the sovereign individuals of capitalism as shoppers rather than citizens and presented the choice between competing brands as the central right of modern life. A sense of shared fate and mutual responsibility was edged out by the promise that for every personal blemish and social problem there was a purchasable solution. The new commodities presented themselves less as useful objects and more as declarations of identity. They whispered and murmured about who their owners were and wished to be, papering over the familiar map of social divisions with brightly coloured images of market segments. Discussion of life chances was eclipsed by the promotion of lifestyles. To cement these new allegiances advertising waged a ceaseless evangelical crusade to persuade people that they could be born again through the benedictions and blessings of consumption.

Broadcasting arrived, then, to find itself faced with the problem of situating itself in relation to two competing visions of the connections between culture and communality. In the United States, despite a spirited defence of various forms of public and community enterprise, broadcasting was mostly delivered into the hands of private corporations and used to generalize the emerging culture of mass consumption. In the United Kingdom, what began as a commercial monopoly granted to a consortium of radio set manufacturers was converted (after two public inquiries had considered the matter) into a public enterprise—the British Broadcasting Corporation—with a mission to provide resources for the responsible exercise of citizenship to every radio set owner for the cost of a single, universal, licence fee. After a few early experiments with sponsorship it carried no commercial speech.

It set out to pursue Matthew Arnold's paternalistic project, by developing a new integrated 'culture in common'. It was to be a museum, library, theatre, seminar room, and church without walls.

Graham Murdock

As C. A. Lewis, the first organizer of programmes, was quick to emphasize in 1924, when the BBC was still a commercial monopoly seeking to convince sceptics that it could be trusted to act responsibly in pursuing this project, senior management saw the 'middle ground' as their natural home. Their 'general policy' was 'to keep on the upper side of public taste [and] at all costs avoid offence in any shape or form to the widely varying susceptibilities of the vast public which it serves' (Lewis 1924: 48–9). Accordingly, they favoured the voices of political figures from the major parties supplemented by the views of legitimized intellectuals and experts and they constructed shared experience around a strongly selective tradition of cultural expression which ruled anything raucous, risqué, or disrespectful out of order. At the same time, as a new and experimental medium, it also attracted programme-makers with a commitment to interrogating contemporary social conditions and providing spaces for voices and testimonies grounded in everyday experiences and dilemmas. The strong echoes of the schoolroom and the pulpit in its paternal mode of address also fuelled rising demands from audiences, for greater access and participation. As in the earlier tussle over the proper uses of Hyde Park, there were running battles over how the communal space of public broadcasting should be deployed. Officialdom favoured the radio equivalents of bracing walks, rowing on the lake, and bandstand concerts. Groups pressing for greater representation lobbied for soap box speakers, spontaneous play and picnics, and gramophones brought onto the grass to play popular music. The resulting tensions between a top-down 'culture in common' and a bottom-up common culture were played out on a daily basis in the Corporation's institutional and creative life. With the introduction of regular television services balancing representation against participation became even more problematic. Questions about who was entitled to picture other people's lives and in which forms were added to long-standing debates about who was entitled to speak. They were also complicated by the arrival of competition.

When commercial television was finally introduced into Britain its 'licence to print money' was over-stamped by a strong regulatory requirement to continue the public service project of providing resources for citizenship as well as meeting advertisers' demands for guaranteed access to mass audiences. This circle was not always easily squared. Attempts to engage with the rapidly shifting conditions of national life through new forms of current affairs and documentary programming and realist forms of television fiction were continually cross-cut by the seductive dramas of consumption mounted in the advertising breaks and game shows. Gritty images of rain-washed streets and blighted lives were surrounded by a 'visual, visceral dazzle, and absorbing sense of pleasure in the act of perusal' (Marling 1994: 5). These competing images of post-war settlement were pitched against each other most consistently in a succession of situation comedies which subjected aspirations for betterment and style to the gravitational pull of blocked mobility and frustrated hopes. These programmes—*Hancock's Half Hour*, *Steptoe and Son*, *Only Fools and Horses*—remain among the most popular ever shown on British television and offer a portrait of London life peopled with characters worthy of Dickens or Mayhew; spivs, wide-boys, gangsters, self-made men, street sweepers, market traders, rag and bone collectors. Although they have attracted far less critical attention than the single plays produced at the same time, they arguably offer a richer guide to the collisions between consumerism and political promise, affluence and disappointment, in post-war British life. We can see this structure of feeling embedding itself ever more securely as Tony Hancock's pretensions to cultural capital rub up against Sid James's get-rich-quick schemes, Harold Steptoe's ambitions for self-improvement are dashed on the rocks of his father's crudity and fear of loneliness, and Del Trotter's dreams of becoming a millionaire are buried under the piles of second-rate goods crowding his flat and filling his battered three-wheeler van. In these fictional lives, the open horizons of consumerism are continually undercut by the broken political promise of substantive equality and opportunity.

If, for the twenty or so years that the regulated dual system lasted, British television at its best moved some way towards constructing a cultural commons in which top-down initiatives confronted grounded experience, albeit one that was differentially open to contest and variably responsive to pressures for wider representation, with the arrival of cable and satellite services this provisional and incomplete democratic settlement began to be dismantled and the process of corporate enclosure was resumed.

Pay-per Cultures

With the launch of subscription channels, television ceased to be a cultural space available to all and moved towards being a commodity. For the first time, access to programming depended on cash payments. Cable relay companies had long offered clear signals on subscription, but the arrival of commercial cable and satellite services marked a break with past practice. This move was publicized by its promoters as a welcome extension of customer choice. They saw it as breaking the cultural dictatorship of broadcasters by allowing audiences to dismantle the set schedules and draw on an array of thematic channels to assemble a menu of viewing tailored to their particular requirements. As the economist Alan Peacock argued forcefully, in a key government report on broadcast finance:

British broadcasting should move towards a sophisticated market system based on consumer sovereignty ... which recognises that viewers and listeners are the best judges of their own interests, which they can best satisfy if they have the option of purchasing the broadcasting services they require from as many alternative sources of supply as possible. (Home Office 1986: para. 592)

However, it quickly became clear that not all interests were equal in this new marketplace. As Michael Green, the chair of the consortium that won the franchise to run one of Britain's new array of digital television channels, candidly admitted a decade later, on hearing of his company's success, 'I fully accept that [the main rival bidder] DTN's programmes were more innovative—but we must have programmes that people want to watch. A bird-watching channel, or opera-watching channel, will not attract viewers' (quoted in Culf 1997: 11).

In a multi-channel world, based on sound commercial principles, entitlement to service and representation depend on a minority's size and their attractiveness to advertisers. But Green's comment is also revealing in another way. Its map of social segmentation is organized entirely around differences in consumption and leisure preferences. It is indelibly consumerist in orientation. There is little or no place for interests grounded in shared social circumstances. Norman Tebbit, one of Mrs Thatcher's closet confidants, had made this abundantly clear over a decade earlier when he berated Jeremy Isaacs, the first chief executive of Channel 4, which had been established expressly to represent interests not adequately catered for elsewhere in the broadcasting system, at an embassy dinner; 'You've got it all wrong you know', he said, 'doing all these programmes for homosexuals and such. Parliament never meant that sort of thing. The different interests you are supposed to cater for are not like that at all. Golf and sailing and fishing. Hobbies. That's what we intended' (Isaacs 1989: 65). In the coming age of proliferating channel choice and pay-per-view ushered in by digital compression's multiplication of television services, viewers are constituted even more forcefully as markets rather than moral communities. In this emerging audio-visual economy public service programming ceases to be a universally accessible space in which the cultural resources for citizenship are continually redefined and struggled over and becomes another form of special interest, a niche market.

Supporters of this new market-driven system admit that some interests will remain unserved and that this poses a problem for a modern democratic polity. Consequently they concede a residual role for public subsidy. As the Peacock Report put it, there 'will always be a need to supplement the direct consumer market by public finance for programmes of a public service kind supported by people in their capacity as citizens and voters but unlikely to be commercially self-supporting in the view of broadcasting entrepreneurs' (Home Office 1986: para. 133). His list of programmes that fit this criterion includes most of the categories that are central to sustaining the access to knowledge, diversity of representation and open debate essential to contemporary citizenship; current affairs and documentary programmes which 'contribute to responsible citizenship'; 'critical and controversial programmes covering everything from the appraisal of commercial products to politics, ideology, philosophy and religion'; and popular programming which experiments with different forms of presentation from 'the ones which viewers would have demanded unprompted' (Home Office 1986: para. 563–5).

Digital Dividends

Public broadcasting has not yet moved entirely from constructing a cultural commons to servicing a market niche, but the BBC's decision to launch a series of subscription channels and to enter into partnerships with commercial companies to develop new programming and services marks a significant step in this direction. Contemporary defenders of the commons therefore find themselves in much the same position as enthusiasts a hundred years ago. Just as turn-of-the-century aspirations for an extended democratic conversation centred on the potential of radio so present-day hopes have migrated to the Internet.

Optimists read the Net's short history as an unexpected victory for grass-roots activism and do-it-yourself culture. They see a system that originated in the heart of the military-industrial complex, built to ensure secure official communication in the event of a nuclear strike, being taken up in universities and research institutes as a medium of scholarly exchange, and finally entering the public domain as the creation the World Wide Web introduced a single, simple, system of use. The Net's supporters take every opportunity to sing the body electronic. Like earlier enthusiasts of the telegraph and of radio, they see communication on the Net released from the 'corruptions attendant to the process of moving information attached to *things*—from paper to brains—across, over, and under the vast and bumpy surface of the earth' and flying free 'in the soft hail of electrons that is cyberspace' (Benedikt 191: 3). They also celebrate its dismantling of established communication hierarchies. Whereas conventional broadcasting is constructed as a vertical, top-down, distribution system with limited possibilities for popular participation, they present the Web as a horizontal network in which each participant can produce as well as consume. Within this system exchange is not organized by paternalism or price but rooted in reciprocity, 'a back-and-forth giving and taking, moderated by all participants in a discourse to their mutual advantage' (Jacobson 1995: 198).

Pessimistic observers, on the other hand, are inclined to highlight the Net's segmentation rather than its communality. As Todd Gitlin has argued, it clearly 'enriches the possibilities for a plurality of publics—for the development of distinct groups organised around affinity and interest. What is not clear is that the proliferation and lubrication of publics contributes to the creation of a public-and-active democratic encounter of citizens who reach out across their social and ideological differences to establish a common agenda of concern and to debate rival approaches' (Gitlin 1998: 173). So, rather than offering a simple solution to the problem of building a contemporary cultural commons, the Net raises the possibility that the most open system of communication so far invented may 'at worst . . . encourage a whole range of closed cultures' (Eagleton 2000: 129). Against this, more optimistic observers argue that although the Net's decentralized nature poses problems for the creation of shared experiences, stable bonds, and continuing commitments, since in the continually shifting conditions of contemporary democracy the achievement of enduring consensus is unrealistic and, arguably, undesirable, facilitating 'sustained dialogue and temporary agreements' may be the only feasible option (Dahlberg 1998: 71).

Recently, however, this utopian dream of extended democracy and revivified mutuality has been comprehensively undermined by the familiar dynamics of corporate enclosure (see Bettig 1997). After an initial period of scepticism, the major communications and consumer goods companies have moved onto the Net in force, fencing off the free use of cultural resources with new intellectual property rights and establishing ticket-of-entry sites in the expectation that it will rapidly become a major medium for distributing cultural and other goods. Advertisers, too, have recognized the Net as a significant new arena for commercial speech, where the gap between promotion and purchase can be progressively closed by new forms of electronic commerce allowing goods to be ordered directly from the screen. Digitalization is confidently expected to deliver sizeable dividends for trade.

As a consequence of this concerted commercial push, the Net is now the site of a deepening conflict between opposed visions of its potentials and uses. Maps of horizontal networks confront models of hierarchy. Systems of reciprocity develop alongside the principle of payment for use. Gift relations are juxtaposed against commodity exchange. The collective conversation required to sustain democracy's habits of the heart is continually edged out by invitations to euphoric moments of individual consumption. Co-operative cultural production is displaced by pre-packaged pleasures, interaction is directed towards commercial transactions.

Building the Virtual Commons

We are now entering the age of communicative convergence. This is partly the outcome of digital technology's translation of all forms of cultural expression into the single universal language of 0s and 1s, and partly the result of the progressive removal of the regulatory barriers that separated one medium from another and prevented companies from crossing these demarcation lines. Now these walls are coming down we see a rapid consolidation within the communications system as the major corporate players in the computing, telecommunications, and cultural industries compete to position themselves to best advantage within the emerging digital arena. This corporate convergence is a powerful force for enclosure. It needs to be matched by an equally strong commitment to build a digital commons modelled on the Athenian agora, which was a much richer and more varied cultural space than many accounts present. 'Far from being architecturally impressive, [it was] a jumble of crowded downtown streets and irregular open spaces where . . . public buildings stood in the midst of workshops, market stalls, and taverns' (Jackson 1987: 119). The digital agora needs to keep that diversity, balancing deliberation against enjoyment, publically sponsored initiatives against spontaneous constructions.

The basic building blocks for this new cultural space are already to hand. All the major public cultural institutions—museums, libraries, schools and universities, and public broadcasting organizations—are in the process of developing Internet sites that make their holdings and expertise more widely available and encourage users to talk to their staff and to each other. At the same time, an increasing number of social groups and movements are using the Net to launch debates, construct exchange networks, and co-ordinate activities. Building the digital commons requires these multiple initiatives to be integrated into a new communal network that operates not as an extended system of distribution or commercial exchange but as a new space of encounter and collaboration between professional organizations and social movements, established and emerging cultural forms, expertise and grounded experience, and as an enlarged forum for debate over the terms on which differences will be recognized and respected and our collective future defined and organized. For work to proceed on this project, two basic conditions have to be met; universal access and the provision of a readily available point of entry and navigation.

Up until now, Internet access has been routed through personal computers and the relatively high price of machines has severely limited participation. Access will increase as digital television systems replace the PC as the modal point of entry, but even then many low-income households will not be able to afford to buy into the 'digital revolution'. They will be excluded by the price of converting from an analogue to a digital set and by the costs of telephone connections to the Net. These barriers can be relatively easily addressed, first by giving everyone a set-top box that allows digital signals to be displayed on an analogue set, and secondly by abolishing all charges for the local telephone calls that connect the set to the Net. This last initiative would also benefit organizations developing paid-for sites and electronic commerce services. However, they could be required to contribute to the costs of developing the digital commons through a small levy on transactions. This would provide a continuing income stream that could be used to support the digitalization of key public holdings, to finance developments proposed by social groups, and to fund points of access in public locations. Once connected, however, users still face the problem of finding their way around the proliferating array of available sites.

The most obvious host for a gateway and navigation system for the digital commons is the BBC. For the Corporation, following its viewers onto the Net is a precondition of survival as a central cultural institution and a logical extension of public broadcasting's obligation to provide cultural resources for contemporary citizenship. For the public, having access to a comprehensive and easy-to-use guide to non-commercial Internet resources that is free at the point of use is a basic cultural right in the digital age. The BBC has already laid the foundations for this by building its public web site into the most visited content site in Europe. At the moment, however, it operates primarily to cement audience involvement with the Corporation in an increasingly competitive marketplace. It is an exercise in brand enhancement. As a result, it is too narrowly based and self-referring to provide the basis for a genuinely open digital commons. It needs to go beyond its present role as a point of entry into the BBC's own institutional and creative activities and become a first port of call for anyone wishing to find their way not only to the resources offered by other public cultural institutions but to the myriad creative, community, and campaigning groups who are producing materials that extend and challenge the cultural maps drawn up by these officially sponsored sites. A digital commons would aim to provide a permanent point of intersection between top-down initiatives and bottom-up interventions, fomenting continual encounters and dialogues between sponsored 'cultures in common' and self-produced 'common cultures'.

In 1930, observing that broadcasting had become a top-down instrument of commercial and bureaucratic organization, Bertold Brecht called for the development of its popular interactive, dialogic, potential, and challenged his listeners to ask themselves, 'If you should think this is utopian . . . consider why it is utopian' (Brecht 1979: 26). Now, more than half a century later, if we listen attentively to the buzz and roar of traffic on the information highway, over the thunder of commercial freight we may just catch the faint sound of the iron wheels on that hackney coach as it rumbled onto Streatham Common that morning in 1794, reminding us that enclosure is always contestable and that even the most solid-looking fences can be taken down if the will is there.

Further Reading

Buscombe, Edward (2000), *British Television: A Reader*, Oxford: Clarendon Press.

Marvin, Caroline (1988), *When Old Technologies Were New: Thinking about Communication in the Late Nineteenth Century*, New York: Oxford University Press.

Naughton, John (1999), *A Brief History of the Future: Origins of the Internet*, London: Weidenfeld and Nicolson.

Graham Murdock

Price, Monroe E. (1995), *Television, the Public Sphere, and National Identity*, Oxford: Clarendon Press.

References

Arnold, Matthew (1966), *Culture and Anarchy*, Cambridge: Cambridge University Press (1st pub. 1869).

Benedikt, Michael (1991), 'Introduction', in Michael Benedikt (ed.), *Cyberspace: First Steps*, Cambridge, Mass.: MIT Press.

Bettig, Ronald (1997), 'The Enclosure of Cyberspace', *Critical Studies in Mass Communication*, 14/2, June.

Brecht, Bertold (1979), 'Radio as a Means of Communication', *Screen*, 20/3–4, Winter.

Briggs, Asa (1977), 'The Pleasure Telephone: A Chapter in the Prehistory of the Media', in Ithiel de Soal Pool (ed.), *The Social Impact of the Telephone*, Cambridge, Mass.: MIT Press.

Culf, Andrew (1997), ' "Second-best" wins Digital TV Fight', *Guardian Weekly*, 6 July.

Czitrom, Daniel (1982), *Media and the American Mind: From Morse to McLuhan*, Chapel Hill: University of North Carolina Press.

Dahlberg, Lincoln (1998), 'Cyberspace and the Public Sphere: Exploring the Democratic Potential of the Net', *Convergence*, 4/1.

Dover Wilson, J. (1966), 'Editor's Introduction', in Matthew Arnold, *Culture and Anarchy*, ed. J. Dover Wilson, Cambridge: Cambridge University Press.

Eagleton, Terry (2000), *The Idea of Culture*, Oxford: Blackwell.

Frost, Stanley (1922), 'Radio Dreams That Can Come True: Here is What the Radio People Can Give You if You Want It', *Colliers*, 69, 10 June.

Gitlin, Todd (1998), 'Public Sphere or Public Sphericles?', in Tamar Liebes and James Curran (eds.), *Media, Ritual and Identity*, London: Routledge.

Home Office (1986), *Report of the Committee on Financing the BBC* [The Peacock Report], London: HMSO, Cmnd. 9824.

Isaacs, Jeremy (1989), *Storm over 4: A Personal Account*, London: Weidenfeld & Nicolson.

Jackson, J. B. (1987), 'Form follows Function', in N. Glazer and M. Lilla (eds.), *The Public Face of Architecture*, New York: Free Press.

Jacobson, Robert (1995), 'Reciprocity versus Interactivity: Principles of Democracy and Control for an Information Age', in Slavko Splichal and Janet Wasko (eds.) *Communication and Democracy*, Norwood, NJ: Ablex Publishing Corporation.

Lewis, C. A. (1924), *Broadcasting from within*, London: George Newnes Limited.

MacGregor, Neil (1997), 'A National State of Emergency: If Britain's Museums Start Charging Admission, the Doors Will Close to the People', *New Statesman*, 7 Nov.

Marling, Karal Ann (1994), *As Seen on Tv: The Visual Culture of Everyday Life in the 1950s*, Cambridge, Mass.: Harvard University Press.

Morus, Iwan Rhys (1996), 'The Electric Ariel: Telegraphy and Commercial Culture in Early Victorian England', *Victorian Studies*, 39/3, Spring.

Porter, Roy (1994), *London: A Social History*, London: Hamish Hamilton.

Rifkin, Jeremy (1998), *The Biotech Century: How Genetic Commerce Will Change the World*, London: Phoenix.

Ross, Edward A. (1910), 'The Suppression of Important News', *Atlantic Monthly*, 105.

Sconce, Jeffrey (1998), 'The Voice from the Void: Wireless, Modernity and the Distant Dead', *International Journal of Cultural Studies*, 1/2, Aug.

Standage, Tom (1998), *The Victorian Internet: The Remarkable Story of the Telegraph and the Nineteenth Century's Online Pioneers*, London: Weidenfeld & Nicolson.

Thompson, Edward P. (1991), 'Custom, Law and Common Rights', in E. P. Thompson, *Customs in Common*. London: Merlin Press.

Wordie, J. R. (1983), 'The Chronology of English Enclosure', *Economic History Review* 2nd ser. 36/4, Nov.

30

Blair and 'Britishness'

STEPHEN DRIVER
AND
LUKE MARTELL

Today I want to set an ambitious course for the country. To be nothing less than the model twenty-first century nation, a beacon to the world. It means drawing deep into the richness of the British character. Creative. Compassionate. Outward-looking. Old British values, but a new British confidence.

(Blair 1997)

New Labour, New Britain

The Labour Party led by Tony Blair was elected to government in May 1997 promising to create a 'New Britain'. The slogan, unveiled at Blair's first party conference as leader in 1994, sought to portray 'New Labour' as a political force in tune with modern times. New Labour would complete the modernization of the Labour Party; and then in government it would modernize Britain: 'The party renewed, the country reborn', as Blair closed his speech to Labour's party conference in 1995 (Blair 1994, 1995). But what are the attitudes, values, and ways of life that New Labour is promoting in its New Britain? What identity does it envisage for the British nation at the turn of the millennium?

Appeals to national identity are normally associated with Conservative politics: whether the 'putting the Great back into Britain' variety of Margaret Thatcher in the 1980s or the Baldwinesque images of village cricket and warm beer from John Major in the early 1990s. The current Tory leader William Hague has staked his party's future on the 'common sense' values of the British people, including personal liberty and defence of private property (Hague 1999a).

To Labour modernizers these recent Conservative appeals to Britishness are seen as exclusive, nostalgic, and nationalistic, as well as being attached to traditional institutions, like the House of Lords, that have had their day. By contrast, Labour's modernization programme has been projected as being more in tune with what it really is to be British and with what 'New Britain' might be. Labour modernizers claim that Britain's national identity at home and abroad is stuck in the past; and in a version of the past that plays on the identity of the British as insular and conservative rather than as free traders open to new ideas and new ways of living (Dodd 1995; Leonard 1997). If Britain is to be modernized—*New Britain*—its identity needs renewing as part of the process of modernization. What Blair calls the 'forces of conservatism' include those who persist in remembering the glories of British times past. Moreover, for Labour modernizers, moral and cultural renewal is required to underpin the economic and social renewal of a divided nation (Blair 1995). The task of government is to rebuild the moral basis for a more cohesive society by identifying the values and identities that people can unite around. Social exclusion, the central metaphor for the Labour government, is as much about culture—values and identities—as it is about economics.

The Labour government's devolution programmes for Scotland, Wales, and Northern Ireland, as well as Britain's membership of the European Union, have brought the question of national identity to the foreground of contemporary politics. Blair has spoken of the Conservatives' 'false promise' of 'narrow nationalism'; and prefers to equate New Labour's sense of Britishness with tolerance, openness, and internationalism—especially regarding Europe. 'Enlightened patriotism' Blair calls it (Blair 1998). Blair wants Britain to be a 'beacon to the world': a leader in European Union politics and an active—and ethical—player in world affairs.

In the rest of this chapter we shall focus on Blair's sense of Britishness: what does the Prime Minister think being British is? Then we shall look at three questions. First, is Blair playing with the fire of nationalism? Secondly, are New Labour's notions of Britishness in tension with its inclusionary politics and with the diversity of local identities in Britain and the pluralism of its political reforms? And thirdly, does New Labour's ambition to modernize

Britain sit uneasily with its emphasis on traditional values and institutions?

Patriots and Populists in the 'Giving Age'?

The Labour Party's second political broadcast during the 1997 general election campaign starred Tony Blair and a fifteen-month-old pedigree bulldog called Fitz. During the broadcast, a listless Fitz is roused from his slumber by Blair talking about New Labour's plans for New Britain. As Blair announces that he is 'a British patriot' and that he wants 'the best out of Europe for Britain', Fitz breaks free of his leash and bounds off! Peter Mandelson, one of the main architects of New Labour's media strategy, said: 'The Labour Party is the patriotic party. *New Labour is the party of one nation and the bulldog is a way of saying this*. It is an animal with a strong sense of history and tradition' (*The Times*, 15 Apr. 1997, our emphasis).

New Labour's one-nation politics has involved the search for inclusive symbols of national identity: images which reach beyond Labour's traditional working-class support; and which are seen as more in touch with popular opinion. Blair has cast himself as a 'new patriot' who identifies with, and understands, modern British people and their everyday lives. 'I love my country', 'I am a patriot', and 'enlightened patriotism' are among the sentiments he evokes in speeches. Blair perceives that the decline in community can be reversed with a renewal of pride in the shared identity of being British—'one nation, one community', as he suggests. A strong sense of British identity underpins the collective values and institutions, such as social justice and the National Health Service, which bind the community—the nation—together. Devolution of government to Scotland, Wales, and Northern Ireland has been paralleled by a reassertion, by leading Labour modernizers, of the shared political and cultural state that, it is argued, is the United Kingdom (Blair 1998; Brown 2000).

Blair's speeches, then, are an attempt to inspire a sense of community by appealing to national pride. Labour modernizers also project New Labour as the 'People's party'. Blair's sense of being British—just as Thatcher before and Hague currently—seeks to evoke the 'real' values of 'the People'. The almost ubiquitous use of 'people' as a prefix to government policies ('the people's budget', the 'people's parliament', etc.) involves a kind of populism that attempts to identify Labour with the British people and what it means to be British. As Blair puts it: 'New Labour is the political arm of none other than the British people as a whole. Our values are the same: the equal worth of all, with no one cast aside; fairness and justice within strong communities' (Labour Party 1997a).

Politically, New Labour's populism is a response to the party's contracting social base and its declining electoral fortunes. Since the 'Labour listens' events after the party's 1987 General Election defeat, Labour has spent a lot of time with focus groups and opinion polling trying to regain a broad social basis of support and swing its values more into line with public opinion. The populist appeal to Labour's values and conception of national identity as those of the people is part of this process of reidentifying with voters and making the party electable.

Blair's ability to strike a chord with popular sentiments was strikingly illustrated as the news broke of the death of Diana, Princess of Wales, in 1997. Blair spoke with apparent emotion, *prefiguring* widespread displays of public grief. He called her 'the People's Princess' and negotiated a public funeral incorporating members of the charities she represented. The widespread emotion at her death was said by Blair to be partly a result of identification amongst people with her compassion and humanitarian values. In his first Labour conference speech as Prime Minister weeks after Diana's death, Blair claimed that New Labour was expressing a more 'giving age'. He described the crowds that greeted his journey to Buckingham Palace on 2 May: 'Theirs were the smiles of tolerant, broad-minded, outward-looking, compassionate people . . . And with them I could see confidence returning to the British people, compassion to the British soul, unity to the British nation' (Blair 1997). The implication was that New Labour like Diana and the British people shared the same 'compassionate agenda'. As MP Chris Smith put it: 'No-one who has lived through the last tragic weeks here in Britain [following the death of Diana, Princess of Wales] can doubt, either, that there is such a thing as a national cultural sense . . . of compassion and commitment to those who are marginalised and disadvantaged . . . What a change this represents from the go-getting, me-first, thrusting Thatcherite world of 1980s values' (Smith 1998: 36–7).

'Creative Britain'

The use of Fitz as a symbol by Labour may seem incongruous. The bulldog, a traditional symbol of British national identity dating back to the early eighteenth century, is hardly an image of a party in tune

Stephen Driver and Luke Martell

with modern times. Nonetheless, New Labour has embraced what it sees as the modernity and youth in British national identity. Labour modernizers offer the British as an inherently creative people. As Blair put it: 'We are one of the great innovative peoples. From the Magna Carta to the first Parliament to the industrial revolution to an empire that covered the world; most of the great inventions of modern times came with Britain stamped on them . . . Even today we lead the world in design, pharmaceuticals, financial services, telecommunications' (Blair 1997; see also Labour Party 1997b and Smith 1998). So New Britain is 'creative Britain' in tune with the developments of a post-industrial information society. It has particular strengths in creative work and innovation, whether in science or in the cultural industries, industries crucial to a post-industrial economy dominated by services and the new information and communication technologies—an economy which New Labour aspires for New Britain.

The symbol of creative Britain, the Millennium Dome in Greenwich, London, was intended to celebrate British achievements in innovation in science and technology. The Dome was to be, Labour hoped, a symbol of a creative and confident New Britain, as Blair suggested when he unveiled the models of it. It would, he said, be the 'envy of the world' and 'it will bring the nation together in common purpose'. The Dome was to be the Labour government's *grand projet*, combining a sense of national unity with that of modernization. Instead, its critical and commercial failure left 'rebranded Britain' with a brand that didn't work (see Bayley 1999).

The 'Young Country'

The creative aspect of New Britain is one feature of what Blair has called many times 'a young country' (Blair 1996). Many of the qualities New Labour wishes to promote as part of New Britain's identity are often associated, rightly or wrongly, with youth—creative, inventive, dynamic, forward-looking . To New Labour, the attraction of the icons of 'Cool Britannia'—such as Britpop and Damien Hirst (one of whose prints adorns the cover of Chris Smith's *Creative Britain*)—is their association with youthfulness, creativity, and self-confidence. Blair himself is a young Prime Minister: born in 1953, the first PM to have grown up in the 1960s and the first to be young enough to play rock guitar (Wilkinson 1996). Similarly, many of the areas of cultural concern for Labour are those in which young people are perceived to be the key producers and consumers, such as film, broadcasting, pop music, fashion, and the new media. The Labour government has made better access for young people a priority in arts policy—for example free entry to museums and art galleries and proposals for a national endowment for science, technology, and the arts (NESTA) aimed at young talent. This appeal to the interests of the young is seen by some modernizers as important because it is they who are thought to be disproportionately alienated from politics.

The 'young country' is an attempt by New Labour to be *modern* and focus on contemporary culture and the industries of the post-industrial information society, with a corresponding downplaying of culture as heritage. Thus, the Department of National Heritage has become under Labour the Department for Culture, Media, and Sport not, Culture Minister Chris Smith argued, 'because heritage is unimportant . . . but because we wanted to capture something more forward-looking, a name which captured more accurately the new spirit of modern Britain' (Smith 1998: 2). So, while traditional cultural institutions such as museums, art galleries, opera, and theatre all have their place in current Labour thinking on the arts (and Labour argue that access to such institutions must be 'for the many not the few'), there is greater excitement than in the past about modern cultural industries, such as film, broadcasting, and the new media, seen to be undergoing rapid change, largely because of innovations in digital technology.

But does New Labour's sense of Britishness provide an opportunity for drawing the country together? To what extent does New Labour offer the basis for reconstruction of community around a new sense of British identity? In the rest of the chapter, we shall address three concerns. First, in emphasizing the positive qualities of British identity is New Labour in danger of fuelling the kind of 'narrow nationalism' it accuses others of? Second, to what extent is New Labour's sense of Britishness inclusive? And third, is New Labour's programme of modernization shackled by its attachment to traditional values and institutions?

Rebuilding Community or Narrow Nationalism?

New Labour's interest in promoting national virtues and symbols of national pride will cause many concern. The Left in particular has tended to support the view that the nation—as both a polity and an identity—is a construction of the modern historical period. As such the nation overlays those economic and social relations that

Stephen Driver and Luke Martell

the Left views as the fundamental building blocks of society—primarily class but also gender and ethnicity. For the Left, nationalist politics endangers the 'real' politics of class by cutting across the lines of working-class community and solidarity. This perspective challenges the core theory of nationalism: that the nation is the 'natural' unit for social, political, and cultural life. It also presents patriotism—the love of country—as irrational, dependent on romantic and often racist notions of people, place, and ethnicity. By giving weight to the significance of national identity—of being British—is Blair in danger of being sucked into the arena of nationalist politics that he so often accuses others of indulging in?

Recent attempts, for example, by David Miller, to link nation and community to progressive politics have tried to make the case that national territories—and the 'common sense of nationality' (Miller 1989, 1995)—provide a framework for citizenship within which social justice is possible: in particular, because the national community offers a set of already existing shared meanings which give people a sense of communal identity. If the Left wants to foster greater community feeling the national community is the one we can most easily identify with. Anthony Giddens, the sociologist who has been an influential figure in New Labour thinking, shares this view that national identity can provide the basis for rebuilding community. Giddens argues that 'people who feel themselves members of a national community are likely to acknowledge a commitment to others within it' (Giddens 1998). Both Giddens and Miller are anxious to steer clear of charges of nationalism. Giddens supports the notion of a 'cosmopolitan nation'. Miller believes that questions of national identity can be separated from nationalist politics: identity is simply a question of shared beliefs rooted in history, not a set of objective characteristics; and what is shared in common need not preclude other forms of identity. Indeed, Miller believes that nationality provides a balance to the diversity characteristic of modern society—providing the 'essential background' to citizenship in a pluralist society.

Labour modernizers, then, are not alone in thinking that the nation might be used for progressive ends. Blair's Britishness is meant to be different from, say, the Tories' 'narrow nationalism' because it is tolerant and outward-looking. There is, to be sure, some hazy thinking in New Labour's conception of 'New Britain'. It might be seen as essentialist: are national virtues like creativity and compassion natural or products of history? Rhetorically, at least, New Labour promise that 'New Britain' will be inclusive, pluralist, and internationalist. But can an aspiration to patriotic pride, national strengths, and identifications really avoid racist and discriminatory possibilities towards 'outsiders'? Home Secretary Jack Straw's tough stance on asylum seekers suggests that New Britain isn't always as compassionate and cosmopolitan as we are led to believe by New Labour.

'My Vision of a Young Country': a Vision for Everyone?

So can New Labour articulate a sense of Britishness that is sensitive to the pluralist character of British society, as well as to the regional and national identities of the United Kingdom (Thompson 1995)? New Labour's vision of a creative, young country with a post-industrial economy is unlikely to apply evenly across the United Kingdom. It reflects a rather narrow view of British society and of being British. It is hardly representative of the British economy, British society—or even British demographics. Indeed, it plays to the view, skilfully put forward by the Countryside Alliance (and taken up by Hague's 'common-sense' Tories), that New Labour is elitist, exclusive, and metropolitan and not reflective of the people of the British Isles more widely. As such, Blair's sense of Britishness—at least his 'creative Britain' version—is unlikely to carry the same resonance in other parts of the United Kingdom and across British society as a whole.

But if 'creative Britain' has failed to embrace British farmers and manufacturers, among others, New Labour appears equally ill at ease with identity politics and with more pluralist conceptions of British society. Where many on the Left have sought to celebrate the 'expressive revolution' and what are seen as the multiple iden-tities of postmodern society, Labour modernizers reject the result-ing 'rainbow' politics, worried about the erosion of the institutions and values which, they argue, provide the bedrock for social cohe-sion. New Labour's response to the perception of fragmentation has been less to celebrate it and more to appeal to institutions (the nation, the family) and values (work, duty, obligation) that it is hoped can provide the basis for greater social cohesion in 'strong communities'. But concerns have been raised that New Labour is too traditional, too conservative, too white, too male, paying lip-service to the cultural diversity of Britain (see Parekh 1998; Wilkin-son 1998; Alibhai-Brown 1998). In the pursuit of middle English votes, New Labour has forgotten that middle England is not England let alone Britain; and in its search for legitimacy it has exchanged pluralism for populism.

Stephen Driver and Luke Martell

Labour modernizers clearly hope that 'New Britain' will offer an inclusive sense of community which acknowledges diversity and which matches the notion of Britain as a hybrid, multinational state (Phillips 1997; Kelly 1997). But the dilemma New Labour faces is that if it tries to project a more pluralist identity that is sensitive to the many different voices of the United Kingdom (which is what some on the progressive Left would like it to do), it could miss out on genuine bases of common identity. This is especially true if its pluralism is simply pragmatic in the sense that it talks to different parts of Britain in different ways (Hassan 1995). In response to the centrifugal political forces unleashed by devolution, New Labour has, for example, responded in Scotland to the challenge from the Scottish Nationalist Party by asserting a sense of Britishness rooted in values and institutions such as social justice and the welfare state likely to go down well with a Scottish audience (see Blair 1998). But as political pluralism becomes embedded in the political culture post-devolution, there are already signs that such pluralism is reinforcing regional and national identities within the UK (see *Scotsman*, 22 Feb. 2000). This is likely to make New Labour's designs for a New Britain all the more difficult. It is certainly the case that constitutional devolution is provoking national and regional questions (such as the identity and representation of England and English regions) that play into the hands of Labour's political opponents (see, for example, Hague 1999*b*).

The Traditional and the Modern

Labour modernizers insist that renewing British identity will be on the basis of 'old values' (Blair 1997). But does New Labour's attachment to traditional values and institutions constrain its ambitions to create a modern New Britain? Stuart Hall, for example, has written: 'On crime, on family values, on one-parent families, on questions of sexuality, on the particular variant of communitarianism which he [Blair] espouses, one can find no echo at all of the underlying sociological analysis that one would expect of a so-called "modernizer".' Hall added that New Labour's 'commitment to the monogamous nuclear family as the only credible and stable family form, gives "modernity" such a deeply conservative inflection that it hardly deserves the name' (Hall 1995: 19–33, 31; see also Driver and Martell 1999).

Certainly there is much to the view that New Labour's modernization programme has strong socially conservative elements in

terms of the family, education, and law and order. So there is substance to the argument that New Labour's commitment to traditional values and institutions shapes and limits modernization. But
sometimes the policy, on the family for example, doesn't actually
match the rhetoric (see Driver and Martell 2000). Indeed, New
Labour could just as easily be accused of playing fast-and-loose with
traditional values and institutions as it sends New Britain hurtling
into a global post-industrial age. New Labour's policies are, if anything, undermining of traditional structures and identities,
embracing as they do economic globalization and e-commerce.

On these two charges—that New Labour is too traditional and
that it is not traditional enough—some care is needed. New Labour,
like Thatcherism before it, is a heterogeneous political formation.
The 'project' does encompass more liberal and progressive stances,
concerning, for example, the gay age of consent, the Human Rights
Act, early years childcare and education provision, and wider constitutional reforms. In these policy areas it is not obvious that New
Labour's modernization programme is traditional in any real sense
or constrained by conservatism. In other public policy areas, notably education (especially pedagogy and the curriculum) and law
and order, New Labour is more conservative and traditional.

Tony Blair is not the first Prime Minister—nor the first Labour
leader—to appeal to the distinctive qualities of the British nation,
and he is unlikely to be the last. And just as Margaret Thatcher
wrapped her policies of market modernization in the Union Jack—
they would make Britain great again!—so Blair has made New
Labour's programme of modernization one of national renewal
and patriotic pride: 'New Labour, New Britain.' In New Labour's
identity politics, there is clearly an attempt to offer a range of
images about what it means to be British. There is 'creative Britain';
the hard-working family Britain; and the socially just Britain supported by the welfare state. Blair's Britain is a series of audiences
that require different messages: what goes down well in Middle
England may not touch Labour's heartlands. And each New Britain
reflects different parts of the Blair project. But there are dangers in
all of this—not least the lack of any coherent narrative to Blair's
New Britain. In particular, post-devolution, the appeal to Britishness
will become increasingly problematical. Certainly, the latent (and
sometimes not so latent) nationalist forces in the devolution settlement will make such appeals so. Moreover, the Labour government's response to asylum seekers appears to confirm that New
Britain can be just as exclusive as Old Britain ever was.

Further reading

For a collection of Tony Blair's pre-election speeches, see *New Britain: My Vision of a Young Country* (London: Fourth Estate, 1996). For his current output, see the Downing Street website (*www.number-10.gov.uk*). For rebranded 'creative Britain' (and the Dome), see works by Chris Smith, Mark Leonard (who both love it), and Stephen Bayley (who loathes it). For a collection of (largely critical) articles on the Blair government, see *Marxism Today* (Nov./Dec. 1998). Everything you ever wanted to know about devolution can be found in Robert Hazel (ed.), *Constitutional Futures: A History of the New Ten Years* (Oxford: Oxford University Press, 1998).

References

Alibhai-Brown, Yasmin (1998), 'Nations under a Groove', *Marxism Today* (Nov./Dec.).

Andrews, Leighton (1995), 'New Labour, New England', in Mark Perryman (ed.) *The Blair Agenda*, London: Lawrence and Wishart.

Bayley, Stephen (1999), *Labour Camp*, London: Pan.

Blair, Tony (1994), *Speech to the 1994 Labour Party Conference*, London: Labour Party.

—— (1995), *Speech to the 1995 Labour Party Conference*, London: Labour Party.

—— (1996), *New Britain: My Vision of a Young Country*, London: Fourth Estate.

—— (1997) *Speech to the 1997 Labour Party Conference*, London: Labour Party.

—— (1998), 'Speech on Scottish Parliament', Strathclyde University, Glasgow, 12 Nov.

Brown, Gordon (2000) 'This is the Time to Start Building a Greater Britain', *The Times*, 10 Jan.

Dodd, Philip (1995), *The Battle over Britain*, London: Demos.

Driver, Stephen, and **Martell, Luke** (1998), *New Labour: Politics after Thatcherism*, Cambridge: Polity.

—— —— (1999), 'New Labour: Culture and Economy', in Larry Ray and Andrew Sayer (eds.), *Culture and Economy: After the Cultural Turn?*, London: Sage.

—— —— (2000), 'New Labour, Work and the Family', in Helen Wilkinson (ed.), *The Family Business*, London: Demos.

Giddens, Anthony (1998), *The Third Way: the Renewal of Social Democracy*, Cambridge: Polity.

Hague, William (1999a), 'Identity and the British Way', speech to the Centre for Policy Studies, London, 19 Jan.

—— (1999b), 'Strengthening the Union after Devolution', speech to the Centre for Policy Studies, 15 July.

Hall, Stuart (1995), 'Parties on the Verge of a Nervous Breakdown', *Soundings*, 1 (Autumn).

Hassan, Gerry (1995), 'Blair and the Importance of Being British', *Renewal*, 3/3 (July).

Kelly, Jude (1997), 'The Single Currency of the Imagination', in Michael Jacobs (ed.), *Creative Futures: Culture, Identity and National Renewal*, London: Fabian Society.

Labour Party (1997a) *New Labour: Because Britain Deserves Better*, London: Labour Party manifesto.

—— (1997b) *Create the Future*, London: Labour Party.

Leonard, Mark (1997), *Britain™: Renewing our Identity*, London: Demos.

Miller, David (1989), *Market, State and Community*, Oxford: Oxford University Press.

—— (1995), *On Nationality*, Oxford: Oxford University Press.

Parekh, Bhikhu (1998), 'Home at Last?', *Marxism Today* (Nov./Dec.).

Phillips, Trevor (1997), 'British Identity and Cultural Renewal', in Michael Jacobs (ed.), *Creative Futures*, London: Fabian Society.

Smith, Chris (1998), *Creative Britain*, London: Faber & Faber.

Thompson, Paul (1995), 'Nations, States and Identities', *Renewal*, 3/3 (July).

Wilkinson, Helen (1996), 'The Making of a Young Country', in Mark Perryman (ed.), *The Blair Agenda*, London: Lawrence & Wishart.

—— (1998) 'Still the Second Sex', *Marxism Today* (Nov./Dec.).

Endnote

To London: The City beyond the Nation

KEVIN ROBINS

The true identity of London is in its absence.
(Patrick Keiller, *London*)

THE chapters in this volume have been concerned with the changing culture and identity of Britain—concerned with it at a time when old truths and certainties about what it is to be British seem to have been considerably disturbed. Of course, Britain is far from being alone in its contemporary experience of national cultural discomfort—in recent years, both the meaning and the claims of national belonging have been called into question in new ways right across the world. But in the British case there are evidently particular complexities to the new national question—the question concerning 'who we are' and 'what we stand for'. And there are also particular difficulties that stand in the way of a more accommodating cultural resolution. Here, in this endnote, I want to make a few last observations concerning the particular dilemmas of contemporary British culture—which are, in the end, dilemmas to do with the growing complexity of cultural life in the British space. And I want to do this somewhat provocatively. In this final intervention in this volume, I actually want to work against the grain of the national cultural agenda. In reflecting, briefly, on the way forward, I shall suggest that much of the difficulty in the way of a new cultural settlement in Britain is a consequence of the predominantly national way of thinking about the problems of the national culture—it is a way of thinking that tends to imagine cultural complexity in terms of disorder and loss of coherence. To think otherwise about cultural complexity, I shall suggest, it is necessary to think from another—a counter-national—perspective. And this will lead me eventually to London—that great provocation to the clarity and coherence of British national culture. From London, I think, it is possible to think differently—more productively—about cultural interactions in contemporary Britain.

The National Imagination

First, however, we should consider how the national imagination understands and responds to the problems of the national culture. A useful starting point is provided by the work of the political scientist David Miller, and I want to spend some time here considering his arguments, for they seem to me to offer a strong, clear, and cogent national response to the contemporary challenges to British cultural integrity. In his book *On Nationality* (1995), Miller reflects on what he sees as a significant and problematical decline in the self-confidence and self-image of British people now. He seems to thinks of it in terms of a weakening of national affect. In the particular British context, Miller suggests, one very significant factor in this new national problem is a crisis of historical continuity. 'The post-war experience of people in Britain', he argues, 'has directly undermined the main elements out of which British identity was originally constructed': 'indeed, the main problem of British national identity today is that the understanding of that identity which has emerged over the past centuries seems no longer appropriate to today's world' (1995: 172, 166). When he invokes this shared historical legacy, Miller is thinking of the early grounding of British imagined community in anti-French sentiments (here he invokes the work of Linda Colley); of the associated historical importance of Protestantism (and anti-Catholic sentiments); of what was for long regarded by many as the 'civilizing' project of empire; and of the symbolic ideal of 'limited, constitutional monarchy'. It is the binding and bidding force of these cultural references and symbols that has been dramatically eroded in the post-war period, Miller suggests. These have all taken 'a severe bruising in recent years, to the point where many Britons may wonder whether there is anything distinctly valuable left in British identity at all' (1995: 170). The vital narcissistic element in British culture has been diminished, in Miller's account, and the present time is one in which Britons are consequently left with confused feelings about their national culture and values. 'On the one hand,' he says, 'there is a strong sense that the British do have a separate identity, and that this matters a good deal; on the other hand, it is far from clear what this separate identity is supposed to consist in' (1995: 172). Britons are clinging to the wreckage of their drifting historical identity.

Kevin Robins

But it is not just a question of Britain's relationship to its past. The national identity is being subverted by other developments too. What we now have to take into account, says Miller, is 'the impact of multiculturalism internally and the world economy externally . . . societies are becoming more culturally fragmented, while at the same time they are increasingly exposed to the homogenising effects of the global market' (1995: 185). What are at issue here, then, are the consequences for the nation of globalization (on this, see Robins 1989). Miller recognizes that the processes of globalization, which are both cultural and economic—involving accelerating global flows of people and of commodities—represent a fundamental challenge now to the ideal of national cultural integrity—'a challenge to the idea that people need to have the kind of map that a national identity provides' (1995: 165). First, there is the question of new 'ethnic minorities', as a consequence of new patterns of migration, and the problems they increasingly pose (or are imagined to pose) for the cultural integrity of the nation. The problems here are to do with the proliferation of discourses concerned with 'the quest for cultural diversity'—the desire, as Miller disparagingly puts it, 'to celebrate diversity, bolster ethnic pride and encourage people to pick and choose among the array of cultural identities that global culture makes accessible' (1995: 186). And, second, there is the matter of new global markets—the coming into existence of a new economic order 'in which each operates solely as a free chooser' (1995: 178). Miller profoundly regrets the cultural consequences of such an order, in which people

are happy to think of themselves as individuals who happen to be working in this job, consuming these goods, married to this partner, and so on . . . Along with this goes a view of the world as a kind of giant supermarket in which different goods and services are on offer in different places and in which it is perfectly reasonable for individuals to gravitate to whatever place offers them the best package. On this view, national ties should count for nothing except perhaps in so far as they affect the range of cultural goods on offer in a particular place. (1995: 165)

This is a cultural prospect that, to Miller, seems no less than 'pathological'. What he is drawing attention to, then, is the, for him discomforting, reality that 'national identities now have to compete with a wider range of other potential objects of loyalty' (1995: 178). His problem is that there is a now a new competition for loyalties, in which national institutions are having to contend with both new particularistic and new consumer identities. And, under these conditions of partialized and fragmented allegiances, British people are losing, or giving up on, 'the deeper resources of a common historical identity' (ibid.)—with deeply problematical consequences, Miller believes.

On Nationality provides a useful reference point for my broader reflections. David Miller acknowledges the real and very difficult challenges to national identity in the contemporary era. 'Nationality', he makes clear, 'can no longer remain a diffuse, taken-for-granted cultural matrix, something one acquires simply by living in a place, breathing the air, being exposed to particular ways of doing things' (1995: 178). And, this being the case, Miller sets himself the task of providing a reasoned and coherent defence of 'nationality' (which he carefully distinguishes from 'nationalism', let us note)—a national agenda for national cultural reintegration. As he does so—aiming to establish 'the appeal of national identity to the modern self'—Miller seeks to identify what he himself calls the 'inner logic' of nationality (1995: 12). What become apparent in his exposition, then, are the established motifs and tropes of the national imaginary—tropes that we must consider as significant in so far as they have indeed appealed to, and found resonance in, the 'modern self'. *On Nationality* is a useful text because of what it tells us about—and because of its commitment to—the discursive themes and images that have been at the heart of the national way of thinking and feeling—the images that have been associated with the 'emotional loyalty' (1995: 160) demanded by national belonging.

Among the core images of national discourse—and they are images to which Miller gives his wholeheartedly approval—are ones to do with wholeness, coherence, and integrity. The prevailing imagery within Miller's argument is one of bonds and binding: his overriding concern is with a 'common national identity' that 'binds [people] together in the face of their many diverse private and group identities' (1995: 188); with 'the ties that bind us to our fellow nationals' (1995: 14); with 'the melding together of "races"' (p. 25); with 'what holds nations together' (p. 32); and so on. An imagined community is a unitary community, characterized by a common culture and by mutual understanding—'its existence', says Miller, 'depends on a shared belief that its members belong together, and a shared wish to continue their life in common' (1995: 23). A national identity, in Miller's view, 'requires that the people who share it should have something in common . . . a common public culture' (1995: 25). And this 'something' is not something that exists in the present alone. The national community should, we are told, be 'solidly based in history' (1995: 36)—the shared characteristics and common culture of the imagined community should be sustained through time. When we talk about the national community,

we are talking not merely about community of the kind that exists between a group of contemporaries who practise mutual aid among themselves, and would dissolve at the point at which such practise ceased; but about a community that, because it stretches back and forward across the generations, is not one that the present generation can renounce. (1995: 23–4)

'People value the rich cultural inheritance that membership of a nation can bring them,' Miller asserts, 'and they want to see continuity between their own lives and the lives of their ancestors' (1995: 184). This concern with the coherence and integrity of the national culture also has a historical dimension, then, where it translates into a preoccupation with transmission and continuity.

What is at issue in the imagined community thus conceived is not only the stability of a shared identity and belonging. A second core theme in Miller's defence of national belonging concerns the relationship between shared identities and the ethical and political life of the community. The point he makes is that it is the shared culture and beliefs of the community that provide the very basis for ethical and political action. 'A shared identity', says Miller, 'carries with it a shared loyalty, and this increases confidence that others will reciprocate one's own co-operative behaviour' (1995: 92). The imagined community is 'a community of obligation' (1995: 23). It is in—and only in—a culturally homogeneous order, then, that it is possible to create the conditions of trust and reciprocity that are necessary for collective life to function effectively—through mutual commitments and obligations. In the national community, Miller is telling us, cultural sameness and moral-political solidarity are interdependent variables—'people have an interest in shaping the world in association with others with whom they identify' (1995: 88). The national community is not only 'the source of personal identity', then, but also 'an obligation-generating community' (1995: 82). In the context of the imagined community we come to know, not only 'who we are', but also 'what we stand for'.

A third set of ideas in Miller's argument is centred on the idea of necessity—the necessity of national cultures as such, and also the necessity of what particular nations have become. Miller adamantly resists the idea of national identities as arbitrary or fictitious. It is simply not possible, he says, that people 'should regard their nationality as merely a historic accident' (1995: 184).

It is incompatible with nationality to think of the members of the nation as people who merely happen to have been thrown together in one place and forced to share a common fate, in the way that the occupants of a lifeboat, say, have been accidentally thrown together. There must be a sense that the people belong together by virtue of the characteristics that they share. (1995: 25)

There is a historical dimension to this sense of necessity. 'In national communities,' says Miller, 'people are more tightly bound to the past than the denizens of our imaginary lifeboat ... Language, social customs, holidays and festivals, are all equally the sediment of a historical process which is national in character. So one is forced to bear a national identity regardless of choice, simply by participating in this way of life' (1995: 42). The weight of history exerts a compelling force, then, binding compatriots together into a trans-historical community of fate. But Miller's argument concerning necessity is to do with more than just historical gravity—there seems also to be an assertion of what we might call the logical necessity of national belonging. He is concerned with 'the part played by nationality in making someone the person that he or she is', maintaining that 'national culture is in this sense *constitutive*' (1995: 86, our emphasis). Or as he puts it later, again mobilizing the nautical metaphor, 'cultures, unlike ships, are not vessels to be boarded and abandoned at will'—a national culture is a 'condition for a person's having an identity and being able to make choices in the first place' (1995: 110). Without nationality, Miller seems to be telling us, there can be no meaningful culture, either collective or individual.

In the immediate context of what is happening in and to Britain now—primarily as a consequence of globalization, in both its economic and cultural aspects—Miller's response is a conventional one; his suggestion and proposals for cultural and political reform are quite predictable, because preordained—because he responds precisely as someone who could never regard himself as the denizen of some imaginary lifeboat. To be consistent with his own underlying *beliefs* about the value of nationality, Miller's response must involve the defence of the national culture, in the face of whatever new cultural complexities are threatening it—for 'everyone has an interest in not having their inherited culture damaged or altered against their will' (1995: 86–7). Miller must be committed to conserving the sovereignty and integrity of the national community. Unsurprisingly, then, what Miller envisages and recommends, in response to the present 'decline in confidence' in British nationality, is a 'revived project of nation-building' (1995: 180). But, in making his recommendations, he is no dogmatic nationalist—that is why I have felt

Kevin Robins

that it is worth reflecting on his careful arguments—and the national response that he proposes to global cultural change is reasonably open and constructive. National identity and solidarity are the core values in Miller's political philosophy—nationality remains the most 'appropriate' form of social solidarity (1995: 184)—but, in order for these values to survive, he recognizes, the national community must 'adapt' to the new global environment. What Miller proposes, then, is a reconstituted and revitalized national order—one that incorporates (and thereby domesticates, I would suggest) some at least of the new cultural complexities: 'A historically transmitted identity . . . must adapt to new circumstances, especially to increasing cultural pluralism' (1995: 179). 'The project of nation-building, pursued so energetically in the eighteenth and nineteenth centuries, must', says Miller, 'be carried forward in a way that takes account of revitalised ethnic, regional, and other such identities' (1995: 182).

Nation Culture and Multiculturalism

I have thought it worthwhile to reflect at some length on the arguments put forward in David Miller's *On Nationality* because they provide a clear statement of one particular way of responding—and, in the context of *British Cultural Studies*, a particularly important way of responding—to the challenges of global and transnational change. What Miller offers us is a clear and consistent response to the new cultural complexities from the perspective of nationality—a response, that is to say, from the perspective of what seems to be particularly under threat from global change. And, through his arguments, I think, one can very clearly see how the national imagination organizes its thinking and orders its categories in response to what is happening in the contemporary world. The national mentality begins from the point of view of singularity—unity, integrity, coherence, consensus, commonality, and so on—which it holds to be a positive value, both culturally and politically—a value to be protected and defended. The imagined community, as 'a source of identity and as a source of obligation' (1995: 12), functions most efficiently when it is a unitary community. And, given this commitment to a foundational unity, the national mentality—which may be taken as both a way of thinking and a way of feeling—regards diversity, difference, and complexity as a problem. Diversity is a problem because it is associated with the (imagined) dangers of cultural and political 'fragmentation' and 'disorder'. But, of course, diversity is—increasingly, it seems—a part of the everyday reality that contemporary nations have to live with and deal with. Mechanisms have to be found, therefore, for managing and containing plurality and its disorganizing consequences. Miller's discourse makes apparent what has been the historical project of the national community—to negotiate a way between an ideal unitarianism and a pragmatic pluralism.

This question of the relation between solidarity and diversity has become one of the key political and cultural issues of our time—and it has a particular acuity in the British case. And we may say that the processes of globalization have made accommodation or reconciliation more and more difficult. A variety of possibilities have been suggested for how it might be possible to sustain the national compromise, from both conservative and radical perspectives. David Miller's own proposition, coming from the moderately conservative end of the spectrum, might be characterized as a revisionist cultural nationalism. His argument is motivated by a rejection of what he calls 'radical multiculturalism'. But Miller is certainly prepared to recognize the significance of cultural diversity, and he is open to the claims of 'ethnic minorities' ('Indeed,' he says, 'it is possible to regard ethnic mixing as the source of a nation's distinctive character' (1995: 25)—a position that is put forward in some quarters with respect to the historic creation of a British collective identity). His moderate concession to diversity is tempered, however, by the more insistent and overriding belief in the need for some kind of binding mechanism—a 'common ethos' (1995: 74). In going on to reflect on what this unifying principle might be in contemporary, multicultural Britain, Miller is quick to dismiss the idea, put forward by some political thinkers, that unity should be predicated on some political principle, on some conception of British citizenship, 'where this is understood in terms of subscription to set of political principles: tolerance, respect for law, belief in the procedures of parliamentary democracy, and so forth' (1995: 175). Miller is outrightly rejecting the idea of a 'constitutional patriotism', as a substitute for national identification of the more familiar and involving kind.

Miller dismisses the principle of civic nationalism as the basis for a common identification because, he says, 'the national identities that support common citizenship must be thicker than "constitutional patriotism" implies' (1995: 189). This civic principle is, simply, too insubstantial: it 'does not explain why the boundaries of the political community should fall here rather than there; nor does it give you any sense of the historical identity of the community, the links that bind present-day politics to decisions made and actions performed in the past' (1995: 163). There must be a more robust bond, argues Miller, one that takes into account citizens' need for a sense of both their historical location and their proper place in the contemporary world. Historically, he maintains, a British identity was forged 'to aid the integration' of Scots, Welsh, and Northern Irish populations, thereby sustaining 'a sense of common nationality alongside an equally powerful sense of difference' (1995: 173). Although the Scots, Welsh, and Northern Irish people 'are not properly described as ethnic groups', Miller goes on, 'they may serve as a vivid reminder of the fact that there are many distinct and equally legitimate ways of "being British"' (1995: 174). What is being advocated, then, is a renewed project of integration (on the old basis, it seems), in which the 'new minorities' are now given their 'opportunity to participate in the continuous redefinition of national identity' (1995: 180)—given the opportunity of 'being British' in their own ways. What Miller conceives as the revitalization of British national identity turns out to be an accommodating form of cultural incorporation—a renewed and revitalized integrationism.

An alternative approach to the possibility of reconciliation between the principles of solidarity and diversity is that associated with the idea of a new 'constitutional patriotism'—the idea that Miller was so quick to dismiss for its lack of emotional 'thickness'. This idea of 'constitutional patriotism' has been developed particularly by Jürgen Habermas, in his attempt to think through the relationship between the national and republican dimensions of democratic culture in Europe. Habermas argues that the republican principle is undermined 'when the integrative force of the nation of citizens is traced back to the prepolitical fact of a quasi-natural people—that is to something independent of and prior to the political opinion- and will-formation of the citizens themselves' (Habermas 1998: 406). Under conditions of increased diversity in the European space, says Habermas, the 'organic' nation, with its myths of cultural homogeneity, has become ever more problematical. The question occurs, then, as to 'whether there exists a functional equivalent to the fusion of the nation of citizens with the ethnic nation' (1998: 407). Habermas's answer is that a 'constitutional patriotism' can be that equivalent. He recognizes that many political commentators find this idea of constitutional loyalty to be too weak a bond, but his own belief is that democratic societies can be held together by political culture if that political culture is also inclusive of social and cultural rights:

The citizens must . . . be able to experience *the fair value of their rights* in the form of social security and the reciprocal recognition of different cultural forms of life. Democratic citizenship can only realise its integrative potential—that is, it can only found solidarity among strangers—if it proves itself as a mechanism that actually realises the material conditions of preferred forms of life. (1998: 409)

What is productive in Habermas's argument, I think, is the disentangling of the idea and concept of the 'real nation of citizens' from that of the 'imagined ethnic-cultural nation' (ibid.).

In the context of debates around British culture and politics, a somewhat similar approach has recently been put forward by the historian Linda Colley (1999). Hers is a less elaborated and a less consistent (and sometimes fudged) argument, I think—in large part, no doubt, because it was put forward in a political policy context, at a Downing Street lecture. Like Habermas, however, Colley regards the distinction between identity and citizenship as being crucial. And she is anxious, too, to play down the identity dimension of national culture, in her case, of course, Britishness ('which is more ancestral and visceral')—with criticism particularly reserved for conservative and nostalgic forms of historical consciousness, with their often 'erroneous and incomplete views of [the] past'. 'Instead of being so mesmerised by debates over British identity,' ventures Colley, 'it would be far more productive to concentrate on renovating British citizenship, and in convincing all of the inhabitants of these islands that they are equal and valued citizens, irrespective of whatever identity they may select to prioritise.' She goes on to suggest that British history could now be rewritten to give a new prominence to civic—rather than national-mythical—events, arguing that a revisionist history of Britain could and should find ways of 'connecting our radical and reforming past with the extension of citizen rights being implemented now'.

There is something positive, then, in Colley's idea of 'a revivified citizen nation' as an answer to her question 'What is Britain for?' Her eschewal of a national culturalism, in favour of a concern with 'more inspiring and more accessible definitions of citizenship', should be seen as constructive—particularly if we take into account the audience for her lecture. But in the end, I feel, Colley fails to go the last mile. She raises the question of diversity and multiculturalism, yet, in the end, she seems reluctant to envisage the possibility of that important 'functional equivalent' (to use Habermas's term) that might replace the fusion of the nation of citizens with the ethnic nation. Indeed, her argument with respect to 'ethnic minorities' ultimately collapses into something that is rather like David Miller's position. In some respects, says Colley,

the position of ethnic minorities in this country is a powerful argument for the enduring utility of Britishness. Unlike Englishness, Welshness or Scottishness, Britishness is a capacious concept with no necessary ethnic or cultural overtones. Consequently, large numbers of non-whites seem content to accept the label 'British' because it doesn't commit them to much.

At this point, it seems as if we might be back to square one in the debate on British national culture. Colley has opened up an interesting possibility, but she is unable or reluctant to push the argument forward consistently, and to connect up with the European republican agenda of Habermas and others (in fact, she considers herself 'radical' for proposing 'a twenty-first-century citizen's monarchy'). Her Anglo-Saxon compromise leaves Colley still caught up in the dilemmas of the imagined ethnic-cultural nation.

Beyond the revisionist cultural nationalism of David Miller and the attenuated civic nationalism of Linda Colley, I want now to consider a third contribution to the debate on the relation between diversity and solidarity in the national culture. This is the contribution made by the Runnymede Trust's Report on *The Future of Multiethnic Britain* (2000), chaired by Bhikhu Parekh—in my view one of the most important and radical contributions to the contemporary debate on British culture. The Parekh Report comes at the issues in a rather different way from the other approaches to national culture and identity that I have been considering. Most discussions begin with the singularity of national cultures and then move on to consider the 'problem' of diversity and complexification. The Parekh Report resists this essentially national formulation of what is at issue. It actually takes as its starting point what it regards as the problem of (imagined) singularity and homogeneity—the 'shared cultural meanings, the common national story, [that] weld a nation of individuals into a social unity' (2000: 16). What it argues—quite lucidly, and in contradiction to the myths of integrity—is that 'British national identity has always been more diverse than it is normally imagined to be' (2000: 23). And what it then recognizes is that contemporary global transformations are making this diversity both more apparent and more unmanageable: 'They have shaken the unified conception of Britishness hitherto taken for granted and have injected a sense of fluidity and uncertainty into what was formerly experienced by many as a settled culture' (ibid.). In these circumstances, say the members of the Runnymede Commission, we need to reflect on the state of our national community:

How has the imagined nation stood the test of time? What should be preserved, what jettisoned, what revised or reworked? How can everyone have a recognised place within the larger picture? These are questions about Britain as an imagined community, and about how a genuinely multicultural Britain needs to reimagine itself. (2000: 15)

The report goes on to suggest that there are fundamental difficulties in the way of this necessary reimagination. 'Britishness', it says, 'as much as Englishness, has systematic, largely unspoken, racial connotations'; and so long as these are not dealt with—so long as the imagined ethnic-cultural nation is treated as a sleeping dog—then 'the idea of a multicultural post-nation remains an empty promise' (2000: 38–9).

The Parekh Report rejects the illusory ideal of cultural singularity, and is constantly working against the prevailing ideology of 'One Nation'. Whilst they have a clear awareness of the need to maintain shared values and social cohesion (see 2000: ch. 4), the Commissioners are keen to explore, and put a positive value on, diversity and difference in British society. The Report thinks of Britain as being a 'community of communities' What the members of the Commission want to convey is a sense of the cultural complexities of everyday life in Britain—complexities that actually make life here more interesting now. As they do so, they recognize that the language that we have available to us is rather limited and limiting: the language we use with respect to both the national imagined community and 'minority' communities is problematical precisely because it is a language of community—one that conceives of cultural groups in terms of 'bounded, homogeneous groupings, each fixedly attached to its ethnicity and tradition' (2000: 26):

There are two things wrong with this mental picture of a large homogeneous majority and various equally homogeneous minorities. First, Britain is not and never has been the unified, conflict-free land of popular imagination. There is no single white majority. Second, the 'minority' communities do not live in separate, self-sufficient enclaves, and they do display substantial internal differences. They too must be reimagined (ibid.).

What is particularly valuable in the Report, in my view, is the attempt to shift the discourse of culture in order to change the way in which cultures are imagined and conceived. Cultures are characterized as 'interacting and overlapping' (2000: 3); as involving 'competing attachments' (p. 23); as being 'more situational' (p. 25); as 'constantly adapting and diversifying' (p. 27); as 'open and porous formations' (p. 37); and so on. The Commissioners are searching for a more subtle and complex language that will make it possible to reimagine community and communities in Britain in terms of more cosmopolitan possibilities—they are trying to stretch our imagination, at least, towards the possibility of new 'post-national' cultural arrangements in British society.

In this part of my discussion, I have considered how some recent contributions to the debate on Britain and Britishness have been concerned with the tension between diversity and solidarity (and I have chosen to focus on contributions that are, in different ways and to different degrees, open to the possibilities of diversity). What is clear is that—in the intellectual domain, at least—new and interesting agendas are being developed (around the notions of constitutional (or civic) patriotism and cosmopolitan multiculturalism, for example). But what is also apparent—in both the intellectual and political arenas—is the continuing force and resonance of the imagined ethno-cultural nation. The resilient appeal of the organic nation was evident, for example, in the critical and often hostile responses to the publication of the Parekh Report. The New Labour Home Secretary, Jack Straw (2000), reacted immediately and spontaneously by 'standing up for Britain', standing up for 'patriotism', standing up for 'pride in our country', and standing up for the 'enduring British values of fairness, tolerance and decency'. In a somewhat more measured way, in the pages of *Prospect* magazine, Alan Wolfe and Jytte Klausen (2000: 32) accused Parekh of 'underestimating the extent to which social solidarity requires strong national cultures'. In a period of change and disruption, they argued, 'Britons still need a unifying idea of Britishness that can encompass diversity but is not eclipsed by it' (2000: 33) (and, with this, we are back once again to the discursive frame of David Miller). The Report from the Runnymede Trust tried to move our thinking about multicultural Britain on somewhat—the new migrant communities 'are familiar strangers', they argued, 'not an alien wedge' (Runnymede Trust 2000: 36). What is more apparent than ever, in the wake of their Report, is that thinking on questions of culture and identity in Britain does not move easily.

To London

In this endnote, I have reflected at some length on what is being said at the present time about the condition of British culture. My starting point was the apparent predicament that the national culture now finds itself in—what some think of as a decline in confidence, and others are inclined to characterize as some kind of cultural crisis. What I have wanted to put into focus is the national mentality—the distinctively national form of thinking and feeling. In its own ideal self-image, I have suggested, the nation regards itself in terms of singularity, as a unified and coherent whole—'the people' bound together in a single cultural and political body. To be part of a nation is to participate (with one's compatriots) in a common culture and in a community of trust and obligation—belonging to that community is the fundamental social relation and social value. And, whilst the imagined community is to a large extent an arbitrary construct, this arbitrariness is always disavowed—the nation regards itself as a community of fate, to be sustained in its essential unity through the course of historical time.

But, of course, the nation can never actually exist in the form of its ideal image of itself. It is always bound to be compromised by disorderly realities. Thus, the imagined unity of the nation has always been under threat—or has always been imagined as under threat—from a real world characterized by its multiplicity and complexity. The imagined unity of the nation has always struggled to cope with actual diversity and difference. In recent years, however, through the accelerating logic of globalization, national communities have felt themselves to be more and more under siege, and they have found it increasingly difficult to defend the integrity and coherence—the always imagined integrity and coherence, let us note—that is at the heart of their narcissistic self-imagination. As we have just seen, much of the debate around Britishness in recent years has been to do with a perceived conflict between the claims of solidarity and unity, on the one hand, and those of pluralism and diversity, on the other. In recent years, the united kingdom has been struggling—increasingly and vainly, it often seems—to deal with issues of migration and ethnicization, transnationalization, and multiculturalism.

And it has been struggling, I suggest, because these disordering transformations, associated with the processes of globalization, simply cannot be dealt with in the national frame. They cannot be made sense of within the national mentality. And so, in this final part of my discussion, I want to introduce a shift of focus, and to move from the national frame to an urban frame—and, thereby, to move the discussion to London. London is the hub for all the global flows that are now profoundly complicating our established models of cultural coherence and order. London is where the processes of global change that now appear to be subverting the integrity of the nation have their most intense and dynamic existence. What is significant for me is that London has generally been left out of discussions of the national culture and identity—as if London were not properly, or purely enough, or manageably enough, British (or English, at that). And on those occasions when London has been referred to, then it has commonly been with feelings of resentment—resentment and hostility towards a city that seems to have a disproportionate share of national resources, and that dramatically overshadows the economic and cultural life of the rest of the country. London has never fitted easily into the national mould. Its nature has been anomalous—and for that it has been resented. And now, in times of global change and cultural disordering, it may be that the national resentment is deepening. This is certainly the message that Hywel Williams (2000) conveys in a recent article in the *Guardian*. London, he says, 'has always been seen as a foreign place—and one that is out of synch with the English nation's temper'. And, says Williams, 'to the settled political-historical differences we must add London's present mood of capitalist glee and cultural pride in which it imagines itself to be an imperium receiving tribute from every subject race'. There is the clear sense here that London's foreignness is increasing: 'The differences between Londoners and the English are now as great as those between the British and the Italians.' Now, that is an interesting proposition! We really ought to reflect on how it is that London could have come to be such a foreign-seeming place. Hywel Williams's observation here might help to put the hostility towards London into what could actually be quite an interesting and productive new context.

I think that there are new kinds of possibilities when we move on to London. In and from London, you can gain a different perspective on global change and its implications for contemporary British society. Hywel Williams's complaints are directed against what he chooses to call 'London nationalism'. 'This is not a city,' he says, 'It is a nation.' But the point about London is precisely that it is *not* a nation—but a city, a metropolis. And, as such, it allows us to reflect on the cultural consequences of globalization from an other than national perspective—to extend our cultural and political concerns from the national question to urban questions (Saskia Sassen (2000: 143–4) discusses this possibility in terms of an intellectual movement beyond the theoretical assumptions of 'embedded statism'). This is not at all a proposal for abandoning the debate on national culture and identity. My earlier discussion should have made quite clear my concern with British nationality—and my support for the important challenges that are now being made to nationalism of the ethnic-cultural kind. I agree with Stuart Hall (2000)—who was one of the Commissioners responsible for producing the Runnymede Trust Report—that it is 'worth continuing to ask the awkward question, how is the nation imagined?' The point about shifting to an urban perspective, however, is that it permits us also to open up some alternative cultural and political possibilities— possibilities that go beyond the limiting vision of the national imagination. In the context of this quite different kind of cultural space, I suggest, it might be possible to pick up on the cosmopolitan and post-national possibilities that are briefly adumbrated in the Parekh Report. From the perspective of London, there is a certain potential to think about culture differently, more openly, in more complicated ways.

What I am trying to say, following Bogdan Bogdanović (1995: 64, 46), is that the city can function as a 'cognitive model', as a 'tool for thought'. And that it can function as a more interesting tool than the nation and the nation-state. Let me just be clear about what I am not saying here. I am *not* saying that people who live in London will necessarily think about cultures differently—with more open-ness towards cultural complexity—than people living elsewhere in Britain. I believe that London can actually serve as a cognitive model *for all of us*—and that, in terms of thinking cultures now, it might be that we all have need of London. And I am *not* by any means saying that London exists at the present time as some kind of ideal cultural space—an achieved cosmopolitan order. I am all too aware of the coexistence, for example, of both multicultures and multiracisms—of 'the contradictions between the vibrancy of hybridisation and the pervasiveness of racism' (Phoenix 1998: 87; see also Sibley 1998). What I *am* wanting to propose is that London might serve as a tool for thinking in different ways about questions of cultural complexity, confrontation, interaction, negotiation, and so on. Following Bogdanovic's idea that the city has always func-tioned as 'a highly complex and highly fruitful epistemological model' (1995: 46), I would argue that now, in the context of the new order of cultural complexity being brought about by the processes of globalization, London provides a crucial intellectual framework for British people to rethink and redescribe their relation to culture and identity.

Let me try to evoke, in what can only be an indicative way here, what it is that I mean when I say that the city provides the possi-bility to think about cultures differently and more productively. There are, I suggest, two key aspects to what makes 'being urban' different from 'being national'. The first concerns the nature of our subjective engagement and involvement with these different kinds of cultural spaces. One does not exist in the city in the same way that one exists as part of the nation. If the nation is fundamentally about belonging to an abstract community, associated with what Paul James (1992: 332, 326) calls 'relations of disembodied extension' or 'disembodied-extended integration', then the urban arena is about immersion in a world of multiplicity, and implicates us in the dimension of embodied cultural experience. As Olivier Mongin (1995: 44) puts it, urban culture is experienced 'at ground level' (*à ras de terre*), and involves bodily engagement with the complex realities of the urban space. What urban experience entails, says Bogdanović (1995: 46), is 'the consciousness of the actual presence of people in the city space that they know and whose very existence . . . provides them with the chance to give responsible answers to eternal human questions like, who am I? what am I? where am I? and why am I where I am?' (very different questions— particularly this last one—from the national questions 'who are we?' and 'what do we stand for?'). The nation, we may say, is a space of identification and identity, whilst the city is an experiential and existential space.

If the first distinction between national and urban frames concerns the nature of the relation to culture, the second has to do with what it is that is being related to. It has to do with the crucial difference between abstract community and the complexity and density of the urban space. In reflecting on this difference, we may usefully draw on the cultural and political division that Michael Hardt and Antonio Negri foreground in their book *Empire* (2000). Their concern is with what is problematical about the idea of 'the nation' and 'the people'. The category of 'the people'—the national people—tends 'toward identity and homogeneity internally while posing its difference from and excluding what remains outside' (2000: 103). The identity of 'the people' has been constructed, Hardt and Negri argue, 'on an imaginary plane that hid and/or eliminated differences'; what it has involved has been 'the eclipse of internal differences through the representation of the whole population by a hegemonic group, race or class' (2000: 103, 104). Against this unifying cultural logic, they counterpose the category of 'the multitude'. 'The multitude is', for Hardt and Negri, 'a multiplicity, a plane of singularities, an open set of relations, which is not homogeneous or identical with itself and bears an indistinct, inclusive relation to those outside of it' (2000: 103). (The cultural logic of nationality—and, even more so, nationalism—has involved transforming the multitude into a singular people.) Hardt and Negri's insistence on this division between the nation/people and the multitude seems to me to be valuable and productive—in the context of the present discussion, it can help us to establish what differentiates the urban space from the national cultural space. For the category of the multitudinous corresponds to the principle of urbanity: it is in the urban context that people have continued to be able to experience their existence in terms of being a multitude, an open and changing multiplicity. The city is not a space that can be conceived (actually, misconceived) as a unitary and coherent entity (which is why, *pace* Hywel Williams, it is not at all meaningful to talk about 'the London nation'). The city stands for an entirely different kind of cultural configuration and operation, which we have more difficulty in grasping, both intellectually and imaginatively. Zygmunt Bauman captures something of what the city is about through his image of 'the clash between independently composed and used maps of the city space.' 'The under-determination of the city space', he says,

its amenability to many, also mutually contradictory, interpretations, its hospitality extended to many different and uncoordinated cartographic efforts, and the resulting opacity, ever negotiated yet ever anew reborn, do not generate 'chaos' . . . The ostensible disorder . . . is in fact a specific form of equilibrium which is perpetually created and reformed through intermittent frictions and negotiations, in the course of which the autonomous actions of free agents are simultaneously the source of initiative, the moving force and the evaluating authority. (Bauman 1999: 184)

It is precisely the idea of a plane of singularities, and of open sets of interactions and relations, that is being evoked in this ground-level understanding of the meaning and resonance of urban space.

It is in terms of their multitudinousness that cities are culturally significant. Because of their multitudinous qualities, cities can pose different kinds of cultural questions from nations and states. And London—as a multitude of multitudes—can articulate these questions with particular dramatic force. 'It is in the nature of the city to encompass everything,' says Peter Ackroyd (2000: 778–9). 'It is illimitable. It is infinite London.' London—where 200 (and growing) languages are now spoken, and where there are around fifty different 'ethnic communities', as well as numerous other more or less transient populations—has always been a city of migrant destination (see Merriman 1993; Hebbert 1998: ch. 7). And now, as a consequence, says Ackroyd (2000: 777), 'there are different worlds, and times, within the city'. As he recounts, London has always been

Babylon ('Babylondon'), 'a city loud with many disparate and unintelligible voices'. To name London as Babylon, he says, 'was to allude to its essential multiplicity' (Ackroyd 2000: 576). And, in the context of these plural worlds and times, there exist cultural possibilities of a kind that national cultures cannot make available. One can become a Londoner very quickly, and one can easily cease being a Londoner, too, if one wishes: one 'belongs' to the city in a very different sense from that in which one belongs to the nation. Urban cultures and identities are more provisional, more transitory and negotiable—less constraining and less sustained—than national ones. In his 'biography' of London, Peter Ackroyd evokes this relative contingency and openness of life and encounter in the multitudinous city:

The elements of innovation and of change are subtly mingled, together with the sheer exhilaration of being one among a numerous company. One could become anybody. Some of the great stories of London concern those who have taken on new identities, and new personalities; to begin again, to renew oneself, is one of the great advantages of the city. It is part of its endlessly dramatic life. It is possible, after all, to enter if only for a moment the lives and emotions of those who pass by. (Ackroyd 2000: 775–6)

Here the concern is no longer with culture as a binding mechanism—'what binds ["the people"] together into a single body', as David Miller (1995: 30) would have it: London is regarded as a huge cultural reservoir and resource—valued for its numerousness, its complexity, and its incalculability. While the nation is about stability and continuity, the city offers important possibilities for cultural unsettling and transformation.

London provides a vast space—bigger in some senses than the nation—in which cultures can be differently imagined and conceived—and differently imagined and conceived by all who are engaged with its reality. And it is a space, consequently, in which the relation between the diversity of cultures might be reimagined and reconceived on a more complex basis. My argument is not intended to idealize what London is now—I take heed of Paul Gilroy's note of caution about the 'automatic multiculture thesis', and of his insistence that 'London's multiculture will not necessarily take care of itself as a private phenomenon' (Gilroy 1999: 60, 59). What I am suggesting is, rather, that London might allow us to think differently and more productively about issues and problems of multiculturalism. The city poses 'the eternal impossible question of how we strangers can live together' (Donald 1997: 182; cf. Robins 1997)—and the metropolitan city, Babylon-London, clearly poses this question of coexistence most profoundly and intensely. And, in the urban and metropolitan context, I would argue, it is a question that must necessarily be posed in ways that are both more grounded and more complex than the national imagination can accommodate. Trevor Phillips (2000: 19) puts forward the image of multicultural London in terms of 'the sound of a hundred cultures softly clashing, sometimes melding, occasionally grating uncomfortably'. What he is evoking here (with a certain romanticism, admittedly) is a complex of spatially distributed cultures, side by side, overlapping, hustling, jarring, negotiating, constantly moving and jostling—a physical and embodied coexistence that defies any abstract (national) schemes of integrationist or assimilationist ordering. In posing his objections to London, Hywel Williams (2000) is aware of, but at the same time resistant to, this kind of social and cultural co-presence: 'London is more tolerant of eccentricity, of differences of race, faith, colour and sexuality than the rest of England. But it is a tolerance which is born of indifference.' What Williams here interprets and dismisses as 'indifference' might, however, be interpreted differently—as something far more positive about the workings of urban complexity 'at ground level'. Perhaps we might regard it in terms of the opacity that Zygmunt Bauman regards as necessary in the urban cultural scene, involving 'the readiness to accept new, often unpleasant and sometimes painful ... meanings and to face up to the situations not fully under one's control and not likely ever to lend themselves to one's control' (Bauman 1999: 184). What is being suggested here is a very different basis for coming to terms with multicultural complexities from the national basis—one that moves beyond the comfort of identity to an entirely different kind of social and cultural project. For Bauman, the inherent disorder of cities might help to 'discourage the doomed yet tempting attempts to fix once and for all one's own relation to the world using the allegedly unchangeable and non-negotiable traits of group identity as the glue'. Cities might 'prompt the effort to define one's identity in terms of the acts that a person is capable of performing, rather than in terms of a given and predetermined set of attributions and received traits' (ibid.).

Might we not productively consider the city in terms of David Miller's lifeboat metaphor? In terms of Londoners as 'people who have been thrown together in one place and forced to share a common fate'? And where what matter are far more the acts that they are capable of performing, rather than the binding traits of collective identity? What I have wanted to do in this endnote is to question the self-evidence of the national question, and then to suggest that there are possibilities for transposing the discussion about what is happening to cultures and multicultures in Britain now into a different—and more productive—register. To see the nation through the prism of London.

References

Ackroyd, Peter (2000), *London: The Biography*, London: Chatto & Windus.

Bauman, Zygmunt (1999), 'Urban Space Wars: On Destructive Order and Creative Chaos', *Citizenship Studies*, 3/2.

Bogdanović, Bogdan (1995), 'The City and Death', in Joanna Labon (ed.), *Balkan Blues: Writing out of Yugoslavia*, Evanston, Ill.: Northwestern University Press.

Colley, Linda (1999), 'Blueprint for Britain', *Observer*, 12 Dec.

Donald, James (1997), 'This, Here, Now: Imagining the Modern City', in Sallie Westwood and John Williams (eds.), *Imagining Cities*, London: Routledge.

Gilroy, Paul (1999), 'A London Sumting Dis . . .', *Critical Quarterly*, 41/3.

Habermas, Jürgen (1998), 'The European Nation-State: On the Past and Future of Sovereignty and Citizenship', *Public Culture*, 10/2.

Hall, Stuart (2000), 'A Question of Identity', *Observer*, 15 Oct.

Hardt, Michael, and **Negri, Antonio** (2000), *Empire*, Cambridge, Mass.: Harvard University Press.

Hebbert, Michael (1998), *London: More by Fortune than Design*, Chichester: John Wiley.

James, Paul (1992), 'Forms of Abstract "Community": From Tribe and Kingdom to Nation and State', *Philosophy of the Social Sciences*, 22/3.

Merriman, Nick (ed.) (1993), *The Peopling of London*, London: Museum of London.

Miller, David (1995), *On Nationality*, Oxford: Clarendon Press.

Mongin, Olivier (1995), *Vers la troisième ville?*, Paris: Hachette.

Phillips, Trevor (2000), 'London—the Multicultural City', *Observer Magazine*, 23 Apr.

Phoenix, Anne (1998), ' "Multicultures", "Multiracisms" and Young People: Contradictory Legacies of Windrush', *Soundings*, 10.

Robins, Kevin (1989), 'Tradition and Translation: National Culture in its Global Context', in John Corner and Sylvia Harvey (eds.), *Enterprise and Heritage: Crosscurrents in National Culture*, London: Routledge.

—— (1997), 'The City in Question: Re-imagining Urban Life', *Renewal*, 5/1.

Runnymede Trust (2000), *The Future of Multi-ethnic Britain* [Parekh Report], London: Profile Books.

Sassen, Saskia (2000), 'New Frontiers Facing Urban Sociology at the Millennium', *British Journal of Sociology*, 51/1.

Sibley, David (1998), 'The Racialisation of Space in British Cities', *Soundings*, 10.

Straw, Jack (2000), 'Blame the Left, not the British', *Observer*, 15 Oct.

Williams Hywel (2000), 'Capital Offence', *Guardian*, 27 Dec.

Wolfe, Alan, and **Klausen, Jytte** (2000), 'Other People', *Prospect*, Dec.

Afterword

SUSAN BASSNETT

EDITING a book of essays on British Cultural Studies is an heroic task to undertake, because the odds on there being consensus among readers are slight. Someone will always argue that the emphasis is weighted too heavily in one direction as opposed to another, or that crucial lines of enquiry have not been pursued or that significant figures do not appear on the contents list. But such charges, which are inevitable in a volume of this scope, can be rebutted by making the simple point that such controversy is fundamental to this undertaking. Just as there is no consensus at the present time as to how to define Britain and Britishness, so no book on British Cultural Studies could fail to reflect the absences, gaps, and lacunae in any attempt to conceptualize Britain today. The very terminology has been called into question: in 2000, the Parekh Report on the future of multi-ethnic Britain caused an outcry in the popular press by suggesting that *Britain* was a word with racist connotations (Runnymede Trust 2000). Tabloid comments on the report focused simplistically on the terminological debate, but nevertheless some important issues were brought out into the open. What, in the twenty-first century, does it mean to define oneself as British? This question has become even more loaded since devolution: few Scots or Welsh citizens would be likely to declare themselves as British, despite carrying British passports, but Britishness is clearly something that extends beyond the geographical boundaries of England. We have a conundrum here, and one that is impossible to resolve.

A century ago, such questioning of basic terminology would have been absurd. When Queen Victoria celebrated her Diamond Jubilee in 1897, the British Empire was at its zenith. Britain controlled roughly a quarter of the surface territory across the planet; British territories on maps in schoolrooms were coloured red, and red was to dominate those maps until after the Second World War.

Between 1870 and 1900, Britain annexed another thirty-nine territories. The death of Queen Victoria in 1901 was marked by mourning not only across the British Isles, but also across the globe. The power of the British Empire was reflected in a sense of security, in a patriotism that brought people out onto the streets to show their respect to the dead queen or to celebrate the relief of the siege of Mafeking in 1900.

Yet the roots of that sense of security were shallow: the Boer War was expensive, the economy was far from sound. The comfortable middle-class Britain of the Edwardian era concealed appalling poverty and social divisiveness. Even as Beatrix Potter published her beautifully illustrated little books on furry animals (*The Tale of Peter Rabbit* first appeared in 1900) millions of children were living close to the breadline in London's East End, in rural areas, in the industrial cities of England and Scotland. Campaigns for Irish independence and universal suffrage became increasingly violent. Abroad, relations with other European states were also uneasy, for although Britain had beaten France, Belgium, Germany, Portugal, and Italy in the struggle to take over the African continent, all those states continued to challenge British supremacy in the colonies and were rapidly developing as competing industrial powers. The policy of splendid isolation began to seem more precarious than reassuring, as other states, particularly Germany, built up their military and naval power.

In February 1913 the survivors of Captain Scott's ill-fated Antarctica expedition were finally able to sail through the loosening icepacks and reach safety in New Zealand. News of the death of Scott's party was telegraphed around the world. If the loss of the *Titanic* in April 1912 had been seen as an ill omen, casting doubts on the invulnerability of British technology, the death of Scott and his companions horrified the nation. Scott's diary, which was quickly published, gave details of the slow deaths of himself and his men, but presented these deaths in terms of heroic endurance and selflessness. We shall never know what drove Captain Oates to crawl out of the tent and die in the snow, whether desperation, delirium, or a genuine desire to help his comrades survive, but Scott wrote his death in terms that have become mythical: 'We knew that poor Oates was walking to his death, but though we tried to dissuade him, we knew it was the act of a brave man and an English gentleman' (Scott 1913). Scott's last words fix the myth of English heroism in terms that have been cited throughout the twentieth century in relation to moments of crisis: in the trenches of the First World War, at Dunkirk, during the Blitz, at all times when Britain

Susan Bassnett

has felt threatened. 'Had we lived,' Scott wrote, 'we would have had a tale to tell of the hardihood, endurance, and courage of my companions which would have stirred the heart of every Englishman.' Yet after this inspiring sentence comes a slightly discordant note, a reminder not to forget the families of the heroes: 'These rough notes and our dead bodies must tell the tale, but surely, surely a great rich country like ours will see that those who are dependent on us are properly provided for.'[1] Reading this moving document today, the contrast between Scott's assertion of an intrinsic English heroism and his plea to the great rich country not to forget his dependants reveals the fissure between myth and reality that was always present. The myth conceals all kinds of divisions: social, economic, regional, and political. Diversity has always been the key to understanding British cultures (I use the plural deliberately). Dying of malnutrition in his freezing tent, Scott exemplified the heroic spirit of self-sacrifice that had built the British Empire, but he was also realist enough, sufficiently aware of his relatively lowly place in the class system, to want to remind his superiors of their responsibilities. The welfare state was still a distant ideal in the minds of utopian dreamers.

Today, the welfare state is rapidly receding into memory in Britain, though in the 1950s the health service and education system were models of their kind. Though still rich by comparison with many of its former colonies, the United Kingdom today is economically less successful than many of its European neighbours. The huge success of Ireland, the booming Celtic Tiger, reflects the affiliation of that country's economy with the European community, whilst the United Kingdom hovers uncertainly on the fringes of Europe. As debates about Europe have raged over three decades, no British political party has dared go to the polls on a solid pro-European platform. There is uneasiness about British relations with Europe, and even greater uneasiness since devolution in 1999. For Scotland has always had different links with Europe historically, and the prospect of Scotland drawing closer to Europe, with Wales benefiting from European policies directed at minority cultures, only serves to emphasize the uncomfortable relationship that the English have with the Continent. The establishment of the Scottish Parliament and the Welsh Assembly gave official sanction to a process that had long been under way and that is also linked to relations between Europe and the component nations of the British Isles. That process accelerated in the 1980s, as high unemployment across Britain emerged in a disturbing pattern which saw some regions suffering excessively and others becoming richer than ever

1 There is a vast body of material on Scott. See in particular, for a range of perspectives: Evans (1921); Huntford (1993); Preston (1997).

before. The upstairs–downstairs class divisions of the early twentieth century were being replaced by huge economic divisions, altering the social map and making easy analysis impossible.

The 1980s saw the end of British manufacturing industry, the end of the great industrial era upon which the empire had been built. The miners' strike of 1984 stands as a landmark because it represents a massive symbolic shift from one age into another. Captain Scott would probably have recognized a great deal in the Britain of the 1960s and 1970s, but once the industrial base disappeared, the entire structure of the state as he had known it was changed. When Humphrey Jennings made his great propaganda films about Britain in the 1940s, he chose to emphasize the lasting quality of two great myths of Britishness: the endurance and heroic stoicism that cut across class boundaries and united officers and men in situations of crisis and the power of working-class communities to build the foundations of a strong state. In his vision, miners, factory women, steelworkers, and shipbuilders were the representatives of the true Britain, of Britain as homeland. These images served briefly to unite the nation, but by the 1980s unity was over. In trying, and succeeding, to modernize Britain, the Conservative government under Margaret Thatcher relied on the power of one myth of Britishness, even as they destroyed the other. The result was the demise of both.

That demise was hastened, however, by the collapse of another aspect of British life that seemed destined to last forever in 1900: the empire. In the second half of the twentieth century, citizens of that dwindling empire came to settle in Britain, bringing with them different languages, traditions, and religions and invigorating a cultural base that was increasingly nostalgic, yearning for a lost golden age. That such an age had never existed does not matter, for like all myths the golden age of Britishness has acquired a life of its own. Significantly, it was the Labour government of 1997 who reintroduced the ritual of a two-minute silence on Remembrance Day, 11 November. Throughout the 1990s there developed virtually an industry of books and films about the First World War, characterized by a sense of grieving for the past. The Second World War is increasingly receiving the same treatment, and the time spent by British children from primary school through to A levels studying the war is worthy of study in its own right. Why is it that notions of Britishness and of Englishness in particular are so characterized by nostalgia and by a sense of loss, exemplified in the two world wars?

Through the 1980s, a new phenomenon began to be observed in British streets: the creation of impromptu shrines to accident victims. Within hours of the Clapham rail crash in 1987 dozens of floral tributes had been laid on the embankment. Today, violent deaths are immediately marked by neighbours with flowers, a practice that reached its peak with the death of Diana, Princess of Wales, in 1997, when shrines sprang up all over the country. We might speculate on why this should be, and hypothesize different answers. It might be a manifestation of the collective grief for a lost time that we have been discussing, or it might reflect a desire to find a substitute for the dwindling state religion, the Church of England, as people seek to express their spiritual needs in a form that is not associated with established religious practice. Or it might be yet another example of the ways in which the new British citizens, those who can trace their ancestry back to the Indian subcontinent, to Africa, to the Caribbean, or, today, to eastern Europe, have influenced contemporary British culture at the most basic, grass-roots level.

The most obvious example of the power of this influence is in British eating habits, which have changed beyond recognition since the early 1980s. Schoolchildren still eat baked beans on toast and fish fingers, but they also eat pasta and pizza, curries and naan bread, chicken tikka masala, and Chinese takeaways, all of which are seen as basic British foods. School assemblies, still obligatory in Britain, celebrate a variety of different religions, so that Christian festivals coexist with other great religious festivals in the minds of the younger generation of British children. In short, in terms of everyday patterns of living, Britain is an increasingly pluralistic society, with a range of religions, languages, customs, and rituals all part of what can rightly be termed British. Linda Colley, in a lecture on Britishness in the twenty-first century given at Downing Street in November 2000, makes this point well. She points out that the Fourth National Survey of Ethnic Minorities found two-thirds of most ethnic groups from the former colonies 'felt themselves British at some level', and notes that British cities are not ghettoized to the same degree as cities in the United States (Colley 2000). Despite the ongoing struggle against institutionalized racism and explicit links between poverty, poor housing, crime, and some ethnic minorities, Britain is increasingly not only multinational, but also multicultural.

Colley argues that the way forward for Britain in the twenty-first century is to set aside out-dated arguments about identity issues and to focus instead on the question of citizenship and citizen's rights. She goes so far as to hypothesize about a Britain that is a 'Citizen Nation' with a charter of contract of citizen rights. Such a contract would incorporate English, Scottish, and European law, and would therefore fundamentally shift the perspective away from nostalgia for a vanished imperial past onto a future based on collaboration and a new set of political and cultural alliances.

Colley's idealism has a solid core of common sense, for it acknowledges the diversity that has always existed in Britain. Geographical and regional distinctions are striking, given the relatively small spatial area occupied by these islands off the coast of mainland Europe. It is important to stress the fact that there are so many islands, for one of the most misleading British myths has been the idea of the single island. It has been a useful myth, for in creating the image of the single island people against the rest of the world, the divisions within Britain could be papered over, and English, Scots, Welsh, and Irish packaged as a cohesive unit. One of the best-known portrayals of the island myth can be found in John of Gaunt's famous speech in Shakespeare's *King Richard II*:

> This royal throne of kings, this sceptred isle,
> This earth of majesty, this seat of Mars,
> This other Eden, demi-paradise,
> This fortress built by Nature for herself
> Against infection and the hand of war,
> This happy breed of men, this little world,
> This precious stone set in the silver sea,
> Which serves it in the office of a wall,
> Or as a moat defensive to a house,
> Against the envy of less happier lands,
> This blessed plot, this earth, this realm, this England
>
> (II. i. 40–50)

Encapsulated in the speech is the basis for the mythologizing that was to grow to its most powerful point in the heyday of the empire: not many islands, but one island only, a natural fortress against threats from other envious nations, a small island but peopled with a 'happy breed of men' who recognize their own good fortune in belonging to the island community. Throughout John of Gaunt's speech, the island is idealized, differences are erased and the sense of insiders versus outsiders is developed strongly.

But the lines cited here represent only part of the whole speech and are, in any case, lifted out of context. For in the play, the dying John of Gaunt is railing against what he sees as the destruction of England by a corrupt ruler. The image of the precious stone set in a silver sea is not a reality, it is a fantasy conjured up to highlight in the most bitterly ironic manner the gap between what is and what should be. For the reality, both of the historical Richard II's reign

Susan Bassnett

and of Shakespeare's depiction of that period, was a different story. During the reign of Richard II civil unrest led to armed conflict, while the spread of reformist religious views sowed the seeds of what was to become the Reformation. Shakespeare chose deliberately to write about Richard II in 1595 in order to highlight the debate about good and bad governance in the troubled latter years of Elizabeth I's reign. So controversial was the play that on the eve of the abortive rebellion led by the Earl of Essex against the Queen in 1601, his friends paid to have the play staged in London. Two years later, when Elizabeth died, the Scottish King James VI became James I of England, uniting the two nations politically. They were to remain ever more closely bound together until devolution in 1999. Significantly, in the late 1990s the single island myth was also challenged by the setting up of the Council of the Isles that sought to divert attention away from Westminster and towards the historic links between the north Celtic regions of the British Isles.

At the start of the twenty-first century we can see how the process of fantasizing about British unity and singularity has grown and developed from the sixteenth century onwards and is only now being set aside. There never was one little island peopled with a race of indomitable courage; there were always many islands, loosely bound together through waves of conquests (the Viking outpost of the Isle of Man, for example, continues to be outside some aspects of British law, particularly fiscal law) and speaking different languages. Regional variations are immense: Cornwall and Northumberland, at the extreme south-west and north-east of England, are totally different in terms of landscape, history, language, religion, and European links. During the nineteenth century it was expedient to present a unified front to the world and pull the threads of imperial possessions tightly together to bind them to what had to be seen to be a single, powerful state, untouched by the revolutionary movements that swept Europe, its energies focused on becoming the greatest manufacturing power on earth. In this period, the process of mythologizing an England that was synonymous with Britain erased the other components of that ideal state.

Today, with manufacturing industry only a memory, with the colonial age gone forever, with new alliances being built with European neighbours, with devolved assemblies and a multi-ethnic, multi-faith culture in most urban areas, Britain has entered a new era, one in which plurality, not singularity, is the norm. Personally, I welcome this change. I can understand the nostalgia, I can see where it comes from, but I can also see that it is not constructive, for it laments the loss of a mythical unity which not only excludes people but was never authentic in the first place. The process of unravelling the roots of the myth, along with the process of building a new pluralistic Britain with its component nations and complex relationships with Europe and the Commonwealth, is well under way. Like all processes of radical change, it involves pain and self-doubt, it involves questioning everything, from terminology to legal frameworks, but it cannot be reversed. Hence the need for a volume such as this, which offers a wide range of perspectives on a truly fascinating period of British history.

References

Colley, Linda (2000), 'Britishness in the 21st Century', *10 Downing Street Magazine*, 14 Nov.

Evans, Capt E. R. G. R. (1921), *South with Scott*, London: Collins.

Huntford, Roland (1993), *Scott and Amundsen*, London: Weidenfeld & Nicolson.

Preston, Diana (1997), *A First Rate Tragedy: Captain Scott's Antarctic Expedition*, London: Constable.

Runnymede Trust (2000), *The Future of Multi-ethnic Britain*, London: Profile Books.

Scott, R. F. (1913), *Scott's Last Expedition*, introd. J. M. Barrie, London: John Murray.

Chronology

1505   'Gypsies' first recorded in Scotland.

1514   'Gypsies' first recorded in England.

1534   Under King Henry VIII, the monasteries are suppressed and the English Church separates from the Roman hierarchy with the reigning monarch at its head.

1535   Incorporation of Wales into England.

1604   Publication of the first monolingual English dictionary, Robert Cawdrey's *A Table Alphabeticall*.

1611   Authorized King James version of the Bible first published.

1707   Treaty of Union between England and Scotland creates the Kingdom of Great Britain.

1712   John Bull appears in the first of a series of satires by the Scottish writer, John Arbuthnot (1667–1735), as the embodiment of the typical Englishman.

1755   Publication of Samuel Johnson's *Dictionary of the English Language*.

1789   *The Interesting Narrative of the Life of Olaudah Equiano, or Gustavus Vassa, the African* (Equiano's Travels), chronicling the horrors of enslavement and the Middle Passage, is published in London.

1801   Act of Union results in the establishment of the Kingdom of Great Britain and Ireland.

1815   Ending of the Revolutionary and Napoleonic wars with France. The terms of the Vienna Peace Settlement marked a significant expansion of the British Empire.

1824   Royal Society for the Prevention of Cruelty to Animals is formed.

1833   Emancipation Act abolishes slavery with effect from 1 August 1834, following a major campaign against slavery in Britain and slave rebellions in the Caribbean.

1840   Treaty of Waitangi and subsequent proclamation of British sovereignty over New Zealand.

1845–7   New Zealand 'Maori' Wars.

1847   Vegetarian Society founded.

1851   Great Exhibition takes place at the Crystal Palace.

1857	Indian Mutiny breaks out.
1858	Government of India Act abolishes the East India Company and establishes direct rule.
1861	Palgrave's *Golden Treasury of English Verse* is published with the aim of establishing a national canon.
1865	Morant Bay Rebellion takes place in Jamaica. Several hundred black peasants are killed in a ruthless campaign of repression by Governor Eyre.
1866	Jamaica becomes a Crown Colony.
1884	Publication of the first part of the *Oxford English Dictionary*.
1885	Formal creation of the Scottish Office to administer Scotland.
1898	British Union for the Abolition of Vivisection (BUAV) founded by Frances Power Cobbe.
1900	Arthur Quiller-Couch's *Oxford Book of English Verse* first published.
1911	First Indian eating house, Salut e Hind, opened in Holborn, London.
1916	Easter uprising against British rule in Dublin.
1921	Anglo–Irish Treaty leads to partition of Ireland.
1922	British Broadcasting Company set up.
	Establishment of the Irish Free State leaving the Kingdom of Great Britain and Northern Ireland.
1922–3	Civil War in the Republic of Ireland.
1925	Plaid Cymru, the Welsh nationalist party, is formed.
1926	First commercial Indian restaurant, Veeraswamy's, opened in Regent Street, London.
1927	On 1 January the British Broadcasting Company becomes the British Broadcasting Corporation (the BBC), a public broadcasting service, funded by a compulsory licence fee payable by all receiving set owners, with a remit to inform, educate, and entertain.
1928	Publication of the final part of the first edition of the *Oxford English Dictionary*.
1932	English Folk Dance and Song Society formed by the merger of the Folk Song Society and the English Dance Society formed by Cecil Sharp in 1911.
1933	British Film Institute established by Royal Charter 'to encourage the development of the art of film in the United Kingdom' and 'to promote its use as a record of contemporary life and manner'.
1934	Scottish National Party founded.
	J. B. Priestley's *English Journey* published.
	The British Council formed to promote cultural, educational, and technical co-operation between Britain and other countries.
1936	BBC Television Service makes its first broadcast on 2 November to around 400 households with TV sets. The service is suspended during the war, but reopens in 1946.
1937	Coronation of George VI.

1946	Arts Council of Great Britian emerges from the wartime Council for the Encouragement of Music and the Arts (CEMA) established by Royal Charter in January 1940.
1947	Indian Independence is accomplished.
1948	SS *Windrush* brings young men from Jamaica, marking the beginning of a large flow of labour migration from British Empire and Commonwealth territories in the Caribbean, Asia, and Africa.
1951	Festival of Britain takes place to celebrate 'one continuous, interwoven story of British contributions to world civilisation in the arts of the people'.
	The Archers, a daily radio drama based in the fictional village of Ambridge, takes to the air for the first time. By the beginning of 2001 over 13,100 episodes have been broadcast.
1953	Coronation of Elizabeth II.
1955	On 1 September the first advertising-supported commercial television service is launched in Britain, as part of the new Independent Television network (ITV).
	Scottish Unionist Party (Conservative) wins 50 per cent of the popular vote in Scotland.
1956	War with Egypt and the Suez Crisis.
	Riots break out in London's Notting Hill area when Teddy boys attack the recently arrived West Indian community.
1957	Publication of the Wolfenden Report recommending changes in the law around homosexuality.
	Treaty of Rome establishes the EEC.
1961	The film *Victim*, is released, the first mainstream and sympathetic film about homosexuals in the UK.
1963	Minister of War, John Profumo, is forced to resign after an affair with Christine Keeler, who had also been involved with an alleged Soviet spy, Eugene Ivanov.
1964	BBC2 television starts broadcasting.
1966	England win the football World Cup, playing every match at home.
1967	Northern Ireland Civil Rights Association established.
	Sexual Offences Act decriminalizes much homosexual activity.
	Winnie Ewing wins the Hamilton by-election for the SNP.
1968	South Asian political refugees start to arrive from East Africa.
	Enoch Powell makes his 'Rivers of Blood' speech in which he predicts that England will be overrun by non-white Commonwealth immigrants who will eventually outnumber and oppress the native white population.
1969	Troubles commence in the North of Ireland.
1970	First Women's Liberation Workshop held in Oxford and attended by around 600 delegates.
	Passing of the Equal Pay Act.
	Gay Liberation Front holds its first meetings at the London School of Economics.
	First Glastonbury Festival held attracting an audience of 1,500.

1973	Britain enters the EEC.
1974	Prevention of Terrorism Act passed.
1975	Sex Discrimination Act passed.
1976	Opening of Britain's first purpose-built shopping mall at Brent Cross in north-west London.
	Pressure by Horace Ove, a film about the children of Caribbean immigrants, becomes the first black feature film made in Britain.
1977	Completion of the Regent's Park Mosque, Central London, twenty-three years after the opening of the Islamic Cultural Centre, established to recognize the sacrifice of thousands of Indian Muslims in the world war.
	The Break-up of Britain by Tom Nairn is published.
1979	Referendums take place on Scottish and Welsh devolution. In Scotland, the 52 per cent Yes vote falls short of the required two-thirds majority. In Wales, the proposal is defeated by a four-to-one margin.
	Thatcher government elected at May general election, marking the beginning of eighteen years of Conservative rule.
1980	Founding of Field Day cultural political initiative and theatre in Derry, Ireland.
	First National Heritage Act passed.
1981	At a time of record unemployment and urban riots in Brixton, Bristol, and Toxteth, Liverpool, the Specials' single 'Ghost Town', about the social and economic deterioration of British cities, goes to number 1 in the charts.
	Hunger strikes take place among republican prisoners in Long Kesh prison over political status.
	Marriage of Prince Charles and Lady Diana Spencer takes place.
	Brideshead Revisited, with its elite country house setting, is a great hit on British TV, in the same year that the British period film *Chariots of Fire* caps its critical and box-office success with the Oscar for Best Picture.
	Animal Liberation by Peter Singer is published.
1981–2	Identification of Aids and emergence of the Terrence Higgins Trust, the first major gay-run Aids organization in the UK.
1982	Channel 4 television starts broadcasting.
1983	House of Lords legal ruling on *Mandla* v. *Lee*, recognizing Sikhs as an ethnic group, requires schools and employers to modify dress codes so that Sikh men may wear turbans.
	Commercial cable television services launched in Britain, breaking the BBC/ITV duopoly control over broadcasting services and ushering in the age of subscription television and themed channels.
	Second National Heritage Act passed.
1984	Council of Europe Equal Pay Directive No. 75/117/EEC incorporated into British law to define equal pay 'for the same work or for work to which equal value is attributed'.
	Leading pop and rock acts record the charity single 'Do They

Know it's Christmas Time?' under the name Band Aid. It is followed by the Live Aid concerts of July 1985.

Foundation of the organization English Heritage, as a result of the 1983 National Heritage Act.

Greenham Common occupation protesting at the siting of cruise missiles in Britain begins.

1984–5 A year-long strike by the National Union of Mineworkers, led by Arthur Scargill, fails to stop a massive programme of pit closures introduced by the Conservative government.

1985 Levi's launderette adverts, featuring model Nick Kamen, first aired in the UK on Boxing Day.

Anglo-Irish agreement leads to increase in number of Protestant Orange parades.

Around 1,000 police drawn from five police forces brutally attack and destroy a convoy of Travellers heading for Stonehenge to mark the solstice in what became known as the Battle of the Beanfield.

Film *My Beautiful Launderette*, written by Hanif Kureishi and directed by Stephen Frears, tells 'a tale of the eighties' as it unpicks the story of a young Asian entrepreneur and his white working-class boyfriend.

1986 *Arena* magazine for men launched by independent publishers Wagadon in autumn.

Release of *A Room with a View*, Merchant–Ivory's adaptation of the E. M. Forster novel.

Car manufacturer Nissan becomes the first Japanese company to build cars in the United Kingdom. Production of its 'Bluebird' model commences at its Sunderland plant in the north-east of England.

Two films by black British directors, *Handsworth Songs* (John Akomfrah) and *The Passion of Remembrance* (Maureen Black-wood and Isaac Julien), receive West End premières.

1987 Publication of Robert Hewison's *The Heritage Industry: Britain in a Climate of Decline*.

Four black MPs, Bernie Grant, Dianne Abbott, Paul Boateng, and Keith Vaz, are elected to the House of Commons.

1988 *Freeze* exhibition in Docklands, curated by Damien Hirst, marks the first collective showing of 'young British artists' (yBas).

Publication of Salman Rushdie's novel *The Satanic Verses* angers Muslims in its depiction of the Prophet Muhammed and his wives. This leads, in February 1989, to the pronouncement of a fatwa on the author by the Iranian Ayatollah Khomeini, proclaiming that Rushdie is an apostate and deserves to be killed.

UK version of publisher Conde Nast's magazine for men GQ (*Gentlemen's Quarterly*) launched.

Section 28 of the Local Government Act makes it an offence to 'promote homosexuality'—the cause of much protest and continued debate into the twenty-first century.

Third Claim of Right asserts sovereignty of the Scottish people, and argues for setting up a Scottish parliament within the Union.

1989   'Second summer of love' as rave culture reaches its peak, with illegal and semi-legal parties organized all over the country.

Scottish Constitutional Convention established to promote setting up of Scottish parliament.

1990   Tory MP Norman Tebbit sets his infamous 'cricket test' in which he questions the nationality status of black and Asian Britons who cheer for India, Pakistan, or the West Indies against England.

European international football championship, 'Italia '90', takes place and soccer becomes fashionable.

1991   UK version of *Esquire* magazine launched in January.

Term 'new lad' coined by Sean O'Hagen in *Arena*.

John Major's newly elected Conservative government establishes new ministry—the Department of National Heritage.

1992   English Football Association Premier League launched.

Howards End, the third Merchant–Ivory adaptation of an E. M. Forster novel, released.

1993   Tim Berners-Lee, a British scientist working at the CERN high energy research laboratory in Geneva, develops the computer protocols for the World Wide Web, opening up the Internet to non-specialists.

1994   First National Lottery draw held on 19 November.

IPC's *Loaded* magazine launched in May.

Northern Ireland peace process begins.

Interracial dance music genre, 'jungle' enters the mainstream with music-press and national media coverage.

Labour Party in Scotland changes its name to Scottish Labour Party.

Criminal Justice and Public Order Act introduced. It includes sections to outlaw impromptu raves and music festivals, protests, and unofficial Traveller encampments by criminalizing trespass and increasing police powers to seize property.

Series of demonstrations attempts to stop the export of live animals at Brightlingsea, Essex.

Arts Council of Great Britain's responsibilities and functions are transferred to three new bodies, the Arts Council of England (ACE), the Scottish Arts Council, and the Arts Council of Wales.

1995   Shri Swaminarayan Mandir, the first Hindu temple in Europe, opened in Neasden, north-west London.

Peak of the 'Britpop' phenomenon; Blur and Oasis occupy number 1 and number 2 in the August singles charts.

'Austenmania' reaches its height with the success of *Pride and Prejudice* on British TV and *Sense and Sensibility* at the cinema.

1996   BBC start a comedy series by young second-generation Asians, *Goodness Gracious Me*; its national success on radio leads to a television version and live theatre performances.

1997   On 1 May, a Labour government elected under the leadership of Tony Blair. Department of Culture, Media, and Sport created, which draws up new guidelines for 'The People's Lottery'.

Sensation exhibition at the Royal Academy establishes young British artists' key position within the contemporary visual arts.

Social Exclusion Unit established by the New Labour government. Main issues addressed so far have been Truancy and School Exclusion; Rough Sleeping; Neighbourhood Renewal; Teenage Pregnancy; and New Opportunities for 16–18-year-olds not in Education, Employment, or Training.

Death of Diana, Princess of Wales, in a car accident in Paris.

Publication of the Demos pamphlet *Britain*™: *Renewing our Identity*, launching the debate on the 'rebranding of Britain'.

Conservatives win no seats in Scotland at British general election.

Referendum on devolved Scottish parliament: 74 per cent vote yes to the principle; 63 per cent vote yes to it having tax-varying powers.

Twyford Down is occupied by a protesters' encampment in an attempt to halt the building of the Newbury bypass.

1998   New Deal for single mothers phased in after pilot schemes in 1997.

Remix version of *Brimful of Asha* by Cornershop becomes the first record by a British Asian band to top the British pop music charts. The original version reached number 60 in 1997.

Release of *Elizabeth*, a revisionist costume drama about Queen Elizabeth I.

Devolution referendums in Scotland and Wales achieve necessary levels of support.

After a series of protests in opposition to Mike Foster's Hunting with Dogs Bill, the Countryside Alliance is formed by the amalgamation of the British Field Sports Society, the Countryside Movement, and the Countryside Business Group to campaign for country sports and 'to promote and protect the rural way of life'.

1999   Nasser Hussain becomes the first ethnic minority cricketer to captain the England team after the 1999 cricket World Cup.

Establishment of Northern Ireland Assembly.

July sees the publication of *Teenage Pregnancy* report presented to Prime Minister Tony Blair by the Social Exclusion Unit.

First elections held in May for the new devolved institutions in Scotland and Wales. The Scottish Parliament and Welsh Assembly are opened.

Release of *Shakespeare in Love*, a romantic comedy in period costume and a major international critical and box-office success.

The Stephen Lawrence Inquiry headed by Sir William Macpherson produces its report into the black teenager's death and the subsequent failed police murder inquiry.

2000   British Medical Association report *Eating Disorders, Body Image and the Media* published in May.

In June Body Image summit held at Cabinet Office, Women's Unit, to discuss the impact of the media and advertising on eating disorders among young girls.

'Generation Sex' series appears in June on Channel 4 TV exploring questions of teenage sexuality, teenage pregnancy, earlier onset of puberty, and sex education.

On 1 January the Millennium Dome opens and immediately runs into problems. It closes on New Year's Eve.

Film Council, responsible for the British film industry, founded.

Tate Modern opens in the former Bankside power station and receives a million visitors in just six weeks.

Runnymede Trust releases the report of the Commission on the Future of Multi-ethnic Britain.

2001   Sven Goran Eriksson becomes the first foreign manager of the England football team.

Parliament votes to abolish fox-hunting as the Home Secretary, Jack Straw, proposes measures to halt the activities of animal rights protesters.

The issue of 'race' dominates the run-up to the June general election. Denouncing Labour policies that might surrender more power to the EU, Conservative leader, William Hague, argues that Britain is in danger of becoming a 'foreign land'; Conservative MP, John Townend, attacks multicultural Britain by claiming that the British have become a 'mongrel race'; the Labour government proposes tough measures to deter 'asylum-seekers'.

Index

253 (Ryman) 314

1066 and All That (Sellar and Yeatman) 43

Abercrombie, Patrick 153
abjection 81–6
abortion, right to and Christian right 202
Abse, Leo 112–13
Absolutely Fabulous 268
accession, Act of Union (1707) 45
Ackroyd, Peter, London 490–1
Adams, Gerry 85
Adidas (trainers) 406, 407
Adonis, A., with S. Pollard, Super Class 139
Adorno, T. W. 411
Adventures in Capitalism (Litt) 313
aesthetics, Other 335–6
agriculture
   economy 146, 148
   Englishness 147
Ahern, Bertie 86
Aids *see* HIV/Aids
Albion 438
Aldiss, Brian 235
Alexander, C. E. 403
alienation 230
All that Dwell Therein (Regan) 434
American Telegraph Magazine 447
Americanization
   consumerism and escape from tradition 331–2
   see also USA
Amis, Martin 9, 313
Anderson, Brett 275
Animal Liberation (Singer) 434
Animal Machines (Harrison) 435

animal welfare 432–5, 437, 440
   and environmentalism 323–4
Anti-Corn Law League 37
Archers 153
Arena, new lad image 380–1, 382, 383
Arnold, Matthew 445, 450
arts
   culture and heritage 7–8
   funding of 237
   subsidy of 176
   young artists 287–303
   young British artists (yBas) 179–80
   see also culture; literature; music
Arts Council 236–9
Ascherson, Neil, xenophobia and nationalism 8
Asians *see* British Asians
Asquith, Viscount 130
asylum seekers 468
Atlantic-centred history 157–69
Attitude, new lad image 383
Au Naturel (Lucas) 300, 302
Austen, Jane 28, 250–1, 252, 305
Austria 43
avant-garde, and consumerism 288

Babymother (Henriques) 64
Back, L. 403
Baddiel, David 405
Baldwin, Stanley 136
   Englishness 4
Balfour, A. J. 400
Balfour, Lady Eve 433
Banham, Reyner 242
Barcelona, and Catalonia 141
Barnes, Julian 313
Barnett, Anthony, Englishness and Britishness 101–2

Barry, Gerald 244
Bassnett, Susan 495–502
Battersea Park Pleasure Gardens 244
Baudrillard, Jean 328
Bauman, Zygmunt, London 490, 492
BBC, origins 450–1
BBC (television) 264, 265
   and the internet 457–8
   see also television
Beattie, James, standard speech 184, 190
Belich, James, New Zealand 33–4
Benjamin, Walter 328
Bennett, Tony 242
Bernstein, Basil 173
Betjeman, John, Englishness 4
Betterton, Rosemary
   young artists 287–304
   young British artists (yBas) 179–80
Bew, P.
   with E. Meehan, European Union and Northern Ireland 91
   with H. Patterson and P. Teague 89
Big Women (Weldon) 363
Billig, Michael 228, 231
   media and the monarchy 215, 218
Birmingham, and the empire 29–30
Birmingham Journal 30, 35
birth control 369
Bitter Cry of Outcast London, The (Mearn) 148
Black, Adam 381
Black Album, The (Kureishi) 309–10
black British
   Black Britishness 57–65
   blackness and Asian identity 68–70
   music 281–4
   religion 198

black British—contd
  and sport 403
  see also race
Black English Vernacular (BEV), and
    politics of standard English
    190–1
Black, Maria 375
Blair, Tony 86, 175, 228, 361
  attitude to Europe 164
  British confidence 461
  Britishness 461–70
  heritage industry and 'Cool
    Britannia' 259
  modernity 235, 236
Blanchett, Cate 253, 254
Bloch, Maurice 224
  hierarchy 228
Blunkett, David 246
Blur 276
Boer War 496
Boffin, Tessa 392
Bogdanović, Bogdan 488, 489
Border Country (Williams) 307
Borrow, George 419
Bourdieu, P. 401
Branson, Richard 236
Brathwaite, K., on T. S. Eliot and Jazz
    168
Brent Cross, consumer culture 337
Brideshead Revisited 249–50
Britain
  creation of United Kingdom 97
  and England 130–3
  forging of 98
  as state-nation 22, 97–8
British Asians
  funding of Muslim schools 75
  identity 67–77
British Grammar (Buchanan) 190
Britishness 7
  and consumer culture 338–9
  and Englishness 24, 41–4, 102,
    130–3
  identity, British Asians 67–77
  and popularity of Asian food 332–3
  rituals and black Britishness 57–65
  and tea 333–4
  Tony Blair 461–70
  see also Englishness; national
    identity
Britons: Forging the Nation (Colley) 98
Britpop music, and indie music 275–8
Brittas Empire, The 269

bro 111
Brown, Gordon 124
Brown, James 381, 382
Bruce, Steve, religious cultures 174,
    195–206
Bruges Group 52
Bruno, Frank 406
Brunt, R., ideological function of the
    monarchy 216
Brylcream, advertisement 373–4
Buchan, John, monarchy 228
Buchanan, James, standard English
    190
Buffalo image, new man image 377,
    378
Burger, Peter 301
Burke, Edmund 164
Burning an Illusion (Shabazz) 61–2
Burton, Antoinette, identification
    with nation and empire 37
Butterfield, Herbert, Whig
    interpretation of English history
    50

Campbell, Beatrix
  masculinity in the police force 355
  masculinity in the workplace 352
Campbell, George, standard language
    185
Cannadine, D., monarchy 210
Car and Country (Prioleau) 152
Caravan Sites Act (1968) 419, 421, 425
Carey, Hugh 90
Carrington, B. 406
Carson, Rachel 435, 440
Carter, Ronald, sociology of proper
    English 187, 191
cartography, Britain's position 157
Cartwright, Garth 427
Carvel, John, Little Englanders 60
Case for Animal Rights, The (Regan) 434
Castells, Manuel 349
  network society 140, 230
Casualty 268
Catalonia, and Barcelona 141
Catholicism
  Northern Ireland 200
  see also Northern Ireland
CBI (Confederation of British
    Industry), changing attitude to
    Welsh devolution 116
celebrities, royalty as 221–32
Chamberlain, Joseph 29

Chambers, Ian 331
Champion, Sarah 312
Chaney, David, monarchy 175, 177,
    207–19
Channel 4 453
Chapman, Dinos 289
Chapman, Jake 289
Chariots of Fire 249–50, 253, 254, 258
Charles I, King
  Hyde Park 444
  statue in Trafalgar Square 158
Chiapinini, Jean-Ange 374
Christianity
  decline of traditional Christianity
    195–8
  see also Catholicism; Protestantism;
    religion
Christie, Linford 57, 406
Christies (auctioneers) 288
Church Gibson, Pamela 256
Churchill, Sir Winston 160, 163, 168
cinema
  black British identity 60–4
  heritage cinema and television
    249–59
  and television 177
  see also television
citizenship 449–50
city culture, and industrial North
    136–9
civil rights campaign, Northern
    Ireland 81–2
civil society, Northern Ireland 80, 88
Civil War 45
Clarion movement 151
Clarke, Jonathan 52
Clary, Julian 391
class
  gender and the New Meritocracy
    364
  heritage culture 259
  literature 311
  national identity 349
  nationalism 467
  and pregnancy 364, 368–71
  rambling and cycling, working class
    151, 152
  see also employment; work
Clinton, Bill 90
Cloonan, Martin 277
Coca-Cola 331–2
Cohen, Robin, British identity 103
Cold Comfort Farm (Gibbons) 153

Colley, Linda
 Britishness 499–500
 culture 482–3
 emergence of nationalism 45
 forging of Britain 8
Collin, M. 279
Collings, Matthew 179
Collini, Stefan, literature and national
  identity 49
Colls, Robert, with P. Dodd
 Englishness 129
 ruralism 149
Common Ground (Cowan) 308
commons, fight against enclosure
  443–5
communes 436–7
community, soap operas 267–8
Connell, Bob 353
Conservative government, impact on
  Wales 113–14
Conservative Party, Scotland 106
constitutional patriotism 481
consumerism 138–9, 450
 and art 294–5
 and avant-garde 288
 consumer culture 319, 327–39
 identity 2, 10–12
 sport 10, 322–3
Cooke, Lynne 291
Cooke, W. F. 446
'Cool Britannia' 259
Cooper, Cary 350
Corner, John
 television 177–8, 261–72
 with S. Harvey, Thatcherism 2
Coronation Street 267
Couldry, Nick 224
 monarchy 175–6, 221–33
Council for the Encouragement of
  Music (CEMA) 236–7
countryside
 control of 323
 see also rurality
Countryside Alliance 147, 154
 fox-hunting 146
Cowan, Andrew 308, 309
Coward, Rosalind 217, 375
Crang, Philip, with P. Jackson,
  consumer culture 319,
  327–42
Creative Industries Task Force 236
creativity, and Britishness 464–5
Crick, Bernard 50, 130

crime, and slipping standards of
  speech 192
Criminal Justice and Public Order Act
  (1994) 12, 323, 418, 422, 424–6
Cromwell, Oliver 161
 establishment's view of 158
Crouch, C., with D. Marquand 423
Crown Heartland 134
culture 306, 344
 cultural policy and heritage 235–47
 heritage and the Arts 8–9
 and multiculturalism 479–85
 see also arts; Britishness;
  Englishness; heritage; literature;
  national identity
Culture and Anarchy (Arnold) 445, 446
curry 333
Curtice, John 60
cyclists, war memorial to 151

Dabydeen, David 310–11
D'Aguiar, Fred 310
Daily Mail 362
 Princess Diana 231
Daily Post 111
Daily Star 333
Daniels, Stephen, heritage culture 258
Davey, Kevin, Northern Ireland 79–95
Davies, Ron 109, 113–14, 123
 attitudes to Welsh language 115
 Welsh devolution and the economy
  117
Dedman, Peter 435
Deep England 148
Deepwell, Katy 298
deindustrialization, erosion of
  collectivist work identity 320
demography
 Northern Ireland 83
 rural districts 146–7
Dennis, N., with F. Henriques and
  C. Slaughter 349
Department of Culture, Media and
  Sport 235, 259
depoliticization, women's issues 367
devolution
 Scotland 105–6
 Wales
  1979 referendum 110–13
  1997 referendum 113–17
  changing identities 123–4
  elections to National Assembly
   121–3

generational divides in opinion
  113, 120–1
 geographical divides in opinion
  117–20
Diana, Princess of Wales 8, 175,
  215–16, 222, 251, 464, 499
 celebrity status 223, 231
 ordinariness 226–7
 People's Princess 228
 populism 225
 rebellious royalty 229–30, 231
diaspora
 Birmingham and the empire 31–9
 Ireland 89
Dickens, Charles 28, 31, 251, 305
Dictionary of the English Language, A
  (Johnson) 187
direct rule, Northern Ireland 79–80,
  87–8, 90
Disco Biscuits (Champion) 312
dissent, and the media 324–5
docusoaps 269–70
Dodd, Phillip, with R. Colls
 Englishness 129
 ruralism 149
Doherty, Willie 291
Dome *see* Millennium Festival
Dongas 439
Douglas, Sylvester, standard speech
  190
downsizing 436
Dreaming River (Attille) 63
Driver, Stephen, with L. Martell
 Blair and Britishness 461–72
 New Labour 325
Dryden, John, English grammar 187
Du Gay, Paul, cultural change 350
Duchamp, Marcel 300–1
Dufresnoy (Dryden) 187
Dwyer, Claire 332
Dyer, Richard 229, 401

earnings
 discrimination against women
  366–7
 gender differences 351–2
economy
 agriculture 146, 148
 globalization 140–1, 331–4
 industry 47, 82, 347
 Northern Ireland 93
 restructuring 355
 Wales 115, 117

economy—*contd*
  wealth of City of London 139–42
  see also employment
education
  gender and the New Meritocracy
    363–8
  Northern Ireland 91
Edwardian Englishness image, new
    man image 378
Eliot, George 251, 305
Eliot, T. S.
  Englishness 4–5
  establishment's rejection of 168
  sport 399
Elizabeth 251, 254, 256
Elphinston, J. 190
emigration, to New Zealand 32–9
Emin, Tracy 288, 295–8, 302
empire 47
  legacy of and cultural identity
    27–39
  power, Britain's rise and fall 158–60,
    162
  state and identity 43–4
employment
  changing nature of 343–58
  see also work
Enchanted Glass, The (Nairn) 221–2
enclosure, struggle against 443–5
Endless Pressure (Pryce) 199
Enfield, William, standard speech 182
England
  and multinational Britain 130–3
  see also Britain
England, England (Barnes) 313
English Journey (Priestly) 43
English National Opera, funding 238
English Woman's Journal 37
Englishness 4–5, 19–20, 129
  and Britishness 24, 41–4, 102
  devolution 133
  emergence of 44–51
  nationalism 51–3
  religion 46–7
  rurality 145–56
  see also Britishness
environment
  environmentalist and animal rights
    activism 323–4, 433–5
  green politics 431–41
  Millennium Commission 240–1
  politics of 12
Esquire 380

ethnicity
  British Asians, identity 72–4
  and Britishness 499
  ethnic identity and racism 21
  and national identity 475
  and race 20–1
  religion 198–201
  sovereignty 164
Europe, and USA, Britain's
    relationship with 157–69
European Union (EU)
  Fortress Europe and Little
    Englandism 7–8
  Northern Ireland 90
  Scotland 106
  Wales 116
Everybody I've Ever Slept With:
  1963–1995 (Emin) 296, 297
Ewen, S. 403
Eyre, Edward John, rebellion at
    Morant Bay 31

Face 294
  new man 376–7
Falwell, Jerry 202
family values, and consumerism 10–11
Famished Road (Okri) 310
Fanon, Frantz 38–9
fashion, ordinariness and royalty 226
femininity, and masculinity 321
feminism
  art 295, 297
  feminists and the empire 37–8, 39
  women under New Labour 362–3
  young women in workforce 320–1
  see also gender
Festival of Britain (1951) 241, 242,
    243–4
Fever Pitch (Hornby) 404, 405
FHM 409
Fiction and the Reading Public (Leavis)
    166
Fight for Manod, The (Williams) 307
film *see* cinema
financial sector, masculinity 352–3
Fireman, Paul 406
Fitzroy, Robert 34, 35
flags
  identity, St George's Cross and
    Union Jack 57–60, 64
  St George's Cross 20
flexibility, and uncertainty 345
'fly-on-the-wall', television 269–70

folk-songs 150
football
  Manchester United 407–8
  Northern Ireland 86
  professionalization of 402
  racism and English nationalism
    58–9
  style 404–5
Football Factory, The (King) 312
Forster, E. M. 250
fourth world 350–1
Fowler, H. W., British and English 42
fox-hunting, and rurality 145
France, Churchill advocates
    unification with 163
Free State (Ireland), establishment 133
Freedland, J., changing nature of
    employment 345–6
Freeze 287, 292
Frith, S. 274
Fukuyama, Francis 3
Future of Multi-ethnic Britain, The
    (Runnymede Trust) 6, 21, 64–5,
    483–4, 488

Gamble, Andrew 423
Garner, R. 434
Gascoigne, Paul 405
gay culture 321–2, 387–96
  see also gender
Gay Liberation Front (GLF) 322, 388,
    390–1, 393
Gay News 394
Gay Pride Marches 393
Gay Times 394
gender
  art 294–302
  changing nature of employment
    344–6, 347
  employment rates and earnings
    351
  feminization of workforce 320
  gay culture 321–2, 387–96
  gender identities 11
  New Meritocracy 361–72
  politics of in Northern Ireland 83–4
  technological change, changing
    work opportunities 344–5, 352
  see also feminism; masculinity
generational divides
  black British 62–3
  British Asians 71–2
  Welsh devolution 113, 120–1

George VI, King, coronation: media
  presentation 213
Georgian Poetry 150
Germany 160
Gerrard, Nicci, country life and urban
  life compared 146–7
Gibbons, Stella 153
Giddens, Anthony
  class cultures 347
  national identity 467
Gill, John 186
Gillespie, M. 331–2
Gilroy, Paul 58, 63–4
  black culture and racialism 282
Girouard, Mark 244
Gitlin, Todd 455
Giuliani, Rudolf 289
global context 25–6
globalization
  global consumer 331–4
  and the North–South divide
    140–1
  see also economy
Golden Treasury of English Verse
  (Palgrave) 49
Goldthorpe, J. 347, 348
Goliath (Campbell) 355
Good Friday agreement 81, 87
Goulbourne, H.
  Labour Party and Britishness 101
  subjects of the Crown 101
Gowrie, Lord 239
GQ, new lad image 379–81, 382
GQ Active 409, 410
Graham, Ben 312–13
Grainger, J. H. 130
grammar *see* speech
Grant, Hugh 253
Grant, Linda 440
Great Exhibition 445
Green, Michael 453
green politics 431–41
Greenberg, Clement 180
Greenhalgh, Liz, impact of Jamie
  Bulger case 11
Grey, Brylcream advertisement 373
Grey, Sir George 34, 36, 37
Guardian 277, 333, 440, 487
  fox-hunting 145
  new lad image 383
  royalty 231
Gudgin, Graham 93
Guest, Jo 382

Gurnah, Abdulrazak 310
gypsies
  discrimination and policing
    418–19, 427
  migrations and control of the
    countryside 323
  see also Travellers

Habermas, Jürgen 216
  national identity 481–2
Haggard, Sir Henry Rider, city as
  unnatural 19
Hague, William 114, 462
Hain, Peter, Welsh devolution 116–17
Hall, Catherine, cultural identity and
  the empire 19, 27–39
Hall, M. 88
Hall, Stuart 63, 76, 411
  culture 344
  on Labour as modernizers 469
  national identity 488
  tea and Britishness 333–4
  Wolfenden Report 388
  with T. Jefferson 361
Hancock's Half Hour 452
Handsworth Songs (Akomfrah) 62
Hansen, Alan 409
Haraway, Donna, concept of home 11
Hardt, Michael, with A. Negri,
  national identity 489–90
Hardy, Thomas 152, 250, 251
Hargreaves, John 405
Harrison, Ruth 435
Hart, John 182, 183
Harvey, David 329
Harvey, Marcus 289
Harvey, Sylvia, with J. Corner,
  Thatcherism 2
Harvie, C. 348
Hatoum, Mona 291
Have I Got News for You 427
Hazelton, W. A., direct rule 88
Heath, Anthony 60
Hebdige, Dick 331
Heelas, Paul 203
Hello magazine 175
Henriques, Julian 64
Henriques, F. *see* Dennis, N.
heritage
  and cultural policy 235–47
  culture and the Arts 8–9
  heritage film and television 249–59
  see also culture; national identity

heroism 496–7
Hesmondhalgh, David, popular music
  178–9, 273–86
Hewison, Robert 8
  official culture 239
hierarchy *see* monarchy; ordinariness
Higden, Ranulph, standard speech 182
high-tech sector, masculinity 353–4
Higson, Andrew
  film and television 177
  heritage cinema and television
    249–60
Himid, Lubaina 291
Hirst, Damien 179, 287, 291, 465
history
  Atlantic-centred 157–69
  England and Britain 130
  Thatcher on teaching of 6
HIV / Aids 322, 389
  and Princess Diana 223
Hoberman, J. 403
Hobsbawm, Eric J., with T. Ranger,
  change and rituals 209, 210
Hodge, Sir Julian 113
Hoggart, Richard 131, 133, 166–7, 344
Holbrook, B. *see* Miller, D.
Holford, Alison 354
Holt, R. 401
Home Rule 81, 99
Honey, John 192
hooks, b. 335
Hornby, Nick 404, 405
hours, work culture 350
Houseman, Laurence 152
Houshiary, Shirazeh 291
Howard, Frankie 391
Howard, Michael 425
Howards End 252–3, 254, 258–9
Howkins, Alun 49–50
  rural culture 24–5, 145–56
Huizinga, Johans 244
Humanitarian League 432
Hume, John 90
hunger strike (Northern Ireland),
  impact 90
hunt saboteurs 422–3
Hussain, Nasser 409
Hutchinson, Robert 237
Huyssen, Andreas 298, 299
Hyde Park 444

I Saw Two Englands (Morton) 135
ID 294

identity
  British Asians 67–77
  consumerism 2, 10–12
  Muslimness 68
  nationalism 5–8
  Northern Ireland 79–93
  rituals and Black Britishness 57–65
  Scottish and British 97–107
  Wales 109–24
  see also Britishness; Englishness;
    national identity
ideology, and the monarchy 215,
  216–18, 229
imperialism *see* empire
Importance of Being Ernest, The (Wilde)
  390
In Search of England (Morton) 137
income *see* earnings
Independent Television Authority
  264–5
Indian Mutiny (1857) 28
indie music, and Britpop 275–8
individual, and network 230
industrial North, and city culture
  136–9
industry 347
  deindustrialization and the
    struggles in Northern Ireland 82
  Industrial Revolution 47
Infinity Wholefoods 435, 436, 437
Information, The (Amis) 313
Intended, The (Dabydeen) 310–11
internet 454–8
Ireland 497
  establishment of Free State 133
Isaacs, Jeremy 453
Ishiguro, Kazuo 250
Italian image, new man image 377,
  378
ITV 264–5

Jackson, Colin 58
Jackson, Peter
  with P. Crang, consumer culture
    319, 327–42
  see also Miller, D.
Jacques, Martin 344
Jamaica, rebellion at Morant Bay 31
James, C. L. R. 399
James, Henry 66, 165, 251
James, Paul 489
Jefferson, T. *see* Hall, S.
Jerry Springer Show, The 270

John Bull, origins 46
John, Elton 388, 393
Johnson, S. 187
Johnstone, Brian 400
Jordan, Michael 405
Joseph, J. E., standard English 186,
  192
Jowell, Tessa 361, 366–7
jungle music 283–4

Kean, Hilda 432
Keane, Roy 409
Kearney, R. 91
Keiller, Patrick 473
Kennedy, Edward 90
Kensington Gardens 444
Kent, Sarah 300
Kevin Davey, Northern Ireland 21–2
Keynes, Lord 236–7
King, John 312
King Lear (Shakespeare) 183
King Richard II (Shakespeare) 500–1
Kingsford, Anne 432
Kinnock, Neil, opposition to
  devolution 111, 112
Kipling, Rudyard 152
Klausen, Jytte, with A. Wolfe, national
  culture 485
Koolhaas, Rem 245
Krishna Consciousness movement 435
Kristeva, Julia 22
  Northern Ireland, identifications
    and abjection 80–1, 85, 88
Kumar, Krishan 239
  Englishness 19–20, 41–53
Kundnani, Arun, English nationalism
  57
Kureishi, Hanif 9, 76, 305–6, 309–10

Labour Party
  Britishness 101, 461–72
  and Home Rule 105–6
  and the Millennium Festival 241–2
  New Labour 3, 320, 343
  Wales, devolution referendum
    (1979) 111–12
  Welsh National Assembly elections
    121–2
  see also New Labour
Labov, William 173
language
  British Asians 71
  and Englishness 48

politics of standard speech 181–92
  and Welsh devolution 115
  see also speech
Lawrence, D. H., English as
  undeveloped citizen 138
Lawrence, Stephen, inquiry into
  murder of 21, 64
Leader Scouts 151
League against Cruel Sports 439
Lean, David 250
Leavis, F. R. 278
Leavis, Q. D. 166
Leeson, Nick 352
legislation
  Act of Union (1707) 45, 104
  British Nationality and Aliens Act
    (1914) 101
  Caravan Sites Act (1968) 419, 421,
    425
  Commonwealth Immigration Act
    (1962) 101
  Criminal Justice and Public Order
    Act (1994) 12, 323, 418, 422,
    424–6
  Immigration Act (1971) 101
  Local Government Act (1988),
    (section 28) 322, 389, 390
  Nationality Act (1948) 100
  Nationality Act (1981) 101
  Patriality Act (1981) 101
  Sexual Offences Act (1967) 388, 390
lesbian cultures, and gay cultures
  321–2
Lewis, C. A. 451
Lewis, Carl 58
Lewis, Michael 353
Linguae Britannicae vera Pronunciatio
  (Buchanan) 190
Lion and the Unicorn, The (Orwell) 43
literature 305–15
  emergence of nationalism 48–50
  literary fiction 180
  urban-rural divide 152–3
  see also arts; culture
Litt, Toby 313
Little Englandism 20, 53, 60
  and Fortress Europe 7–8
Littlewood, Joan 244–5
Lloyd, Kathy 381–2
Loaded 409
  new lad image 381–2, 384
Local Government Act (1988),
  (section 28) 322, 389, 390

Locke, John 181
London 485–93
  wealth of City of London 139–42
London Chamber of Commerce,
    women in professional jobs 351
London's Burning 268
Longest Memory, The (D'Aguiar) 310
Lottery *see* National Lottery
Louis-Dreyfus, Robert 407
Lowe, R., with W. Shaw 420
Lucas, Sarah 287, 299–302

Maastricht Treaty 116
McCabe, Colin 192
McClintock, Anne 336
McCrone, David, Scotland 22–3,
    97–108
McDonald's 331
McDowell, Linda
  meaning of work 319–20
  work culture 343–60
McGee, Alan 236
McGeough, Gerry 90
McGuigan, Jim 242
McKay, George 437–8
McKittrick, David 87
Maconie, Stuart 275
Macpherson Report 21, 64
McQueen, Steve 291
McRobbie, Angela 403
  feminization of workforce 320–1
  meritocracy, women under New
    Labour 361–72
Maginnis, Ken 83
Magna Carta, myth of 50
Major, John 6, 136, 424, 462
  British nation 52–3
Man without Qualities, The (Musil) 43
Manchester United 407–8
Mandelson, Peter 236, 243, 463
Mandler, Peter
  ruralism 149
  urbanity 148
Mangan, J. A. 400, 401
manufacturing 347
Maoris 33–9
Marquand, David
  British state 99–100, 104
  with C. Crouch 423
marriage, British Asians 72
Martell, Luke, with S. Driver
  Blair and Britishness 461–72
  New Labour 325

Martin Bernadette 84
Martin, S. 354
Marx, Karl 2
masculinity
  and art 299
  discrimination in the workplace
    352–5
  and femininity 321
  new man and new lad images
    373–84
  see also gender
mass culture, and modernism 298
Massey, Doreen 347, 353, 354
maternity, and role of women in New
    Meritocracy 363
May, Jon 334–5
Mearn, Andrew, problem of the city
    148
media
  and dissent 324–5
  and the monarchy 210–11, 212–16,
    222
  royalty and inequality 229
  see also cinema; newspapers;
    television
Meehan, E., with P. Bew, European
    Union and Northern Ireland 91
Melody Maker 275
Memory of Departure (Gurnah) 310
Men Behaving Badly 268
Mercer, K. 408
Merchant-Ivory 250
meritocracy, women under New
    Labour 361–72
Merricks, Linda
  animal rights and
    environmentalism 323–4
  green politics 431–42
metaphysics, and Englishness 50
Methodism, and banishment of fun
    244–5
Michael, Alun 121
Millennium Commission 240
Millennium Festival 241–2, 243
  Dome at Greenwich 9, 236
  Dome to celebrate British creativity
    465
Miller, David
  common sense of nationality 467
  London 491, 492
  national identity 474–81, 483, 485
  with P. Jackson, N. Thrift, B.
    Holbrook and M. Rowlands 336

Mirza, Safia, education 365–6
Mitchell, George 86
Mo, Timothy 308–9
Modern English Usage (Fowler) 42
modernism
  and mass culture 298
  and ruralism 153
modernizers, New Labour as 469–70
Modood, Tariq
  British Asian identities 67–77
  ethnic identity and racism 21
monarchy 175–6, 207–9
  celebrities, royalty as 221–32
  changing role of 209–11
  ideology 216–18
  loss of support in Wales 116
  as narrative 211–16
  subjects of the crown 100
  see also royalty
Mongin, Olivier 489
Monk, Claire 256
Monster Raving Loony Party 202–3
Moreno scale 102
Morgan, Rhodri 122
Morley, David, with K. Robins,
    national culture in global context
    1–13
Morley, John 49
Morris Owner 152
Morris, William 50
Morrison, Blake, Englishness 4, 5
Morrison, Herbert 243
Morse, Samuel 446
Mort, Frank, masculinity 374–5
Morton, H. V. 134, 137
  two Englands 135–6
Mowlam, Mo 84
Moynihan, Daniel 90
Mugglestone, Lynda 177
  politics of Standard Speech 181–94
  'Proper English' 173–4
Mulgan, Geoff
  Englishness 5
  with K. Worpole, private enterprise
    and culture 290
multiculturalism 58–9, 76
  Channel 4 265
  and consumerism 331–3
  heritage culture 258
  national identity 479–85
  and ruralism 154
  writers 308
  see also culture; race

Murdoch, Rupert 407–8
Murdock, Graham
  media 324–5
  struggle for access to resources
    443–60
Murray, James, English language 48
music
  popular music 178–9, 273–5, 284–5
    black British music 281–4
    electronic dance music 278–81
    indie music and Britpop 275–8
  see also arts
Musil, Robert 43
Muslims
  and state funding of Muslim
    schools 75
  see also religion
My Beautiful Laundrette (Kureishi) 309
Myra (Harvey) 289

Nairn, Tom
  Crown Heartland 134
  monarchy 221–32 passim
  race and nationalism 60
  state and identity 42–3
Nast, Conde 379
nation
  British history 161–2
  see also state
National Anthem, Northern Ireland
    83
National Endowment for Science,
    Technology and the Arts
    (NESTA) 236, 241, 466
national identity 474–9
  and class 349
  and London 485–93
  and multiculturalism 479–85
  see also Britishness; Englishness;
    identity; patriotism
National Lottery 235–41
  funding of arts 176
National Survey of Ethnic Minorities
    in Britain (Fourth) 68
National Telegraph Review and
    Operator's Companion 447
nationalism
  and class 467–8
  and identity 5–8
  rise of in 19th century 48
  and social justice 466–8
  see also Britishness; Englishness;
    national identity

'Nationalization of British Culture'
    (Kumar) 239
Nature 447
naturism 437, 438
Nead, Lynda 300
Neale, Mary 149
Negri, Antonio, with M. Hardt,
    national identity 489–90
Nelson, Horatio, Viscount, Trafalgar
    Square column 158
network, and the individual 230
network society 140–1
New Age religion 203–4
New Age Travellers 323, 438
  see also gypsies; Travellers
New Deal 356, 357
New Labour 3, 320, 343
  and Britishness 461–72
  see also Labour Party
new lad image 379–84
new man image 373–9
New Musical Express (NME) 275
New Right 370–1, 423–4
New Statesman 370
New Zealand, immigrants and natives
    32–9
New Zealand Company 32, 33
Newbolt Report, teaching English
    186–7, 188–9
Newbould, Frank 153
Newman, Francis, pronunciation 188,
    189
News from Nowhere (Morris) 50
newspapers
  devolution 111
  race and empire 30–1
  see also media
Nike (trainers) 406, 407
Nixon, Sean, femininity and
    masculinity 321, 373–85
North, industries and cities 136–9
North–South divide, and rural–city
    divide 127–42
Northern Ireland 21–2
  abjection 81–6
  Christianity 199–200
  identities and abjection 79–93
Norton, Graham 391
nostalgia see heritage

Oasis 276
Oates, L. E. G. 496
Odone, Christina 370–1

Ofili, Chris 289, 291
O'Hagan, Sean 380
Okri, Ben 310
Olympic Games 402
On Nationality (Miller) 474–81
One Foot in the Grave 268
O'Neill, Tip 90
Only Fools and Horses 452
Onslow, Sir Cranley 423
Onwuhra, Ngozi 63
Oprah Winfrey Show, The 270
ordinariness
  and royalty 224–8
  see also populism
Orwell, George, Englishness 4, 6, 43,
    305
Osmond, John, Wales 23–4, 109–25
Other, consumption 335–6
Outrage 395
Ove, Horace 21, 60–1
Oxford Book of English Verse (Quiller-
    Couch) 49
Oxford English Dictionary on Historical
    Principles (Murray) 48

Paisley, Ian 84, 200
Palgrave, Francis Turner 49
Paltrow, Gwyneth 254
Palumbo, Lord 239
Panorama, Princess Diana 227
Paradise (Gurnah) 310
Parekh Report 483–5, 488, 495
Parkes family
  Bessie Rayner Parkes 37–8
  Birmingham and New Zealand
    32–8
Passion of Remembrance, The
    (Blackwood and Julien) 63
'Pastoral Interlude' (Pollard) 154
Patiz, Tatjana 380
patriotism
  New Labour 463–4
  and racism 467
Patterson, H., with P. Bew and
    P. Teague 89
Paxman, Jeremy
  absence of English urban tradition
    138
  Englishness 5
pay see earnings
Peacock Report 454
Pearson, Geoffrey 422
Peel, Sir Robert 445

Penn, Roger 365
Pentecostalism 199
Penthouse 382
People of the Black Mountains
    (Williams) 307, 313
Pepper, David 434
period drama *see* heritage
Perverts Undermining State Scrutiny
    (PUSSY) 392
Peter Rabbit (Potter) 496
Petri, Ray 376–7, 378, 384
Phillips, Trevor 492
Phoenix, A. 356, 369
Phyfe, William 181, 186
Pines, Jim
    black Britishness 57–65
    race and ethnicity 20–1
Plaid Cymru, National Assembly
    elections 121–2
Plummer, Ken, gay culture 321–2,
    387–98
Poirier, R. 404
police force
    masculinity 354–5
    Northern Ireland 92
politics, and religion 202–3
Pollard, Ingrid, ruralism 154
Pollard, S., with A. Adonis, Super
    Class 139
popular music 178–9, 273–86
population *see* demography
populism
    and royalty 224–8, 231
    television 264
Portillo, Michael 52
Potter, Beatrix 496
Powell, Enoch 52, 104
pregnancy, and social class 364,
    368–71
Pressure (Ove) 60–1
Price, Cedric 245
Pride and Prejudice 251, 254, 255, 256
Priestly, J. B. 43
    Englishness 4
Prinjha, Suman 333
Prioleau, John 152
private enterprise, and culture 290
pronunciation *see* speech
proportional representation, Wales
    122
Propriety Ascertained in her Picture
    (Elphinston) 190
Prospect 485

Protestantism
    alienation from society 199
    and Englishness 46, 47
    Northern Ireland 200
    see also Christianity; Northern
        Ireland
Pryce, Ken, Protestantism and society
    199
public provision, discredited 13
public sector, Northern Ireland 82
puritanism 245, 246
Puttenham, George, standard speech
    184

Queer as Folk 393
Quiller-Couch, Sir Arthur 49
Quim 392

race
    Black Britishness 57–65
    consumer culture 336–7
    discrimination in education 366
    and the empire 30–1
    Englishness and the Other 335–6
    and ethnicity 20–1
    literature 305–6, 309–11, 312
    racist abuse in Northern Ireland
        85
    see also black British; British Asians;
        multiculturalism; xenophobia
racism
    Britain 495
    British Asians 74–5
    commodity racism 336–7
    discrimination 69
    and ethnic identity 21
    and patriotism 467
radio 447–9
rainbow politics 468
Rake, Katherine 366
Ranger, T., with E. J. Hobsbawm,
    change and rituals 209, 210
Ravenhill, Mark 246
raves 421–2
Redfern, Simon 440
Redwood, John 114, 277
Reebok 406
Rees-Mogg, Sir William 239
referenda
    Welsh devolution 109–17
        (1979) 110–13
        (1997) 113–17
Regan, Tom 434–5

Reith, Sir John 264
religion
    and Englishness 20
    identity, British Asians 70–2, 73–4
    religious cultures 174, 195–206
    see also Catholicism; Methodism;
        Muslims; Protestantism
Remains of the Day 250, 253
reunification, struggle for in Northern
    Ireland 82
Reynolds, Simon 283
rituals, and black Britishness 57–65
Riviere, Joan 299
road-building, campaigns against 439
Roberts, John 294–6
Robins, Kevin
    national identity and London
        473–93
    with D. Morley, national culture in
        global context 1–13
Robinson, Gerry 239
Rogers, Sir Richard 246
Romanticism 49–50
Rosenthal, Norman 289
Rowlands, M. *see* Miller, D.
Royal Black Institution 84
Royal Opera House, funding 238
Royal Ulster Constabulary (RUC) 92
royalty *see* monarchy
RSPCA *see* Society for the Prevention
    of Cruelty to Animals
Rubinstein, W. D., ruralism 149
Runnymede Trust, *The Future of
    Multi-ethnic Britain* 6, 21, 64–5,
    483–4, 488
rural culture, and Englishness 24–5
*Rural England: A Nation Committed to a
    Living Countryside* (White Paper)
    147
rurality
    control of countryside 323
    and Englishness 145–55
    North–South and rural–urban
        divides 136–42
    see also countryside
Rushdie, Salman 9, 310
Ruskin, John 242
Rutherford, Jonathan 332
Rye, Maria 38
Ryman, Geoff 314

Saatchi & Saatchi 382
Saatchi, Charles 179, 287, 288–91

sadomasochism (SM) 392
St George's Cross see flags
Sales, Roger 256
Salisbury, Lord 447
Samuel, Raphael 8, 133
   heritage culture 258
   urbanism and modernism after
      WW II 153
Sanderson, Lesley 291
Sartre, Jean-Paul 309
Satanic Verses (Rushdie) 310
*Saturday Night or Sunday Morning?
   From the Arts to Industry: New
   Forms of Cultural Policy* (Worpole
   and Mulgan) 290
Scannell, P. 216
Schlegel, Margaret 254
Schoenberger, E. 350–1
Schwarz, Bill
   Atlantic-centred history 157–69
   Britain in global context 25–6
Scotland 497
   and the British state 22–3
   Britishness 468–9
   devolution 105–6
   and the Union 45, 97–107, 131
Scott, Sir Robert F. 496–7, 498
Second Generation (Williams) 307
secularization 201
Sedgwick, Eve K. 387
Seeley, J. R. 159
Select 275
Sellar, W. C. 43
Sennett, Richard, alienation 230
*Sensation: Young British Artists from the
   Saatchi Collection* 179, 288–90,
   292
Sense and Sensibility 251, 253
Sexual Offences Act (1967) 388, 390
sexuality, and heritage culture 259
Seymour, John 436
Shabazz, Menelik, black cultural
   identity 61–2
Shakespeare in Love 251, 254, 256
Shakespeare, William 183, 251,
   500–1
Sharratt, Bernard, literature 180,
   305–16
Shaw, W., with R. Lowe 420
Sheridan, Thomas, standard speech
   183, 188, 189, 190
Shields, Rob 135
   North–South divide 128–9

Shirlow, Peter, new identities in
   Northern Ireland 91
Shonibare, Yinka 291
Shopping and Fucking (Ravenhill)
   246
Sibley, David
   control of the countryside 323
   travellers, youth and drug cultures
      417–30
Silent Spring (Carson) 435
'Simpsons' 380
Singer, Peter 434
Sinn Fein 84
sitcom, television 268
Sivanandan, A. 310
Slaughter, C. see Dennis, N.
slavery, antislavery movement 30
Smart, Benjamin, standard speech
   185, 187, 190
Smith, Barbara Leigh 37–8
Smith, Chris 246, 464, 465, 466
Smith, Joan 296
Smith, Paul 236, 246
Smith, Sheila Kaye 152
Smith, Zadie 9
soap operas, television 267–8
social change, role of women under
   New Labour 361–72
social control, travellers, youth and
   drug cultures 417–29
Social Democratic and Labour Party
   (SDLP) 90
social justice, and nationalism
   466–8
social relations, consumption 329
Society for the Prevention of Cruelty
   to Animals (SPCA) 433, 437
Soil Association (SA) 433
Sour Sweet (Mo) 308–9
Southwell, Tim 381
sovereignty 164
Sparks, R. 217
special relationship, UK and USA
   163
speech
   'Proper English' 173–4, 181–92
   see also language
sport
   and consumerism 10, 322–3
   football 58–9, 86, 402, 404–5
   Northern Ireland 86
   and style 399–415
Sproat, Ian 402

state
   Britain as state-nation 22, 97–103
   and Scotland 22–3
   see also nation
status see ordinariness
Stedman Jones, Gareth, urban
   degeneration 148–9
Steele, Tom 242
Steptoe and Son 452
Stockholm Exhibition (1930) 241
Stoke Newington, consumer culture
   334–5
Stone, Norman 52
Stonewall 395
Straw, Jack 485
   asylum seekers 468
   Left's lack of patriotism 6
Streatham Common, fight against
   enclosure 443
Sturridge, Charles 250
style, and sport 399–415
subsidized arts 290
suffrage, Northern Ireland 87
Sun, Prince William 225–6
Sunday Sport 300
Sunday Telegraph 254, 259
Super Class 139–40
Surrey Anti-Litter League 154
Swainson, Mary, New Zealand 32,
   34–8
Swampy 427, 439
Sweet, Henry, pronunciation 188
Sweet, Matthew 357
Syal, Meera 9, 313
symbolism
   institutional symbolism and change
      209
   monarchy 224

talk shows 270, 296
Tanner, Jo 382
Taylor, Elizabeth, celebrity status
   compared to Princess Diana
   223
Taylor, Peter 90
   Britishness and Englishness 24
   North–South divide 127–42
Te Rangihaeata, Wairau massacre 34,
   36
Te Rauparaha 34
tea, and Britishness 333–4
'Teaching of English in England, The'
   (Newbolt Report) 186–7

Teague, P., with H. Patterson and P. Bew 89
Tebbit, Norman, Baron 6, 52, 192, 453
technology, change 344–5
telegraph 446–7
telephone 447–8
television 177–8
  heritage television and cinema 249–59
  introduction of 451–2
  split over Welsh devolution 118
  sport 401
  subscription channels 452–3
  see also BBC; cinema; ITV
Terrence Higgins Trust (THT) 389
Thackeray, William Makepeace 305
Thatcher, Margaret 52, 53, 241, 461, 470, 498
  attitude to Europe 164
  cut-back on the state 111–12
  Department of National Heritage 176
  family values 389–90
  teaching of history 6
Thatcherism
  consumerism and identity 2
  impact on Scotland and Wales 106
Theatres of Memory (Samuel) 153
There Ain't No Black in the Union Jack (Gilroy) 58
third space 348–9
Thirsk, Joan 432
This Time: Our Constitutional Revolution (Barnett) 101–2
Thomas, Dylan 41
Thomas, Keith 231–2, 431
Thompson, E. P. 347
Thompson, Emma 251, 253
Thornton, Sarah 279
Thrift, N. see Miller, D.
Thurman, Uma 382
Tidrick, Kathryn, empire and Englishness 47
Time Out 288
Times, The 38, 447
  race 30
Today (BBC Radio 4) 368
Tomkin, Boyd 404
Tomlinson, Alan, sport and leisure 322–3, 399–415
Tonypandy, Viscount 113
tourism, Northern Ireland 92–3
Toynbee, Jason 281

tradition
  break with in consumption 331–2
  and the monarchy 209–11
  and New Labour as modernizers 469–70
Trafalgar, Battle of 159
Trafalgar Square, as centre of Britain 158
Trainspotting (Welsh) 312
Transcendental Meditation 203
Travellers 420–1, 427
  New Age Travellers 323, 438
  see also gypsies
Treaty of Waitangi 33
Trollope, Anthony 305
Trudgill, Peter 191
Tudorbethan 152
Turner, Mark 214
Turner Prize 9, 291
Two Fried Eggs and a Kebab (Lucas) 300, 301

Ulster Unionist Party (UUP) 87
Under Milk Wood (Thomas) 41
unemployment, Northern Ireland 82–3, 91
Union, England and Scotland 45, 97–107, 131
Union Jack see flags
unionism, Northern Ireland 87–8
unions, Winter of Discontent 110
United Kingdom
  creation of 97
  see also Britain
urbanity, urban–rural divide and Englishness 136–42, 145–55
USA
  Americanization, consumerism and escape from tradition 331–2
  Britain's loss of America 28
  Christian Right 202
  and Europe, Britain's relationship with 157–69
  involvement in Northern Ireland 89–90
Use or Ornament? The Social Impact of Participation in the Arts (Matarasso) 237
Uses of Literacy, The (Hoggart) 166–7

values, consumerism and identity 2
Vauxhall Pleasure Gardens 243, 244
Vegetarian Society 432

vegetarianism 432, 435–6
  see also environment
Victim 390
Victoria, Queen 432, 495–6
Vidal, John 145
Video Diaries 269
Village People 391
villages, and Englishness 134–6
Vincent, John 52
violence, as unEnglish 422
Voice for Wales, A (White Paper) 117
Volosinov, V. N. 6
voyeurism, and art 296, 298

wages see earnings
Wairau massacre 34
Wakefield, Arthur (Captain) 34
Wakefield, E. G., emigration to New Zealand 32–3
Wales
  1979 referendum 110–13
  1997 referendum 113–17
  changing identities 123–4
  devolution 23–4, 109–25
    division of opinion on 113, 117–21
    elections to National Assembly 121–3
  Wales TUC 112
Walker, A. 250
Walsh, Viv 382
War Graves Commission 151
Warde, Alan 440
Washington Post 250
Waugh, Evelyn 250
Wearing, Gillian 294
Webb, Mary 152
Welcome II the Terrordome (Onwuhra) 63–4
Weldon, Fay 363
welfare benefits 356
  Northern Ireland 91
  Scotland 105
Wellington 33–4
Welsh Development Agency 112
Welsh, Irvine 312
Welsh Office 112, 114
Western Mail 111
Whannel, G. 401
Wheatstone, C. 446
When Memory Dies (Sivanandan) 310
Whig interpretation, English history 49, 50–1
Wiener, Martin J., ruralism 149

Wight, Daniel 348–9
Wilde, Oscar 390
William IV, King 446
William, Prince, populism 225–6, 227, 228
Williams, Hywel 487, 492
Williams, Kenneth 391
Williams, Raymond 42, 313, 314, 347
  common culture and culture in common 445–6
  culture 306–7, 344
Williams, Vaughn 237
Willis, P. 407
Wilson, Robin, peace process in Northern Ireland 88
Winslet, Kate 253
Winter of Discontent 110
Winterson, Jeanette 380
Wolfe, Alan, with J. Klausen, national culture 485
Wolfe, James 159
Wolfenden Report (1957) 322, 388

women
  franchise 449
  New Labour's policy 361–72
  see also feminism; gender
Wood Green, consumer culture 337
Woolf, Virginia 251
work
  meaning of 319–20
  work culture 343–58
  see also class; employment
working class see class
World Wars 498
  World War I, Englishness and ruralism 151
  World War II
  Englishness and ruralism 153
  and Welsh devolution 120–1
Worpole, Ken
  arts, subsidy of 176
  Englishness 5
  heritage and cultural policy 235–48
  impact of Jamie Bulger case 11
  town centres 13

with G. Mulgan, private enterprise and culture 290
Wright, Patrick
  Deep England 148
  heritage culture 8

xenophobia
  and nationalism 8
  see also race

Y Fro Gymraeg 118, 119–20
Yeatman, R. J. 43
York, Peter 382
York, Sarah, Duchess of 215
Young, Brett 152
Young British Artists (art exhibition) 287, 292
young British artists (yBas) 179–80
youth
  and Labour's New Britain 465–6
  youth counter-culture 435
  see also education; generational divides